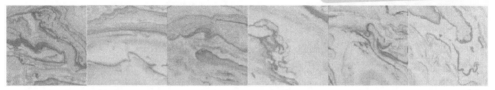

Management and Economics of Organization

Felix R. FitzRoy
(University of St Andrews)

Zoltan J. Acs
Daniel A. Gerlowski
(both Merrick Business School, University of Baltimore)

FINANCIAL TIMES
Prentice Hall

An imprint of **Pearson Education**

Harlow, England · London · New York · Reading, Massachusetts · San Francisco
Toronto · Don Mills, Ontario · Sydney · Tokyo · Singapore · Hong Kong · Seoul
Taipei · Cape Town · Madrid · Mexico City · Amsterdam · Munich · Paris · Milan

Pearson Education Limited
Edinburgh Gate
Harlow
Essex CM20 2JE
England
And Associated Companies throughout the world
Visit us on the World Wide Web at: http://www.pearsoneduc.com

Typeset in 10/12pt Plantin Light
by Wyvern 21 Ltd, Bristol

Printed and bound in Great Britain by
T. J. International Ltd, Cornwall

Library of Congress Cataloging-in-Publication Data

FitzRoy, Felix R.
  Management and economics of organization / Felix R. FitzRoy,
Zoltan J. Acs, Daniel A. Gerlowski.
    p.   cm.
  Includes bibliographical references and index.
  ISBN 0-13-231952-7 (alk. paper)
    1. Industrial organization.   2. Industrial management.
3. Organizational learning.   4. Managerial economics.
I. Gerlowski, Daniel A.   II. Acs, Zoltan J.   III. Title.
HD31.A285   1997
  658—dc21   97-42859
                                                              CIP

British Library Cataloguing in Publication Data

A catalogue record for this book is available from
the British Library

ISBN 0-13-231952-7 (pbk)

---

10 9 8 7 6 5 4 3
04 03 02 01 00

Management and Economics
of Organization

For our children

Olga and Jamie
Ashley and Annabel
Danny and Drew

Contents

Preface

The business environment that will carry us into the twenty-first century is driven by global competition in quality as well as price, innovation and the flexibility of organizations. In our rapidly changing world the diverse areas of modern economics have much to offer in preparing tomorrow's managers.

Traditional economics courses in universities are beginning to change. Managerial economics is no exception. The quantitative tools emphasized in most managerial economics courses have progressed in scale and scope, very often finding a home in specified 'tool courses' leaving the way open for innovation. Business and economics courses are being revised from a traditional mix of quantitative tools and economic theory towards an understanding of the role of management in economic organizations.

Management and Economics of Organization presents the most up-to-date research on economics of organization at the undergraduate and MBA level, without mathematical or other prerequisites, with a focus on how European and international organizations are evolving in today's highly competitive, global and technology-driven economy. The pioneering spirit in this endeavour was first embodied in *Economics, Organization, and Management* by Paul Milgrom and John Roberts (Prentice Hall, 1992). Although representing a remarkable achievement, parts of the book are above the level of most undergraduate students. Moreover, certain themes warrant more detailed exposition in order to make the subject more applicable in a global economy, such as the role of technological change and international comparisons of institutions and organizations.

Subject matter

Relying on many years of experience in teaching managerial economics, we have created an exciting treatment of the subject that is (a) reflective of the changing business environment and (b) more integrated with other traditional business disciplines.

Traditional aspects of our text include a detailed treatment of supply and demand, and the basic theory of the neoclassical firm, cost and efficiency. We also offer an accessible introduction to many of the more recent contributions of economics in the areas of coordination, motivation, organization and strategy. Thus we have provided undergraduate and graduate students with a set of tools to manage diverse and rapidly changing business organizations.

Management and Economics of Organization bridges the gap between traditional approaches to managerial economics and the more modern study of organization. Traditional courses in economics provided an analytical framework of the market environment but viewed the firm as a black box. The study of organization and strategy, although concerned with re-engineering, outsourcing, teaming, venturing and empowering, failed to provide managers with a systematic and comprehensive framework for examining organizational problems. This book uses economic analysis to develop such a framework. The material is presented in a organized, integrated and easily accessible manner. This evolving framework is now being adopted by an increasing number of our colleagues because of its relevance to the real world and its integrative nature. We hope that our efforts to tailor the material in terms of content and level towards the prototypical undergraduate and MBA student will contribute to this development.

Unique features

1 *Management and Economics of Organization* is the first textbook to integrate the economics of organization into undergraduate management or economics and MBA courses with a systematic European and internationally comparative perspective. The text starts with the economics of exchange and systematically develops the theory of economic organization. This makes managerial economics much more relevant for management education in today's global economy.

2 The text has four highly original and yet easy-to-understand chapters on the economics of organization. Building on transaction cost economics we examine efficiency and coordination within organizations. We develop the theory of contracting to discuss issues of motivation and discourse. Finally we develop the theory of distribution. This allows us to explain why firms exist in the first place.

3 The text is written in simple, understandable language. It is easy to read, requires no mathematics or prior knowledge of economics, yet maintains a high level of rigour and analytic content. The text uses numerous real-world examples drawn from the pages of the business press and explains them with organizational tools. The students enjoy the text, are more motivated and find learning rewarding.

4 The text examines organizational issues in a changing international

environment. Organizational dynamics are examined from historical, technological and global perspectives. For example, we examine the evolution of the firm from mass production using semi-skilled workers to the high-valued-added corporation using knowledge workers.

5 Our text is more integrated with traditional business disciplines such as finance and human resource management than with traditional managerial textbooks. Drawing upon the economics of organization we study the markets for corporate control, human resources and the changing boundaries of the firm.

Organization of the book

The book is organized into five parts: The efficiency of markets; The economics of organization; Organization, ownership and control; Managing human resources; and Innovation, technology and organization.

In effect, these four themes allow the student to explore managerial issues from an economic vantage point. Drawing upon the theory of economic organization we develop relevant examples from business to study issues of human resource management, financial structure and organizational dynamics.

For the instructor

Management and Economics of Organization is targeted towards undergraduate students of management and economics and MBA students. In order fully to appreciate the relevance of the topics in this text it is likely that students should have had at least an exposure to principles-level economics; however, the text is self-contained and begins with the economic prerequisites. There is no formal requirement that students already have mastered, or will learn, algebra, calculus or statistics. We have also had great success in the classroom involving students in discussion rather than simply conducting lectures.

This book represents an exciting and rewarding approach to teaching managerial economics. The material has been classroom tested over a four-year period. We have found that students are genuinely excited about what they learn, acquire the ability to apply the material to their real-world situations, and also begin to apply the concepts to other courses. Students can easily discuss moral hazard, asset specificity and the principal–agent problem in class.

The wide variety of topics included in *Management and Economics of Organization* would make it nearly impossible to cover each and every chapter fully in a single course. When designing this text, we fully appreciated this constraint and suggest the following alternatives.

Business students who may have a relatively weak background in principles-level economics, or who may have taken these courses long ago (a common feature given the changing student demographics), could be taught, on the basis of the first four chapters, a preliminary 'refresher' course of traditional economics of the firm, but including some modern ideas of game theory and imperfect competition. The remaining chapters (5–17) could be covered in a semester, with a wide range of emphasis possible according to the preferences of the instructor.

The second model course outline is more applicable when students already have a good understanding of the material covered in principles-level economics. It provides more of an organizational perspective and the emphasis is more on how 'firms' change in response to past and current forces, and are likely to continue evolving. This course could simply omit Chapters 3 and 4, which review the standard economics of the firm. Chapters 5–9 cover the modern theory of contracts and organization, and form the foundation for the following 'applications' chapters (10–17). However, there is no need to include all the applications in a single course. Depending on emphasis and other components of the curriculum, instructors may choose to omit selected chapters from the applications parts of the text without any loss of continuity.

For the student

This book is written for you. It is written to help you learn about the world in which you live and the organization in which you will work. Every page of the book is filled with interesting information that will be of use to you for years to come. The introductory chapter is your road map to the book. Each chapter has an introduction to make sure that you will find your way. The sections of each chapter are clearly marked and easy to follow. There is a large glossary with clear definitions at the end of the text, and the vocabulary necessary to understand management and economics of organization is bold faced within the text at the point where the term is introduced and defined.

Acknowledgements

A project like this does not take place overnight. Many people have helped us with it. First and foremost we express our gratitude to our students, without whom this project could not have been completed. We have benefited from comments by John Kay, Oxford School of Management and London Economics; Angela Black, University of St Andrews; Margaret Blair, Brookings Institution; Neil Kay, Strathclyde University; Steve Thompson, Nottingham

University; Hank Chesbrough, the University of California at Berkeley; Sharon Gifford, Rutgers University; Josh Lerner, Harvard Business School; Robert Wendle, the University of Maryland at College Park; Donald Siegel, Arizona State University-West; Bo Carlsson, Case Western Reserve University; Thomas Klier, Chicago Federal Reserve Bank; Frank Giarratani, University of Pittsburgh; and David Levy, University of Baltimore. We would like to thank our editors at Prentice Hall Europe, Economics Editor, Tony Johnston, and Production Editor, Joanna Pyke, for their help and patience throughout the project. Finally we are grateful to Wendy Seath for expertly typing and retyping much of the manuscript at St Andrews.

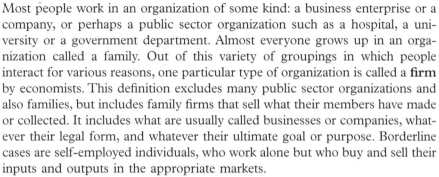

CHAPTER 1

Introduction: Firms and managing them

A. What is a firm?

Most people work in an organization of some kind: a business enterprise or a company, or perhaps a public sector organization such as a hospital, a university or a government department. Almost everyone grows up in an organization called a family. Out of this variety of groupings in which people interact for various reasons, one particular type of organization is called a **firm** by economists. This definition excludes many public sector organizations and also families, but includes family firms that sell what their members have made or collected. It includes what are usually called businesses or companies, whatever their legal form, and whatever their ultimate goal or purpose. Borderline cases are self-employed individuals, who work alone but who buy and sell their inputs and outputs in the appropriate markets.

In short, the firm is a productive organization, whose most important characteristic is that members cooperate under some form of agreement. This agreement may be based on a formal **contract**, on quite informal, mutual expectations, or just on bonds of kinship as in a (possibly extended) family. Cooperation or interaction inside an organization do imply more than an 'arm's length' market exchange, though a productive organization also has to interact with markets, as when inputs are purchased and outputs are sold.

Relationships within the firm

What exactly does this intrafirm interaction involve? Most people who have ever worked as an employee in some organization know that at least two different kinds of interaction are involved. First and foremost, you have to accept some ultimate authority, a boss who tells you what to do. Even a detailed contract of employment can never specify your work tasks in all possible circumstances, so a boss is necessary. Indeed, the existence of an **authority relationship** could (almost) be taken as one of the defining characteristics of organization. The exception is the case of an equal partnership, where, say, two or three professionals (lawyers or accountants perhaps) jointly make the ultimate decisions.

The second kind of interaction in an organization does not directly involve authority, but relates only to communication and cooperation between workers at the same level. Again, this is a non-market exchange of information, advice or material components in a workshop or factory. Of course, these 'horizontal' interactions do take place under the authority of the organization in the form of immediate supervisors, even when there is some scope for individual initiative. Finally, many employees can or must exercise authority as part of their job, managing or monitoring subordinates in the organizational hierarchy.

The firm has been described as a 'nexus of contracts', but the home owner who signs contracts with craftsmen for repairs or improvements to her house is at the centre of a nexus of contracts without thereby becoming a firm. There are invariably some formal contractual agreements that help to hold a firm together, but these generally last beyond the completion of one particular task – the building contractor will hope to construct or repair more homes than just yours.

Firm creation

The rather abstract nature of the firm that we have outlined so far can be made more realistic by following some typical life-histories or representative case-studies of firms from birth to death. The founder of a firm is usually called the 'entrepreneur', who initiates the contractual agreements that follow. The entrepreneur first needs to have an idea, some vision of a new or better product or service. It helps if the entrepreneur has some capital or accumulated savings, or at least if the spouse has a steady job to tide them over the early phase of setting up the new business. However none of these is strictly necessary.

If our fledgling entrepreneur is persuasive enough, he may be able to convince another party, perhaps a relative who has confidence in the entrepreneur's ability, to invest the required initial capital in the new enterprise, in the return for a share of future profits. This agreement with the pure capitalist will have to be 'nailed down' by a formal contract, say giving the capitalist 50 per cent of all future profits. In exchange for his savings, the capitalist has now become part-owner of the new firm, entitled to one half of the residual income after all contractual obligations have been fulfilled. He will also expect to share ultimate decision-making authority, or residual control, with the original entrepreneur in order to protect his capital stake.

The entrepreneur retains the other half of the expected profits, and thereby becomes the second owner, which is a different role from his prior work initiating the contract. The entrepreneur at this stage also has to assume a third role, namely working for the firm of which he is part-owner, say developing the innovative computer software that was his original idea.

The capital may be used to purchase necessary inputs such as other computer software and hardware, or to pay for marketing expenses. An expert programmer may have to be hired to assist in the development, and an employment contract specifying wages and working time is then appropriate. The founder of the firm has now been transformed from entrepreneur and part-owner into a manager as well, telling his new employee what to do from time to time, paying her salary out of the initial capital, and helping to develop and market the new software as well. As additional motivation he may offer his programmer a contractual share of his equity or profit.

After the first year of operation, much of the initial capital has probably been used up. If there are no firm orders for the new software, additional capital may not be forthcoming and the firm may suffer the fate of most entrepreneurial start-ups, namely bankruptcy and liquidation. The capitalist will then lose his stake, and the entrepreneur will have wasted a year of very hard work with no reward. Even the sole employee may have taken a low salary in the hope of benefiting from future profits and promotion, though finding a new job should not be difficult for a mobile, skilled employee whose talents are widely demanded.

If the firm is lucky, and the new product comes on stream in time, revenue will begin to flow and the entrepreneur can begin to pay himself a salary as managing director and perhaps a dividend for the outside capitalist or equity holder. Most profits will be ploughed back to expand the business, and more employees may be hired. Only in very exceptional cases – a small minority of all new start-ups – does rapid growth of sales and employment persist and propel the firm from the ranks of the small to the medium sized, let alone into the major league of their industry.

Even large and successful companies can be taken over or fail and be broken up and liquidated. Sometimes an entrepreneur–inventor is so successful that the firm outgrows the founder's managerial abilities. A wise entrepreneur then hands over to professional management, while retaining perhaps a seat on the board of directors and an equity stake. Otherwise a founding entrepreneur may be ousted by his own managers, directors and outside investors, a fate that befell Steve Jobs, the founder of Apple Computers. Family firms often run into trouble over succession, like kingdoms of old. Eldest sons in the second or third generation after the founding father may prefer life as a playboy, leaving other relatives and outsiders to squabble over control and direction.

The basic, simple story of entrepreneurship and the birth of a firm can be varied in many ways. If collateral is available, perhaps the entrepreneur's house where the firm starts life in a basement workshop, then a bank or individual may provide capital in the form of a fixed-interest loan. The creditor, who provides capital under such terms, need not become involved in residual control and decision-making unless the firm (or debtor) defaults on contractual obligations. As we have already seen in the example, conceptually distinct roles in the firm, such as entrepreneur, capitalist, manager and worker, can overlap in different ways. The contractual structure that emerges and defines the firm also defines one of a number of legal forms that a firm can adopt.

The legal entity

Although the precise legal framework and terminology differ from country to country, there are a few basic legal structures and distinctions that are found almost everywhere. The **sole proprietorship** is a business owned by a single individual. This form is very simple to set up, subject to few government regulations and exempt from company tax; the owner pays only income tax on her income from the business (and other sources). However, proprietorship has major disadvantages. The proprietor bears unlimited personal liability for debts incurred by the business, though, unless collateral can be provided, it is difficult to raise capital for this type of business.

Various forms of **partnership** between two or more individuals also suffer from the same problems of unlimited liability. To gain protection derived from limited liability status, a company must fulfil various conditions and regulations, as well as pay company tax. To become a public limited company (plc) or a publicly traded corporation whose shares are quoted on the stock exchange, subjects a business to the most demanding conditions. These include publication of detailed accounts and the appointment of a board of directors, which in some countries must include employee representatives under co-determination laws.

Corporations are recognized by all legal systems as legal entities or individuals. Although formation, or 'going public', may be quite a costly and lengthy process, this legal form has major benefits. Ownership and capital provision can be completely separated from employment in the firm, with liability restricted to each investor's initial capital stake. Transfer of ownership shares or certificates is then easy in established stock markets, and a corporation can, in principle, have an unlimited lifetime, lasting long after its original owners and founders are dead and gone.

The giant multinational corporations that dominate the world economy are hardly conceivable without the protection of limited liability for their millions of often widely dispersed stockholders. The sheer remoteness and multiplicity of these owners raise problems, for the managing director or chief executive of a large corporation can then pursue his own goals, perhaps 'empire building' at the cost of the shareholders. The chief executive is appointed by a board of directors, who are supposed to represent the interests of owners, and also of employees under codetermination laws in European countries such as Germany and Sweden. Conflicts of interest between owners, directors, managers and workers when there is much uncertainty and limited information will be major topics addressed throughout the rest of this text.

The parties listed above are often described as the firm's stakeholders. This term means that they expect to receive more in the form of current and future dividends, salaries and wages, respectively, than they could earn in their next-best opportunity. Customers too may feel better off than they would buying competing products, and so also have a stake in their firm or suppliers.

An existing corporation can raise capital for new investment and expansion in three different ways: (a) funds can be borrowed either from a bank or directly from investors through a bond issue; (b) the corporation may issue new shares of stock; (c) profitable corporations can be (to an extent) self-financing, that is by retaining a portion of their earnings rather than by paying them out to shareholders (owners) in the form of dividends. The best choice for financing a firm's operations depends upon many factors and is closely linked with the organizational form chosen. Some economists go so far as to argue that these decisions are made simultaneously with the choice of organizational form.

B. Three attributes of firms

In the developed economies of the world today, the dominant feature on the economic landscape is clearly the existence of firms. Most goods and services are produced by firms in the private, for-profit sector.

The field of economics has provided a number of theories explaining why these firms exist and, it is hoped, explaining their behaviour and future evolution. A brief review of these theories appears in the next section. For now, it is instructive to consider three attributes of firms identified by Alfred D. Chandler (1992) after a lengthy historical study.

1 **A legal entity**. As explained in the previous section, firms are able to enter into contracts with suppliers, distributors, employees and customers. This is the most general attribute of firms in our society.

2 **Administrative units under a central authority**. Recall our working definition of a firm. Perhaps the basic idea behind firms is that a group of persons engage in some form of collective behaviour; in larger firms each member is able to specialize in some task (or set of tasks) that is a smaller part of the whole. Because of this, firms and organizations consist of administrative units under a central authority. The benefits of specialization have been well known since Adam Smith, particularly his major work, *The Wealth of Nations* (1776). Organizations hope to capture these benefits, at the expense of having

to coordinate the actions of some group of individuals. In this light, firms are concerned with coordinating, motivating, and monitoring the actions of others.

3   **A pool of resources**. Once established, a firm becomes a pool of physical facilities, learned skills and perhaps liquid capital. In the previous section we learned that one aspect of legally recognized corporations is that they exist as a legal individual, and further that they can outlive their original owners. Once created, there are several pieces that make up this 'thing' that we call a firm. First, there are tangible components such as plants, distribution networks, patents, copyrights, and investment holdings. Secondly, there are intangible components to be considered: proprietary technical knowledge, consumer goodwill, reputation, and the personal relationships developed through years of interaction. Third, firms may have liquid assets such as cash deposits at the bank.

If we divide all economic activity into three sectors – for-profit firms, not-for-profit firms and government – it is clearly the case that most economic activity in most countries occurs in the for-profit, private sector.

C. A review of traditional theories of the firm

Given the state of economic knowledge today, there are four identifiable, separate and established theories concerning the existence of firms.[1] The differences among the theories largely concern the unit of analysis, the availability of information and the operational environment assumed.

The black box

The neoclassical theory of firm organization is perhaps the oldest and most established view. In its simplest form, the firm is regarded as a 'black box' or a **production function**, without internal structure but able to produce a large variety of output(s) using different combinations of inputs. Every economic agent has **perfect information**; that is, all agents know all technically feasible production and consumption plans and all prices in every market.

It follows that information is distributed symmetrically; that is, every party has access to the same data. The role of managers, given their (and everyone else's) full information in the neoclassical theory, is simply to maximize the profits or market value of the firm by choosing the optimal production plan. Standard courses in microeconomics go into great detail about the neoclassical theory of firms.

The agency view

The principal–agent theory of firms and their organization introduces asymmetric information into the mix. **Asymmetric information** exists when at least one party to an agreement has better information concerning some dimension of the agreement that some others are lacking. At the heart of the firm is a series of contracts, in many of which a principal hires an agent to act on her behalf. Usually, the agent has better information regarding his own performance and effort as well as the true prospects for advancing the principal's interests.

Within the principal–agent theories it is important to understand one very basic difference between the principal and the agent. The principal is best thought of as the 'superior party' in the relationship, frequently cast as the owner or controller of the concern. The agent is best thought of as the employee. The principal then bears some of the underlying risks facing the concern, and the agent is insulated from certain kinds of these risks by the contractual obligations of the principal.[2]

What makes the principal–agent theory particularly relevant and attractive to the study of firms is that, in many situations, the interests of the agent do not align with those of the principal. Classical conflicts between owners, managers and workers can be analyzed with the help of this theory.

Focus on costly interactions

The basic unit of analysis in the neoclassical theory of the firm is a form of exchange, namely the production function that describes the transformation of inputs into outputs. In the principal–agent methodology, the unit of analysis is the contracts between the parties and their resulting behaviour. In the transaction cost theory of firm organization, the unit of analysis is the individual transaction underlying the contractual agreements between parties. The last two approaches clearly overlap and complement each other.

Many of the important elements of the transaction cost theory also concern the availability and accuracy of information, and the possibility that those involved will act selfishly. The most basic assumption in transaction cost theories is that individuals and organizations have the property of **bounded rationality**, which means that information is costly (perhaps tremendously so) to acquire. As such, agreements are made with less than full information available.

From the transaction cost vantage point it is possible that parties to an agreement will engage in opportunistic or plainly dishonest behaviour, that is, act in their own selfish interests at the expense of others, perhaps involving fraud and deception. Exchange in such an environment gives rise to what are called **transaction costs** above and beyond contracted prices, including the acquisition of costly information, the costs of monitoring performance, the costs of committing specific assets, and the costs of handling complexity and uncertainty in reaching agreements. The proponents of the transaction cost theory of firm organization argue that transaction costs determine the structure of agreements upon which organizations are based; as such, they greatly affect the ultimate form of organization itself.

By now you have probably come to understand the importance of contracts to the transaction cost theory of firm organization. One of most interesting questions addressed by transaction cost analysis is the question of whether the firm should 'contract' or decide to fill a particular need within the organization, or contract to fill that requirement with a party outside of the organization. **Internal 'contracting'** will be chosen over **external contracting** (other things being equal) if the transaction costs of so doing are relatively smaller. This issue is so central to the problems facing managers of organizations that it has come to be called the **make-or-buy decision**; i.e. should a firm make an **intermediate good** in-house or should a firm secure the intermediate good in some competitive market?

The learning organization

The **evolutionary theory** of the firm is the newest and least developed of the accepted theories of firm organization. The unit of analysis under this view is clearly the firm and its productive processes. This theory focuses on three related aspects of organizations: their structure, their strategy and their **core competency**. A firm is said to have a core competency in a business area if it not only has an advantage in producing a good or service, but also has a similar advantage in the production of innovation and new, related products.

Firms are able to survive only if they change appropriately in response to changing market demands and technologies; in short they must adapt and find new productive scope for their core competencies – the things they do well. Evolutionary theory also emphasizes the role of historical accidents in giving one firm (or country) a dominating position in a particular market. On the other hand, firms and whole economies may also become 'locked' into an inefficient technology by accident or tradition.

D. A short history of capitalist firms

The industrial revolution began in England at around the time that Adam Smith wrote his famous book *The Wealth of Nations* (1776). This work is generally regarded as the starting point of modern economics, the first social science. Smith described how the division of labour and specialization were transforming early manufacturing and displacing traditional craft production.

In his example of pin-making, one worker cut the wire, another sharpened the points, and a third made the head of the pin. Productivity was much greater and yet each worker earned less than the skilled craftsman who had mastered all the tasks required to complete a pin. Work also became repetitive and monotonous, but low wages made long hours necessary for subsistence. Competition between manufacturers increased output and sooner or later cut the price of pins and other products.

The nineteenth century

In the early stages of the industrial revolution another modern practice was widespread, in the form of subcontracting. In the putting-out system, cottage workers and their families made components such as yarn or cloth for small workshops – the early manufactories. But a series of breakthrough inventions such as the spinning jenny and the mechanical loom, as well as the development of steam power in the late eighteenth and early nineteenth centuries, led to increasing **concentration** of the various stages of production under one roof and the stern discipline of factory organization. Outworkers with a modicum of independence and irregular working habits could not match factory productivity and reliability, where women and children worked long hours under harsh supervision to supplement family incomes with their minuscule wages.

The factories that accounted for most industrial employment by the middle of the nineteenth century were generally owner managed, as sole proprietorships or small partnerships. Capital was invested from savings or retained profits, or borrowed from close friends and relations. It was only with the ascendancy of heavy industry in the latter half of the century that the joint stock or public company, with limited liability for shareholders who were not involved in management, became important. Drawing on the savings of a growing middle class, the much greater capital requirements of steelworks, railways, shipbuilding and heavy engineering could be met only by these organizational and financial innovations. At the same time, managerial talent could be employed to oversee the growing administrative hierarchy of larger firms, without requiring capital ownership and the risk of unlimited liability, as in the traditional partnership.

By about 1870, Britain's industrial supremacy had peaked, apparently unchallengeable at the centre of a global colonial empire. But now two newly industrializing countries, Germany and the United States of America, were starting on a period of even more rapid expansion that would ultimately eclipse the first and oldest industrial nation.

The early twentieth century

Fuelled by abundant natural resources and an expanding flow of highly motivated immigrant labour, industry in the continental United States boomed, led
by the giant new railroad companies, which were among the pioneers of large-
scale integrated industrial and financial organization. The sheer scale of the
market favoured the early entrepreneurs such as Rockefeller, Morgan and
Carnegie, and in the first great merger wave the world's largest corporations
or 'trusts' came to dominate the American economy. By 1902, the United
States Steel Corporation, with 60 per cent of the market, employed 168,000
workers. In this context of giant bureaucratic organizations, it is perhaps not
surprising that the engineer Frederick Taylor tried to push the division of labour
down to the smallest definable task with his concept of 'scientific management', and Henry Ford introduced mass production with the first assembly
line in 1914.

In Europe, the new German empire that followed the Franco-Prussian war
of 1870–1, was rapidly overtaking the old leader, Great Britain, in most
branches of industry and technology for rather different reasons. Interestingly,
it was for very similar reasons that West Germany overtook Britain again a
century later. One of the reasons sometimes put forward by historians was
simply Germany's late start with industrialization. This allowed more modern
capital equipment and technology (as in reconstruction during the 1950s),
which, it is argued, may have helped Germany to gain a competitive advantage over older rivals using less advanced technology. However, this argument
does not explain why Germany was more successful than many other late
starters. The key to understanding Germany's historical (and current) economic success lies in two distinct policy areas, rather than in historical accidents or abundance of natural resources. First, modern technical training and
education in cooperation with industry was pioneered in Germany. New technical universities grew rapidly in the late nineteenth century. Craft traditions
inherited from the pre-industrial era were adapted to the needs of industry in
a system of vocational training and apprenticeship that remains unsurpassed
to the present day. Skills in the blue-collar labour force thus complemented
the abilities of scientists and engineers in the manufacture of high-quality, technically advanced products, particularly in the new growth industries of chemicals and electrical engineering.

The other key to rapid German growth was the role of 'universal' banks in
the organization of industry. Bradford De Long, a leading expert on their role,
writes:

> These 'Great Banks' were the largest corporations in the pre-World War I
> Germany and were at once commercial banks, investment banks, stockbrokers
> and investment councillors. They placed their representatives on the boards of
> most industrial corporations, repeatedly extended loans that provided long-term

capital for German industrial development, and appeared to exercise the dominant influence on the choice of top managers and executives, and over dividend and expansion policy on main corporate boards. (De Long, 1992, p. 10)

The banks also stabilized share prices on the stock market, avoiding the speculative bubbles and excess volatility that plagued most other stock markets. They channelled savings into industrial investment, rather than lending to foreign and colonial governments, as British banks and savers preferred. As a result, Germany's share of world manufacturing exports grew from one-third of Britain's share in 1880 to two-thirds in 1913 on the eve of World War I, and about twice the UK share today. The banks also helped to organize cartels that avoided cut-throat competition in Germany's rapidly expanding industries, and were tolerated by the authorities. Cartelization also helped to avoid wasteful duplication of investment and research and development (R&D) activity, and by raising profits encouraged a higher rate of investment and faster growth. Price-fixing agreements by the cartel may have harmed consumers in the short term, but they probably resulted in lower prices and higher wages in the long run, owing to the effects of enhanced growth.

Among the pioneers of German industrialization, men such as Bosch, Daimler, Krupp, Siemens and Zeiss founded companies that grew to become household names the world over. Although leading banks such as Deutsche and Dresdner are no longer as dominant as they were in the nineteenth century, they are still part of a tradition of industrial groups that maintain stability with the help of long-run mutual shareholding and business relationships. The pervasive short-termism of the Anglo-American, stock market dominated economies has thus been avoided, though banks have come under increasing criticism for their role in some spectacular business failures in the 1990s.

The German economy still has relatively few publicly quoted companies compared with the United Kingdom or the United States. Closely held family firms are common, as are large corporate shareholders, including the banks, which promote long-term investment strategies. Non-voting shares are still widely used in Germany, and minority shareholders with at least 25 per cent of a firm's outstanding share capital are protected by legal rights that allow them to veto major decisions. Hostile takeover attempts can thus be effectively blocked, and are indeed essentially unknown in Germany and also in Japan. This gives managers the freedom to concentrate on long-term investment strategies, and reduces wasteful speculation. Top management balances the interests of all stakeholders – employees, customers and owners – rather than pursuing an exclusive goal such as maximization of shareholders' value.

Large and long-standing corporate shareholders, including banks, can usually monitor managers more effectively than widely dispersed shareholders, and they are usually more inclined to understand the need for long-term investment in R&D and new technology. In the United Kingdom and the United States, where most large corporations are not subject to active control by major stockholders, underperforming managers can be replaced after a takeover or by the board of directors. However, the predominant role of the Anglo-American stock market is thought by many observers to discourage long-term investment projects and to divert resources to essentially speculative activity – trying to 'outguess' the market for quick capital gains in the United Kingdom and the United States. In all the major economies, most investment is actually financed by retained profits rather than by new share issues or by credit.

From mass production to flexible manufacturing

For more than a century, the productivity of an American manufacturing worker has been around twice the level of his British counterpart. This advantage even preceded the modern system of mass production that was pioneered by Henry Ford before World War I. It was based on **economies of scale**, or the benefits of large-scale production of standardized products, combined with greater capital intensity and more specialized machinery. Ford's assembly line also helped to reduce the skills needed by most production workers. A combination of specialized capital equipment and detailed planning by managers and supervisors essentially replaced craft skills in the industrial labour force, leaving most workers with repetitive, simplified tasks. Skilled maintenance work was reserved for trained engineers.

Starting with Ford's payment of $5 a day in 1914, premium wages were needed to keep workers under the numbing monotony of the line and the harsh rule of supervisors. Yet standardized products from Ford's model T to the flood of consumer durables in the booming 1960s were fabricated in ever vaster quantities at ever lower prices. As the giant oligopolistic corporations that dominated most American industries integrated backwards to control their suppliers, more layers of hierarchical management were added, to form increasingly unwieldy bureaucratic organizations. In Europe, smaller national markets and much stronger craft traditions combined to delay the adoption of mass production and scientific management. The apprentice system of on-the-job training provided a plentiful supply of skilled labour. Lower production volumes (units of output per day or week) could not justify replacement of skills with American levels of investment in specialized machinery and managerial control.

After World War II, British manufacturers embraced American mass-production methods with enthusiasm. Apprentice training declined precipitously, mergers were encouraged to gain scale economies, and efforts were made to introduce scientific management. However, professional and technical management training lagged far behind that of competitors, and investment was inadequate to re-equip obsolete, multiple establishments in the new conglomerates. Trade unions defended craft traditions and restrictive work rules in embittered confrontation with employers, and Britain's share of world manufacturing experts dropped from 25 per cent in 1950 to 9 per cent in 1973. In the same period, Germany's share tripled to 22 per cent, Japan's share quadrupled to 13 per cent, and the US share declined from 27 to 15 per cent (Broadberry, 1994).

In post-war Germany, industrial development took a very different course, and set a pattern for the rest of Europe commonly referred to as an economic miracle or *Wirtschaftswunder*. In contrast to Britain's unsuccessful attempt to copy American mass-production methods without the appropriate inputs or markets, Germany succeeded in combining the craft tradition with modern technology. Vocational and apprentice training were built up with extensive state support rather than cut back, and Germany's unique codetermination system helped to maintain cooperative labour–management relations. Highly skilled blue-collar master craftsmen or *Meister* could rise to supervisory positions, and worked harmoniously in cooperation with technically trained professional managers, helped by ubiquitous and powerful works councils.

The Volkswagen Beetle was a famous example of a mass-produced, standardized product that attained worldwide competitive success through design attributes such as economy and reliability. However, much of Germany's early export leadership was in the field of industrial products rather than consumer goods. These products gained their reputation through quality and design, and were often custom-made, individually or in small batches. Shop-floor skills, nurtured in the craft tradition, complemented scientific, engineering and managerial expertise in this early development of **flexible production**. This represented a significant departure from minimizing cost through high-volume production; instead the goal was the optimal solution to individual customer needs, which required rapid response to both changing demands and evolving technology.

At the same time, the absence of a speculative market for hostile takeovers meant that German managers and corporations were more likely than their Anglo-American competitors to focus on their core competencies, the things they could do best. There were no conglomerate merger waves in Germany, but stable networks of corporate alliances, supported by major banks, encouraged long-term, relational contracting and high levels of trust and cooperation. Many of the traditions of Germany's rapid industrialization at the end of the nineteenth century were thus maintained and adapted to modern conditions in the post-war West German resurgence to European economic preeminence (see Goodhart, 1994).

Although there were also major differences, many features of (West) German economic and industrial organization resembled elements of the Japanese system of flexible production. The growth of Japanese exports in the 1970s and 1980s was even more spectacular than the German 'economic miracle', and was followed by the wave of **transplants** or Japanese-owned manufacturing plants established particularly in the United Kingdom and the United States. These establishments demonstrated that important aspects of the Japanese model of flexible production were not culture bound, as sceptics had claimed for a long time, but rather represented fairly universal principles of effective organization.

The most important principles were pioneered by Toyota, which developed the use of flexible, multi-purpose machines operated by highly skilled teams of workers, who participated in a process of continuous improvement or incremental product and process innovation. Like other Japanese manufacturers, Toyota was not vertically integrated but depended on a close network of 'first-tier' suppliers for all major components. In contrast to the arm's-length market relationship with numerous suppliers that was favoured by manufacturers in the United States and the United Kingdom, Japanese parent companies developed long-term alliances with a relatively small number of suppliers. Relational contracting, including exchange of personnel and technical know-how, allowed all parties to invest heavily in specific skills and other specialized and complementary assets, geared to each other's particular requirements. The risk of disagreement or conflict was reduced by the long-term nature of the relationship, which put a premium on reliability and reputation, and elements of competition such as dual sourcing for key components. Each supplier thus had to match a similarly situated competitor's performance, but was also assisted by its main customer or parent corporation in the process of continuous improvement, and rewarded with an ongoing partnership.

In the 1980s there was growing recognition of the importance of flexible manufacturing in Britain and the United States. This recognition was driven by a number of factors. First and foremost were probably the inroads of Japanese and German competitors and the influence of Japanese transplants. Accelerating technological change and the rise in demand for customized rather than standardized products in the mature economies also contributed. However, the demise of craft traditions and neglect of vocational training, as well as traditionally adversarial labour relations, all served to delay the transition from Taylorist work organization and mass production to flexible manufacturing in the United Kingdom and the United States.

From 1979 to 1996, UK manufacturing employment declined by one-third, to about 20 per cent of the labour force. This unprecedented collapse helped to raise productivity more rapidly than in earlier decades, because the least productive workers were shed, and those remaining often had to work harder to counter the threat of future job loss. But by 1996, manufacturing output exceeded its 1979 level by only 10 per cent. At the same time, import penetration was increasing rapidly, in spite of restrictive quotas on Japanese car imports.

Declining union membership and the abolition of restrictive working practices were viewed as major achievements of the Thatcher government in 1980s' Britain. Yet R&D expenditure, training and industrial investment continued to lag behind those of competitors, and UK manufacturers tended to export cheaper, lower-quality products, whereas imports tended to be of higher quality and embody newer technology.

In the mid-1990s, a declining pound and recovery from widespread recession among trading partners gave a much-needed boost to UK exports, which now included the output of many Japanese transplants. Increasing adoption of flexible production had helped to reduce producers' costs and raise private sector profits during the upswing, but has also imposed substantial social costs on the UK economy. Part-time and temporary or 'contingent' work enhanced employers' flexibility and grew more rapidly than full-time employment throughout the 1980s and 1990s, while many employees could no longer find full-time work. Part-time jobs are usually unskilled, paid at a lower hourly rate than full-time comparable positions, and provide little or no opportunity for training and career advancement. Job security and job satisfaction tend to be minimal, in what is often termed the secondary sector, which also has to compete with outsourcing to low-wage countries in the developing world. The growth of part-time work in the United Kingdom and the United States has been linked to increasing numbers of the 'working poor', whose wages are insufficient to raise families above the poverty line. The real income of the poorest 10 per cent of the UK population actually fell by 17 per cent between 1979 and 1992, and income inequality grew more rapidly than in all other industrial economies. No less than one-third of British children are growing up in poverty in the 1990s, and one-fifth of all households have no wage-earner (Rowntree Foundation, 1995).[3]

E. The global 1990s: Reorganization, joint ventures and strategic alliances

The decade of the 1990s is a time of turbulent change for business and labour throughout the world. The most significant tendencies can be summarized as follows:

- Lean and flexible production is evolving into 'agile manufacturing' that can offer 'mass customization' in place of mass production of standardized goods. Supplier networks, including low-wage sources in developing countries, and global strategic alliances are blurring the boundaries of firms and even of nations.
- The explosive growth of information and communication technology has accelerated global linkages far beyond the material exchange of traditional trade, and has helped to break down conventional barriers and boundaries.
- The combination of rapid technological change and global market penetration has increased competitive pressures to such an extent that secure, protected markets and safe jobs are becoming rare.
- Even the biggest and most powerful corporations that missed crucial trends and developments, such as IBM or Philips, have been forced to undergo drastic reorganization and downsizing, losing hundreds of thousands of jobs.

Big changes at big companies

In the United States, which pioneered mass production and giant, **vertically integrated** corporations such as General Motors (GM), the impact of reorganization on ailing dinosaurs and erstwhile technological leaders such as GM or IBM has been most dramatic. The 500 largest manufacturing corporations shed a quarter of their workforce between 1980 and 1993.

While former leaders have everywhere been losing market share, part of the reorganization simply represents **decentralization**. Components that were formerly produced under the control of central management are increasingly outsourced to subcontractors, who can provide a more flexible and **efficient** service as independent organizations. In Japan, where the system of subcontracting has been a source of competitive strength for decades, close relationships between subcontractors and their main customers have been built up, fostering trust and communication. More short-term, arm's-length market relationships such as are often still found in the United States and the United Kingdom may be less effective in the long run, unless they, too, evolve towards some kind of partnership between large firms and their suppliers.

As different relationships among firms develop, including subcontracting, joint ventures and strategic alliances over differing time-scales, the boundaries between markets and firms (and also between firms) are becoming increasingly blurred. Formally and legally independent subcontractors may be more closely linked to a dominant partner both economically and practically than is a wholly owned subsidiary.

There are, however, striking differences between countries. In the United Kingdom in the 1980s, manufacturing employment plummeted, and the number of the smallest firms outside agriculture – that is self-employed individuals – grew from 7 to 12 per cent of total employment. Many of them were people made redundant by the downsizing of large companies, who used savings and redundancy payments to set up new entrepreneurial ventures. In Germany and other continental countries, the share of small-firm employment has traditionally been much higher than in Britain and, in particular, firms with 5–49 employees have increased their share quite rapidly. The largest firms (with over 1,000 employees) have stopped expanding since 1970, but have declined only slightly since then. The share of establishments with 1–4 employees has not increased in Germany (Stockman and Leicht, 1994).

As part of overall reorganization, process re-engineering has also been fundamentally changing the way work is organized and companies are managed. Best-practice firms in the West frequently follow the Japanese example, using 'total quality management' (TQM) and work teams to solve problems jointly and to motivate members. As managerial hierarchies are trimmed down, workers are empowered to make decisions without going through a bureaucratic, hierarchical decision-making process, thus gaining vital speed of response and enhancing flexibility.

Downsizing

Unfortunately, when top management has been too slow to respond to changing markets and technologies, the quickest and simplest way to stem the resulting losses and boost the bottom line is drastic **downsizing**. Most of the employees who lose their jobs have not been responsible for the strategic errors and failures to anticipate future trends that led to their plight. Those workers who retain their jobs are expected to work harder than ever before for fear of losing them in the future, in a climate where expectations of job security based on seniority, according to past practice, have been widely and rudely shattered.

Without more fundamental change, fighting current losses with even radical downsizing is often merely a retrospective strategy or rearguard action that offers little promise for the long-term future. Consultants Gary Hamel and C K. Prahalad (1994) have shown how the most successful companies surge ahead of much larger and more powerful competitors by anticipating or even defining customers' future needs. Sometimes however, radical reorganization coupled with appropriate new initiatives does hold promise for the future, as Box 1.1 on Philips suggests.

Box 1.1 Reorganizing Philips

In 1990, Europe's second-largest electrical goods manufacturer (after Siemens) seemed close to collapse. A loss of nearly 4½ billion guilders, or over $2 billion, the largest loss in the firm's 100-year history, and declining sales from over 300 production facilities world wide represented a seemingly insoluble problem for management. But a new chief executive, Jan Timmer, slashed bureaucracy, closed dozens of factories and cut the workforce by nearly 50,000. In 1994 operating profits rose to about 2 billion guilders and sales exceeded 60 billion guilders for the first time since 1985. Innovative new products, flexibility and customer-friendliness, reinforced by a string of global joint ventures, have combined to shake up the Dutch giant's lack-lustre image of quiet tulip fields around corporate headquarters in Eindhoven. For example, Philips leads a European joint venture, the Flat Panel Display Company, for making active liquid crystal display units, a field dominated by Japan. The European LCDs use thin-film diodes as their main switching device, instead of the transistors favoured by their Japanese competitors, which need three electrical connections instead of only two for the diode. This simplification should allow for lower-cost manufacturing, and the European venture is hoping to open a second, Asian plant as production at their original, Eindhoven facility expands rapidly. Ironically though, the specialized glass used in the LCD screens still has to be imported from Japan, because it cannot be supplied by any European manufacturer. In 1996, however, profits fell again.

(Based on 'Alles auf eine Karte', *Der Spiegel*, 8/1995, pp.106–7, and 'Europe's liquid assets', *Financial Times*, 22 December 1994)

There is also increasing evidence that motivating workers through the fear of job loss may be counterproductive. As Hamel and Prahalad point out,

> The social costs of restructuring are high. Although an individual firm may be able to avoid some of these costs, society cannot . . . One of the inevitable results of downsizing is plummeting employee morale. Employees have a hard time squaring all the talk about the importance of human capital with seemingly indiscriminate cutting . . . What employees hear is that they're the firm's most valuable assets; what they know is that they're the most expendable assets. (1994, p. 10)

In this situation, the incentive for most employees to raise productivity is blunted. Unless the firm achieves growing sales, higher productivity means fewer jobs and every member of the workforce feels threatened. Job security, as enjoyed by core workers in large Japanese corporations, is thus an important factor encouraging collaborative effort and teamwork to increase the overall efficiency of the organization. The Morgan Stanley bank's chief economist, Stephen Roach, a leading proponent of downsizing, has recently admitted that 'maybe I went too far . . . Tactics of open-ended downsizing and real wage compression are ultimately recipes for industrial extinction' (*Financial Times*, 14 May 1996).

Though downsizing has been less drastic in continental Europe and state-supported retraining schemes have helped to cushion the impact, long-term unemployment and also withdrawal from the labour market remain major problems. Indeed, lack of new jobs has kept unemployment and non-employment in the European Union at much higher levels than in the United States in the 1980s and 1990s. Employers would like to see the European labour market deregulated, so that they could adjust their workforces and working practices more freely and restrain labour costs, although such measures have not been overwhelmingly successful in Britain. There have been some striking cases of successful corporate reorganization in Europe, however, as Boxes 1.1 and 1.2 on Philips and Nokia show.

Manufacturing and the transplants

In 1980s' Britain under the Conservative government of Margaret Thatcher, union influence was rolled back and labour markets were deregulated. The lowest-paid, unskilled workers saw little growth in their real wages while the highest-paid executives enjoyed a five-fold increase in their total real compensation. In the mid-1990s, both total labour costs (hourly wages plus non-wage costs) and productivity in British manufacturing were among the lowest in Europe.

Japanese automobile manufacturers have made major investments in Britain, following the first move by Nissan in 1984. Toyota announced it was doubling

Box 1.2 Cellular core competence

One of Europe's rare high-technology success stories come from its northern-most capital, Helsinki. Only in 1991 the Nokia conglomerate lost $40 million on a wide range of often unrelated products. In 1992 a new chief executive, Jorma Ollila, was appointed. He decided to concentrate on the core competence developed a decade earlier, when the Finnish corporation pioneered early cellular phone technology. Ollila sold off dozens of the loss-making product lines, and brought the company to second position in the worldwide market for mobile phones, behind only Motorola. Nokia was first to produce a digital phone with a fine-line screen for e-mail and fax operation, and is now credited with a technology lead over Motorola. Nokia designs cellular phones with interchangeable parts to reduce manufacturing costs at its network of production plants, in spite of differing standards in Europe, Japan and the United States. R&D centres are integrated with production to implement continuous improvement. Even such spectacular success is no guarantee for the future, though, and Nokia cannot rest on its laurels as global competition continues to intensity, and profits fell sharply in 1996.

(Based on G. Edmondson, 'Grabbing markets from the giants', *Business Week*, 19 December 1994, p. 27, and 'Scared of growing fat and lazy', *Financial Times*, 10 July 1995, p. 11).

capacity at its Burnaston factory to 200,000 cars a year in 1995, following plans by Ford to produce Mazda cars at its Dagenham plant. The South Korean Daewoo Company plans to build 100,000 cars a year in Britain, and Samsung has announced a large new electronics plant on Teesside.

These developments have been encouraged by union weakness as well as by the declining competitive threat from the remaining British automobile industry. Japanese transplants in the United Kingdom are now the most productive car manufacturers in Europe, and Rover's success follows extensive collaboration with Honda, prior to its takeover by BMW in 1994. Japanese demands on subcontractors and suppliers are coupled with cooperative efforts to improve their performance. These efforts have had a considerable impact on British manufacturing efficiency. As Toyota Motor Europe's vice-chairman Alan Marsh has explained, 'Toyota works as a partnership: if a supplier has a problem we work with them to overcome it – at no charge' (see Kay, 1995, p. 3).

Other British suppliers still lag far behind best practice in quality, reliability and productivity. In their 'Worldwide Manufacturing Competitiveness Study' (Oliver *et al.*, 1994), Andersen Consulting investigated 71 automotive component plants in Europe and North America. In spite of improvement among suppliers to Japanese transplants, UK plants averaged the lowest productivity, second-worst quality and second-highest unit labour costs in Europe after Germany. Although productivity in the UK and other European plants rose, the performance gap with Japan actually increased over the recession period of 1992–4.

Andersen Consulting and their collaborators at the University of Cambridge and Cardiff Business School identified 13 'world-class' plants (out of the sample of 71) that were 'high performing' in both quality and productivity. The world-class plants consistently outperformed the rest of the sample by a factor of 2:1 over a wide range of measures. Five of the world-class plants were located in Japan, three in France, three in the United States and two in Spain. None of the German or UK plants was in the world class.

The Andersen Consulting researchers draw a number of conclusions from their detailed study:

> • Benefits from supplying Japanese transplants in the United Kingdom have not been sufficient to overcome traditional problems in much of the industry.
> • Germany's poor results may surprise many people, but 'one should be wary of confusing the quality and prestige of the finished product with the efficiency and sophistication of the process which produced it'.
> • No less than 40 per cent of the world-class plants were Toyota suppliers. 'Being a supplier to a world-class customer does not guarantee world class performance, but it certainly helps.'

The European Union as well as the North American Free Trade Area and the General Agreement on Tariffs and Trade have given a major boost to cross-border activity. Mergers, acquisitions, joint ventures and strategic alliances are multiplying, often driven by the realization that traditional, national companies are ill equipped to compete in the new European – let alone the global – market place. And emergence of a growing technology gap between even Europe's leading corporations and the pacemakers in Japan and the United States has prompted a wave of strategic alliances between traditional rivals. Agreements between Siemens and Matsushita, Daimler-Benz and Mitsubishi, or Philips and Motorola give the Europeans access to advanced technology such as 'mechatronics', the wedding of mechanical and electrical engineering pioneered by Japan. Japanese and American companies, on the other hand, hope for access to Europe's huge, newly integrated but protected market.

Europe's high-technology deficit

In the most rapidly advancing, 'highest'-technology areas, Europeans appear to be lagging dangerously far behind. US patent applications in microelectronics, biotechnology and medical technology doubled between 1987 and 1993, whereas European applications declined by 50 per cent in microelectronics and stagnated in the other fields. The four leading American suppliers of personal computers – Compaq, IBM, Apple and Hewlett-Packard – held nearly 40 per cent of market share in Western Europe in 1994. Italy's Olivetti ranked fifth with only 5 per cent, less than half its share a decade ago, and after a 25 per cent cut in its global workforce.

Major blocks to building the information superhighway or *Infobahn* in Europe are thought by many to be too little venture capital and too much government regulation. In 1994, only about 5 per cent of European 'venture capital' went to start-ups, so that 'the term is something of a misnomer'. On the other hand, monolithic government telecommunications monopolies in all European countries except the United Kingdom and, until 1996, Germany, have stifled innovation in the vital information and communication technology (ICT) areas. Planned deregulation of European telecom by 1998 still faces political minefields, and may be too late for European players to catch up with their more dynamic rivals in the United States and Japan.

In some ways, the troubled state of continental Europe's high-technology sectors is surprising. European institutions (with the exception of the United Kingdom) are closer in structure and tradition to those of Japan than to the Anglo-American *laissez-faire* model. Germany and other countries already have well-functioning supplier networks that maintain long-term relationships with large corporations as in the Japanese Keiretsu. A high proportion of family firms and dominating ownership interests by large corporate investors maintain a focus on long-term investment. With little threat of hostile takeover, and less stock market pressure for short-run profitability, the long-run interests of all stakeholders – employees, customers and shareholders – are explicitly recognized in corporate policy, as in Japan. Higher standards of training and blue-collar worker skills are envied by UK and US employers.

Strategic alliances in various guises (including cartels) have in fact long been part of continental corporate strategy, often under the umbrella of a major bank or leading corporation. By contrast, anti-trust policy in the United States has been criticized by leading industrial and business economists as fundamentally hostile to any kind of horizontal agreement or alliance between potential competitors. In his important study of industrial policy, Bennett Harrison of Carnegie Mellon University castigates 'the deeply ingrained prejudice against all forms of interfirm cooporation, going back to the origins of the antitrust movement in the last quarter of the Nineteenth Century' (1994, p. 230). Harrison and others such as Berkeley's management strategist David Teece recommend that US anti-trust law should be modified to encourage innovation through the formation of networks and strategic alliances.

Europe does have one striking example of what Harrison (1994, p. 169) calls 'a particularly successful public–private production network', in the shape of Airbus Industrie. Launched in 1971 by a French, British, German and

Spanish government-backed consortium, the Airbus has been catching up with formerly dominant Boeing in the wide-bodied passenger jet market. Massive government investment has generated some major innovations such as the first all-electronic cockpit. Although there may well be other technological spillovers through the network of subcontractors, it is still not clear whether there has yet been a positive return on the taxpayers' investment in strictly accounting terms. The consortium plans to become a public limited company, and to challenge Boeing in the lucrative jumbo jet market, both risky ventures.

On the other hand, the record of almost all government involvement in high-technology and other industries in Europe has been uniformly disastrous for the average taxpayer. Nuclear power is the worst example, absorbing a substantial share of total civilian R&D budgets in the United Kingdom, France and Germany, and remaining uncompetitive with other energy sources even when the costs of future decommissioning and nuclear waste disposal are concealed or ignored. The concentration of scientific and engineering resources in this industry has generated a formidable lobbying power that survived even Chernobyl, and has been little affected by more mundane considerations such as cost–benefit analysis. The existence of some 60 unsafe, Soviet-designed nuclear reactors in Eastern Europe and the former Soviet Union imposes literally incalculable risks on Western Europe. There, the nuclear industry is actively seeking government support for involvement in upgrading – or building new – Eastern nuclear facilities. In the meantime, urgent repairs and safety measures at Chernobyl and other installations remain stalled, while government support for safe and clean solar power remains negligible.

Quite generally, and indeed not surprisingly, government R&D funds often seem to flow to the most effective lobbyists, which are usually large established industries or corporations. Newer, untried ventures with inherently higher risks of failure are 'crowded out' and face severe shortages of investment capital. Arguments involving national prestige or very long-term commercial benefits are invoked to justify support for expensive white elephants such as the Anglo-French Concorde, or the German 'maglev' high-speed rail project. By their very nature, such claims can be proved wrong only after prolonged expenditure of public funds.

Although governments have not been good at picking commercial winners in the technology race, public support for basic science and university R&D has yielded significant spillovers to industrial innovation and high-technology employment in the United States (see Acs *et al.*, 1996). Localized clusters of interaction between academic research centres and entrepreneurial networks such as Silicon Valley's growth near Stanford University have no parallel in Europe.

With changing technologies and the opening of a more global economy, most markets are becoming much more risky. A common response to this risk is the emergence of organizations and arrangements that permit the 'pooling' or sharing of this risk; even historical rivals are seeing the benefits of cooperation. In some instances, joint ventures and strategic alliances are created as firms seek to enter new industries. Technologies are now emerging that will create whole industries in the years ahead. The corporate form that will organize production, distribution and marketing in these new industries is emerging as well. In the past, large firms were created via acquisition and internal investment; in these emerging markets it appears that the major players will be consortiums of firms, each investing in the project so as to bid for entry into the market while avoiding some of the risks involved. The consortiums are usually made up of similar firms, sometimes even competitors. There is a definite pattern of teamwork and necessary mutual trust that was absent in the corporate world of the past.

One example of a number of players participating in a global joint venture into a new market is General Magic, an organization producing hand-held communicators and electronic notebooks. The early versions of this product were called Newton. General Magic started as a venture by Apple Computers. In 1993, General Magic was joined by American Telephone and Telegraph (AT&T), Sony, Motorola, Philips Electronics and Matsushita Electric Industrial. As an incentive, each member of the alliance would have access to the underlying software (Telescript and Magic Cap) that would likely become the industry standard in a market projected to be worth $3.5 trillion by the year 2000.

One pledge made by General Magic in securing the participation of these industrial giants (some of which compete in other markets) was to keep this technology open to anyone who wants to adopt it. This pledge was somewhat compromised when AT&T obtained exclusive rights to General Magic software over its direct competitors. However, all in all, the credibility of the General Magic pledge was sufficient to attract many investors.

Competitors emerged quickly. As of 1993, the most promising competitor was EO, another Californian firm, which shares two principal investors with General Magic – AT&T and Matsushita. Interestingly, by 1994, EO had ceased to exist and was replaced by other alliances and joint ventures. This pattern of strategic alliances forming to access new and growing markets is historically unique. Its hallmark seems to be an atmosphere based on firms exploiting their core competencies, and of trust and cooperation. For another example of strategic alliance-building to serve a market that did not yet exist upon alliance formation, see Box 1.3

A somewhat different rationale for cooperation is emerging as well, as cooperation among independent companies is being substituted for a single corporate form. A value-adding partnership (VAP) is a developing form of organizing economic activity. The VAP form is a collection of independent companies jointly managing the flow of goods and services along the value-added chain. The relationship is in stark contrast to the historically prevalent highly vertically integrated corporations because of the many ownership interests involved. It also differs markedly from a single entity hiring outside

Box 1.3 High-density television: The grand alliance

In the early 1990s, a high-stakes race was taking place to establish an industry standard for the technology underlying high-density television (HDTV). The competition was international, with firms in the United States, Japan and Europe vying to become leaders in this, as of then, non-existing market place.

In the early going, it seemed as though the Japanese had an advantage with an analog-based system that was operational at the time. Similar systems were proposed by European firms as well. Both the Japanese and the various European governments heavily promoted their producers' offerings. The US firms were concerned more with a less well-developed system based on digital signals, similar to those used in computers.

The Federal Communications Commission (FCC) sponsored an impartial competition to determine the standards in the American market place. Nearly every entrant into the competition itself was sponsored by several firms; thus, the competition was entirely between joint ventures. During the competition, more alliances were formed until only three were left.

Those three entities in effect merged into a single entity that came to be called, somewhat appropriately, the Grand Alliance, after they had already agreed jointly to share future royalties from the one chosen system. The members of the Grand Alliance are mostly American companies – AT&T, General Instruments, Zenith, the David Sarnoff Research Center, and the Massachusetts Institute of Technology – plus Holland's Philips and France's Thomson.

This outcome was attributed both to a desire to avoid the costs of subsequent testing before the FCC, which would reduce future gains for the winner and further losses for the losers, and also to a fear that the FCC's choice might be challenged in the courts in a lengthy (and costly) legal battle.

suppliers to produce the component parts of final goods provided to the consumer. Thus, the VAP represents a true horizontal network of producers involved in production.

In spite of the growing importance of decentralization and small firms, in many cases size is still important. Two economists can easily decide to open a firm and print a textbook; they do not however have the resources to build multi-billion dollar oil refineries or paper production mills. Japan has increasingly become the model for high-technology, innovative manufacturing success, and it is notable that this success has been driven by large corporations run for the benefit of all stakeholders and working closely with networks of smaller and small subcontracters, based on long-term cooperative relationships. Japanese structures of organization, both interfirm and intrafirm, are much closer to continental European practice than to the American model of stock market dominance, cut-throat competition and entrepreneurship. Though

Europe lags behind both Japan and the United States in many respects, it is not obvious that simply emulating US institutions is the optimal route for European firms and government policy (see Box 1.4).

One indicator of Europe's problems is the index of world competitiveness published annually by a leading Swiss business school, IMD of Lausanne. In 1996 the top four countries were the United States, Singapore, Hong Kong and Japan. Germany dropped from rank 6 in 1995 to 10 in 1996, with the United Kingdom, France and Italy far behind in positions 19, 20 and 28, respectively. The index is a subjective aggregation of a number of differing indicators. Though derided by some economists, indicators of national competitiveness do reflect widely held perceptions of relative economic performance and, above all, future prospects (see IMD, 1996).

Box 1.4 (still) The importance of size

Despite the success of small firms there are still industries in which size is a necessity for survival. In each of these industries, large investments of various types are clearly required.

Classic production. Industries: commodity chemicals, paper, oil refining, and concrete. Mass production setting is still important for these standardized commodities. Companies: ICI, Shell, Hoechst.

Marketing–distribution intensive. Industries: beverages, athletic footwear, consumer goods. Brand name and consumer familiarity and loyalty are made important by the existing producers' marketing budgets and distribution networks. Companies: Unilever, Proctor & Gamble.

Volume buyers. Industries: automobile manufacturing, food processing, and retailing. Block buying is transferred to lower per-unit costs, a distinct advantage to retail outfits and firms buying components for finished products. Companies: Toyota, Nestlé.

Technology-intensive businesses. Industries: semiconductors, electrical, aerospace, pharmaceutical. Big corporations may have more funds for research and development when product lives may be short. Companies: Philips, Siemens, Bayer, Daimler-Benz.

(Adapted from James B. Treece, 'Sometimes you still gotta have size', *Business Week*, Enterprise 1993, p. 200.)

F. Our pathway to an understanding of management and the economics of organizations

What we want to teach you in our book is new, exciting and, most importantly, useful in your real life: those years after you graduate from business school. However, we must in fairness point out that much of the material is abstract and only recently fully developed by economists. Further, our approach is different from what has been traditionally 'accepted' for the economics component of your business education.

Box 1.5 Two views of the 'new way' of doing economics

Unlike most other people, businessmen love not only to give advice, but to take it too. Management gurus proliferate. Consultants earn fat fees. A flood of books on management pours off printing presses every year. And yet the one group of people to whom most businessmen rarely turn are economists. Big firms ask economists to predict the ups and downs of national economies, but when it comes to finding ways to run their own company better, many managers would sooner consult an astrologer.

In the past this was understandable. Most economists assumed all firms responded in much the same way to incentives and obstacles. To any practising manager it is not the similarities between firms that matter, but the differences – specifically those that explain why some firms succeed and others fail, even though all are seeking to survive and prosper.

Nevertheless, the gulf between economists and managers should be closing.

('Quacks and coaches', *The Economist*, 17 April 1993, p. 65.)

What defines business-oriented economics is its focus on what economists call 'the firm' – and the rest of us call 'the company' – as the unit of analysis. Traditional microeconomics, by contrast, is concerned with markets and prices. It looks at the economy or at an industry, but rarely peeks inside the individual enterprise. Indeed anyone who wandered into the usual course in microeconomics would discover only that the firm sells everything it produces at a market price that it does not control. Says Yale economist Bengt Holmstrom: 'There was nothing there for a manager to learn.'

A series of conceptual breakthroughs in microeconomics and game theory over the past dozen years has set the stage for today's work . . .

The new ideas tend to be commonsensical notions with forbidding-sounding names like 'bounded rationality,' 'asymmetric information,' and incomplete contracts.'

('A new tool to help managers', *Fortune*, 30 May 1994, p. 136.)

Economics is, after all, the science of exchange and resource allocation. All economic activity results from transactions between multiple parties. Ultimately, such exchanges build upon themselves to create things like partnerships, joint ventures, firms and virtual corporations. The tools developed in this textbook enable you to understand the way in which transactions are carried out across and within firms. The culmination of this study is a valuable insight into the development of corporate strategy, which we argue must reflect both the internal and external environments of organizations.

Several interrelated themes permeate all of the individual chapters in this book. At this point, we can only describe these themes to you; their importance will be demonstrated in later chapters.

Theme 1: Exchange. Economic activity is really about exchange. We focus on the conditions surrounding exchange more so than the exchange itself. Many exchanges, or transactions, occur in markets and are well understood. Many take place outside of the protective realm of markets; it is our purpose to understand the course of events in these instances as well.

Theme 2: Organization. Firms exist to organize economic activity. We must keep in mind that, to a certain extent, organizations replace markets. A firm is really a series of contracts linking various parties. The circumstances surrounding these contracts may be termed the environment of the firm. Over time this environment changes, which implies that organizations will change as well.

Theme 3: Imperfect information. Uncertainty and imperfect information exist in all contracts. No transaction is made under conditions of complete certainty because nobody can predict the future. It is difficult for us to monitor the behaviour of our contracting partners, and it is always wise for us to have a clear understanding of all commitments made to a given deal. Trust becomes a valued commodity.

Theme 4: Opportunistic behaviour. In framing and carrying out agreements governing exchange, rational parties may engage in self-serving behaviour – possibly at the expense of other involved parties. Contracting, because it is the building blocks of organizations, must address this through the establishment of trust, incentives and provisions for monitoring. As a guiding principle, efficiency dictates that agreements will be crafted keeping these things in mind.

The book is organized into five parts. Part I (The Efficiency of Markets) is the most straightforward part of this text because it is concerned with traditional, neoclassical economic analysis and some of the problems of applying the teachings of this school of thought in the real world. This chapter has introduced the subject and provides a useful starting point for our explorations. Large parts of Chapters 2 and 3 are probably familiar to most students. In these chapters we present the basic tools of analysis of traditional economics: the functioning of competitive markets and the competitive profit-maximizing firm. We review price determination by supply and demand, and highlight some useful managerial implications of demand analysis. What is interesting and unique in our coverage of material that is frequently found in other economics textbooks is our emphasis on the underlying assumptions behind the workings of the price system. The profit-maximizing firm in the short run and the long run is then considered in light of competitive markets governed by supply and demand.

Chapter 4 contains a systematic discussion of realistic departures from the 'benchmark' case of perfect competition. The polar case of monopoly and degrees of market power are considered. The basic modern tool of game theory to describe strategic intervention between small numbers of large firms in oligopolistic competition is introduced here. As unrealistically stringent assumptions required for the benchmark case of perfect competition are dropped, we set the stage for the study of real-world organizations and markets in the rest of the text.

Chapter 5 explores a rapidly growing literature in economics on property rights, that is, the effects of asset ownership on exchange. We view the approach in this chapter as a bridge between the 'new' and the 'old' economics. Much of this material is from the work of Nobel Laureate Ronald Coase, who showed the world that, even if a market were to fail, an efficient outcome can still occur if all interested parties are able to bargain with each other.

A very different view of exchange is presented in Part II (The Economics of Organization), where we begin to develop a different approach to understanding exchange, contracts and the structure of economic organizations. The logic behind all of Part II centres on transaction costs, which represent 'frictions' preventing the smooth functioning of exchange. In some markets, transaction costs do not inhibit the functioning of the powerful forces of supply and demand. The emphasis of the Coase theorem introduced in Chapter 5 is clearly that bargaining can lead to an efficient outcome if the costs of doing so are relatively small. The material in Part II is applicable to the huge number of exchanges lacking coverage by either competitive analysis or Coasian bargaining.

Chapter 6 addresses transaction costs and their impact on exchange. We explore the various dimensions of transaction costs in order to provide a useful terminology for later application of these ideas. Students are made aware of two major ways in which transaction costs can arise. Firms in the economy operate with less than perfect information about the exchanges in which they engage. Also, firms have ample reason to hesitate to make a deal from which the other parties can walk away whereas they cannot. From a managerial vantage point, this chapter considers what has come to be called the 'make-or-buy' decision in organizations; i.e. should the organization purchase or produce components of its final product.

Chapter 7 is all about the 'sticky stuff' that holds organizations together – contracts. The important idea to remember is that contracts are made reflecting various transaction costs. Usually one thinks of contracts as being highly rigid and very legalistic; in practice contracts are often less formal and more relational, stressing the underlying dynamics of the relationship between the parties. Contracting problems arise under conditions of asymmetric information, and when **opportunistic behaviour** is an option. Opportunistic behaviour means advancing your own interests at the expense of other party/parties under an existing contract by less than perfect honesty.

In Chapter 8 we turn to one important issue in relational contracting, **moral hazard**. Transactions take place in this type of environment when one party to the transaction can only imperfectly monitor the behaviour of the other party to the transaction. We begin by relating the organization to the property rights material presented in Chapter 5. We need to think about organizations as teams. Two important questions are: who should 'own' the team, and who should reap the rewards from good team behaviour? We also consider certain types of contracts in which moral hazard is a particular problem: insurance and employment contracts. Once a firm understanding of the basic issue of moral hazard is in place, we turn to considering how contracts may be structured to eliminate some of the moral hazard and to minimize the risks posed to different parties.

In Chapter 9 the importance and role of rents in economic exchange and organizations are made clear. We explore the initially surprising concept of **economic rents**, which, for now, can be defined as benefits going to a party engaged in an activity that are in excess of what is required to attract that party to that activity. Thus, in a sense, economic rents represent 'something for nothing'. Economic rents serve many purposes in our economic system. First, because they are desirable to those receiving the rents, individuals and organizations will strive to earn them. Secondly, rents provide one way to reward good behaviour in a world strewn with transaction costs. In organizations, rents abound and much effort is expended by members in securing these rents for themselves, an activity termed rent-seeking behaviour. Usually these efforts are counterproductive to the goals of the organization and we discuss ways to minimize the impact of such behaviour.

Parts I and II contain all of the building blocks needed to understand the organizational theory of economics. Economic activity may be organized by markets or by contracts within organizations. Beginning with the premise that all economic activity occurs through exchanges carried out in an environment of imperfect information, firms respond by contracting with their owners, workers and related firms in a rich variety of ways. The remainder of the book focuses on these relationships by addressing issues in firm financing, in relationships with workers, and in relationships between firms addressed from the strategic alliance vantage point.

In Part III (Organization, Ownership and Control) we attempt to gain some understanding of the financing activities of firms. The emphasis here is on a sometimes imprecise relationship between the 'owners' of a firm and those who 'control' the firm.

Chapter 10 concentrates on understanding some basic tools and issues of financial analysis. At the beginning of the chapter we present the key building block of discounting and present-value calculation with perfect information. There is a striking resemblance between this theoretical setting and the traditional neoclassical analysis of economic markets. We summarize the growing body of evidence that real-world financial markets may not be efficient, but rather subject to fads and fashions leading to excess volatility and 'bubbles'. From a social point of view, excessive resources are spent on trying to obtain information about firm prospects before others do so, in order to gamble on changing stock prices. And, contrary to widespread perceptions, stock markets are nowhere a major source of new investment funds.

Chapter 11 covers problems caused by the separation of legal, equity ownership of large corporations by many different shareholders from the control exercised by top managers who are theoretically agents of the owners, at least in Anglo-American terms. In continental Europe and Japan, managers are generally required to exercise a broader responsibility to various stakeholders including employees and customers as well as shareholders. This can lead to more efficient governance of the corporation when employee skills are specific to their job or firms and less valuable elsewhere.

Part IV (Managing Human Resources) applies our understanding of exchange to the management of human resources. Put in the simplest terms possible, employment is a contract. As with all contracts, it is made under conditions of uncertainty, imperfect information, complexity and imperfect commitment. Employers offer a wage and a certain amount of security; they are concerned with motivation and productivity, employee fit, and turning a profit on operations. Workers offer their skills, knowledge and some degree of loyalty; they are concerned with earning a good living and, presumably, in having a job in the future.

Chapter 12 summarizes modern approaches to some of the basic questions. Employees must be motivated by the prospect of promotion and higher pay, or by the threat of dismissal. Wages are less variable than profits, and so offer some insurance to risk-averse workers, but the major risk of job loss remains. This risk, but also attendant motivation, is enhanced if pay includes a rent component exceeding the worker's best alternative wage.

Chapter 13 examines the actual tasks people perform in different jobs and firms. Division of labour or specialization replaced craftsmanship to culminate in Fordist mass production, which was in turn supplemented by Toyota's lean manufacturing. Changing patterns of demand and technology require increasing employee skills, flexibility and involvement. Manufacturing and unskilled employment have been declining everywhere as service sectors expand, but significant international differences remain.

In the concluding Part V we first review the production of innovation and technological progress and follow this with an account of the new flexible production technology and its impact on firm organization. As information technology helps to blur the boundaries of the firm, strategic alliances between independent firms are replacing vertical hierarchies and chains of command. In spite of global markets and talk of convergence, fundamental international differences in technological performance and organizational style seem to persist or even grow, as we summarize in the final chapter.

Chapter 14 begins with the often misunderstood relationship between pure science and (applied) technology. The systematic production of innovation has been organized in different ways in different countries, and we document and explain the remarkable ascendency of Japan in high technology, now rivalling the United States but without an entrepreneurial sector.

Chapter 15 surveys the essential complementarities between new technology in the production process and the organization of manufacturing firms. The strategy of concentration on core competencies is being increasingly enforced by the intensity of global competition. The accelerating pace of innovation described in the previous chapter as well as shifting demand require the flexibility that can be attained only with highly skilled and empowered workers in 'flatter' hierarchies, reversing the earlier trend towards diversification and vertical integration of production.

Chapter 16 reviews the economic foundations of these increasingly common joint ventures. We apply the earlier tools of incomplete contracting and transaction asset analysis to explain the expansion of institutions that lie somewhere between the 'markets and hierarchies' of Oliver Williamson and are eroding the traditional boundaries of the firm.

Chapter 17 is essentially a summary of a major recurrent theme, the comparison of management and organization in the three most distinctive economic systems today. We review the salient features and distinctive elements of the (stock) market dominated Anglo-American economic systems, the more regulated social market economy of Germany, and the Japanese economy based on stakeholder firms and long-term relationships.

G. Of particular interest to managers

Just what do economists do at large corporations today? Most frequently they are asked to forecast movements in interest rates, price levels or overall economic activity. A smaller number of economists are consulted regarding the impact of various regulatory changes. Among business people, then, economists are viewed in a special way: very good at working in the abstract realm of theory, sometimes moderately good at predicting the future course of events, but rarely consulted for strategic managerial decisions. The purpose of this book is to introduce managers to the many powerful tools available in the so-called 'dismal science'.

We have presented in this chapter a fairly brief history of industrial evolution in the leading economies. The decline of the mass-producing firms and the subsequent rise of smaller, nimbler and flatter corporate forms linked into networks to produce more efficiently in today's globally competitive market place. It is our aim to study change such as this on the organizational level. Towards that end we turn our attention throughout this book back to the ultimate building blocks of all economic activity: the exchanges themselves, and the contracts and customs (both formal and informal) that regulate economic interaction. Although the economic theories behind this approach are not new, the implications are far-reaching. It is now time to bring them into the business area for wider exposure.

 ## Key words

asymmetric information	flexible manufacturing systems
authority relationship	intermediate goods
bounded rationality	internal contract
concentration	make-or-buy decision
contract	moral hazard
core competency	opportunistic behaviour
corporation	partnership
decentralization	perfect information
downsizing	production function
economic rents	real
economies of scale	sole proprietorship
efficient	transaction costs
external contract	transplants
firm	vertical integration

 ## Notes

1 The number of 'unestablished' theories of the firm is undoubtedly very large.
2 The principal–agent relationship is so important in modern economics that we devote an entire chapter to it (Chapter 8). For those of you with some background in this area we now point out that the agent is risk averse towards the underlying risks of the concern. If this were not so, the optimal, or efficient, solution would be to make the agent the residual claimant in the relationship.
3 Although the lowest wages rose slightly, the number of households with no wage

earners as well as homelessness increased rapidly. See also the survey of Britain's problems and suggested solutions by a leading economist, Richard Layard (1997).

References

Acs, Z., F. FitzRoy and I. Smith (1996), 'High technology employment and the achievement of R&D spillovers', Chap. 7 in A. Belcher, J. Hassard and S. J. Procter, *R&D Decisions*, London: Routledge.

Broadberry, S. N. (1994), 'Technological leadership and productivity leadership in manufacturing since the industrial revolution: Implications for convergence', *Economic Journal*, 104, pp. 295–302.

Chandler, A. D. (1992), 'Organizational capabilities and the economic history of the industrial enterprise', *Journal of Economic Perspectives*, 6, pp.79–100.

De Long, B. (1992), 'Growth, industrialization and finance', *NBER Reporter*, Summer.

Goodhart, D. (1994), *The Reshaping of the German Social Market*, London: IPPR.

Hamel, G., and C. K. Prahalad (1994), *Competing for the Future*, Boston: Harvard Business School Press, 1994.

Harrison, B. (1994), *Lean and Mean*, New York: Basic Books.

IMD (1996) *World Competitiveness Year Book 1996*. Lausanne, Switzerland: IMD.

Kay, W. (1995), 'Japanese spur suppliers in two-speed U.K.', *Independent on Sunday*, 19 March, p. 3.

Layard, R. (1997), *What Labour Can Do*, London: Warner Books.

Newsweek (1994), 'Lost on the Infobahn', 31 October.

Oliver, N., *et al.* (1994), 'The Worldwide Manufacturing Competitiveness Study: The Second Lean Enterprise Report', London: Andersen Consulting.

Rowntree Foundation (1995), *Inquiry Into Income and Wealth*, York: Joseph Rowntree Foundation.

Smith, A. (1976[1776]) *An Inquiry into the Nature and Causes of the Wealth of Nations*, Chicago: University of Chicago Press.

Stockman, R., and R. Leicht (1994), 'The pattern of changes in the long term development of establishment size', *Small Business Economics*, 6, December, pp. 451–64.

PART ONE

The efficiency of markets

CHAPTER 2

Demand and supply

> Nobody ever saw a dog make a fair and deliberate exchange of one bone
> for another with another dog. (Smith, 1976, Book 1, ch. 2)

A. Chapter outline and student goals

This chapter explains activity in a competitive market. The forces of demand
and supply are explained as representing the activities of many interrelated
buyers and sellers whose interaction determines market prices. The perfectly
competitive model we describe is important because it is the best understood
and most powerful (when used correctly) tool with which to study, explain
and predict activity in the business world. This chapter covers material that
you should be familiar with from your introductory economics class.

Exchange is the unit of analysis in this chapter. We consider two types of participants in our analysis: the consumer and the entrepreneur. The consumer is
the head of the household, and the entrepreneur is the head of the firm. We define
a **market** as the interaction of one or more buyers with one or more sellers.

In competitive markets, it is competition that limits and guides the behaviour of market participants and forms the basis of efficiency upon which the
whole economy rests. When competition is present, and all market participants
are omniscient, it is not necessary for governments to intervene. The impersonal forces of supply and demand will motivate firms to produce the goods
and services people value and to produce them in the most efficient, least
costly way. Market reactions, not public policies, will eliminate shortages or
surpluses. There is no need for government regulatory agencies or bureaucrats
to make arbitrary decisions about who may produce what, how to produce it,
set standards of quality, or how much it is permissible to charge for the product.
Within the competitive model, the public good is best promoted by individuals pursuing their own self-interest.

In the admittedly abstract and rarified, impersonal decision-making world
of **perfect competition**, neither private firms nor public officials wield economic power. Adam Smith, perhaps the most famous economist of all time,
used the metaphor of the 'invisible hand' to describe how self interest led to
the social good:

> It is not from the benevolence of the butcher, the brewer, or the baker, that we expect our dinner, but from their regard to their own interest. . . . He intends only his own gain, and he is in this as in many other cases, led by an invisible hand to promote an end which was not part of his intention. (Smith, 1976, p. 18)

First, this chapter develops the elements of competitive exchange and provides some guidance as to when it is appropriately applied. It is a logical statement about the functioning of the price system. Second, it is also a 'set of tools' for later use to help you understand the working of the market environment in which real firms actually exist. These tools have been developed over many years and will be invaluable for understanding the external environment facing firms.

After reading this chapter, you should be able to:

- briefly explain the methodological features of economic analysis;
- explain in your own words what perfect competition is;
- explain the difference between supply, demand and price;
- understand how market equilibrium works and why markets clear;
- understand the difference between elastic and inelastic demand;
- understand the difference between point and arc elasticity;
- explain the relationship between demand and total revenue.

B. The methodology of economics

The scientific method in economics

The **scientific method** is a way of thinking about problems and formulating a solution to or explanation of them. We can briefly outline the steps involved in scientific enquiry. A schematic diagram, such as Figure 2.1, may be used to represent these steps in a meaningful way.

The first step is to observe some phenomena occurring in the real world. This may amount to something simple like the legendary account of Sir Isaac Newton dozing under an apple tree and 'discovering' gravity when an apple fell from the tree to the ground. In economics, such an initial observation might be a relationship between the amount of money in an economy and the price level; or the so-called 'flattening' organizational restructurings common in large corporations in the 1990s.

The second step is to consult existing knowledge and logical systems related to the initial observation. The economist might turn to the written literature on a given topic in a variety of academic fields. Further, the economist might, and often does, consider a mathematical representation of the circumstances surrounding the initial observation.

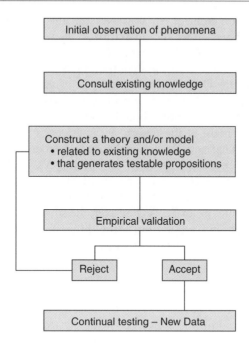

Figure 2.1 Schematic sketch of scientific method.

The third step is to construct a *theory* that explains the initial observation, and all other related events. A theory, or hypothesis, is nothing more than an attempt at an explanation for some phenomena. Quite often, a theory is interpeted with the help of a specific model, which may be defined as an abstract description of reality. Such a model might be a system of mathematical equations, a series of graphs or a verbal description. A model might depend on one or more theories in an attempt to explain, analyze and predict behaviour. The requirements for a model are that it offer an explanation reducible to an existing and known body of knowledge and that it generate testable propositions that can validate or reject the model and/or its underlying theory/ theories.

The fourth step in the scientific method is to seek empirical confirmation, confronting the model and its testable implications with activity in the real world. At this stage, we would then gather data from the real world and use it to confirm or reject the stated theories. Usually such tests are statistical in nature. Unfortunately, it is rather common for the statistical tests to generate ambiguous results that neither completely reject nor completely accept the theory. A good case in point of statistical tests not being able to settle a theory's validity is in macroeconomics, where there is a constant and long-standing difference of opinion between the Monetarist and Keynesian views regarding appropriate stabilization policies. If, however, the theory is rejected by the empirical evidence, the scientist should return to step 3 and re-examine the basic assumptions and construction of the theory.

The scientific method also calls for a continuing test of theory by new experience in the real world. Quite often, a theory is originally tested with data from one period or place, and it is found to be less than suitable for another period or place. Again, the scientist should return to step three and critically reconsider the development of the theory.

Perhaps you are familiar with this general approach to problem-solving from prior coursework in chemistry, biology or physics. Most of these courses involve a laboratory section where the experiments done by students have been designed with this type of approach in mind. Many people do not immediately recognize economics as a science; however, the subject is best approached as one. In the next section we point out some differences between economics and the more commonly recognized sciences.

Some differences between the sciences

Like any science, Economics is concerned with the explanation and prediction of observed phenomena. When most people think about science, they relate the concept only to the so-called **hard science**s, those concerned with the interactions and physical properties of matter: chemistry, physics and engineering. Economics, like psychology, sociology and political science, is a so-called **soft science**, one that explains the interactions resulting from human behaviour. There are two basic differences between the hard and soft sciences.

1 The hard sciences have the benefit of the controlled experiment. Two chemists can conjecture as to the exact shade of green that will result when certain yellow and blue chemicals are mixed. Their conjectures can be proven in the laboratory. Economists do not have this luxury; it would be inhumane to, for example, place a thousand people on a desert island and tinker with various systems that would allocate them food, clothing and shelter.
2 In the hard sciences, there is a stochastic, or random, component, however it is quite small and can often be identified. In economics, the random component of behaviour is usually not negligible. A fact of life is that, when the same individual is confronted with exactly the same stimuli, he will act differently on different occasions.

These differences have been identified and known for centuries and, as such, greatly affect the way in which economists approach problems vis-à-vis their counterparts in the hard sciences.

More on the practice of good economics

The method of enquiry adhered to by most economists is **logical positivism**. According to logical positivism, the basic axioms or assumptions of the theory are not subject to independent empirical verification. However, no theory, whether it be in economics or physics, is perfectly correct. Therefore, it is important to test the deduced hypotheses and thereby to test indirectly the system of axioms underlying economic theory. The usefulness and validity of a theory depends on whether it succeeds in explaining and predicting the set of phenomena that it is intended to explain.

Economists put primary emphasis upon the predictive powers of a model. If the predictions derived from one model prove better than the predictions drawn from another model, the former is tentatively selected as preferable. If a subsequent theory is advanced that explains more of the relevant facts the new theory is deemed superior to the one previously accepted.

The study of managerial economics and organization deals with both **positive** and **normative economics**. Positive questions have to do with explanations and predictions of what is, or is expected to be. Normative questions entail some moral or ethical basis within the issues to be addressed, dealing with what ought to or should be.

Positive economics is crucial to economic theory. It tells us what will happen to the price of cars when autoworkers' wages increase, or what will happen to productivity if wages are increased at Ford or Volkswagen.[1]

There may be times when we, as economists and human beings, want to go beyond explanation and prediction. We may wish to explore the normative implications of certain decisions. For example, what are the consequences of paying competitively determined wages in a developing country? Within this arena of intellectual exchange we may identify instances in which the predicted outcome of our models may not be what is in the best interests of society.

The assumption of rationality

Though different economists employ different models of the economy, they all use a common, basic set of assumptions as a point of departure. The basic model of the economy has three components: assumptions about how firms behave, assumptions about how consumers behave, and assumptions about the market in which these consumers and firms interact. Underlying much of economic analysis is the basic assumption of **rationality**. This assumption is based on the expectation that individuals and firms will act in a consistent manner, with a reasonably well-defined notion of what they like and what their objectives are, and with a reasonable understanding of how to attain those objectives.

For individuals, the rationality assumption is taken to mean that he or she makes choices and decisions in pursuit of his or her own self-interest. Different people will have different goals and desires. Bill may want to own a Porsche, have a large house in the country and work the long hours needed to provide for his family. Andrew prefers a less harried life-style. He is willing to accept a lower income for longer vacations and more quality time with his family.

The rationality assumption it taken to mean that firms operate to maximize their profits. The principle of rationality applies to decisions about gathering information as well. Rational firms and consumers decide whether to spend money and time to become more informed, for example about new technologies, or new products.

Exchange and the circular flow

Figure 2.2 is a broad schematic diagram showing the economic flows, which together constitute a market economy. Goods and services go from the business sector to consumers in exchange for payments, labelled 'consumer spending' in Figure 2.2. Consumers provide labour and funds, in the form of hours of work and stock purchases (or loans), to firms. Money payments in the form of wages and dividends are returned to households for these productive resources, providing households with incomes with which they will purchase more from the business sector.

This figure also shows a self-contained loop within the business sector, labelled 'intermediate goods'. The importance of this loop is growing by leaps and bounds, with far-reaching repercussions for the way in which economic activity is organized. Notably absent from our diagram is government activity.

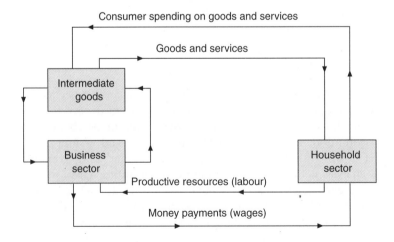

Figure 2.2 Relationship between households and business in the economy.

This simplification enables us to focus on the role of exchange. The 'consumer spending' and 'goods and services' flows result from activity surrounding the exchange in final goods markets. Of course, behind these aggregate flows are many, many individual markets. There is, for example, a market for cars, one for refrigerators and one for beds. Likewise the 'productive resources' and 'money payments' flows represent activity in different labour markets and in different capital (money, stock and bond) markets.

We now more clearly focus on our view of the economy and describe the forces operating in each of these markets.

C. The market mechanism

One of the best ways to appreciate the relevance of economics is to begin with the basics of supply and demand. Supply and demand analysis is a fundamental and powerful tool that can be applied to a wide variety of interesting and important problems.

In order to appreciate the workings of exchange, we begin by focusing on the case where there are many buyers and sellers, all buying and selling basically the same thing. This case is termed the *basic competitive model* by economists. Each firm is a price taker, which simply means that, because it cannot influence the market price, it must accept that price. On the other side of the market are rational individuals, each of whom would like to pay as little as possible for goods and services. The consumers also take the market price and quality as given.

The market economy revolves around exchange between individuals, who buy goods and services from firms, and firms, which buy productive resources, in particular labour and capital, from households. Many firms also sell their goods and services to other firms. This intermediate goods market is becoming even more important today.

The law of demand

Demand is the quantity of a good or service that customers are willing and able to purchase over a given period of time. For managerial decision-making, the primary focus is on market demand. Market demand, however, is merely the aggregation of individual demands, and insights into market demand relations is gained by understanding the nature of individual demand. Individual demand is determined by two factors: (1) the value associated with using the good or service, and (2) the ability to acquire it. Both are required for effective individual demand, and, hence, for market demand.

There are two basic types of individual demand: direct and derived demand. **Direct demand** is the appropriate concept for analyzing individual demand for goods and services that directly satisfy buyer desires. In this model the value of a good or service lies not in the product itself; but rather in the satisfaction provided by the good.

Other goods and services are acquired not for their direct consumption value but because they are required to produce, distribute or market other products. Engineers, production workers, natural resources and airplanes are all examples of goods and services demanded not for direct final personal consumption but rather for their use in providing other goods and services. We say that their demand is derived from the demand for the products that they help produce. The demand for all inputs used by a firm is **derived demand**.

Regardless of whether a good or service is demanded by individuals for final consumption or as an indirect factor used in providing other goods and services, the fundamentals of economic analysis provide a basis for investigating the characteristics of demand. When we make this relationship explicit, and define it over a range of prices, we create a **demand function**. It is customary to view the relationship with price determining quantity. We could state a demand function as follows:

$$q = f(p) \tag{2.1}$$

where q is the quantity of the good or service demanded, and p is the price of the good or service, other things being equal. The law of demand states that there is an inverse relationship between price and quantity.

A distinction must be made between the amount demanded at a given price and the whole schedule of quantities demanded at all relevant prices. If the price of a good or service falls, and nothing else changes, then the quantity demanded will increase, but the change in price will not affect the demand schedule. When we say that the quantity demanded is a function of price we state simply that, for every price, there is a corresponding quantity demanded. Though this is a convenient abstraction from all the other changes that normally take place at the same time, it is plausible that in general, sooner or later the consumer's ability and willingness to buy will be enhanced by a reduction in the price of a good or service. This is known as the *law of demand*.

The demand curve

How can the relationship between quantity demanded and price be represented? One method is to use a demand schedule. This is a numerical tabulation showing the quantity that is demanded at selected prices. Table 2.1 is a hypothetical demand schedule for computer chips. It lists the quantity of chips that would be demanded at various prices, other things being equal.

A second method of showing the relationship between quantity demanded and price is by an equation. Suppose that the demand curve is given by the following linear equation:

$$q = 10 - p \tag{2.2}$$

Table 2.1 Hypothetical demand schedule

Price	Quantity demanded
10	0
9	1
8	2
7	3
6	4
5	5
4	6
3	7
2	8
1	9
0	10

where q is the amount demanded and p is the price of computer chips. Instead of a general functional relationship between the amount demanded and the price, we now have a specific relationship between the amount demanded and the price. That is, we now have a specific demand by particular consumers for a given good. By substituting different values of p in equation (2.2), we can determine the amount that would be demanded at any price.

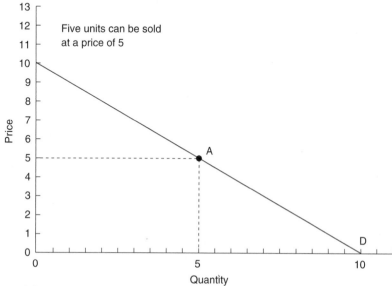

Figure 2.3 Demand curve.

Demand can also be represented geometrically by a **demand curve**. The linear demand curve or schedule in Figure 2.3 represents the complete relationship between quantity demanded and price, other things being equal. A single point on the demand curve indicates a single price–quantity combination. Notice that, while any point on the demand curve presents a specific quantity demanded, the demand curve as a whole shows all such combinations.

Before we continue with our study of demand functions, we must make sure we understand what a demand function shows. Consider once again the demand schedule shown in Table 2.1. Basically we may view the situation as follows: there are nine people, each willing to buy one unit of the good at prices ranging from 9 units of the notional currency down to 1. Suppose that we could get these nine people to stand in a line, with those who value the good the most in front of those who value the good the least. If we asked the first person in line what value she placed on her unit of the good, she would respond '9'. The second person would value the good at 8. The last, or ninth person in line would value the good at 1.

We can conclude, then, that every point on the demand function shows the value placed on one unit of the good by some buyer. This important interpretation of the demand function is frequently overlooked. It will become extremely useful to us in Chapter 5 when we consider externalities and their implication for a smoothly functioning price system.

If q number of computer chips can be sold at price p, then, if the price falls to p', the number of computer chips that will be demanded will increase.

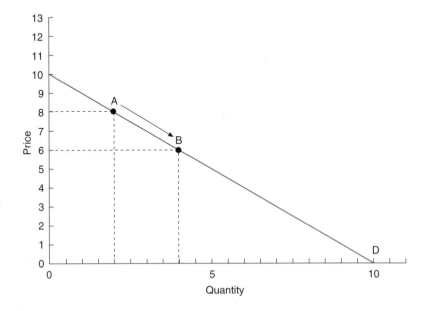

Figure 2.4a Movement along a given demand curve.

This variation in the number of chips sold is refered to as a **change in quan-tity demanded**, defined as a movement along a given demand curve as shown in Figure 2.4a (from point A to point B, or from $p=8$ to $p=6$).

A demand schedule (such as that in Table 2.1) and a demand curve are always defined with the assumption of *ceteris paribus*, a Latin phrase meaning all other things being constant. The other things that are constant are anything else that may affect buyer behaviour besides the good's or service's own price being held constant. A change occurs when any of the variables previously held constant shifts the entire demand curve to a new position. A shift to a new demand curve implies that the quantity demanded at each price has changed.

A **change in demand**, or shift from one demand curve to another, reflects a change in one of the non-price determinants of demand: income, the price of other goods, consumer tastes, population, advertising expenditures, etc. In Figure 2.4b, the rightward or upward shift in the demand curve from D_1 to D_2 indicates an increase in the quantity demanded at each and every price. Such a shift in the demand function indicates that consumers are willing to pay more for any unit of the good.

A leftward (downward) shift in demand would be termed a decrease in demand. A decrease in the demand for a good is consistent with consumers' willingness to pay less for any unit of a good.

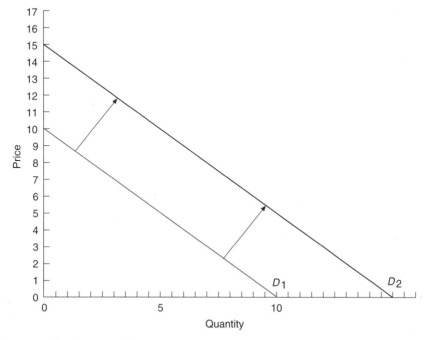

Figure 2.4b Change in demand.

Non-price determinants of demand

We should keep in mind that price is not the only factor that influences demand. For most goods and services there are a number of non-price determinants of demand that, if changed, will cause a shift in the demand function. Generally speaking, the effects of the non-price determinants of demand are felt in two ways: a change in the willingness and/or ability to pay, of existing consumers; or, a change in the number of consumers. The European Union (EU) has eliminated tariffs and other barriers between member states, and as new countries join the EU, the demand for good and services will grow.

After one of the most intense debates in recent years, the American House of Representatives approved the North American Free Trade Agreement (NAFTA) on 18 November 1993. The 234 to 200 vote was a huge victory for President Clinton, who pushed for the trade deal with Mexico and Canada that was actually negotiated by his Republican predecessor. A majority of Democrats – 156 – opposed the treaty, which would eliminate most barriers then in place to the export and import of goods and services among the United States, Canada and Mexico over the next 15 years. The treaty places 360 million consumers in the three countries, with a total annual economic output of $6 trillion, into a single, open, barrier-free market. The agreement took effect on 1 January 1994. What are the non-price determinants of demand, and how do they affect the demand curve?

One of the most important effects of NAFTA on demand will be the increase in the number of consumers in the market. Mexico alone adds over 100 million consumers. Mexicans who in 1993 purchased $40 billion worth of US exports will be buying more consumer goods, financial services, autos and agricultural goods, especially corn, grains, meat and soybeans. NAFTA integrates the US market with a large and growing Mexican consumer base. This will shift the demand curve to the right for a large number of consumer and capital goods.

Population is also an important determinant of demand. Population growth does not by itself create new demand. The additional people must have purchasing power before demand is changed. Extra people of working age, however, usually means extra output, and if they are productive, they will earn income. When this happens, the demand for all the commodities purchased by the new income earners will rise. A rise in population will shift the demand curves for goods and services to the right, indicating that more will be bought at each price. Both the additional income of Mexicans and the larger number of wage-earners should increase the demand for US products in Mexico.

The European Union (EU) represents a similarly large free trade area on the other side of the Atlantic based on the long-standing Common Market. A European monetary union (EMU) with a common currency (the ECU) is planned.

The law of supply

You now have a basic understanding of demand and the behaviour of consumers. The other half of the picture is supply and the behaviour of sellers. The term 'supply' also means something different to the economist from the meaning attached to the word in popular speech. **Supply** is the relationship between amounts of a commodity that sellers would be willing and able to make available for sale at alternative prices during a given time period, all other things remaining the same. As with demand, it is customary to view the quantity determined by price, holding all else constant. It too may be stated in mathematical terms:

$$q = f(p) \qquad (2.3)$$

where q is the quantity supplied and p is price. This expression does not indicate the nature of the price–quantity relationship; it simply says that, for any price, a corresponding quantity will be supplied. But this time common sense tells us that the relationship is a direct one. Unlike the demand curve, the supply curve slopes upward from left to right (as price increases). This property illustrates what is known as the *law of supply*.

The general relationship just discussed can be illustrated by a supply schedule that shows various price–quantity pairs. Table 2.2 represents a hypothetical supply schedule for computer chips. No chips will be offered for sale for prices at or below 2.50. We call 2.50 the **reservation price**. We may also consider the **supply function** in an explicit mathematical form. The values in Table 2.2, for example were created using the following equation:

$$q = 2p - 5 \qquad (2.4)$$

where q is the quantity supplied. The quantity supplied can be obtained by

Table 2.2 Hypothetical supply schedule

Price	Quantity supplied
10	15
9	13
8	11
7	9
6	7
5	5
4	3
3	1
2	0

supplying different values for price. For example, at the price of 8.98, 12.96 units per time period would be supplied.

The supply curve

The supply schedule can also be represented geometrically as a **supply curve**. The supply curve is the part of the supply function that expresses the relation between the price charged for a good or service and the quantity supplied, holding constant the effects of all other variables.

Before we go on to the more detailed workings of the supply concept we need to address one frequently overlooked issue of supply functions: namely when they exist. Interestingly enough, this issue has been addressed only at the higher levels of economic theory, although the ideas are very intuitive.

We now note that sellers hold the idea of the supply price for a given unit of output very near and dear to their hearts. A supply price is, of course, the price shown by the supply function. While this supply is important it only shows the minimum price at which a unit will be offered for sale. We know that sellers are greedy but, since this term has a decidedly negative connotation, we instead say that sellers are rational. Why would sellers provide the good at the lowest price? Only if they are pushed.

In short, a supply function exists only under conditions of perfect competition. Consider a market with only one seller. Does she have a supply function? No, she does not. In a market with a single seller, that seller is concerned with costs only in so far as costs are covered; that seller sets her price based solely upon what the market will bear.

A shift in the supply curve means that, at each price, a different quantity will be supplied than previously. As with the demand function, **changes in supply** occur when the supply function shifts to a new position in response to a change in one of the non-price determinants of supply. Production, distribution, marketing and selling are all processes that may affect the supply function in this way. A change in any costs related actually to providing the good or service to consumers will cause a change in supply. This is somewhat different from a **change in quantity supplied**, which occurs in response to a price change and involves a movement along a fixed supply function.

An increase in supply is shown as a shift in the supply function downward and to the right. Figure 2.5 shows an increase in supply from S_1 to S_2. If we adopt the logic that each point on the supply function shows the amount producers must be paid to bring a given unit of output to market, then we can claim that an increase in supply (such as shown in Figure 2.5) means that each unit is supplied to the market at a lower price. Similarly, a decrease in supply would be shown as an upward and leftward shift, implying that each unit brought to market appears at a higher price.

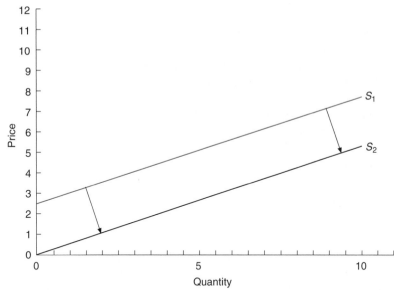

Figure 2.5 Change in supply.

Non-price determinants of supply

What will shift the whole supply curve? The concept of a supply curve pertains to things that affect the production, distribution, marketing and selling costs. If changes occur that decrease the final, total cost of providing consumers with a good or service, this will cause an increase in supply.

The price paid for a factor of production (or input) is a cost to the firm that uses it. A change in factor prices changes the price at which producers will be willing to sell any unit of output because it changes firm profitability. Just as profits are increased by an increase in the good or service price, factor costs remaining constant, so are they increased by a fall in factor prices, the price of the good or service remaining constant. An increase in factor prices reduces the profitability of a commodity at any given price of that good or service.

At any time, what is produced and how it is produced depends on what is known. Over time this knowledge changes. The enormous increase in production per worker that has been observed in industrial societies for the past 200 years is largely due to improved methods of production. Discoveries in computers have led to lower costs in the production of many goods and services. The invention of the microprocessor has revolutionized production of televisions, computers and satellites. Today many companies gather daily sales records so that inventories can be changed and production plans altered nearly as often.

D. Market equilibrium

Integrating the concepts of demand and supply establishes a framework for understanding how they interact to determine market price and quantities. When the quantity demanded and the quantity supplied of a good or service are in perfect balance at some price governing exchanges, the market for the good or service is in **equilibrium**. Another way of saying that a market is in equilibrium is to say that equilibrium has been achieved when there is no tendency for the price to change due to some unsatisfied (or excess) demand or supply at that price.

Surplus and shortage

There is only one price in equilibrium. Table 2.3 brings together the demand and supply schedules from Table 2.1 and Table 2.2. The quantities to be supplied and demanded at each price can be directly compared. There is only one price at which the quantity demanded and the quantity supplied are equal. At any price above equilibrium the quantity supplied will be greater than the quantity demanded. This is often refereed to as a situation of **surplus** or excess supply. The tendency for buyers to offer, and sellers to ask for, lower prices when there is excess supply implies a downward pressure on price. In many markets, consumers have come to expect excess supply at special times. For example at the end of summer, retailers often put air conditioners, swim suits and some sporting goods on sale.

Table 2.3 Market equilibrium, shortage and surplus

Price	Quantity demanded	Quantity supplied	Market status
10	0	15	Surplus
9	1	13	Surplus
8	2	11	Surplus
7	3	9	Surplus
6	4	7	Surplus
5	5	5	Equilibrium
4	6	3	Shortage
3	7	1	Shortage[a]
2	8	0	Shortage[a]
1	9	0	Shortage[a]
0	10	0	Shortage[a]

[a] There is technically a shortage at prices below 2.5, but no exchange occurs. Similarly, there is no exchange at prices equal to 10.

At prices less than equilibrium the quantity demanded will be greater than the quantity supplied and there will be a **shortage**. The tendency for buyers to offer, and sellers to ask for, higher prices when there is excess demand implies an upward pressure on price.

Neither surplus nor shortage will occur when a market is in equilibrium, since equilibrium is defined as a condition in which the quantities demanded and supplied are exactly in balance at the current market price. Surplus and shortage describe situations of market **disequilibrium** because both will result in powerful market forces being exerted to change the price and quantities offered in the market. At the equilibrium price there is no tendency for price to change as long as demand and supply remain unchanged.

The equilibrium price is determined by locating the price at which the quantity demanded is just equal to the quantity supplied. It terms of our algebraic model, we want to determine where the supply and demand functions have the same values for p and q. We can accomplish this by setting the two functions equal to each other and solving for p:

$$S = D$$
$$2p - 5 = 10 - p \qquad (2.5)$$
$$3p = 15$$
$$p = 5$$

Therefore,

$$Q_d = 10 - 5 = 5, \text{ and } Q_s = 10 - 5 = 5,$$

where Q_d is the quantity demanded and Q_s is the quantity supplied.

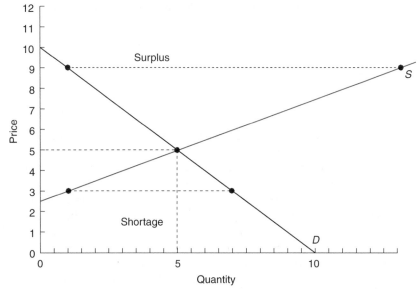

Figure 2.6 Market equilibrium.

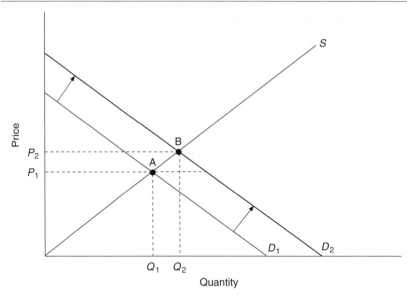

Figure 2.7 A new equilibrium: Increase in demand.

The above situation is depicted in Figure 2.6. The price of 5 is the equilibrium price because there is neither excess supply nor excess demand. All other prices are disequilibrium prices and, if they occur, the market will not be in a state of rest. At prices below the equilibrium, there will be shortages and rising prices. At prices above the equilibrium, there will be surpluses and falling prices.

Shifts in demand

Now let us look at the effect of an increase in demand on price and quantity. Figure 2.7 shows an increase in demand caused, for example, by an increase in income. With greater disposable income, consumers can spend more money on any good or service, and some consumers will do so for most goods. If the market price were held constant at P_1, we would expect to see excess demand. Facing this shortage, sellers would raise prices towards that level indicated by P_2. In Figure 2.7 this is shown as an increase in demand from D_1 to D_2.

In general, neither price nor quantity remains constant when disposable income increases. Rather, the market responds with a new equilibrium price and quantity, as the new demand force interacts with the existing supply force. In Figure 2.7 at point B we would expect to see consumers pay a higher price and firms produce a greater quantity, as a result of an increase in disposable income.

Shifts in supply

Now let us look at the supply curve. Suppose that there is a change in technology of production, lowering assembly costs. How does that affect supply? Lower production costs make production more profitable, encouraging existing firms to expand production and enabling new firms to enter the market and produce. So, if the market price stayed constant at P_1, we would expect to observe a greater supply of output than before. In Figure 2.8 this is shown as an increase from A to B. Output increases no matter what the price happens to be, so the entire supply curve shifts to the right, which is shown in the figure as a shift from S_1 to S_2. As a result the market price drops from P_1 to P_2, and the total quantity produced increases from Q_1 to Q_2. Lower costs result in lower prices and increased sales.

Comparative statics analysis

The approach above is referred to as **comparative statics**. That is, the theory is static rather than dynamic. Static theory compares different equilibrium points, for example the shift from equilibrium point A to B in Figure 2.8. Static theory assumes prompt adjustments to changes in the economic environment, and it is not concerned with the time required for changes to take place, or the organizational and managerial structure needed for the change. Static theory is concerned with determining the direction in which economic variables move in response to

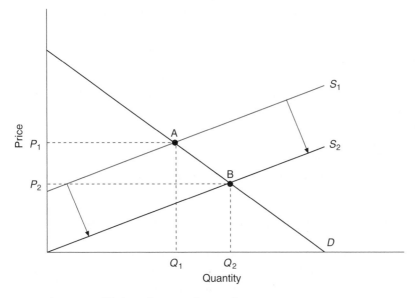

Figure 2.8 A new equilibrium: Increase in supply.

other variables. This is important since economic variables are seldom directly observable or easily manipulated. The comparison of the original equilibrium with the new equilibrium provides the economist with one of the most powerful tools at his disposal. Comparative statics analysis is designed to provide some of the tools which will assist the economist in his analysis of economic variables.

Algebraic example of shift in equilibrium

Suppose now that, with no change in supply, demand increases because of a change in income of consumers. The new demand function, denoted D', will be given by:

$$Q_d = 13 - P. \tag{2.6}$$

The new demand curve represents an increase in demand because, at any price, more units will be demanded now than previously. We may then determine the new equilibrium price as before by setting the supply function equal to the new demand function, D', and solving for P.

$$
\begin{aligned}
S &= D' \\
2P - 5 &= 13 - P \\
3P &= 18 \\
P &= 6
\end{aligned} \tag{2.7}
$$

Therefore $Q_d = 13 - 6 = 7$ and $Q_s = 12 - 5 = 7$

We can briefly review the concepts of supply and demand. The law of demand states that the quantity demanded of a good varies inversely with its price, other things remaining constant. The law of supply states that the quantity supplied of a good usually varies directly with its price, other things remaining constant. The intersection of the supply and demand curves indicates the equilibrium market price and quantity. A change in demand or a change in supply is represented by a shift of the curve to a new position. Such shifts may occur as a result of changes in any of the non-price determinants otherwise assumed to be constant. Finally, if the demand or supply curves remain fixed, a movement along the curve from one point to another denotes a change in the quantity demanded or a change in the quantity supplied.

E. Elasticity, total revenue and marginal revenue

As we have seen above, the relationship between price and quantity is one of causation. For example, a rise in price will cause a decrease in the quantity demanded. It is time that we turn out attention towards describing by how much the quantity demanded changes in response to variations in price.

Elasticity defined

Elasticity is a general economic concept that measures the change in one variable caused by changes in other, related variables. In short, elasticity measures sensitivity. What is interesting about the concept of elasticity is that it is a pure number, i.e. one to which no units are attached.

We can consider and compare elasticity measures for very different commodities. The quantity demanded of both apples and oranges depends on the prices of apples and oranges respectively. Elasticity enables a useful comparison to be made between the sensitivity of apple demand to changes in the price of apples and the sensitivity of orange demand to changes in the price of oranges.

We will be concerned with three types of demand elasticity in this section; price elasticity of demand, income elasticity of demand, and cross elasticity of demand.

Elasticity is a measure of responsiveness of one variable to changes in another. Specifically, it is a number that tells us the percentage change that will occur in one variable in response to a 1 per cent change in another variable. Remember that, for example, quantity demanded is a function of price, where price is an independent variable; that is, price determines quantity demanded. We can define a simple mathematical expression quantifying the concept of the price elasticity, ε_p, of demand. This expression is shown below in Equation 2.8, with the symbol Δ meaning change in:

$$\varepsilon_p = \frac{\% \, \Delta \, Q}{\% \, \Delta \, P} \tag{2.8}$$

Since price and quantity demanded are inversely related, ε_p is, technically speaking, a negative number. However, this measure is more easily interpreted if we ignore the minus sign and treat it as a positive entity. Economists consider three cases depending on the value for ε_p. Shortly, we will explain how numerical values are actually obtained for ε_p; for now, we concentrate on its intuitive meaning.

First, the case of weak percentage response of Q to a change in P is put in the category of **inelastic demand**. The numerator of ε_p is (very) small relative to the denominator. Thus, for goods with an inelastic demand, ε_p will be a (very) small number: between 0 and 1. Put more simply, goods whose demand is inelastic with respect to price are goods whose prices can drastically change with a (very) small resultant change in quantity demanded.

For goods with an **elastic demand**, a change in P causes a large change in the quantity demanded. The numerator of ε_p is (very) large relative to the denominator. Thus, for goods with an elastic demand, ε_p will be relatively large: between one and infinity. Put more simply, goods whose demand is elastic with respect to price are goods whose quantity demanded changes drastically for some change in price.

The in-between case, where the percentage change in P is equal to the percentage change in Q is called **unitary elasticity of demand**. In this case $\varepsilon_p = 1$.

The above equation for ε_p, Equation 2.8, is a mathematical equation that can be rearranged to the following:

$$\varepsilon_p = [(\Delta Q)/(\Delta P)] \times [P/Q] \tag{2.9}$$

Thus, the price elasticity of demand is the product of two terms. The first term shows the ratio of the change in quantity to the change in price. This concept is very similar to the concept of the slope of a function. In the traditional graphical representation of demand functions, price is put on the vertical axis and quantity is put on the horizontal axis. The expression $(\Delta Q)/(\Delta P)$ is then the inverse of (i.e. one divided by) the slope of the demand function. The second product in the expression for ε_p is the ratio of price to quantity.

In general, as we move along a given demand curve, the price elasticity of demand will change. Both the price–quantity ratio and the slope of the demand function may change. Therefore, the price elasticity of demand must be measured at a particular point on the demand curve; or, at the least, over a very small region of the demand curve.

Beware of a very common mistake. Often the slope of a curve is confused with its elasticity. You might think a steep slope must mean inelastic demand, and a flat slope must mean elastic demand. This is not quite true. Why not? Because the slope of the demand curve depends upon the absolute change in P and Q, whereas elasticity depends on the percentage change.

This can be easily demonstrated with a linear demand curve of the form

$$Q = a - bP \tag{2.10}$$

where a and b are numerical constants. As an example consider the following demand curve ($a = 10$ and $b = 1$):

$$Q = 10 - P \tag{2.11}$$

For this curve, $(\Delta Q)/(\Delta P)$ is constant and equal to -1. However, the curve does not have a constant elasticity. As shown in Figure 2.9, as we move down the demand curve the ratio P/Q falls, therefore the elasticity decreases in magnitude. Near the intersection of the curve with the price axis, Q is very small, so elasticity is large in magnitude. When $P = 7$ elasticity is greater than 1. When $P = 3$ elasticity is less than 1. As the demand curve approaches the vertical axis, the ratio of P/Q gets to be quite large, and elasticity approaches infinity. As the demand curve approaches the horizontal axis, the ratio P/Q approaches 0, causing elasticity also to approach 0. At the midpoint of the demand curve, $(\Delta Q)/(\Delta P) \times (P/Q) = -1$. This is the point of unitary elasticity.

If a demand curve is perfectly elastic throughout, or if it has an elasticity of zero at all points, it is not inappropriate to speak of the elasticity of the curve because the elasticity is uniform at all points or between any two points. The case of the perfectly elastic demand curve is an important one for economics,

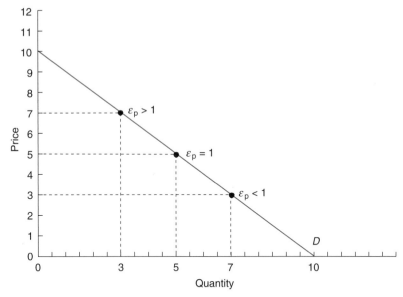

Figure 2.9 Elasticity and the demand curve.

and such a demand curve is just a horizontal line. It is infinitely elastic. A perfectly inelastic demand curve is said to have an elasticity of zero and is a vertical line.

Measurement of elasticity

Let us stop for a moment to examine the numerical details of the elasticity of demand calculation. There is always a slight ambiguity about percentage changes. Fortunately, when it comes to very small percentage changes, as from 99 to 100 or from 100 to 101, the difference between 1/99 and 1/100 becomes hardly worth talking about. For small changes, it matters little how you calculate the percentage change. For larger changes, it may make quite a difference. Unfortunately, no single approach can be declared to be the right one. Elasticity can be measured two different ways, point elasticity and arc elasticity. **Point elasticity** measures elasticity at a given point on a demand function and **arc elasticity** is a measurement done over a range of a function.

We have already obtained an equation, 2.9, that can be used to calculate the point elasticity of demand:

$$\varepsilon_p = [(\Delta Q)/(\Delta P)]\ [P/Q]$$

Recall that this implies that ε_p is the product of two ratios: the inverse of the slope of the demand function and the price-to-quantity ratio. In Figure 2.10, we show a linear demand function with the equation

$$Q = 100 - 5P \qquad\qquad (2.12)$$

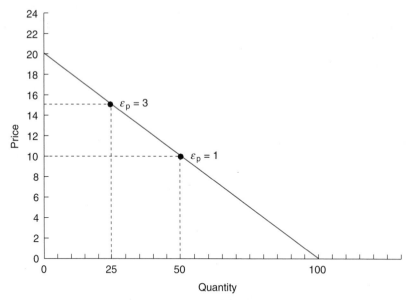

Figure 2.10 Measuring point elasticity.

To calculate the price elasticity of demand at various points on the demand function shown in Figure 2.10 we need three pieces of information: a price, a quantity and $\Delta Q/\Delta P$. At a price of 10, the quantity demanded is 50. Also at a price of 10, the $\Delta Q/\Delta P$ ratio is −5. Thus, the point elasticity of demand at $P=10$ is given by $[(\Delta Q)/(\Delta P)]\ [P/Q]$, or $(-5)\ (10/50) = -1$. Thus, when $P=10$, the demand function in Figure 2.10 has unitary elasticity. At a price of 15, the quantity demanded is 25, and the $\Delta Q/\Delta P$ ratio remains equal to −5. The point elasticity of demand when $P=15$ is then given by $(-5) \times (15/25) = -3$. At a price of 15, the demand function in Figure 2.10 is price elastic.

In general, for all linear demand curves of the form

$$Q = a - bP \qquad (2.13)$$

where a and b are numerical constants, the point elasticity of demand can be shown to be equal to

$$(-b)\ [P/(a - bP)] \qquad (2.14)$$

Notice that, for linear functions, the $\Delta Q/\Delta P$ term is constant, that is, does not vary with P or Q.

Arc elasticity is an alternative measurement of the price elasticity of demand. The calculation of arc elasticity requires far less information than does the calculation of point elasticity.

When calculating arc elasticity, it is important to determine the percentage change based on the averages of the price and quantity ranges. For example, consider the calculation of the elasticity of demand for movie tickets between 8 and 9. If you calculate the percentage change with 8 as the base the percentage change will be 12.5 per cent. However, if you calculate the same change with 9 as the base the percentage change will be 11 per cent. What is a good rule to use? A good rule to use is to calculate the price change relative to neither the higher nor the lower of the two prices, but to their average. Arc elasticity measures the average elasticity over a given range of a demand curve. We assume then that we know two points on the demand curve. Let those two points be (Q_1,P_1) and (Q_2,P_2). The arc elasticity formula is:

$$\frac{\Delta Q/\text{average } Q}{\Delta P/\text{average } P} \quad \text{or} \quad [(Q_1 - Q_2)/(P_1 - P_2)] \div [(P_1 + P_2)/(Q_1 + Q_2)] \quad (2.15)$$

Arc elasticity can be estimated from the following demand curve:

$$Q_d = 30 - 5P \qquad (2.16)$$

Assume that the price is increased from 2 to 4. At the 4 price, the quantity demanded is 10, and at 2, the quantity demanded is 20. The change in Q, ΔQ, is 10, the average Q is $(20+10)/2 = 15$; the change in P, ΔP, is 2; and the aver-

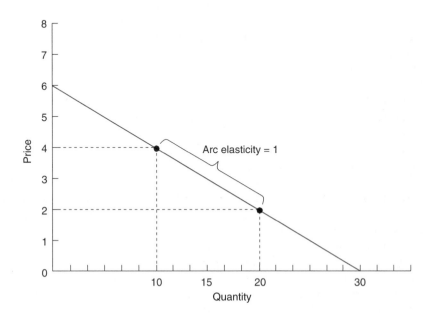

Figure 2.11 Measuring arc elasticity.

age P is 3. Substituting these values into the equation for arc elasticity yields

$$\frac{10/15}{-2/3}$$

which simplifies to –1, in Figure 2.11.

Which measure, point or arc, to use depends on the problem to be studied, and the amount of information available to the decision maker. When the range of change is small and approaches zero, the point elasticity formula is preferred. However, when the range is greater than, for example, 5 per cent, it is appropriate to use the arc elasticity formula. We also point out that using the point elasticity formula requires that the analyst know the exact demand function, or at least its slope. If it is assumed that the demand function is not stable, that is, has shifted over time, using the arc formula may pose a problem because the analyst might end up comparing two points on two separate demand functions.

Price elasticity of demand

What determines the price elasticity of demand for particular goods? While it is important to be able to quantify the various measures of elasticity, there is a great deal of intuition involved in finding what factors cause a good to have an elastic or inelastic demand.

Far and away the most important factor in determining elasticity is the availability of substitutes for a particular good. As more substitutes are available, demand becomes more and more elastic. As fewer substitutes are available, demand becomes more and more inelastic. The demand for the experimental AIDS drug AZT is probably very, very inelastic. Even though the price of AZT could conceivably increase greatly, there would be little variation in the quantity of the good demanded by AIDS patients. However, if the price of potato chips were to increase substantially, consumers would very likely shift their consumption towards pretzels and nachos.

Also related to the availability of substitutes is the width of the definition used in defining the good. For widely defined goods, demand will tend to be more price inelastic than for more narrowly defined goods, since there are few close substitutes. For example, the demand for meat is probably price inelastic. The demand for beef or chicken is probably more responsive to changes in the prices of these goods, and, hence, more elastic.

A third dimension which affects the price elasticity of demand concerns the percentage of a consumer's budget spent on a commodity. If consumers spend a very small portion of their budget on a commodity, there is a tendency for demand to be price inelastic. We probably spend an almost negligible percentage of our incomes on salt; the demand for salt is likely to be very price inelastic.

Price elasticity and total revenue

One of the most useful features of the concept of price elasticity is that it can be used to predict the effect of price changes on total revenue. Remember that elasticity can be equal to 1, greater than 1, or less than 1. Depending on the degree of price elasticity, a reduction in price can increase total revenue, decrease it, or leave it unchanged. If we have a good estimate of price elasticity, we can estimate quite accurately the change in total revenue.

Recall from your principles of economics course that **total revenue** (TR) is equal to price (P) times quantity (Q). If we change price in one direction, there will be a change in quantity in the opposite direction; the net effect on total revenues depends on which effect dominates. Say, for example, that price increases and quantity decreases. The higher price, by itself, will tend to raise total revenues; the lower quantity sold, will tend to reduce total revenues. The resolution of these opposing forces on total revenues depends on the price elasticity of demand.

If demand is price elastic, then ε_p is greater than 1, and the %Δ in Q is larger than the %Δ in P. If price increases when demand is price elastic, the impact of the quantity effect dominates the impact of the price effect, and total revenues will fall. Likewise, if demand is price elastic, a price decrease will cause total revenues to increase.

A summary of the effects on total revenues from price changes is shown below in Table 2.4.

A more mathematical treatment of the price elasticity of demand and its relationship to total revenues is also possible and is contained in the appendix to this chapter.

Income elasticity of demand

We may be interested in elasticities of demand with respect to other variables besides price. Income is another important determinant of demand. For example, demand for most goods usually rises when income rises. The **income elasticity of demand** measures the responsiveness of demand to changes in

Table 2.4 Elasticity and total revenue

The case of	Implies	Following a price increase, revenue	Following a price decrease, revenue
1. Elastic demand, $\varepsilon_p > 1$	%ΔQ > %ΔP	Decreases	Increases
2. Unitary elasticity, $\varepsilon_p = 1$	%ΔQ = %ΔP	Is unchanged	Is unchanged
3. Inelastic demand, $\varepsilon_p < 1$	%ΔQ < %ΔP	Increases	Decreases

income, holding constant the effect of all other variables that influence demand.

The income elasticity of demand is the percentage change in the quantity demanded, Q, resulting from a 1 per cent change in income (I):

$$\varepsilon_I = \frac{\%\Delta Q}{\%\Delta I}$$

(2.17)

Income and the quantity purchased usually move in the same direction; thus ε_I is usually greater than zero, although it may conceivably be negative. When ε_I is positive, the good is said to be a normal good; when ε_I is negative, the good is said to be an inferior good. Automobiles, jewellery and housing are normal goods. Some examples of inferior goods are generic potato chips, public transport and beer.

Cross-price elasticity of demand

The demand for most goods is also affected by the price of other goods. For example, because butter and margarine can easily be substituted for each other, the demand for each depends on the price of the other. As the price of chicken rises so does the demand for beef. The **cross-price elasticity of demand**, $\varepsilon_{x,y}$, for goods x and y, refers to the percentage change in the quantity demanded for good x resulting from a 1 per cent increase in the price of another good or service, y. So, for example, the cross price elasticity of demand for butter with respect to the price of margarine would be written as

$$\varepsilon_{b,m} = \% \; \Delta \text{ quantity of butter}/\% \; \Delta \text{ price of margarine}$$

(2.18)

F. Gains from competitive markets

We would like to examine how exchange in a free and competitive market leads to gains for both buyers and sellers. Consumers buy goods because the purchases make them better off. However, because different consumers value particular goods and services differently the maximum they are willing to pay for these goods and services will also vary. **Consumer surplus** is the difference between what a consumer is willing to pay for a good and what he actually pays. For example, suppose that one consumer values a good much more highly than another. However, they both will pay the same price for the commodity in competitive markets because then there is only one price. In other words, some consumers would pay more for a good or service than they had to.

Suppose, for example, that there are two consumers in the market, Danny and Andrew. Danny values the one unit of the good he purchases at 15; Andrew

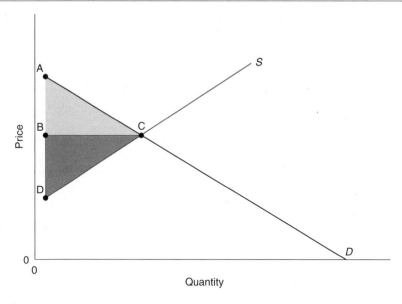

Figure 2.12 Benefits of exchange.

values his one unit of the good at 10. If the market price of the good is 10 then Danny earns a consumer surplus of 5 and Andrew earns no consumer surplus. Andrew is not hurt by the transaction; he will still buy his unit for 10. The total consumer surplus in this market is then 5.

In a more general sense, the consumer surplus in a free, competitive market is all of the area under the demand function and above the market price. In Figure 2.12, the amount of consumer surplus is shown as the area of the triangle ABC. Notice that triangle ABC is bounded above by the demand function and below by the horizontal line at the market price.

An analogous concept to consumer surplus exists for the supply curve called **producer surplus**. Producer surplus is the area above the supply curve and below the market price. It is measured by the triangle DBC in Figure 2.12. Some producers are producing goods and services just at the market price. At a lower price these producers would not be in the market. However, there are some producers who would be willing to produce if the price were below the market price. These producers would sell even if the market price were lower because their costs are lower.

Therefore, consumer surplus and producer surplus measure the welfare benefits of a competitive market. The total gain from exchange is measured by the area between the supply curve and the demand curve.

Considered jointly, consumers and producers are made as well off as possible by exchange in free, competitive markets. Technically we would say the sum of producer and consumer surplus is maximized under free, competitive exchange.

G. Chapter summary and key ideas

This chapter has explained how competitive exchange works. First we examined the scientific method. Economists rely on the scientific method to study markets. Economists use both normative and positive economics to examine the economy. The economy is organized by markets that facilitate exchange between households and firms.

The main force operating on exchange in the economy is competition. When competition is perfect, government will not have to intervene in the market. The basic competitive model in the economy studies demand, supply and price. Demand is the quantity of goods or services that customers are willing and able to purchase. Supply is the quantity of goods and services that firms are willing to supply. The equilibrium price is when the quantity demanded and the quantity supplied are in equilibrium. If the quantity demanded is greater than the quantity supplied there will be a shortage in the market. If the quantity demanded is less than the quantity supplied there will be a surplus in the economy.

A change in demand is a shift from one demand curve to another, reflecting a change in one of the non-price determinants of demand. A change in supply is a shift from one supply curve to another, reflecting a change in one of the non-price determinants of supply. The study of two equilibrium points is comparative statics.

Elasticity is a measure of responsiveness of one variable to another. Price elasticity of demand is the percentage change in the quantity demanded of a good resulting from a 1 per cent increase in the price of that good. Demand for a good may either be elastic, inelastic or unit elastic. Two other measured elasticities of demand are income elasticity of demand and cross-price elasticity of demand.

One of the most useful features of elasticity is that it can be used to predict the effect of price changes on total revenue. If demand is elastic a decrease in price will result in an increase in revenue. If demand is inelastic an increase in price will result in an increase in revenue.

Competitive exchange leads to the concept of consumer and producer surplus. These gains from exchange are an important outcome of the market economy.

Appendix A: Price elasticity, demand and total revenue

In this appendix we use some of the tools available from mathematics to shed some light on the relationship between the price elasticity of demand and total revenue.

We begin with a general statement of a demand function that is inverted; that is, it expresses P as a function of Q rather than Q as a function of P.

Notice that P and Q are still negatively related and that an increase in Q can be obtained only by a reduction in P.

$$P = a - bQ \qquad\qquad (2A.1)$$

The notation implies that a and b represent any positive, constant values. We will refer to a as the vertical intercept, because it reveals the value for price, P, when Q is zero. Likewise, b is termed the slope of the function because it shows the change in P for a one-unit change in Q. When the demand relationship is written in this way, it is referred to as the *average revenue*, or *AR*, function because it shows the revenue received for each of Q units sold.

Because total revenues, TR, are equal to price times quantity, we can multiply each side by Q to obtain:

$$TR = ARQ = PQ = (a - bQ)Q$$

or,
$$\qquad\qquad (2A.2)$$
$$TR = aQ - bQ^2$$

Marginal revenue, MR, is defined as the change in total revenue resulting from a one-unit change in output, Q. As such, we can write the marginal revenue function, also expressed in terms of Q, as: [2]

$$MR = a - 2bQ \qquad\qquad (2A.3)$$

Some additional intuition is possible by looking at all of these relationships in a graphical context. This is accomplished in the two panels of Figure 2.13. Panel (a) shows a total revenue function of the form discussed above. In panel (b) you will find the corresponding average and marginal revenue functions. In these displays, the values for a and b are 100 and 0.25, respectively. Thus, the functions are

Average Revenue or *AR*: $P = 100 - 0.25Q$
Total Revenue: $TR = PQ = 100Q - 0.25Q^2$
Marginal Revenue: $MR = 100 - 0.5Q$

In panel (a) of Figure 2.13, notice that total revenues are maximized when $Q = 200$ at point C. In panel (b), notice that marginal revenue equals zero whenever $Q = 200$. A comparison of equations 2A.1 and 2A.3 displayed for the sample values of a and b in panel (b) yields some insights as well. Both the average revenue and the marginal revenue share the same vertical intercept, 100 in this example and a in general. Also note that the marginal revenue is twice as steep as the average revenue function. Thus, given the same starting point, the *AR* function hits the horizontal axis twice as fast as does the *MR* function.

It is also true that total revenues are maximized whenever marginal revenue equals zero. We can easily argue this point without the use of mathematical techniques. First, the marginal revenue function is decreasing. Secondly, when the

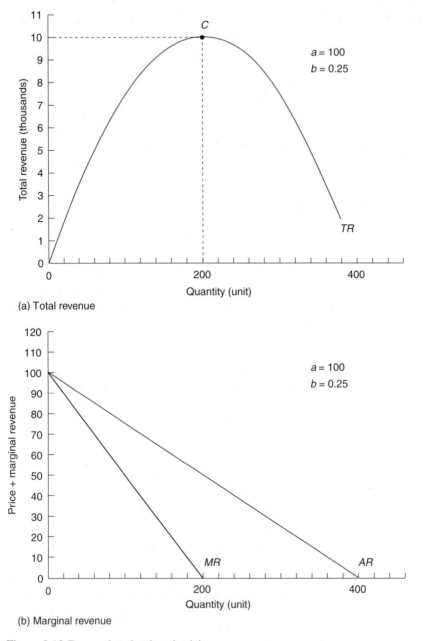

(a) Total revenue

(b) Marginal revenue

Figure 2.13 Demand and price elasticity.

MR function is positive, additional output causes an increase in total revenues. Likewise, when the *MR* function is negative, additional output causes a decrease in total revenues. Thus, for total revenues to be maximized, *MR* must be zero.

Appendix B: Price elasticity and optimal pricing policy

A bit of knowledge relating demand, total revenues and price elasticity can be of great help to managers in determining an appropriate pricing policy. The simple relationship between marginal revenue, price and point elasticity of demand may be one of the most useful pricing tools managerial economics has to offer. The relationship between marginal revenue, price and point price elasticity of demand can be stated as follows:

$$MR = P(1 + 1/\varepsilon_p) \qquad\qquad (2B.1)$$

where ε_p is the point elasticity of demand.

To illustrate the usefulness of this relationship, recall from your introductory course that the firm maximizes profits by producing when $MR = MC$. By equating marginal costs with marginal revenues, the profit-maximizing level of output can be determined.

Suppose that your local supermarket ran a sale on hamburgers last week and found that a 4 per cent discount resulted in a 12 per cent increase in weekly sales. The point elasticity of demand for hamburgers is:

$$\varepsilon_p = \frac{\% \ \Delta \ \text{in} \ Q}{\% \ \Delta \ \text{in} \ P}$$
$$= 12/{-4}$$
$$= -3$$

What is the optimal price for hamburgers if the supermarket's relevant marginal cost per unit for hamburgers is 1.50? Working with equation 2B.1, we can build the following relationship:

$$MC = MR$$
$$MC = P(1 + 1/\varepsilon_p)$$

which implies that the optimal or profit-maximizing price, $P^{\star}$, equals

$$P^{\star} = \frac{MC}{(1 + 1/\varepsilon_p)}$$

With marginal cost of 1.50 and $\varepsilon_p = -3$, the profit-maximizing price is then

$$P^{\star} = \frac{1.50}{(1 + 1/{-3})}$$
$$= 2.25$$

Therefore, the profit-maximizing price on the supermarket's hamburgers is 2.25 a pound. The preceding equations can be used to calculate the profit-maximizing price under current cost and market conditions as well as under a variety of conditions.

Table 2.5 Demand, total revenue, marginal revenue and elasticity.

Price (P)	Quantity (Q)	Total revenue (TR = P*Q)	Marginal revenue (MR = ΔTR/ΔQ)	Point price elasticity ($\varepsilon_p = (\Delta Q/\Delta P)\ \varepsilon_p\ (P/Q)$)
10	0	0	0	
9	40	360	80	−9.00
8	80	640	60	−4.00
7	120	840	40	−2.33
6	160	960	20	−1.50
5	200	1,000	0	−1.00
4	240	960	−20	−0.66
3	280	840	−40	−0.43
2	320	640	−60	−0.25
1	360	360	−80	−0.11

Sometimes managers are interested in maximizing total revenues rather than profits. Equation (2B.1) can also be used to help managers achieve these ends. We can clearly see that if, at the price charged, demand is price elastic and marginal revenues are positive, lowering price will increase total revenues.

In Table 2.5 we display a numerical example drawn from the sample values of Appendix A. The demand relationship is shown in the first two columns. A price of 6 in this example is seen to be too high because lowering it to 5 increases total revenues.

Key words

arc elasticity	derived demand
change in demand	direct demand
change in quantity demanded	disequilibrium
	elastic demand
change in quantity supplied	elasticity
change in supply	equilibrium
comparative statics	hard sciences
consumer surplus	income elasticity of demand
cross-price elasticity of demand	inelastic demand
	logical positivism
demand	market
demand curve	normative economics
demand function	perfect competition

point elasticity	soft science
positive economics	supply
producer surplus	supply curve
rationality	supply function
reservation price	surplus
scientific method	total revenue
shortage	unitary elasticity of demand

Questions and problems for review and discussion

1 Construct (i.e. draw) a supply and demand model to explain the
   following three situations. Please include with each picture a brief
   paragraph of explanation.
   (a) Consider the market segment for cars that contains the Ford
       Taurus and Honda Accord. Explain what you expect to happen to
       the price of Ford Taurus if the exchange rate between the dollar
       and yen changes substantially. Suppose that the dollar becomes
       much stronger relative to the yen.
   (b) Show the effects in the market for cigarettes if President Clinton's
       health plan is passed and a tax is imposed on a package of
       cigarettes that approximately equals its current price.
   (c) Show the effects in the market for 'lunch' in the area near your
       university if a new restaurant featuring cheap and fast food opens
       directly nearby.
   (d) Consider the market for generic paper towels. This is the paper
       towel market for those of us consumers who lack the purchasing
       power to buy Kleenex or some other name brand. Suppose that, as
       a result of an economic expansion, real consumer incomes increase
       by 30 per cent. Show the effects of this increase in real income in
       the generic paper towel market.
2 Explain whether the following goods and services have a demand that
   is either price elastic or inelastic. Be sure to explain clearly why you
   have chosen your answer.
   (a) Secretaries.
   (b) Strawberries.
   (c) Gasoline.
   (d) Cigarettes.
3 Advertising serves many goals in our economic system (some of these
   are noble). One purpose of advertising in consumer goods markets is
   to differentiate products. There are, for example, about a billion
   different types of laundry soaps; each is nearly equally able to clean

your clothes. Explain, using the concept of the price elasticity of demand, one rationale for this practice. Be sure to use all the relevant concepts and frame your discussion in language that a layperson could understand.

4 Assume for this question that the necessary competitive assumptions are fulfilled and that the market for used cars is blessed with competition among and between sellers. Information is not freely distributed in this market. For any given used car, the seller would have a tremendous informational advantage over any potential buyer. Explain how the supply and demand functions would differ because of this uneven spread of information. In any diagram that you may (should) draw, make one demand and supply function where information is not a problem. On that same diagram (if you draw it), include curves that show the effects in the market of the uneven distribution of information.

5 Suppose that I am selling cans of beer to people on a beach. Because I am concerned about my income (and because I am the only beer seller), I decide to sell the beer in the following way. I will not tell the people on the beach how many cans of beer I have. I will sell the cans of beer individually, or one at a time, to my customers. Each can of beer will go to the highest bidder, and the person who buys the can of beer from me will be required to consume the beer. As such, I am basically holding an auction for the beer. The first can of beer sells for 3.70. The second can of beer sells for 3.40, the third for 3.10, the fourth for 2.80, the fifth for 2.50, and the sixth for 2.20.

   (a) In either tabular or graphical form, show the demand for beer function for the consumers on the beach.
   (b) If I offer to sell the beer at a single price of 2.80 (i.e. do not follow my auction scheme), how many cans of beer will I sell?
   (c) If I sell the beer at a single price of 2.20, what is the consumer surplus in the market?
   (d) If I sell the beer individually according to the rules of the auction, what is the consumer surplus?

6 (a) Draw a supply and demand curve for the market for beer for people on the beach of problem (E) if I am going to sell the beer according to rules stated there for the auction.
   (b) Is there a supply function? Explain why or why not.

Notes

1 The art of economics is the application of the knowledge learned in positive economics to the achievement of the goals determined in normative economics. This three-part distinction dates back to John Neville Keynes.

2 For those who know some calculus, the marginal revenue function is obtained by taking the derivative of the total revenue function with respect to Q. If you don't know calculus, take our word for it.

Reference

Smith, A. (1976 [1776]), *An Inquiry into the Nature and Causes of the Wealth of Nations*, Chicago: University of Chicago Press.

Neoclassical firms in perfectly competitive markets

A. Chapter outline and student goals

How will we, as a society, look back on the changes in economic activity in the past 20 to 25 years of the twentieth century? There is a tendency to identify eras with various products or markets that dominated conversation at that time. We may, for example, look back at the reorganization in control and ownership dimensions of firms: the busting up of the conglomerates and the spinnings offs of the early 1980s and the subsequent trend in the mid- to late 1990s of strategic mergers. There was, arguably, an even more dominant trend in the organization of economic activity over that time; one that we even today take for granted – the advent of the silicon chip.

The rate of advance in computing power was so apparent that a rule-of-thumb widely accepted by industry professionals and analysts was developed. According to the principle known as Moore's Law, at any given price level, microchips, the building blocks for the 'brains' of a computer, double in performance every 18 months. As computers become more powerful, they also become less expensive. Advances in hardware lead to even more impressive and usable software, which, in turn, leads to increased communication capability.

How did producers react to the increased computing power? Machines were created that could do what no machine had ever done before. In other words, machines were created that could do many of the tasks done only by hand before.

Clearly the prices of inputs available to producers of goods and services changed drastically. Firms had to determine the optimal mix of technology and labour in order to remain competitive in their industries. Granted, the situation was somewhat clouded by an aversion to simply replacing living, breathing humans with cold, hard machines. However, even for the most compassionate managers, some changes were clearly called for.

In this chapter we address the issue of input substitution in the appropriate theoretical context. Furthermore, we raise and address many other issues that are important to managers in today's firms.

In the perfectly competitive economy, there are many firms and each is a price taker responding freely to prices set by the market. No single firm has any market power or control over the price of its product. Individual producers are passive quantity adjusters who respond to market signals.

The analysis of this chapter differs from that found throughout the remainder of the book. In the neoclassical model considered here, the firm is a black box. It is a black box in the sense that a computer chip is a black box. You may know what it does, but you have very little understanding of how the microprocessor in your computer actually works. Before you become smug and revel in your expertise, answer a simple question, 'If it broke, could you fix it?' Representing the black box in the neoclassical view of the firm is a production function. In later chapters as we consider the organizing influences on the behaviour within firms – the principal–agent model and the transaction costs model – the makeup of the black box becomes more complex as components are added. Fortuitously, we know something about the production function component in the black box. This knowledge is useful to us because most firms and organizations in the economy either actually produce something or add value for their customers, which is something very similar to production.

After you have finished reading this chapter you should be able to:

- understand what economists mean when they speak of a production function as it relates to both the long and short run;
- understand the intuitive nature of the rule determining the optimum level of use for variable inputs to production – in particular, be able to explain why the demand for labour curve slopes downward and what guidelines firms follow regarding substituting inputs for each other as an input price changes;
- identify the various managerial cost measures provided by economic analysis;
- relate the unit cost and output relationships back to the production process in which they arise;
- understand the mechanics operating in what economists call perfectly competitive markets;
- adopt the neoclassical view of firm behaviour in explaining firm behaviour in perfectly competitive markets.

B. The theory of production: I

Production functions

Defined: outputs and inputs
The theory of production is concerned with the way in which physical resources are employed to produce a firm's products. 'Production' refers to the process by which one group of goods and services called 'inputs' is converted into another group of goods and services called 'outputs'. We can divide

inputs into the traditional broad categories of labour, technology, materials and capital. Labour inputs include skilled workers and unskilled workers, as well as the efforts of the firm's managers. Technology encompasses the level of knowledge available to a given firm. Materials include steel, plastics, electricity, water and so on. Capital includes what we usually think of fixed inputs: buildings, machines, trucks, computers and inventories.

A **production function** is a descriptive statement that relates inputs to outputs. It specifies the maximum output that can be produced for given amounts of inputs. The actual production function is determined by the given state of technology (i.e. a given state of knowledge about the various methods that might be used to transform inputs into outputs). Any investment in technology – for example a new, faster computer chip – that permits the firm to produce a given output with fewer inputs results in the determination of a new production function. Thus, it is useful (though not perhaps technically absolutely 100 percent correct) to think of technology as 'shifting' a production function in much the same way that changes in income shift a consumer demand function.

The production function describes what is technically feasible when the firm operates in a technically efficient way. **Technical efficiency** refers to the situation in which the firm uses each combination of inputs in a manner that produces the largest possible output.

A production function may be expressed in many ways. One of the more common ways is a mathematical representation where a single output Q is related to a number of inputs, say K, the amount of capital available, L, the amount of labour available, and M, the amount of materials available. In mathematical terms the expression could look like this:

$$Q=f(K,L,M). \tag{3.1}$$

To 'read' the production function we would make a statement such as the following. If you tell me the amounts of the inputs K, L and M that are available to the firm, I can tell you Q, the maximum attainable outputs from those inputs per unit time. Suppose, for example, that in a consulting firm the amount of consulting services produced, S, is dependent on A, the number of accountants available, and C, the number of networked computers available in the firm. The production function might look like this (where output S is measured in thousands of hours of services):

$$S = 300 \ A^{1/2}C^{1/2} \tag{3.2}$$

Then, if 10 accountants are used with 10 networked computers, the firm could, if everything goes right, produce 3,000,000 hours of consulting services per year.

Returns to scale

The concept of **returns to scale** refers to the relation between the changes in output caused by a proportional change in all inputs. There are three possible ranges to consider.

Under conditions of constant returns to scale, if all inputs are simultaneously increased by some percentage, then output will increase by precisely that percentage. Within the idea of constant returns to scale there are no bonuses or penalties involved in adding inputs. If all inputs are increased by, say 5 per cent, then output will expand by that same 5-per cent.

Using the notation above, where S refers to the thousands of hours of consulting services, A refers to the number of accountants and C refers to the number of networked computer workstations, the production process indicated above in equation (3.2) exhibits constant returns to scale. When 10 accountants and 10 networked computer workstations are used, output is 3,000,000 hours of accounting services. If all inputs are increased by 10 per cent then the 11 accountants using the 11 networked computer workstations can produce 3,300,000 hours of consulting services per year.

Sometimes it appears as though there are benefits to size in production, at least over some wide range of input usage. **Increasing returns to scale** exist in production if an equal percentage change in all inputs yields a proportionately larger change in output. If there are increasing returns to scale in production, then a 10 per cent increase in all inputs used by the firm will result in a greater than 10 per cent increase in output. Using the notation from the example above (in equation (3.2)), consider the production function:

$$S = 30 \ AC \qquad\qquad (3.3)$$

If 20 accounts are used ($A = 20$) along with 20 networked computers ($C = 20$) then 12,000,000 hours of consulting services can be produced. If the amount of all inputs is increased by 10 per cent, then 14,520,000 hours of consulting services are produced. Notice that the increase in output (2,520,000) is greater than a 10 per cent increase in the output when 20 units of each unit are employed. One could think of increasing returns to scale in production occurring in the production of very complex items requiring many specialized steps in their creation, such as the production of motorcycles. At low levels of input usage, inputs, including human labour, must be forced into multiple tasks. At higher levels of input usage, inputs, including human labour, are able to specialize in production, resulting in some efficiency gains.

The remaining possible case of returns to scale is **decreasing returns to scale**.[1] There are said to be decreasing returns to scale if an increase in all inputs of, say, X per cent results in a less than X per cent increase in output. The likelihood of a firm experiencing decreasing returns to scale may seem counterintuitive and subject to deserved debate. Typically one could expect any firm to replicate (perhaps allowing for a period of learning) itself and achieve at least constant returns to scale. Another set of problems with which we will concern ourselves in later chapters could also theoretically lead to decreasing returns to scale. If increases in inputs occur, the job of management in terms of managing and coordinating the increased level of activity may become very complex. The size of firms may lead to certain efficiencies if workers or suppliers to the firm are able to hide less than perfect performance behind the bureaucracy inherent in the size of the firm itself.

Timeframe

We engage in an analysis of production that is dependent upon the choices available to the firm in terms of altering its use of inputs. More specifically, it is important that we know whether or not we are talking about a period of time over which the firm can alter its inputs. In the **short run**, there is usually at least one **fixed input**, that is, an input whose supply to the firm is constant. Regarding a fixed input, the firm's choice is either to use the input to some degree or not. A university building, for example, represents a fixed input. The university cannot expand the amount of space available in the short run, nor can it reduce the space available in the short run. The entire building, or portions thereof, may be left vacant however. Although it is reasonable to assume that the shortest run describes a period in which all inputs are fixed to the firm, there is then really nothing left to analyze. We will assume that the short run is not so short that there is at least one input that is not fixed. A variable input is one that the firm can alter its supply of. Thus, in the short run, if a firm chooses to expand output it may do so only by increasing the amount(s) of the variable input(s) it has to work with.

The **long run** refers to a period of time over which there are no fixed factors of production. In the long run, the firm may build additional plants, renovate existing ones, close some plants down, or any combination thereof. The concept of returns to scale introduced above is clearly a long-run concept.

Returns to a factor

To understand the ins and outs of production and production functions better it is necessary to learn some terminology. We turn our attention to a problem couched in the traditional notation used in economic analysis. We consider a production process where units of output, Q, are produced by combining two inputs, K and L. Such a function is given below:

$$Q = f(K,L) \qquad (3.4)$$

Assume that a firm starts with a fixed amount of capital, K, and contemplates applying various amounts of labour, L, to it. The output of the variable and fixed inputs will be referred to as **total product**. Clearly the manager knows that in this short-run situation changes in Q require changes in the variable input L, with the amount of K fixed.

Table 3.1 shows the information our hypothetical manager faces. The amount of the variable input is shown in column 1. The second column shows the amount of the fixed factor, K. The third column is total product. Notice that, when labour is zero, total product is also zero. You cannot produce without

Table 3.1 Production with one variable input

(1) Labour	(2) Fixed capital, K	(3) Total product, Q	(4) Average product, Q/L	(5) Marginal product, ΔQ/ΔL
0	20	0	–	–
1	20	10	10	10
2	20	30	15	20
3	20	60	20	30
4	20	80	20	20
5	20	95	19	15
6	20	108	18	13
7	20	112	16	4
8	20	112	14	0
9	20	108	12	-4
10	20	100	10	-8

any variable inputs. As variable inputs increase, total product is initially increased, but eventually declines. For any given production process it is important to understand the relationship between the amount of variable input usage and changes in total product.

The **marginal product** of an input is the change in total product resulting from the use of one more unit of the variable factor, holding all other factors constant. The marginal product can be expressed as:

$$\text{Marginal product} = \frac{\text{Change in output}}{\text{Change in variable input}} = \frac{\Delta Q}{\Delta L} \qquad (3.5)$$

The marginal product of the input L in our hypothetical example is shown in column 5 of Table 3.1. For example, with capital fixed at 20, when labour is increased from 3 to 4 units total product increases from 60 to 80, creating a marginal product of 20 ((80-60)/(4-3) = 20/1).

Another useful managerial production measure in the short run is shown in the fourth column of Table 3.1. The **average product** of a variable input is defined as total product divided by the number of units of the variable input employed. In our hypothetical example, at 6 units of labour input, the average product of labour is 18 (108/6). Mathematically, average product is given by equation (3.6):

$$\text{Average product} = \frac{\text{Total product}}{\text{Units of variable input}} \qquad (3.6)$$

The law of diminishing marginal returns

The variations in total product that result from applying more or less of a variable factor to a given quantity of a fixed factor are the subject of a famous economic law called the **law of diminishing marginal returns**. The law states that, if increasing amounts of a variable factor are applied to a fixed factor, eventually a situation will be reached in which each additional unit of the variable factor adds less to total product than did the previous unit. Stated differently, the law of diminishing marginal returns (also known as the law of eventually diminishing marginal productivity) states that the marginal product (MP) of the variable factor must eventually decline if enough of it is combined with some fixed quantity of one or more other factors in a production system. The hypothesis predicts only that sooner or later the MP will decline. The law is usually applied to the short run, although it can, as we will shortly see, be applied to the long-run process of firm planning.

The key to understanding the intuitive appeal of the law of diminishing marginal returns is to consider what is going on in the production process regarding the fixed factor of production. Consider a manufacturing plant producing heavy construction machinery. With only a few workers, production is difficult because each worker must not only master several pieces of machinery, but also coordinate his activities with other workers, each of whom also runs several pieces of machinery. As more workers are added, each worker is better able to focus his energies on fewer tasks; further, scheduling will become less of a problem. The plant will experience the gains from specialization. Eventually, however, adding workers causes smaller increases to total product. Workers begin getting in each others' way; the increase in the level of management bureaucracy may itself cause inefficiencies. It is even possible to be in a situation where adding additional workers will actually cause total product itself to diminish.

The neoclassical theory of firm production is evidenced by the above example. At low levels of input usage (and hence output), marginal product may be high. At higher levels of input usage (and hence output), marginal products will begin to decline. So long as marginal product is positive, adding units of variable input will increase total product. If, however, marginal product is negative, additional units of variable input usage will cause decreases in total product.

In Figure 3.1 we show the short-run relationship between total product (TP) and variable input usage. The total product curve has an elongated 'S' shape. Beginning at the origin, up until the input amount L_A, total output increases quickly. We say that, in this range, output is increasing at an increasing rate. When the variable input usage is between L_A and L_C, additional units of the variable input L cause additions to total product; however, these incremental gains are growing smaller as successive units of L are added to the production process. When more than L_C units of the variable are used, each additional unit of L causes output to decrease.

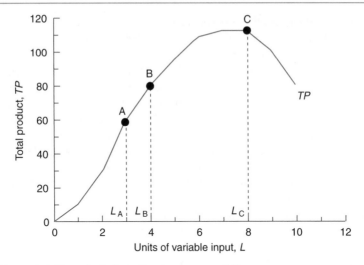

Figure 3.1 Hypothetical production process: TP curve.

In Figure 3.2 we show the marginal product (MP), and average product (AP) curves that correspond to the total product function used in Figure 3.1. Thus, the amounts of input usage denoted by L_A and L_C in Figure 3.2 correspond to those amounts labelled in Figure 3.1. We see that, up until L_A units of input usage, marginal productivity of labour is increasing. When the labour usage is between L_A and L_C, marginal product is declining but positive. Beyond L_C units of the variable input, L, marginal product is negative.

We now turn our attention to the point we have ignored so far in both Figures 3.1 and 3.2: point B, corresponding to L_B units of input usage. Notice

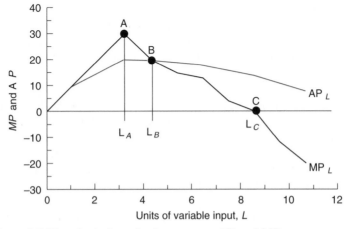

Figure 3.2 Hypothetical production process: AP and MP curves

at this point the average product of labour is maximized. This highlights a very important technical detail, whose derivation is not important, but whose understanding is. Regarding average and marginal relationships: when the marginal is above the average, the average must be increasing. Likewise, when the marginal is below the average, the average must be decreasing. For example, consider your performance in college as measured by your grade point average (GPA). You have two that are relevant: your cumulative GPA, recording your academic performance over your academic career, and your current term GPA. Consider your cumulative GPA as the 'average' and your current term GPA as your 'marginal'. Suppose your cumulative GPA is a 3.1; if this term you expect better grades in the form of a current term GPA of 3.8, then your average (cumulative GPA) must increase. If, on the other hand, you expect to have an 'off' term with a lower GPA, then your cumulative GPA must decrease.

Using one variable input

The demand for a variable input

The decision facing the manager in the short run is clear: create as much profit as possible. In practice this involves determining the right amount of the variable inputs to purchase. Some of the important forces motivating firm managers can be identified in a very constrained problem, which we consider now. The conceptual approach taken here is useful for understanding how the demand for a variable input of production is determined in the short run.

In the short run, the firm is in a situation in which the price of its output is fixed; let us consider the case where there is one variable input. The decision on how many units to produce is equivalent to determining how many units of the variable input to hire. If all inputs except one are in fixed supply to the firm, then this is equivalent to saying that output is determined by the amount of variable input used.

As an example, suppose that beer is produced using two inputs: a capital input (K), representing the physical and technological characteristics of the brewery, and a labour input (L), representing the number of brewery workers used in any week. Let the relationship be as follows, where Q represents the number of barrels of beer produced in any week:

$$Q = f(K,L) = \sqrt{K} \times \sqrt{L} \qquad (3.7)$$

Now, because we know that the capital input is fixed, we can simplify the production function. Suppose that the brewery has 2,500 units of K, no more and no less, available for beer production. Then the above production function becomes:

$$Q = 50 \times \sqrt{L} \qquad (3.8)$$

The total barrels of beer produced for alternative levels of L are shown in

Table 3.2. If the brewery decides to produce 300 barrels of beer during the third week of July, 36 weekly brewery workers are required.

To highlight the issues facing managers at the brewery, consider the determination of the optimal quantity of beer to produce. For simplicity, suppose that the firm is already producing some amount of output. Clearly, producing more output involves hiring (at least) one more unit of input, in our example one more unit of the variable input, L. The question then becomes: Should the firm hire one more unit of the variable factor of production? For the sake of argument, suppose that it does. The change in costs to the firm is clear from this action: total costs increase by the amount that must be paid to hire this additional unit of L. Within the competitive context we define the market price of L as w, the weekly wage for this kind of labour.

We must also consider the marginal benefits of hiring that additional unit of L. On the margin, the benefit of hiring one more unit of L is equal to the market value of the output produced by that additional unit; that is, the market value of the marginal product of L. If all units produced by the firm are sold at the price of p, then the benefits of hiring an additional unit of L are given by pMP_L. We refer to these additional benefits as the marginal revenue product of labour, or the MRP_L.[2]

To determine whether the firm should expand output, the relevant comparison to make is between the market wage, w, and the MRP_L. If MRP_L exceeds w, expanding output will add more to total revenue than it will to costs; thus, total profits will increase. As additional units of L are added to the production process, MRP_L declines owing to the diminishing returns of labour. Thus, if we initially were in a situation where MRP_L exceeded w, as more labour is hired we move towards a position of equality between MRP_L and w.

If, on the other hand, MRP_L is less than w, expanding output will add less to total revenue than it will to costs; thus, total profits will decrease.

Table 3.2 Beer produced with variable input L

Number of weekly brewery workers	Barrels of beer produced
33	287.2
34	291.5
35	295.8
36	300.0
37	304.1
38	308.2
39	312.2
40	316.2
41	320.1
42	324.0

Accordingly, if MRP_L is less than w, the signal to the firm's managers is to reduce the amount of labour being used. As less labour is being used, the marginal product of labour will increase, moving us to equality between MRP_L and w.

This mechanism determining the optimal amount of labour to use provides the theoretical underpinnings for the firm's demand for labour curve. Any demand curve relates the quantity to the maximum amount a party is willing to pay, per unit, for that quantity. Using the same logic as used above, suppose that the firm is currently producing some level of output using some amount of labour input. How much will the firm pay for the next unit of labour input? The MRP_L of course. Since this simple experiment can be repeated for any given level of input usage we can conclude that the firm's demand for labour functions shows, for every quantity of labour, the MRP_L.

We can illustrate some of these points using the brewery example discussed earlier. Suppose that the market price for a barrel of beer from the brewery is ECU 70 and that the going wage rate for workers doing jobs similar to those at the brewery is ECU 294 per week.[3] We can easily demonstrate profit-maximizing behaviour and our rule that $MRP_L = w$ is, in fact, true using the information in Table 3.2.

Begin with the possibility that the brewery initially produces 287.2 barrels of beer and employs 33 workers. Should another worker be added? The marginal cost of hiring that worker is the market wage of ECU 294. The marginal benefits of hiring that worker are the marginal product of the 33rd worker, 4.4 barrels of beer, times the market price of ECU 70. Then, the marginal revenue product of labour exceeds the wage. Hiring that 33rd worker increases profits by ECU 14, so that worker should be hired. The 34th and 35th workers likewise increase profits, each doing so by ECU 7. Further gains are exhausted, however, by hiring the 36th worker.

C. The theory of production: II

More than one input

Isoquants of production
In order to understand how firms make production decisions we need to analyze cases in which there is more than one variable input. Our approach is to consider the case of two inputs to production and to produce a result that generalizes to the more-than-two input case in an intuitive way.

The term **isoquant** – derived from the Greek *iso*, meaning equal, and *quant*, the root word of quantity – refers to all of the possible combinations of two inputs, say K and L, that yield the same maximum amount of output. Traditionally, isoquants are shown in graphical form, with the amount of capital input, K, on the vertical axis and the amount of labour input, L, on the horizontal axis.

Hypothetical production data are presented in Table 3.3. In this table, the amounts of capital (K) and labour (L) inputs required to produce three output levels ($Q = 55$, $Q = 60$ and $Q = 65$) are shown. It should be remembered that the input amounts represent the minimum amounts of inputs required to produce each level of output, or, in other words, that production is **technically efficient**. In Figure 3.3 we show three isoquants in graphical form from the production data of Table 3.3.

Limiting cases of isoquants
One characteristic evident in the production process whose isoquants are shown in Figure 3.3 is that, holding output constant, one input may be substituted for the other. In practice, production functions vary in terms of how easily one input can be substituted for another. In some instances, termed **fixed proportion production**, inputs can be combined only according to a fixed ratio. An example common to most kitchens is the baking of a cake. Regardless of the output, or number of servings produced, the same proportionate amounts of flour, sugar and milk must be used; if not, output suffers. When the production process is characterized in this way, the isoquants take the form of right angles emanating outwards from the origin.

Alternatively, the inputs may be perfectly substitutable. In this case any given level of output can be produced by freely substituting one input for another.

Table 3.3 Hypothetical production data, isoquants

Q = 55		Q = 60		Q = 65	
L	K	L	K	L	K
10	391	10	473	10	563
11	355	11	430	11	512
12	325	12	394	12	469
13	300	13	364	13	433
14	279	14	338	14	402
15	260	15	315	15	375
16	244	16	295	16	352
17	230	17	278	17	331
18	217	18	263	18	313
19	206	19	249	19	296
20	195	20	236	20	281
21	186	21	225	21	267
22	178	22	215	22	256
23	170	23	206	23	244
24	163	24	196	24	235
25	156	25	189	25	225

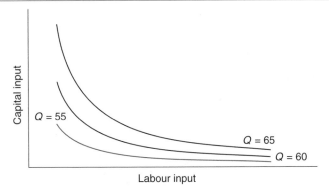

Figure 3.3 Three isoquants.

The fixed proportion production technology is considered as extreme case in one direction. Perfect input substitutability is considered an extreme case in the other direction. Most production processes represent neither extreme but are somewhere in the middle. In Figures 3.4 and 3.5 we illustrate the isoquants relevant to both extreme cases.

The $MRTS_{LK}$

With two inputs, managers want to substitute between inputs, perhaps as one input becomes relatively more expensive than another. Isoquants provide a unique way to analyze this substitution. The slope of each isoquant is in terms of $\Delta K / \Delta L$, that is, the change in K divided by the change in L. Economists refer to the slope of an isoquant as the **marginal rate of technical substitution** of labour for capital, or $MRTS_{LK}$.

As we move rightward along an isoquant we observe that the amount of capital (measured on the vertical axis) is decreasing and the amount of labour (measured on the horizontal axis) is increasing. When the effects of these two

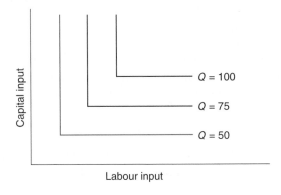

Figure 3.4 Isoquants: Fixed proportion production.

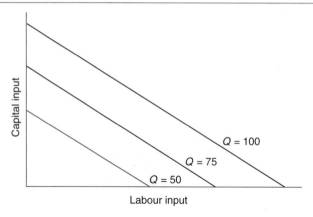

Figure 3.5 Isoquants: Perfect substitutes.

changes are taken separately we see that one offsets the other. The reduction in the amount of capital, K, implies less output, while the increase in the amount of labour, L, implies greater output. Furthermore, each of these separate effects must cancel the other one out because the amount of output is assumed to be constant as we move along a given isoquant.

The $MRTS_{LK}$ provides a measure of the amount of capital that must be added (substituted) when one less unit of labour is used so as to keep output constant. It is always negative, although, for simplicity, we will ignore the negative sign. This relationship can be stated as follows,

$$MRTS_{LK} = \Delta K / \Delta L, \tag{3.9}$$

where ΔK is a small change in capital and ΔL is a small change in labour for a fixed level of Q.

The $MRTS_{LK}$ is not constant but diminishes as one moves down (from left to right) the isoquant. Or, put another way, the isoquant becomes flatter. In slightly more precise language, we say that isoquants are convex, that is, 'bowed in' toward the origin.

Consider once again the input substitution that occurs as we move rightward along an isoquant, that is, holding output constant. There is an increase in the amount of labour available to the firm; this should work to increase output. The increase in output caused by having more labour available for production equals the number of units that labour is increased times the amount produced by those added units. Mathematically,

$$\Delta Q = MP_L \times \Delta L \tag{3.10}$$

where ΔQ represents the change in output, MP_L is the marginal productivity of labour and ΔL equals the increase in the number of units of labour available to the firm.

As mentioned earlier, the increase in output does not happen in isolation, however. Recall that we are moving along a given isoquant and that capital must decrease so as to keep output constant. The reduction in output attributable to the lower amount of capital can be written as:

$$\Delta Q = MP_K \times \Delta K, \tag{3.11}$$

where MP_K represents the marginal productivity of capital and ΔK the change in the number of units of capital.

Recall that the definition of an isoquant requires that output be constant all along the curve. The increase in output caused by the greater amount of labour must be offset by the reduction in output caused by the lower amount of capital. Put another way, we may take the two previous mathematical expressions, add them together, and set the result equal to zero.

$$MP_L \times \Delta L + MP_K \times \Delta K = 0 \tag{3.12}$$

When we showed the graph of isoquants above in Figure 3.3, capital was shown on the vertical axis and labour on the horizontal. Thus it follows that the slope of the isoquant must be in terms of $\Delta K/\Delta L$. Solving equation (3.12) for this expression reveals the slope of the isoquant to be:

$$MP_L \times \Delta L = -MP_K \times \Delta K$$

Dividing through by ΔL and MP_K, we obtain:

$$-MP_L/MP_K = \Delta K/\Delta L \tag{3.13}$$

The expression in equation (3.13) reveals that the slope of the isoquant equals the ratio of the marginal product of labour to the marginal product of capital. Although this result will become quite a bit more important in the next section, we can also use it here for a technical treatment as to why isoquants are typically thought of as being convex to the origin.

As we move rightward along a given isoquant, the amount of labour available to the firm decreases and the amount of capital available to the firm increases. As the amount of labour available decreases, the marginal product of labour increases. Thus the numerator of the slope of the isoquant gets larger. Likewise, as the amount of capital available to the firm diminishes, the marginal product of capital increases. Both of these forces ensure that the isoquants become steeper as we move towards the vertical axis and more horizontal as we move towards the labour axis.

Measuring input usage: Isocost lines

Definition
The standard definition of productive efficiency used by economists includes a cost minimization dimension. In fact, from the producer's standpoint, efficiency means that a firm is getting the most output given what it spends on inputs; or,

put another way, that the firm cannot rearrange its input usage to produce more output at the same, or lower, cost. To capture this effect we need to add another graphical device to our analysis. An isocost function shows all the different combinations of labour and capital that a firm can purchase for a given sum of money.

The total cost by definition must be equal to the sum of the amounts spent on each input. Since we are considering the case of two inputs, total cost will be equal to the (money) expenditures on labour plus expenditures on capital. We assume that each unit of labour costs the firm w and that each unit of capital costs the firm r.[4] If the firm hires L units of labour, then total expenditure on the labour input equals $w \times L$. Likewise, total expenditure on the capital input equals $r \times K$. The total costs, C, may then be written as:

$$C = w \times L + r \times K \tag{3.14}$$

Suppose, for example, that a firm has 1,000 to spend on inputs, that the price of labour is 100 and that the price of capital is 200. Then the firm can purchase 4 units of capital and 2 units of labour, 3 units of capital and 4 units of labour, or any one of a number of combinations of labour and capital that involve a 1,000 expenditure. In Figure 3.6 we show the isocost line, C_{1000}, that corresponds to these prices for labour and capital.

With the basic concepts of an isocost line derived, we can now move on to two more important issues: the isocost line's position and its slope. Equation (3.14) can be rearranged to yield:

$$K = C/r - (w/r)L, \tag{3.15}$$

which says the same thing but in a different form. We have written the equation with the variable measured on the vertical axis on the left-hand side. On the right-hand side is the variable on the horizontal axis, L, multiplied by the expression $-w/r$. If you are familiar with basic geometric concepts then you know that the expression C/r represents the vertical intercept of the line and $-w/r$ represents the line's slope.

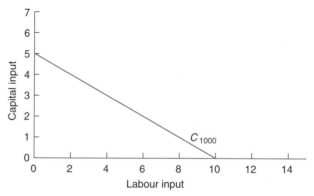

Figure 3.6 Example isocost line.

Alternative cost levels

The isocost line's position is determined solely by the level of total cost, C. Consider our example isocost line discussed above, where the total cost was said to be 1,000. How many units of capital could the firm buy if it bought only capital? 1,000 divided by the unit cost of capital = 1,000/200, or 5 (in general this would be C/r). If the firm bought only labour, it could purchase 1,000 divided by the price of labour = 1,000/100, or 10 (in general this would be C/w). Clearly, if the firm were to increase its total expenditures on inputs to, say, 2,000, then it could purchase 10 units of capital and 20 units of labour. If total costs increase, then the isocost line shifts outwards and parallel to itself. This situation is shown in Figure 3.7, where C_{1000} shows all combinations of K and L that can be purchased for a total outlay of 1,000. Similarly, C_{2000} shows all combinations of K and L that can be purchased for a total outlay of 2,000.

Changing the cost of one input

Whereas the position of the isocost line depends on the level of total expenditure by the firm, its slope is determined by the ratio of the input prices.

Continuing with our previous example, where the price of labour is 100, the price of capital is 200 and total expenditures are 1,000, what would happen if the price of labour were to increase to 125? If the firm bought only capital, it could purchase 5 units, just as many as it could before the price of labour increased. On the other hand, the firm could now purchase only 8 (1000/125) units of labour. The isocost line representing the new price of labour will connect the two points (5 capital, 0 labour) and (0 capital, 8 labour). The effect of this change is shown in Figure 3.8.

In more general terms, the slope of the isocost line is equal to $-w/r$. As labour becomes more expensive relative to capital, the isocost line becomes steeper.

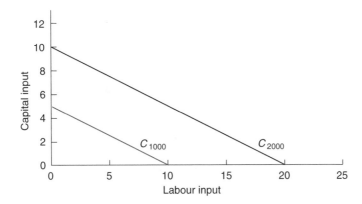

Figure 3.7 Isocost lines: Alternative total costs.

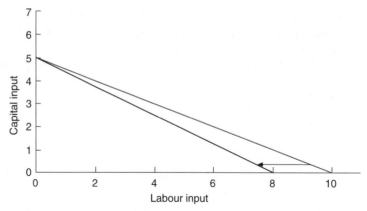

Figure 3.8 Isoquant lines: Increases in w.

The opposite is true for capital. Notice, however, that if the prices of both inputs increase by the same percentages the isocost line is unchanged.

Cost minimization

A graphical explanation
Regarding our productive efficiency puzzle, we now have two of the major pieces of the puzzle and it is time to put them together in a meaningful way.

The manager of the firm wishes to produce Q units of output at the lowest possible cost. Suppose further that the firm wishes to spend a fixed amount of money. The problem facing the manager is shown in Figure 3.9.[5] Here, equilibrium in production occurs at point E, where the isocost line C_{1260} intersects isoquant Q_{55}. We must develop an understanding as to why point E is an equilibrium and why it is efficient.

Definitionally we say that a firm is in productive equilibrium when it maximizes output for a given cost outlay. In this example, the isocost line C_{1260} shows all combinations of capital and labour that the firm can purchase for its total outlay of 1,260 (the price of labour, w, is 42, the price of capital, r, is 2). Notice that the firms could purchase the combination of inputs associated with point F and use them to produce the output associated with Q_{50}, or 50 units. However, this outcome would be neither efficient nor an equilibrium. Notice also that the firm would like to attain point G on Q_{60}, and produce 60 units. However, this combination of inputs would require an expenditure that would exceed the firm's outlay.

We can then argue that productive equilibrium and efficiency must occur at the unique intersection, or tangency, of an isoquant and isocost line. Only when this is true will the firm be producing all that it can given its outlay on inputs. Although this result may seem a little forced and reliant on our graph-

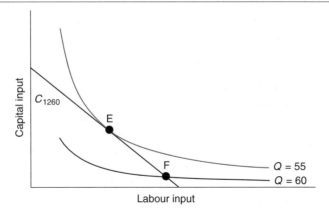

Figure 3.9 Production equilibrium.

ical tools, the intuition behind it can provide an even greater understanding.

One property of geometry is that, at the point where two curves are tangential, their slopes must be equal. We have argued that the slope of the isocost line is equal to w/r, the price of labour divided by the price of capital. We have also shown that the slope of an isoquant is equal to MP_L/MP_K, the ratio of the marginal product of labour to that of capital. Mathematically, we may write this as

$$MP_L/MP_K = w/r \qquad (3.16)$$

Some rearrangement yields:

$$MP_L/w = MP_K/r, \qquad (3.17)$$

which we refer to as the single firm condition of productive efficiency. Each side of equation (3.17) identifies the amount of output provided by the last ECU spent on an input. Consider the left-hand side which refers to labour. The units of the marginal product of labour are $\Delta Q/\Delta L$, and the units of w, the price of labour, are ECU. If we ignore the Δ's (which is appropriate if we consider the magnitudes fixed), the units of MP_L/w simplify to Q/ECU, or units of output per ECU. Efficient production requires that a firm choose the level of its inputs so that, for every input, the ratio of marginal productivity to input price be equal.

An intuitive explanation

The single firm condition of productive efficiency maintains that the last ECU spent on each input must yield the same amount of output. What would happen if this were not true? Then, the firm could reallocate its resources and increase output holding total cost constant.

Suppose, for the sake of argument, that the single firm condition of productive efficiency were not met. Let the marginal product of labour be 200, the price of labour be 50, the marginal product of capital be 125 and the price of capital be 25. At these values, the equation becomes:

$$MP_L/w = 200/50 < MP/r = 125/25$$

From this point, the firm can increase output without incurring any additional cost. Let the firm eliminate one unit of labour, in effect freeing up ECU 50. Eliminating this unit of labour will cause output to fall. By how much? By 200 units, because this is the marginal productivity of labour. With the ECU 50 now let the firm purchase 2 units of capital, which will cause output to increase by 250 units (2 units of capital times the marginal product of 125). Clearly more is added to output by the extra capital than is lost by the reduced labour. We can conclude then that the single firm condition of productive efficiency must imply efficient production.[6]

As a brief review we need to take a look at what we have recently accomplished. We began with a production function of a single producer and determined guidelines to lead this firm to producing efficiently. The tools we relied upon were isoquants and isocost lines. In one sense, the output of our discussion is embodied in the single firm condition of productive efficiency. What we now need to do is determine what efficiency, as a requirement, implies for the input choice of more than one producer. This will prove invaluable in our understanding of productive efficiency and enable us to continue our efforts in describing general equilibrium behaviour throughout the economy.

D. The costs of production

Sources and types of costs

Having examined the firm's production technology, the method by which inputs are turned into outputs, we now turn to the firm's costs. The production technology together with the cost of factor inputs will determine the firm's cost of production. Before we move into detailed descriptions of the cost measures used in economic analysis, it is useful to consider a differing perspective of costs from a broader, more general level.

Opportunity costs versus accounting costs
Accountants and economists have different views of costs. Accountants take a historical view of costs; that is, they are concerned with money that has already been spent. Economists, and managers, have a forward-looking view of the firm. Therefore, they are concerned with what costs are expected to be in the future. The cost in this sense of a 'thing' is what must be given up in order to acquire it. For example, the total cost of a college education is the income that must be forgone while in school plus tuition fees and other expenses. The cost of living in a house you own is the rent that you forgo by

not renting it out. This forward-looking view of costs is known as **opportunity cost**. These are costs that are forgone by not putting a firm's resources to their best use.

Costs are of importance to managers because profits are the main motivating force in a market economy. And profit is the difference between total revenue and total cost:

$$\Pi = TR - TC$$

where Π is profit, TR is total revenue, and TC is total cost. Opportunity costs are a part of total cost. Opportunity costs are costs associated with opportunities forgone. For example, an owner who manages her own business but chooses not to take a salary forgoes an opportunity to earn a salary somewhere else. Although no monetary costs have been incurred, and no costs appeared on the accounting statement, an opportunity cost has been incurred by forgoing income from another occupation. The **opportunity cost of capital** is the rate of return that one could earn by investing in a different project with similar risk. Another cost of doing business may be the return to one's own funds invested in one's business which could earn an income if invested elsewhere.

From the point of view of the manager, all costs can be classified as either short-run or long-run costs. In the short run some costs can be varied with the rate of production, while others are fixed.

Allotting and defining unit costs

Total measures
Total cost (TC) means the total cost of producing any given level of output. The total cost of production is divided into two parts: **variable cost** (VC) and **fixed cost** (FC). Fixed costs are those that do not vary with output. These costs which include insurance, plant maintenance and some staff, will remain the same no matter how much is produced. All costs that vary directly with output, rising as more is produced and falling as less is produced, are called variable costs. Variable costs include expenses for wages, raw materials and utilities.

Average per-unit measures
There are three types of average costs. **Average total cost** (atc) is the total cost of production, at any level of output divided by the number of units produced, TC/Q. **Average fixed cost** (afc) is fixed costs divided by the level of output, FC/Q, and **average variable cost** (avc) is variable cost divided by Q, VC/Q. Average fixed cost plus average variable cost equals average total cost.

Table 3.4 Costs as a function of output Q

Q	FC	VC	TC	MC	afc	avc	atc
0	4	0	4	–	–	–	–
1	4	5	9	5	4	5	9
2	4	8	12	3	2	4	6
3	4	15	19	7	1	5	6
4	4	32	36	17	1	8	9
5	4	65	69	33	0.8	13	13.8

Marginal costs

Marginal cost (MC) – sometimes called incremental costs – is the increase in total cost resulting from raising production by one unit. Because fixed costs do not change with output, marginal cost is just the increase in variable cost that results from an extra unit of output. It can be written as $\Delta VC/\Delta Q$. Marginal cost tells us how much it will cost to expand output by one unit. These figures are shown in Table 3.4.

Short-run costs can be summarized as follows:

$$afc = FC/Q$$
$$avc = VC/Q$$
$$atc = TC/Q$$
$$atc = (FC + VC)/Q$$
$$atc = afc + avc$$
$$MC = \Delta VC/\Delta Q$$

Let us look at an algebraic example. These three measures of cost are simply different ways of looking at the same phenomenon. They are mathematically interrelated. For example, suppose that we are given the following total cost function

$$TC = q^3 - 4q^2 + 8q = 4.$$

Because the last term, the number 4, is the only term that does not change as q (output) changes, the fixed cost must be 4.

$$FC = 4$$

Total cost minus fixed cost is variable cost. The terms in the total cost function which contain the variable q will comprise total variable cost:

$$VC = q^3 - 4q^2 + 8q$$

If we know the total cost function and it is continuously variable, then the marginal cost is the slope or derivative of the total cost function, which is also equal to the derivative of the variable cost function. (Students with a background in calculus will see this right away. If you do not know calculus, just take our word for it.) We may write:

$$MC = \mathrm{d}TC/\mathrm{d}q = 3q^2 - 8q + 8$$

The average cost curves can also be derived by dividing *TC*, *VC* and *FC* by *q*:

$$atc = q^2 - 4q + 8 + 4/q.$$

Similarly,

$$afc = 4/q$$

and

$$avc = q^2 - 4q + 8$$

Relating costs of inputs to output: Short run

The production process as a filter
In our analysis, the role of the firm is to organize the production of some output for marketable sale. Towards this end the firm's actions are both guided and constrained by the production function. Recall that the source of all costs to our firm is the provision of inputs to the production process. If we are interested, and we are, in the relationship between the various cost measures and units of output, we must always remember that this relationship will be dependent upon the costs of acquiring inputs and the way in which these inputs are combined in the production process. Figures 3.10 and 3.11 plot the cost curves from information in Table 3.4 and the above equations. Total costs are shown in Figure 3.10; the average cost functions are shown in Figure 3.11.

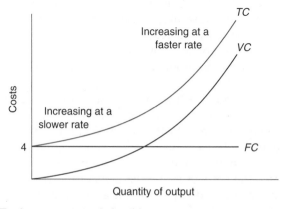

Figure 3.10 Total cost–output relationship.

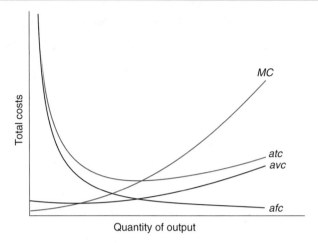

Figure 3.11 Unit cost–output relationship.

Total costs of output

Fixed cost does not vary with output (q), and therefore is a horizontal line at ECU 4. Variable cost is zero when there is no output (q). Therefore, the variable cost function goes through the origin. Total cost is variable cost plus fixed cost $(VC + FC)$ and therefore sits on top of the fixed cost curve. When output is zero, total cost is also ECU 4. The distance between the two curves is always equal to 4, the level of fixed costs.

The nature of per-unit costs as output changes

The average fixed cost *afc* falls as q is increased. This is because, as long as the denominator is increasing, *afc* will be smaller with each additional unit of output. Such a curve is described by mathematicians as a rectangular hyperbola. As q increases, *afc* approaches but never reaches the q axis. It is apparent that, if we have large fixed costs, for example in mass production industries, average fixed costs will decrease over a wide range of output. Suppose that the die to stamp out the left front fender of an Acura Legend costs ECU 5 million. If the die used to produce only one car, the die cost per car is ECU 5 million. If 1 million cars are produced, the die cost per fender will be only ECU 5.

Next we turn our attention to the relationship between total variable cost and average variable cost. Within this comparison we will call to mind the important principle from section B, the principle of diminishing returns.

Consider a production function in the short run with one variable input. If more output is to be produced, then more input must be used. Consider the relationship between the costs of hiring the units of the variable input necessary for producing the expanded output and a measure of the output itself. As the initial units of variable input are added, variable costs increase with output. However, if marginal product is still increasing, the variable costs will increase less rapidly than output. Thus the ratio of total variable costs to output, or *avc*, will fall. If, on the other hand, the marginal product of the variable output is diminishing, variable costs will increase more rapidly than output. In the face of diminishing marginal productivity, average variable costs will increase. This is the reasoning behind the U shape attributed to the *avc* function.

With the shape and form of the *avc* and *afc* curves determined it is an easy matter to determine the shape and nature of the average total cost, *atc*, curve. Because *avc* + *afc* = *atc*, adding the *avc* and the *afc* curves will yield the *atc* curve. Put another way, the distance between the *avc* and the *atc* curves equals *afc*. Thus, the shape of the *atc* should be U shaped like the *avc* curve. At low levels of output both *afc* and *avc* are declining. When the diminishing returns manifest themselves for the variable factor of production, the *avc* curve begins to go up as average variable costs begin to rise. Whether or not the *atc* begins to turn up immediately at this point or shortly thereafter depends on the slope of the *afc* curve. Eventually, however, the *atc* curve will begin rising.

The nature of marginal costs as output changes

The marginal costs arising in the firm relate the cost of the marginal unit produced to the number of units produced. Thus, by definition, it is a unit cost measure. As with the *avc* curve discussed above, the shape and character of the *MC* curve relies on the principle of diminishing returns.

Consider again adding units of a variable input sufficient to produce one more unit of output. The marginal cost of that additional unit of output will be, of course, the cost of obtaining those units of variable input. Is that cost rising or falling as more and more units of output are produced? If marginal productivity is increasing, then fewer units of input are required to produce an additional unit of output. Under conditions of increasing marginal productivity then marginal costs must diminish; the firm is getting more 'bang for its buck'. The situation is reversed if marginal productivity is decreasing. When marginal productivity is decreasing, more units of variable input are required to produce that additional unit of output. Hence, the marginal cost of production must be increasing.

Relating costs of inputs to output: Long run

Background

We defined the concepts of 'short run' and 'long run' in the context of production. These same distinctions are relevant in an understanding of cost issues. The distinction is based not on calendar time but rather on the flexibility open to the firm in terms of fixed inputs: in the long run the firm has complete flexibility; there are no fixed inputs. For a janitorial services firm operating out of a rented office front, the long run may be, and probably is, at most the length of time left on the rental lease. For a manufacturing firm with millions of dollars invested in machinery and other fixed capital items, the long run may be decades. For this reason short-run cost curves are sometimes called **operating curves** because they are useful in making near-term production and pricing decisions. Long-run cost curves are often referred to as planning curves because they play a key role in longer-run planning decisions relating to plant size and equipment acquisitions.

The mechanics of planning

In the long run all factors can be varied. When this is the case, there are alternative ways of achieving the same total output, and it is necessary to choose among them. Any firm that is trying to survive in a competitive environment must minimize its costs in the long run. Therefore, it must choose to produce at the lowest possible cost. If the level of output is known, along with factor costs, the firm can select the optimal level of output. However, today's variable factors are tomorrow's fixed factors. If the firm does not choose wisely it may not be at the minimum level of costs. Long-run decisions are among the most important that the firm makes.

For example, a utility executive decides to build a coal-fired plant because the price of coal is expected to be cheaper than oil in the future. The firm is planning to be the low-cost producer. After the plant has been built there is a strike in the coal fields and the miners demand higher wages. Similarly, peace is achieved in the Middle East, and the price of oil declines significantly. Oil now costs 20 per cent less than coal, and the coal-fired utility plant is no longer producing at the lowest average total cost.

The size choice

A second decision facing managers is about the level of future demand, and therefore the size of plant to build. If a plant is built that is too large, the firm may be saddled with excess capacity and higher short-run average cost. In the long run what is important is the firm's long-run average cost curve. The long-run average cost curve is usually called the envelope curve showing all the possibilities of short-run cost curves. The relationship between long-run and short-run cost curves is shown in Figure 3.12. Assume that the firm is uncertain about the future demand for energy and is considering three alternative plant sizes. The short average cost curve for the three plants is given by SAC_1, SAC_2 and SAC_3. The decision, just like the type of plant to build, is important because once made it cannot be easily changed.

If the firm thinks that it will have long-run demand of Q_1, this can be produced with either SAC_1 or SAC_2. This level of output is produced at a minimum for plant number 1. It is at the minimum point on the short-run average cost curve. However, if the firm increased output too much with plant 1, average cost would be higher than with plant 2. However, neither of these plants

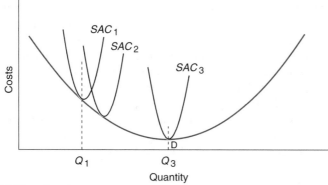

Figure 3.12 The planning curve.

achieves the minimum average cost at point D with plant 3. To achieve this you would have to build a larger plant.

U-shaped long-run costs

What determines the shape of the long-run average cost (LRAC) curve? The most important determinant is returns to scale in the underlying production technology. The LRAC typically declines over some range of output owing to increasing returns to scale in the underlying production technology. The same factor – ignoring the role of fixed costs – that is thought to cause a diminishing region on the short-run *avc* function manifests itself across increasing levels of plant size. An industry is said to be characterized by **economies of scale** if long-run average total cost diminishes over a very broad range of output. Quite naturally, significant economies of scale can limit the degree of competition in the industry. The minimum efficient scale for a firm refers to achieving an output level at which long-run average total costs are at a minimum. This concept is important for long-run planning purposes. For example, if the minimum efficient scale for tyre plants is 20 per cent of the market, then there is room for only five tyre makers in the industry. All of this is not to say that a large minimum efficient scale will result in non-competitive industries; it may be enough that the threat of entry exists, especially in a rapidly changing technological environment. We turn to this question in the next chapter.

E. Perfectly competitive markets

Industry types

Having looked at a firm's cost and production technology we would now like to examine under what conditions some firms will survive, and under what conditions others will not. To sort out the question of who is competing with whom and in what sense, it is useful to distinguish between the behaviour of individual firms and the type of market in which the firm operates.

Economists use the term 'market structure' to refer to the market type. The degree of competitiveness of the market structure refers to the extent to which individual firms lack market power over price or some other variable. The degree of competitive behaviour refers to the degree to which individual firms actively compete with one another. Perfect competition is an exacting concept forming the basis of the standard neoclassical view of firm behaviour. Other environments of interaction between firms that are less exacting but usually more realistic are considered in the following chapter.

Characteristics

The essence of the perfectly competitive market concept is that the market is entirely impersonal. There is no rivalry among suppliers in the market and buyers do not recognize their competitiveness with one another. Before we examine the behaviour of firms it will be important to look at the assumptions of perfect competition.

- *A large number of small firms.* The number of buyers and sellers in the market is so large that no single seller can affect the price. The demand curve confronting the individual is perfectly elastic. The firm can sell in the market period any quantity it wants at the market price. However,it cannot affect the market price. Both seller and buyer are price takers in a competitive market.
- *Homogeneous output.* The products sold in a perfectly competitive market must be identical. That is, the product of one firm is in no way differentiated from the product of other sellers in the market. The word is used very strictly. Every feature of the product must be the same. If the product is not homogeneous, the producer has a degree of control over the product.
- *Freedom of entry and exit in product and factor markets.* All factors of production have perfect mobility. Workers can and will move promptly and quickly from low-wage to high-wage jobs, and land will be quickly diverted from low-rent to high-rent uses. Moreover, firms will not face any barriers to either entry or exit from an industry. Finally, both entry and exist must be costless.
- *Perfect information.* All producers, factors of production and consumers in a perfectly competitive market have perfect information on present and future prices. A worker, for example, would not accept a lower wage because of ignorance of the going market wage rate, and consumers would never pay more than the current market price. Furthermore, all products sold are basically well-known commodities of clearly under- stood quality, each sold at a known price. All of this information is transmitted costlessly and perfectly to all market participants.

Individual firm demand

Relative to market demand and supply

One must be careful not to confuse the individual firm demand curve under perfect competition with the market demand curve for the product. In Figure 3.13 the market demand curve is downward sloping. In perfectly competitive markets, the price of the good or service is determined exclusively by the intersection of the market demand curve and the market supply curve for the good or service. The perfectly competitive firm is then a price taker and can sell any amount of the good or service at the established price. Because the firm is a price taker, the demand curve facing an individual firm is a horizontal line over the range of output we need to consider for all practical purposes. The implication of the horizontal demand curve for the firm is that its output will leave market price unaffected by any changes the perfectly competitive firm may make.

Per-unit revenue measures

In Figure 3.14, the firm's demand curve corresponds to a price of 8 for a computer chip. The horizontal axis measures the quantity of chips that the firm can sell and the vertical the price that it can charge. Figure 3.14 shows conditions in the chip market. The market demand curve shows how much all consumers are willing to buy. At lower prices consumers will buy more. The demand curve facing the firm is horizontal because the firm's sales will have no effect on price. If the firm increases its sales of chips from 100 to 200, this would have no effect on the market because the total market for chips is in the millions. Under perfect competition a firm can sell an additional unit of output without lowering its price. Therefore its average revenue curve is the same as its marginal revenue curve. If the firm sells an additional chip, its total revenue will go up by 8. In this case marginal revenue is 8. Therefore, for the

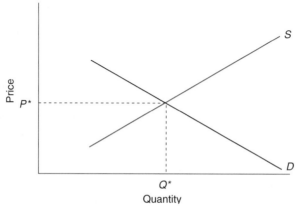

Figure 3.13 Market supply and demand.

Figure 3.14 Competitive firm's demand function.

firm, average revenue is the same as marginal revenue and price along the demand curve.

F. The firm in a perfectly competitive market

The actions of the firm

Profit-maximizing behaviour

The first rule of profit maximization is to decide whether to produce or not. If the firm produces nothing it will have a loss equal to fixed cost. If the firm decides to produce, it will add the variable cost of production to fixed cost. If at some point the level of revenue, PQ, exceeds variable cost, it will pay the firm to produce. If, however, revenue is less than variable cost, it will not pay to produce. The first rule of **profit maximization** is that the firm should produce if the revenue from selling its product exceeds the variable cost of production.

If the firm decides to produce it must decide how much to produce. The second rule of profit maximization is that the firm must produce to the point where marginal revenue equals marginal cost.

$$MR = MC$$

That this condition must be true should be intuitive. For the perfectly competitive firm, marginal revenue is simply market price, and marginal cost is given by the production technology and the input prices. It was argued above that, in most cases, marginal costs can be expected to be increasing. If price exceeds marginal cost, profits are increased if an additional unit is produced and sold – the benefits of doing so, MR, exceed the costs of doing so. After the next unit is produced, MC will be increased. The firm would continually expand output, unit by unit, until the further marginal gains from doing so were at most equal to the marginal costs of doing so.

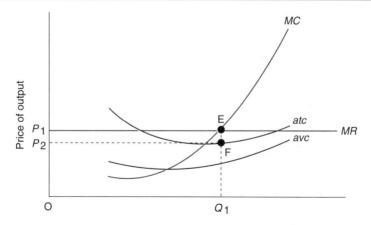

Figure 3.15 Perfect competition: profit maximization.

Short-run equilibrium

As shown in Figure 3.15, profit maximization occurs at point E, where *MR* = *MC*. The firm will produce Q_1 units of output, and its total revenues will equal the rectangle area P_1EQ_1O. The firm's total costs are given by the area of the rectangle P_2FQ_1O. Given the revenues and costs, we are in a position to determine whether or not the firm is earning an economic profit. The area of the economic profit is given by P_1EFP_2. The firm whose profit-maximizing decision is depicted in Figure 3.15 is in a **short-run equilibrium**.

The profit function can be derived using the total revenue and total cost curves. **Total revenue** is equal to the price of the good or service, *P*, times the number of units sold, *Q*. In other words, total revenue is equal to the number of units sold times the price of each unit. The cost of production is also dependent on the level of output. Profit is the difference between total revenue (*TR*) and total cost (*TC*). To maximize profits the firm selects the level of output for which the difference between total cost and total revenue is the greatest. A hypothetical depiction is provided in Figure 3.16.

The firm's supply function

Varying price

Using the concept of a short-run, profit-maximizing equilibrium for perfectly competitive firms, we can appreciate the derivation of the firm's supply function. Consider a situation where a perfectly competitive firm faces three distinct market prices: a low price, P_c; a medium price, P_b (which coincidentally equals the minimum *atc*); and a high price, P_a. Each of these three prices will result in a different profit-maximizing short-run equilibrium for the firm. We will analyze each one separately in descending order. To help with our

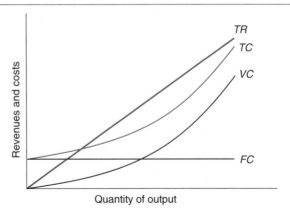

Figure 3.16 Perfect competition: total profits.

analysis please refer to Figure 3.17. We have created three versions of Figure 3.17, designated 3.17a, 3.17b and 3.17c. In these three versions of Figure 3.17 we add one of the three prices to our story.

If the market price is P_a (Fig. 3.17a), the optimum level of production is at point A, at which $MR = MC$. If the firm sells at lower price than P_a, any economic profit it currently enjoys would decrease. If the firm sells at a higher price than P_a, its sales would drop to zero because customers would switch purchases to one of the many other sellers. You will notice that at price P_a the firm is earning a positive economic profit because revenues per unit exceed average total costs per unit.

On the other hand, suppose that the market price is established at P_b (Fig. 3.17b). The firm will maximize profits by producing at point B, where $MR = MC$. At point B the demand curve is exactly tangent to the average total cost curve. At this price the firm is exactly covering its average total cost and is earning no economic profit.

The final situation we now consider is when price equals P_c (Fig. 3.17c). Notice that the price P_c is below average variable cost. The profit-maximizing rule requires production at point C, where $MR = MC$. However, will the firm continue production at this short-run equilibrium? Consider the costs and revenues per unit. On every unit produced, the firm is clearly earning a loss. Furthermore, this loss, on a per-unit basis, exceeds the average fixed costs. Put another way, the firm is not only losing its fixed costs by producing, it is losing money on every unit produced. Clearly at a price such as P_c the firm will minimize losses by closing down.

The shut-down point

This raises a very important point. A rational firm will produce only so long as price exceeds average variable costs; this guarantees that the firm has some revenues left over after paying the variable inputs to apply to its fixed costs, which it must pay no matter what it does.

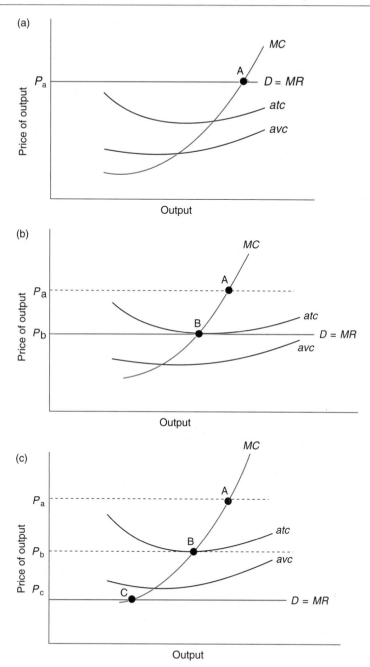

Figure 3.17 The firm supply function.

By definition, the firm's supply function must show the units of output provided at various prices. Using the logic of the profit-maximizing short-run equilibrium, this collection of points is given by the firm's marginal cost function. For, no matter what the price, profit maximization dictates that the output produced be determined by the intersection of the *MC* and *MR* (price) functions. However, the entire marginal cost function is not the supply function.

The point at which the marginal cost function intersects the average variable cost function is the minimum of the average variable cost function and is termed the **shut-down point**. This is so because no firm will ever produce when price is less than average variable cost.

A firm need not always make an economic profit in the short run. Why would a firm operate at a loss in the short run? A firm might operate at a loss because it expects the market price to change. In other words, it fully expected to make a profit in the future, and therefore will operate at a loss in the short run. The firm has two choices here. It can continue to operate at a short-run loss, or it can shut down. If price is above average variable cost and below average total cost, some production is appropriate. It is cheaper to operate the firm than to produce no output because price exceeds average variable cost. Each unit produced yields more revenue than cost, therefore producing higher profits than if the firm were shut down. In other words, the firm can minimize losses by continuing to produce at a loss.

Long-run equilibrium

A bleak entrepreneurial scenario
Although in the short run a firm may break even or earn an economic profit or loss, in the long run all of these positions are not possible equilibrium positions. The key to **long-run equilibrium** under perfect competition is entry and exit. We have seen that, when firms are in short-run equilibrium, they may be making profits or losses or just breaking even. Since costs include the opportunity cost of capital, firms that are just breaking even are doing as well as they could if they invested their capital elsewhere. Thus there will be no incentive for existing firms to leave the industry. Neither will there be an incentive for new firms to enter the industry, because capital can earn the same return elsewhere in the economy.

The mechanics of long-run adjustment
If existing firms are making a negative economic profit they should consider leaving the industry because higher returns can be earned elsewhere. As firms leave the industry, there is a reduction in the market supply function (a shift upward and leftward) and the market price for the good will rise. As the price rises, the firms that remain will see their losses getting smaller. Economic the-

ory would predict that the market price will continue to rise so long as firms in the industry are making losses and exiting. When the firms are earning zero economic profits, the exit will stop, the price will stabilize and, for every firm, a situation of long-run equilibrium will prevail. Naturally the only difference between the long-run and the short-run equilibrium from the firm's perspective is that the long-run outcome involves zero economic profits.

This turn of events is shown in Figures 3.18 and 3.19. In Figure 3.18 the initial market price is P_L. In Figure 3.19 the initial market supply and demand functions, labelled S_1 and D_1 respectively, intersect at this price. The exit of some firms from the market causes a reduction in market supply and a higher market price. These are labelled as S_2 and P_H respectively. Notice that, for the firm, the price P_H represents a short-run equilibrium involving zero economic profits and a long-run position of equilibrium.

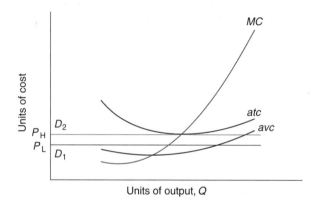

Figure 3.18 Exit: firm losses.

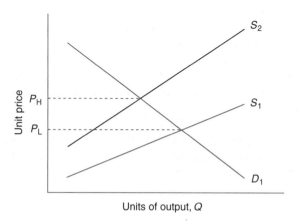

Figure 3.19 Exit: market losses.

The counterpart of this story is likewise true. If existing firms are earning positive economic profits, new capital will enter the industry. If economic profits are being earned in the industry, price will be above average total cost. This will encourage entry into the industry. Over time the industry supply curve will shift to the right and downward, and market price will fall. This will put downward pressure on prices, thereby competing away economic profits in the long run.

G. Chapter summary and key ideas

This chapter examined the neoclassical theory of the firm. The neoclassical theory of the firm is a black box. The firm is described by a production function where inputs are turned into outputs. The production function specifies the maximum amount of outputs that can be produced with given inputs.

We first looked at production with one variable input to examine total product, marginal product and average product. The production function is characterized by the law of diminishing returns. The law states that, if increasing amounts of a variable factor are applied to a given amount of a fixed factor, eventually a situation will be reached in which each additional unit of the variable factor adds less to the total product.

Next we examined the cost of production. Costs are divided between short-run costs and long-run costs. Short-run costs can be varied with the cost of production. Total cost is the cost of producing any given level of output. Costs are important because they are used to calculate profits. Profit is the difference between total revenue and total cost. A firm maximizes profit by producing where marginal revenue equals marginal cost.

Economists use the term 'market structure' to refer to the type of market in which the firm produces. In a market where firms are price takers, markets are referred to as being perfectly competitive. Perfectly competitive markets are characterized by a large number of firms, homogeneous output, easy entry and exit, and perfect information.

In short-run equilibrium firms will produce where marginal revenue equals marginal cost. Under these conditions a firm may earn excess economic profits or may incur short-run losses. In long-run equilibrium a firm will earn zero economic profits.

In the long run, all inputs are variable. Therefore a firm will stay in business only if it has the appropriate size plant or capacity and can produce the appropriate level of output. In the long run, firms adjust to changes in supply and demand by either entering or exiting an industry.

Key words

average fixed cost	marginal product
average product	operating curves
average total cost	opportunity cost of capital
average variable cost	opportunity costs
constant returns to scale	perfect input substitutability
decreasing returns to scale	planning curves
economies of scale	productive efficiency
fixed cost	production function
fixed input	profit maximization
fixed proportion production	returns to scale
increasing returns to scale	short run
isoquant	short-run equilibrium
law of diminishing marginal	shut-down point
returns	technical efficiency
long run	total revenue
long-run equilibrium	total cost
marginal rate of technical	total product
substitution	variable cost
marginal cost	variable input

Questions and problems for review and discussion

1 Consider a production function which describes the production of
your earned grade on an upcoming economics examination. Call the
output P, for percentage of correct answers. Carefully consider what
the inputs of this production process would be. Please include the
following as inputs: IQ, your academic ability as measured by your
individual IQ; W, your parents' level of income; T1, the average
number of hours you have spent studying economics per week so far
this term; and T2, the number of hours you spend studying for this
particular test.
  (a) Please list and fully explain two additional inputs to the produc-
       tion process.
  (b) Explain which of the inputs are fixed and which are variable in
       the production of your test grade.
  (c) For each input that you determine is a variable input, discuss the
       marginal productivity of that input. In particular, explain when,
       and under what conditions, the marginal productivity of that input
       would begin to decline.

(d) For each input that you determine is a variable input, explain when, and under what conditions, the marginal productivity of that input would become negative.

(e) Suppose you must choose this evening whether you should go to a rock concert or study for the upcoming economics exam. Use the principle of marginal productivity in your explanation of which choice to undertake.

2 A firm has 3,000 currency units to spend on production in this period. The firm uses only two productive inputs, K and L.

(a) If the price of inputs K and L are 200 and 150 currency units respectively, graph the firm's isocost line.

(b) On the diagram you created for 2a, draw in a set of isoquants describing a production process characterized as being of fixed proportions. Label the efficient point as point Z.

(c) Also on the diagram you created for 2a, allow the price of the input K to change from 200 currency units to 150 currency units. Label the new efficient point as point W.

(d) Explain the movement from point Z to point W mentioned above.

3 In a production process with two variable inputs (K and L) a situation is observed where the marginal product of K is 50 and the marginal product of L is 25. Furthermore, the per-unit prices of K and L are 4 and 5 currency units respectively. Include in your explanation the marginal productivities of each input.

(a) Fully explain, using the single firm condition of productive efficiency, why the current allocation of K and L is not efficient.

(b) Fully explain how the firm should move to a point where the single firm condition of productive efficiency is met. Include in your explanation the marginal productivities of each input.

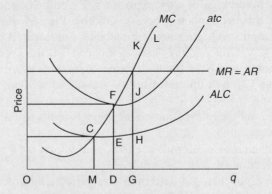

4 Circle the correct answer in each instance:

(a) Most profitable output: OA, OB, OM, OG.

(b) Market price: BK, AF, GK, MC.

(c) Average revenue: OB, BK, OG, DF.
(d) Marginal revenue: OA, AF, GK, DF.
(e) Average total cost at most profitable output: OB, OD, MC, GJ.
(f) Average variable cost at most profitable output: GH, GJ, MC, DF.
(g) Profit per unit at most profitable output: AB, JK, JH, EF.
(h) Average fixed cost at most profitable output: EF, JH, AB, MC.
(i) Long-run equilibrium output: OD, OM, OG, ON.
(j) Short-run supply curve: OM, CI, AF, BK.

5 Given: $TC = x^3 - 4x^2 + 8x + 4$
           $TR = 4x.$

(a) What is the equation for the firm's average revenue curve?
(b) What is the equation for the firm's marginal revenue curve?
(c) What is total revenue at $x = 4$?
(d) What is the equation for marginal cost?
(e) What is the equation for the average total cost curve?
(f) What is the firm's total fixed cost?
(g) What is the firm's average fixed cost at $x = 5$?
(h) What is the firm's total variable cost at $x = 3$?
(i) What is the y-intercept of the firm's demand curve?
(j) What is the equation for the firm's total profit?
(k What is the most profitable output?
(l) At what price can the most profitable output be sold?
(m) What is the elasticity of demand at the most profitable price?
(n) What is marginal revenue at the most profitable output?
(o) What is total revenue at the most profitable output?
(p) What is total variable cost at the most profitable output?
(q) What is total cost at the most profitable output?
(r) What is total profit at the most profitable output?
(s) What is total profit at $x = 2\frac{1}{2}$?
(t) In what kind of market does this firm sell?

6

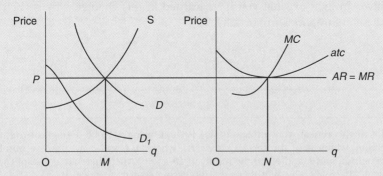

In the above figure the market price is established at OP, the industry is producing OM units of output per time period, and each firm is selling ON units. Assume that market demand shifts from D to D'.

(a) Indicate on the figure the new market price as OP', the new output of the industry as OM', and the new output of each firm as ON'.

(b) Each firm is now (making a profit, suffering a loss, breaking even), and as a result there will be in the long run (an entry of new firms into the industry, an exit of firms from the industry, no change in the number of firms); this will result in a shift in the industry's short-run supply curve to the (right, left).

(c) Assume that this is a constant-cost industry. Draw the short-run supply curve that will re-establish long-run equilibrium, and label it S'.

(d) The new long-run equilibrium price is—?

(e) The output of each firm under the new equilibrium condition is—?

(f) The output of the industry under the new equilibrium is (equal to, less than, greater than) the original equilibrium output because the number of firms has (increased, decreased, remained the same).

(g) Label the long-run supply curve, LRS.

7 A firm pays its accountants an annual retainer of 10,000. Is this an explicit or an implicit cost?

8 The owner of a small retail store does her own accounting work. How would you measure the opportunity cost of her work?

9 The supply curve for a firm in the short run is the short-run marginal cost curve (above the point of minimum average variable cost). Why is the supply curve in the long run *not* the long-run marginal cost curve (above the point of minimum average total cost)?

10 In long-run equilibrium, all firms in the industry earn zero economic profit. Why is this true?

11 What assumptions are necessary for a market to be perfectly competitive? In light of what you have learned in this chapter, why is each of these assumptions important?

Notes

1 A lot of theoretical work in economics is done using a Cobb–Douglas production function, which is of the form $Q = aL^bK^c$, where a, b and c are positive numbers, Q is output, and L and K are the inputs. If $(b+c) = 1$, then there are constant returns to scale. If $(b+c) > 1$, then there are increasing returns to scale. If $(b+c) < 1$, then there are decreasing returns to scale. For a fuller discussion see Pindyck and Rubinfeld (1992).

2 If all units of output are sold at the same price, then MRP is equal to the current

marginal revenue times the marginal product. Although this distinction is important in some applications, it somewhat clouds our analysis at this point.

3 This may seem to be a very high price for a barrel of beer, but remember two things: first there is a good deal of beer in a barrel, and, second, it is very good beer.

4 This follows the language developed by economists in the historical development of these ideas where w refers to a wage rate and r refers to a rental rate.

5 For Figure 3.9, the equations of the isoquants are from Table 3.3 and the equation of the isocost line is $K = 61-21L$. This equation was found by determining the slope of the isoquant at $K = 315$, $L = 15$, which is 21. The new price of labour is 42, the new price of capital is 2.

6 Note also that this rearrangement by the firm will move it closer to meeting the condition of productive efficiency so long as marginal productivity declines. Fewer units of labour will raise the marginal product of labour. More units of capital will increase the marginal product of capital. Thus, these adjustments will occur until the condition of productive efficiency is met.

Reference

Pindyck, R. S. and D. L. Rubinfeld (1992), *Microeconomics*, New York: Macmillan.

CHAPTER 4

Market structure

A. Chapter outline and student goals

The analysis of Chapter 3 provided one view of firm behaviour. That view is useful because it provided us with some of the basic knowledge we need to have, as economists, to understand the behaviour of firms. Although useful, in that it illustrated many of the basic forces operating in competitive atmospheres and within a firm's production process, it was limited in that it represented a very narrow viewpoint of the firm. In this chapter we shed some of the assumptions concerning product differentiation, interaction of competitors and the firm's control over its own long-run destiny. All of this is not to say that understanding the perfectly competitive model is a waste of time; rather it should be viewed as a starting point in understanding more complex industries.

The massive reorganizations in global businesses of the past 10 years have been driven by a number of interacting forces. First, and foremost, is the heightened level of competition in historically sedate industries caused by increased opportunities for international trade. Secondly, not only is technology redefining production and distribution, it is also redefining the actual goods and services themselves. Thirdly, in many industries, particularly in the European and US economies, firms are merging into larger and larger business units. One aspect of these mergers is an attempt to harness economies of scale. A second aspect of these mergers is to provide more market power to the newly created firms. Indeed *Business Week*, a major US business periodical, recently asked, 'Is the U.S. economy becoming a private party?' The answer offered is: 'One commercial aircraft maker. Three major defense contractors. Five big railroads, soon to be four. Fewer banks, electric utilities, phone companies, hospitals' (Mandel, 1997, p. 34).

The domination of big firms is nothing new in industry. What is new is the rate at which these big firms are being formed. The obvious observation is that these large firms are a clear departure from the perfectly competitive firms considered in the last chapter. Typically, such firms have control over market price; limit, distort and otherwise obfuscate information reaching consumers; and not only are successful at preventing entry into the market but also are reluctant to exit.

Perfectly competitive firm
homogenous product
no control over price
entry a certainty
zero long-run profits

Pure monopoly
unique product
control over price
entry precluded
positive long-run profits

Figure 4.1 The spectrum of possible market structures.

To help us come to grips with understanding these large firms, we now turn our attention towards a more general enquiry into what economists term **market structure**, the description of the arrangement of buyers and sellers in an industry and their interaction. We can think of market structure as a question of degree of competitiveness, envisioning a spectrum of possibilities (see Figure 4.1). At one end of the spectrum is the perfectly competitive firm, producing a homogeneous output, having no control over price, facing entry in response to profitable conditions, and earning zero economic profits in the long run. At the other end of the spectrum is the **monopoly**, a market structure featuring a single seller serving the entire market. The monopolist produces a unique good, has absolute control over its price, completely thwarts entry, and earns potentially substantial profits in the long run. As is the case with most economic and political debates, the most interesting truth lies somewhere in the middle.

The markets that are not perfectly competitive and not monopolistic may be the most interesting. However, they are the most difficult to deal with. We consider market structures that blend certain elements of both extremes. There may be, for example, product differentiation and 'limited' entry. Alternatively, the current and future number of competitors may be fixed and we may seek to model competition centred on something other than price. To understand firm behaviour in these exchange environments we need additional analytical tools.

Economists define a **game** as any exchange environment in which participants, called players, must choose a course of action when there is a large degree of uncertainty regarding what choices other participants, or players, will choose to do. **Game theory** is the formal modelling of a game highlighting the interaction resulting from choices made by all the players. In the setting of a game, the decisions made by the players are said to be **strategic** in that not only do they affect other players, they affect the choices made by the other players. In some market structures, game theory offers an elegant description of the exchange environment and enables economists to make predictions regarding firm behaviour.

After reading this chapter you should be able to:

- describe the four market structures identified by economists;
- identify ways that firms may work to act in a less than competitive manner;
- explain the two categories of barriers to entry and understand how firms use them to preserve market power;
- explain the differences among the market structures;
- understand, on a very basic level, what game theory is and how it can be applied to study competitive, strategic interaction by firms;
- define some basic concepts of game theory such as the payoff matrix, strategy identification, and the three types of equilibria in this chapter;
- comment on the economic efficiency of the different market structures relative to the perfectly competitive market structure.

B. Departures from the competitive ideal

Market structure

Less than perfectly competitive markets

When an economist considers events in a market or, to use a synonymous term, industry, the most important characteristic is the market structure. In many industries the perfectly competitive model of Chapter 3 is not applicable and the competition one sees is far less than 'perfect'. As already discussed in the introduction to this chapter, a monopoly is the case completely orthogonal to the perfectly competitive firm.

The market structure termed **monopolistic competition** features fewer firms than found in perfectly competitive markets, but more than the single firm of monopoly. In the monopolistically competitive market, products are differentiated but similar. Given the large number of firms in this type of market, each firm can ignore the actions of any single competitor. If one company lowers its price, for instance, it may expect to increase its market share; however, the number of customers it captures from a typical competitor is small enough not to evoke a reaction from that competitor. As is the case in perfectly competitive industries, the monopolistically competitive firm acts with a view of the market in mind, thus its pricing and output decisions are not likely to be strategic in nature.

The **oligopoly** market structure features fewer firms than monopolistically competitive industries. The most compelling feature of oligopolistic markets is that each of the limited number of firms is directly concerned with how its rivals will react to any action that the firm takes. The oligopolistic firm may very well feel, for example, that rivals will match price cuts in a fairly direct way, but not price increases.

Each of the less than 'perfectly' competitive market structures shares two common elements, which may be considered as differences from the perfectly competitive market structure. These common elements are what make the industries what they are. First, each has fewer firms owing to some ability by firms in the market to keep other producers out. Secondly, under each market structure firms enjoy at least some degree of market power, or control over their own price. For the oligopolists and monopolistically competitive firms this control is due largely to some form of product differentiation – practised more heavily in the former and a little less in the latter.

Still MR = MC

You are probably beginning to ask, 'If these market structures are so different from perfect competition, what analytical devices can we bring to bear?' The answer is, quite a few. Firms are still assumed to face the same type of production process characterized by diminishing marginal productivity, U-shaped average unit cost curves and increasing marginal costs. From an analytical perspective, the different market structures affect the revenue side of the profit equation.

When a firm has market power, it can no longer sell as much as it wants at the going market price. Instead, the firm faces a downward-sloping demand function: if it raises (lowers) its price, its quantity demanded falls (increases). This implies that marginal revenue is different from price in these market structures. In fact, marginal revenue must be less than price. To see why, suppose that a firm wishes to sell an additional unit. To do so it must offer that additional unit to the market for sale at a lower price than the preceding unit because the market was already purchasing all it wanted at the initial price. It also follows that, if the firm sells all of its output at the same price (an assumption we will relax later in this chapter), the prices of all those other units must fall too. All of this to sell an additional unit! The net result is that, from the firm's perspective, the marginal revenue received from selling that additional unit – all things considered – is not only less than price, it is also less than the marginal revenue of the preceding unit.

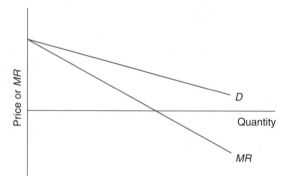

Figure 4.2 Demand and marginal revenue with market power.

In Figure 4.2, we show the demand curve of a firm with some market power and its associated marginal revenue curve. Although a linear form is shown, the results generalize to form more complex than this simple linear approximation. The hypothetical firm's demand function is labelled *D*, and its marginal revenue curve is labelled *MR*. Recall from the argument in Chapter 2 that marginal revenue can become negative, indicating that further price declines to increase quantity demanded may decrease total revenue.

Measuring market power

Measuring industries

Firm behaviour in markets in which they have market power will be very different from behaviour of firms in markets where no firm has substantial market power. These differences in behaviour will affect the entire industry. When economists measure market power they usually rely on industry measures, for this and another reason. The second reason for measuring market power on an industry basis is a reluctance of most statistical agencies to present data clearly identifying individual firms.

The market structure in an industry refers to the number and size distribution of firms. Most theories of competition suggest that market-wide behaviour depends more on the characteristics of its largest firms, than on those of its smallest, or fringe firms. Accordingly, attempts to measure market structure or the availability of market power stress the importance of the largest firms in the market. Markets are described as **concentrated** if they have just a few, dominant sellers. We can expect to see very little semblance of the perfectly competitive firm in concentrated markets.

N-firm Concentration Ratio

A widely used and easy to calculate measure of market structure is the **N-firm concentration ratio**, which shows the combined market share of the *N* largest firms. For example, the four-firm concentration ratio in the soft drink industry in the United States is approximately 0.90, which indicates that, taken together, the four largest firms in the soft drink industry account for 90 percent of sales.

In Table 4.1, *three-firm concentration ratios* for a number of industries in a number of different nations in the 1970s are shown. Although the data are somewhat old, we present them for two reasons. First, they provide a clear example not only of the underlying concentration ratios, but also of some international comparisons. Secondly, we can think of these industries today and compare them with how they were in the past.

Some compelling features are presented in Table 4.1. First, concentration ratios can vary substantially across industries. Secondly, concentration levels for a given industry are roughly comparable across nations. This would

Table 4.1 Three-firm concentration ratios

Industry	United States	United Kingdom	Sweden	France	West Germany	Canada
Brewing	39	47	70	63	17	89
Cigarettes	68	94	100	100	94	90
Paints	26	40	92	14	32	40
Shoes (except rubber)	17	17	37	13	20	18
Portland cement	20	86	100	81	54	65
Refrigerators	64	65	80	100	72	75
Storage batteries	54	75	100	94	82	73
Ordinary steel	42	39	63	84	56	80

Source F. M. Scherer, A. Beckenstein, E. Kaufer, and R. D. Murphy, T*he Economics of Multi-Plant Operations: An International Comparison Study*, Cambridge, Mass.: Harvard University Press, 1975, pp. 218–19 and 426–8.

suggest that the underlying technology of production and the ownership of the rights to certain factors of production are more important in determining industry competitiveness than are regulatory environments or some randomized lottery. Thirdly, markets in the United States are seemingly less concentrated than markets in other countries.

Herfindahl index
The **Herfindahl index** equals the sum of the squared market shares of all the firms in the market. Although the Herfindahl index is more complex in terms of data requirements (one needs data on all firms in the market) and calculation, it represents an alternative to the more standard N-firm concentration ratio. If S_i denotes the market share for firm i in the market, then the Herfindahl index for any industry is defined as:

$$H = \Sigma_i (S_i)^2$$

In a market with two equal-sized firms, the Herfindahl index is equal to $(0.5)^2 + (0.5)^2 = 0.5$. This simple example points to both an interesting mathematical property of the Herfindahl index, and also the importance of comparing the actual size distribution of firms with some benchmark, or standard. If an industry has N equal-sized firms, then the Herfindahl index for that industry equals $1/N$. For this reason, the inverse, or reciprocal, of the Herfindahl index is referred to as the numbers-equivalent of firms. Thus, for an industry with a Herfindahl index of 0.25, the numbers-equivalent for that industry would be 4. As with N-firm concentration ratios, calculated Herfindahl indexes that are larger are consistent with more market power held by some firms and a lower degree of competition in the market.

In an applied sense, the Herfindahl index offers an advantage over the N-

firm concentration ratio because it weights firms by their relative sizes. For example, consider an industry of 30 firms dominated by 4 large firms for which both measures of concentration are calculated. If the largest firm in the industry captures half the market share of the second-, third- and fourth-largest firms in the industry the four-firm concentration ratio will not change, whereas the Herfindahl index will. The major weakness inherent in using the Herfindahl index to measure market power is the volume of data required in its construction.

Barriers to entry

What can be protected and how
The perfectly competitive equilibrium described in Chapter 3 is useful as a benchmark against which to judge other types of industries. One has to admit, however, that its ultimate result (that free entry will eliminate economic profits by all firms) is a rather gloomy proposition from the firms' point of view. Notice however that, without the prospect of free entry, firms could continue to earn positive economic profits indefinitely. In some markets this indeed occurs, and in every case one can identify at least one reason potential competitors are precluded from entering the market. Economists define **entry barriers** as some factors that limit the entry of new firms into a market, even though the existing firms are making economic profits in that market. The existence of barriers to entry is a necessary condition for market power to exist.

To understand barriers to entry we can put ourselves into the position of a firm contemplating entry into an existing market. Its decision to enter will be affected by three separate issues. First, a potential entrant to the market will be concerned about price and output levels after its entry. The state of the industry after entry will, in turn, depend on at least two factors. Will the entry result in such a large increase in market supply that prices are depressed to uneconomic levels for firms? The other factor affecting the state of the industry after entry relates to the expected reaction of already existing firms. If the previously established firms follow a strategy of accommodating the entry, then, potentially, a new equilibrium will be established at which all firms make a satisfactory economic profit. On the other hand, the previously established firms may seek to punish the entrant through a price war, for example, to drive the entrant away from the market. The value of this type of strategy by the established firms is that it sends a clear message to other firms contemplating entry into the industry.

The potential entrant into a market is concerned about two more factors that are at least as important as the first. Secondly, potential entrants will want to recognize any and all incumbent advantages. Existing firms may possess certain advantages unavailable to market entrants. Potential entrants may face a daunting task in acquiring their own advantages to compete with the established sellers. Thirdly, the potential entrant will be concerned about the costs of exiting the industry. More concretely, if entering the market requires a substantial expenditure on resources that have no value if not used by the entering firm in that industry, then exit costs may be large. Whether or not they are too large depends ultimately on the potential entrant's opinion of profitability.

Classifying entry barriers

The creation and maintenance of entry barriers is essential if firms are to expect to earn positive economic profits in the long run. We turn our attention to examples of barriers to entry, focusing on how exactly those barriers are created and maintained by firms.[1] One may think of barriers to entry as being factors of production that are *required* for the production, distribution and sale of a good or service. This type of barrier is referred to as an **exogenous barrier** to entry if any firm wanting to enter the market must, because of the physical nature of the production, distribution or sale of a good, acquire a set amount of resources to accomplish this task. Consider an airline for example. The airline must spend millions of pounds to establish airport hub operations before it can efficiently transport passengers. Since any firm wishing to enter must acquire these resources, the hub operations represent an exogenous entry barrier.

Endogenous barriers to entry on the other hand are those resources that may be necessary to enter an industry but are not necessary for the production, distribution and sale of the good by an incumbent who is not trying to create such barriers. Research and development expenditures aimed at product improvement and advertising expenditures aimed at increasing consumer awareness of the product are good examples of endogenous barriers to entry. One could perhaps produce, for example, a drink superior to Coca-Cola; getting consumers to notice it, however, may be an entirely different story. In short, many of the fixed costs involved in entering an industry are not, strictly speaking, necessitated by considerations directly related to the production, sale and distribution of the goods in the market place. Endogenous entry barriers are those that are created by the firms populating an industry. Exogenous entry barriers are those that exist in the absence of any conscious effort by incumbent firms.

The economics profession is not in unanimous agreement on what terminology to use when discussing entry barriers. Some follow the terminology set up by Joseph Bain in his seminal writings (Bain, 1956). Others focus on incumbent advantages, which most closely tie to the concept of exogenous barriers to entry as used here, and also incumbent reactions, which most closely tie in the concept of endogenous advantages used here.[2] Still other economists adopt other ways to classify barriers to entry.

Exogenous advantages

Perhaps the most interesting (from a strategic viewpoint) exogenous barrier to entry is the presence of economies of scale or economies of scope in the provision of a good in the market. Other exogenous advantages that are turned into entry barriers through the market process are cost reductions that manifest themselves because of experience producing a good, and pioneering brand advantages. A more obvious exogenous barrier to entry is the control over some physical resource necessary for the production or distribution of the good or service.

We discuss economies of scale explicitly; a similar argument for economies of scope is left to the reader. In some industries, large-scale production may be required to produce output at reasonably low unit costs either because of large fixed costs required in the production process, or because of the nature of the production process itself. The reader may be troubled by the use of the word 'large' because it is a relative term. Two metres may be a long way for a snail to travel, but it is but two large steps for a professional athlete.

In order to talk in a meaningful way about large outputs we need to revisit the concept of **minimum efficient scale** (MES), which represents the efficient level of production. If, in an industry, the MES is large relative to market demand, then economies of scale will represent an entry barrier. Such a situation is pictured in Figure 4.3. At the other extreme, MES may represent a very small portion of industry output, a situation depicted in Figure 4.4.

Separate and apart from economies of scale and scope, firms may develop cost advantages that are transformed into entry barriers if experience in the production or sale of a good or service translates into lower unit costs. Economists speak of **learning curve** effects if unit costs depend in a significant way on cumulative (over many periods) output. Learning curve effects may result from actual human learning or from adaptations of the production process owing to experience.

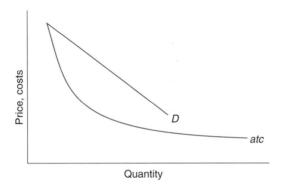

Figure 4.3 Small demand relative to costs.

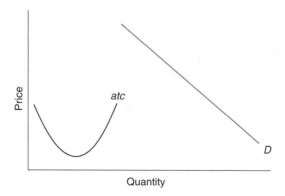

Figure 4.4 Large demand relative to costs.

Just as there are experience benefits in production, there may also be experience effects in consumption. A firm often benefits from being the first to enter an industry because their product, by default, becomes the standard against which all others are judged in consumers' minds. We could then say that there may be a first-mover effect in consumption that elicits in consumers a sense of brand loyalty or familiarity that results in market power for the firm. A good example is provided by the over-the-counter medicine market: if a consumer is happy that the cold remedy Sneeze-B-Gone will mitigate the effects of a flu virus, that consumer may be unwilling even to try other cold remedies as they enter the market.

A very obvious exogenous barrier to entry is the control, by some firm, over a key physical resource necessary for the production or distribution and sale of a good. A good example is the technology necessary to make advanced computer chips. Only a handful of companies in the entire world possess this technology and are quite unlikely to share it with other firms for fear of inviting competitors into the market place.

Endogenous advantages
Established firms often have long-term contracts for necessary raw materials, distribution networks and the like that preclude the availability of these resources to competitors. Potential entrants may in effect be locked out of competing in the market owing to an inability to capture the use of certain assets, even though those assets may not be absolutely necessary to the production, distribution or sale of the good. Such **precommitment contracts** are illegal in some countries owing to their anti-competitive effects on the market place. Several examples of such devices are discussed in section 14 of this chapter.

Government action, at the request of the established firms in an industry, may create an endogenous entry barrier. The most common devices are licences, patents and copyrights. The regulating bodies often justify legal entry barriers on two grounds. First, they may protect product quality or purity. Secondly, they may promote innovation because licences, patents and copyrights in effect increase the potential rewards of innovative efforts. From an applied viewpoint, the effectiveness of government action as an entry barrier may be, and often is, circumvented by clever engineering and design changes. While policing copyrights and patents in a single country is a tough enough task, it becomes even tougher in the international market place.

Sometimes firms in an industry create excess productive capacity. At normal operating ranges, average units costs may be quite high depending on the slope of an average cost curve. When faced with entry, however, the established firms may simply expand output, lowering unit costs and market prices either to deter entry or to drive the new entrant out of the market. The use of excess capacity may represent a good strategy to deter entry if fixed costs are large. Under such a scenario, for the entrant all costs are avoidable, meaning the entrant will want to price at average total costs. For the established firms however, all costs are not avoidable; quite likely the incumbent has some of its costs sunk. Put another way, the established firms will permit prices to fall to average variable costs.

In markets with differentiated products it is useful to think of individual brands having some market power over those consumers who most prefer their brand over all other brands. The market power arises because, although consumers are willing to switch brands if compensated, the costs in terms of a mismatch between the characteristics of their most preferred brand and the characteristics of competing brands outweigh any price differential between their most preferred and the competing brands. In such a scenario one firm could conceivably launch a number of competing brands. The purpose of seemingly competing with itself is to flood the market and to prevent any entrant to the market from capturing a sufficient product niche to make their entry worthwhile. A good example of this is in the United Kingdom and the United States, where the ready-to-eat cereal industry features many, many brands and few producers. The incredible variety of brands leaves every conceivable market niche 'covered'. Not surprisingly, there has been only one minimal entry into this market in the past five decades.

C. Monopoly: A polar case

Monopoly mechanics

Firm demand
Since there is only one firm in the market, consumers are not able to substitute among different brands. As such, the demand curve facing the monopolist is equivalent to the market demand function. It is downward sloping and

the monopolist has complete freedom from fear of competitor reaction in setting its price. This is not to say that the monopolist can charge 'whatever price
it wishes'; rather, the monopolist's pricing decision is governed by the strengths
and weaknesses of market demand.

Profit maximization
Even though the monopolist is the only seller in the market, the basic mechanics of profit maximization remains the same: produce where marginal revenue
equals marginal cost. When viewed as a function of quantity produced, marginal revenue decreases and marginal cost increases, ensuring that profits will
be maximized when $MR = MC$. The situation facing the firm is shown in
Figure 4.5. The marginal revenue curve lies everywhere below the demand
curve. Profits are maximized when $MR = MC$, at output level Q_1. Given the
absence of the threat of entry, we might expect substantial economic profits
to be made.

  Facing the market demand function D, the monopolist will sell units of output for as much as the market will bear, P_1. On a per-unit basis the economic
profits are given by the difference between P_1 and atc_1, the level of the average total costs of production. The total profits earned by the monopolist are
given by the rectangle P_1EFatc_1.

The inefficiency of monopoly
Over the years economists have noted a number of inefficiencies arising from
monopolies. These include restricted output, managerial waste and non-
optimal levels of research and development.

Restricted output In considering the inefficiencies of monopolies restricting
output we will compare the monopolistic outcome with that of the perfectly

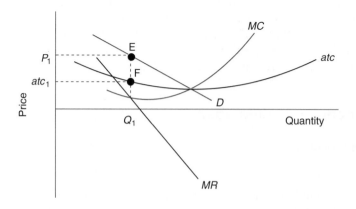

Figure 4.5 Monopoly: Profit maximization.

competitive firm. Although we may not expect to see any given industry best characterized as a perfectly competitive one, it provides a useful benchmark from which to address questions of efficiency. All firms are in business to create profits. The monopolist has a very useful tool in this regard, the ability to restrict output and to drive up price.

When a monopolist sets marginal revenue equal to marginal cost to determine its level of output it is necessarily producing less than a perfectly competitive firm would. In Figure 4.6 we show the monopoly output and price as Q_m and P_m, respectively. For comparison purposes we may ask at what level of output and price a perfectly competitive industry would supply this same market. Recall that for perfectly competitive firms $P = MR$, and that the industry supply function is simply the summation of individual firm supply functions. We then argue that a perfectly competitive firm would provide the market with Q_{pc} units at a price of P_{pc}.

It is necessary to understand why the output and price combination chosen by the monopolist is too little. The price of the last unit of the good sold represents the amount one individual is willing to pay for that marginal unit of output. It measures, in other words, the marginal benefit to society of that marginal unit. Under perfectly competitive conditions that price also equals the marginal cost of producing that unit. Thus, under perfectly competitive conditions, further efficiency gains are impossible. There is no way that, if one could force the production of an extra unit, then the gain to society would exceed the costs. For the monopolist, however, further efficiency gains are possible. If one could force the production of an extra unit, beyond the monopolist's chosen level of output, the marginal benefit of that additional unit would clearly exceed the marginal cost of providing it. Thus, with reference to Figure 4.6 below, the marginal benefits of the Q_m + 1 unit exceed the costs. You may then ask why, if the gains exceed the costs, the monopolist doesn't produce

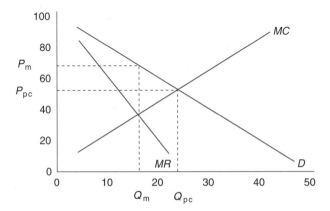

Figure 4.6 A monopolist restricting output.

that extra unit. The answer is that the gain is experienced by consumers; only a loss would be had by the monopolist because such an increase in output would move it away from the profit-maximizing choice.

The fact that monopolists typically restrict output and raise price in their own markets is an obvious reason why economists usually object to monopolistic market structures. Quite generally, consumers object as well. Still, there remains a potentially more serious economic effect from the monopolist restricting output to an amount less than the competitive ideal. For an economic system to operate in an efficient manner, **allocative efficiency** has to be attained. Allocative efficiency refers to the economy's ability to produce the quantities of the good and services that consumers desire to buy. There is a tendency to view allocative efficiency as solely a price problem; however, it may be viewed as a quantity problem as well.

Figure 4.7 reintroduces you to a concept with which you were made familiar in your prior economics coursework – the production possibilities frontier, which shows the maximum amount that an economy can produce given available resources. Given a statement of consumer preferences and a functioning market system, all economic agents, producers and consumers alike, will have an optimal point on the production possibilities frontier (PPF). In Figure 4.7 we assume, for simplicity, that there are only two goods in the economy: guns, measured on the horizontal axis; and butter, measured on the vertical axis. The optimal consumption point for the economy might be point A, the point at which allocative efficiency is reached. Suppose however that the gun industry is, in fact, a monopoly and the single gun producer restricts output to preserve its own profits. In this case the economy might be moved to point B on the PPF, which is efficient in that the economy is on its PPF, but which may not represent a point consistent with allocative efficiency.

Managerial waste In Chapter 3 we argued that, in competitive markets, producers want, as part of making profits as high as possible, to minimize costs.

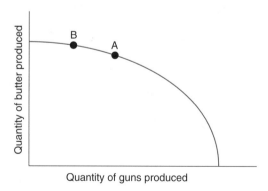

Figure 4.7 Monopoly and the PPF.

Indeed, a competitive atmosphere will cause companies to make costs as small as possible. A monopoly may not face this pressure to the same degree.

Non-optimal levels of research and development A competitive market place encourages innovation by producers. In fact, in many of today's high-tech markets the process has reached the point where companies are producing totally new products and convincing consumers that there is, in fact, a need for them. In some industries where competition is not an issue however, this pressure may be lacking.

Natural monopolies
In some industries, the technology underlying the production process may be expected to result in having one firm serve the market. The most common feature of these industries is huge fixed costs in production resulting in economies of scale. More technically we would say that if the average total cost curve declines over the relevant range of market demand, then the industry is called a **natural monopoly**. The situation would be like that pictured in Figure 4.8. If left alone, the natural monopolist would produce the amount Q_m, charging a price of P_m.

This cost structure is typical of many industries. Railroads, for example, have a large portion of their costs fixed: once the track is laid and the locomotives and rail cars are bought, it costs only a small amount to run a train. Electrical generation and distribution is another industry best called a natural monopoly. Again, most of the costs are fixed: once the generation facility is built and the transmission lines are installed, it costs very little to provide the electricity necessary to turn on the light in your study. These industries are termed natural monopolies because there is some intuitive sense in having only one firm serve the market. The argument goes that, if two firms were to serve the market, each would have to capitalize the necessary huge fixed costs. In

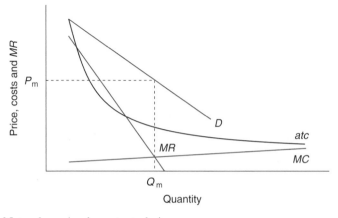

Figure 4.8 Natural monopoly, output choice.

the limit, each of the potential two firms would have to incur the fixed costs borne by a single firm serving the market. The inefficiency here is obvious and the only question is under what condition one firm will be permitted to serve the market.

Dealing with natural monopolies

Public policies differ marketedly regarding attempts to deal with natural monopolies.[3] In most economies, policy makers understand the efficiencies from not having two producers incur the necessary fixed costs, and weigh these efficiencies against the granting of monopoly power to a firm. We identify two categories of policies often employed by governments in dealing with this market structure: adopting regulatory boards and nationalizing firms. For each we attempt to recognize the strengths and weaknesses arising in that approach.

Adopting regulatory boards In some cases, natural monopolies are left to exist as private firms, so as to encourage any competitive market discipline there, and regulated in terms of output levels, types of output and price. In the UK and many other countries, for example, local utilities (providing natural gas and electric service) are heavily regulated private firms.

The goal of the regulation is to ensure that prices are kept as low as possible. In practice, this equates price to average total cost, ensuring the monopolist a normal return on investment. This type of regulatory environment is shown in Figure 4.9 as setting price equal to P_R and output to Q_R.[4]

A regulatory scheme that forces the producer to sell at average unit cost has two widely recognized weaknesses. First, because the owners of the underlying capital are ensured a fair and safe return, they have incentive to invest in more capital than they otherwise would. Secondly, in this regulatory environment pressures may be brought to bear on the regulators to provide output

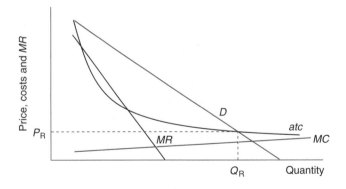

Figure 4.9 Regulated natural monopoly.

or services to some customers at a price below either marginal or average total costs. It is relatively inexpensive, for example, to extend an existing electric or gas distribution grid in a heavily developed urban area to, say, a new housing development. If the housing development is built in a relatively secluded rural area, the situation may be quite different, necessitating the establishment of additional trunk lines and substations to service the new residential development. Yet it is common practice for all customers to pay the same utility rates within the jurisdiction of the regulated monopolist. When this occurs, one group of users/customers must in effect subsidize another group, a practice termed **cross-subsidization**.

Nationalizing firms In many European countries the governmental response to natural monopolies has been to take ownership of the firms. The United Kingdom and France, for example, nationalized their electric power, telephone, and gas and water companies, the United Kingdom has privatized them recently. On the plus side, any monopoly profits earned are returned to customers in indirect ways via the central governments, who own these potential profits. Further, governments will have little incentive to restrict output or services, wanting to act instead as benevolent monopolists.

There are some potential weaknesses in this approach. First, governments may not be efficient managers. Political pressures may affect key business decisions such as adopting technological standards or where to locate a new facility. Secondly, the government managers may be under pressure to provide some services far below either marginal or average total cost. Like the regulatory approach to dealing with natural monopolies, nationalizing these firms may also result in cross-subsidization. As an example of a nationalized natural monopoly engaging in cross-subsidization, consider any national postal service, which relies heavily on cross-subsidization because the heavy volume of easy-to-deliver mail in urban areas undoubtedly pays for the low volume of hard-to-deliver mail in rural areas.

D. Pricing practices reflecting market power

Some definitions

Surplus and capturing it

As explained in Chapter 2, **consumer surplus** is defined as the difference between what consumers will pay for a unit of a good and what they actually do pay for that unit of the good. To illustrate this concept further, envision a market where every consumer purchases only one unit of output. Suppose, hypothetically, that we had some device to force consumers to reveal their individual **reservation prices** (the maximum amount they would be willing to pay for their unit of the good). We could then think of the market demand function of the good corresponding to a lining up of the customers by decreasing values of their reservation prices. Clearly, then, the height of the demand function at any point shows the marginal benefit to one consumer from consuming the good. Now suppose that the good is sold at a single price. Consumers whose consumer surplus is greater than or equal to zero purchase the good; for those whose consumer surplus is negative there is no purchase. If we aggregate all the individual consumer surpluses across the market we obtain the total consumer surplus.

In Figure 4.10 there is a hypothetical demand function whose equation is $P = 20 - 2Q$. For illustrative purposes we can assume that a good is being offered for sale at a price of 10. Again thinking of the market demand function as an ordering of consumers by decreasing reservation prices, we can see that the person with the highest reservation price for the good will offer 18 for her unit of the good. The second person will offer 16, the third 14, the fourth 12, and the fifth 10. The sixth to tenth individuals in our hypothetical line-up will offer less than the price of the good and can hence be ignored. The consumer surpluses for the first to fifth consumers are 8, 6, 4, 2 and 0, respectively. In more general terms we can say that the consumer surplus in the market is equal to the shaded area of the triangle ABC in Figure 4.10.

Economists have long recognized that consumer surplus represents one of the basic benefits of free, voluntary exchange. Given that there is, in this sense, a gain to be had, it is not unrealistic to assume that some sellers will attempt to transfer the gain from consumers to themselves. We will investigate two mechanisms to do this: price discrimination and two-part tariffs.

Different buyers, different prices
Price discrimination occurs when different buyers pay different prices for similar goods and the difference in prices is more than any cost difference in serving the separate buyers. It is not price discrimination if a lumber merchant sells lumber at one price in his store and at a higher price at the buyer's

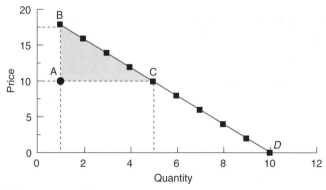

Figure 4.10 Consumer surplus.

location, so long as the price at the buyer's location does not exceed the in-store price by more than shipping charges. Three conditions are required for successful price discrimination. First, the seller must be able to separately identify groups of buyers. Secondly, the buyer groups must have price elasticities of demand that are different. It is generally true that buyers with a greater price elasticity of demand will pay a lower price than those buyer groups with more inelastic demands. Thirdly, the seller has to be able to prevent resale of the good; if not, the low-price buyers would arbitrage on behalf of the high-price buyers at the seller's expense. In all cases, the seller equates marginal revenue and marginal cost in each sub-market.

There are three cases of identified price discrimination, differing in terms of the seller's ability to capture consumer surplus. Under **first-degree price discrimination**, each individual consumer is charged a price equal to their reservation price, making the consumers indifferent between purchasing the good or not. In the above example the first buyer would be charged 18, the second 16 and so on. The firm would sell to all consumers whose reservation prices exceed the marginal costs of production. If successful, first-degree price discrimination would completely transfer consumer surplus to the seller, implying that all the gains from trade go to the seller. Price discrimination of the first degree is rare, although we have seen attempts at least approximating it. Consider the typical auction setting where sellers do not have to be concerned with resale, owing perhaps to protocol or perhaps to individuals leaving the auction after their purchase. A clever auctioneer will not reveal how many of a set of identical items he has. Instead he will, most preferably, sell them off one at a time, each to the highest bidder.

Second-degree price discrimination involves setting smaller prices for additional units purchased. A common example of this occurs at the grocery store where the larger-sized packages of many items sell at a lower per-unit price than smaller packages. Large-quantity users, for example a mother shopping for her six children, are likely to be more price sensitive than a childless couple, representing a small-quantity user. When such quantity discounts are used, **blocked pricing** is said to occur, with high prices charged for the first unit and lower prices for subsequent units.

Whereas price discrimination of the first degree is somewhat rare, second- and third-degree price discrimination are much more common. In a pricing scheme adopting **third-degree price discrimination** buyers are separated into several sub-markets, each paying a unique price. Examples include airlines identifying business and recreational fliers and computer manufacturers providing student discounts.

Mathematical example of third degree Cheryl Osbourne manages a publishing company that is planning the marketing of a new book, *Woodworking in the Twentieth Century*. Market research and prior experience have shown that two groups of buyers are interested in this book: members of the Fisbane Woodworking

Society, and the general public. Ms Osbourne feels that the demand from the members of the Fisbane Woodworking Society will be a little less sensitive to price than from the public at large and wants to plan a separate marketing strategy through the *Fisbane Splinter*, the official newsletter of the Fisbane Woodworking Society. The demand from the readers of the *Fisbane Splinter* is known to be (where Q^{FWS} denotes the quantity demanded by this group):

$$Q^{FWS} = 100 - 2P^{FWS} \tag{4.1}$$

The demand for the book by the general public at large, Q^{GP}, is:

$$Q^{GP} = 160 - 4P^{GP} \tag{4.2}$$

Aggregating the quantity demanded at each price level across the two groups of buyers reveals the total market demand, Q^{TOT}, to be:

$$Q^{TOT} = 260 - 6P^{TOT} \tag{4.3}$$

where P^{TOT} denotes the single price charged in the market if separate groups of buyers are not identified.

The cost structure faced by Ms Osbourne is assumed to be somewhat simpler than those described in Chapter 3 to allow us to focus on this example. There is a constant marginal cost of 5 and fixed costs of 20 associated with this project. Figure 4.11 shows the market demand by all consumers of *Woodworking in the Twentieth Century*. The demand attributable to members of the Fisbane Society is shown in Figure 4.12, and general public demand is shown in Figure 4.13.

Ms Osbourne should engage in third-degree price discrimination. If she sells the books at a single price to all buyers, the publisher profits by 2,184.13. If, on the other hand, she isolates the buyers in each market, her earnings, on behalf of the publishing company, are greater. Sales to Fisbane Woodworking

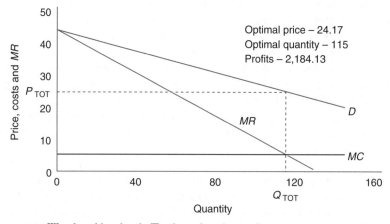

Figure 4.11 Woodworking book: Total market demand.

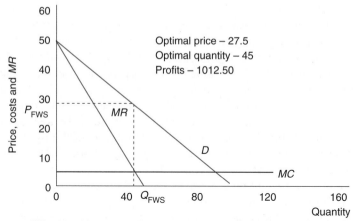

Figure 4.12 Woodworking book: Demand from members of Fisbane Society.

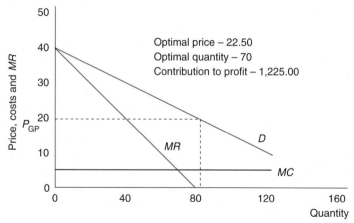

Figure 4.13 Woodworking book: General public demand.

Society members through their newsletter will result in a price of 27.50, 45 books will be sold, and profits from that market, exclusive of fixed costs, will be 1,012.50. In sales to the general public, 70 books will be sold at a price of 22.50, resulting in a contribution to profit of 1,225. Total profits from the third-degree price discrimination would then be 2,217.50.

Applying the formulas for the price elasticity of demand from Chapter 2, we can see that, where demand is more elastic with respect to price, the price will be lower. Applying the point elasticity formula at the optimal price in each sub-market reveals that for society members the price elasticity of demand is 1.22 and for the general public the price elasticity of demand is 1.29.

Two-part tariffs

A second method enabling sellers to pursue consumer surplus, although more restrictive in its application, is a **two-part tariff**, where buyers are charged an up-front fee granting them the right to purchase the product and then charged a per-unit fee as they use the product.[5] This approach is generally taken in amusement parks, where there is a fee to enter the park and a charge per attraction, or ride, visited. Some professional sports teams in the United States, notably those in the National Football League, require those wishing to buy season tickets first to purchase a seat licence granting them the right to do so. These seat licences are not cheap, on average nearly $2,000 – a large amount given that the season ticket itself averages $320.

The mechanics of instituting a two-part tariff pricing scheme are somewhat complex. A shortened algorithm would be as follows. The 'first part' of this pricing scheme is to charge buyers an amount equal to their consumer surplus from the transaction conducted, hypothetically, at marginal cost. The 'second part' is then to charge the consumer an amount equal to marginal cost for actual use of the good.

A two-part tariff is easier to envision and apply when consumers can be expected to consume more than one unit of the good. In Figure 4.14 we show the demand curve for a hypothetical consumer visiting an amusement park called Econoland. All of the attractions in Econoland are provided at the same marginal cost, 20. For illustrative purposes suppose that the representative consumer's demand function has equation $P = 100 - 10Q$. The marginal cost curve intersects the demand function at 8 units of output. The first part of the two-part tariff aims to capture the entire consumer surplus for each buyer, shown in the diagram as the shaded triangle ABC. The area of triangle ABC is easily calculated and the consumer surplus is seen to be $(\frac{1}{2})(80)(8) = 320$. This amount would be paid up front upon admission to Econoland. Each attraction in Econoland would be visited for a price of 20.

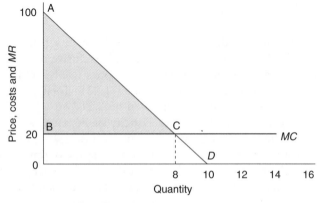

Figure 4.14 Two-part tariff at Econoland.

The difficulty in applying the two-part tariff is identifying an appropriate amount to charge to capture the consumer surplus. Quite possibly this amount differs markedly across individuals. Usually one observes some type of price discrimination accompanying the first part of the two-part tariff-pricing scheme. Amusement parks sometimes distribute discount tickets for local consumers and make arrangements with hotels and visitor centres, setting up package plans.

Competitive considerations

Both price discrimination and two-part tariff-pricing schemes require that the selling firm have some market power. Naturally, if the firm is a monopolist, this requirement is met. However, pure monopolies are not as common as we might think and many firms face, at least, limited competition. Whether or not a firm can engage in attempts to capture consumer surplus is severely limited by the amount of competition the firm faces. Consider how a rival would, for example, react to discriminatory pricing. If the competition is intense, the rival will easily undercut the price charged to the consumers paying more for the good. On the other hand, it is quite possible that rivals may act in concert, preserving the profits of all producers and sellers. In a sense, the perfectly competitive and monopolistic market models represent limiting cases. We now turn our attention to the market structures that are in effect hybrids of these two polar cases.

E. Monopolistic competition

Differentiated products

A hybrid market structure

In 1993, Edward Chamberlin of Harvard University envisioned a market structure that shared certain features of the perfectly competitive and monopolistic market models. The unique result of the theory of **monopolistic competition** is that each seller has some market power, yet, in the end, economic profits are driven to zero. The two main features of Chamberlin's model were that there were many sellers and that the product of each seller is slightly different from the rest.

With many sellers in the market, it is reasonable to suppose that no single seller can take an action that will significantly affect other sellers. For example, consider the women's retail clothing market in a major city such as London. There are easily hundreds of such merchants. If any single seller were to lower its prices, it is quite unlikely that other sellers would react. In fact, most sellers would probably fail to notice. Even if some sellers of women's clothes in London recognized the drop-off in sales, they could easily attribute it to any one of a thousand different factors.

Notice however that each seller of women's clothes in London strives to be different from its competitors. Different retailers may target younger or older women; others may cater to professional women, etc. Further differentiation may, and probably does, occur regarding location. If the wares of each seller were homogeneous, consumers would willingly switch from one to the other. We say that two products, X and Y, are **differentiated products** if there is some common price for the two products at which some consumers prefer to purchase X and others prefer to purchase Y. Furthermore, there is a limit to the degree of product differentiation. At equal prices, if a consumer, Mr Kimball, prefers product X over product Y, then there may well be a pair of unequal prices for goods X and Y at which Mr Kimball prefers product Y over product X.

Economists further distinguish between **vertical differentiation** and **horizontal differentiation**. When producers make a product of higher quality than competing products, they are exploiting vertical differentiation. When producers make a product more distinct from competitors they are following horizontal differentiation. A toothpaste becomes vertically differentiated when it has greater power to fight cavities and to prevent plaque build-up. Toothpaste becomes horizontally differentiated when the producer adds minty-fresh flavour capsules. In discussing monopolistic competition, the nature of the product differentiation is not important; what is important is that we recognize that the quantity demanded of a firm's output does not fall to zero when its price is raised while competitor's prices are held constant.

In Figure 4.15 we show the situation facing the monopolistically competitive firm. Notice that the demand function is downward sloping. It represents a share of the total market demand faced by all of the sellers in the monopolistically competitive industry. The exact way in which the individual firm demands aggregate into market demand is a complex concept and would require a thorough understanding of not only all the firms in the industry, but their prices, advertising efforts and the exact way in which products are

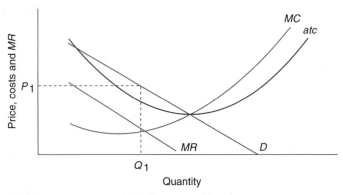

Figure 4.15 Short-run monopolistically competitive firm.

differentiated in that industry. If the firm were to lower its price below P_1, it would capture some customers from its rivals. Likewise, if the firm were to raise its price above P_1, it would undoubtedly lose customers to rivals. It is important to recognize that each firm takes the prices of its competitors as given in its pricing decisions.[6]

To determine the optimal price and quantity, the monopolistically competitive firm acts like a monopolist, setting marginal revenue equal to marginal cost and taking price from its demand curve. As shown in Figure 4.15, the firm is earning profits. In some respects the outcome could be referred to as a mini-monopoly, where each firm has positive economic profits on its own brand, or at its own location, or within its own market niche.

When entrants come
In monopolistically competitive markets, entry is not precluded by any significant entry barrier. If existing firms are earning positive economic profits, new firms will seek to enter the industry, driving down price and reducing market shares. Under the monopolistically competitive market structure, the effect of this entry is felt by all firms. The firm demand functions diminish, shifting towards the origin. The entry stops when profits are equal to zero for all market participants.

The situation is shown in Figure 4.16. In long-run equilibrium, the firm's demand function, D_{LR}, must be tangent to the average total cost curve. Not shown are the firm's marginals revenue and marginal cost curves, which necessarily intersect at the quantity associated with the tangency between the demand and average total cost curve. This is so because, at any other point, average costs exceed price, so profits are less than zero.

There are some interesting features of this equilibrium. First, price equals average total cost but exceeds marginal cost. Thus, one could criticize the equilibrium as inefficient, just as the monopolistic outcome is inefficient. However, there is a feature of this equilibrium that cannot be overlooked. Consumers

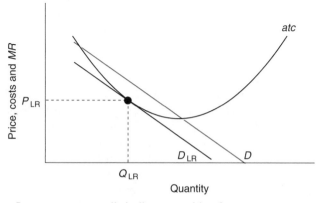

Figure 4.16 Long-run monopolistically competitive firm.

generally prefer variety and are willing to pay a higher price to get it. Buyers in monopolistically competitive markets benefit not only from the existing variety of products available, but also from innovative attempts (perhaps successful attempts) by entrants seeking to define and fill an existing niche by offering a unique product.

F. Game theory: A new tool

Definition and applicability

Uncertainty
Firms in the perfectly competitive, monopolistically competitive and monopolistic market structures make few decisions in the context of their industries. Furthermore, in each case, the reactions of other firms are largely ignored. In many situations firms make more than pricing and output decisions. They have to make decisions regarding advertising, marketing plans and how to develop new products. More importantly in many cases, none of these decisions can be made ignoring the reactions of other, related firms.

A natural way to account for the reactions of other firms is to assign probabilities to their likely actions and to act so as to maximize your expected profits. This approach incorporates risk into decision-making and is widely used in the field of finance. Concerning the competitive interplay between a small number of large firms in an industry, however, such an approach may not be appropriate. The results of any risk-based analysis are severely dependent on the probabilities assigned concerning the likely course of action taken by rival firms. If there is some error in assigning these probabilities then the goal of optimizing expected profits may not be met with any large degree of certainty.

What is needed is an approach to analyzing a competitive situation under conditions of uncertainty, i.e. when the actions and reactions of participants can be identified, but no assessment of probabilities concerning their actions is made. We seek an approach that first attempts to identify the self-interest of your competitor in light of their actions and, secondly, allows you to maximize according to this identified self-interest.

Players and strategies
Economists define a **game** as any exchange environment in which participants, called players, must choose a course of action when there is a potential degree of uncertainty regarding choices by other participants, or players. **Game theory** is the formal modelling of a game, highlighting the interaction resulting from choices made by all the players. In the setting of a game, the decisions made by the players are said to be **strategic** in that not only do they affect other players, they affect the choices made by the other players. The participants in the game are said to be the **players**, and their possible courses

of actions, or behavioural options, are termed **strategies**. In some market structures, game theory offers an elegant description of the exchange environment and enables economists to make predictions regarding firm behaviour.

Depicting the game

The payoff matrix

Applications of game theory recognize the circularity of the situation at hand. One player is attempting to predict what a second player is going to do, while the second player is attempting to predict what the first player will do. To keep the discussion in a manageable format economists pay great attention to how they depict the game. One widely used depiction of a game is the use of a **payoff matrix**, whose rows and columns represent the strategies available to the players. The elements in the payoff matrix show the benefits received by each player when the appropriate strategies are chosen.

Consider the examination game played between yourself and your economics instructor. The exam could be either an easy exam or a gruelling experience. The instructor's payoff takes the form of glee points and depends on your performance in the exam. If the instructor gives a hard exam and you had not prepared adequately, then the instructor 'earns' 15 glee points. If the instructor gives a hard exam and you earn a good grade because you had prepared for it, then the instructor receives a payoff of 25 glee points. The instructor values an easy exam quite differently because the only reason she will give you an easy exam is if she is too busy with her research pursuits competing for the Nobel Prize to take the time to prepare a hard one. Thus, if the instructor gives an easy exam that you had prepared adequately for she earns a payoff of 30 glee points. If, on the other hand, the instructor prepares and gives an easy exam and you didn't prepare for it, the instructor will never know the obvious (your lack of preparation) and in a state of blissful ignorance she receives 32 glee points.

Your payoffs are rather different in meaning but are also expressed in glee points. If you are given a difficult exam and had prepared for it then your payoff is 40 glee points. If, on the other hand, you were given a hard exam and had not prepared, then you receive 15 glee points. If the exam proves to be an easy one and you had prepared, then your payoff is 20 glee points because you are shaking your head wondering why you had to study so long. If the exam proves to be an easy one and you had not prepared, then your payoff is 45 glee points.

We now turn to the question of how to set up the situation in a format that is easy to analyze. The payoff matrix for this game will have two rows and two columns. The rows will depict the student's strategies, of your instructor: prepare a hard exam or prepare an easy exam. At the intersection of any two strategies are two numbers separated by a comma. We follow the convention in the field and denote the player's payoff whose strategies are shown in the rows of the payoff matrix as the first number. The second number is then, of course, the payoff going to the player whose strategies are shown in the columns of the payoff matrix. Thus, in Figure 4.17, if a hard exam is given and the student prepares, the student earns 40 glee points while the instructor earns 25 glee points.

All players in a game assume rational behaviour on the part of all other players. This assumption is crucial if we are to focus on the interplay between simultaneously determined strategies. A given strategy is said to be a player's **dominant strategy** if it offers the player the highest payoff regardless of what the other player does. Thus, in the exam game, the student lacks a dominant strategy. However, for the instructor, the easy exam strategy dominates the hard exam. A clever student who knows (or guesses) all the payoffs could actually deduce that the instructor will set the dominant, easy exam strategy. Uncertainty is then removed, and the student's best choice is not to prepare. Each player's choice is now optimal, *given* the other player's choice of strategy.

Nash equilibrium

Description of setting
The concept of an equilibrium in a game where each participant does the best it can given the actions of other participants is known as a **Nash equilibrium** after the Nobel Laureate John Nash. In many games that are of interest to economists the interaction between the players takes a unique form. The players may, in some sense, cooperate, making all players better off; or they may tend to act in what they perceive to be their own selfish interest, attempting to raise their payoff while lowering the payoff of the other players. Given this structure, the Nash equilibrium often involves an outcome where parties exhibit behaviour hardly consistent with a sense of community. The existence of Nash equilibria are of particular interest in **non-cooperative games**, where players act in their own self-interest, assuming their opponents to do the same,

		Instructor's strategies	
		Hard exam	Easy exam
Student strategies	Prepare	40, 25	20, 30
	Not prepare	15, 15	45, 32

NOTE: All amounts are expressed in glee points.
The student's payoff is shown first.

Figure 4.17 The exam game.

and precluding the possibility of some concerted effort to make all players better off.

A common example in economics is the capacity game where two firms, Smith and Wesson, produce competing products. Each firm is deciding whether or not to expand production capacity in the coming year. We will assume that each firm always produces at full capacity. If one firm expands its capacity, market prices will undoubtedly fall somewhat, but the firm that expands its capacity will earn a larger market share and, hence, larger profits. The second possible outcome is that neither firm chooses to expand its capacity and both firms stay at current production and profit levels. The third outcome is that both firms expand capacity, putting sharp downward pressure on market price and resulting in lower profits for both firms.

The payoff matrix is shown in Figure 4.18. Each firm makes its capacity decision independently and simultaneously. There is a Nash equilibrium that represents the 'likely outcome' of this game.

Consider the decision to be made by Smith. If Wesson does not expand capacity, Smith receives 36 if it does nothing and 40 if it expands capacity. Clearly Smith is better off expanding capacity if Wesson does not. Now consider how Smith fares if Wesson expands capacity. In the face of Wesson's capacity expansion, if Smith does not expand it receives 30; if Smith also expands it receives 32. Again Smith is clearly better off expanding capacity. For Smith, expanding capacity is a dominant strategy. A check of Figure 4.18 reveals the same type of decision-making by Wesson as it contemplates its fate under different scenarios defined by Smith's actions.

The Nash equilibrium is identified as occurring when both players expand. The non-cooperative nature of the likely outcome is evident, in that both firms could be made better off if some cooperative agreement could be reached under which each firm would agree not to expand. This characteristic of the Nash equilibria is what first attracted economists to this type of outcome. In the next subsection we consider the famous example of the **prisoners' dilemma game**.

| | | Wesson's strategies | |
		Not expand	Expand
Smith's strategies	Not expand	36, 36	30, 40
	Expand	40, 30	32, 32

NOTE: All amounts are expressed as profits earned by Smith or Wesson. Smith's payoff is shown first.

Figure 4.18 The capacity game.

The prisoners' dilemma game

As the story goes, two suspected criminals, Dan and Stan, are apprehended and detained by the police authorities. The evidence against them for the suspected crime is not strong enough to obtain a conviction on the strongest possible grounds. A confession would, however, convict either or both of Dan and Stan. On the other hand, there is a benefit of the confession to consider: by confessing, the individual shows remorse and can expect at least some leniency.

The police immediately separate the two suspected criminals. An officer goes into each room and informs Dan and Stan independently of some options they have. Consider what Dan is told: 'If your partner confesses and you remain silent, you'll get 2½ years in prison. If you confess and your partner remains silent, you will receive a sentence of 3 months in prison. If both you and your partner confess, you'll get only 1½ years in prison. If you and your partner both remain silent, we can send you to prison for 6 months.' To determine the likely outcome, and to verify that it is a Nash equilibrium, consider Figure 4.19.

A glance at Figure 4.19 reveals why it is referred to as the prisoners' dilemma. Clearly the prisoners are both in a bad situation. We can expect each prisoner to confess and to spend 18 months in jail. Notice if each could trust the other not to confess they would spend the least total time in jail. The prisoners' dilemma arises in a number of settings. During the years of the cold war, the arms race between the United States and the former Soviet Union caused each side to expend massive resources on building weapons systems. Sometimes these expenses were to the detriment of each country's national economy. Each party understood two things. First, if the other side built weapons, it needed to match the buildup. Second, if the other side did not build weapons, it could acquire an advantage by building.

		Stan's strategies	
		Confess	Not confess
Dan's strategies	Confess	1.5, 1.5	0.25, 2.5
	Not confess	2.5, 0.25	0.5, 0.5

NOTE: All amounts are expressed in years of jail time.
Dan's payoff is shown first.

Figure 4.19 The prisoners' dilemma.

G. Oligopoly

Competition among the few

In the monopolistically competitive market structure, firms could safely ignore the pricing and output actions of any single competitor. In a somewhat indirect way the same could also be said for the perfectly competitive firm and the monopolist by reason of default. Consider, however, when this may not be the case, such as in the automobile, cigarette and computer chip industries. On a much smaller scale consider the market served by the petrol stations in any reasonably sized city. Any given station will consider itself in competition with the station on the next intersection, or even on the other side of the street. Firms such as these are clearly in a touchy and tenuous position considering the strategic implications of their actions. If they lower price in an attempt to increase market share they may well find their competitors doing the same, resulting in an equal-sized market served at a lower price – hardly a way to boost profits. Price wars, if sustained, typically benefit consumers not producers; a point not lost on entities trying to maximize profits. The alternative may be even more bleak. Raising price to increase profits may damage the firm of its direct competitors do not match the price rise.

An **oligopoly** is a type of market structure in which there is competition among a few firms. How many is a few? Just enough so that the actions of one firm can be expected to evoke a response from its rivals. The oligopolist is best understood as being between a rock and a hard place. On the one hand, cooperating with competing oligopolists will avoid destructive actions such as price wars and massive advertising campaigns. In a way, then, cooperation can be understood as providing an oligopolist with some portion of the monopoly profits 'available' in the market. On the other hand, each oligopolist knows full well that, if all oligopolists cooperate except themselves, their own individual profits increase tremendously. When firms cooperate so as to emulate more closely the monopoly outcome, they are said to **collude**.

The prevalence of collusion was commented on long ago by Adam Smith, who clearly was not naive about where business men's self-interest would lead them. Smith wrote: 'People of the same trade seldom meet together, even for merriment and diversion, but the conversation ends in a conspiracy against the public, or in some contrivance to raise prices' (Smith, 1976, Book 1, Chapter 10, Part II). A group of companies that formally operates in collusion is said to be a **cartel**. OPEC, the Organization of Petroleum Exporting Countries, for example, acts collusively to restrict the output of oil in order to raise oil prices, and hence the profits of member countries.

Collusion and other forms of agreement

Relationships between competitors

To help us more fully understand the costs and benefits of collusion let us consider a hypothetical example based in a market with which we are somewhat familiar, computer software. Adopt the abstraction that there are only two software manufacturers: Macrohard and Shovell. Significant barriers exist to prevent others from entering the industry; some of these barriers are due to the technological nature of the market, others are due to the actions of Macrohard and Shovell themselves. Both firms are sure about the demand conditions existing in the software market.

Under these conditions, a marriage between the two firms might very well be in the pipeline. Certainly, it would be difficult to pull off; however, the gains from this exchange would be large indeed. Suppose that Macrohard and Shovell merged, then there would only be one firm serving the market, and we know full well that certain things would happen. First, the single entity, perhaps named HardShove, would act as a monopolist by restricting output and raising price. Secondly, the new company would earn positive, and possibly significant, economic profits. Both of these outcomes beg the question: what would it take to convince each of them to merge?

Could Macrohard purchase Shovell (or, equivalently, could Shovell purchase Macrohard)? Macrohard would have to offer Shovell's current ownership more than the discounted stream of profits Shovell could expect to earn in the absence of the merger. This is because everyone would know that the combined company would earn excess economic profits. The most that Macrohard would have to, and be able to, offer Shovell's current owners is an amount equal to the discounted stream of profits earned by the merged entity. It is unclear between this minimum and this maximum amount exactly at what price the merger would be consummated. All that is clear is that the amount would, in all probability, split the future profits of the newly created corporate entity between the two ownership groups.

Given that the marriage between Macrohard and Shovell might not come about, let us explore a relationship more along the lines of cohabitation. Is there any way that the two firms could be expected or, more importantly, persuaded to act as one? If you thought ironing out the details of the merger was a difficult task, consider the problems here. Suppose the Macrohard and Shovell came to some agreement so that together they would emulate the actions of the hypothetical monopoly firm HardShove. Once again the debate would be about profits; however, the strategic interplay between the two firms greatly complicates the situation. The two computer giants seeking to become one fact two sorts of problems.

First, the two firms must decide how the monopoly profits will be split between them. If Macrohard and Shovell each produce one-half of the market output, or are responsible for one-half of the value created in the joint enterprise, then an equal split would probably make sense. Deviations from this symmetrical position are costly to negotiate. Each firm can take the position that the other firm is better off with them than without them and increase the difficulty of reaching agreement on how to set up the cartel.

Secondly, under any agreement crafted between the two separate companies, it generally pays one cartel member to cheat on the agreement. If the cartel is formed on the premise of restricting output, each member's self-interest will lead them to desire to expand output beyond their quota. Similarly, if all the other members of the cartel have set their prices at a high level, it pays any single member to undercut that price slightly, thereby stealing customers away from other members and increasing its own profits. In either event, the cheating firm is said to be free-riding on the cartel – the other firms pay the price of collusion while the free-rider gets the advantages.

Collusion may take two forms. **Explicit collusion** is said to occur when competing firms explicitly craft agreements that in effect increase prices, decrease output and stymie competition. In most countries explicit collusion is illegal and subject to penalty. **Tacit collusion** is said to occur when competing firms simply recognize that cooperation may well be in everyone's best interest. Tacit collusive schemes are generally weaker than explicit schemes; however, they avoid some of the legal difficulties in the latter and are more likely to occur when the gains from colluding are small relative to the gains from not colluding.

Applying game theory

Description of the setting

The situation facing oligopolistic firms can be generally stated as follows. The actions of one firm affect the market directly and indirectly. The direct effect is the change in consumer behaviour that it causes. The indirect effect is much more interesting because it includes the changes in the market environment caused by competitors' reactions to one competitor's actions. Economists have three separate approaches to this problem, all within the realm of game theory.

The Cournot model

In the Cournot model, each firm treats the output level of all other firms as fixed, and then decides how much to produce. One can think of this as the firm fixing its demand function based on assumed competitors' quantities, equating marginal revenue to marginal cost and maximizing profits. For the Cournot oligopolist, the marginal revenue equals marginal cost condition (based on assumed competitors' quantities) generates a relationship termed a **reaction function** for each firm. The reaction function for firm j, will show the best, profit-maximizing amount for firm j to produce given the production levels of all other firms k. In equilibrium, no firm has an incentive to alter its output level, given the other firms' choices. Thus, any Cournot equilibrium will also be a Nash equilibrium.

To illustrate the derivation of the Cournot equilibrium, we analyze the case of two similar competitors: Firm Blue and Firm Red.[7] Just as an industry with a single firm is termed a monopoly, an industry with two firms is termed a duopoly. Together, Firms Blue and Red face the market demand function:

$$P = 420 - 2Q \tag{4.4}$$

where P is the average market price. Market output, Q, is equal to the sum of Blue's output and Red's output: $Q = Q_B + Q_R$. We will ignore, for simplicity's sake, the law of diminishing marginal productivity and assume that each firm faces constant marginal costs of 20.

$$MC_B = MC_R = 20 \tag{4.5}$$

Consider the problem from Firm Red's perspective. Let $Q_B{}^\star$ represent Firm Red's expectation of Firm Blue's output. Its demand function will be:

$$P_R = 420 - 2 \, (Q_B{}^\star + Q_R)$$

or:[8]

$$P_R = (420 - 2 \, Q_B{}^\star) - 2 \, Q_R \tag{4.6}$$

The marginal revenue equals marginal cost equation for Firm Red becomes:

$$MR_R = (420 - 2 \, Q_B{}^\star) - 4 \, Q_R = 20 = MC_R \tag{4.7}$$

which can be rearranged to yield

$$Q_R = 100 - 0.5 \, Q_B{}^\star \tag{4.8}$$

A similar analysis for the Firm Blue reveals (where $Q_R{}^\star$ is Firm Blue's expectation of Firm Red's output):

$$Q_B = 100 - 0.5 \, Q_R{}^\star \tag{4.9}$$

To determine the amount produced by Firm Red and Firm Blue, we must find the point at which each firm's expectation of its rival's output is met. This is done by finding the pair of firm outputs, Q_B and Q_R, that jointly satisfy equations (4.8) and (4.9). Calculations reveal that each of the Firm Red and Firm Blue will produce 133⅓ units of output. The price charged by each firm is seen to be, from equation (4.4), 153⅓. The situation can be approached graphically, as is done in Figure 4.17. Each reaction function is shown. The equilibrium, which happens to be a Nash equilibrium, is shown at the intersection of the individual firms' reaction functions.

We would expect to see a Cournot equilibrium emerge in industries where it takes firms time to adjust productive capacity and also in which capital costs represent a large portion of all production costs.

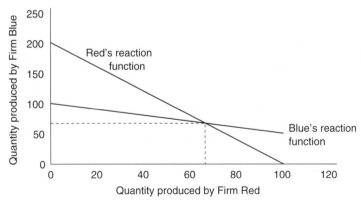

Figure 4.20 Cournot duopoly reaction functions.

The Bertrand model

In Cournot competition each firm makes its output calculation based on an assumed level of output of its rival firms. In some industries, those in which it is fairly easy to expand output, we may expect to see a different type of competition, termed **Bertrand competition** after the French economist Joseph Bertrand, who first studied this form of competition in 1883. In a situation characterized as Bertrand competition, each firm can be thought of as choosing a price assuming that the prices of its rivals are fixed. Following the logic of a Bertrand competition, if two firms collude to charge a price P, then each firm will desire to cheat by charging a price slightly less than P and capture large amounts of the market. Thus, under Bertrand competition, the demand curve facing each oligopolist is very elastic. If firms have the same marginal cost, the price will be pushed down to the competitive level, equal to marginal cost, even if there are only two competitors. A third model, due to German economist Heinrich von Stackelberg, assumes that one firm, the price leader, sets the price, and others follow. This case is analyzed in texts on microeconomics and industrial organization, but will not be pursed here.

H. Weaker forms of collusion

Anti-competitive practices

Impeding competition

Outright collusion by members of an oligopoly may be difficult to coordinate for a number of reasons. First, any explicit agreement is, in most countries, illegal. Secondly, the oligopolists would have to come to some agreement about how the economic profits would be divided among the members if collusion were to take place. Thirdly, as mentioned above in the prisoners' dilemma example, there is typically a stability problem because each cartel member has an incentive to cheat – indeed, this is the Nash outcome in a game theoretic sense. Since oligopolists wish to, in some sense, act as a monopoly, not only do they desire to prevent competition among themselves, they should desire to prevent other firms from entering the industry.

We now turn our attention to **restrictive practices**, which are a weaker form of behaviour than outright collusion. Restrictive practices are those that may serve to restrict competition both among existing oligopolists and also with regard to future potential competitors. We may think of restrictive practices as arising in two ways. When one firm buys or sells another's goods or services the two firms are said to have a vertical relationship. Accordingly, **vertical restrictions** are impediments to competition that arise in these vertical relationships. **Horizontal restrictions**, on the other hand, are said to occur when different firms selling competing products act to reduce current and future competition in the market place.

Exclusive territories

One common example of a restrictive practice is when a producer grants a reseller (either a wholesaler or a retailer) the exclusive right to sell its output in a specified geographical area. Such agreements are called **exclusive territories** and represent an attempt by the producer to avoid intra-brand competition, or the competition between alternative sellers of a particular brand. This practice is prevalent in the United States for soft drink manufacturers. Coca-cola for example, manufactures the syrup for its product and sells it to geographically based bottlers (who mix in water and other additives); the bottlers, who are granted exclusive territories, in turn sell it to retailers. Of course, a retailer in a geographical area cannot buy its Coca-Cola from a bottler in another geographical region.

Exclusive territories may also be used to dampen inter-brand competition. They could serve as a horizontal restriction to competition if different brands are granted, in effect, local monopolies. Suppose that we consider a product whose production entails significant economies of scale, and which also can be shipped distances only at a tremendous cost. Such a product could be something like asphalt, which must be manufactured and kept hot while being shipped to where it will ultimately be used. In a sense, we would expect to see, looking across broad geographical areas, a patchwork-like arrangement of asphalt producers. Only when demand, within any single geographical area, was large would there be more than one asphalt producer. Granted, one could argue that each asphalt firm owned a natural monopoly; however that explanation fails to recognize any cognizant effort on the part of neighbouring asphalt producers not to impede on each other's markets.

Exclusive dealing

A manufacturer engages in **exclusive dealing** when it insists that any reseller selling its products shall not engage in the selling of competing products. When you pull your car into the local Shell petrol station you can be assured that the Shell station will sell only petroleum refined at a Shell-owned refinery. Exclusive dealing is always a vertical restriction on competitive behaviour. The presence of so-called insurance brokers in most insurance markets is an example where some sellers recognize the value signal they can send regarding their encouragement of competition. An insurance broker typically represents several competing insurance carriers, whereas the more well-known insurance agent represents a single insurance carrier. The power of exclusive dealing arrangements is most obvious in franchises. McDonald's, for example, makes exclusive use of this type of arrangement.

Other restrictions

Product tie-ins are used to restrict competition when consumers must purchase more than one product to fulfil a particular need. Manufacturing oligopolists may insist that purchases of their product be accompanied by purchases of another, related product.

A final example of a restrictive practice is **resale price maintenance**. An oligopolistic producer of a good or service engages in resale price maintenance when it posts, or otherwise makes known, a price at which resellers are suggested to sell the product.

Enforceability

Exclusive territories, exclusive dealing, product tie-ins and resale price maintenance all share one common element beyond their ability to denigrate competition. They all are highly visible and easily verifiable. The importance of this point is easily understood within the context of the inherent instability of any collusive arrangement. Each single oligopolist has incentive not only to cheat but also to hide their actions from their rivals to avoid costly retaliation. The high visibility of these horizontal and vertical restrictive practices may then be thought of as reducing the incentive to cheat on any explicit or implicit arrangement among oligopolists. In this sense, restrictive practices, although falling short of outright collusion by oligopolists, may serve to reduce the instability inside any cartel.

Overall impacts of restrictive practices

Justifications versus consequences

Economists are not so quick to agree that the horizontal and vertical restrictive practices described above represent an efficiency loss to society. Instead, they see that there may be benefits of these practices even though there are losses in the sense that they minimize the degree of competition in the market. There are many possible arguments to be made both in favour of these types of practices and against these practices. Our purpose here is to outline some of the major points.

The creation of exclusive territories may enhance efficiency in that this practice can lead producers to better cultivate and provide customized services and product offerings in a given market. These may represent efficiency gains in that consumers receive products more closely tailored to the unique needs of consumers found in their territories. The cultivation of a market can provide both producers and consumers with a sense of stability that is lacking in more competitive, changing environments.

Whether or not these efficiency gains will lead to lower prices for consumers is a matter of debate among economists. Producers in a stable market may be less inclined to charge higher prices than producers in an unstable, competitive market if the stability translates into lower production or distribution costs. The claims regarding better, more customized, products and services also contain at least some truth.

Exclusive dealing likewise may also provide benefits. When one reseller can focus on the products of a given producer, consumers may benefit from that reseller's knowledge of the product offerings. In certain franchising settings, consumers may likewise benefit from exclusive dealing in that it offers a uniform product across multiple points of potential purchase. Customers at McDonald's can expect the same level of cleanliness, service, product characteristics and product quality across all locations.

The obvious main argument against restrictive practices deals with how the practices may limit competition and thereby restrict quantity and raise price. A related argument is that restrictive practices may also restrict product variety and curtail the selection available to consumers at a given point of sale, as in product tie-ins and exclusive dealing, or within a geographical area, as in the creation of exclusive territories.

A more subtle argument against restrictive practices on economic efficiency grounds is that they may prevent some producers from experiencing economies of scale. In the granting of an exclusive territory, for example, producer quantities may be so low as to encourage an inefficient use of capital. Or it could very well be that potential economies of scale in shipping and distribution are not available at the regional (local) level.

I. Chapter summary and key ideas

When economists, business analysts, and managers discuss firm strategy they must consider the business environment in which the firm finds itself. One of the key components of that business environment is the structure of the market in which the firm operates. By and large the market structure refers to the amount, type, and degree of competition in that particular industry. An entrepreneur, for example, entering the dairy industry will consider one particular market environment while a second entrepreneur entering the computer software industry will consider quite another.

In the previous chapter we considered the perfectly competitive market structure, a rather bleak prospect in terms of long-run expected profitability. In this chapter we considered alternatives to this competitive ideal, hopefully illuminating them by comparison. In the perfectly competitive market structure it is somewhat ironic that the competition among firms is so intense that the question of individual competitor interaction is simply not relevant given that the market allows for aggregated, anonymous competitive forces. The alternative market structures presented in this chapter are quite different.

The most important factor limiting or encouraging the degree of competition in the market is the presence of entry barriers. We have offered one taxonomy of entry barriers in this chapter, while in the literature different taxonomies are to be found. What is important about these different characterizations of entry barriers is that some entry barriers are created by the firm or firms involved and some are, in a sense, just there waiting to be exploited. When entry can be completely blockaded by a single firm, monopoly will result. It is useful to keep in mind the inefficiency created by a single monopolist in the market. It is also useful to keep in mind that these inefficiencies harm buyers while they promote the well being of the monopolist. Both the inefficiencies and the monopolist's profits are increased by the various pricing practices we considered in this chapter.

The importance of the monopolistically competitive market structure is that it permits an analysis of markets where consumers view the output of the various sellers as substitutes. We see then that, like so many things in life, market power is not an absolute question but one of degree.

Perhaps the most interesting market structure, oligopoly, is also the one least understood. The so-called competition among the few highlights the strategic behaviour of firm interaction. When the firms are agreeable, economic theory tells us to expect some form of collusion under which the firms act in concert as a perfect monopoly. Economic theory also highlights the instability of these collusive arrangements as there is a definite difference between what is good for the individual and what is good for the group.

One very interesting branch of economics has sprung up to analyze oligopolistic competition: game theory. While this body of knowledge has many interesting twists, turns, and complexities it provides two very useful concepts applicable in many areas: Nash equilibria, and the prisoners' dilemma. Intuitively, the concept of a Nash equilibrium is appealing: in a strategic situation act as if your competitor(s) are doing the best they can while they make the same assumption about your own behaviour.

Clearly this chapter has expanded our viewpoint of the firm by allowing a more careful consideration of the business environment in which the firm operates. Granted, some complexity has been added; however the gains are numerous and evident. This broader view of one component of the firm's business environment will carry us through into later chapters where we consider topics like the firm's relation to the capital and labour markets, and the choice of pursuing activities in the firm or acquiring them in some form of market exchange.

 Key words

allocative efficiency	monopoly
entry barriers	N-firm concentration ratio
Bertrand competition	Nash equilibrium
blocked pricing	natural monopoly
cartel	non-cooperative games
collude	oligopoly
concentrated	payoff matrix
consumer surplus	players
cross-subsidization	precommitment contracts
differentiated products	price discrimination
dominant strategy	prisoners' dilemma game
endogenous barriers	product tie-in
entry barriers	reaction function
exclusive dealing	resale price maintenance
exclusive territories	reservation price
exogenous barriers	restrictive practices
explicit collusion	second-degree price
first-degree price discrimination	discrimination
game	strategic
game theory	strategies
Herfindahl index	tacit collusion
horizontal differentiation	third-degree price
horizontal restrictions	discrimination
learning curve	two-part tariff
market structure	vertical differentiation
minimum efficient scale (MES)	vertical restrictions
monopolistic competition	

Questions and problems for review and discussion

1 Price discrimination requires that the seller be able to characterize and identify different groups of consumers and also that the seller be able to prevent arbitrage between the different consumers or groups thus identified. Explain how price discrimination can arise in each of the following situations. Be sure to explain how, in each situation, the

different consumer groups are identified and how the seller knows to which group to charge the higher price.
  (a) Selling a consumer appliance with an attached coupon that can be sent to the manufacturer to obtain a significant rebate.
  (b) Offering temporary price cuts on a non-durable item such as bathroom tissue.
  (c) Charging high-income patients more than low-income patients for plastic surgery.
  (d) The requirement made by airlines that to obtain a different fare the traveler must spend one Saturday night away from home.
2 Compaq computer is one of the largest producers of computer systems in the world. Suppose that they hire you to advise them on their pricing policy. One of the things the company would like to know is how much a 5 per cent increase in their price is likely to reduce sales.
  (a) What types of information would you need to help the company with their problem?
  (b) Explain why each of these types of information would be important to you.
3 Explain why there is no market supply curve under monopoly.
4 The table below shows the demand curve facing a monopolist who produces at a constant marginal cost of 20.

Price	Quantity
54	0
48	4
42	8
36	12
30	16
24	20
18	24
12	28
6	32
0	36

  (a) In either tabular or graphical form show the firm's marginal revenue function.
  (b) What are the firm's profit-maximizing output and price?
  (c) At the optimal level of output what are the firm's profits? Do you need more information to answer this question? If so, exactly what information do you need?
  (d) What would the equilibrium price be if this were a competitive industry?
  (e) Identify the efficiency gains if this monopolist were forced to produce at the 'competitive' price.

5 Explain fully the concept of a Nash equilibrium.
6 Construct a payoff matrix for the game between the following two firms. Firms 1 and 2 both produce soft drinks. Each has the ability to produce a new drink that will have one main characteristic. The new drink will be either sweet or sour. If both produce a sweet drink the payoffs will be –5 to each firm. Similarly if both produce a sour drink the payoffs to each firm will be –5. If one firm produces a sweet drink and the other produces a sour drink then the payoff to the firm producing the sweet drink will be 10 as will the payoff to the firm producing the sour drink.
  (a) If Firm 1 somehow signals to Firm 2 that it (Firm 1) will produce a sweet drink, what is Firm 2's best response?
  (b) Identify any and all Nash equilibria in this game.
7 (a) What are the characteristics of a monopolistically competitive market?
  (b) What happens to the equilibrium in a monopolistically competitive industry if one firm introduces a new, improved product? Fully explain the effects on other firms.
8 The OPEC oil cartel has succeeded in colluding to raise worldwide oil prices substantially while other cartels have failed. One example of a failed attempt at forming a cartel is CIPEC, the French acronym for International Council of Copper Exporting Countries.[9] Given that there are many substitutes for copper (aluminium, for example) and no substitutes for oil explain how the elasticity of demand in the output market may affect the stability of any collusive scheme.

Notes

1 This argument builds upon that of Sutton (1992) and also upon that of Besanko *et al.* (1996), pp. 212–14.
2 A good example of this is found in Brickley *et al.* (1997), Chapter 6.
3 We offer here a brief survey view of the broader topic of regulating monopolies. For a more complete view please see Spulber (1989).
4 Another interesting regulatory approach is for the regulatory board to simulate the competitive market outcome, price equalling marginal costs. Although this approach is laudable on economic grounds, it faces two distinct obstacles. First, there is tremendous technical difficulty in identifying exactly what marginal costs may be. Secondly, it is entirely possible, perhaps even likely, that, given the declining nature of average total costs, the marginal cost curve may even lie below the atc for the output levels in question, so that subsidies would then be required.
5 The original work on which we and others have built is Oi (1971).
6 If this were not the case then the firm's demand function would possibly shift around each time its competitors changed their prices.
7 The analysis generalizes to more than two firms; however, it becomes less tractable.

8 Notice the way this equation is written: when the output of Firm Blue changes, the demand function of Firm Red shifts (its vertical intercept changes).

9 See Pindyck, R. S., 'The Cartelization of World Commodity Markets', American Economic Review 69, May 1979, pp. 154–158.

References

Bain, J. S. (1959) *Industrial Organization*, New York: John Wiley & Sons.

Besanko, D., D. Dranove and M. Shanley (1996), *Economics of Strategy*, New York: Wiley.

Brinkley, J. A., C. W. Smith and J. L. Zimmerman (1997), *Managerial Economics and Organizational Architecture*, Chicago: Irwin.

Carlton, D. W. and J. M. Perloff (1994) *Modern Industrial Organization*, 2nd edn, New York: Harper-Collins College Publishers.

Chamberlin, E. H. (1993), *The Theory of Monopolistic Competition*, Cambridge, Mass.: Harvard University Press.

Greerer, D. F. (1980) *Industrial Organization and Public Policy*, 2nd edn, New York: Macmillan.

Mandel, M. J. (1997), 'A pack of 800-lb gorillas', *Business Week*, 3 February, p. 34.

Oi, W. (1971), 'A Disneyland dilemma: Two-part tariffs for a Mickey Mouse monopoly', *Quarterly Journal of Economics*, 85, pp. 77–96.

Sheperd, William G., *Public Policies Toward Business*, Seventh Edition, Richard D. Irwin, Inc., New York, 1985.

Sheperd, W. G. (1985) *The Economics of Industrial Organization*, 2nd edn, Englewood Cliffs, NJ: Prentice-Hall.

Shy, O. (1995) *Industrial Organization: Theory and Applications*, Cambridge, Mass.: MIT Press.

Smith, A. (1976 [1776]). *An Inquiry into the Nature and Causes of the Wealth of Nations*, Chicago: University of Chicago Press.

Spulber, D. F. (1989), *Regulation and Markets*, Cambridge, Mass.: MIT Press.

Sutton, J. (1992), *Sunk Costs and Market Structure*, Cambridge, Mass.: MIT Press.

Wysocki, B., Jr. (1997) 'In Some Industries, Executives Foresee Tough Times Ahead', *The Wall Street Journal*, 7 August, page A-1.

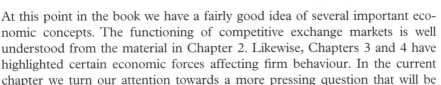

CHAPTER 5

Efficiency in organizing economic activity

A. Chapter outline and student goals

At this point in the book we have a fairly good idea of several important economic concepts. The functioning of competitive exchange markets is well understood from the material in Chapter 2. Likewise, Chapters 3 and 4 have highlighted certain economic forces affecting firm behaviour. In the current chapter we turn our attention towards a more pressing question that will be addressed throughout the remainder of the book. How good a job does a system of firms and markets do in allocating economic resources?

From an economy-wide, macro-oriented view this question refers to a society's ability to produce the goods and services that are needed. This is not an easy task. When individuals specialize in production their activities must be coordinated so that they produce the right things and are able to exchange their output for the goods and services they wish to consume. The need to achieve coordination arises from the division of labour. Separate, yet interconnected, markets coordinate the activities of millions of individuals and firms in the economy. Economists refer to the collection of related markets in a capitalistic economy as the price system. The price system achieves coordination by answering three basic economic questions: what to produce, how to produce it, and for whom to produce. One basic criterion used in determining the adequacy of the price system is whether allocation of resources by the price system happens efficiently.

From the organizational view we can apply similar reasoning to the way in which economic activity is organized within firms, or within individual transactions. The concepts put into place in this chapter lead us to address questions such as: 'Should a firm have a high or low degree of vertical integration?' and 'Should workers be paid a flat wage or a wage that depends on some measurement of their productivity?' Whether addressing the question from the economy-wide vantage point or from the point of view of the individual transaction, the important concept is efficiency.

Put very simply, efficiency is the process of getting more for less. For example, today many people are interested in the efficiency of their hard disks and their household appliances such as their refrigerator, furnace, or car. Any person who has worked with computers for 15 years has to be amazed at the size of today's hard drives. However, we all know we should follow the advice of computer manufacturers when they tell us to optimize the performance of our hard disk by frequent disk maintenance such as deleting old, unused files, protecting it from viruses, and defragmenting the drive.

Similar arguments apply to economic issues. An economy is efficient when it is impossible to get more output from existing resources. Efficiency is what all economic systems strive for, whether they are individuals, organizations or countries. How a system of related, competitive markets (the price system) achieves economic efficiency is the subject of this chapter. Firms, in their quest to organize economic activity, likewise are efficient when it is impossible to improve the welfare of the firm's stakeholders by some alternative plan to organize economic activity.

The most common reasons for markets not achieving efficient coordination are: market power, imperfect information, increasing returns in production, and externalities. When any of these conditions prevail, the market may be inefficient. When people have found that markets were inefficient in coordinating economic activities, often they organized firms. Recall the functional component in the definition of firms presented in Chapter 1.

The fundamental question of why firms exist was first asked by Ronald Coase. According to Coase there are costs of carrying out transactions in a market setting. These will be different depending on the product, the industry or the market. In order to achieve efficiency, the tendency will be for activities to be carried out so that the costs of conducting transactions and/or the costs of coordinating individuals' activities will be the lowest. Coase argued that production is coordinated within markets when the organization costs are low, and in firms when the costs of using the market are high. This, in and of itself, is an interesting question and we will return to in Chapter 6.

After reading this chapter you should be able to:

- explain, in an intuitive way, the concept of economic efficiency;
- understand that the competitive supply and demand equilibrium introduced in Chapter 2 represents an efficient allocation of resources;
- identify four broad categories of reasons why market exchange may fail to yield an outcome that is efficient from the point of view of society;
- use the mechanics of the supply and demand model to explain why externalities and public goods will lead to an inefficient allocation of economic resources when markets are used to coordinate exchange;
- state the Coase Theorem and understand how it provides an alternative way in which an efficient outcome can be obtained in a market setting;
- provide some implications of these concepts for managerial behaviour.

B. Economic efficiency

The concept of efficiency

A promising future realized

Ukraine, a country of 52 million people, gained independence from the former Soviet Union in 1991.[1] At that time, its prospects seemed promising, to say the least. After all, it was the breadbasket of the former Soviet Union, it was rich in natural resources, and it possessed a warm-water port on the Black Sea. However, it has not worked out that way. At least up to 1994 the country's economic and social systems appeared in deep collapse, with inflation running at 70 per cent a month, bread lines in Kiev, and fuel so scarce that many factories had shut down. Indeed, Ukraine made other 'new' nations such as Poland and Russia seem like success stories.

What caused the misfortunes of Ukraine's economy? There are two reasons. First, the economic environment had changed. When Ukraine declared independence, it severed long-standing ties with Russia, forcing a push towards a new and unfamiliar equilibrium in the economy. Oil and gas became much more expensive than before, and markets for exports had dried up. With a new equilibrium, the basic questions of what to produce, how to produce it and for whom to produce had to be answered again.

Secondly, and perhaps much more important, the country inherited an ideology from its former communist rulers that assumed that people are fundamentally good; unfortunately, they are not – they are fundamentally selfish (Sinn and Sinn, 1994). Prior to independence from the Soviet Union a system of government was in place where the lines of authority were set up to suit the convenience of party officials. As of 1994, there was no clear rule of law and no effective banking system, and huge unprofitable state enterprises dependent on state subsidies played a major role in the Ukraine economy. Tight export and price controls were liberalized only in late 1994, but in spite of some progress since, Ukraine still lags behind many other transition economies of Eastern Europe.

Trying to avoid the shock therapy Mr Yeltsin applied in Russia, the country failed to restructure its economy. Privatization, for example, was almost non-existent. Market prices and market incentives that come with privatization were also non-existent. The economy was seen to be hopelessly inefficient in part because the prices needed to coordinate economic activity were non-existent.

Definition of a criterion

The concept of efficiency is related to the concerns and well-being of those affected by economic exchange. Efficiency is to be judged by the ability of the system or mechanism allocating economic resources to satisfy the wants and needs of individual human beings. Efficiency is therefore important for

resource allocation. From an economic standpoint, the resources to be allocated could be the assets of separate divisions within a vertically integrated firm, or all the resources in the economy. Resource allocations that have the property that no one can be made better off without making someone else worse off are said to be efficient. If someone can be made better off without making someone worse off then the system is inefficient. When economists refer to Pareto efficiency this is what they usually mean (after Italian economist Vilfredo Pareto). We offer the following formal definition:

> **Efficient**: An economic arrangement is said to be efficient if it is impossible, given available resources, to implement an alternative arrangement under which all parties involved are at least as well off, and some are strictly better off.

The concept of efficiency can be easily illustrated. If two individuals with different endowments specialize in production and agree to trade thereafter, each will be better off than before. Suppose that individual A specializes in farming and individual B in hunting. They both like bread and meat equally. Allowing these two people to trade potentially makes both better off. In other words, if individuals are willing to specialize according to their comparative advantages and trade according to their preferences, each has the capability to become enriched beyond what he could accomplish on his own. However, we must remember that, although specialization may make people better off, each could, if he so desired, remain completely self-sufficient. Mr A, instead of allocating his time to farming for Mr B, could use that time to hunt on his own. The point is that Mr A may be a very poor hunter compared with Mr B, while Mr B is likely to understand little about farming, which is why autarky or self-sufficiency is inefficient.

Markets and efficiency

Efficient coordination and motivation
Do markets provide an efficient mechanism for allocating economic activity? The answer is mixed, but positively a 'yes' for the most part. Casual empiricism certainly is in favour of answering this question in a positive way. We are all aware of the chronic shortages that plagued the planned socialist economies under their former communist rule. We are also well aware that such shortages are indeed rare in the more capitalistic economies. In a market-based economy, prices serve to *coordinate* economic activity in that they determine what is produced, how it is produced and who receives the goods and services produced.

There used to be a riddle in communist societies. The riddle was: Why can't you have socialism in every country? The answer is that you need one country to set the prices. The implied punch line of this somewhat dark riddle is that any government could coordinate the actions of all the participants in its economy if they knew what the prices should be. Of course no economy approaches either one of these extremes, relying on only the market or the state. The US government dabbles in setting prices; even the communist economies left some decisions to individual consumers.

Although there is not only some evidence, but also certain grounds of reasonableness, to believe that markets can lead to an efficient outcome, there is one other piece of information we must not overlook. The market economy coordinates all the individual pieces of economic activity with a minimal amount of information. A market-based system does not require a nation to have elaborate bureaucracies equipped with supercomputers to answer the allocation question. Rather, all it requires is that all participants have access to some basic information. In short, knowing only local information and system-wide prices is enough for each producer and consumer to make the choices required for efficiency.

Like the DNA in our bodies that carries all the genetic information to create life, prices carry all the necessary *economic* information for organizing an economy. As Milgrom and Roberts point out, 'There is no need to transmit detailed information about preferences, technological possibilities, resource availabilities, and the like that would be needed to achieve a centralized solution because the prices summarize all the relevant information. Furthermore, when conditions change, detailed local knowledge of these changes need not be transmitted to achieve effective responses' (1992, p. 27).

A price system will also provide the motivation necessary to encourage individuals to act in a coordinated way towards a goal of economic efficiency for all. The second remarkable feature of the price system is that it provides the incentive for individuals to help themselves in a socially beneficial way. As Adam Smith put it in his famous metaphor of the 'invisible hand' to describe how self-interest led to social good: 'He intends only his own gain, and he is in this as in many other cases, led by an invisible hand to promote an end which was no part of his intention' (1977, Book 1, ch. 2).

The public interest is promoted by individuals pursuing their own self-interest. People do not have to be artificially induced or forced to work in a well-functioning economy. People led by impersonal market forces will take the action necessary to achieve efficiency. Economics has progressed a long way since Adam Smith, but his fundamental argument relating to the ability of a price system to motivate individuals has had great appeal over the past two centuries.

A few years ago, airports all over the United States installed trolleys to help people carry their luggage. The trolleys could be rented for $1 and used throughout the airport. When they were returned, the customer would receive a 25 cent refund. The trolleys were an instant success. Most people used them to take their luggage to the parking lot. A difficulty arose, however, when individuals did not return the trolleys to the vending machine. The parking lot was littered with abandoned trolleys and consumers wanting them at the advertised prices could find none for hire. The 25 cent refund was not enough of an incentive to return the trolley. Whereas few executives returned the trolleys for the reward, dozens of people found it profitable to spend the whole day at the airport collecting trolleys. Indeed, it was a common sight at Kennedy Airport in New York City to see people pushing up to 50 carts. In Europe trolleys are usually provided free, and attendants collect them. This service also works quite effectively.

Is the market allocation good?

Now you are left wondering what this has to do with the concept of an equilibrium in a competitive exchange market. How would you answer the following question: 'Is the price of food in your city too high?' One answer is that we know that in most cities in the United States, and to a lesser extent in Europe, it is an unfortunate fact that many poor people go without adequate food. An extension of this answer is that, yes, the price of non-junk food should be lowered so that everyone can eat a healthy diet. This answer coupled with its logical extension is a normative economic argument. A positive economic answer to this question would contain some description of what could be done to increase either the supply of food to the disadvantaged or their incomes.

Both of these answers dodge the main issue. We need to answer the question with another question: 'Does the food market work well?' It is easy enough to see that the food market works; at the very minimum food is being exchanged between buyers and sellers. The hard part is determining whether or not the food market works well.

We centre our economic analysis on the efficiency of the equilibrium reached by the food market. The food that is transferred from sellers to buyers represents an allocation. Notice also that, within the supply and demand model we have developed, each allocation of food brought to the market is uniquely characterized by a price. This is a very relevant point to make given that in our market-oriented economy the role of prices is to act as signals, determining whether more or less of a good or service is to be produced. Figure 5.1 illustrates a standard supply and demand model of the market for food. At the lowest price depicted, P_L, the allocation called forth by the market represents an excess demand for food. Likewise, at the price P_H, the market allocation results in an excess supply of food. Only at the price P_E does the allocation of food transferred from sellers to buyer represent an equilibrium.

The efficiency of supply and demand markets

Now that we know precisely what the supply and demand market allocation is, we can begin to determine if the market for food works well in allocating food. Put another way, we can see if the allocation of food, at the equilibrium price, is economically efficient.

Suppose that the food market reaches an equilibrium. Let us continue with

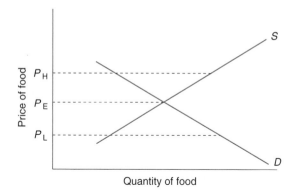

Figure 5.1 The allocation produced by the food market.

the implicit assumption that we can talk about one market for food; that is, all the relevant sub-markets (i.e. hamburgers, steaks, green beans, etc.) have been aggregated into some meaningful single entity.[2] To help further in our interpretation we have changed Figure 5.1 to include numbers (see Figure 5.2). We can see that the market reaches an equilibrium (or determines an allocation) with a price of 50 c.u. (currency units), at which 25 units of food are exchanged.

Asking whether or not the market works is equivalent to asking whether or not the equilibrium price of 50 c.u. produces an efficient allocation of food. The easiest way to argue that the allocation is, in fact, economically efficient is to consider all allocations not represented by the equilibrium and to show that you cannot move from the equilibrium without violating the criterion of economic efficiency.

Suppose that we were able to increase the amount of food to 26 units. Clearly that 26th unit of food would be of benefit to somebody, as shown by the height of the demand curve at 26 units. Somebody's benefit of that 26th unit of food can be seen in Figure 5.2 to be nearly 50 c.u. (but slightly less). Clearly, changing the allocation can make at least one person better off. But can this be done without harming somebody?

The cost, on the margin, of increasing food available on the market is given by the height of the supply curve at 26 units. Clearly this cost is slightly above 50 c.u. The move to 26 units of food production simply cannot be accomplished as a move towards an efficient allocation in the food market. If the 26th unit of food were brought to the market, true somebody would benefit. However, somebody would be harmed because, even if that unit of food were able to be sold for nearly 50 c.u., nobody would be willing to pay the marginal cost of producing that 26th unit of food.

A similar argument can be made for reducing the quantity of food in the market to 24 units, and this is left to the reader.

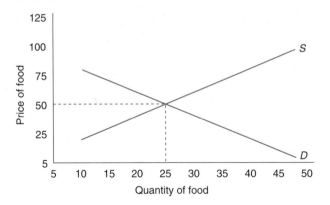

Figure 5.2 Does the food market work?

From all of this we can then conclude that the allocation of food produced in our hypothetical food market is, in fact, economically efficient because it is impossible to help someone without harming someone else. Recall that the costs of production of that extra unit of food could never be recouped, implying a loss for at least one food producer.

This raises a very interesting point regarding some of the material presented in this chapter: although the existence of markets allows the setting of prices necessary for the attainment of an efficient allocation of economic resources, the existence of markets does not guarantee than an efficient allocation of resources will happen.

Economy-wide efficiency

An introduction
Efficiency in a single market or in some form of non-market exchange is a very interesting concept and one with which we shall concern ourselves throughout much of the remainder of this book. A much bigger question arises when we consider whether or not the economy, as a whole, reaches an efficient allocation of resources. At the beginning of this chapter we presented evidence that perhaps Ukraine did not in the early 1990s.

Partial equilibrium analysis refers to a type of economic analysis that is concerned with events in separate, isolated markets. Concerning the outcome in the food market earlier, it is clear that several other important markets were simply not considered. **General equilibrium analysis** takes into account all of the interactions and interdependencies between the various parts of the economy, examining the allocation of all goods and services. General equilibrium analysis, for example, seeks an understanding of the wages, interest rates and prices at which the markets for labour, capital and goods and services clear simultaneously. In general equilibrium analysis, all markets must clear simultaneously for equilibrium to be achieved. This equilibrium is then open to being questioned as being efficient or not.

Conditions for economy-wide efficiency

Economic theorists have identified three conditions that must be met in order for an economy to reach an efficient equilibrium. **Exchange efficiency** analyzes the behaviour of consumers who can trade goods between themselves. In an efficient allocation of goods, no one can be made better off without making someone else worse off. **Production efficiency** looks at the economy from the perspective of inputs into the production process. A particular allocation of inputs into a production process is technically efficient if the output of one good cannot be increased without decreasing the output of another good. **Product mix efficiency** requires that the goods produced are those that consumers want, at the right prices; or, in other words, that all markets clear.

A great deal of the economics profession has explored the question of efficiency in an economy. Unfortunately a rich treatment of this important topic would require, in and of itself, a very advanced graduate-level course.[3] What is important here is to recognize the basic outline of what has come to be termed the general equilibrium model of economic activity.

The basic assumptions of the model are that rational, perfectly informed households interact with rational, profit-maximizing firms in competitive markets. Thus we rule out any instances of market power such as those introduced in Chapter 4. Furthermore, all exchanges take place in an environment where all economic agents have all the information they need about any exchanges they need to make. Market failures are simply ruled out. We now turn our attention to reasons why the celebrated market mechanism might in fact fail to reach an efficient allocation of economic resources.

C. Why markets may fail to reach efficiency

Monopoly

Those discussed earlier

Firms are said to have market power whenever their own actions can influence the market price of their output. Market power is not, however, something that every firm simply has; rather market power arises out of some barrier that precludes other sellers from capturing a given firm's customers. In the previous chapter we characterized barriers to entry as being either exogenous or endogenous. Exogenous barriers are those attributable to a factor of production that is necessary for th production, distribution or sale of a good. Exogenous barriers do not arise because of any conscious effort on the part of incumbent firms. Endogenous barriers are those that are, at least in part, created by existing firms in an industry.

Economies of scale are one of the most familiar barriers to entry. If MES (minimum efficient scale) in an industry is sufficiently large relative to market demand, firms will have some market power, enabling them to raise prices beyond competitive levels. Indeed, increasing returns in production, which would clearly result in economies of scale, are one well-known force working to disrupt the beneficial aspects of competitive economy-wide equilibrium. Some endogenous entry barriers are perhaps more interesting because they are created by firms and have the effect of thwarting competition by both existing sellers and potential market entrants. Advertising and research and development aimed at product improvement are two widely cited endogenous entry barriers.

The plethora of work available dealing with business strategy presents a somewhat different look at the creation and maintenance of entry barriers. One of the more widely known arguments calls for the creations of a **core competency**, which is an advantage not only in current production of a good or service but in the creation of new, related goods and services. In their best-selling book *Competing for the Future*, Hamel and Prahalad (1994) encourage firms to set a strategy that enables them to preserve future market share. Some of the tools of business strategy (including product niching, research and development leadership, and market penetration) create, at least to a certain extent, a set of endogenous entry barriers.

As we said in the previous chapter, entry barriers are often not absolute; they do not typically create pure monopolies. In the usual economic discussion of market power, the conversation goes along the lines of anti-competitive behaviours restraining free trade. In oligopolistic markets, the efficiency effects of firms having market power are similar to those effects in a monopolistic market: output is restricted and prices are inflated. Thus, to see formally the effects of market power on economic efficiency, we turn to the model of pure monopoly.

The deadweight loss of monopoly

A barrier to entry will keep a monopolist operating free from fear of competition. In order fully to appreciate the efficiency implications arising from monopolistic behaviour we ask that you once again consider the market situation as faced by a monopolistic firm. In Figure 5.3 we show the demand, marginal revenue and marginal cost curves facing a monopolist. Of course, the monopolist produces Q_m units of output, which it sells at a price of P_m. This outcome is not efficient because, hypothetically, some well-meaning, benevolent dictator could rearrange the market allocation to make at least one person better off without making anyone worse off.

To see how, consider Figure 5.4. In Figure 5.4 we reproduce the curves from Figure 5.3. However, we also show the costs and benefits of producing

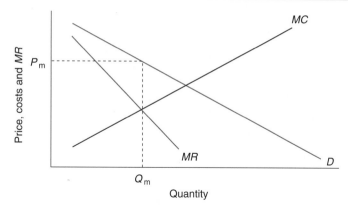

Figure 5.3 The monopolist in the market.

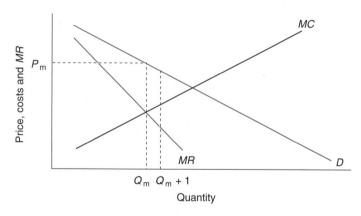

Figure 5.4 Enhancing the efficiency of the monopoly outcome.

one additional unit of output, say the Q_m + 1 unit. The benefits of making that unit available to the market, given by the height of the demand function above the Q_m + 1 unit, clearly outweigh the costs of doing so, given by the height of the marginal cost function above the Q_m + 1 unit. In fact, this graphical result is true for any number of additional units beyond Q_m so long as the height of the demand curve exceeds that of the marginal cost curve.

In Figure 5.5 we show the total loss to society, in efficiency terms, of having a monopolist operate in the market place. In Figure 5.5, the triangle ABC represents the **deadweight loss,** in terms of unrealized gains of permitting the monopolist to produce. Another name given to this widely cited result in economic theory is the 'welfare triangle', because it represents the decline in societal welfare due to the operation of a monopolistic seller in the market place.

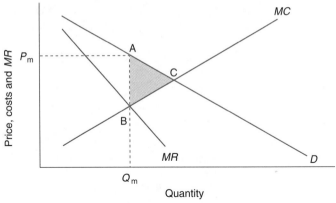

Figure 5.5 Deadweight loss of monopoly.

Externalities and public goods

Issues relating to resource ownership

If we think of a very common object, say a car, we have a clear view of who owns the car. Imagine if your car and my car manage to bump into each other at an intersection; I will undoubtedly ask why you decided to run into my car. Ownership, however, may not be a so clearly defined isuse.

One interesting recent development in microeconomics is a re-examination of what ownership means. In very many situations, this seemingly simple idea requires much more than a simple yes or no answer to the question, 'Does some party own an asset?' According to the economic view, ownership translates into a group of **property rights**, or the rights to decide how, when, for how long and under what conditions an asset may be used or sold. In the developed economies of the world, property rights are typically established and maintained by legislative mandate, and may typically be rented, discarded or sold.

The Osbournes are a four-person family living in Anytown, UK, just outside of Liverpool. The Osbourne children are 5 years old and 18 years old. The family has two cars. Mr Osbourne typically takes the train to work each day; Mrs Osbourne commutes to work by car and drops Brian, the 5 year old, off at day nursery each day. The oldest Osbourne child, Heather, drives the other car to college each day and to her job at the shopping mall. As is typical in most households, the cars are registered to the parents, one each respectively. In practice, all four family members refer to the cars driven by Heather as 'Heather's car'. Exactly who 'owns' Heather's car? To determine this we have to examine some of the property rights associated with the vehicle.

The right actually to drive the car on a daily basis has been assigned to Heather. Brian also has property rights because Heather has agreed to drive Brian to soccer practice and Cub Scouts every Tuesday and Thursday evening respectively. Mrs Osbourne also has property rights for 'Heather's' car because she routinely drives it to the golf course on Saturday mornings. Mr Osbourne rarely drives 'Heather's' car but is usually directly involved in servicing it and financing repairs. The property rights of insurance coverage do not help to define the situation any better either because Mr and Mrs Osbourne have declared Heather to be a 'secondary' driver of her car.

This simple example illustrates some basic points surrounding any question of ownership. First, property rights are often a question of degree. Some party may hold 'limited' property rights. Secondly, property rights can be shared among a group. Thirdly, properly rights may be exchanged or altered. What we did not mention in our example is that Heather's use of the car is permitted, or agreed to, by Mr and Mrs Osbourne as the outcome of some exchange process. Heather's permission to use the car is subject to certain specified minimum grade averages achieved in college, and also to completion of an expanded set of household duties. We must also point out in all fairness that, as parents of a teenager, Mr and Mrs Osbourne are not exactly sure that they would ever completely curtail Heather's use of the car.

Property rights and the profit motive
In a capitalistic economic system, property rights and the profit motive work together to lead markets to make economically efficient allocations of resources. The reasoning is very basic. If firms and individuals are going to be productive, they must be rewarded. A failure to reward will cause a reduction in effort in an economy. One way for this reward to fail to appear is if firms and individuals do not have property rights in the results of their efforts. A firm will willingly invest money in innovative activity if it feels not only that it will be profitable but also that those profits cannot be stolen away by, say, a firm copying their product or service. It is the role of the legal system in our capitalistic economy to ensure property rights. If an individual has defined property rights to an asset or to their own efforts, and also to the benefits of using that asset or their own efforts, they can reliably be expected to act in an economically efficient way. Clearly defined and established property rights are then necessary for economic efficiency.

Individual market failure
Ownership is, in practice, a very central question to consider when exploring the issues surrounding the attainment of an economically efficient equilibrium. Consider, briefly, two seemingly abstract examples. The underlying details of these examples will be made abundantly clear later in this chapter.

First, consider a resource that is owned by party A. In using this resource, party A affects the well-being of party B. Quite possibly there will be no compensation going from either party A to party B, or from party B to party A in response to party A's using of the resource in question. You may ask why there is no compensation. Well, suppose that both party A and party B are aware of the impact of party A's actions, but that one party refuses to compensate the other. Furthermore suppose that proving the existence of the impact simply cannot be done in a court of law or to justify some governmental action. The situation gets more complex if, for example, party B is not a single entity but some aggregation of individuals. In this case, it may be impossible for bargaining to proceed to allow the two parties to reach an agreeable, and hence efficient, outcome.

Even if bargaining were possible between party A and party B, the situation may never be straightened out. Quite possibly the impact of party A's actions on party B's well-being is transmitted through some third resource. If this were the case, and neither party A nor party B had ownership claims on the (third) resource, we could never be sure that bargaining would result in an efficient outcome. This is essentially the problem encountered when there are **externalities** associated with some economic activity. An externality is a cost or a benefit involuntarily imposed on another party that is not regulated by any system of prices. We examine this problem in much greater detail in section D of this chapter.

Another way that ownership may cause a problem in attaining an efficient outcome in market exchange is if all parties involved in a transaction own the underlying resource. Suppose there were a resource to be jointly owned by two people: say Mr C and Mr D. Furthermore, suppose that once this resource were obtained Mr C's use of it would not impose a direct burden on Mr D. For efficiency purposes, Mr C and Mr D must agree not only on the purchase of the asset but also on its use. Will Mr C and Mr D be able to do this? There are a lot of issues here involving the relationship between Mr C and Mr D. Even if you feel that Mr C and Mr D could agree to purchase and use the asset, how about if there were three people, or four, or even more? Eventually some individual, say Mr H, involved in the transaction will realize that all the other parties are better off with Mr H than without Mr H. The incentives facing Mr H are then clear: he may offer to pay less than his 'fair share' for the resource, or he may use more than his 'fair share' of the resource once it was created. This is essentially the problem encountered when some economic good has properties making it a public good. We examine this problem in much greater detail in section E of this chapter.

Transaction costs

A definition
Economic interaction may be costly, or it may be cheap. Consider two alternative transactions: buying a hamburger for lunch and buying a house. What does the hamburger cost you? This is an easy question and you can probably quote the price of a hamburger as a certain number of pounds. If we go one step further we can also see that purchasing the hamburger is an easy transaction: the commodity is well defined, the relationship between you and the

hamburger provided is well defined, and the transaction is short lived. You, as a hamburger consumer, can also rest assured that the hamburger market is relatively competitive and that if one hamburger seller behaves in a way that causes you question, another hamburger provider is readily available.

Buying a house is not so easy a task. What does the house cost you? Clearly the house costs you some amount for the land and the property; it also costs you time researching the house and probably different financing mechanisms to enable you to purchase it. As any home owner will tell you, the house is not easily defined. It has many different characteristics – too many to list here in fact. Different buyers may value the particular bundle of characteristics of any given house quite differently. The relationship between you and the seller of the house is also more ambiguous than the relationship between you and the hamburger provider. As part of the sales contract, research will have to be done on possible claims against the house, or structural problems in the house may impart some liability to the seller after the sale. Furthermore, the housing market is not perfectly competitive. Market figures are used to provide the buyer and seller with information about the value of the house, but not the exact value of any individual house. In the housing market, sellers clearly jockey and attempt to manipulate the transaction so as to earn for themselves some market power. Housing is a very durable commodity and trading it, as you the home buyer well know, is not easy.

In short the transaction allowing you to purchase a house is quite different from the transaction of buying a hamburger. The purchase of the house requires you to devote sufficient resources to investigate the transaction. Furthermore, a prudent seller of any given house will also invest significant resources to investigate the exchange. Economists have recognized the types of issues involved in this simple example, and have come to some startling conclusions about market exchange.

The term 'transaction costs' refers to costs incurred because of economic interaction. **Transaction costs** are the costs above and beyond contracted prices, including the costs of acquiring costly information, monitoring performance, committing specific assets and handling complexity. The term may seem broad and ambiguous at this point and we expand greatly on this concept in Chapter 6. For now, however, we offer an admittedly brief breakdown of this concept, asking you to consider transaction costs as arising out of an environment of informational problems and out of commitment.

Informational deficiencies

The perfectly competitive model described in Chapters 3 and 4 of this book reached a very strong conclusion: if all of the assumptions supporting the economy-wide perfectly competitive model were met, an efficient equilibrium would exist throughout the entire economy. One of these assumptions was the existence of what is termed **perfect information**, i.e. that every buyer and seller (and potential buyer and seller) becomes aware of all relevant information in the market place. In practice, the distribution of information is nearly always imperfect. Under an environment characterized by **imperfect information**, at least one market participant, or potential participant, is less than perfectly informed. Although the effect of imperfect information on an efficient economy-wide equilibrium is interesting, it is far beyond what we need here. Our interests are merely to know how imperfect information can give rise to transaction costs that can directly affect the attainment of an efficient equilibrium in a single market.

Consider the home-buyer example discussed earlier. Suppose that the minimum amount the seller is willing to let the house go for is less than the maximum amount a buyer is willing to pay. Call the difference between the two the reservation gap. From the vantage point of economic efficiency, the house should be sold. But it is an open question whether or not the house will be sold. There are a lot of reasons why this may be so. Consider a fairly obvious and typical one: suppose the seller has some private information about the house that he doesn't want the buyer to determine. The buyer has a hunch that the seller is withholding information. Naturally the buyer can obtain the hidden information through other means, and there is some cost to this. Suppose that the buyer has to pay a third party some amount greater than the reservation gap to determine whether or not the seller has some type of private information. Now, from the buyer's perspective the situation may be viewed as a game resulting in a prisoners' dilemma where the Nash strategy is to not purchase the house. What the buyer is concerned about, of course, is that her cost in trying to determine the seller's private information reduces the net benefit, reflected in the maximum amounts she is willing to pay for the house below the minimum amount the seller is willing to accept for the house. Whether or not the seller's private information will negatively affect the buyer's valuation of the house is not relevant. All that is relevant is that the buyer has a hunch. The acknowledged existence of imperfect information will create transaction costs that will prevent an efficient exchange.

Commitment

One of the factors that make one exchange easier than another is the level of commitment required to the transaction. By commitment we mean here that participation in one transaction precludes participation in other transactions, a kind of measure of the opportunity cost of a particular transaction. Commitment may be beneficial or it may be destructive. One transaction party may fear that other parties are not committed to the exchange and this fear may create the need for costly bargaining between the two parties.

As an example, consider the printing and publishing industry. In particular consider two published articles: this textbook and a daily newspaper. There are virtually no exogenous entry barriers to either type of publishing. The equipment is readily available, and in each case there is a ready supply of printers available actually to do the dirty printing work. But what of the commitment level required in the transaction where the book publisher and the daily newspaper publisher seek to get their product printed?

Most of the larger publishing houses hire outside vendors to print their books. Most of the larger daily newspapers do not have the printing done by outside vendors, relying instead on employees of the newspapers to do the printing on machinery owned by the newspaper. The reason is commitment and fear of exploitation. If you were the editor of the large daily newspaper you would have a great fear that the printer would lack your commitment to the exchange. Let us say that, on a Monday, evidence of intelligent life on other planets is found. Clearly, this can sell a lot of newspapers. Your staff is busy writing stories about the new-found aliens; you are busy supervising your staff. The phone rings and the printer you have contracted with says it is urgent. You speak to the printer, who basically wants to renegotiate the deal you have so that the printer gets a hefty raise. At this point, you have a problem. The printer knows full well that there is simply no way for you to acquire the services of another printer in time for Tuesday's edition. Very likely, the printer will get his raise.

How can the situation be avoided? The obvious choice is for the newspaper publishing company to own the printing capability. This conclusion is drawn with absolutely no consideration of efficiency concerns. In fact, this same conclusion is drawn even if the printer were able to produce a higher-quality, lower-cost output than the newspaper publisher. Even if efficiency were to dictate that the printer produce the newspaper for the newspaper publishing company, the newspaper publisher will be fearful of such a deal. The fear of committing to a particular printer may keep the newspaper publisher from doing so. From the newspaper publishing company's perspective, it may very well be deemed too costly to reach a negotiated agreement under which its fears of exploitation will be sufficiently small. Put another way, the presence of commitment in and to the transaction by involved parties may prevent an otherwise efficient exchange from occurring.

D. Externalities and market failure reconsidered

Decision-making with externalities

Private versus social costs and benefits

Consider, for a moment, your decision to commute to work or school. A variety of options is open to you in a number of different dimensions. You might pick (subject to your requirements) the time you commute, your route, and your mode of transportation. Let us focus on the mode dimension – exactly how will you get there? You have several options: you may drive your own car; you may take public transport; you may cycle or walk; or you may opt to car pool with others living near you.

This decision is clearly yours, but your choice will affect others. It may even affect others in different ways than it affects you. Let us briefly examine the effects of your mode choice on all involved parties. If you drive, you maximize convenience (no coordination with others). You also add to traffic congestion, thus making everyone else on the road with you take a little longer. If you take public transport, you deal with the inconvenience of being subject to an externally created schedule, and also may have to stand in a crowded aisle for a long period of time. By taking public transport you will have reduced the amount of congestion. If you car pool, you face a schedule over which you can presumably exert some influence, and you do a little less to reduce the amount of congestion on the road.

Once again, notice that the decision is yours; and you will make it in your own interests, with maybe no concern given to the effects of your decision on others. For most of us, the decision we make is to drive our own cars. Each of us then makes a contribution to traffic congestion and pollution. The commuting decision then involves an externality, in this case a cost imposed on other members of the commuting public, termed a negative externality. Analogously, a positive externality imposes a benefit on another party.

Because of this, the outcome is not **efficient** because of a difference between our benefit from the choice to drive our own car and the costs to society of our having made this choice. Inefficiencies typically occur with externalities because decision makers do not take full account of all the costs and benefits involved with their choices. Namely, they fail to recognize those costs and benefits that accrue to other parties.

The commuting mode choice example clearly points out two different types of costs to be considered in analysis based on efficiency: **private costs** are the total costs borne by the initiator of some activity; **social costs** are the total costs borne by all members of society. Because individuals decide on what type of transportation to employ, their actions are based only on the private costs of their choice. Clearly, in choosing to drive their own cars, to the individual the private costs are far less than the social costs of their actions. With the idea of externalities causing a difference between private and social costs, we now turn our attention back to markets and to supply and demand analysis.

Market failure in a supply and demand context

A negative production externality
Kimball is a small, relatively isolated, fictitious town in northern England. Although there are several small manufacturing firms in Kimball, most economic activity there is in the agricultural sector. Cummings is an international producer of ball bearings. In the past couple of years, it has become clear that Cummings needs to close its older existing plants throughout the United Kingdom and Europe and, because of technological innovation in ball bearing

production, consolidate manufacturing in a single new facility. Cummings decides to locate in Kimball because of low labour costs in the area relative to other regions and counties in Western Europe.[4]

The townsfolk of Kimball are abuzz over the new decision, and many are overjoyed at the prospect of having a new industry in their town. CEO Stanley Beckwith and Cummings construct their new plant, bring many Cummings' employees into town, and also hire a very large number of Kimball residents. Business in Kimball is good: there are plenty of jobs to go around, and lots of infrastructure development and construction taking place.

For Cummings (which, incidentally, is a major player in the ball-bearing market) the national price of the ball bearings is shown in Figure 5.6 as P_c, and at this price Cummings produces Q_c units of ball bearings. The supply curve in Figure 5.6 reflects the costs to Cummings of producing, distributing and marketing their ball bearings in the United Kingdom.

After about a year, some of the other local employers begin to complain about the presence of Cummings in 'their' community. Donald Smith, a farm equipment dealer is quoted in the *Kimball Gazette*, the local newspaper, saying 'I know that Cummings has brought a lot of good things into Kimball; but I have some concerns. Ever since the ball bearing plant has opened, it is harder for me to hold on to my staff. I am a fair guy, and would not begrudge somebody fair pay for hard work. You see though, since the plant opened I have had to raise my people's wages by about half to keep them.' Similar sentiments are voiced by the owners of the area brewery, bakery and bus company.

The other employers in Kimball are affected by an externality created by the presence of Stanley Beckwith's Cummings; namely, the higher wages they must pay to attract and keep workers. Make no mistake about the role of the price system in this example. The labour markets transmit the externality to local employers. The price system also fails in forcing Cummings to bear the

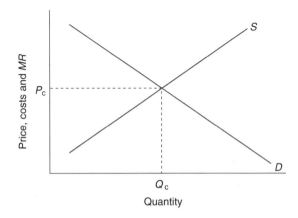

Figure 5.6 Cummings: Supply and demand.

full cost of the higher wages in the local area labour markets. It is true that Cummings' presence raises labour costs to itself, but this is a separate issue from raising the labour costs of other producers in the Kimball area.

Once again, the issue here is a difference between the private and social costs of ball-bearing production by Cummings. If we define society here as all economic activity surrounding Kimball (maybe not a bad assumption for a relatively isolated town), the social costs of Cummings' actions include the increase in wages experienced by other employers in the Kimball area on account of the presence of Cummings. In Figure 5.7, the supply and demand curves of Figure 5.6 are reproduced. A second curve, above and to the left of the original supply curve, labelled S_C, also appears. The S_C curve includes the increased labour costs borne by other employers in the Kimball area. The socially optimal, and efficient, level of output for Cummings is found by the intersection of the demand and S_C curves, Q_S.

This diagram illustrates one important very general result concerning externalities generated by producers. Under a market system, a negative productive externality will result in overproduction of some good or service.

A positive production externality

The situation is a little different, but still not optimal, if the production of some good or service generates a positive externality. As an example, consider the production of widgets, a hypothetical good. Because of the production of widgets, others in the economy benefit. Consider the market depicted in Figure 5.8. The supply function, S, accounts for all of the production costs incurred by the industry of widget producers. The demand function, D_1, shows the market demand for widget consumers. Recall from Chapter 2 that the height of the demand function at any point shows the value placed on that unit by the marginal consumer of widgets. The market will clear at the price P_m, and Q_m units will be produced and purchased.

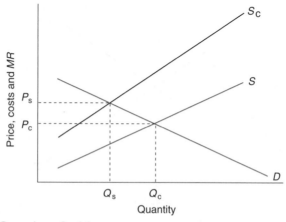

Figure 5.7 Cummings: Social cost.

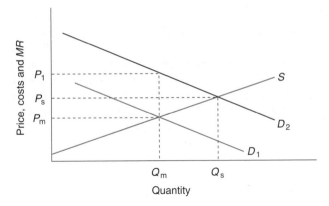

Figure 5.8 Positive production externalities.

The market demand function, D_1, does not reflect the total value placed on widget production by society. Because of the benefits to others in the economy who do not produce widgets, and possibly do not even consume them, the total benefit of producing any quantity of widgets will exceed the amount shown by the demand function. The demand function labelled D_2 is drawn so as to represent these positive externalities. At the output level Q_m, for example, the marginal consumer (that willing to pay P_m at most for a widget) experiences benefits equal to P_m from consuming a widget, or else he would not purchase it. However, there are other benefits. The production of the widget consumed by the marginal consumer created certain benefits for others in the economy; in Figure 5.8 these benefits are shown as the difference between P_1 and P_m, i.e. ($P_1 - P_m$). The socially efficient level of output in the widget market is Q_s, which would sell for a price of P_s.

When markets function in the presence of externalities, substantial distortions may exist precluding a socially efficient outcome. In the context of the general equilibrium ideas presented in Chapter 4, we say that market failure has occurred. This implies that the prices relayed to producers and consumers lead them to the 'wrong' quantity sold at the 'wrong' price;.

With a negative externality in production, too large a quantity is produced. You may ask what the harm of this is. The answer is perhaps subtle. The injured parties would prefer less to be produced; if we add to the costs of production the value lost by the injured parties, we obtain the total social cost. Presumably, if some redistributive authority existed, the price that would equate the total social cost to the demand function could be charged, the socially optimal level of output would be produced, and the source of the externality could be made to compensate those injured by its actions (the 'polluter pays' principle). ·

With a positive externality, too small a quantity is produced. Society, as a whole, could benefit from additional production. Unfortunately, the only information acted on by producers is the demand function, which ignores these benefits.

Although externalities represent a rich field of exploration for economists interested in market failure, we will end our discussion of them for now. Suffice it to say that some very prominent economists use externalities as a justification for increased government involvement in markets. Although this solution to the problems caused by externalities has its merits, we explore another solution in this chapter. Before we do, it will be helpful to explore another common source of market failure. We will then turn to a solution to these and other causes of inefficiencies in the functioning of markets. This solution is the much-heralded Coase Theorem.

E. Public and private goods

An example

For a brief moment put aside thoughts of school work, examinations and term papers. Let us suppose that it is early July and you set off, blankets and coolers in hand, to the local fireworks display. You select the best spot, spread out the blanket and wait. As you are waiting, an ice-cream vendor appears and you purchase a treat – after all, it had been a hot day. Pretty soon the fireworks are lighting up the night-time sky.

Reflecting for a moment, you realize that you have consumed two goods that go very well together. Each is quite different though. The ice-cream was purchased in an organized market, you pay for it and you have the right to determine who will consume it. The situation with the fireworks is very different: they may have been paid for by the local government or by some civic organization such as the Chamber of Commerce. Equally striking is the idea that, while you are consuming the fireworks, plenty of other people are too. Goods such as fireworks present problems to a market-oriented approach to economic analysis.

Two characteristics

A **public good** is a good that can be consumed by one person without diminishing the amount that other people consume of it, and also that no individual can be barred from consuming. More technically, we may say that public goods have two very special features. First, they exhibit **non-rivalrous consumption**, that is one party's consumption does not detract from (rival) full enjoyment by other parties. Secondly, **non-excludability** means that, once a public good is produced, it is impossible to exclude others from consuming it.

Public goods tend to be relatively indivisible; they often come in such large units (or lumps) that they cannot be broken into pieces that can be bought or sold. The two above-mentioned characteristics of public goods make them separate and distinct from private goods, which are most of the goods and services exchanged in the economy.

Usually, the supply and demand models described in Chapter 2 are applicable to the markets for private goods. The benefits and additions to utility from consuming a private good are directly assignable in a price-based system of exchange. At the fireworks display, you (or your designee) can consume the ice-cream cone because you contracted with the vendor and provided payment.

The community fireworks display itself is clearly a public good. Up to an ambiguous crowd size limit, the rockets' red glare can be enjoyed by all. Other examples of public goods include national defence, parks and the environment.

The free-rider problem

Many, but not all, public goods are provided by government. The reason is that the characteristic of non-rivalrous consumption encourages the market mechanism to fail. Suppose that the fireworks were to be financed by asking everyone in the crowd to contribute whatever they wished. It is in your own interests grossly to understate the value you place on the fireworks. Being a business student, you clearly recognize that, so long as others are more altruistic and generous than you, your enjoyment of the fireworks will not suffer. This reasoning embodies what economists call the **free-rider problem**, which should ensure market failure or the attainment of an inefficient outcome in the market.

The market for fireworks

As was the case with production externalities, the attainment of non-optimal outcomes in the market with consumption externalities can be exhibited in a supply and demand model. The 'market' for fireworks displays is depicted in Figure 5.9. In this diagram, the supply function shows the costs of providing fireworks. For simplicity we assume that there is a wide variety of quantity of fireworks available, with larger quantities – better and longer displays – costing more to produce. We attempt to measure these attributes of fireworks

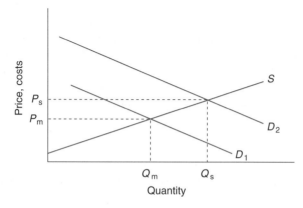

Figure 5.9 The market for fireworks.

displays in a single dimension. Thus, as we move rightward on the horizontal axis in Figure 5.9, we increase the quantity of fireworks.

The market demand in Figure 5.9 is the lower downward-sloping curve labelled D_1. It shows, for a given quantity, the maximum amount the crowd would be willing to pay in a market setting for their right to watch the fireworks. Herein lies the free-rider problem. Sound, rational (and perhaps shrewd) individuals would never let their true valuations of the fireworks become known. After all, once the fireworks are produced, they cannot be excluded from consuming them. Further, their consumption does not detract from the consumption by others.

The higher downward-sloping curve, D_2, is drawn to reflect the true, unknown, valuation placed on fireworks. Naturally, one could never actually construct a demand curve such as D_2, because it would be difficult to induce consumers to reveal their true valuations of fireworks.[5] The implication of the fireworks example is well in accordance with standard economic theory: markets provide far too little of public goods.

Ownership of public goods

Now that we have somewhat of an idea of what a public good is, we want to emphasize one way of examining market failure in the context of public goods, the related issues of ownership and property rights. Expressed somewhat parenthetically, in one sense everyone owns a public good and has certain property rights to its use. However, it is also true that nobody owns a public good: that is, because of the free-rider problem, no one has any incentive to create a public good, to maintain a public good or to provide it in sufficient quantity to maximize the welfare of all members of society.

National defence is clearly a public good. A national government cannot protect one person in one part of a country and fail to protect another person in another part of that same country. Clearly, this provided some of the incentive for the formation of NATO in Europe during the Cold War. However, national defence is not provided by a market; it is provided by national government. Why is this the case? Everyone owns national defence once it is provided; would any individual, group of individuals, or firm voluntarily provide this service? Suppose one did. Also suppose that you decided to not contribute, reasoning that defence could not be provided to your neighbour and not yourself. Surely, the good would not be provided or would be provided in a limited quantity. When the government provides the good, it can circumvent the functioning of the market by levying taxes and forcing you to pay them.

The tragedy of the commons

The ownership and property rights issues associated with public goods have long been recognized by economists. One of the oldest and most widely used examples of property rights and the incentives of ownership is the tragedy of the commons, a situation experienced throughout England in prior centuries.

Garrett Hardin (1968) describes the tragedy of the commons in this way. There is a small town that is economically dependent on the agricultural sector for its economic and practical existence. Part of the output of this town is cattle; owing to historical forces there is a large pasture, or commons, freely available for grazing to each herdsman's cattle. The situation is good for years, barring the occasional minor dispute between herdsmen.

As time passes the town grows and develops. Stresses and strains emerge in the arrangement with the commons. Simply put, the commons is over-grazed, hurting each cattle owner. The reason for this failure is evident. Each herdsman advances his own interests by maximizing the size of his herd; it is rational for each to expect a positive gain by adding one more animal. The cost of adding each additional animal is, of course, the effects of overgrazing, which are borne by *all* cattle owners. Hardin states it more eloquently:

> the rational herdsman concludes that the only sensible course for him to pursue is to add another animal to his herd. And another; and another . . . But this is the conclusion reached by each and every rational herdsman sharing a commons. Therein is the tragedy. Each man is locked into a system that compels him to increase his herd without limit – in a world that is limited. Ruin is the destination toward which all men rush, each pursuing his own best interest in a society that believes in the freedom of the commons. Freedom in the commons brings ruin to all. (1968, p. 1244)

In this set-up, which was prevalent for several centuries throughout England, the commons are clearly a public good. It is equally clear that externalities play a role in the allocation of grazing rights on the commons. Each individual rancher acts on the private costs of grazing his herd on the common land while ignoring the social costs of his actions. In this example, the free-rider problem manifests itself, bringing disaster to the community – the destruction of the common grazing land.

The free-rider problem also causes trouble in the fireworks example. In that case, however, the results were not as damaging. We do not need a detailed, highly technical study to determine whether or not communities regularly enjoy fireworks displays. These yearly celebrations anchor events at many backyard barbecues, but are seemingly never as long or as good as we wish they were.

The problems illustrated above with public goods are some of the most severe incentive problems in economic management. When a resource is freely available to all, overuse will likely result. It also stands to reason that, when many people share the obligation to provide some resource, it will be under-supplied.

The environment
The ultimate public good is perhaps what we have come to call the environment: the relatively thin layer of nitrogen, oxygen, ozone and other gases that surround our planet, the salt and fresh water available for human use, and the large number of biological forms found therein. Given that the environment exists, everyone has access to it (exclusion is viewed as equivalent to murder

in most societies); and, within reason, one person's consumption of it does not impinge upon another person's enjoyment of it. Further, the environment is one of the greatest causes of concern in the world today.

For years, we discharge Freon gas into the atmosphere; in the late 1980s we learned that these discharges were causing a great thinning of the layer of ozone surrounding the earth that keeps us safe from the dangerous ultraviolet radiation put out by the sun. This is an example of a negative worldwide externality. The problem is that, because nobody owns the atmosphere, no one party had incentive to curb the use of Freon gases, which had valuable commercial properties. Notably, a treaty (The Montreal Protocol) was signed in 1987 and extended in1992 calling for the eventual removal of these gases from the market place.

A similar example is provided by the so-called greenhouse effect, where the emissions of carbon dioxide from burning carbon are ultimately raising the average temperature on the planet. The list of environmental threats goes on and on: acid rain, water shortages and oil spills on the world's oceans.

There is also concern, widely described, regarding a number of species of fish in the ocean. Of particular concern is the overfishing of whales by commercial fishermen from a variety of countries, particularly Japan and Norway. Again the problem is that nobody clearly owns the whales.

Property rights, ownership and incentives
In each of these examples of public goods, the story is the same. There is a lack of clearly defined property rights for certain resources. Whereas all can enjoy the fireworks display, nobody holds the property rights enabling them to sell viewing rights to others. The payment issue seemingly dominates the example of national defence as a public good; only the government can force people to pay for it through taxation. If one cattleman owned the grazing resource called the commons, he would have an incentive to ration its use in order to secure his own income next year. Similarly, no one person has the incentive to restrict access to the environment so as to preclude other individuals from damaging or even destroying it.

With the importance of property rights established, we will next turn our attention to a solution to the problems of externalities and public goods in markets. Although these solutions are interesting in their own right, they also provide critical insights into managing economic organizations.

F. The Coasian approach to market failure

The Coase theorem

The 1991 Nobel Prize in Economics was awarded to Ronald Coase; the 1993 Nobel Prize in Economics was awarded to Douglas North. The work of both

of these men is important to understanding managerial economics and organizations; we shall, however, mainly concern ourselves in this chapter with the
work of Ronald Coase. In fact, we will pretty much focus on only one piece
of Coase's work contained in an article written in 1960 entitled 'The Problem
of Social Cost'.[6] A number of arguments made in this article have grown into
what is now called the Coase theorem. Just how important can this one theorem be? Consider the purposes in which it may be put.

One of the most celebrated contributions to economics in this century is
also one of the simplest. The **Coase theorem** states that if there are no legal,
strategic or informational barriers to bargaining, and if property rights are
clearly defined, then people can always negotiate themselves to an efficient
outcome. Furthermore, civil liability rules will have no effect on the allocation
of economic resources.[7] The Coase theorem implies that, if parties bargain to
an efficient agreement then the activities chosen will not depend on the bargaining power of the individuals, and are not influenced by what assets each
owned when the bargaining began. Efficiency alone determines the selection
of the activity by the group.

Part of the appeal of the Coase theorem to economists is the minimal role
allotted to government. The task of government is simply to assign clear property rights; theoretically it does not even matter to whom the property rights
are assigned.

In practical applications of the Coase theorem there are two common stumbling blocks. First, in many cases bargaining may be expensive. The costs of
reaching agreements are commonly called transaction costs, an idea introduced
in Chapter 1. Reflecting the importance of transaction costs, we devote a whole
chapter, Chapter 6, to their discussion. The second stumbling block is that the
actual assignment of property rights will cause redistributive effects; i.e. one
party will end up paying another party.

An illustrative example

In order to illustrate the application of the Coase theorem to an economic
problem, we refer to the example provided by Ronald Coase himself in his
article, 'The Problem of Social Cost'. In advance we apologize for the size of
the numbers used in this example; we modified the numbers used originally
by Coase in order to facilitate the exposition.

Imagine a railroad that owns a pair of tracks passing through the middle of
a farmer's land. The farmer must decide how much crop to plant on his fields
and the railroad must decide how many trains to run per day along these tracks.
The issue of concern are the sparks sometimes produced by each train as it trav-
els down the track; the sparks can create fires that destroy the farmer's crop.

Perhaps your immediate response is to recognize that the trains impose a
negative externality on the farmer and to call for the railroad to reimburse the

farmer for any damage caused by the passing trains. However, we can safely point out that there are two ways to solve this problem: either the railroad could run fewer trains, or the farmer could plant his crops further back from the tracks. At this point, more facts are needed before the most efficient solution is identified.

The basic facts are as follows. If the railroad runs one train per day, the total value of these transportation services to consumers is 300 currency units (c.u.) per year. Two trains per day result in a total value of 500 c.u. per year, and three trains in a total value of 560 c.u. per year. The marginal cost of running each train equals 100 c.u. per year. If the railroad acts in its own interests, it will run two trains per day. The first train generates a profit for the railroad of 200 c.u. If a second train is run, revenues increase by 200 c.u. and costs by 100 c.u.; since the marginal revenues exceed the marginal costs, the second train will increase profits. For the third train, however, marginal revenues are less than marginal costs and running it will decrease profits by 40 c.u. per year.

Concerning the profitability of farming in this example, the market value of the crops produced by each of the farmer's two identical fields is, if there is no fire damage, 1,000 c.u. The marginal cost of putting one field into production is 700 c.u., and the marginal cost of putting the second field into production is 980 c.u. Clearly the farmer will choose, in the absence of the threat of fire damage, to plant and harvest both fields.

It is by no means certain that a fire will ever occur. However, it one does, on either plot of land, the value of the crops that remain is only 40 c.u. In the event of a fire, all other production costs are lost. A fire on the first plot causes the farmer a loss of 660 c.u., a fire on the second causes a loss of 940 c.u. A fire in both plots causes a loss of 1620 c.u. Since it is random whether or not a fire occurs, we can only characterize the possibility of one occurring. We will assume that the probability of a fire on either plot is the same and increases with the number of trains run each day. This probability is zero if no trains are run, 12.5 per cent ($\frac{1}{8}$) if one train is run, and 25 per cent ($\frac{2}{8} = \frac{1}{4}$) if two trains are run.

To determine the socially optimal number of trains to run and number of fields to plant, let us calculate the net expected social benefit from all of the possible combinations of number of trains and number of plots. If no trains are run and no plots are planted, the expected total social benefit is zero.

If one train is run and one plot is cultivated, the calculations are a little more involved. The net benefit to society of running one train is the market value of the services provides less the costs of providing that train for service: 300 c.u. − 100 c.u. = 200 c.u. To this figure we will add the expected net social benefit of the farmer having planted a single field.

If the farmer plants a single field, the expected net social benefit reflects the net benefit if there is and if there is not a fire. To form the expected benefit, the benefit in each case is multiplied by the probability that each occurs. If there is no fire, the social benefit of one field's production equals 1000 c.u., the market value of the crops produced, minus the costs of providing that one field, 700 c.u. The difference is 300 c.u. If there is a fire, the market value of the one field is reduced to 40 c.u., but the costs of cultivating that field remain at 700 c.u.; the benefits are then negative, 40 c.u. − 700 c.u. = −660 c.u. The probability of there being a fire, given that one train is run, is 12.5 per cent; the probability of there not being a fire is 87.5 per cent. The expected benefit of planting one field, given that one train is run, then equals:

$$(0.125) \times (-660 \text{ c.u.}) + (0.875) \times (300 \text{ c.u.}) = -82.5 + 262.5 = 180 \text{ c.u.}$$

The total expected net social benefit is then found by adding the net benefit of running one train to the expected net benefit of planting one field: 180 c.u. + 200 c.u. = 380 c.u. The total expected net social benefit for all possible pairings of numbers of plots cultivated and number of trains run is shown in Table 5.1.

With some of the facts of this example laid bare, we can see how each party can best participate in reaching the socially optimal, and efficient, outcome. Society is made as well off as possible when there is one train per day and one plot of land cultivated. Two questions remain. First, can the farmer and the railroad operator be expected to reach this conclusion on their own? Secondly, what are the property rights issues involved? Both of these questions are now addressed. We assume that the parties can bargain and that the costs of this bargaining are negligible. Concurrently we will make assumptions about which party has the property rights. What will be seen, and this is part of the attraction of the Coase theorem to economists, is that the efficient outcome will emerge regardless of which party is granted the property rights.

First, suppose that the farmer is granted the property rights, i.e. that the farmer has the final say about what happens in the field, and that the railroad must reimburse the farmer's fire damages. What will the farmer decide: zero, one or two trains, and zero, one or two plots cultivated?

Since zero plots result in zero income for the farmer, this option may be ruled out. So let the farmer plant one plot. Now we examine the number of trains chosen by the farmer. If there are zero trains, the farmer earns profits of 300 c.u. In fact, because the railroad is liable for any fire damage to the farmer's crops, his profits are the same regardless of the number of trains being

Table 5.1 Total net expected social benefit (in hypothetical currency units)

Farmer	Railroad		
	0 trains	1 train	2 trains
0 plots	0	200	300
1 plot	300	380	360
2 plots	320	280	140

run, always 300 c.u. Now, will the farmer permit one train to run? He would be willing to do so if it earned him more profits than 300 c.u.

If the railroad runs one train, its profits depend now upon whether or not there is a fire, so we must construct the railroad's profit of running one train. If there is no fire, the railroad's gain in running one train is simply revenues (300 c.u.) less operating costs (100 c.u.), or 200 c.u. If there is a fire, the railroad's gain includes damaged paid to the farmer. These damages equal the lost value of the farmer's crops, 960 c.u. Then if there is a fire, the railroad's gain is revenues (300 c.u.) less operating costs (100 c.u.) less reimbursement to the farmer (960 c.u.), or −760 c.u. Since we know that the probability of a fire when one train is run equals 12.5 per cent and the probability of there being no fire when one trail is run equals 87.5 per cent, the expected gain to the railroad can be calculated as

$$(0.125) \times (-760 \text{ c.u.}) + (0.875) \times (200 \text{ c.u.}) = 80 \text{ c.u.}$$

Will the farmer be willing to permit the railroad to operate one train? Well, the running of one train allows 80 c.u. of value to be created even when the fire losses of the farmer are covered by the railroad operator. If the parties are free to bargain, this 80 c.u. can be allocated between the two parties to induce the farmer to permit one train to run. Presumably, if the railroad pays the farmer 1 c.u. for the right to run one train under the liability rule, the farmer would then earn profits of 301 c.u., and the railroad 79 c.u. It is also possible that the farmer could wind up with profits of 379 c.u., and the railroad with 1 c.u. So it is clear that social benefits can be increased to 380 c.u. when one train runs from the level of 300 c.u. when no trains run. The cause of this gain is the profit earned by the railroad operator.

At this point, the farmer holds the property rights concerning activities in the field. He may permit the railroad operator to run trains if so doing raises the total value created, and if some of this increase in value is paid back to the farmer. The source of this incremental value is the profit earned by the railroad. In Table 5.2 the profits earned the railroad under all possible combinations of plots cultivated and trains run are shown.

The calculations behind Table 5.2 are somewhat cumbersome and are left as an exercise to the reader. The figures indicate, however, that the railroad's

Table 5.2 Railroad profits when farmer holds property rights
(in hypothetical currency units)

Farmer	Railroad		
	0 trains	1 train	2 trains
0 plots	0	200	300
1 plot	0	380	60
2 plots	0	−40	−180

profits are maximized by running two trains if zero plots are cultivated, by running one train if one plot is cultivated, and by running zero trains if two plots are cultivated. When the railroad incorporates crop damage as a cost of doing business, the largest social value is created if one plot of land is cultivated and if one train is run. Recall that we showed earlier that this mixture was socially optimal.

An alternative arrangement would assign property rights to the railroads, making the farmer liable for any damage caused to his crops. In this arrangement, the railroad is guaranteed 200 c.u. by running one train and 300 c.u. from running two trains. The farmer could bribe the railroad not to run any trains at all by paying the railroad 300 c.u.[8] The farmer could bribe the railroad into running only one train by paying 100 c.u., the value to the railroad of the second train.

Under this alternative liability rule, the profits of the farmer now depend on the expected fire loss. To see how these profits are calculated, suppose that the railroad will be running two trains per day. If the farmer does not cultivate either of his fields, his profits are zero. If the farmer cultivates only one of his fields, his expected gains can be calculated. If there is a fire (the probability of a fire with two trains run is 25 per cent), the net gain to the farmer is –660 (40–700). If there is no fire (the probability of no fire with two trains is 75 per cent), the gain to the farmer is 300 c.u. The expected gain to the farmer is then:

$$(0.25) \times (-660 \text{ c.u.}) + (0.75) \times 300 \text{ c.u.} = -165 + 225 = 60 \text{ c.u.}$$

The expected net gains to the farmer under all the possible combinations of number of plots and number of trains are shown in Table 5.3. The figures show that, when the railroad owns the property rights, the number of trains run directly affects the costs to the farmer of doing business. Once again, we can see how exchange will occur. To start, suppose that the railroad intends running two trains. If it is in the farmer's interests to pay the railroad to eliminate one of its trains, will the railroad accept the bribe? If the farmer considers planting only one plot of land, his well-being increases by 120 c.u. as the number of trains is reduced from two to one. The railroad values the second train at only 100 c.u., so some exchange is possible. Perhaps the parties could split the difference, with the farmer paying the railroad 100 c.u. to eliminate the second train. Can the farmer induce the railroad to go from one to zero trains? No, because the gain to the farmer from such a move does not exceed the loss by the railroad.

Continuing our analysis of the bargaining situation described by the figures in Table 5.3, we point out that the farmer will not rationally ever plan on using both of his plots when two trains are run because he loses 160 c.u. in this situation and can lose nothing by planting neither of his fields.

We can now conclude which outcome will be chosen by the farmer and the railroad if the railroad is not legally liable for the fire damage caused by its

Table 5.3 Farmer profits when railroad holds property rights (in hypothetical currency units)

Farmer	Railroad		
	0 trains	1 train	2 trains
0 plots	0	0	0
1 plot	300	180	60
2 plots	320	80	−160

trains. The farmer will plant on one of his plots and the railroad will run only one train. As shown earlier in Table 5.1, this is exactly the outcome that maximizes the total expected social net welfare. The granting of property rights, in this case the right to use the fields, affects only the relative well-being of the farmer and the railroad operator.

Several points are central to this conclusion. First, we assumed that there were no large bargaining costs for the exchange between the farmer and the railroad. Communication was easy and cheap. Secondly, we assumed that somebody held the property rights. If both parties held the property rights, then in effect neither of them would and it would be impossible to predict the outcome. In practice, what would happen is the railroad system would run two trains and the farmer, if a fire occurred, when pursue the railroad through the court system – a situation where the emphasis could very well end up on bargaining costs in the form of legal fees.

Before moving on to other ways of dealing with externalities, we need to make one more point with our farmer and railroad example: if the two entities were to be joined under a common ownership, perhaps by a merger or by simultaneous purchase by some third party, the newly created organization would choose the socially efficient outcome. After all, the new entity's profits would be equal to the net total social benefit shown in Table 5.1. If, for some reason, property rights could not be assigned, or if bargaining costs were too high, a merger would create total value for the concerned parties.

G. Externalities and public goods: Other solutions

Coasian analysis provides one solution to the problem of market failure in the presence of externalities and public goods. Three other approaches have been identified: cooperation, regulatory responses, and tax and subsidy measures.

Cooperation and group ownership

Cooperation involves, in one way or another, an element of group ownership. If all parties involved in the externality or in the use of a public good can in effect be joined in some fashion then they would be forced to equate the social and private costs of their actions. Consider the forces behind the ocean fisheries off the coasts of Europe. As a group, all fishermen of different nationalities have an interest in preventing overfishing. As individuals, all fishermen have more of an interest in their own incomes. If ownership of the current and future fishing harvests could be granted to all fishermen simultaneously, then the incentives would be in place to eliminate overfishing.

In practice, however, this level of cooperation would fail for much the same reason as would the Coase theorem, namely the bargaining involved would not be costless. Some issues that could be resolved only with great difficulty would be: defining the relative shares of ownership across all fishermen, identifying who should receive the shares, determining whether the shares should be sold or given away, and policing members to see that cheating (in the form of overfishing) did not occur.

Regulatory responses

Regulatory responses to negative externalities are sometimes called the application of the command and control approach. In its strictest application, the government simply outlaws the negative externality. Although this approach may be appealing, the example above with the farmer and the railroad shows that it may be possible to increase social welfare if some agreed amount of the externality is permitted.

The command and control approach applied to pollution typically defines some uniform standard that all sources of pollution must meet. Certain inefficiencies result, however, because of the different marginal costs faced by different firms. Furthermore, once a company meets the uniform standard, they have little economic incentive to find innovative ways to reduce pollution even further.

In 1993 the federal government of the United States began another approach to reduce pollution, a system of marketable permits. Firms can purchase (or are granted) a permit allowing them to emit a certain level of pollution. Enough permits are issued to take the pollution levels in total to some desirable level. Under this system, companies are allowed to sell their permits. This programme is clearly an attempt by the federal government to assign property rights, namely the right to pollute. This system provides many incentives to create the best possible anti-pollution devices, rather than simply meeting the government-imposed targets for emissions.

Taxes and subsidies

The third response to the presence of externalities in markets is some form of tax and subsidy programme instituted by the government. Subsidies, in a sense, are the carrot used to drive firms towards some standard; taxes are the stick. Subsidies, in the form of tax credits for the purchase of pollution-reducing equipment, are fairly common and are favoured by businesses. Such subsidies will not affect firm output because they represent a change in fixed costs and not a change in firm managerial costs. Because subsidies reduce the level of pollution, they lower the social marginal costs of production, driving them closer to the private marginal costs of production. In effect, the difference between the socially optimal outcome and the market outcome is diminished.

Economists tend to focus on the difference between social and private marginal costs as being the major cause of the inefficiency created by an externality and favour taxes as the appropriate policy response. Taxes equate private and social marginal costs and grant firms some leeway in deciding how to react to a demand for pollution reduction. In the best world, a per-unit tax on pollution would be levied. In the absence of this, the tax would be placed on units of output at a rate sufficient to reduce pollution to some desirable level.

H. Implications for managers

Approach to economic problems

Ownership, property rights and the reasoning behind the Coase theorem provide managers with many useful tools to be used in solving economic problems.

The concept of ownership for some assets is clear. You may own your car, giving you the right to operate as you wish subject to some legal restrictions; you also have an incentive to take proper care of your car. The concept of ownership of organizations is not so clear, but can be understood in terms of what are called residual rights.

The residual rights of control to an asset give the holder the opportunity to employ the asset as she wishes, subject to legal constraints and all prior contractual commitments. In firms, the residual rights of control would include the selection of suppliers and advertising medium and price setting. In short, the holder of the residual right of control determines how the firm will act. In most large corporations, the residual rights of control belong, in large part, to the chief executive officer (CEO) and some levels of their management teams. In smaller enterprises, the residual rights of control belong to the owner.

The **residual claimant** has the rights to the **residual returns**. An organization may be seen as an entity that takes in revenues (determined in part by luck) and, out of these revenues, makes specified payments to the factors of production, or inputs. Any amounts left over are said to be residual returns and belong to the residual claimant. Under the corporate structures mandated by state and federal laws, the residual claimants in corporations are the stockholders.

The improper matching of the residual rights of control with the interests of the residual claimant forms the basis for one of the fundamental problems in managing economic organizations. In large corporations, the linkage between the stockholders and the CEOs is the corporate board of directors, which is supposed to pick a CEO and monitor her performance in light of the stockholders' interests. There are many ways in which this linkage has been strained. In Chapter 11, we provide detailed discussion of this problem.

On a much lower organizational level, this mismatch is also apparent. It may not be practical to assign every employee a portion of the rights to the residual return. Thus, in the absence of the favourable incentives provided by ownership, employees must be motivated in some other way. One response is to monitor employee performance. In practice, however, this process may be rife with measurement errors.

One of the classic papers in organizational economics, by Alchian and Demsetz (1972), treats the very nature of firms as creating the linkage between residual control and residual claims. They consider an environment of team production, in which firm output is a joint effort of many individuals' efforts, which cannot be uniquely identified. In a sense, the output of the team becomes a public good; and a free-rider in this context is a worker who decides to put in little effort. This problem is discussed in detail in Chapter 12.

The Coase theorem is also important to understanding patterns of economic activity. The emphasis of the Coase theorem is the importance of costless bargaining. Even if markets fail, efficient solutions may be obtained regardless of bargaining position. The Coase theorem also provides essential insights when the theorem fails to hold, because it emphasizes the importance of bargaining costs.

Application to vendors

One area of application of the Coase theorem is the use of outside suppliers by firms. Quite often, markets fail to provide the intermediate goods needed by firms. What supplier will willingly commit himself, in a major way, to the needs of a particular customer? If we understand the cost of this commitment by the supplier and the total value created by this horizontal relationship, Coasian analysis may provide clues to how this value may be shared by the parties involved.

The problem facing firms in lining up other firms as outside suppliers may be considered one of property rights. With some form of cooperation, the total value of the relationship may be increased substantially. The critical point of contention is who should lay claim to this value, or who has the property rights to it. If the bargaining costs prove too high, then there are two options: either the extra value will not be realized, because the two firms will fail to come to an agreement; or one firm will try to purchase the other, thus internalizing the relationship. Recall that, in the example of the farmer bargaining with the rail-road company, some form of merger would result in the socially optimal outcome. These questions are addressed in great detail in the first two chapters of Part II.

I. Chapter summary

The concept of economic efficiency is one of the broadest and most far-reaching tools provided to economic analysis of firm behaviour. In its simplest form economic efficiency relates to the well-being of some collection if individuals who, if behaving efficiently, may not be making all group members as well off as possible but who collectively agree that it is impossible to make one person better off without harming someone else. One of the unstated rules of efficiency is how the group of individuals is defined. For example, if efficiency were defined only for the well-being of you and your classmate Chester, it may well be efficient for all your other classmates to pay you and Chester one-third of their monthly incomes. Such a turn of events would be very unlikely to be efficient if the relevant group were defined as all of your classmates.

In terms of organizing economic activity we maintain that efficiency, or least tendencies towards efficiency will emerge as part of some Darwinistic, evolutionary process. A great example is provided by the role of money in our economy. Historians tell us that even in primitive societies something functioned as a generally accepted medium of exchange, or money. On some small islands in the Pacific Ocean for example various shells were accepted in trade. More recently gold emerged as a standard of exchange evidenced by its prominent role as coinage over the years. Later on other forms of money emerged that were backed by gold, only to be replaced by forms of money that are backed only by the faith and credit of the issuing government. In more recent times we would argue that credit cards are effectively money. Clearly along each of these steps the forms of money emerged that were in some sense 'better' or more likely to facilitate trade and exchange. Also, each form of money replaced the prior form in an evolutionary process. The money currently floating through the world's economies is far from perfect: it may be lost, counterfeited, or stolen. None the less our current money represents a tendency towards efficiency. Internet and World Wide Web users are currently looking for some device to play the role of money in that medium of exchange.

There is a very broad theme in economics stating that competition will promote efficiency in terms of allocating goods and services in the economy. In fact much theoretical work exists proving this. The problem however lies not in the mechanics of the models describing economic exchange but rather in the assumptions supporting the models. The presence of monopoly power by firms, externalities in production and consumption, public goods, and significant transaction costs can each preclude the attainment of an efficient equilibrium.

In the progression of economic theory in the understanding of the issues surrounding economic efficiency a problem became apparent. On the one hand, economists had historically celebrated the proposition that competitive markets will reach an efficient allocation of resources. On the other hand, some economists had shown that things could cause markets to fail. The work of the Nobel Laurate Ronald Coase was truly heroic. Because of his work all did not seem lost – voluntary exchange could result in an efficient allocation of resources if transaction costs were suitably low.

While these topics are interesting within the context of markets and how they may fail to reach an efficient allocation of goods and services, they are more interesting in the context of a firm's attempts to organize economic activity, and make money, in an efficient manner.

Within the context of team production we see a situation where a group of separate individuals act simultaneously to produce output. If the payoffs to all team members are the same, some serious incentive problems emerge threatening the possible benefit of having a team perform a task in the first place. Put simply, individual team members have incentive to shirk because of the free-rider problem. Further compounding the issue is that attempts to pay individual team members differently face great difficulty because of the measurement issues involved. We will return to this important issue later in the text when we discuss moral hazard and some of the agency problems in a contracting environment.

Of far more interest to us in our ultimate quest to understand the behaviour of the firm is that the existence of significant transaction costs may well preclude efficient exchange. This single issue is important enough to us that we devote a full chapter towards an understanding of transaction costs.

Key words

Coase theorem	perfect information
core competency	private costs
deadweight loss	product mix efficiency
efficient	production efficiency
exchange efficiency	property rights
externalities	public good
free-rider problem	residual claimant
general equilibrium analysis	residual returns
imperfect information	resource allocation
non-excludability	social costs
non-rivalrous consumption	transaction costs
partial equilibrium analysis	welfare triangle

Questions and problems for review and discussion

1 Consider an example of a family run steel mill in Belgium. Even though the mill is the largest employer in the area in which it is located and enjoys 'good community relations,' the mill has faced protest and criticism lately for the pollution it causes. Rod Biddinger, a bright, young graduate student being trained to be an economist at a nearby university remarks: 'the problem is not that there is too much pollution, the problem is that there is too much steel being produced at the Salinas family steel mill'. Mr Patterson, publisher of *Today, Our Town*, a local paper, has taken offence at this comment in an editorial appearing in that newspaper. While Mr Patterson is understandably upset by the whole affair, dismissing Mr Biddinger's comments as more 'useless, academic drivel' this has created a series of public exchanges between Mr Patterson and Mr Biddinger. Suppose that you were hired as a consultant to work to resolve the debate.

   (a) Can you explain Mr Biddinger's comments in light of the material presented in this and earlier chapters?

   (b) Can you anticipate Mr Patterson's reaction?

   Use the following information for questions 2 to 7

   For the purpose of this discussion example suppose that in a small town there exist two firms: a cafe and a printing press. Each business is somewhat successful. The cafe draws a large number of 'upscale' patrons from a local business school. The printing press is kept busy by the numerous orders received for *Management and Economics of Organization* by FitzRoy, Acs and Gerlowski. There is, however, a conflict between these two entities to which we now turn our attention.

   The operation of the printing press is a very noisy activity. This noise drives customers away from the cafe depending on how severe the noise is. The printing press can run for 25 minutes out of each hour, the remaining 35 minutes are needed for maintenance. The printing press can operate at any level between 0 and 25 minutes in 5 minute increments. The net revenues (expressed in h.c.u.'s or hypothetical currency units) received by the press operator in excess of costs is 5 h.c.u. for each minute the press runs. Thus if the press operates for 5 minutes, the owner receives 25 h.c.u., 10 minutes yield the press owner 50 h.c.u., etc.

   Activity at the cafe is far less stressful when the printing press is not operating the full 25 minutes. The cafe owner knows that if the press runs for 5 minutes one customer is lost; at 10 minutes of press time three customers are lost. Each customer lost at the cafe is valued by the owner at 7 h.c.u.. That is, each customer yields the cafe owner 7 h.c.u. net of expenses. The table below shows the minutes of press time and the corresponding lost cafe customers, lost cafe revenue, and total revenue received by the press operator.

Minutes of press time	Lost cafe customers	Lost cafe revenue	Press total revenue
5	1	7	25
10	3	21	50
15	6	42	75
20	10	70	100
25	15	105	125

2 Suppose that there are no laws concerning noise pollution in existence.
  (a) What is the resource in the example to which property rights are not assigned?
  (b) If there is no bargaining between the cafe owner and the press owner, or if that bargaining breaks down, what is the expected outcome in terms of minutes of press time?
  (c) In the answer you provided in (b) how do the press operator and the cafe owner fare? Identify the revenues of the printing press operator (if any) and any lost revenues to the cafe owner.

3 Again, suppose that there are no laws concerning noise pollution in existence. What is the socially efficient number of minutes for the press to operate? The answer must be between 0 and 25 (inclusive) minutes. An answer of 0 minutes of press time implies that the printing press is effectively shut down. Explain fully.

4 Again suppose that there are no laws concerning noise pollution in existence. If the cafe owner and the press owner are able to costlessly bargain, what number of minutes of press operation will result? Again your answer must be between 0 and 25 (inclusive) minutes.

5 Suppose that a number of laws are passed to the effect that noise makers have to compensate those hurt by their noise.
  (a) To whom are the property rights to the resource in question now assigned?
  (b) What number of minutes of press time will the parties bargain to if bargaining is costless? Explain fully how the bargaining will proceed.
  (c) One aspect of the Coase theorem is that the efficient outcome is obtained regardless of who holds what assets when the bargaining begins. How is this aspect relevant in what we have determined about this problem so far?

6 If a single entity were to own both businesses and if that entity were concerned with maximizing its joint profits, how many minutes would

that entity run the press (if at all)? What profits would be contributed individually by the cafe and by the printing press to the joint effort? Explain fully.

7 Suppose, once again, that there are no laws in existence concerning the noise pollution generated by the printing press. Also, suppose that the ownership of the cafe and printing press are separate entities. We already know that mutually beneficial bargaining will take place as the cafe owner has incentive to approach the printing press operator. Now, suppose that these interactions are not costless. More specifically, suppose that it costs the cafe owner 8 h.c.u. for each meeting with the press operator and that a separate meeting is required for each 5-minute reduction in press time. Put another way, to get the press operator to reduce press time from 25 to 15 minutes would require two meetings each of which would cost the cafe owner 16 h.c.u. total (2 meetings at 8 h.c.u. each). If bargaining is permitted between the cafe owner and the press operator, what will be the outcome of this bargaining?

8 The amount of training that firms make available to their employees varies greatly across firms and across occupations. Some firms will pay the employment and training costs or tuition for employees, regardless of the content of the knowledge gained; others are more choosy. Consider the following two individuals. Pete Simpson is a computer analyst for BigChip plc; his job involves writing code to integrate multi-media capability throughout BigChip's operations. Mike Wallace also works for BigChip. However, Mike Wallace works as a sales representative.

(a) BigChip has offered to pay Pete Simpson's tuition as he pursues a Masters Degree in Systems Design from a major university, Big U. BigChip has denied Mike Wallace's request for tuition payment for an M.B.A. degree programme at Big U. What can you say about BigChip's rationale behind paying for Pete Simpson's degree while denying Mike Wallace's request?

(b) Which degree, Pete Simpson's Masters in Systems Design, or Mike Wallace's M.B.A. has more characteristics of a public good to the pool of current and future employers?

Notes

1 For a good account of the problems facing the Ukraine and other transition economies see World Bank (1996).
2 This assumption may appear to be an oversimplification. It does not, however, affect the outcome of our analysis.
3 For starters the interested reader is referred to Edgeworth (1953) and Milgrom and Roberts (1992).

4 Although this tongue-in-cheek example may make some drastic simplifications to make its point, it is only fair to point out that firm location is often quite unpredictable.
5 A good discussion of this issue in a very different context can be found in Silberman *et al.* (1992).
6 This article is arguably the most often cited research work in economics; its importance has been recognized not only by economists but also by legal scholars and, more recently, by management professionals. It is strongly recommended that you read this article as part of your general education.
7 There is actually one additional assumption to the Coase theorem. This assumption is that there are no 'wealth effects' in the implementation of decisions for the involved parties. A wealth effect occurs when changes in an individual's wealth cause a change in her behaviour.
8 Bribe is a very strong word; typically economists prefer the term 'side payment'.

References

Alchian, A. and H. Demsetz (1972), 'Production, information costs, and economic organization', *American Economic Review*, 62, pp. 777–97.

Brickley, J. A., C. W. Smith, Jr., and J. L. Zimmerman (1997) *Managerial Economics and Organizational Architecture*, New York: Richard D. Irwin.

Coase, R. (1937), 'The Nature of the Firm', *Economica*, 4, November, pp. 386–405.

Coase, R. (1960) 'The Problem of Social Cost', *Journal of Law and Economics*, 3, October, pp. 1–44.

Douma, S. and H. Schreuder (1992) *Economic Approaches to Organizations*, Hemel Hempstead: Prentice Hall International.

Eatwell, J., M. Milgate and P. Newman (1989) *Allocation, Information, and Markets*, New York: W. W. Norton.

The Economist (1994), 'Ukraine: The birth and possible death of a country', 7 May.

Edgeworth, F. Y. (1953), *Mathematical Psychics: An Essay on the Application of Mathematics to the Moral Sciences*, New York: Augustus M. Kelley.

Garrett, H. (1968), 'The Tragedy of the Commons', *Science*, 13 December, pp. 1243–8.

Hamel, G. and C. K. Prahalad (1994), *Competing for the Future*, Boston: Harvard Business School.

McCormick, R. E. (1993), *Managerial Economics*, Englewood Cliffs, NJ: Prentice Hall.

Milgrom, P. and J. Roberts (1992), *Economics, Organization and Management*, Englewood Cliffs, NJ: Prentice Hall.

Pindyck, R. S. and D. L. Rubinfeld (1992), *Microeconomics*, 2nd edn, New York: Macmillan.

Putterman, L. and R. S. Kroszner eds. (1996), *The Economic Nature of the Firm*, Cambridge: Cambridge University Press.

Silberman, J., D. Gerlowski and N. Williams (1992), 'Estimating existence values for users and nonusers of New Jersey beaches', *Land Economics*, 68, pp. 225–36.

Sinn, G. and H.-W. Sinn (1994), *Jumpstart*, Cambridge, Mass.: MIT Press.

Smith, A. (1977 [1776]), *An Inquiry into the Nature and Causes of the Wealth of Nations*, Chicago: University of Chicago Press.

Varian, H. R. (1987), *Intermediate Microeconomics: A Modern Approach*, 2nd edn, New York: W. W. Norton.

Williamson, O. E. (1983), 'Organization Form, Residual Claimants, and Corporate Control', *The Journal of Law and Economics*, 26(2), June, pp. 351–366.

World Bank (1996), 'From plan to market', *World Development Report 1996*, Oxford: Oxford University Press.

PART TWO

The economics of organization

CHAPTER 6

Organizational tools

The normal economic system works itself. For its current operation it is under no central control, it needs no central survey. Over the whole range of human activity and human need, supply is adjusted to demand, and production to consumption, by a process that is automatic, elastic and responsive. (Alfred Slater, quoted in Coase, 1937, p. 387)

The main reason why it is profitable to establish a firm would seem to be that there is a cost of using the price mechanism. The most obvious cost of 'organising' production through the price mechanism is that of discovering what the relevant prices are. The costs of negotiating and concluding a separate contract for each exchange transaction which takes place on a market must also be taken into account. (Coase, 1937, p. 391)

A. Chapter outline and student goals

Adam Smith and specialization

Economic efficiency is enhanced and the opportunities for exchange are created by specialization in production. The idea of specialization, or division of labour, was first expressed by Adam Smith in 1776. Smith argued that specialization increases resource productivity, causes larger amounts of output and, hence, raises standards of living. Since a finer division of labour reduces self-sufficiency, exchange is beneficial and indeed necessary to both producers and consumers.

In Chapters 2, 3 and 4 we visited the perfectly competitive neoclassical world from which many economic theories are drawn. In this scenario, Adam Smith's 'invisible hand' ensures that transactors are efficiently coordinated and motivated by the price system. In the previous chapter we saw how the Coase theorem predicts that an efficient outcome *can* happen even when the perfectly competitive market may fail. Of course, according to the Coase theorem, to achieve this outcome property rights must be clearly assigned and bargaining costs must be zero. In this chapter we return to this line of enquiry by examining what happens regarding efficiency if bargaining costs are not zero.

In standard economic analysis very little is said about firms and why they exist. In the standard story, there is a mysterious thing called 'the firm' acting to maximize profits subject to production and market constraints. The firm has been viewed as a car speeding down the highway. Economic theory could often predict the car's destination; it could not, however, explain the body style, speed or route selection.

Inside the firm looking out

It is our task to examine the firm from the inside out rather than from the outside in. We hope that by looking under the bonnet of the car and understanding the functions of the engine, transmission and brake system we can see how the driver (the firm manager) can best coordinate and motivate the individual pieces under the bonnet to reach the driver's objectives.

This useful vantage point from which we view economic organization is not possible within traditional economic thought largely because traditional economic thought assumes away many of the basic issues we are concerned with. We begin our study by recognizing that there are significant, additional costs associated with transactions and hence all economic decisions. Using an analogy from elementary physics, these costs represent frictions restricting the free motion of economic agents.

Buyers and sellers freely interacting?

Economists such as Nobel Laureates Ronald Coase, George Stigler and Kenneth Arrow have focused attention on these costs, and Coase concluded that firms exist where a central coordinating authority is more efficient than market exchange. Oliver Williamson has continued this line of enquiry and his work leads us to recognize that several significant differences exist between transactions handled entirely within a firm and those made between the firm and outside parties.

Information is costly and limits exist on market-based transactions; thus, buyers and sellers do not freely interact. The additional costs incurred by economic interaction are called **transaction costs** – costs above and beyond contracted prices including the acquisition of costly information, the costs of monitoring performance, the costs of committing specific assets and the costs of handling complexity. Out of the limitations of the price system, firms emerge to organize economic activity efficiently handling these transaction costs.

After reading this chapter, you should be able to:

- explain, in your own words, what transaction costs are;
- discuss various ways in which the task of coordinating economic activity gives rise to transaction costs;
- interpret the necessity of motivating parties to contractual agreements and how this gives rise to costs;
- understand the importance of asset specificity to contractual agreements; and why commitment is a particular concern;
- recognize that certain transactions occur frequently and that institutions emerge to lower the costs behind these transactions;
- acknowledge that, from an organizational perspective, some transactions are 'stand alone' in that they affect only a small segment of the organization, whereas others have a wide impact on many parties;
- interpret the implications of complex transactions possibly involving great uncertainty;
- recognize that it may be quite difficult for the parties to a contract or transaction to evaluate the performance of other parties;
- apply information and transaction costs analysis to a variety of managerial problems, including the so-called 'make or buy' decision of firms.

B. An example of transaction costs

Some problems for business

There are two adages often tossed about by successful entrepreneurs in business today: 'Necessity is the mother of invention' and 'If you build a better mousetrap, the world will beat a path to your door.' Let us suppose that there is a brilliant inventor, Joe Zinpack. Joe is a man of modest means, supporting his wife, Rose, and two children, Ashley and Daniel, on his salary as a staff engineer at a large chemical corporation. Joe is deeply concerned about the environment and the prospects of a better life for his two children.

Working in the basement of his family's home, Joe accomplishes some wondrous things. To Joe's astonishment he stumbles on a process that converts standard household waste, hedge clippings and old newspapers into clean-burning ethanol. Joe soon realizes that his discoveries have enormous implications for society. A single, and relatively simple, process can reduce pressure on overcrowded landfills and nearly eliminate a major source of air pollution plaguing the world today – automobile emissions.

In a nutshell, Joe's process works like this. Fifty pounds of standard household garbage are placed in a large metal container, called a reactor vessel, along with 4 gallons of a chemical mixture. The reactor vessel is sealed and then basically left alone for a week. One pipe allows a second chemical mixture to flow into the reactor vessel. A second pipe allows pure, clean-burning ethanol to flow continuously out of the vessel. At the end of the week, 30 gallons of ethanol will have been produced, ready for use in the family car. At that time, the reactor vessel contains only water, which is available for household use or can be safely dumped into any household drain.

Joe shares his news with his neighbour Doug, a venture capital specialist, who quickly outlines the financial benefits now possible for Joe, Rose, Ashley and Daniel.

Not wanting to trust others with his significant knowledge, Joe sets out to produce and sell his device on what he envisions as a fairly large scale – 1,000 units. Joe is brimming with confidence; after all, he has proven his technical competence and superiority. As he begins making arrangements, Joe becomes less enthusiastic; and, as Rose confides to a family friend, he begins to wonder if his dream will ever become a reality. Let us examine the sources of some of Joe's headaches.[1]

In his basement workshop Joe fashioned a reactor vessel out of a standard metal garbage can and copper tubing available at any hardware store. Clearly, fashioning 1,000 of these devices would not be possible. Joe contacts three local metalworking shops concerning the production of a suitable reactor vessel. The prices submitted by the metalworking shops vary considerably. None of the potential suppliers is overly enthusiastic about retooling their factories even temporarily to meet Joe's needs. Furthermore, despite his technical background and nature, Joe is dumbfounded by the exotic-sounding materials and detailed quality assurance measures each potential subcontractor is proposing.

Production is not the only concern. In order to sell his invention, Joe has begun negotiating with four marketing consultant firms. Each has examined the relevant market data and, to Joe's consternation, four unique and separately distinct market assessments have been produced. A bewildering array of pricing schemes and advertising strategies adds to Joe's confusion.

Another possibility Joe considers is licensing his technology to an established firm in a related line of business. He contacts two likely prospects but is dismayed when each seems less than enthusiastic about getting Joe's invention to market. It also becomes clear that, with a new technology such as his, any licensing agreement would involve giving up control and ownership of his process for future products.

In order to avoid some of these issues, at least for a little while, Joe decides to do some gardening. His neighbour Doug comes over to borrow a rake and strikes up a conversation. Joe discusses the difficulties he is facing and conveys two deeper concerns to Doug. First, Joe is concerned about being taken advantage of in one or both of the relationships. Secondly, Joe is afraid of the **opportunity cost** of choosing any one supplier/consultant over any other. The opportunity cost of an action is the value of the next-best alternative to that action. Joe asks: ' How will I know that this supplier or that consulting firm did everything possible for me?'

A system of markets exists for Joe to exploit. Reactor vessels can be bought from any number of sellers. There is an even longer queue of marketing specialists eager, and probably even competing, to guide Joe through the effort of selling his wares. How close these markets come to the neoclassical ideals discussed in Chapters 2, 3 and 4 is not the real issue here. Even if the 'metal workshop' and 'marketing services' markets were perfectly competitive (or least approximately so), in practical terms they still present some problems to Joe, who must expend considerable effort simply to make contacts in them.

From a broad perspective, Joe faces two types of obstacles in reaching his goal of producing and selling 1,000 units of his invention. First, Joe must coordinate the activities of several parties: his design must be communicated to the reactor vessel producer, whose output must be in line with a marketing firm. Secondly, Joe must motivate and evaluate three parties: himself, in his role of entrepreneur; the reactor vessel maker; and the marketing firm.

Our hypothetical situation facing Joe may be simplistic in a number of ways, but it does pinpoint a central concern of many businesses and their managers. Like Joe, they may have a better idea, and they may have even proven their ability to produce or implement their idea. However, actually organizing the necessary resources may be too tall a task. Or, put into the language of economics, transaction costs may be very high.

C. Transaction costs: A broad perspective

Just how informed?

The pursuit of economic goals across multiple parties involves numerous agreements made with various levels of knowledge available in different amounts to different parties.

Information, or the lack thereof, plays a central role in the theory of economic organization. A market is characterized as providing **perfect information** if every participant (and potential participant) becomes aware of every price, product specification and buyer and seller location at no cost. Perfect information does not imply costless processing of this information; only that it be freely available to all who desire to have it. Agreement and exchange are said to occur under **imperfect information** if at least some buyer or seller has less than perfect information. Contracting parties operate under **informational asymmetries** if one party to the transaction possesses knowledge that other parties do not.

Information increases the efficiency of exchange and facilitates the market mechanism in smoothly handling transactions. Nowhere is the value of timely information more apparent than on the stock exchanges. Several major publications such as the *Financial Times*, and the *Wall Street Journal* have arisen to facilitate the flow of information between buyers and sellers. On the stock exchanges, thousands of shares, involving millions of pounds or dollars are commonly bought and sold on the faintest rumours and informed speculation.[2]

No market is likely ever to be characterized as having perfect information. The major stock and commodity exchanges probably come closest to this ideal. Two classic examples of the uneven distribution of information are the market for used cars and the market for life insurance. A buyer of a used car cannot be expected to possess the same amount of information about the car as the seller. A number of states have enacted 'Lemon Laws' designed to protect used car buyers; these require the seller to provide certain information about the vehicle to the buyer. In most insurance markets the situation is reversed, in that the insured are likely to have better information concerning the risks they experience.

Expensive information, poor individuals

Most exchanges in business today occur under conditions of imperfect informational availability. The reason is simply that information is costly to obtain and interpret. This fact has given rise in economics to the concept of **bounded rationality**, which states that, since there are positive costs to gathering and evaluating all information, economic agents will always bear some kinds of uncertainty because eliminating it would be prohibitively expensive. Nobel Laureate Herbert Simon is the economist who developed the concept of bounded rationality and explored its implications for economic analysis.

Although the concept of bounded rationality seems straightforward, its implications are far-reaching and have caused economists to reconsider some of the basic assumptions made in their modelling efforts. Because individuals are boundedly rational, transaction costs will exist; or, put another way, no agreement will ever be made under conditions of perfect information. This puts economic agents in the position of making a trade-off. Transaction participants must weigh the benefits of gathering more information against the costs of doing so.

Organizing economic activity is generally a costly proposition. At a very abstract level we can distinguish between **coordination** and **motivation costs** above and beyond the simple monetary costs of agreements. Coordination costs entail the determination of prices, the costs of acquiring information concerning the location, quality, reputation and availability of different parties, and other costs associated with allocating workers to specific tasks and with bringing transacting participants together. Motivation costs are less direct but arguably more important to business managers today. They arise on two broad fronts: informational incompleteness and imperfect commitments. **Imperfect commitment** is said to exist when the parties come to an agreement that one or both would later like to abandon. Consider, for example, a municipality that promises a major manufacturing concern that it will construct a four-lane road to a site if the manufacturer agrees to locate a new facility and many jobs there. Once the road is built (in the absence of any enforceable guarantees), the manufacturing plant manager has ample incentive to attempt to extract further concessions from the municipality. The ability of the municipality to extract resources from the manufacturer may be limited if there is ample social and political pressure to create jobs, or if the municipality is concerned about its reputation in future dealings with other firms wishing to locate there.

D. Distinctive dimensions of transaction costs of agreement

By now we hope to have made you aware of the importance of transaction costs in the study of economic organization on both the theoretical and more intuitive level. Up until now we have offered two very broad categories of such costs: coordination and motivation costs. In this section, we will provide a more detailed terminology based on more specific exchange characteristics. We refer to this grouping as the distinctive dimensions of transaction costs.

Asset specificity

In order to complete a transaction, at least one of the parties may be required to tailor some of its resources to very specific needs. **Asset specificity** refers to the degree to which an asset is committed to a specific task, and thus cannot be redeployed to alternative uses without sacrificing the majority of its productive value.

When you pull your car into your favourite petrol station, your commitment to the transaction is, in all likelihood, very low. By contrast, when Westinghouse's Nuclear Reactor Division signs a construction and 30-year service contract to supervise and maintain a nuclear electric generating facility, it must commit the services of an army of very specialized engineers and technicians. Likewise, when a coal-fired electricity generating facility enters into an arrangement with a coal mine, each party commits assets in such a way as to greatly lessen their value in any alternative use.

Because of the importance of asset specificity in our understanding of the management and economics of organization, we will 'fine-tune' our asset specificity dimension of transaction costs along the lines commonly made by economists.[3]

(a) site specificity
(b) physical asset specificity
(c) human asset specificity
(d) dedicated asset specificity
(e) brand name capital specificity

Site specificity refers to an asset that becomes committed to a particular use owing to its location. A key consideration when General Motors chooses a site for one of its major production plants is the existing or future proximity of suppliers. As just-in-time inventory management has become more widespread, the geographical proximity of suppliers has become a major concern in locating large manufacturing plants.

As another example, consider site specificity from the demand side of the market. Certain retail concerns will open stores only in the up-scale shopping centres spreading through large urban areas and in prime town centre areas. Furthermore, one rarely finds antique stores in depressed areas.

Physical asset specificity represents investment in machinery or equipment that has one narrowly defined purpose. Consider, for example, the construction of a movie set by a Hollywood studio that has contracted with a production company to produce a futuristic, science fiction movie. The set is likely to have only one use, unless, of course, the movie proves immensely popular and sequels can be made.

Human asset specificity arises when individuals develop skills with narrow applications as a result of learning by doing or specialized training courses. Economists refer to the experience, abilities, training and knowledge held by individuals as **human capital**, which like physical capital (plant, machines, etc.) may be committed to specific uses. For example, certain jobs in our economy limit their holders in terms of outside opportunities. The recession of 1990–3 resulted in many corporate downsizings and a well-publicized purging of the middle management ranks. These mid-level managers did not have a wide variety of jobs to choose from and many were forced to 're-tool' significantly in pursuit of employment. Likewise, as armed forces shrank during the early 1990s, many military personnel found themselves in a position of being very good at things that few employers were looking for.

Dedicated asset specificity entails investments in general-purpose plant that are made at the behest of a particular customer. The specificity here refers to committing funds to a specified transaction that might have been used elsewhere.

Brand name capital specificity refers to becoming affiliated with a well-known 'brand name' and thus becoming less free to pursue other opportunities. Perhaps the most colourful example of brand name capital specificity occurs with actors on popular television shows. During the 1980s, *Dallas* was a very successful prime-time soap opera. Two of the main characters were the Ewing brothers, J. R. and Bobby, played by Larry Hagman and Patrick Duffy. The personage of these actors in effect became brands, and this identification in the public's eyes prevented these actors from being taken seriously in other parts.[4] Being so intimately related to *Dallas* significantly reduced their ability to find other acting work.

Asset specificity is a major theme of transaction cost based economic analysis for a very basic reason. The more committed one becomes to a transaction, the more one stands to lose from unforeseen events and the possibility that contracting partners may find it in their interests to renegotiate more favourable terms from you given that you have committed (or sunk) assets. The various forms of asset specificity make transacting parties fearful of making a commitment that might later prove to be 'one way'. The other dimensions of transaction costs are more closely tied to the importance of informational availability.

Assessing the benefits of the transaction

Contractual exchange or relationship is made possible by all parties being convinced that they are made better off by the deal. In nearly every contract, party A's well-being is tied directly to the actions of party B. In most realistic settings party A will have doubts about whether party B lived up to her promises. It is entirely likely that A will expend considerable effort in determining whether B has performed as promised in the contract whenever the results leave some room for ambiguity about the actions taken.

Consider, for example, your hot dog and soft drink purchase at the football match. It is very easy for you to check to see whether or not the vendor had performed as promised. Of course, the bun is soggy, the drink is flat and the hot dog is cold. But, the vendor had performed to your satisfaction and met or exceeded your (rather modest) expectations.

As another example, consider your hiring of a paid tax adviser. You are at first pleased with her services because she informs you that your refund this year will be 3,000 c.u. A part of you is not happy however. You ask yourself the question, 'If she was able to get me a 3,000 c.u. refund, maybe I was due for a 3,500 c.u. refund?' In short, you may never be completely sure that the tax adviser had done as good a job as she was able.

In assessing the benefits of a transaction, an economic organization faces difficulties in three areas. First, participation in an agreement involves some form of opportunity cost. If I hire one accountant I will always wonder if another accountant would have achieved a larger refund for me (within the dimensions of the tax regulations of course).

The second area of difficulty in assessing the benefits of a transaction lies in the organization's ability uniquely to identify the impact of that transaction on the organization's performance. A great example of this is when a firm hires a single employee. One could reasonably ask what effect that single employee has on a large, complex organization.

The third area of difficulty involves a mixture of not being able to perfectly monitor the actions of other parties to a deal and the incentives that those other parties face. To provide a clearer initial look at this difficulty we briefly return to the example of Joe Zinpack from earlier in this chapter.

Suppose that Joe's business is operating and he hires a manager, Barry Stein.

Sure, Joe owns the business and is Mr Stein's boss; but how can Joe be sure that Mr Stein is advancing his interests rather than Mr Stein's own interests. Maybe Mr Stein will pay himself far too generously. Maybe Mr Stein will act so as to pursue short-term rather than long-term gains to make himself look good. It is even possible that Mr Stein will put in very little time as manager and blame circumstances beyond his control when Joe's profits begin to fall.

The difficulties of assessing the benefits of a transaction greatly influence both the underlying exchange and the agreement crafted to organize it. This dimension of transaction costs is, as expected, very problematic. We have barely hinted at its importance, instead deferring more detailed inspection to later chapters.

Complexity and uncertainty

Given that individuals are boundedly rational, agreements are expected to be made in which the parties have not planned for every possible contingency. Within this context, economists say that in every transaction there is a degree of complexity and uncertainty that presents costs to the transactors.

Consider, for example, a standard futures contract for Treasury Bills. The parties agree to exchange money today in return for a promise to provide a specified amount of Treasury Bills at some future date. There is very little complexity in this transaction: the rights and responsibilities of each party are clearly stated. There is uncertainty about the outcome, however, and most of this uncertainty is the force behind the creation of the transaction in the first place (a differing perspective on the future course of interest rates). No unforeseen event is likely to cause ambiguity about the *terms* of the exchange.

In contrast, Rockwell Inc.'s contract with the US government in the early 1980s to provide a fleet of space shuttle vehicles was both complex and uncertain in many ways. Rockwell knew it would be put in a position of dealing with many specialized subcontractors. Furthermore, Rockwell was often working with technology that it was actively developing as it constructed the spacebound vehicles we are so proud of today. Most importantly, Rockwell knew that it would be affected by changing political opinions, if the public began questioning the massive spending on space exploration.

Familiarity with the transaction

Some transactions, such as daily shopping, are repeated quite often and span a relatively short time-period. Other transactions, such as a contract for life insurance or marriage, occur once and are designed to last for many, many years. We would expect that the transaction costs for frequently repeated transactions, such as grocery shopping, are much lower than the transaction costs behind the 'exchange' of marriage or life insurance. We would also expect that individuals have devised mechanisms, or institutions, to lower the costs of exchange for frequently repeated transactions.

If, in your household, you are responsible for the grocery shopping, you probably have devised a routine. Using another, more technical sounding word, we could say that you have created an institution. The institution may involve a designated shopping day where your schedule and the expected crowd at the store provide the best mix.

The purchase of life insurance is quite different. We face a dazzling array of options: the amount of the insurance, term or whole life, cash value, survivability, etc. Granted agents exist who can further explain your options and perhaps even make recommendations. However, any reputable agent will leave the final decision up to you. Very likely, you will devote a lot of time to this single exchange.

Generally, when at least one party expects to be involved in many similar transactions, it is in that party's interests to acquire information and create an institution to manage the transaction. The first division soccer players and team owners provide a good case in point. When disputes arise concerning player salaries, the vast majority are turned over to approved arbitrators. The costs of this arbitration may seem large when viewed alone, but are small in light of the large amounts of major player contracts.

The familiarity of transaction participants with the transaction and with each other has another effect. In situations where transactions are frequent and repeated over a long period of time, parties have motives and opportunities to withhold or grant favours, to help (or hinder) each other, in informal, implicit ways. The ability to cooperate and learn over time can reduce transaction costs and increase efficiency because parties will grow to understand what is expected of them, and also because the need for formal institutions to enforce arrangements may be greatly lessened. Further, within this scenario, parties may attain mutual trust and reputations that would be costly to jeopardize.

Relationship to other transactions

Some transactions occur in relative isolation, with little connection to other transactions. Other transactions exert broad influences across the organization, being connected to other transactions. As transactions become more intertwined and interconnected, the cost of evaluating and enforcing them increases dramatically. These effects are thought to be magnified as the number of people involved increases.

The choice of industry standards for the high-density television signals and transmission equipment is an example of a very connected transaction. The entire industry will be adversely affected by a poor choice today, because future contracts for peripheral equipment will be affected.

E. Efficiency and economic organizations

The idea of efficiency

In order to best understand the role of transaction costs in economic analysis it will prove useful to ignore them, for the time being. In this section we first lay down some of the ground rules concerning the assumed behaviour of economic agents and examine how these agents pursue a set of goals, or objectives. Once this is understood, we consider the role of transaction costs and how these costs interfere with agents' pursuit of goals.

Economic analysis, as a science, follows a well-established pattern in explaining rational behaviour by economic actors. First, assume that the economic agents strive to achieve some well-defined goal(s). Secondly, examine and operationalize the constraints faced by the economic agents. Thirdly, produce behavioural statements by optimizing choices to best meet the goals in light of constraints. Consumers, for example, strive to maximize utility, or well-being, subject to well-defined budget and liquidity constraints. Likewise, in determining an optimal portfolio of financial investments, a financial institution will diversify and mix investments of different risk and return.

In our study of economic organization we have yet to formally state the goal of agents in our economic analysis. In standard business theory there appear a variety of goals for organizations. Our analysis will be based on the premise that economic agents will act efficiently. Recall from our discussion in Chapter 5 that an allocation of goods and services is inefficient if there exists another feasible allocation that lowers the well-being of no party and raises the well-being of (at least) one party.

Many familiar business relationships and economic institutions are framed by efficiency. Consider the role played by money in facilitating exchange. If money were absent, even the simplest transaction would take place by barter, the direct exchange of one good for another. Each party has a collection of goods to trade for objects that they desire to acquire; exchange will take place only if those who have the desired goods are willing to accept the goods offered in exchange. The Big Mac produced at the local McDonald's would trade for perhaps one video rental, or two ice-cream cones, or any one of an almost limitless list of goods, rather than for a well-defined amount of money. The use of money obviously promotes efficiency despite several drawbacks: occasional counterfeiting, ability to be lost, and the practice of governments of issuing it in excessive amounts.[5] Later in the text we will examine several transactions whose organization may appear strange at first pass, but which do a nice job of promoting efficient exchange.

The concept of efficiency is important for at least two reasons. First, it provides a minimal set of rules governing the behaviour of economic agents. We can always assume, at a minimum, that rational economic agents acting voluntarily will try to promote efficiency according to their knowledge and abilities. Secondly, it provides a decision criterion in ruling out certain outcomes. When faced with analyzing the decision of some group of economic agents, we may consider all the feasible possibilities and begin by ruling out those that are not efficient.

The role of transaction costs in reaching efficient agreements is probably a little unclear at this point. In the previous chapter, we introduced the Coase theorem, which predicts the attainment of efficient outcomes in the absence of transaction costs. As a reminder we outline this logic now.

If the parties are free to bargain voluntarily to a binding agreement and resulting allocation, then it follows that this resulting allocation must be efficient. Suppose that bargaining resulted in an inefficient allocation; then by definition there is another allocation that is efficient that could replace the first. Moving from the inefficient to the efficient allocation, nobody would be made worse off, and at least one person would be made better off. These gains could be awarded to the losers under the inefficient allocation; and then all parties would support the efficient allocation and voluntarily agree to it.

When the Coase theorem won't do

The existence of transaction costs and the property of bounded rationality may, strictly speaking, preclude the existence of an efficient outcome. However, the notion of efficiency remains important to us. We offer an alternative behavioural axiom.

> **The Constrained Efficiency Postulate**: If individuals are able to bargain voluntarily to an enforceable allocation, then the result of their efforts will tend to be efficient, subject to their generally limited information, resources and bounded rationality.

In one sense, what the constrained efficiency postulate does is to pick up where the Coase theorem fails in meeting the costly bargaining of the real world.

Transaction costs and the pursuit of efficiency are interesting concepts to help us understand firm behaviour. These ideas are very far-reaching and provide a rich vantage point from which to view exchanges as the building blocks of firms. Efficiency is, however, in certain circumstances equivalent to **total value maximization**. We define **total value** as the complete set of benefits accruing to the participants in a transaction. It may include regularly defined profits of firms, employee rents and consumer surplus; it may also include elements of risk minimization, strategic gains and non-market benefits.

The relationship between efficiency, value maximization and transaction costs is not always clear and distinct. Value maximization does not necessarily imply transaction cost minimization; in other words, the allocation that minimizes transaction costs may or may not be the allocation that maximizes total value.[6] If benefits can be defined in money terms and added up across all participants, then total value maximization is equivalent to efficiency.

Later in this chapter we will explore in detail the 'make or buy' decision, using, as an example, the use of outside suppliers by the large domestic automobile makers. The outside suppliers contribute expertise and skills associated with experience in making very specific components; basically they contribute the benefits of specialization in production. The automobile makers contribute their ability to manufacture a complicated finished product for consumer use. Efficiency, and hence value maximization, in this example requires more than the provision of low-cost components; it requires a degree of trust and an environment of cooperation.

However, it is reasonable to argue that reducing transaction and other costs holding output constant serves to promote efficiency and, hence, total value maximization. Thus, our approach will be to examine the underlying exchanges and make recommendations on how the activities of the parties should be organized on efficiency and value maximization grounds.

F. Firm organization and transaction costs: A historical example

Long-term changes in the automobile industry

In 1921 General Motors (GM) was in dire straits. The recession that began in 1920 had decimated the market demand for automobiles. To make matters worse, a more efficient competitor, Ford Motor Company's Model T, was rapidly eroding GM's market share. Alfred Sloan was appointed to run GM in that year and, as they say in the movies, 'the rest is history'.

Sloan envisioned a number of marketing and organizational improvements that would propel GM to the forefront of the automobile market at that time. Sloan wished to capitalize on GM's size while offering a variety of products to different market segments. What Sloan accomplished was to coordinate many aspects of the different GM divisions (Cadillac, Buick, Oakland, Oldsmobile and Chevrolet) from within a single corporate entity (see Sloan, 1964, and Chandler, 1962).

Under the new organizational setting, GM moved to take full advantage of the large scale of its operations by including the same parts in many of the automobiles produced by the various divisions. When large numbers of such parts were required for the organization, **scale economies**, or the reduction in average unit costs as the number of units produced increases, became available for exploitation. This organization created by Sloan was also able to exploit

scope economies, a reduction in unit costs due to the production of related goods. With almost unlimited access to capital, General Motors was able to achieve a high degree of **vertical integration,** or the control over various stages of production.

Thirty years later, a relatively small Japanese manufacturer, Toyota, embarked on an entirely different path to challenge GM. Toyota lacked the 'bigness' and ready access to capital that its American competitors enjoyed. Thus, it developed a new organizational approach better suited to its needs.

Many believe that Toyota's rise to a positions of market leadership (and that of the other Japanese auto firms) was due to a favourable treatment by the Japanese government and lower labour costs. These advantages existed but were far from the only ones. The stark difference between the operations of US and Japanese firms was that the Japanese firms relied heavily on outside suppliers for many of the parts used in their automobiles.

The important innovation was the development of '***kanban***', or a '**just-in-time' (JIT) manufacturing system.** A great amount of coordination and trust was required between Toyota and its suppliers as inventories were reduced to minimal levels. The effect of JIT was to eliminate much of the slack in the production process. The absence of inventories meant that Toyota had to be linked to suppliers on a day-to-day basis. At the same time, broken equipment had to be fixed quickly, so that shortages did not occur at later stages of production. Toyota began training its workers to maintain and repair the machines they ran, and to help each other in teams. Toyota and its Japanese counterparts were able to use their smallness in promoting flexibility for use against their larger, less dynamic competitors in the United States.

A number of interesting points concerning transaction cost analysis can be made by comparing General Motors' strategy in the 1920s and the strategy used by Toyota in the 1950s. When General Motors underwent the massive change under Alfred Sloan, the automobile industry was in its infant stages. Precision manufacturing at mass production levels was still a fairly new concept for firms in the economy. Many of the parts used by GM in its cars might have been available through market transactions; but it is likely that the transaction costs associated with this approach would have been high.

Difficulties would also be foreseen by the potential suppliers themselves. Given GM's size and the potential economies of scale available, supplying GM would require a massive investment in specific assets. As one of the corporate icons of industrial America, General Motors would enjoy an advantage in terms of cost of capital over its potential suppliers. Given GM's cost advantage in securing capital and the asset specificity required of suppliers, one could argue that the emergence of a vertically integrated firm was efficient and consistent with a desire to maximize total value by GM.

The situation was quite different in Japan in the 1950s for a number of reasons. Primarily, large amounts of technology and manufacturing know-how were available. The automobile industry was already established, providing a pool of information and resources. In this environment, entrepreneurs would be able to harness this available technology and serve as outside suppliers, producing goods for Toyota. Furthermore, the Japanese culture with its emphasis on consensus and cooperation would foster a spirit of trust between Toyota and its suppliers under which the suppliers would be less afraid of engaging in highly specific investment.

G. Transaction costs and outside suppliers: Analysis of the make-or-buy decision

Specialization and specificity

One of the purposes of this textbook is to provide some insights into the economic factors behind the organizational strategies of firms. Logically, this involves identifying which activities will be carried out inside the firm and which will be provided by the market. A quick look at business organizations today provides quite a mixture of firms regarding in-house versus outside acquisition of goods and services. Although clearly no universal rules are followed, and recognizing that in some organizations entropy and historical precedence may be the only justifications, we will analyze the problem from a transaction cost perspective. As usual, we will suppose that, in pursuit of value maximization, economic actors will pursue efficiency.

Perhaps the most obvious characterization of the in-house versus outside supplier choice involves the degree of asset specificity. This idea is so important to us that we spend a great deal of time on it in the next chapter.

Looking at the major metropolitan areas of European countries and the United States we would observe that most local or national daily newspapers own their own printing presses and operate their own distribution process. However, the publishers of most textbooks liberally subcontract the actual printing process. Both textbook and newspaper publishers provide information and data via the printed page. The difference between them lies in the specificity of the content. For the newspapers, content is specific for a given day; for a textbook, the information will be relevant for a number of years.

Chrysler, Ford and GM

A better example designed to show the many dimensions of transaction costs is the 'make or buy' decision in the automobile industry in the late 1980s and early 1990s. The most dynamic American player in the market at this time was clearly Chrysler Corporation, which developed its new LH line of cars (Chrysler Concorde, Dodge Intrepid and Eagle Vision) at this time. As with General Motors in the 1920s, Chrysler acted in response to a fairly desperate financial situation.

There are a number of new features in Chrysler's LH series of cars. For consumers, there is plenty of high-tech wizardry along with the new 'cab forward' design, which moves the car's windshield further to the front of the vehicle and moves the rear wheels back. This design change produces more interior space, provides better visibility, enhances aerodynamics and yields a smoother ride for rear passengers owing to the vehicle's longer wheel base.

From the organization's standpoint, changes were equally drastic. Ford, in producing the Taurus and Mercury Sable, had followed Honda's example and used the team concept of production and design, allowing suppliers some input. Chrysler has carried the concept of teamwork the furthest by actually letting outside firms influence the design process. This level of cooperation had previously been unheard of in the industry. To facilitate speedy development, Chrysler established a $1billion technology centre for itself and its suppliers.

The larger role played by the outside suppliers was clearly evident because 70 per cent of the LH series was made by outside suppliers. By contrast, Ford and GM bought 50 per cent and 30 per cent, respectively, of their parts from outsiders (see Taylor, 1991). Recognizing its critical dependence on outside suppliers, Chrysler has extended its partnership model outside of its corporation.

Because the US automobile makers faced severe global competition earlier than most industries did, executives at the Big Three were early converts to the partnership model. As far back as 1979 they were murmuring about switching to long-term contracts, taking advantage of their suppliers' know-how, and forging supplier relationships that valued more than just the lowest bid. By the mid-1980s that murmur had become a chorus. To compete, the automobile makers needed higher quality, lower costs and more innovation. In all of those things, they needed suppliers' help. So the car companies promised a new era of supplier relationships. On the one hand, the Big Three needed to reduce their supplier bases, but the companies they kept would be trusted. The trade-off would consist of using suppliers' ideas about improving product design and price cuts in exchange for long-term contracts. That was the theory. All three major domestic car companies did switch to long-term contracts with suppliers and did receive price cuts. However, when the US recession deepened in 1990 and 1991, two of the Big Three requested bigger cuts. Chrysler, in a more cooperative mode, asked suppliers to come up with cost-saving suggestions.

Rather than simply demanding that their key suppliers cut costs overnight, as GM and Ford had done, Chrysler enlisted supplier support to make design and engineering changes that would add value and boost productivity. As a result, Chrysler's parts suppliers have turned in 3,900 suggestions that have saved the company an estimated $156 million in production costs.[7]

The transaction costs components of these contractual arrangements are illuminating. From a strict marginalist standpoint the decision to use an outside supplier or rely on a more vertically integrated source is based on a consideration of costs and benefits. For the larger firm, the component can be made in-house or purchased on the market at a given quality and cost.

Standard economic thinking dictates that, if a better part is made by a supplier at a lower cost, then in-house production would be curtailed. The transaction costs relevant for this decision cloud the issue and are missing from a strict marginalist interpretation of the situation.

Asset specificity is an issue for both the supplier and the larger firm. The supplier should have reservations about committing highly specific assets, machinery and the human capital of engineers and technicians to the needs of the larger company. The bigger company has grounds to fear relying exclusively on the outside supplier for integral parts, believing that the outside supplier may withhold delivery at the last moment and desire to renegotiate the contractual relationship. Given the recession-battered state of the industry and the rough handling by GM and Ford, the suppliers may have been willing to trust the maverick Chrysler Corporation, which may have been willing to trust the suppliers for the same reasons.

The complexity and uncertainty dimensions of transaction costs also come into play in the 'make or buy' decision. The daunting task of building a car seems to favour an in-house solution. However, given the new assisting computer technologies and large pool of engineering talent, there are incentives and opportunities for compartmentalizing the production and design process. Chrysler clearly seeks to coordinate the activities and value-adding abilities of many bright, innovative companies rather than relying on its own, more static, resources. The use of outside suppliers would prove advantageous if they can provide cost reductions and quality improvements.

Chrysler is also in a position adequately to assess the benefits from its contracts with its outside suppliers. With the required integration of the activities of many firms, Chrysler can easily monitor the performance of its contracting partners. Congruence to specifications can be checked through mechanical means and by simply seeing if all the pieces fit together. It may also be easy to determine if the suppliers are putting forth their best efforts. Involving firms outside of Chrysler means letting them share in the risks and rewards of the LH product line. Chrysler has shown a willingness to share the rewards, through long-term contracts and by rewarding cost-saving suggestions. The suppliers must clearly recognize this for the transaction cost advantages of outside suppliers to manifest themselves in the long run.

The truly startling thing about Chrysler's decision to rely extensively on outside suppliers is not the technical challenges it successfully overcame, but the implication that this form of organization was chosen over the more vertically integrated operation scheme of its American counterparts. It must be believed that Chrysler was aware of all the alternative organizational arrangements. Chrysler managers have often been both praised and criticized in the business press for ordering endless 'what if' analyses when they tackle problems.

The coordination and motivation costs associated with extensive use of outside suppliers at first pass appear huge. Chrysler has taught us that, yes these costs may be large, but, on balance, they may be far less than in-house production.

The greater reliance on outside suppliers is not tied exclusively to the automobile manufacturing industry. The early 1990s saw the application of this organizational technique by many high-tech firms.[8] Hewlett-Packard had dominated the laser printer industry for a number of years in terms of quality, value and durability. It did not, however, follow the leadership example of the two dominant US computer-making firms, International Business Machines and Digital Equipment, and rely on a high degree of vertical integration. Hewlett-Packard, in fact, obtains the heart of its printers, the laser engine, from Canon of Japan.

The arrangement is clearly beneficial to both parties. Canon sells its own line of printers that compete with the Hewlett-Packard products. The US-based concern has protected itself by denying Canon the rights to its printer software, termed PDL by the industry. Furthermore, Hewlett-Packard handles all production of its less expensive line of ink jet printers. Clearly, it is efficient and value creating for Hewlett-Packard and Canon to contract. Furthermore, mechanisms exist to overcome the transaction costs.

Hewlett-Packard is not alone in combining its relative strengths with those of other firms with complementary advantages. In the early 1990s, Apple Computers had manufacturing pacts with two Japanese companies, Sharp and Sony, to manufacture some of its hand-held and laptop computers.

For these firms in the computer industry, the pattern of exchange happens to follow nationalistic lines. US-based firms typically are stronger in systems design and software creation. Their Japanese counterparts enjoy advantages in the more mechanical components, notably memory chips and monitors. Contractual exchanges permit each entity to add value in terms of what it does best.

H. The virtual corporation: A limiting case?

Corporations today are involved in many diverse activities. In many instances, teams are formed with competitors and suppliers alike, all as an attempt to promote efficiency and maximize value through exchange. A new corporate model has emerged termed the **virtual corporation**, a temporary network of companies that come together quickly to exploit fast-changing opportunities.[9] In a virtual corporation (VC), companies can share costs, skills and access to global markets, with each partner contributing what it is best at.

The possibility of opportunism or misbehaviour by one of the contracting parties is minimized because companies team up to meet a specific market opportunity and then usually fall apart once the need evaporates. An expanding technology will encourage the development of VCs as information networks link geographically dispersed entrepreneurs and enable them to work together. A VC form encourages excellence and efficiency because each partner offers what it does best. Potentially, a VC arrangement would be 'world class', something that no single company could achieve. The VC relationship heightens the reliance between companies and will require far more trust than in the past. Most interestingly, VCs redefine the boundaries between corporations by blurring them. More cooperation among competitors, suppliers and customers makes it harder to pinpoint where company A ends and company B begins.

The possibilities allowable under a VC would be exceptionally attractive for smaller corporations and entrepreneurs. Significant start-up costs for manufacturing capacity and basic research results may be available from the market. Key components can be purchased from existing manufacturers, saving even more there. Engineering services in particular can be purchased, saving the small firm large amounts in human capital development and/or hiring costs.

I. Of particular interest to managers

Consider, once again, our definition of firms from Chapter 1:

> Cooperative interaction and agreement among any number of people, in order to produce some marketable output, define a firm.

Of course it is important to note that a firm is nothing more than a collection of contracts. Transaction costs are important to us because they are extremely relevant for the environment in which contracts are crafted.

Traditional microeconomics is concerned with things external to the firm such as the behaviour of markets. The transaction cost view of economic organization, on the other hand, attempts to look at the situation from within the firm. Of course this is a relatively new approach, filled with scary-sounding names like bounded rationality, asymmetric information and asset specificity. However, all of the ideas represented by these terms are very intuitive and will, we hope, move economics back into the realm of interest for business managers.

The most interesting problem we approached in this chapter with the tools provided by transaction cost analysis was the 'make or buy' decision faced by firms. We are all well aware of trends in this area, beginning with the breakdown of the mass-producing firms in the late 1970s. The prudent use of outside suppliers provides the benefits of specialization weighed against the transaction costs of market exchange. In the athletic footwear industry, this way of doing business is even more entrenched. One of the major players in this market, Nike, owns one small factory, and Reebok, one of its competitors, owns none. In 1992 both Nike and Reebok earned a return on assets of 16 per cent, ranking them fifth and sixth, respectively, in *Fortune* magazine's list of best service companies in that year. (Tully, 1993).

J. Chapter summary and key ideas

The theme of this chapter is that economic exchange is often costly for the participants in that exchange. Every day we make very simple exchanges; for example, we purchase a cup of coffee. A number of factors cause us to think of this as a simple exchange: both buyer and seller are probably aware of other prices in the market; the market is very competitive; there are few complexities in the transaction; and the exchange does not involve a large degree of commitment by either party. For other exchanges made by individuals and organizations, none of these things is true and some resources must be expended to provide a clearer picture of the environment in which the transaction takes place. We refer to these costs as transaction costs.

Individuals and organizations have the property of bounded rationality, which rules out the possibility of ever becoming completely informed owing to the costs of doing so. As we study the principles of economic organization we must keep this idea clearly in mind. There will always be costs to acquiring information and attaining commitment as individual parties try to coordinate and motivate economic exchange.

We have introduced five distinctive dimensions of transaction costs to further our understanding of this important topic. Two of the most important ones are asset specificity and assessing the benefits of the transaction. As we continue into the next chapter we begin thinking about how to deal with these types of transaction costs.

From the firm's perspective, the most important aspect of transaction costs may very well be as forces affecting the make-or-buy decision. In this decision the firm must balance the potential gains from specialization in production against the costs of using a market (as opposed to an internal) source to fulfil certain needs. As more outside suppliers are used, the degree of vertical integration falls in the firm. Clearly this is a prevalent trend in the recent evolution of most Western corporations as they seek to become competitive in a global sense.

When people think about what economists do, they are likely to conjure nightmarish equations and computer simulations and all manner of indigestible Greek-letter salad. For the most part, they are right.

But exceptions are often more interesting than the rules. And few are as interesting as the work of Ronald H. Coase, the 81-year-old retired University of Chicago Law School professor who last week won the Nobel prize for economics. His ideas have swept through legal scholarship like a fresh breeze. It is likely – some would argue, inevitable – that the Coasian way of thinking will influence policies ranging from access to transplant organs to the control of corporations.

Mr Coase (whose name rhymes with dose) has made a career asking basic questions about the minuet of the markets – how people organize to advance their economic interests, and when government is needed to choreograph the dance. And what a career: his penetrating yet disarmingly simple answers have become the stuff of myth to a generation of scholars more at home in multi-variate regression analysis than in English.

For a sample of vintage Coase, consider his 1974 article on lighthouses. For decades, textbooks used the lighthouse as an example of a 'public good', a service that private markets could not deliver efficiently because there was no practical way to exclude consumers who refused to pay.

But the British-born Mr Coase noted that lighthouses began as private enterprises in Britain, and that the system worked well. For in spite of the 'free rider' problem, enough people who profited from the ship traffic through British ports were willing to support the lighthouses because they did not trust government to provide adequate service on its own. New Yorkers may note that what worked in Britain also works closer to home: hundreds of city block associations now pay for the extra protection the city's police department cannot or will not provide.

Mr Coase reserved his broadest brush for an analysis of why business companies exist. Companies, he argued, are really contractual hierarchies that shelter collections of workers from the uncertainties and costs of relying on markets to meet their needs. When a professional wants a letter typed, she can hand it to her secretary rather than looking for typists on the street or in the Yellow Pages. And when a typist wants to sell his skills, he can trade flexibility, independence and perhaps a higher income for a guaranteed salary.

Businesses grow, Mr Coase concluded, to the point that the costs of internal sources of inefficiency – the myriad conflicts between individual workers' interest and that of the organization as a whole – equal the costs of coping with the endless headaches of buying and selling what you need, when you need it. This may not seem an earth-shaking insight. But his ideas lurk behind serious analyses of contemporary business issues ranging from corporate control to workplace discrimination. Indeed, they have proved so fruitful that one of his disciples, Oliver Williamson of the University of California at Berkeley, may yet win his own Nobel prize for extensions of the framework.

For all its impact, however, Mr Coase's theory of the firm must take a back seat to his 1960 article, 'The Problem of Social Cost.' When first submitted to the University of Chicago's Journal of Law and Economics, it evoked the wrath of the entire economics department, which was then home to giants including the future Nobel prize winners Milton Friedman and George Stigler. But in a famous seminar, Mr Coase converted them one by one. Thirty years later it has probably become the single most cited article in modern economics.

Again, the point is simple. It had long been the conventional wisdom that markets generating 'externalities' – costs not borne by producers – would inevitably be wasteful without a little help from government. If, for example, soot from a factory chimney ruined the paint on neighboring houses, some sort of tax or regulation would be needed to get the factory to take account of the soot damage in choosing a lowest-cost method of production.

Mr Coase was skeptical. If the damage created by the soot exceeded the cost of curtailing it, why couldn't the homeowners bribe the factory to clean up its act? In a world where the practical problems of making deals (what economists call the transactions costs) were tiny, he concluded, government would not be needed to insure least-cost solutions to problems of externalities.

By the same logic, of course, pigs could fly if only they had wings. But as Guido Calabresi, dean of the Yale Law School, points out, Mr Coase was not trying to make a practical case for keeping government out of regulating pollution. Rather, he was arguing the true source of market failure is not the externalities but the transactions costs that prevent waste-reducing deals. For purposes of clearer analysis, he was separating the problem of coping with the nuisance from the question of who was at fault. In a Coasian world of 'causal agnosticism,' Mr Calabresi says, one could as easily speak of the paint getting in the way of the soot as the soot getting in the way of the paint.

Michael E. Levine, the dean of Yale's School of Management, offers an example of the way such analysis can change established legal thinking. In a hoary Minnesota case often cited in law texts, a Great Lakes steamer tied up at the nearest wharf to avoid sinking in a storm. The dock was badly damaged, and the owner sued to cover the repair costs.

At the time (1910), the court floundered its way through a logical thicket of assigning liability where common sense said no one was truly at fault. If Mr Coase had been on the bench, however, he might well have focused on the next accident rather than the last.

A Coasian scholar would want to give both the owners of docks and the owners of boats the incentives to minimize the total damage to life and property. And that probably would have meant billing the boat owner, who was in the better position to weigh the risks.

The Coasian way of thinking, Mr Calabresi says, offers opportunities for analyzing questions in everything from bankruptcy to environmental law. Even novel legal issues, like balancing the wishes of grieving families against society's interest in making body organs available for transplant, give way easily to Mr Coase's brand of analysis. Such Coasian techniques have found a firm niche in legal scholarship.

But Richard A. Posner, a Federal appeals court judge and disciple of the Nobel prize winner from his days as a University of Chicago Law professor, thinks the best is yet to come. 'Ideas filter gradually into the real law,' he said. 'It will be another generation' before the shock waves fully penetrate the system.

(Source: Peter Passell, 'For a Common-Sense Economist, a Nobel – And an Impact in the Law', *New York Times*, 20 October 1991, p. 2E. Copyright © 1991 by The New York Times Company. Reprinted by permission.)

Key words

asset specificity	motivation costs
brand name capital specificity	opportunity cost
bounded rationality	perfect information
constrained efficiency postulate	physical asset specificity
coordination costs	scale economies
dedicated asset specificity	scope economies
human asset specificity	site specificity
human capital	total value
imperfect commitment	total value maximization
imperfect information	transaction costs
informational asymmetries	vertical integration
just-in-time manufacturing system	virtual corporation
kanban	

Questions and problems for review and discussion

1 Suppose that your university was currently trying to fill two empty positions: marketing department secretary, and Professor of Economics. The job description for the secretarial position lists the major duties as: answering faculty phones, forwarding mail and messages to faculty, providing administrative support, typing letters, examinations and research papers, and serving as departmental receptionist. The job description for the faculty position lists the major duties as: working with existing faculty in a variety of research projects, collaborating with faculty of all departments regarding curriculum development, and serving and enhancing the visibility and reputation of the university in the local and national communities. For which position would the university expect to incur more transaction costs? Frame your answer along the lines indicated by the dimensions of transaction costs.

2 There are basically two ways to purchase the stocks of US corporations directly: through a full service broker or through a discount broker. One of the main differences between them is that the full service broker makes available to you advice by 'market professionals'. What is the role of transaction costs in the different services offered by the firms that buy and sell stocks for investors?

3 Suppose for the purposes of this problem in transaction costs analysis that a university very much like the one you are attending exists not very far, perhaps on the other side of town, from your own university.

Parallel University is similar in size, function, mission and quality to your own university. There are six divisions at Parallel University: Registration/clerical, Library, Faculty, Pure Administration, Support Staff and Secretarial Services. There is no central authority at Parallel U. The distinct divisions exist to permit specialization and the resulting productivity gains. The only interaction between the divisions, outside of functional communications, is a system of contracts binding them all. It is from this system (or nexus) of contracts that Parallel University exists.

(a) How many pairs of contracting partners are there at Parallel U?

(b) Comment on the efficiency of the Parallel U arrangement from a transaction cost perspective.

(c) Propose a second organizational scheme for Parallel U that would be more efficient. How does your proposed organizational scheme differ from that used at Parallel U?

4 The large consumer products corporations consume large amounts of business services in order to conduct their affairs. Three particular services come to mind: legal, advertising, and accounting/financial control. Most of the large, established firms contract out advertising, with little effort from 'in-house' talent. The firms typically have their own legal and accounting/financial staffs. The services of outside legal and accounting firms are often used, however.

(a) What factors could explain the use of both outside and inside legal resources by these firms?

(b) What does transaction cost analysis have to say about the differences in the outside provision of advertising services and the mixture of inside and outside firms used in legal and accounting matters?

Notes

1 In our example we concentrate on certain aspects of Joe's problem and ignore financing at this time. The financial decisions are indeed complex and introduced in Chapter 10. In a very practical way, financing would be, perhaps, Joe's biggest problem; we do not consider it here so that we may focus attention elsewhere.

2 Despite all the resources dedicated to the transmission and analysis of information it is interesting to note that a randomly chosen portfolio of stocks often outperforms highly regarded market professionals.

3 These are summarized in Williamson (1989, p. 145).

4 Some may argue that this is an example of human capital specificity, and this argument has some validity. However, this validity is questioned when it is recognized that it is not the skills of the actors that bind them to *Dallas*, but rather the recognition by television viewers.

5 By printing too much money, governments can cause inflation and erode the real value or purchasing power of money.

6 An interesting example of this point is the use of 'second sources' by computer chip manufacturers. This example is found in Milgrom and Roberts (1992, p. 34).
7 For an interesting description of these events see Mangelsdorf (1991) and McWhirter (1992).
8 A more detailed description can be found in Zachary (1992).
9 An excellent viewpoint on the purposes and scope of this organizational form is presented in *Business Week* (1993).

References

Business Week (1993), 'The virtual corporation: The company of the future will be the ultimate in adaptability', 8 February, pp. 98–102.

Chandler, A. (1962), *Strategy and Structure: Chapters in the History of the American Industrial Enterprise*, Cambridge, Mass.: MIT Press.

Coase, R. (1937), 'The Nature of the Firm', *Economica*, 4, pp. 386–405.

McWhirter, W. (1992), 'Chrysler's second amazing comeback', *Time*, 9 November, p. 51.

Mangelsdorf, M. E. (1991), 'Broken promises', *Inc.*, July, pp. 25–7.

Milgrom, P. and J. Roberts (1992), *Economics, Organization and Management*, Englewood Cliffs, NJ: Prentice Hall.

Sloan, A. (1964) *My Years with General Motors*, Garden City, NY: Doubleday.

Taylor, A., III (1991), 'Can Iacocca fix Chrysler – Again?' *Fortune*, 8 April, pp. 50–4.

Tully, S. (1993), 'The modular corporation', *Fortune*, 8 February, pp. 106–11.

Williamson, O. (1989), 'Transaction Cost Economics', Chapter 3 in Schmalensee and R. Willig (eds), *Handbook of Industrial Economics*, New York: North-Holland.

Zachary, G. P. (1992), 'Getting help: High-tech firms find it's good to line up outside contractors', *Wall Street Journal*, 29 July, p. A–1.

Contracts and contracting

A. Chapter outline and student goals

Contracting: An economist's viewpoint

One of the most commonly used words in business is 'contract'. Almost every issue of the *Financial Times*, the *Wall Street Journal*, *Business Week* or any other business publication contains mention of labour contracts, executive contracts, futures contracts and T-bill contracts. Other references to contracts are more subtle: merger, strategic alliance, hostile takeover and production networks are examples of contracts created by participating parties. Activities closer to your everyday course of events are also subject to contract. Newspaper delivery, utility services, purchasing petrol with a credit card and watching cable television also represent contracts. If you are a parent, there is a contract with which you are even more familiar: you will do it (whatever it is) and your child expects it 'because you are the mum (dad)'.

From an economist's viewpoint, contracts are useful because they are the 'stuff' that binds. But even more important, from an organizational perspective, contracts serve to govern transactions defining relationships between parties. We analyze the crafting of **incomplete contracts**, agreements that fail fully to specify actions under every conceivable course of events. When a contract is crafted, the involved parties are forced to forecast future events and acquire costly information. Individuals will never become fully informed because doing so is prohibitively costly. In economic terms we say that individuals are subject to **bounded rationality**; that is, they know that large transaction costs will prevent them from becoming fully informed.

Throughout this chapter we emphasize transaction costs and the importance of eliminating opportunistic behaviour. An understanding of these issues is essential in helping us to appreciate the importance of economic efficiency in organizing economic activity. Economic efficiency comes into play here because improvements in the contracting process through minimizing transaction costs will increase organizational productivity.

Definition and properties of contracts

Despite the wide usage of the term 'contract' and the even wider spectrum of activities that are undertaken to fulfil contracts, it is rather difficult to provide a working definition of what we will mean when we use the term 'contract'. Our working definition is very general and somewhat ambiguous so that it can be applied to a very diverse range of situations.

> Contract: an interlocking set of mutual promises that are enforceable and acknowledged by some disinterested third party. Generally, a contract specifies actions that each party will take and may assign decision-making powers.

Although this definition is workable, it may create a certain amount of confusion through its ambiguity. To help further clarify the term 'contract', we list the properties common to most contracts.

Contracting, or economic exchange, is a process of voluntary exchange.[1] Although this property of contracting may seem obvious, it has an interesting implication. For any group to reach an agreement voluntarily, the expected result of that agreement must be both individually and mutually advantageous. All parties together and each individual party must expect to benefit for an agreement to be reached. Considering the voluntary nature of contracts, it is important to recognize that the parties expect to benefit; these expectations rely on limited information available in different amounts to the involved parties, on the level of commitment of each of the parties and on the honesty of each of the parties.

Another property of contracts is that they attempt to provide motivation to the parties. Many contracts contain enforcement mechanisms outlining performance criteria and means for measuring that performance. Motivation also implies a specifying of the reward structure identifying levels of payment if some minimum level of performance is achieved.

The set of promises comprising a contract may be explicit or implicit. When dealings occur under an **explicit contract**, there is a written record of the agreement. With an **implicit contract**, there is no formal statement of the terms and conditions agreed to by the parties.

Contracts can be made highly transaction specific, with **fungible** terms; that is, they can be crafted to meet very unique individual needs and circumstances. Standard form contracts exist for frequently occurring transactions whose terms change little from transaction to transaction. Such forms exist as well for more complex dealings, such as buying a house or purchasing life insurance. However, in standard business practice it is not uncommon for items in these standard form contracts to be crossed out, or for the contracts to have blanks inserted where the money amounts or additional text are pencilled in.

The final property of contracts is that they are relational and incomplete in nature. It would be rare for a contract to specify a mutually agreeable set of actions for every possible contingency that may arise over the life of the contract. This last property is very important and gives rise to a number of contracting problems. A more detailed explanation of **relational contracting** will come shortly.

Do contracts replace markets?

All of these properties of contracts indicate what you may have already guessed – that contracts are a basic tool used to organize economic activity. Do contracts replace markets? The answer is hidden in the slippery terminology. All market transactions are governed by contracts; although this is obvious, it must be remembered. The difference between contracts and markets is that relational contracting becomes important either when a market does not exist or when the transaction costs associated with market transactions are relatively large.

From a strict economic point of view, competitive markets provide many of the benefits of contracting through **market discipline**. A functioning, competitive market provides discipline if enough buyers (sellers) learn of a particular seller's (buyer's) poor behaviour so as to curtail that seller's activities. Discipline under relational contracting is somewhat harder to identify.

Contracting problems fall into two general categories: those arising from **imperfect information** and those related to **asset specificity**. In an environment of imperfect information and boundedly rational individuals, agreements must be crafted with some effort. Rational individuals will fear being taken advantage of by the situation itself or by other parties to the transaction. We define **opportunism** as individuals pursuing their own interests at the expense of others with less than complete honesty. Opportunism may arise when the contract is being negotiated, within the contract, or through reneging on agreed-upon terms.

Internal versus external contracts
It will be useful to distinguish between internal and external contracts. From an organization's perspective, an **internal contract** governs an arrangement between the firm itself and an employee or owner of that firm. **External contracts** are those covering agreements between the firm and all other parties.

Opportunism and reputation

It stands to reason that in an environment of imperfect information, individuals fear misbehaviour or opportunistic trading partners. It also stands to reason that there should be some reward for good behaviour. To organizations, reputation may be a valuable commodity. It is, and this does play a role in our understanding of economic organizations. We more fully investigate this role in Chapter 9.

Establishing a reputation as an honest and fair trading partner can help an organization craft efficient contracts. Considering an external contract, Craftsman Tools, sold by Sears, are guaranteed indefinitely. Broken hammers, wrenches and saws are replaced on demand. Because of this, Sears sells a great many tools. Considering an internal contract, your employer most probably has an incentive to treat you fairly, although there are unfortunately exceptions. If she imposes difficult work conditions or pays an unfair wage, attracting new employees and maintaining current employees may prove impossible, unless unemployment is high.

After reading this chapter, you should be able to:

- explain, in your own words, what a contract is;
- discuss, in layman's terms, the concepts of relational contracting, incomplete contracts, and bounded rationality;
- understand the problems associated with incomplete contracting in terms of the incentive structure facing parties to a contract;
- appreciate the role played by truthfulness and reputation in reaching agreement;
- identify the role played by private information in encouraging precontractual opportunism and strategic misrepresentation;
- understand the problems created by adverse selection and the potential role played by signalling, screening and self-selection;
- recognize the hold-up possibilities created by asset specificity and offer insights into the ways of achieving commitment;
- acknowledge the presence of opportunities for pre- and post-contractual opportunism and identify strategies to mitigate their effects.

B. Incomplete contracting

Contributing factors

Owing to bounded rationality and the associated transaction costs, most agreements framing behaviour in the business world are incomplete and, as such, fail to determine future actions exactly. Four specific factors are identified by Coase (1937) and Williamson (1975) as contributing to the presence of contractual incompleteness. First, some contingencies that the parties may face are not predictable at the contracting date. Secondly, even if all contingencies could be foreseen, there may be too many contingencies to write into the contract. Thirdly, checking that the other party/parties abide by its terms (i.e. monitoring the behaviour of others) may be costly. Fourthly, enforcing contracts may involve considerable legal costs. Using our terminology, these four factors contributing to contractual incompleteness do so by creating transaction costs.

Summer employment: An example

In order clearly to illustrate some of the issues surrounding incomplete or relational contracting, we turn to an example with which you may share some common experience. Most college students seek full-time employment during the months when the college is not in session. Let us discuss, as an example, the experience of Becky, a full-time student at a major university. Becky obtains a job for the summer at BigFood, a large grocery store near her home, as a stockperson/clerk. Becky's employment contract is an example of an internal contract.

There is no explicit contract detailing Becky's hourly wage rate or weekly schedule. In terms of documents, there is only a job application listing her education, work history and personal information. Part of the application contains a paragraph stipulating that the information she provided was true and correct (to the best of her ability), and asking her to agree to regular company policies. A second paragraph describes company policies regarding pay, promotion and scheduling disputes. According to policy, employee grievances are to be submitted in writing to the store manager, who must reply within seven days. If an agreement is not reached in the following seven days, an outside arbitrator, appointed by BigFoods, will mediate the dispute. Becky's signature on the application recognized her agreement to these terms and her willingness to work.

Most of the agreement between Becky and BigFood was implicit and framed by a 5-minute discussion with her supervisor prior to application. The two agreed that Becky would perform a variety of jobs: stocking shelves, checking out customer orders, bagging groceries for customers, assisting customers in getting their orders to their cars, and icing cakes in the store's in-house bakery. They also agreed on a wage and that Becky would fill in where needed as the store's regular staff went on vacation, and during the extremely busy weekends and summer holidays. Any hours worked above 40 in any week would be compensated at time and a half.

Becky ponders the vagueness of her relationship with the store. There are a number of possibilities that are left unanswered; in fact, there are seemingly infinite possibilities that could cause problems. Becky realizes that some weeks she will work more hours than other weeks, the number of hours in any one week depending on when the regular staff request time off and the level of activity at the store. These, in turn, depend on many, many factors that are not included in the implicit agreement between herself and the store manager. Her exact duties are also unclear. Some of the tasks she will be quite good at; at others she will experience difficulty. Further, she will enjoy some duties more than others. Becky does understand the procedure for settling disputes, and is somewhat comforted that, in serious cases, an outside arbitrator will eventually be called in.

Becky comes to the realization that enumerating any significant portion of these things beforehand would require a lot of thought and negotiation with the manager of BigFood. After her first day on the job she does know one thing: a grocery store is a very busy place and neither she nor her manager has the time to discuss all of her concerns. In more formal terms we could say that Becky and the store manager are both boundedly rational and seeking an efficient way to organize this transaction. Becky is partially appeased by the standard answer of her manager: 'Don't worry Becky, we treat our summer help well because we need you and we need to attract good people during the summer months when many of our year-round staff take time off.'

As the summer progresses, Becky receives a raise in her hourly rate and her manager congratulates her for doing 'a good job'. Becky pauses for a moment and wonders on what this assessment was based. Her supervisor hardly seemed to notice her and never once actually watched her work. The supervisor was usually busy ordering items, programming the store's computer or dealing with specific customers. She did notice that some of the other stockpersons took extended breaks or spent much longer than necessary with customers in the store's parking lot. They never seemed worried about being caught, and had informed her that the manager was far too busy to know exactly what they were doing. Becky concludes that they were probably correct and, thinking back on her one economics course in college, realizes that the opportunity cost for the manager of keeping close tabs on all the employees is much too high.

The contract between Becky and BigFoods is clearly incomplete. As Becky explains to her younger brother, it seems that her job is the result of cooperation between herself and BigFoods, rather than the result of any highly specific list of job duties or activities.

The example of the relationship between Becky and BigFoods illustrates some of the basic elements and causes of incomplete contracting.[2] The idea of foreseeing and unambiguously describing every contingency that may be relevant to the agreement between Becky and BigFoods is obviously ridiculous. Neither Becky nor BigFoods could possibly foresee every contingency in this environment. Furthermore, no language could be precise enough to describe all the eventualities, even if they could be foreseen. If we assumed that either Becky or BigFoods were omniscient and could, somehow, see every possible course of events, by the time Becky had read through the reams of paper, the summer could well be over and Becky would not have worked a single day.

In practice, the complete contracts of standard economic theory that specify what parties will do in every conceivable circumstance are impossible to negotiate and write. People's ability to make plans and contracts are limited by bounded rationality. Relational contracts emerge as a response to the many difficulties of writing complete contracts.

Ex ante and *ex post* environments

In our analysis of contracting we will consider the contracting process as a sequence of three time periods. The first to occur is the period of time prior to reaching agreement. Behaviour in this period, the negotiating phase, will be termed **ex ante**, a Latin phrase that translates roughly as 'before the fact'. *Ex ante* contracting issues concern incentives parties may have to exploit informational advantages, to engage in some sorting or selection activity, or to misrepresent their interests prior to signing the contract. The second event is the actual signing of the contract, or the contract date. The third period will be termed **ex post**, again a Latin phrase that translates roughly as 'after the fact'. *Ex post* contracting issues are centred around the likelihood that one of the parties to the agreement may find it advantageous to fail to perform in agreement with the contract terms.

C. *Ex ante* opportunism

Just what are informational asymmetries?

Prior to signing the contract, the parties involved (at a minimum) must reach a consensus as to what contingencies the agreement will govern. There are said to be **informational asymmetries** when the amount and quality of information held by each party differs, or is believed to differ. One contracting party may be better informed regarding the likelihoods of each of several possible operating environments occurring after the contract date. Possibly, one party may have superior information concerning the net value of the contract to herself and other bargainers. It is also conceivable that information regarding the alternative opportunities, costs of delay and commitment possibilities of the involved parties may be imperfect. Informational asymmetries give rise to transaction costs and, as such, they hinder arrival at an efficient agreement.

We will examine the effects of imperfect information in the form of informational asymmetries within an exchange setting. There will then be a buyer (consumer) and a seller (provider). The setting of such imperfect information gives rise to incentives to engage in opportunistic behaviour. In this section we will consider: private information and the efficiency of markets; strategic misrepresentation and investments in bargaining position; adverse selection; signalling, screening and self-selection behaviour; and measurement costs. Each of these influences gives rise to transaction costs and hinders efficient exchange. In certain situations, the presence of these transaction costs may be so compelling as to prevent trade all together.

Private information and market efficiency

The economic forces underlying exchange allow for analysis centred on the role of imperfect information in a market setting.

In the following example, we consider the pricing options of BigChip, a computer supplier in an environment where private information affects the efficiency of transactions. BigChip has many identical computers for sale that cost 800 currency units (c.u.) to build. Since BigChip has no direct competition, it need not sell at cost.

There are two kinds of potential buyers: those who value the computers at 832 c.u. and those who value the computers at 865 c.u. Half of the potential buyers place a high value on the computers; half place a low value on the computers. Thus, the probability that any given buyer is a high-value consumer is one-half. BigChip has no mechanism to distinguish between the two types of buyers even though its market research can show that two types of buyers exist.

BigChip must set a single price to all consumers in our example. This price is made as a take-it-or-leave-it offer. The risks to the seller are clear. If too high a price is set, sales will be lost to those consumers with low valuations. If the price is set too low, profits are lost because some of the surplus of the high-value consumers is not captured by BigChip. So what price is appropriate?

BigChip will never set a price less than 832 c.u., so this amount provides a starting point. At a price of 832 c.u., every potential buyer makes a purchase, and the profit per potential buyer is 32 c.u. If the price is set at 833 c.u., only the high-valuation consumers purchase. If the price is set at 834 c.u., again only the high-valuation consumers purchase. In fact for any price between 833 c.u. and 865 c.u. only the high-valuation consumers purchase and the profit per sale is the selling price minus 800 c.u. However, the profit per potential buyer is only one-half of this difference because the probability that a consumer is a high-value consumer is 0.5.

BigChip would then set a price of 865 c.u., selling only to high-value consumers so long as there were enough high-value consumers to purchase all of BigChip's stock. To understand why, consider the following. If a price of 832 c.u. is set, every consumer will buy and the profit per sale will be equal to (832–800) = 32. If, however, a price of 865 c.u. is set, only one-half of the buyers will purchase and the profit per potential buyer will equal (0.5) (865–800) = 32.50.

In a retail setting, this would amount to consumers appearing at the BigChip selling location, and only half of them purchasing. The seller, ignorant of how highly any consumer values the product, rationally sets a price that excludes half of the potential buyers.

The efficiency loss is apparent. There still remain mutual gains from further trade; the lower-valued consumers are willing to pay 32 c.u. more per computer than the cost of supplying those computers.

Strategic misrepresentation

One party may try to benefit by being less than truthful about his assessment of an exchange situation. This **strategic misrepresentation** is an attempt to increase negotiating or bargaining power and arises out of an air of uncertainty that surrounds negotiations. If all parties' valuations of a transaction were known with precision, strategic misrepresentation would be impossible.

Consider, for example, labour contracts. Negotiators expend significant resources to determine their opponents' objectives and to conceal their own. Effective labour union negotiators precede the bargaining talks with research to determine the production costs of the firm, the corresponding costs of competing firms, and the financial health of the firm. Concurrently, management's negotiators attempt to survey the subjective mood of workers and to determine the wage workers could obtain elsewhere. Feigned anger, excessive friendliness, exaggerated impatience and personal abuse are sometimes used in labour negotiations as a ploy to get 'the other side' to reveal its true intentions and beliefs.

Strategic misrepresentation also occurs in more common settings. In most retail settings, prices are fixed. For big ticket consumer items however, haggling is common. One reason for the success of General Motor's Saturn Division in selling its automobiles was that their selling practices eliminated haggling. Haggling over a sales price is an attempt by a buyer and a seller strategically to misrepresent their valuation of a transaction. This is possible, given the basic economics behind exchange. Consumers buy an item because it yields them positive utility. Implicitly, buyers place a valuation, termed a **reservation price**, on an item (given their preferences, their income and prices of other goods). The reservation price is equal to the maximum amount a consumer would pay for an item. In Chapter 2 we introduced the concept of consumer surplus; we can now see that, for any given buyer, consumer surplus is equal to the difference between the reservation price and the actual price paid. Consumers strive to maximize the net value of their purchases by paying a price as far below their reservation price as is possible.

A similar option is available to sellers who have a minimum amount in mind, placing a floor on what they will provide the good for. This floor, termed a **minimum supply price**, may be determined by production costs or market conditions. In Chapter 2 we defined the idea of producer surplus, which is simply the difference between the price received by the seller and the minimum supply price.

Bargaining over a sales price typically involves the seller desiring a high price and the buyer offering a low price. Each party is thus attempting to maximize their surplus for the transaction. Clearly, the buyer has an incentive to make the seller believe that her reservation price is lower than it actually is. Likewise, the seller has an incentive to make the buyer believe that his minimum supply price is higher than it actually is.

In Chapter 2, we briefly discussed the practice of price discrimination by sellers. This would occur if sellers had some monopoly power, resale could be prevented and different types of buyers could be identified. Under price discrimination, sellers attempt to appropriate some (if not all) consumers' surplus.

If buyers and sellers are less than truthful about the valuations they place on goods, it is possible that efficient exchanges may not take place. If the buyer claims too low a value, and the seller too high a value, the good will not be transferred from the seller to the buyer even though efficiency dictates that it should be.

Negotiation often involves many factors, and is at least partly an art. There is simply no way that economic theory can provide analysis general enough to be applicable in every case. Forces such as determination, interpersonal communication skills and reputations for shrewdness or leniency could never be explicitly modelled. What economics *can* do is offer insights into that part of negotiation that is a science.

The question 'how much bargaining power does each of the bargainers have' is, in effect, equivalent to the question 'what does my opponent believe about my beliefs and willingness to settle?' We can identify some propositions about how beliefs are formed. We recognize the limitations of these propositions however, because they require one party to have some knowledge (which may be private) about the other parties.

An opponent with strong alternative opportunities will fare better under a negotiated outcome. A standard tactic everywhere is to use a competing job offer in negotiating for a pay rise. Knowing that production members lacked alternative employment opportunities, Caterpillar Tractor (CAT) was able to end a strike by its employees who belonged to the United Auto Workers Union. By reminding the strikers that the unemployment rate in Illinois, where many of CAT's plants were located, was very high, it gained the upper hand. Since a bargainer expects to benefit by having a stronger fallback position, the investment in time, money and energy in developing alternatives is rational. An understanding of the opponent's alternatives will strengthen your own bargaining position as well.

A second way to gain understanding of your opponent's position is to understand the relative costs of delay to each party. In order to capture a larger share of the revenues generated by their efforts, the Major League Players Association voted to strike against the team owners in 1980. The players would refuse to participate in the pre-season exhibition games, then agree to play for the first six weeks of the regular season, and then refuse to play again until their demands were met. Their rationale was clever. The players would lose less fan support than if they planned to strike continuously from the date of the first pre-season game. The players also recognized that the revenues earned by owners were not uniform throughout the year. Attendance and fan interest are fairly low during the first part of the season and pick up markedly as the weather turns warmer, kids are let out of school and baseball begins to stimulate peak interest by fans.[3]

In order to minimize delay costs, most labour unions have strike funds, whose purpose is to make payments to union members during a strike. Likewise, when anticipating a strike, many manufacturing firms stockpile product so as to not lose sales during a strike. In a bargaining situation, delay is a weapon and parties may take actions to diffuse this threat.

Another method to alleviate the possibility of strategic misrepresentation is to use commitment as a bargaining technique. Quite possibly, bargainers view a continuum of possible outcomes: any agreement may be favourable in one dimension and unfavourable in another dimension relative to some other feasible agreement. In short, parties may expect an agreement to represent simultaneous trade-offs in a number of dimensions. One of the bargainers may attempt to manipulate the other's expectations. The strategy here is to be the first party to make a 'take it or leave it' offer. If the 'leave it' option is credible, and if the other party has limited alternative opportunities or cannot withstand long delays, this strategy may confer significant bargaining power. In short, refusing to bargain may represent the best bargaining strategy.[4]

Adverse selection

The role of information
If one party to a contract has private information at the time of contract negotiation that potentially reduces the value of the contract to the other party, we say that the situation is one of **adverse selection**. The used car market provides a good setting to illustrate the efficiency effects of adverse selection.

The used car market: another look at supply and demand
In the used car market, sellers typically hold private information during the negotiation or bargaining stage that potentially reduces the value of the transaction to the buyer. Two related aspects of used cars affect their market demand: quality and price. Of these, only price is clearly communicated to, and known by, the buyer, who must conjecture as to the quality of the car.

In this environment of asymmetric information, it is rational to expect sellers of high-quality cars to demand a premium for them. Thus, as quality increases, price rises. The higher price might reflect some subjective measure (a pleasing paint job or a 'high-performance' appearance) or some objective measure (the amortized value of avoided repair bills). Buyers, however, are unable to gauge quality accurately and have no way of knowing whether the price of a given used car reflects higher quality or opportunistic behaviour by the seller.

Consumers do, however, make inferences about the quality of goods being offered based on the price charged, because this is the only clear information they obtain. They know that on average, if the price of a used car is low, the chance of getting a so-called lemon is high. Sellers know, of course, that consumers know this, and they try to take advantage of that information.

With imperfect information, sellers are not price takers; rather, they set prices based on their beliefs about consumers' expectations concerning the quality of their products. Lowering price may not increase sales, for a lower price might be an indication to consumers of low product quality. When offer price is an indication of quality, the market mechanism may operate in a somewhat perverse way.

The supply of used cars will be increasing in price, and current owners will be more likely to part with their cars if prices rise. One likely argument for a supply function increasing in price is the reason one usually sells a car: to buy a new one. The demand function may not, however, have the standard slope. The reasoning is subtle and depends on the relationship between price and quality. In general, quality increases with price; but there may be diminishing returns. In other words, quality increases with price at a decreasing rate: in the lower price ranges, price increases lead to large quality increases; in the higher price ranges, price increases lead to smaller quality increases. If we define value as the quality–price ratio, then there will be a single quality–price ratio that represents maximum value. We call the price at this combination p_0.

This price in effect becomes the market price for used cars. At any price less than p_0, the quantity demanded falls. The mechanics of this positive relationship between price and quantity depend crucially on the asymmetric information and the notion of value as a quality–price ratio. Lowering price indicates that a given car offers lower quality than other similar cars, thus depressing the value of that car. A similar argument holds for price increases above p_0.

Causal empiricism indicates that the used car market is typically characterized by excess supply at any point in time, confirming buyers' wariness when facing sellers with superior information. However, time spent on searching by buyers, and on waiting for a buyer by sellers, is an integral part of the information dissemination process in all markets of this kind.

In Figure 7.1 the graphical mechanics of this exchange situation are shown. As drawn, the used car market is characterized by excess supply. Note that the normal functioning of markets will not cause the markets to clear. Typically, excess supply is eliminated as competition forces sellers to lower prices. In the used car market, however, lower prices might actually increase market surplus, because price also communicates quality to consumers. In a market such as this we would expect a price of p_0 to emerge as the market price; however, the usual market-clearing mechanism would not function properly, driving us towards this outcome.

Efficiency in insurance markets
Adverse selection is also a problem in insurance markets. The problem facing the insurance companies is fairly simple. Those most likely to file a claim

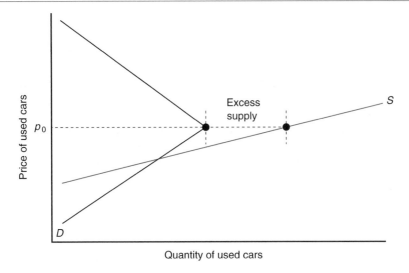

Figure 7.1 Used car market.

against a policy are also those most likely to purchase insurance. Those who are least likely to collect, i.e. those who are safety and health conscious, may still buy some insurance, but will not pay too high a price for it.

In insurance markets, the information regarding policyholder risks is asymmetrically held. The party buying the policy has much more information regarding the potential risks they pose than does the insurance firm. This setting may present serious problems to insurance companies.

Suppose that an insurance company is making losses; that is, that revenues from policy premiums and investments are less than the amount paid out for claims. Can the insurer simply raise rates? Quite possibly the answer is no. Increasing premiums will result in a more serious adverse selection problem for the insurer. At higher rates, those customers who pose lower risks will either opt out of the market, contact another underwriter or purchase less insurance.

High-risk policyholders, on the other hand, are less likely to opt out. The reasoning is subtle but very intuitive. Opting out means that a new insurer will have to be found who will want to assess the risks posed by the client independently. This examination may lay bare the true risks posed by the client and result in even higher premiums for the client.

On balance then, if an insurer wishes to raise premiums, the cost–benefit analysis of policyholders will be altered. Given that some current policyholders are low risk and some are high risk and also that only the policyholders know for sure what risks they pose, low-risk policyholders are more likely than high-risk policyholders to abandon the company in face of higher premiums. Thus, the mix of high- and low-risk policyholders changes because high-risk policyholders comprise a larger percentage of policyholders.

Rationing goods and services

Adverse selection may also occur in markets as a rationing device when price increases are not permitted in order to reduce excess demand. A good example of this phenomenon is the market for loanable funds and credit rationing by banks and other lenders. In this setting of imperfect information, borrowers are more aware of the actual risks they pose than are lenders. An informational asymmetry exists, preventing efficient exchange.

Banks are well aware of the risk–return trade-off characterizing most investment projects. Accordingly, higher returns can be earned only by bearing higher risk. The return on stocks, for example, is typically much higher than the return on government bonds. To a lender, this trade-off presents a unique environment. At low interest rates, potential borrowers representing different levels of risk are plentiful. Notwithstanding the efforts of the bank to identify the risks associated with each borrower, the odds of any borrower presenting a small risk are relatively high. At high interest rates, the pool of potential borrowers is larger; and, further, a significantly larger percentage of these borrowers will pose higher risks. This is because of the aforementioned trade-off; only high-risk borrowers will anticipate the returns necessary to pay the higher interest rates.

The effects of this selection of borrowers are shown diagrammatically in Figure 7.2. There are two offsetting components to the expected returns for the lender. Higher interest rates will (in the low range of interest rates) increase returns to the lender. In the lower range of interest rates, risky borrowers comprise a smaller percentage of the pool of potential borrowers. Thus, defaults are fairly low. In the higher range of interest rates, low-risk borrowers are conspicuously absent from the pool of potential borrowers. As interest rates rise

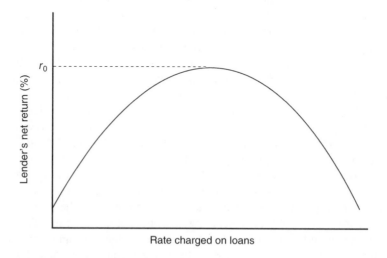

Figure 7.2 Credit rationing with adverse selection.

within the higher range of interest rates, an even riskier pool of borrowers emerges. Thus, at higher rates, the lender can expect more defaults. At some point, the gains from further increases in the interest rate are more than off-set by the increased proportion of riskier borrowers attracted. This rate, labelled r_0 in Figure 7.2, is the interest rate on the lender's loans that maximizes its expected return.

As in the used car example above, it is assumed that lenders are not 'price takers', rather, they are price setters. There is no reason to suppose that the intersection of the market supply and demand curves will occur at or above r_0. Thus, as shown in Figure 7.3, the market may not clear and efficient exchanges may not take place.

Informal solutions to adverse selection
Given that most markets are characterized to some extent by imperfect infor-mation, ways have evolved to promote efficiency in the face of adverse selec-tion. In the next subsection we concentrate on two more formal ways. Before proceeding to them, we might the consider the following less formal approaches to mitigating efficiency declines associated with imperfect information.

Outside appraisers may be called in to inform the information-deficient party. In the used car market, for example, some potential buyers will hire a trusted mechanic to examine the car. In some of the larger metropolitan areas firms exist solely to perform this function. Similarly, before banks lend money to real estate developers (and even home buyers), they often require input from an independent appraiser.

If transacting parties are fairly sophisticated and recognize that they are at an informational disadvantage, they may expend effort towards altering their

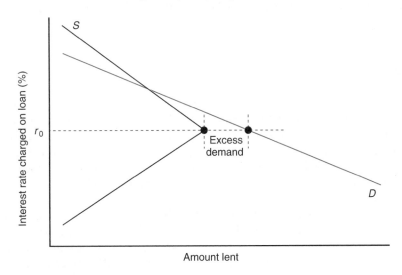

Figure 7.3 Credit rationing.

selection of potential contracting partners. Credit card companies may target a specific demographic group – college graduates, for example – if they believe that the potential future earnings of recent graduates make them reasonable credit risks.

In some instances, however, companies have to expend effort in order to get a more random cross-section of customers. Most holders of health insurance policies in the United States are covered by employer-sponsored group plans. Furthermore, the premiums on group health insurance are markedly lower than the premiums on privately (and independently) purchased policies. There are two interesting viewpoints to explain the price difference between private and group policies. On the one hand, insurers may believe that the employees of large firms represent a 'true' cross-section of individuals. A second, more cynical, viewpoint is that insurers know that, if they tie coverage to a job, then the person holding the job is at least healthy enough to work and thus might pose a lower risk. Whichever point of view you deem more relevant, each admits to the importance of one contracting partner holding an informational advantage and exploiting this advantage.

Credibility and reputation can also alleviate some of the inefficiencies posed by selection problems. Sellers of goods and borrowers of funds often go to great lengths to make their longevity and reputation for honesty known to potential buyers and lenders. Other contractual and regulatory devices also exist to facilitate trade with imperfect information. Warranties are commonly offered with expensive consumer items. Not surprisingly, the fact that not all warranties are offered for free provides information to consumers regarding the underlying quality of the good being sold. In most countries, government laws and regulations specify basic minimums for performance. As another example, consumers' associations offer additional testing and quality reports.

Signalling and screening

In exchange situations with asymmetric information one party is better informed than the other concerning specific attributes of the good being exchanged. Herein lies the problem: 'If I am unsure about the characteristics of this good relative to other goods competing for my scarce resources, what price should I pay?' Economists have identified signalling and screening as two market responses that have emerged to facilitate information flows to the lesser-informed party.

Consider, for a moment, all of the characteristics associated with a product. For most products the list could get rather long. Divide these characteristics into two groups: those characteristics that are desirable to a potential buyer, and those that are observable by a potential buyer. With perfect information and completely efficient markets, each item in the desirable group would also be in the observable group. In practice, however, only some of the items in the desirable group are also in the observable group.

This feature of imperfect information is illustrated in Figure 7.4. Characteristics are either observable, and in the lower box, or unobservable, and in the upper box. Also, characteristics are either desirable, and in the circle, or undesirable, and outside of the circle. Buyers are limited to observable characteristics in their assessments and decision-making.

Consider all the elements in the circle, i.e. the desirable characteristics. There may be some link between the observable and unobservable items that may be exploited. Suppose, for example, that a firm is considering hiring (i.e. buying) a job applicant. The applicant may hold a Masters Degree from a prestigious university; that is observable and verifiable. The fact that she holds a Master's Degree may point to other desirable traits that are unobservable such as perseverance, ability to work with others and intelligence.

Signalling occurs when the better-informed party makes certain verifiable facts known, which, when properly interpreted, may indicate the presence of other unobservable but desirable characteristics. A job applicant may then signal his work ethic by pointing out that he earned his degree with honours while working full-time as a sales person. Similarly, a used car dealership may signal its standing in the community by building a permanent showroom (thus indicating that it would be costly to pack up and leave) or by making its long record of doing business known to prospective buyers.

For signalling to be effective, the receiver must believe that the signal is credible. That is, the observable characteristic must clearly point to the unobservable, desirable characteristic.

This concept is best illustrated in the context of the job applicant and the hiring firm example. Suppose that there are two types of workers: high ability and low ability. The exact level of ability predicts the ultimate productivity of workers but is, unfortunately, not observable. Educational attainment may serve as a signal to employers to differentiate between applicants if two conditions are prevalent within the context of the bargaining and contracting situation.

First, it should be generally true that only high-ability applicants be able to earn the degree marking educational attainment. If low-ability applicants could obtain the degree, then they would do so and pass themselves off to unsuspecting employers as future high-ability workers. Secondly, it should be the case that all high-ability persons hold the degree; i.e. it is in their interests to hold the degree. These conditions work to guarantee that any person with a degree is a promising hire to the firm, and that there are no promising hires to the firm who lack a degree.

When the uninformed parties to an agreement undertake activities in order to cause the informed parties to distinguish between themselves, economists say that **screening** is taking place. In the context of Figure 7.4, screening means that one contracting partner demands certain elements in the set of

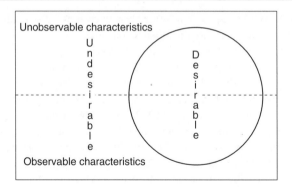

Figure 7.4 Signalling and screening

observed characteristics that are correlated with unobserved but desirable elements. Screening then is a strategy sometimes available to an uninformed party that, if successful, will get the better-informed party to reveal information. In order to help operationalize our understanding of screening we will consider two examples: screening in the labour market, and screening used by sellers to privately informed buyers.

Screening is very prevalent in the job market for many types of workers. Salop and Salop (1976) present a model in which screening is practised by firms in order to reduce employee turnover. Having workers quit is costly for all firms. In the event of a sudden departure, the firm suffers two losses. First, if the employee has undergone training, the cost of that training is lost rather than offset against the future gains in worker productivity occasioned by the more productive worker. Secondly, there are positive costs involved in replacement: advertising, interviewing and selection costs are fairly high. In many circumstances firms have ample incentive to attract workers who are less inclined to change jobs.

Salop and Salop argue that employers may be able to alter the odds that an employee would consider leaving. One possible device is to announce a policy of continuous wage increases. Following this logic, a firm would offer to pay relatively low wages initially, but higher-than-market wages after the employee had been with the firm for an extended period of time. The positive relationship between wages and experience would discourage workers who were likely to change jobs, and would encourage workers who planned on staying with the firm for a substantial portion of their careers.

Screening may also be used by sellers of goods if buyers hold private information concerning their true valuation of the good, and also if the cost of delay to the buyers is higher than the cost of delay to the seller.

Consider once again the used car seller example presented earlier in this chapter. The seller faces two kinds of buyers: those who place a high value on the good and those who place a low value on the good. Obviously, and assuming that the seller is a price setter, buyers have no incentive in revealing their true valuations. All buyers favour purchasing and having use of the car today over purchasing in two weeks. For simplicity we will assume that the seller has no costs of delay.

With the adoption of a price schedule rather than of a single price, the seller may be able to distinguish between the two types of buyers, and in effect to price discriminate against the high-value buyers. One possible strategy for the seller is as follows: Offer the good at a high price today and, if refused, offer the car at a somewhat lower price two weeks hence. If a successful screen is created, the seller can be sure that only low-valuation consumers come back in two weeks and purchase the car. The price in the second period will be the valuation of the low-value consumers. The first-period price must be slightly less than (within several pence of) the price that equates the net return of first-period buyers purchasing two weeks later adjusted for the costs of delay.

Bargaining typically consists of a series of offers and counter-offers, with the seller starting high and the buyer starting low. Eventually, it is hoped, agreement is reached somewhere in the middle. The previous exchange example shows, in a primitive way, an incentive for haggling. The seller is uncertain of any buyer's evaluation and starts with a high price and successively lowers it. Buyers with high valuations are relatively impatient to settle, for they lose more by waiting than buyers with low valuations would. By enduring the costs of holding out, low-valuation buyers credibly prove their starting valuation. Thus, at least in this example, the purpose of haggling is for the seller to get buyers to reveal valuable information.[5]

Measurement costs

As you have read through this chapter so far you have undoubtedly become aware that the availability of information in exchange is a central issue in economics. To this point, we may not have added any ideas that are truly new to your knowledge base; we have however made two important contributions to your overall business education. First, we have provided a terminology for you to use in describing information problems. Secondly, by examining these issues from several vantage points, we hope that we have provided at least some new insights for you.

Strategic misrepresentation and adverse selection are two types of *ex ante* contracting problems. As we discussed these situations it became clear that the best answer is to become better informed. The fear of exploitation by a contracting partner will rationally lead all parties to become as informed as possible. Economists call the costs incurred by parties attempting to become fully informed **measurement costs**. We consider measurement costs to be a subcategory of the more general class of costs associated with exchange transaction costs.

In the traditional supply and demand models, measurement costs are very small if not zero. Since there is a high degree of homogeneity among the wares of competing sellers, buyers have little incentive to assess the quality of a product themselves. Also, in the traditional supply and demand model, there is no incentive to invest in bargaining position. Haggling will not occur because there is a fairly well-defined price known generally by all market participants. Over-anxious sellers seeking higher prices quickly lose buyers. Exceptionally tight-fisted buyers will not find sellers at overly generous terms.

In the real world however, market participants frequently cannot rely on competitive markets and the invisible hand. Consider, for example, hard-to-define goods that change hands infrequently, such as houses. For any given house, there may be no true 'equilibrium' price. The seller must expend resources to determine the 'fair market value' of the house. Buyers, in turn, attempt to determine the value of the house to them given their household size, tastes and the house's locational characteristics.

From an efficiency perspective, these measurement costs represent a burden and a waste. When both parties seek to become better informed, the costs of gathering and analyzing the information are subtracted from the total value of the transaction to each party. The ownership of the asset changes, whether or not the information costs had been borne, just as efficiency requires. It is true that the higher level of information results in an exchange price in line with the true value of the asset; however, to an outside party, price differences represent a transfer from (to) the buyer to (from) the seller.

Strictly speaking, measurement costs are a loss to society as a whole and to transaction participants in particular. In some instances, contracting techniques have emerged to lessen the influence of measurement costs.

Reducing measurement costs

One strategy used in reducing measurement costs is **block booking**. Kenney and Klein (1983) identify block booking in several contexts. In each instance, block booking involves a price-setting seller, with some market power, grouping similar goods together and offering the package to buyers, who had little information. Sellers thus set, in effect, an average price. This practice will eliminate duplicative search costs. Presumably if a buyer could reject part of a package, he would do so after a critical (and costly) assessment of product quality. The seller would then have to verify this assessment and offer the once-rejected product at a lower price to another buyer, who would then incur the same measurement costs.

The practice of block booking does not require a perfect monopoly by the seller, but some monopoly power certainly helps provide the necessary framework. Competition by several sellers would not favour the practice of block booking; undoubtedly competition would entice sellers to abandon the practice. What is required is that both the buyer and seller recognize that the quality of each of the items in the package is somewhat random. They can then expect, on average, to get their money's worth. A definite contributing factor to this practice is that most arrangements of block booking involve many transactions over a long time-period reinforcing the effects of bad 'draws' being counteracted by good ones.

Block booking has been common in the American motion picture industry from as early as 1916. Kenney and Klein (1983) outline the following common scenario for many of the contractual arrangements made by Paramount Studios with theatres. The 'block booked' group of films was offered prior to the films' actual production; thus they were said to be 'blind sold'. Potential exhibitors had some information about production budget estimates, the past year's gross rentals of the studio's films, and the likely acting, writing and directing talent. They could not, however, view the movies they were renting; further, if the exhibitor reneged, they were not contacted by the studio again. The potential for short-term opportunistic behaviour was therefore large, placing an emphasis on reputation and brand name capital of the distributor.

Kenney and Klein also identify the marketing efforts of the Central Selling Organization (CSO) of the De Beers diamond group. Over the past decade, this group has directly controlled about 80 per cent of the world's supply of new diamonds. Each customer regularly informs CSO of the kinds of diamonds it wishes to purchase. The CSO, in turn, puts together a 'sight' of diamonds for the customer. Each buyer examines the sight before deciding to purchase or not for as long as he wishes. Negotiation over the price or composition of the sight is not permitted. If a buyer claims that one or more stones in the sight is incorrectly graded, the sight is adjusted if the sales staff agrees. These occurrences are said to be rare. Buyers rarely reject a sight, because, in so doing, they are offered no alternative and deleted from the list of customers.

The economic rationale for the marketing practices of the CSO and Paramount Studios is clearly to avoid excessive bargaining costs. The transaction costs incurred in haggling over the price of diamonds and movies would be significant. It is interesting to note that De Beer's CSO pursues a different selling strategy for particularly large diamonds. Instead of being sold on a fixed average price basis, very large stones are offered to particular buyers on an individual stone negotiation based basis. The buyers of large stones suffer no consequences if they reject a stone on the basis of price or perceived quality. The rationale for the selling practice of large stones is arguably that estimates of value of larger stones vary significantly across buyers, because they can be put to many different uses.

Block booking, or average pricing, is also common in many less glamorous aspects of economic life. Sports teams typically prefer to sell 'season tickets' requiring customers to attend a number of home games or matches. In the United States major college football programmes have taken the idea one step further; tickets for home games against nationally recognized powerhouses are sometimes sold together with tickets for home games against less prestigious opponents.

A second strategy for reducing the measurement costs is to rely on other interested parties, who may have incurred the measurements costs but whose observable actions can relay that information to others. Economists term this practice 'free-riding' off the information of others.[6]

If you can obtain costly information for free, through observation, then it is in your interest to do so. In a retail setting, it is widely regarded that this practice is often used by fast food chains in determining locations for their restaurants. Conventional wisdom has it that McDonald's is usually first into an area, after having done the necessary research on the site. Soon other competitors follow. In another context, free-riding has been offered as an alternative to deposit insurance at banks and savings and loans. The argument goes as follows: large depositors will have more incentive to monitor the financial health of the institution in which they have placed funds than will small depositors. Further, large depositors often have the resources and technical sophistication to conduct this monitoring. If the actions of the large depositors were made public knowledge, small depositors could mimic their actions and safeguard their investments.

D. *Ex post* opportunism

Ex post disadvantages

The contracts crafted between individuals and organizations have a single purpose and a means of achieving this purpose. A contract is intended to benefit all agreeing parties. This benefit is achieved by aligning the parties' incentives and interests. With contracting, this alignment may be less than perfect. In particular, the possibility of being harmed by the other party's self-interested behaviour may hinder efficient exchange. Opportunistic behaviour occurs when one party selfishly pursues her own interests possibly at the expense of other contracting parties. The threat of opportunism may seriously limit the degree of cooperation that can be expected, especially under bounded rationality and contracts.

In this chapter, we will consider two forms of *ex post* opportunism: reneging and the 'hold-up'. A third form of post-contractual opportunism arising out of imperfect information is reserved for the next chapter. **Reneging** occurs when one or more parties to a transaction simply refuses to honour the agreement. The **hold-up** of a trading partner involves exploiting the inflexibility or captiveness that may result from an agreement. The threats of falling victim to reneging or the hold-up problem present (sometimes significant) transaction costs to be overcome in the pursuit of efficient exchange.

These transaction costs arise from two sources: contract incompleteness and asset specificity. Before examining the second of these sources, we consider the role of contracts and its association with reneging.

Reneging

Contractual incompleteness and bounded rationality imply a trade-off in reaching agreements. On the one hand, relational, (or, in lay terms, imprecise) contracts involve a cost saving over perfect, highly detailed contracts. On the other hand, however, they leave much for interpretation *ex post*. Then it may be easy for one party to complain about the other's performance only to have the second party claim that they are doing as agreed, and that no reneging is going on. Moreover, even if the other party fully believes you are not living up to the agreement, the ambiguity of the contract means that it may be very hard for outsiders to determine exactly who is misbehaving and what actual behaviour is appropriate.

In a well-publicized case in the early 1980s Westinghouse failed to deliver uranium fuel to other utilities at prices set in a long-term agreement. The basis of Westinghouse's position was that appropriate contractual behaviour indicated this to be the reasonable course of action.

If reneging takes the form of a failure to conform to agreed actions, efficiency is not directly sacrificed. For example, consider a magazine subscriber refusing to pay the subscription bill after receiving six months' of issues. All that efficiency required was that the magazines be supplied; payments are merely an income transfer from one party to another. The threat of reneging may affect efficiency indirectly, however, by increasing the belief held by one party that he may be cheated or by tarnishing the reputation of a person or organization. If the magazine subscriber's name in the above example is added to a 'deadbeat' list, then he may have trouble subscribing to other magazines.

A second form of reneging, termed *ex post* renegotiation, may occur if at least one party wishes the contract to remain in force, only on altered terms. When contracts are imprecise, future behaviour under different possible environments may not be stipulated. In fact, it may be impossible to know the environments themselves. If the parties understand at the time they are crafting the original agreement that they will later face these incentives, they may not be able to draft a contract.

Consider, for example, the practice of large corporations of rewarding key executives with stock options. An option gives the holder the right to buy the firm's stock at a specified point in time at a specified price. The executive will earn substantial profits if she is able to purchase the stock in the future at a price well below the market price, only to resell it immediately. This motivation scheme is, theoretically, a win–win situation. For the firm, it costs less than money paid today and provides incentives to the executive to enhance the profitability of the company. For the executive, she is essentially guaranteed a bonus in the future that is larger than the cash bonus she could get now. One essential parameter, however, is the price at which the executive can purchase the stock in the future, the 'execute' price relative to the future market price of the stock. If the execute price is set too high, the stock option may be viewed as an unreachable goal; if the market price turns out to be too low, the value to the executive falls. In this case, it might make sense, *ex post*, for the executive and the firm to renegotiate the option execute price. This is especially true when both sides agree that the stock price may have changed owing to reasons far outside the executive's, or for that matter the organization's, control.

Certain contractual devices and separate institutions have emerged to help remedy some portion of the threat of reneging to individuals and organizations. By and large these remedies involve introducing some flexibility into the relational contract. Within contracts, penalty clauses are sometimes instituted if requirements concerning repayment, quality and timeliness are not met. Further, some contracts guarantee a variety of options at some point in the future. In the home mortgage market during the early 1990s, for example, the relatively low interest rates encouraged both new home purchases and the refinancing of existing mortgages. Many borrowers opted for an **adjustable rate mortgage** (ARM). The interest rates on these mortgages change in response to changes in some specified target rate. This aspect of ARMs makes them attractive to lenders, who have some protection in their earnings against a protracted increase in long-term interest rates. Consumers also have protection against higher mortgage costs in light of increasing interest rates; they often have the right to convert their ARM to a conventional fixed-rate mortgage at some specified point in time.

When parties fear that their trading partners may renege on agreements made, they may rely on the **reputation** of those with whom they make deals. Economists view reputation as an institutional device that may be considered as part of an organization's capital stock. Reputations are formed on past behaviour and, more importantly, on others' perceptions of that behaviour. Choosing trading partners on the basis of their reputation is one defence against being exploited by a reneging trading partner.

You are probably aware of the importance of reputation and perhaps have some experience with devices created to provide information on a potential trading partner's reputation. One very common certifier of reputations is the local credit bureau, which may help determine if a person is going to renege on her promise to repay. Local Better Business Bureaus and Chambers of Commerce often store complaints against retailers, distributors and contractors so that potential customers can assess their reputations. On a much larger scale, Standard and Poor's rates organizations issuing bonds, all in an attempt to determine the possibility that they will or will not repay their financial obligations.

The hold-up problem: Asset specificity revisited

A different and perhaps larger problem caused by imperfect commitment arises when individuals or organizations are required to make significant investments that are (at least somewhat) specific to a particular purpose. **Investment** is the current expenditure of resources that produces a stream of benefits over future period(s). When a firm or individual invests, it creates an asset. There are many types of assets, most usefully categorized by the created asset and its future stream of benefits. Financial investments purchase assets such as stocks and bonds, yielding a future flow of cash returns. For most people, the single biggest tangible investment they will make is in their home, which provides a stream of housing services over a long period of time. Although we most commonly think of physical investments such as houses, factories or buildings, investments need not be tangible. Education is clearly not a physical asset, yet it is an investment we make in ourselves to reap future benefits. Economists term investments in education, skills and training **human capital**, which, it is hoped, leads to higher future incomes, more meaningful lives and better decision-making ability.

When considering the costs and benefits of investments, one problematic dimension concerns the asset specificity of an investment. Assets become specific when they are most valuable in one particular transaction or relationship. Physical assets may be highly specific, such as a large office building becoming part of an area or neighbourhood. Asset specificity is not limited to physical assets however. Human capital may be specific to a particular trade or discipline; blue-collar manufacturing workers faced significant unemployment during the decline of manufacturing in most industrial countries in the 1980s and 1990s. The reputations of firms may also be specific to a particular product line or type of service.

Asset specificity becomes a problem in designing efficient contracts when it puts one party at a disadvantage in potential future *ex post* bargaining situations. The disadvantage arises as a result of a shortage of outside, alternative options.

The opportunities for *ex post* opportunism are especially important when the specificity applies to more than one asset. Two assets become **co-specialized** when they are most productive when used together, and lose much of their value or productivity in the absence of the other. When assets become co-specialized, the value of the investment to one party depends crucially on the behaviour of another asset owner with his own agenda and selfish interests. Thus, the door is left open for exploitative *ex post* opportunistic behaviour. The determination of winners and losers in such exchanges is unclear and determined by unquantifiable factors such as the value of an organization's reputation and the alternative opportunities available.

An organization that places a high value on its reputation is less likely to attempt to exploit its position and hold up a trading partner. A damaged reputation may cause other, future, trading partners to think twice before committing to a joint effort. Co-specialization, like specialization, is a question of degree.

Asset specificity gauges commitment; formally, the specificity of an asset is measured as the percentage of investment value that is lost when the asset is used outside the specific setting or relationship. A higher degree of commitment implies a greater vulnerability to being held up. A higher degree of commitment by your partner is beneficial to you because it lowers the probability that she will attempt to hold you up (this would amount to cutting her own throat). Likewise, the lower the asset specificity, the more likely is one party to hold up the other.

Consider, for example, a municipality wishing to lure a manufacturing facility into its jurisdiction. Indeed, one common economic development strategy is for a state to promise a factory certain inducements: tax forgiveness, road networks, worker training, low interest loans, etc. Suppose that an agreement is reached and the state government constructs a road linking the factory site to a major highway. Both negotiating sides have committed specific assets: the state has constructed a road with limited alternative uses, and the manufacturer has sunk development costs to construct its plant. In this case the road and the plant are co-specialized assets.

In this example, either party could attempt to hold up the other, the specificity of the investments (the road and the factory) being determined by their owners alone. The factory manager could reason that, once the state has laid the roadbed, he could make further opportunistic demands for, perhaps, further tax forgiveness or increased worker training. What factors limit the factory manager? Only two. The reputation of the plant in future dealings with the state and in future dealings with suppliers, labour and other state governments, and the true alternatives to the state for use of the road. If the state could still profit by extending the road to another site perhaps, then at least some of its value could be realized. Likewise the state could notice that the constructed plant is highly specialized and, arguing economic hardship, prematurely end its tax forgiveness or worker training. This would, of course, damage the state's reputation and hinder its attempts in drawing additional employers and contributors to the tax base.

The hold-up problem deserves our attention for two reasons. First, because it is most prevalent within an investment context, the affected transactions typically involve substantial sums of money. Secondly, and again because asset specificity is best exemplified in an investment context, the affected transactions typically span a number of time-periods. Paul Joskow, a well-known economist, has produced a number of studies examining the hold-up problem in the context of the arrangements between coal-burning electricity utility companies and the coal suppliers that serve them. A descriptive account of the bargaining situation facing the mines and the utilities, together with Joskow's findings, which are consistent with the transaction cost approach, appears in Box 7.1.

Box 7.1 Joskow's Case of coal-burning electricity generating plants

The transaction cost theory suggests that the incentives for firms to write long and detailed contracts increase with the lack of alternative *ex post* outside opportunities, and also with the specificity of investments. In a series of related articles, Paul Joskow (1985, 1987, 1988) confronted the transaction cost approach with real-world evidence.

Joskow chose to examine the specifics of the relationships between coal-burning electricity generating plants and the mines that provide the coal (in the mid-1980s coal generated more than 50 per cent of the electricity consumed in the United States). For our purposes, this case is interesting, and the analysis is clear given the apparent and verifiable differences between the coal markets in different sections of the continental United States and the many specificities involved for both buyer and seller.

Coal mines (suppliers) must sink investments in mining capacity. The electricity utilities (buyers) must commit specific investments in the amount of generating equipment and also in the adaption of boilers to a particular type of coal.

Coal reserves are not distributed uniformly across the United States in terms of either quantity or quality. We can roughly distinguish two polar geographical regions. In the east, topography and the nature of coal deposits support underground mining. Eastern coal is relatively homogeneous and there are no significant economies of scale in its production. In the west, strip-mining is more common, providing large economies of scale in coal production. There is more variation, however, in the quality of western coal.

A large component of the effective price of coal to users is transportation or shipping costs. Again a regional difference emerges: given a more developed transportation infrastructure and more shipping agents, transportation costs are much lower in the east.

Joskow's findings are clearly in line with the predictions of transaction cost analysis. Contracts between buyers and suppliers are typically of much shorter duration in the east. In the western region, Joskow found the contracts to be much more complex and for much longer duration. Furthermore, he found that the spot market for coal is very important in the east, whereas it is largely insignificant in the west.

In the language of this chapter, we would conclude that specificity is an issue in this contracting situation. However, the degree of co-specialization in the eastern coal markets is much lower than the degree of co-specialization in the western coal markets.

E. Governance structures and specificity

The contributions of Coase and Williamson

Many economists have studied the role of transaction cost considerations in forming agreements between economic agents. The initial groundwork was laid by the Nobel Prize winning economist Ronald Coase in his 1937 paper. Coase introduced the idea of transaction costs and argued that efficiency would dictate that contractual arrangements be crafted in ways to minimize them.

According to the Coasian logic, individuals and organizations would choose a contractual format, termed a **governance structure**, from a wide variety of possibilities. At one extreme, transactions could take place within a 'market'. This extreme is the realm of most traditional theoretical economic analysis: there is perfect information, lots of competition and little, if any, room for opportunism. At the other extreme is the possibility that transactions could occur entirely within an organization. If the transaction costs were too high in terms of informational asymmetries, selection problems or asset specificity, then organizations would manage these transactions internally, avoiding markets altogether. In the previous chapter, we examined this same problem in terms of major manufacturing firms choosing to make components of their products in-house or to rely on outside suppliers.

This train of thought was picked up by Williamson in his 1975 work, *Markets and Hierarchies*. Williamson used a 'comparative institutional' perspective in which there is a wide range of institutional arrangements that can be used to govern transactions between economic agents. Governance structures emerge in response to various transactional considerations. The boundary between a firm and a market provides a very rough distinction between the two primary institutional arrangements used by economic agents seeking to promote efficiency in defining the relationships between them. Williamson made it clear that firms are able to take on any one of a variety of different organizational structures.

Williamson also argued that market transactions too can be structured in a variety of ways, and he provided a variety of examples. One type is the spot market transaction where buyer and seller come together at one point in time and exchange. A second alternative is for buyer and seller to craft their relationship with a complex long-term contract. For any given transaction, the chosen governance structure could be either of these two extremes, or lie somewhere in the middle.

Of all the different sources of transaction costs, asset specificity has the clearest implications for the form of governance structure chosen by firms. In these instances, spot market transactions can be ruled out. When investment in co-specialized assets is required for efficient exchange, and when these investment costs represent a significant portion of the costs of arranging and implementing the transaction, anonymous spot markets will fail. The reasoning relies on expectations of opportunistic behaviour. Sinking a relationship-specific investment transfers an *ex ante* situation that may be competitive into an *ex post* bargaining situation that is not competitive and is, in fact, a bilateral monopoly. To induce the parties to make optimal investments *ex ante*, some contractual method is needed to constrain the *ex post* hold-up problem. After ruling out spot markets, we are left with eliminating the opportunities for opportunistic behaviour in one of two ways.

The transaction may be designed so that it is entirely within one firm: the vertical integration solution. Alternatively, a long-term relational contract may be written binding the parties together. Any long-term relational contract must preserve individual and joint incentives.

Vertical integration

Logically extending the transaction cost analysis of Coase and Williamson, **vertical integration** is more likely the more specific the investments are. We revisit the work of Paul Joskow, which was highlighted earlier in Box 7.1. Joskow found that, in the western United States, investments by mines and utilities are in effect more specific than investments in the eastern United States. Another feature of the coal market is that some utilities construct coal-burning electricity generating facilities at the entrance to a given coal mine. These so-called 'mine-mouth' plants are nearly completely co-specialized with the utility facility. As a result, the mine-mouth plants and coal mines are always vertically integrated.

The question may be raised as to why more coal mines are not integrated into the utility firms. There are several reasons for this pattern of governance. First, coal producers are aware that energy prices fluctuate and change relative to each other. For example, during the Opec oil crisis of the mid 1970s, coal prices relative to other competing energy sources declined. US coal producers had to find new markets for their product. Secondly, the utility companies may not feel that coal is the permanent technology for creating energy. The utilities are surely aware that technological advances have increased the importance of nuclear energy and that future breakthroughs in solar- and perhaps even fusion-based processes may make them more practical.

Another example of co-specialized assets is provided by Klein, Crawford and Alchian, who examine the US automobile industry in the early part of the twentieth century. As of the early 1920s, General Motors purchased the automobile bodies used by their many divisions from Fisher Body. The threat of competition and the advance of automobile production technology pushed General Motors into constructing a new automobile assembly plant. GM desired greater cooperation from Fisher Body, arguing that product reliability would increase, production could be made more efficient, and massive savings in shipping costs could result if Fisher Body would likewise build a new plant adjacent to the new GM facility. In fact, one plan even suggested that Fisher Body not construct loading docks, road extensions or rail spurs; instead Fisher would directly supply only to the GM production floor. Fisher balked at these ideas. GM eventually solved the obvious threat of the hold-up problem by buying Fisher Body. Klein, Crawford and Alchian offer other examples where firms fearing imperfect commitment opt for the vertical integration solution.

Long-term relational contracts

In his survey of contracts between coal mines and utilities, Joskow (1987) found that future exchange prices were not usually stipulated. Rather, indexing was used. Under price indexing, future prices are tied to changes in some established market price. In the coal market, the spot market price is often used. This is a very familiar concept to many home owners who hold adjustable rate mortgages (ARMs). Under the typical ARM arrangement, only the annual interest rates in the first year or the first and second year of a 15- or 30-year mortgage are stated. The interest rate in the remaining years results from changing the interest rate in the prior year according to changes in some index of mortgage loans, or to changes in a long-term federal government bond rate.

It is also common for the buyer to agree to a change in prices in response to changes in the seller's (supplier's) costs. This practice is common in the construction industry, where the completion of large projects may take several years. A US trade publication, the *Engineering News Record* publishes region-based indexes for the costs of different types of labour, cement, steel and other inputs to the construction process.

An alternative approach that avoids the *ex post* hold-up problem is to introduce *ex post* competition wherever possible. Farrell and Gallini (1988) and Shepard (1986) were the first economists to model this process formally in the context of models of firm behaviour based on transaction cost. Suppose that the buyer invests in specific assets and the seller chooses, *ex post*, some *ex ante* variable (perhaps quality, delivery lag, adaptability or taste) that is not part of the contract. *Ex post*, the seller has an incentive to choose low quality; therefore, *ex ante*, the buyer invests little in the relationship. Dual sourcing consists of having two or more suppliers, who compete *ex post* on quality. This raises the equilibrium level of quality and the *ex ante* investment. Farrell and Gallini argue that this is a persuasive explanation of why Intel licenses its microprocessor technologies and why IBM adopts an 'open architecture' policy in regard to its personal computers.

Reputation

We must also recognize the role of reputation in avoiding future contracting hazards. An excellent article by MacCaulay (1963) found that relations between firms tended to be more informal than would be predicted by theory. In long-run relationships, reputation can sustain efficiency. Any firm that cheats (perhaps by making decisions that are not jointly efficient) runs the risk of losing future profitable deals with its partner. Reputation allows a firm to save on the costs of writing more complete contracts, or even from deciding on some distribution of authority.

F. The importance of contracting for managers

A manager in today's firm faces a number of challanges. A firm understanding of the economic forces operating behind contracting can help today's manager face these challanges in a value-maximizing way. Whereas lawyers are most interested in what a contract is, the economist is most concerned with what a contract does: it is chosen to organize economic activity.

The two themes of this chapter are the role of information and the likely effects of asset specificity. In a perfectly competitive market, neither of these issues is very important or interesting and managers can act in the supply and demand framework taught in basic economics courses. In most exchanges however, the invisible hand of Adam Smith is joined by another or possibly two other hands and today's manager must be aware of things such as bounded rationality, asymmetric information and asset specificity.

The possibility of strategic misrepresentation and adverse selection gives rise to significant transaction costs that can destroy value and impede efficiency. The manager must carefully weigh the costs and benefits of gathering more information and altering the selection of trading partners.

Specialized assets pose another problem more at the heart of today's corporations. The evidence indicates that relational contracts where parties agree on broad goals and objectives and also on some flexibility concerning the involved prices and costs can be a suitable answer.

G. Chapter summary and key ideas

Economics is the science whose duty it is to study the process of exchange. Traditionally, the functioning of markets has been explained within a competitive supply and demand framework. An alternative approach was pursued in this chapter. Our analysis focuses on the relevance of transaction costs in the crafting of contracts, or agreements, between parties that interact. Bounded rationality, contracting, information availability, reputation and opportunism are the recurring themes in our analysis. If we accept the premise offered by Coase and Williamson, economic units should act to arrange their interactions with other economic units in such a way as to minimize the associated transaction costs. We consider such behaviour as a movement toward efficiency.

Bounded rationality implies that some uncertainty will result in any contractual arrangement. Theoretically it may be possible to remove the risks associated with contracting; however, the cost of doing so may quite well be infinite. Most employment contracts are largely relational, containing relatively few provisions in light of the nearly infinite possible environments that may occur *ex post*.

In exchange, information is a very valuable commodity. A number of problems emerge when one party to a transaction holds private information. Strategic misrepresentation is the economist's equivalent to successful bluffing in a poker game. Trade is not likely to be efficient when the threat of strategic misrepresentation exists, and parties will expend significant resources towards learning the truth about their partners. From an individual perspective it pays to acquire information concerning your opponent's outside opportunities and costs of delay.

Insurance markets provide an excellent example of another efficiency-reducing aspect of private information. Adverse selection, to a trading partner, most generally means attracting the wrong type of people with whom to do business. Signalling and screening are two market responses to adverse selection.

Whereas *ex ante* opportunism focuses on the availability of information, *ex post* opportunism centres on the idea of commitment arising from investments in highly specific assets. Market transactions involving highly specific investments are likely to be carried out either with a long-term contract or entirely within the auspices of a firm, i.e. vertical integration.

A governance structure is a feasible way to manage a transaction. Major contributions by Coase and Williamson have emphasized the idea that firms have incentives to choose a governance structure that minimizes the costs of their interaction. Quite often that governance structure is a long-term relational contract.

The effective design of long-term relational contracts requires an alignment of individual and joint incentives that mitigates *ex post* opportunism (hold-ups or reneging), and also is flexible enough to be lived out in an imperfect and unpredictable world. Economics cannot offer any single model of contract design under these conditions. Transaction cost analysis can, however, offer guidelines and suggestions.

Key words

adjustable rate mortage
adverse selection
asset specificity
block booking
bounded rationality
contract
co-specialized assets
ex ante
ex post
explicit contract
external contract
fungible
governance structure
hold-up
human capital
imperfect information
implicit contract

incomplete contracts
informational asymmetries
internal contract
investment
market discipline
measurement costs
minimum supply price
opportunism
relational contracting
reneging
reputation
reservation price
screening
signalling
strategic misrepresentation
vertical integration

Questions and problems for review and discussion

1 Discuss, in general terms, the value of reputation in a contracting environment. Be sure to indicate how reputation can mitigate the negative efficiency effects of:
  (a) strategic misrepresentation
  (b) adverse selection
  (c) the burden of measurement costs
  (d) asset specificity.

2 Measurement costs may affect efficiency in a number of interesting ways. Consider, for example, the sale of a professional baseball team. Recently, some clubs have sold for tremendous amounts of money. In August 1993, for example, the Baltimore Orioles sold for $173 million.
  (a) What do you think some of the sources of measurement costs are in such a transaction? Will they involve significant funds being expended?
  (b) Quite often the sale of a professional sports club invokes a bidding war involving many diverse interests. As in any other form of a bidding war, there is a winner who gets the team and at least one loser who does not. What are the efficiency implications for the measurement costs incurred by the winner? What are the efficiency

implications for the measurement costs incurred by the loser?

3 Characterize the following statements as 'True, false, or uncertain: 'In a market characterized as competitive on both the seller and buyer sides, private information is not an issue.'

4 In the previous two chapters we have discussed many of the issues surrounding asset specificity and its effects on agreement. Is there a direct efficiency effect of the hold-up problem?

5 Adverse selection is a problem of precontractual opportunism; it arises because of the private information held by at least one party to a contract. Consider the market for used cars. There are *good used cars*, which will provide a reasonably expected amount of service. There are also *lemons*, which will provide far less than a reasonably expected amount of service. Explain how, in this situation, adverse selection may in effect close the market, i.e. there will be no voluntary exchanges. An excellent source for the thinking needed to analyze this situation is Akerlof (1970).

6 Suppose that I own DANGER, a small manufacturing plant in northern England. DANGER specializes in finely milling specialty sheet steel to a variety of industrial uses. Business is good despite the recession. I am approached by a representative of Nissan concerning the possibility of supplying the local Nissan plant with product. Mine is the only facility of its type in the area that can do the job Nissan wants done. My reputation and skills are well known. The Nissan deal would require me to add additional capacity to the point of nearly doubling my manufacturing capacity.

   (a) If I accept the deal, what specific assets am I contributing?

   (b) One dimension of transactions costs is 'asset specificity'. Is this relevant here? Why, or why not, for either or both parties?

   (c) Suppose that I accept the deal. What are the aspects of 'the hold-up problem' that each contracting party could exploit?

7 Use the information in problem number 6 above. What additional circumstances *could* reduce DANGER's exposure to being 'held up'? What additional circumstances could reduce the big firm's exposure to being 'held up'? For each of these produce a listing of three, and be prepared to explain and/or defend each list item fully.

Notes

1 There are, of course, situations where agreement is involuntary, such as the contract formed when the thief brandishes a gun and orders the victim to hand over her money and jewellery. The prison sentence given to the thief upon conviction is likewise an involuntary contract between the court system and the thief.

2 There are some missing aspects that may appear in other transactions, however. In

our example, there is no opportunistic behaviour by either Becky or BigFoods. In continental Europe, even temporary employment is subject to more government regulation or even to collective bargaining agreements with trade unions.

3 The facts behind the strike by players against Major League Baseball appear in DeBrock and Roth (1981).

4 Of course, bargaining may completely break down if all negotiators have instruments to make a 'take it or leave it' offer.

5 Haggling to achieve these ends may not always work however. If, for example, the difference between high and low valuations is too large relative to the costs of delay, it will be impossible to determine a first-period price that results in seller profits in excess of those earned by simply setting a fixed price.

6 An interesting perspective on these issues is provided in a fairly sophisticated paper by Milgrom and Roberts (1986).

References

Akerlof, G. (1970), 'The market for lemons: Qualitative uncertainty and the market mechanism', *Quarterly Journal of Economics*, 84, pp. 488–500.

Coase, R., (1937), 'The nature of the firm', *Economica*, 4, pp. 386–405.

DeBrock, L. M. and A. Roth (1981), 'Strike two: Labour management negotiations in major-league baseball', *Bell Journal of Economics*, 12, pp. 413–25.

Farrell, J. and N. Gallini (1988), 'Second-sourcing as a commitment: Monopoly incentives to attract competition', *Quarterly Journal of Economics*, 103, pp. 673–94.

Joskow, P. (1985), 'Vertical integration and long term contracts: The case of coal-burning electric generating plants', *Journal of Law, Economics and Organization*, 1, pp. 33–79.

Joskow, P. (1987), 'Contract duration and relationship-specific investments: The case of coal', *American Economic Review*, 77, pp. 168–85.

Joskow, P. (1988), 'Asset specificity and the structure of vertical relationships: Empirical evidence', *Journal of Law, Economics, and Organization*, 4, pp. 95–117.

Kenney, R. W. and B. Klein (1983), 'The economics of block booking', *Journal of Law and Economics*, 26, pp. 497–540.

Klein, B., J. Crawford and A. Alchian (1978), 'Vertical Integration, Appropriable Rents, and the Competitive Contracting Process', *Journal of Law and Economics*, 21, pp. 297–326.

MacCaulay, S. (1963), 'Non-contract relations in business', *American Sociological Review*, 28, pp. 55–70.

Milgrom, P. and J. Roberts (1986), 'Relying on the information of interested parties', *Rand Journal of Economics*, 17, pp. 18–32.

Salop J. and S. Salop (1976), 'Self-selection and turnover in the labour market', *Quarterly Journal of Economics*, 90, pp. 629–49.

Shepard, A. (1986), 'Licensing to enhance demand for new technologies', mimeo, Yale University.

Williamson, O. (1975), *Markets and Hierarchies: Analysis and Antitrust Implications*, New York: Free Press.

Contractual discourse: Moral hazard

> Boats are pulled upstream by a team of coolies prodded by an overseer with a whip . . . an American lady, horrified at the sight of the overseer whipping the men as they strained at their harness, demanded that something be done about the brutality. She was quickly informed . . . 'Those men own the rights to draw boats over this stretch of water and they have hired the overseer and given him his duties.' (McManus, 1975, p. 341)

A. Chapter outline and student goals

Another important source of transaction costs

The two previous chapters have highlighted the importance of information and commitment in economic exchange. Strategic misrepresentation and adverse selection were seen to negatively impact efficiency in transactions. Asset specificity was shown to be another culprit in affecting efficient exchange. In this chapter we remain in the realm of bounded rationality and incomplete contracting and examine another *ex post* contracting problem.

Before proceeding into the detailed analysis, consider these following examples of agreements gone awry.

> You are a business student at a large university. In order to instil in you the ability to work in teams, your economics professor has placed you on a team of students charged with writing a report that will determine your grade for the semester. You notice that throughout the term some of your team members fail to complete tasks that they agreed to do.

> A child is given an extravagant-looking toy train set featuring a complete layout of TinyTown. The picture on the box is breathtaking. When opened however, the cardboard cut-outs you are provided with seem hideous.

> Banks and building socities are just like any other business: they try to 'buy low and sell high.' They are unique, however, in that the commodity they trade in is money. 'Buying low' means acquiring deposits at low interest rates. 'Selling high' means loaning this same money at higher rates. Financial markets are characterized by a risk–return relation: higher returns are had only by incurring the expense of higher

risks. Bank managers have an incentive to make riskier investments than they otherwise would, putting the solvency of their institutions in jeopardy.

John Rockofellow examines the operations of Acme Corporation and decides that he could make better (more profitable) use of Acme's assets. Rockofellow buys enough shares in Acme to gain control, fires most of Acme's management, spins off some of its assets, and sets the company in his direction.

You take your car to an automobile conditioning specialist who promises to make your car 'showroom new'. One week later your car seems to be just like it always was.

In neoclassical theory, none of these events would arise. In the perfectly competitive and fully informed world, competition would prevent each of these occurrences. Each classmate on your team would put forth more effort; toy train sets would actually look like those pictured on the box they came out of; and very, very few banks and building societies would ever fail.

The problems in the above examples arise out of the arrangement of the exchange between individuals and/or organizations. They are examples of what economists call **moral hazard**. Moral hazard occurs when one party's actions are imperfectly observable and affect the value of the exchange to other parties. It is common to anticipate moral hazard in situations with imperfect information and also in which there is a misalignment of incentives. In describing retail markets, consumer protection groups often use the phrase *caveat emptor*, or 'let the buyer beware'. In many settings it may be impossible for buyers to monitor the quality of the goods and services they purchase. As such, sellers may often substitute lower-quality and less expensive goods, components or delivery systems without the buyer's knowledge. Economists have studied moral hazard in this and many other less obvious contexts.

Situations of moral hazard arise frequently in daily life. If you have ever rented a car, you are likely to exercise more caution if you are responsible for damages than if you purchased the Collision Damage Waiver. The prevalence of huge malpractice awards against physicians has led many to practise what is termed 'conservative' medicine: this is, they order many tests on patients that probably were not worth the cost in order to avoid a negligence or malpractice suit.

The term 'moral hazard' originated in the insurance industry to describe situations where, once an individual is insured against certain risks, she will expend less effort in avoiding those same risks. This context serves to characterize many other situations as well. In the context of bounded rationality and incomplete contracts, a moral hazard framework is useful for analyzing: firm organization, team production, shareholder activism and certain financial characteristics of firms.

Shirking and the principal–agent problem

From an organizational standpoint, moral hazard is a serious problem attributable to the absence of perfect and cost-free monitoring behaviour. Employees may have an incentive to engage in **shirking,** or to put forth less effort than they otherwise might if their actions could be more effectively monitored.

Why might shirking exist? There are two ways to approach this question. One is to consider the question from an ethical perspective and to argue that shirking is morally wrong. This approach is not within the realm of economics and thus not a topic for this book. The question may also be considered from an economic standpoint, which would stress the likely costs and benefits of shirking. Employees recognize that (some) work is distasteful; the benefit of shirking is the avoiding of work, leaving individuals free to pursue other options for their time. To the individual, the costs of shirking may be small, depending on the employer's response and the degree to which the work can be shifted to other members of the organization.

It will often be useful in our discussions to adopt the jargon used by researchers in this field, referring to moral hazard as the **principal–agent problem.** The agent is hired by the principal to act on the principal's behalf. The problem facing the principal is to observe the agent's actions to determine if the agent has, in fact, acted to advance the principal's goals. Quite often, as suggested by the terminology, the principal is the authority figure: the owner of the firm, the employer or the person whose car is being fixed. However, in some instances this appearance vanishes and the principal is, for example, the depositor or an insurance company. It is important to keep straight who is to be acting on who's behalf rather than who is perceived as an authority in some connotative sense.

After reading this chapter, you should be able to:

- describe, in your own words, what is meant by moral hazard, and how this problem emerges in transactions within an informational framework;
- review and understand the concept of property rights, and to apply this concept to the organization of a value-creating firm;
- explain the many problems of team production within a moral hazard context;
- identify the factors contributing to moral hazard in an insurance setting;
- recognize the characteristics of the banking industry in the 1980s, particularly the role of deposit insurance, which made it especially susceptible to the principal–agent problem;
- discuss the principal–agent problem in standard employment contracts, and also regarding the ownership and control of a corporation;
- explain the risks facing agents in the writing of incentive-based contracts;
- discuss the conditions under which suitable contracting structures may minimize agent risk.

B. Property rights, team production and organizations

Team production: A public good?

In Chapter 5 we discussed the issue of property rights. In that discussion we argued that the establishment of well-defined property rights to resources subject to congestion could be seen as an attempt to achieve efficiency gains. The development of institutional structures such as firms can be viewed in the same light. In Chapter 6 we introduced the concept of transaction costs and argued that the firm is a device used to minimize transaction costs. We can add a new viewpoint to the purposes and functions of firms in this section where we emphasize that the contractual relations found within a firm may be viewed as establishing property rights concerning the use of the firm's resources and defining the ownership of what is produced.

This reasoning was first advanced by the economists Alchian and Demsetz (1972)[1] who argued that the creation and allocation of property rights within a firm is a response to transactional problems in general, and in particular to the problem of **team production**, which occurs when an output is produced by the simultaneous cooperation of several team members. However, they were mistaken in explicitly denying the existence of authority in organization, which we shall see to be crucial when information and contracts or property rights are incomplete. The organizational device called 'the firm' then allows people to function as one or more coordinated teams.

As early as Adam Smith, economists understood the benefits of specialization in production. Firms and organizations exist to pool the talents of individuals collectively. An organization may then be viewed as a team. Team production is not a sequence of separate, identifiable stages by members; rather it results from the simultaneous application of effort by team members. There are two complications facing team production. First, the input of individual members is not identifiable and distinguishable from that of others. Secondly, the productivity of any one team member depends crucially on the input provided by other members.

The property rights approach to analyzing team behaviour shares many similarities with the analysis of **public goods** presented in Chapter 5. A public good is a commodity that has two unique properties. First is the non-rivalrous consumption characteristic, which says that one individual's consumption of the good does not detract from another individual's enjoyment of the good, given its existence. The second property is non-excludability, or, in other words, consumers cannot be stopped from enjoying the benefits of the public good once it is produced.

Recall that no individual has an incentive to produce a public good; however, each individual has an incentive to consume it once produced. Its production advances the interests of society. For this reason, public goods are usually provided as one of the functions of government. When asked to pay for a public good, individuals have incentives strategically to misrepresent their valuations of the good. Thus, public goods are generally financed by tax collections.

The concept of team production is subject to these same problems. An agreement by all team members to work harder in order to increase joint output will be difficult to implement and enforce. Individual team members have incentives strategically to misrepresent their intentions by agreeing to some level of performance that is beneficial to the group, and then to shirk and lower their level of performance knowing full well that their input into the joint output cannot be accurately determined. In the absence of perfect and cost-free monitoring, then each person can rationally be expected to shirk and to hope to free-ride on the efforts of other team members.

A monitor as a residual claimant

Alchian and Demsetz (1972) pursue the property rights argument to provide a solution to the moral hazard inherent in team production. Their solution involves the use of a 'monitor' who would be charged with checking on the effort level of members. In many cases, having a full-time designated monitor can alleviate shirking. In other cases, it would be prohibitively costly even for a full-time monitor to assess the efforts expended by team members.

If we assume that a monitor is able to gauge the efforts of individual team members, the problem of determining the pay of the monitor remains. If the monitor is simply a team member who is assigned the monitor role, then he will have the same incentive to shirk as other team members. In common parlance this is equivalent to 'putting the fox in charge of the henhouse'.

To promote efficiency, the role of the monitor must be defined as having some property rights to what is produced. Efficiency dictates that the monitor be made a **residual claimant** to the benefits of joint production. Each member of the team would receive a contractually determined wage for his efforts; after these and all other expenses have been paid, the monitor receives whatever residual is left. The more effectively the team operates, the bigger the residual will be. Thus, the monitor will have a definite interest in promoting the efficiency of the team.

Ownership and control: A connection

Recall our discussion in Chapter 5 of the 'tragedy of the commons'. There is a single resource (grazing land) to be allocated to multiple users. In the absence of established property rights, the land is formally owned by everyone, and in effect by no one. The ruin of the Commons could be prevented by assigning ownership to some party, who would allocate its current use in such a way as to guarantee its future existence. The monitor, in some capacity as a residual claimant, is in effect given property rights to the output produced by the team. If the monitor is also given control over the contractual arrangements then, by pursuing his own selfish interests, the monitor will encourage efficiency in team production.

Although seemingly intuitive, the logic that a strong connection exists between the owners of an enterprise and those who control the enterprise has far-reaching implications. In Chapter 1 we identified the separation of ownership and control as a major organizational problem to be overcome as firms attempt to organize economic activity so as to maximize value. This is the same problem as that facing the common grazing land in that famous example of a public good causing market failure.

There may be some doubt forming in your mind at this point. You may stand ready to question the relevance of our discussion of property rights and team production by pointing out that no one entity could ever simultaneously 'own' and 'control' a firm such as IBM or ICI. Actually your point is right on the mark and well taken. No single entity could ever accomplish this task. The problem facing large and small organizations is to determine the best way to simulate, or approximate, this necessary connection between ownership and control.

In any joint production effort, suppose that one worker is thought to be performing poorly. Her first reply is going to be that she was adversely affected by some random element such as a mechanical defect, poor materials or the receipt of bad data owing to some transmission error. Her second reply is going to be that other team members failed to perform to specification, reducing the effectiveness of her effort. Since both of these replies rely on the importance of random effects, they illustrate the nature of the risks involved in monitoring.

The complex web of contractual relations within an organization may reasonably be expected to exhibit instances of moral hazard. Firm production has been termed team production and presents several difficulties. Any team member's output is determined only with difficulty. One solution that would promote efficiency is to appoint a monitor who is also made a residual claimant to the value created by the firm.

C. Team production: Coordination and motivation

In the previous section, we discussed the issue of property rights and the organization of productive resources accomplished by firms in a team, or joint, production context. In this section we continue along these lines, only now we examine the same situation in more of a managerial context. In addition, we expand the ownership and property rights line of reasoning into several applied dimensions. We now consider: the incentive problem, the horizon problem and the inalienability problem facing managers in team production situations in virtually all companies and organizations.

The incentive problem

For the selfish individual, team production presents incentives to shirk, largely for two, related reasons. First, it is impossible to determine exactly the effort expended by any individual member; hence, management (or the principal) cannot determine exactly which individuals are shirking. Secondly, the individual reaps all the gains from his own shirking, whereas the costs are distributed over all members of the group. The dilemma posed in providing motivation in these situations is termed the **incentive problem**.

Management attempts at dealing with the incentive problem can be categorized into two general techniques: the carrot method, and the stick method. The **carrot method** covers all incentive packages that attempt to encourage individual responsibility by linking an employee's pay to performance. In a sense, commissions assign to employees property rights to the output created by the team. If extra output is created, at least some of this additional value is passed along to the employee. In a limited sense, then, commissions or productivity bonuses assign to the team member some property rights to the residual value of production.

To see why, consider the view of the firm offered by Alchian and Demsetz (1972) and discussed in the previous section. Under this view, the firm organizes productive activity and pays the factors of production a fixed wage. Any value remaining flows to the residual claimant. The main result of the work of Alchian and Demsetz is that an arrangement that places contractual rights in the hands of a 'monitor' promotes efficiency and alleviates some aspects of the principal–agent problem. Clearly, the carrot method of providing commission-based and other performance-based pay schemes is a step in that direction. Who better to fill the role of the monitor than the employees themselves?

The **stick method** implies a less subtle approach. In its crudest form, the stick method may amount to a supervisor yelling at, perhaps even threatening to fire, employees in response to some perceived misdeed. Usually, the stick method amounts to a substantial set of work rules coupled with a great deal of monitoring or supervision.

The question of choosing either a carrot or a stick approach in designing incentive systems is usually one of degree, although for a number of reasons we would expect one or the other to be predominant.

The horizon problem

The **horizon problem** refers to the potential mismatch between the planning horizon of the decision maker and the planning horizon of those affected by the manager's decision. Put another way, the horizon problem highlights the possibility that planners are not inclined to imput into their decision calculus the costs and benefits that their current actions might have after they have left the business.

Analogous to the incentive problem, the horizon issue is also within the realm of property rights, only along a temporal dimension. The manager, or decision maker, has property rights that expire at some date known perhaps only by the manager. If the manager is a residual claimant today, it may be in her interests to alter the current and future stream of costs and benefits. If possible, he/she can cause the benefits to occur prior to the expiration of her property rights, and the costs to occur after. In more common language, the selfish manager may leave others 'holding the bag'.

The inalienability problem

Sometimes efficiency is affected in organizations when the net benefit flows from a business relationship cannot be sold by those who currently hold the rights to those flows. When this occurs, economists say that the manager faces the **inalienability problem**. There is a distinct difference between the inalienability problem and the horizon problem discussed earlier. The horizon problem considered situations when the property rights could be transferred by the current holder and was concerned with the value of those rights. The inalienability problem is relevant when those rights in effect cannot be transferred.

As a simple example, consider the care given to vehicles by those who rent them. The customers of automobile rental firms such as Hertz or Avis are not likely to check oil and transmission fluid levels, tyre pressure, or fuel filter condition. Those who own their own cars are more inclined to check these items themselves, or to contract to have someone else do it regularly.

An asset owner who cannot pass title to assets onto others has much in common with car renters. The owner may be reluctant to consider the future consequences of his current actions. This presents some significant drawbacks to efficient actions. One interesting application of this idea concerns some very successful businesses created largely through the efforts of a single person or some small group of people.

Individual reputations may also be inalienable. The giant retailing chain Wal-Mart was established largely by Sam Walton. Apple Computer began as a small player in the personal computer market place in the early 1980s and rose to become an industry giant challenging even the mighty 'Big Blue', IBM. Steve Jobs was one of the founders of Apple Computers, but was ultimately fired by the board of directors. Similarly, Bill Gates, at one time was reported to own over 40 per cent of the largest software company ever, Microsoft. It is true, however, that Bill Gates' right to future benefit flows is partly inalienable. If he were to leave Microsoft or sell his holding, the value of the firm, and hence the value of the Gates holding in the firm, would undoubtedly decline. In any team production setting, the manager must not only be concerned with monitoring the actions of the team members, but also be made aware of the incentives facing each team member. What we have discussed in this section are managerial problems that occur within the broader realm of moral hazard. The incentive, inalienable asset, and horizon problems are each concerned not only with the monitoring of team members but also with the incentives faced by each team member.

D. Moral hazard in insurance markets

Imperfect information and risk aversion

Moral hazard arises in contracting situations for two reasons: positive measurement costs and misaligned incentives. Insurance markets provide a rich environment for moral hazard. Before we focus entirely on the moral hazard issues, let us briefly review the basic mechanics of insurance markets.

With the exception of the 'Gypsy fortune teller' present at most carnivals and charity bazaars and a few shady characters routinely found near horse-racing tracks, most individuals are unable to predict the future. Everyone faces future risks in the form of possible losses (and, theoretically, gains). Families risk having their homes burgled or burnt down; individuals risk death, poor health, or accidents requiring visits to the doctor; multinational corporations risk changes in exchange rates; farmers risk the loss of their crops. We define **risk averse** individuals as those who dislike risk and are willing to pay some explicit or implicit payment to have the risk removed.

In each of these situations, institutions that serve an insuring function have emerged to transfer the risk from one party to another. Property insurance eliminates a family's risk concerning fire and theft. Life and medical insurance covers individual risks of poor health and early death. A variety of financial contracts consisting of options, forward contracts and futures exist to protect the multinational corporations from sudden, unanticipated swings in the exchange rate, and the farmers from unforeseen bad (and good) weather.

In every insurance situation there is a buyer and a seller of risk. In the above examples the families and individuals sell risk to insurance companies. The multinational firm and the farmer in effect sell risk to investors in the financial markets. The gain to the sellers of risk is clear: they benefit from transferring their risk to another party. The gain to the buyer of the risk is not so obvious.

Insurance companies and other buyers of risk profit for one simple reason: pooling independent risks. Two events are said to be independent if the occurrence of one does not change the probability that the other will occur. For example, the fact that you won last night's card game will not influence the probability that you win tomorrow's lottery draw. More importantly, the fact that Mr Jones, a policyholder of Bangup Auto Insurance Company, is filing a claim to cover a loss from a car accident today does not influence the probability that Mr Smith, a second policyholder of Bangup Auto Insurance Company, will file a claim today (unless, of course, it is known that Mr Jones happened to bump into Mr Smith).

The one basic truth behind the economics of insurance is that, when several parties face independent risks, these risks can be shared and the costs of bearing these risks can be reduced, if not technically eliminated. The **principle of risk-sharing** – the sharing of independent risks reduces the total cost of bearing the risk – underlies all financial insurance arrangements.

Insurance companies can profit by bearing the risk of policyholders and in effect pooling them. Of course, if the risks are not independent, pooling may fail to reduce the risk to the insurance company. Property insurers in Florida made very large payouts in 1993 in response to the extensive damage done by Hurricane Andrew. Many insurers rightly argued that pooling the risks of Florida property owners was unprofitable given that the risk that any one policyholder would file a claim from hurricane damage was not independent from the risk that other policyholders would file similar claims.

Even if an insurer is able to pool the perceived risks in an effort to eliminate them, there are moral hazard problems to be overcome in which the insurer is the principal and the insured the agent. The insured (agent) can affect the benefits from the transaction received by the insurer (principal) in a number of ways. First, the agent can take more risks than he would in the absence of insurance. Secondly, the agent can lie to the principal concerning the terms of the insurance contract. This would be the case, for example, if the agent claims to have taken steps to minimize the risks he poses to the insurer.

Moral hazard is present in insurance markets if two conditions hold. First, after purchasing an insurance policy, the insurance buyer (agent) must be able to take actions that alter the probability of the loss or the size of the loss. Secondly, it must be so costly for the principal (insurance seller) to observe these actions that monitoring the buyer's actions is economically unfeasible. Because of these high monitoring costs, the insuring company cannot change the terms of the policy after the insured acts to change the risks he transfers. The insurance company is then exploited by a consumer.

In the insurance setting it is hard to determine the efficiency impacts of moral hazard. Consider life insurance. It seems unlikely that a great many people would alter their behaviour in such a way as to encourage their own death simply so that their beneficiaries can cash in on their policies. A small percentage of individuals do, however, commit suicide. Insurance companies have taken steps to mitigate the impact of policyholder suicide. All life insurance policies issued in the United States and other countries contain provisions barring payment of claims for suicide before a specified amount of time has elapsed (either one or two years). Milgrom and Roberts (1992, p. 178) report that life insurance statistics show that the probability that a policyholder commits suicide is lowest in the twelfth or twenty-fourth month after the policy has been issued and highest in the thirteenth and twenty-fifth months.

Regarding health insurance, again it is difficult to determine whether or not the moral hazard problem encourages inefficient behaviour. In this context, we would expect individuals to visit doctors more than they otherwise would. At one extreme, some individuals will overuse this resource and visit the doctor for every little (normal) ache, pain and sneeze. For most people, however, there may be a benefit to their health. Clearly, any arrangement that encourages a healthier society has at least some efficiency characteristics and is not, by definition, socially inefficient.

From this perspective, moral hazard in certain insurance markets may not be wasteful, damaging or evil. All it represents is that insurance coverage has lowered the cost of something that people value – medical care. Because individuals are rational, they simply consume more of that good. Regarding medical insurance, it can even be argued that efficiency gains exist from this 'overuse'. In the next section we will discuss a particular financial insurance arrangement plagued by moral hazard. Federally sponsored deposit insurance programmes are typically plagued by principal–agent problems, and it can be easily argued that these inefficiencies and 'perverse incentives' *are* wasteful, damaging and possibly evil from society's point of view.

E. The federal deposit insurance crisis

The prominent role of deposit insurance in the US economic system is best understood by first reflecting on the history of deposit insurance schemes in the United States. The first step in understanding the problems with these programmes unfortunately involves a very simple understanding of the balance sheets of deposit-taking institutions in the US economy. Of particular importance are the items on that balance sheet that represent the position of the owners of the institution.

The second step in understanding the failure of federally sponsored deposit insurance problems in the late 1980s and early 1990s involves an appreciation of the forces at work in and around the banking industry. We can identify the severe moral hazard problems between the principal (the federal government, and all taxpayers) and the agents (insured deposit-taking institutions). As we shall see below, the agents' incentives were not consistent with the interests of the principal, a situation made worse by a failure of monitoring mechanisms.

The federal deposit insurance crisis also shares a key element from the team production reasoning considered earlier: the agents did not share the full costs of their actions; rather these costs were shared by other deposit-taking institutions and eventually by Joe Public.

Sorry, a brief history lesson

In response to the Great Depression, the US Congress created the Federal Deposit Insurance Corporation (FDIC) and the Federal Savings and Loan Insurance Corporation (FSLIC) in the 1930s. The purpose of these programmes was to protect the savings and banking deposits of US citizens in the event of institution failure. All commercial banks were insured by the FDIC, while the FSLIC insured deposits in the nation's savings and loan institutions (similar to UK building societies). Deposit insurance was not a new idea in the United States. Between 1907 and 1924, eight mid-western states had enacted their own deposit insurance programmes; each of these failed quickly and spectacularly.[2] In our discussion, we will not differentiate between commercial banks and savings and loan institutions, referring to each of them simply as banks. There is little harm in this simplification and, when we do focus on events in the savings and loan industry, we will drop this simple terminology.

For the first fifty-odd years, the federally mandated deposit insurance systems seemed to work well. Banks rarely failed. In the mid-1980s, however, bank failures increased markedly: within several years more banks had failed than in the preceding 50 years. The impacts on the FDIC and FSLIC were enormous. The FSLIC went bankrupt in 1986; the FDIC followed in 1990. By bankrupt, we mean that the cost of bailing out failed institutions (claims against the insurance fund) exceeded the cumulative stock of current and past premiums. Differences are borrowed from the US Treasury.

A bank's balance sheet

Before we can fully discuss and explain the underlying forces behind the deposit insurance crisis, it will be necessary to review some of the basic 'mechanics' behind the operations of deposit-taking institutions if we are fully to develop the importance of moral hazard issues in the most direct way.

Consider the balance sheet of a bank. On the one side are the assets, things the bank owns: cash, the bank's deposits at the Federal Reserve, and loans and investments. On the other side are the liabilities of the bank: funds the bank owes to others; for the most part, these are deposit accounts. There is a very important third component, owners' equity, which represents the capital used by the owners of the institution to finance the operation of the bank. According to a basic accounting identity:

$$\text{ASSETS} = \text{LIABILITIES} + \text{OWNERS' EQUITY}$$

A bank is said to be solvent so long as the value of its assets and owners' equity exceeds its liabilities. Recall that a portion (in fact a very large portion) of a bank's assets is the loans and investments it has made. Solvency requires then that, if push came to shove, and depositors demanded their deposits, the bank could pay them. Funds could be raised by selling off some of the bank's assets; if these were not sufficient, funds could be taken from the owners' stake in the institution.

The owners' equity represents the amount of capital invested in a bank or savings institution. The institution's charter is another source of value to the owners of the bank. Not anyone can open and operate a deposit institution; a charter must be obtained from either the state or national banking authorities. Obtaining a charter requires a substantial application process where the authorities must approve the major players in any proposed bank, and where minimum capital requirements and market definition are determined. In the managerial context, a bank's charter represents an inalienable asset, that is, one whose value cannot be transferred from the current holder.

Traditionally, the chartering agencies would not encourage 'reckless' competition among banks, and limited the number of charters in any one market. Thus, the charter became an entry barrier supporting profits for some lucky institutions and functioning much like the certification and licence requirements for practising medicine or, law or for providing certain accounting services. These restrictions deter entry into the medical, legal and accounting industries and, thus, safeguard the incomes of many doctors, lawyers and accountants.

In other words, the charter of a bank may have value. Owners may have an incentive not only to protect their own capital but also to protect the value of their charter.

If depositors are fairly sophisticated and can determine that a bank's assets are quickly falling in value, they may fear for their deposits. This fear is taken away by the presence of deposit insurance; if the depositors know that their funds are safeguarded by some party, then they will not fear bank failure. Deposit insurance is clearly in the interest of the depositors: it protects their vested interest regardless of the health of the deposit institution (up to some maximum amount, currently $100,000). The guarantee in effect removes any incentive depositors may have to monitor the banks that hold their balances.

Although beneficial to the public, the existence of deposit insurance creates quite a different set of incentives for the bank owners.

Bank management knows that because depositors' interests are guaranteed by the government, depositors will not carefully watch the actions of management. They will seek to exploit the risk–return trade-off in order to increase their profits. Their loans will become a bit more speculative. They may even reduce their equity in order to increase the rate of return on their capital. Remember that the owners' equity represents capital they have invested in the organization, and they will always act so as to earn as many rewards as possible.

The environment begins to change

In the late 1970s and early 1980s the environment began to change at both commercial banks and thrifts (savings and loans or building societies). Interest rates began to rise. Institutions that had previously made long-term loans at low interest rates (3–6 per cent) were having to pay double that to attract deposits to support those loans. This proved especially difficult for the nation's savings and loans (or thrift) institutions, which traditionally held a large portion of their assets in residential mortgages. New competitors emerged: life insurance companies and other financial intermediaries offered to lend money to what used to be the customers of banks and savings and loans. Some of the best corporate borrowers were lost to the emerging direct market for corporate debt.

At the same time, restrictions on markets were crumbling. Aggressive institutions appeared in geographical markets that had been profitable for years. Bank expansion was encouraged by economies of scale (the reduction in unit costs at higher levels of output) in banking services. Banks expand by increasing the size of their loan portfolios. Quick expansion means to take on more risk, in terms of either less diversification or lower probability of repayment.

Moral hazard rears its ugly head

For thrifts, the higher interest rates paid for deposits meant, in effect, buying high and selling low, given their emphasis on residential mortgages. Further, many thrifts had expanded their lending in commercial real estate: shopping malls, resorts, and office buildings. Many of these projects were large, glamorous, hyped by publicity – and – unprofitable. Unfortunately, in some regions of the country (notably Florida, California and Texas), land values began to fall, and many development schemes went belly up. Thus, the value of the assets of many thrifts fell drastically.

Using the basic accounting identity above, given that the value of their assets had deteriorated, the value of the equity stake held by management fell as well.

A second, more subtle, factor also contributed greatly to the moral hazard problem faced by thrifts. When an institution is protected from competition, it has market power and will earn significant economic profits. The increased competition fostered by regulations (ironically these regulations were designed to help the industry) eroded the value of their charters.

These events both undermined the incentives for the owners of thrifts to engage in safe banking. With little to lose and deposit insurance to cover the downside, thrift managers increased the riskiness of their loan portfolios. On the upside, if these risky loans paid off, the larger profits would earn them bonuses and restore profitability to their institutions. On the downside, if the new, riskier, loans and investments failed, the owners would lose little more than they already had, and the risk would have been transferred to the deposit insurance programme.

Two regulatory responses

The regulators responded to this crisis in 1980 on two fronts. First was the policy of **regulatory forbearance**, which allowed insolvent thrifts to continue operations in the naive hope that continued operations would restore profitability. Most notably, the regulators allowed thrift institutions to change their accounting methods in evaluating assets – in a way that overstated their values. The insolvent institutions became known as 'zombie' thrifts.

The second part of the regulatory response was to allow thrifts to invest in assets that were previously unallowed. Thrifts were permitted to invest in more non-residential real estate and, most notably, junk bonds.

The justification for these policies was that the cost of the clean-up was much too high. The General Accounting Office estimated in 1982 that, at that time, it would have cost $20 billion to close down all the insolvent thrifts and insure the depositors. Of course, by 1988 the actual cost of dealing with some of the thrift problem was close to $70 billion. Inflation alone accounts for only about 6 per cent of the increase.

Clearly neither of these responses served to mitigate the moral hazard problem facing the thrift owners. By 1988, the FSLIC was unable to keep up with the problem. Monitoring was difficult given the large number of institutions becoming insolvent and also because of staff reductions within the FSLIC caused by the federal budget cuts ordered by President Reagan.

The closer a bank is to insolvency, the more serious the moral hazard problem becomes. The equity and charter values were pretty much gone at many institutions; as such, equity holders had little to lose. The delay in closing these institutions provided the motivation to gamble with depositor money. The lax restrictions on allowable investments gave thrift owners something to gamble with.

By 1988, even the reluctant regulators were willing to admit to a problem. Their initial reply was the passage of the Financial Institution Reform, Recovery, and Enforcement Act (FIRREA) of 1989. FIRREA abolished the FSLIC and moved thrift institutions under the FDIC umbrella of coverage and regulation. The Federal Home Loan Bank Board, which was responsible for thrift supervision, was replaced with a new Office of Thrift Supervision housed in the Treasury Department. Deposits at thrifts were then insured by a new Savings Association Insurance Fund, a division of the FDIC. In addition to these organizational changes, regulatory changes were also instituted.

Under FIRREA, capital requirements at thrifts were doubled, putting them on a par with those at commercial banks. Additionally, assets were grouped according to riskiness; higher-risk assets could be held only if increasingly higher percentages of capital were held to support them. FIRREA also changed the pattern of loans and investments of thrifts. Savings and loan institutions are now required to have 70 per cent of their assets in mortgage-related investments; commercial real estate loans could be no more than four times capital.

Each of these changes was designed to force an institution's owners to have a larger stake in their business. Thrifts were allowed to make risky investments, but only if the owners set aside increasingly more capital to be available if the riskier investments were to fail. Obviously, the new standards are designed to provide incentives to thrift owners to pick their investments more carefully.

FIRREA and later legislation, the Federal Deposit Insurance Corporation Improvement Act (FDICIA) of 1991, did two additional things to eliminate the agency problems at banks and thrifts. First, all institutions would be subject to more careful (and, it was threatened, more frequent) audits by regulatory agencies. Secondly, this legislation gave the FDIC more powers in closing institutions. The legislation prohibits 'zombie' institutions. Additionally, current law phases out the ability of the FDIC to reimburse depositors over the stated maximum amount, currently $100,000. The effects of these laws, it is hoped, will be to remove more of the perverse incentives created by deposit insurance. Insolvent institutions will not be able to undertake undue risk, counting on the deposit insurance system to bail them out. Furthermore, large, institutional depositors will have an incentive closely to monitor the financial well-being of their institutions.

F. Moral hazard: Impact on the organization

Employee shirking

Employment relationships are essentially incomplete contracts written between employers and employees. Owing to their incomplete nature, the vagueness of these relationships has many implications. Now we consider only one dimension of this vagueness, that associated with imperfect monitoring and the misalignment of interests of the principal and the agent. Workers recognize that monitoring is imperfect and that workers may enjoy the full benefits of their shirking while spreading the costs of their shirking around, to be borne by all team members.

The importance of moral hazard in employment situations is evidenced by the large number of incentive pay systems currently in use. As will be argued later in section H, perhaps the most efficient compensation scheme would involve workers being paid for the effort they supply to their employer. Employees provide their intellect, charm, computer skills, knowledge and the sweat off their back. It is, however, impossible to measure this effort directly so employers often base pay on measured output, which itself is subject to random influences.

The problem within the employment relationship is how to motivate workers whose actions the principal can only imperfectly observe. In Chapter 13 we focus on this issue in greater detail. For now suffice it to say that one way of dealing with moral hazard problems in the employment relationship is for management to reward workers who do not shirk, but to withhold these rewards for some period.

Managerial misbehaviour: When the bosses shirk

Although most of us envision shirking as a response of the usual, typical or rank and file worker, it is not at all uncommon at much higher levels in large organizations. We now discuss two aspects of **managerial misbehaviour** that have attracted ample attention in recent years involving the tricky relationship between firm managers and stockholders. Within these organizations, the goals of upper management may be quite different from the goals of the shareholders; given that shareholders have limited ability to monitor the performance of CEOs, the framework is ripe for agency problems. A second source of managerial misbehaviour became evident in the surge of corporate takeovers during the 1980s and early 1990s. The justification for many of these takeovers was simple. A target firm was viewed as having certain assets and a management team that did not make the best use of those assets. The acquiring firm would then have reason to purchase shares in the target firm and put the assets of the target firm to this better use.

The roles of upper management and boards of directors in large corporations are related. Senior executives, in Anglo-American firms at least, are supposed to advance the interests of the firm's owners (shareholders); the board of directors is to supervise these managers. Thus, as is well known, in large corporations there is a **separation of ownership and control**.

The difficult situation is compounded by the incentives of the owners. Frequently, ownership is spread over many different individuals and institutions, none of which may have the resources or interests in any one company in which they invest. Large institutional investors have traditionally taken a hands-off approach and concentrated their efforts on diversification.

Critics of this ownership system maintain that CEOs' interests are quite different from the owners' interests, and that it has become quite difficult for the owners to discipline their management teams. The interests of the managers may well be served by keeping unprofitable operations, resisting takeovers, pursuing short-term profits at the expense of longer-term increases in firm value, and lavishing themselves with perquisites. Additionally, it became common practice at many large firms for the CEO to name some members of the board of directors.

Economists have concluded that it is not at all clear that upper management teams are disciplined when necessary. There are two ways in which the interests of owners and managers may be aligned in a fairly subtle way. First, the managers' compensation packages may provide stock in the firm they manage. Secondly, the reputation of the manager may serve to influence her behaviour. The manager might recognize that ultimately her employment is at the will of the stockholders; it would be wise to maintain some interest in her own marketability. A manager who took undue advantage of imperfect monitoring might find it quite difficult to pursue other employment opportunities.

The ultimate form of discipline occurs when a manager or CEO is displaced by unhappy stockholders. When shareholders take an active role in the firm's operations and attempt to secure drastic changes in the organization, they are said to participate in **shareholder activism**.

Shareholder activism is becoming more of a force in most stock markets. Starting in the 1993, many institutional investors got into the act to influence the decisions of managements in which they have a large stake. The ultimate form of discipline for the corporate managers is of course the threat of corporate takeover, the topic to which we now turn.

There is an efficiency argument behind corporate takeovers. Suppose that the existing management of a firm has operated so that the value of the firm is approximately $2 million. The 50,000 shares of the firm in the hands of the public are routinely bought and sold at prices very close to $40 per share. An alternative management team may feel confident that it can make better use of the firm's resources, perhaps believing that it could raise the value of the firm to $3 million. The alternative management team would then be willing to pay as much as $3million/50,000 per share to own the firm. The acquiring firm would, of course, attempt to keep its actual valuation of the target firm secret.

In this light, takeovers may be viewed as auctions. The shares of publicly traded companies are available for sale, if their current owners can be induced to part with them. Efficiency would dictate that the shares should go to the highest bidder for, in that case, the assets that comprise the target firm will be put to their best use. Some market professionals talk of a **takeover market** where buyers actively identify and pursue firms they deem attractive.

The threat of a takeover provides an important discipline device even for firms not seen as potential targets. A well-managed firm is unlikely to be taken over because the acquiring party would be hard pressed to make better use of the firm's assets.

The efficiency-enhancing aspects of takeovers may seem obvious. The principal–agent problem may imply, in a large corporation, that management is taking advantage of the firm, acting in a way to enrich themselves at the expense of shareholders. The threat of takeover, or takeover itself, may be sufficient to correct this inefficiency; but it may create others.

Very often, takeovers involve a restructuring of the acquired firm: some divisions or facilities are closed, others are sold off. The repercussions of these changes may be quite negative from the employees' view. Nobody likes to have their job cut or moved to some distant location. Recall that behind the concept of efficiency is the idea that everyone can be made better off without making anyone else worse off. In the merger and acquisition game, a new corporate structure represents a different allocation of resources, and displaced employees typically suffer losses, as we discuss in Chapter 11 below.

A second, and more direct argument against the efficiency of corporate takeovers is the creation of **poison pills** by the acquiring firms.[3] A poison pill is a defence against corporate takeover under which the target firm agrees to allow its current shareholders to purchase additional shares in the firm once some designated third party acquires a set percentage of the ownership of the firm. This strategy will raise the cost of acquiring the firm. Although poison pills may seem like a good way to prevent corporate takeover, their value to shareholders is dubious.

First, recall that shareholders may favour takeover, preferring either to sell their shares at the higher price offered by the acquiring firm, or to maintain share ownership and enjoy the larger profits earned by the acquiring firm (of course this second option requires a shared vision of future success). Secondly, notice that poison pills are clearly in the interest of the firm's current managers who may use them as a way to avoid market discipline for inefficient management. Michael Jensen (1988) has collected evidence on the use of poison pills by large corporations and came to some startling conclusions. Once a firm adopts a poison pill takeover defence, the value of the firm typically falls. Also, firms that are more likely to adopt poison pill defences are firms where the managers and members of the board of directors typically hold very few of the company shares.

Other sources of agency problems

Another source of agency problems arising in modern corporations involves how the firm finances its activities. Typically, firms are financed through a combination of **debt** and **equity**. Debt holders are anyone who has loaned the firm money without receiving an ownership stake in return: bond holders, suppliers who offer credit, and banks are some examples. Equity holders, on the other hand, are the stockholders in most corporate structures. Usually, the debt holders receive fixed, stipulated payments while equity holders are residual claimants on current and future profits.

In some instances disagreement arises between those holding debt in the firm and those owning shares of stock. The reason is fairly straightforward. Debt holders normally have no say in the operation of the firm; stockholders do. At times, the interests of these two groups diverge and the debt holders feel at odds with the stockholders. If the firm defaults on payment of creditors, then the debt holders actually become the residual claimants and essentially assume control. During the late 1980s and continuing into the 1990s debt holders began placing demands and restrictions on the firms that borrowed their funds. We will pick up this train of thought again in Chapter 10.

The crisis in federally provided deposit insurance is an excellent example of this in a somewhat related context, so we will not dwell on it again. Basically, the equity holders are those who own the bank; the debt holders are depositors.

G. Adjustments and allowing for moral hazard

Relationship between monitoring and efficiency

Moral hazard in a contracting environment creates so called 'agency problems' in relationships where a principal basically hires an agent to pursue the principal's interests. If it were cost-free to monitor the actions of the agent, and the actions of many agents can be readily checked, then there are no implications for economic efficiency. In some cases however, the actions of the agent are observed imperfectly and the agent and principal do not share the same incentives.

In this section we will discuss some of the issues surrounding efforts to mitigate the efficiency-reducing effects of moral hazard. In all fairness, we point out that moral hazard cannot be eliminated in many situations; rather the parties to a transaction simply adjust to its presence. Throughout this section we will make frequent use of the organizational, insurance, and ownership examples discussed previously.

The logical choice for eliminating agency problems is to improve monitoring activities by lowering their cost. All corporations are required, for example, to have certain financial reports audited by independent accounting firms. Presumably, independent auditors would not share with the audited corporations any gains from the production of false or misleading financial statements.

In the instance of health insurance, the UK national health service and most health maintenance organizations (HMOs) do not allow patients to see highly specialized doctors without a recommendation from a general practitioner. If market charges are any indication, the services of general practitioners are much less expensive than are the services of a doctor with a much smaller area of expertise. Requiring a referral is an attempt at monitoring the patient behaviour. In Germany patients can consult specialists directly and total health care costs are almost double the UK's 7 per cent of GNP. However patient waiting times are much lower in Germany and hospital infrastructure much more up to date.

One of the major problems in the deposit insurance crisis was a lack of monitoring by the regulatory staffs of state and local governments. The alternative incentives of the typical CEO and his shareholders present problems that may be reduced by monitoring. If the shareholders are willing, their efforts may directly influence the actions of CEOs and corporate boards of directors. One interesting truth in the matter is that CEOs often demand to appoint at least some of the members of the boards of directors.

Monitoring is typically a costly behaviour, and may require good faith on the part of the agent in developing an appropriate measurement. Consider the deposit insurance crisis. The insurance-providing agency (the principal) is dependent on the accounting and other records kept by the insured institution (agent). It was not unheard of for banks to lie to regulators, or to misrepresent the value of their holdings. The costs would have been extremely high for the regulators to reconstruct the banks' financial statements from transaction-level documentation; it also would have been exorbitantly costly for the regulators to ascertain the true values of the banks' investments.

It might also very well be that principals expect a certain level of misbehaviour by the agents and simply consider this a cost when conducting their decision-making calculus. Employers might rationally expect a certain amount of shirking by their employees and recognize that eliminating it would be prohibitively expensive. At most commercial research labs, for example, research scientists frequently publish their results in technical and scientific journals. The value of these publications to the labs themselves is questionable; the value to the scientists is clear: enhanced professional reputation and better mobility.

In some situations, monitoring may be provided by an established market. For corporations in reasonably competitive product markets, failure may come quickly. As already discussed, a competitive takeover market will punish poorly behaving CEOs and their management teams. Some proposals for reforming the deposit insurance crisis centred on a larger reliance on market discipline. Large institutional investors often had the resources to acquire the necessary information to accurately predict failures, and the technical savvy to assess this information. If their actions were commonly known, then smaller depositors could be expected to follow suit.

Because of the nature of the moral hazard problem, monitoring may not alleviate (and may even aggravate) tension between principals and agents. This is because measurement, no matter how costly, may be imperfect in a number of ways. Quite often these problems come to light when the agent is motivated by some performance incentive such as a sales-based commission.

Quite often, only the result is measured. There is no leeway for accounting for good luck that may have befallen the agent; likewise there is no way to determine if something outside of the agent's control affected the result. Each of these is a source of randomness that may put the employer and employee at odds with each other.

H. Contractual risks for the agent

The importance of avoiding risks to the agent

Two general characteristics are relevant for our current discussion:

1 Motivating agents through performance-based incentives will enhance efficiency in the principal–agent relationship so long as the performance being rewarded advances the interest of the principal.
2 The measurements necessary in incentive systems are far from perfect; this creates an environment of risk for the agent.

The first of these general characteristics merely points out the benefits of aligning the interests of the agent with those of the principal, and then rewarding the agent for success in pursuing those goals. Recalling the situation surrounding the deposit insurance crisis of the late 1980s, the interests of the bank manager were clearly not in line with those of the deposit insurer. The regulatory reforms (FIRREA and FDICIA) were attempts at aligning the interests of the deposit institutions with the interests of the deposit insurer. Currently, banks are rewarded for making safer loans and investments by having to keep less supporting capital. The environment surrounding deposit-taking institutions is clearly much safer now than in the past; the efficiency gains are well defined.

The second of these general conditions may not be as obvious as the first. Surely we would all agree that agents – be they workers, deposit institutions or CEOs – should have a link between their performance and their compensation. However, actually measuring their performance is costly and, usually, imprecise. This imprecision creates risk for both the principal and the agent.

Once created, this risk can be a source of inefficiencies in the relationship. Put in the simplest terms possible, one reason that some parties are agents instead of principals is because they are risk averse. Recall that we consider individuals to be risk averse if they dislike risk and are willing to pay some explicit or implicit payment to have the risk removed. When you graduate from your business programme, you will have the basic skills necessary to compete in the business world. Notice, however, that very few business graduates become 'their own bosses' upon graduation; most go to work for others. The obvious reason for this is that agents bear less risk regarding the stability of their future incomes.

This is not to say that being an agent completely eliminates risk. Rather, so long as monitoring is costly and imperfect, and so long as earnings are linked to performance, some risk remains.

If principals are to monitor the behaviour of agents, the transaction must recognize the risk imputed to the agent from imperfect measurements. In a contractual framework, the risk takes the form of a wider range of possible outcomes for the agent.

Sources of risk in the principal–agent contract

There are many ways that randomness might enter the picture and affect the process of contracting between principal and agent. We will explore these in this section within the context of one particular principal–agent relationship: employer and employee. Our analysis is germane to the more general principal–agent scenario, but we focus on the employment relationship because of its familiarity, and to help prepare us for the part of the text dealing with managing human resources.

To help set the stage for investigation into the risks involved in an employer–employee relationship, let us pretend that we live in a perfect world. It is not required that employees expend full effort at their jobs. To a certain extent, workers would be able to pick their position on the shirk/don't shirk spectrum. There would be variation in wages expected by workers. Rational individuals would decide, based on their own preferences (and also on how badly they needed the money), how hard to work after they knew their rate of compensation. Employers would be able to determine the effort put in by each employee, and adjust wages accordingly.

Now to drop some of the veneer and move back towards the real world. Employers cannot identify the effort expended by any single employee; at best, employers can observe only very general things: hours at work, work experience, training completed, sick days, etc. Employers also have, at best, a limited idea of individual output, but they may be able to observe team output. The central problem in the employment relationship is then that employers face significant obstacles in observing individual effort. The employer is in the position of assessing the efforts of any one individual from (usually) indirect evidence. This assessment, along with imperfect indirect measurements, forces employees to bear some risk, no longer knowing for certain how their performance is assessed.

The first way that randomness may enter employee evaluations lies in the very nature of team production and is internal to the organization. Earlier we discussed this topic in great detail. For now we recall only the main points: the input of any one team member cannot be determined, and the 'output' of any single team member depends crucially on the inputs of other team members.

A second way randomness may enter into an assessment of employee productivity lies outside the organization. Factors outside of the individual's control may affect their productivity. Consider the petrol station on the corner, which is part of a large national chain. Quite possibly, the station manager's pay cheque may depend on the volume of sales. Sales of petrol at one location of a chain of stations may depend on the traffic flowing by the station, on consumers' experiences with other stations of that chain, or on the national advertising efforts of the parent company. Clearly, the manager does not control any of these other factors.

A third source of randomness may be caused if the performance itself entails some subjective elements by a supervisor. The influence of subjectivities is internal to the firm only in the sense that they represent a human element in conducting transactions. A waitress in a restaurant must be pleasant, welcoming and friendly to customers. Each of these terms involves a degree of subjective evaluation: one person's idea of friendly may, to another person, be insulting or even brash.

A final source of randomness arises when factors internal to the employee, but external to the firm, are recognized. Many organizations are willing to recognize that individuals may face problems affecting their performance. Some larger organizations even go so far as to provide employee programmes aimed at reducing drug dependency or dealing with other traumatic occurrences such as poor health, divorce or child care.

Basing pay on performance is not a risk-free proposition from an employee's point of view. In some situations, the entire risk is in effect shifted to employees. Sharecropping was commonly used in agriculture in many areas, and is still used today in many less developed countries. Under this arrangement, the tenant gives a set percentage of his crop to the landlord. Similarly, many telephone marketing workers are paid solely on commission. In these instances, there is no attempt to account for bad luck, and employees have complete responsibility for their actions. Most employment relationships are not like these however; instead, at least some of the risk is transferred back to the employer. In the next section we consider the mixture of risks and incentives inherent when the employer shares some (if not the majority) of the risk with the employee.

I. Implications for managers

In a complex and changing business environment, moral hazard remains unfortunately as one of the few constants affecting contracts. Economists have been aware for years of the principal–agent problem, yet have only recently become aware of its implications. From a managerial perspective, the two most interesting areas in which agency problems crop up are the external world where the firm interacts in the financial markets and the internal dealings with employees.

When the laws were written outlining the basic corporate form featuring stockholders, boards of directors and chief executive officers, much progress was made possible. Because of limited shareholder liability, huge corporations could be created and financed to accomplish great things. The implied separation of ownership and control was probably not seen as a major issue, given the existence of boards of directors. However, for many reasons, recent history has taught us that moral hazard problems between the owners of a firm (the principals) and the management running the firm (the agents) can poison the relationship. In this chapter we have argued that efficiency dictates a closer relationship between ownership and control interests.

All firms must pay their employees, and the employees must work for the firm. Efficiency seems clearly to indicate that an incentive-based scheme is necessary. However, measurement problems can throw sand in the gears of this machinery. Essentially, the workers are risk averse, and employers (the principals) reduce some of the risks associated with variable incomes in definite ways. By introducing incentive pay systems, the principals may add risk back to the relationship. In the appendix to this chapter a mathematical model highlights some of these issues and provides some guidelines.

The importance of a firm's dealings with its employees and its financial backers is hard to overstate. We have begun to analyze these problems and will consider them in much greater detail in the following chapters of this book.

J. Chapter summary and key ideas

Moral hazard arises in a contracting environment because of incomplete and asymmetric information. This class of contractual frictions has come to be called principal–agent problems, and a typical characterization involves a principal hiring an agent to act on behalf of the principal. The quandary is created because the agent has better information concerning her actions than does the principal. In order for the principal–agent problem to become operationalized, the interests of the agent must differ from those of the principal. This misalignment gives the agent incentives to act counter to the interests of the principal.

One seemingly obvious answer to the problems associated with moral hazard is to have better monitoring. In many situations this may simply prove to be impossible for two very basic reasons. First, monitoring may be a costly process and perhaps physically impossible to accomplish. Secondly, we cannot demand more monitoring without considering the opportunity cost of the principal's time. The principal must allocate time carefully: more time devoted to monitoring necessarily implies less time for other activities.

Another, seemingly obvious, answer to the moral hazard problem is to write most contracts between principal and agent with very strong incentive clauses. The problem with this approach is that in most cases it can be argued that the agent will be risk averse. When contracts are based largely on incentive schemes the agent is exposed to a number of risks. One is from fluctuating demand for the output of the firm. The other is from faulty measurements that reflect things outside of the agent's control. In short, these sources of risk may actually work to reduce efficiency.

When expressed as a form of *ex post* opportunism, one solution to the moral hazard problem is to rely on the reputation of trading partners. Where possible, information on reputations can provide potential trading partners with at least some guidance on whom to contract with and how. This solution may not be applicable to each and every transaction.

The term 'moral hazard' originated in insurance markets, and these markets provide much insight into the functioning of agents in the presence of moral hazard. In the basic insurance setting, the agent purchases some form of insurance to minimize his exposure to various risks. From the insured's point of view, it may now be beneficial to takes less care, or to expose himself to risks, because his potential losses are covered by insurance. Of course, these actions are costly to the principal, and thus the potential for inefficiencies is created.

One of the most analyzed and well-known economic calamities of this century is the crisis in the US federal deposit insurance programmes. In these programmes, many bank and savings and loan managers engaged in risky behaviour as a response to a perverse set of incentives. Money could be lent under risky conditions, earning the manager and institution large profits if the investments were successful. The downside was in effect covered by the federal government. The situation was made worse by market conditions and relatively small capital requirements for owners.

In organizations, moral hazard can take many forms. One can usually easily identify instances of employee shirking. Managerial misbehaviour by chief executive officers may also occur since the standard corporate structure provides for a separation of ownership and control. Market discipline may present an effective control on managerial activities. The basic argument for efficiency of the ubiquitous large corporation is the analogy with Darwinian natural selection applied to competitive markets. In particular, the threat of takeover represents the ultimate constraint on managerial discretion and organizational inefficiency, and so in theory should enforce value maximization.

We are very nearly through presenting the organizational tools needed to analyze firm behaviour. In the next chapter we turn our attention to the last remaining tool. In subsequent parts of the text we begin to apply these tools to better understand a firm in its dealings with the financial markets and with its employees and its position as part of a larger group of firms comprising a sector or industry.

 ## Appendix: The risk–incentive trade-off

A second efficiency function for employers

Employers play a dual role in our society. Naturally, they organize production and provide workers with a pay cheque. In this context, we also tend to attribute to employers a function of providing a type of income insurance to employees. Just as fire insurance transfers the risks faced by a home owner to the threat of fire, the employer in effect insures, via the employment relationship, the employee against randomness in income caused by two types of factors. Fluctuating industry demand would create much larger swings in income than are actually observed. Although this is interesting in its own right, we do not dwell on it now; rather we turn our attention to the second source of randomness in employee income: measurement error.

As our analysis unfolds, you will undoubtedly try to relate our model to your own experiences or knowledge of wage agreements. This is to be encouraged with some warnings. First, our model is intended to be quite general; its application to a given set of circumstances may greatly increase its complexity. Secondly, our model is constructed to emphasize certain aspects of employment relationships, and, as such, other aspects are held constant and do not explicitly appear.

We are concerned with characterizing the risks faced by employees (agents). Our analysis will consider these risks along with the measurement costs from which they arise. An efficient contract is an arrangement that balances the cost of shifting these risks from the employee against the incentive benefits that result.

In our analysis, we will concentrate on one particular measure of risk, the variability in the outcome of employee assessment. As in the choice between buying government bonds and stocks of major corporations, both the expected net return and the variability of net return are relevant. The expected return is the return that investors can rationally anticipate.

Towards a simple mathematical model

The structure of our model is relatively simple. A firm is charged with organizing labour to produce output that is sold in response to a profit motive. To keep the model as simple as possible, we will consider the simplest case imaginable: one firm selling a single product that hires only one employee. Although this assumption is clearly unrealistic it does not make the analysis unreasonable. Using a single employee as an example allows us to ignore different types of employees, which would increase the analytical content of our model exponentially.

The employee chooses the intensity of her efforts on the job. We will characterize these efforts as the employee's level of application or intensity to the job, I. Worker intensity, or energy level, is a personal choice for the individual. In our model, work *per se* is not distasteful; however, the personal cost of working at a high intensity level is greater than working at a lower intensity level. The personal cost associated with each level of intensity is determined by our worker's own tastes, preferences and attitude. We assume that a functional relationship exists and that we can write this relationship as:

$$PC = PC(I).$$

The firm in our model employs the worker and realizes that profits depend largely on the quality of the effort expended by the employee. Greater employee intensity implies larger profits. We write the firm's profit function, *PROF*, also as a function of *I*.

$$PROF = PROF(I)$$

The components of the wage

Next, it is necessary to impose some structure on the wage paid to our worker. We will assume that the worker's compensation is an increasing linear function of what the employer observes. This may seem a little vague now and very soon we will become much more concerned with what the employer observes. For now, let us say that the employer observes a quantity called *O*bserved *E*ffort *I*ntensity, which we will write as *OEI*. In particular, assume that a worker's wage payments in any time-period are of the form:

$$WAGE = B_1 + B_2(OEI)$$

The logic of this linear compensation formula is straightforward. The worker receives a base wage of B_1. To this base amount is added some component that depends on *OEI*. As *OEI* increases by one measurement unit, pay would rise by B_2. The parameter B_2 will be termed the incentive intensity parameter.

We now turn our attention back to a fuller specification of the quantity *OEI*. There are three components to *OEI* and each will add some insight into the problems of efficiently designing wage contracts in the face of imperfect measurement of employee activity.

Of the three components of *OEI*, two are lumped together in a single entity that can be observed by the employee. The direct performance indicator, *DPI*, is a joint observation on *I*, the true employee intensity, and random influences. These random influences, *RI*, are factors that affect employee productivity but are not easily identified as being attributable to any specific cause. For completeness, we include an equation linking *DPI* to *I* and *RI*.

$$DPI = I + RI$$

It will be useful to remember that the firm observes only *DPI* and cannot disentangle either *I* or *RI*.

The remaining component of the observed effort intensity, *OEI*, is the strength of overall conditions, *OC*. Overall conditions might include the strength of the market for the firm's product, overall business conditions or factors inside the firm that might affect employee productivity. We assume that both the worker and firm can observe *OC* without error.

It also seems reasonable that *OC* would receive some weighting in determining the observed effort intensity, *OEI*. This weighting could be either positive or negative depending on the impact of the outside conditions. We will use the notation for the weighting of B_3OC.

We can then write an expression for observed effort intensity as:

$$OEI = I + RI + B_3OC.$$

A negative value for B_3 would be chosen when outside conditions were favourable to employee performance. As such, some of the employee's productivity is attributable to a healthy market or some external factor increasing demand for the firm's output. Likewise, a positive value for B_3 would imply that outside conditions were unfavorable to employee performance. This would be the case if, for example, the market for the firm's output was declining.

A lot has gone on here and it may be useful briefly to review this discussion of employee wages. We began with the idea that our hypothetical employee's wage ought to be linked to her productivity, which we called observed effort intensity, or OEI. We then broke OEI down into three components, two of which were jointly observed and indistinguishable from each other. This joint observation we termed DPI, which was the sum of I and RI. The third component of OEI was overall conditions to which we attached a weight. We can sum up this development with the following three equations.

$$WAGE = B_1 + B_2(OEI)$$
$$WAGE = B_1 + B_2(DPI + B_3OC)$$
$$WAGE = B_1 + B_2(I + RI + B_3OC)$$

A fuller understanding of the last equation for $WAGE$ is obtained if we make the rationality assumption commonly made in economic analysis. In the context of our model, the rationality assumption would provide us with definite expectations concerning the three components of OEI. I is, of course, chosen by the worker; this choice will be explained in the next section. Both the worker and the firm would expect RI and OC to be zero on average. That is, in their planning, random influences cannot be predetermined and no outside influences (in terms of exceptionally strong or weak markets for the firm's output) are anticipated.[4]

What the worker faces

We now have some idea of the wage risk facing the employee and how this risk may affect her choice of I. The worker's job is to take the $WAGE$ that she expects to earn for every value of I and compare this wage with the corresponding increase in her personal cost function, $PC(I)$. Thus, our worker compares the marginal benefits of increasing I, the higher $WAGE$, with the marginal costs of doing so. The level of I that equates, on the margin, the benefits and the costs will be the one that she chooses. These marginal costs are determined by her own tastes and preferences and represent the value of what she gives up by increasing her intensity of employment.

Although this may sound like a simple task for our hypothetical worker, she faces some things that are known and some things that are not. Both the worker and the firm will know the exact values for B_1, B_2 and B_3. Being rational she will assume also that average RI and OC will be zero; but she also recognizes that this may not always be the case. This uncertainty may lead her to provide a level of effort, I, that is not efficient.

If the employee puts greater intensity into her duties (i.e. increases I), she cannot be certain that her wage will increase. In fact, her wage may increase or even decrease. Payments will increase if the combined effects of RI and OC do not counteract the effect of the larger I. Rather than viewing her income as certain, our employee can view it now only as a random entity.

As an example, suppose our worker manages (and operates) an ice-cream store at the shopping mall for an owner. She may increase her efforts substantially: being friendly to all customers, working longer hours, or explaining the beneficial nutritional implications of ice-cream consumption to the clientele. However, if the mall is experiencing less pedestrian traffic owing to the completion of a new mall nearby (a negative RI), and/or if the economy is in recession (a negative OC), then her wage may not increase if tied to the volume of ice-cream products sold.

Four principles to help efficiency

One way to reduce employee risk is to follow the *relevant information principle*, which states that efficient contracts include a combination of parameters (B_1, B_2, B_3) that reduce the measurement error associated with the agent's performance.

To put the relevant information principle into the context of our model, recall the employee's compensation formula.

$$WAGE = B_1 + B_2(I + RI + B_3OC)$$

In our model, the employee treats B_1, B_2 and B_3 as fixed and reacts in her own self-interest in choosing I. Because of this, we can let these measures be fixed and observe that random variation in wages then enters from that part involving RI and B_3OC.

In the interests of efficiency we then seek the conditions under which the measurement risks caused by random influences and outside conditions are minimized. To do so, we have to identify common movements in RI and OC. We still expect, on average, RI and OC to take zero values; however, the parties to the employment contract may very well have ideas about what one of these quantities is likely to be given that the other is positive (or negative).[5]

It is probably most likely, in practice, that RI and OC are positively related.

This means that a positive (negative) value for *RI* would tend to be caused by the same set of broad economic factors that would make *OC* positive (negative) as well. In this case, risk in the form of variation in *WAGE* would be minimized and efficiency in the relationship enhanced if B_3 were negative. Suppose this were not true and B_3 were positive. Then when times were 'good' both *RI* and *OC* would tend to be positive and *WAGE* would increase spectacularly. However, when times were 'bad' both *RI* and *OC* would tend to be negative and *WAGE* would decrease spectacularly. Such variation in *WAGE* exposes the employee to larger risk.

The *incentive responsiveness principle* provides some managerial insights into how sensitive rewards should be to improved (or reduced) performance if an employment contract is to be structured to minimize risk to the agent.

Within the context of our model, our task is to determine factors that influence the size of B_2. Although we do not include a formal mathematical proof, we do offer guidelines with some intuitive explanation.

The size of B_2 should depend on the effectiveness of the agent in causing changes in the firm's profits. If the employee is able, through her choice of intensity level, to increase firm profits greatly, then a large B_2 should be chosen. On the other hand, if there is not a clear link between employee efforts and firm profits, B_2 ought to be smaller. Production workers, for example, could be motivated by incentive schemes tied to amount produced, but only up to a certain level. Overproduction in one division may swamp other divisions with components that are not yet needed.

The responsiveness of wages to effort expended should also depend on two internal (to the employee) characteristics. If the employee is strongly risk averse, i.e. does not like risk, then an intense link between pay and performance will not be desirable. If, on the other hand, the agent is a risk taker, then it is entirely appropriate to motivate with intense incentives.

The *competing activities compensation principle* is meant to apply when one employee is to be motivated to fill several functions that may compete for the employee's time. Suppose that the employer cannot determine how much effort an employee devotes to each of two separate activities. If the marginal benefits of the two activities to the employee are unequal, then the employee will optimally devote time only to the activity with the higher marginal benefit. The consequences of the competing activities principle are enormous for the design of incentive contracts. In particular, if an employee is expected to engage in an activity for which no performance measurement is available, then performance pay cannot be used for any other activities that the employee controls.

At almost every business school in Europe or the United States, faculty members are required to teach classes and expected to pursue an active research agenda. The reason for the teaching duties is simple: without students, society would have little use for universities. The reason for expecting the faculty to conduct research is to benefit both the business school and the faculty member, and indirectly (or even directly) to improve the quality of teaching.

In evaluating faculty members from different universities, teaching evaluations are of limited use: they have been shown to be highly subjective, and there is not a uniform evaluation system across campuses. For these reasons (and many others) a faculty member's reputation depends largely on her research productivity. Quite often, within a given university, a faculty member's raises and ultimate promotion depend crucially on research productivity and somewhat less on teaching abilities.

The typical faculty member must allocate her time among competing uses. The competing activities compensation principle can shed some light on the faculty member's choices and the university administrators' decision to permit this situation to exist. Given the great difficulty in obtaining an objective measure of teaching productivity across disciplines, and even across faculty members within a common discipline, too large a weight given to teaching would present undue risk to faculty members.

The *monitoring intensity principle* adds to the above some responsibilities of the manager, employer or firm. The monitoring intensity principle dictates that if an agent's rewards are to be highly sensitive to her performance, then it will pay the principal to monitor that performance very heavily. If we consider two contracts between pairs of principals and agents that differ only in the size of B_2, the principal involved in the contract with the larger B_2 will expend more resources in measuring agent performance.

 Key words

carrot method	public good
debt	regulatory forbearance
equity	residual claimant
horizon problem	risk averse
inalienability problem	separation of ownership and control
incentive problem	shareholder activism
managerial misbehaviour	shirking
moral hazard	stick method
poison pills	takeover market
principal–agent problem	team production
principle of risk sharing	

Questions and problems for review and discussion

1 Firms today are financed in a multitude of ways. The two largest
   sources of financing are debt and equity. Since debt and equity are the
   two largest sources of financing for firms, a firm's capital structure is
   largely determined by the amount of debt financing relative to the
   amount of equity financing. Suppose that DANBANK is considering
   making two loans to different borrowers that are identical in all respects
   except for their capital structures. DANNY, one potential borrower, has
   a capital structure featuring a low debt–equity ratio. DREW has a
   capital structure featuring low levels of equity relative to debt. Which
   borrower, DANNY or DREW, poses a larger risk to DANBANK? Fully
   explain why and incorporate concepts covered in this course.

2 In many countries, corporations whose shares are publicly traded are
   required to have their financial statements audited by independent
   accountants, who check whether the financial information being
   provided by management to investors is accurate and has been prepared following accepted methods and procedures, and who then
   publicly attest to their findings. The auditors are generally chosen by
   management (perhaps subject to nominal stockholder approval). Audit
   work provides a major source of income for accounting firms.
   Generally, each accounting firm has many clients that it audits. This is
   true even when it might be technically feasible for a relatively small
   accounting firm to audit a large corporation's records. There seems to
   be a reluctance for corporations to use audit firms when a single client
   would represent too much of the accountant's business. Instead, a
   handful of extremely large accounting firms typically do almost all the
   auditing of large corporations, with each having many corporate
   clients. How do you account for this?

3 The 1980s were clearly a go-go decade. Yuppies ruled the consumer
   markets and many critics maintained that in some areas one-half of
   the population got rich selling real estate to the other half. Quite
   predictably there are now many people in those areas with their hats
   in their hands so to speak. Another aspect of the 1980s was the
   invention and widespread use of the hostile takeover in corporate
   finance. A hostile takeover is the acquisition of enough of the shares in
   a company to give a controlling ownership interest in the firm, where
   the offer to acquire the firm is opposed by the target company's
   executives and directors.

   'Managerial moral hazard in the form of managers' pursuing their
   own interests at the expense of others caused the surge in hostile
   takeovers during the 1980s'. True or false? And fully explain your
   position.

4 In all industrial economies, many workers use a computer as a part of their job. In many fields, not only do these machines greatly enhance productivity; they are a necessity. One popular operating system is Windows, produced by Microsoft. A standard feature in most copies of Windows is a version of solitaire, a card game played by an individual. Games such as solitaire represent an opportunity to shirk. In fact in 1993, Wes Cherry, the Microsoft programmer who wrote the solitaire application for Windows, boasted: 'I like to think that I'm partly responsible for the recession.'[6]

(a) What types of monitoring costs do these games pose to employers?

(b) A corporate policy that does not permit these games to be loaded onto company machines is passed. Is this likely to be successful?

(c) Tetris, popularized by Spectrum Holobyte, is another popular game. One popular feature of Tetris is a 'boss key', which, when pressed, quickly displays a spreadsheet that looks like work. What is the effect of this 'boss key' on the employer's monitoring costs?

Notes

1 Another paper is available that is written from a finance theory perspective; see Fama (1980). A critical discussion of these approaches is provided by FitzRoy and Mueller (1984).

2 A history of the deposit guarantee programmes and evidence of regulatory involvement in their failure can be found in Thies and Gerlowski (1993) and Thies and Gerlowski (1989).

3 More will be said in Chapter 10 on poison pills, white knights, raiders, greenmail and golden parachutes in the context of corporate takeovers.

4 Excessively strong or weak overall conditions would be accounted for by revising the values chosen for B_1 and B_2.

5 For those with a firm understanding of statistics, you will be aware that what we are really talking about here is the covariance between RI and OC, two random variables.

6 For an interesting background on this issue, see *Business Week* (11 October 1993, p. 40).

References

Alchian, A. A. and H. Demsetz (1972), 'Production, information costs, and economic organization', *American Economic Review*, 62, pp. 777–97.

Business Week (1993), 'The games people play in the office', 11 October.

Fama, E. (1980), 'Agency problems and the theory of the firm', *Journal of Political Economy*, 88, pp. 288–307.

Fitzroy, F. R. and D. C. Mueller, 'Cooperation and Conflict in Contractual Organization', *The Quarterly Review of Economics and Business*, 24, Winter 1984, No. 4, 24–49.

Jensen, M. (1988), 'Takeovers: Their causes and consequences', *Journal of Economic Perspectives*, 2, pp. 21–48.

McManus, J. (1975), 'The costs of alternative economic organizations', *Canadian Journal of Economics*, August.

Milgrom, P. and J. Roberts (1992), *Economics, Organization and Management*, Englewood Cliffs, NJ: Prentice Hall.

Thies, C. and D. Gerlowski (1989), 'Deposit insurance: A history of failure', *The Cato Journal*, Spring/Summer.

Thies, C. and D. Gerlowski (1993), 'Bank capital and bank failure, 1921–1932: Testing the White hypothesis', *Journal of Economic History*, 53, pp. 908–14.

CHAPTER 9

Distribution, rents and efficiency

> Low wages are by no means identical with cheap labour. From a purely
> quantitative point of view the efficiency of labour decreases with a wage
> which is physiologically insufficient . . . the present-day average Silesian
> mows, when he exerts himself to the full, little more than two-thirds as
> much land as the better paid and nourished Pomeranian or Mecklenberger,
> and the Pole, the further East he comes from, accomplishes progressively
> less than the German. Low wages fail even from a purely business point of
> view wherever it is a question of producing goods which require any sort of
> skilled labour, or the use of expensive machinery which is easily damaged,
> or in general wherever any greater amount of sharp attention of initiative is
> required. Here low wages do not pay, and their effort is the opposite of
> what was intended. (Weber, 1925, p. 61)

A. Chapter outline and student goals

Introducing rents and distribution

In the chapters prior to this, we have encountered a number of issues. In Part
I, our emphasis was on the traditional approach taken by economists in analyzing the organization of economic activity: markets. In Chapters 6, 7 and 8
the emphasis shifted away from markets because imperfect information and
bounded rationality create transaction costs that prevent the smooth and efficient functioning of the market mechanism.

In this chapter we turn our attention to rents and distribution effects. We
define these terms more fully later; for now we offer only broad general definitions. Rents are benefits earned by an economic resource that exceed what
the resource could willingly earn elsewhere. Distributional effects broadly refer
to the resources available to the parties of a transaction both before and after
the transaction is carried out.

Economists became interested in rents long ago. Initially analysis of rents
focused on land and other fixed factors of production. This is not surprising
because long ago most individuals earned their living from the land. In fact,
the term 'rent' today typically evokes images of a cheque sent to your landlord
– a usage evolved from the concept developed by economists. This concept of

rent has been greatly expanded to cover many interesting exchanger situations.

Efficient behaviour can generate rents, a fact that should not be lost on any business manager. Where they exist, rents can be traced back to the mutual benefits of the underlying exchange, which is why two parties would interact in the first place. In a sense, rents represent 'something for nothing', or, at least, an unearned bonus. As such, rational individuals will try to arrange things so that they capture these rents. When viewed in this light rents have the potential of either enhancing or diminishing efficiency.

Distribution, in economic terms, refers to who has (or gets) what. Attention was first paid by economists to the macro economy where distribution referred to the allocation of gross domestic product (GDP) between the owners of land, labour, capital and entrepreneurial ability. Within a transaction, distribution refers to the sharing of costs and benefits. Within an organization, which, we remind you, is really nothing more than a collection of transactions or contracts, distribution refers to how the benefits of production and the required efforts are shared by members of the organization.

It has long been thought by managers, economists and business strategists that the distribution of rents in an organization is simple: they go to the group with residual control. In a changing business environment, rents have taken on a new meaning. This is especially true witnessing the re-emergence of markets as the highly vertically integrated firms created in the first half of the twentieth century are being replaced by the more nimble and responsive organizations created as this century comes to a close.

After reading this chapter you should be able to:

- describe, in your own words, what is meant by rent,
- differentiate between the types of rents considered by organizational economists,
- describe how rents can be used to increase efficiency,
- explain the importance of reputation and 'good behaviour' in overcoming threats of *ex ante* and *ex post* opportunistic behaviour,
- understand the importance of distribution effects in economic analysis of the organization;
- explain what is meant by rent-seeking behaviour and why it is not efficient.

B. The meanings of rents and distribution effects

Types of rents

Economists refer to two different types of rents: economic rents and, a slightly different and new concept, quasi-rents. **Economic rents** are defined as the benefits from an activity going to a resource in excess of what is needed to attract that resource to that activity. **Quasi-rents** are the benefits from an activity going to a resource that are in excess of the minimum required to keep a resource in its current use.

The implication of getting something for nothing in terms of economic rents is fairly clear. Some tremendous examples of economic rents are provided by the earnings of some professional athletes in the United States and elsewhere. Star football players such as Emitt Smith of the Dallas Cowboys, Dan Marino of the Miami Dolphins and Jim Kelly of the Buffalo Bills earn millions of dollars a year,[1] as do tennis stars such as Boris Becker and Steffi Graf of Germany. When each of these players is interviewed they often dwell on how they play sports out of love for the game. If this claim is in fact true then all of their earnings represent economic rent, since, presumably, out of love, they would play the game for free.

Economic rents are relevant for an 'entry' decision regarding some activity. If an individual or organization is attempting to pick one of several activities to undertake with some limited resources, it will always choose the activity yielding the largest economic rent. The concept of quasi-rent is somewhat different; it focuses on an 'exit' decision.

Under the quasi-rent concept, a distinction between **sunk costs** and **opportunity costs** must be kept in mind. A cost is said to be sunk if, once paid, it can never be recouped. An opportunity cost of an action is the value of the next-best alternative. When an individual assesses the quasi-rents of some particular activity, she ignores any sunk costs and focuses instead on payments in excess of what she could earn elsewhere (the opportunity cost).

These definitions may be a little murky at first blush, and we offer the following two examples to help cement them in your thinking.

Two economic examples

Consider the analysis of the neoclassical, competitive firm discussed in Chapter 3. The firm would enter an industry if so doing would yield positive profits. If p represents the market price in some industry and p_{atc} represents the firm's average total cost of production,[2] a firm will enter so long as p is greater than or equal to p_{atc}. In this case, the firm's profits are equivalent to economic rents. On a per-unit basis the economic rents are $(p-p_{atc})$.

It is not necessary for a firm to earn positive economic rents; recall that the long-run equilibrium condition for competitive industries involves zero profits. It is necessary, however, for a firm to earn positive quasi-rents. Regarding the competitive firm, quasi-rents are the difference between market price, p, and the average variable costs of production, p_{avc}. If the market price falls below p_{avc}, then a rational firm will 'shut down', i.e. not produce because producing involves a loss on every unit sold. On a per-unit basis, the quasi-rents earned by a competitive firm equal $(p-p_{avc})$.

Notice that in the simple example provided by the neoclassical, competitive firm, the fixed costs are sunk. This is obviously a simplification because a firm's fixed costs, in reality, might be offset by some salvage value, or might contain some maintenance cost component that is possibly avoidable.

One implication of this discussion relevant for managers that is made clear by the above example is that quasi-rents are not less than economic rents. Even when economic rents are zero (such as for the neoclassical competitive firm in long-run equilibrium), quasi-rents are positive and may be allocated to members of the organization to fulfil numerous efficiency needs.

A second useful example in illustrating the related, but different, concepts of economic and quasi-rents is provided by the wage earned by a hypothetical factory worker, Noel Wheeler. Noel works for a wage of 15.00 currency units (c.u.) per hour; we can assume for simplicity that there are no fringe benefits. We will denote this wage simply as w. Since Noel is a rational individual, he has a definite opinion regarding the highest wage he could earn elsewhere in a similar position. Suppose, in fact, Noel feels that his alternative wage, which we will label if w_{alt}, is 12.00 c.u. per hour. Part of Noel's wage represents an economic rent; this economic rent is equal to $(w-w_{alt})$, or 3.00 c.u. per hour.

Although the rent component of his wage may seem large (20 per cent), his wage has an even larger quasi-rent associated with it. Define w_{keep} as the wage needed actually to keep Noel in his current position. It is important to understand why w_{keep} will be lower than w_{alt}. Associated with job changes are three categories of costs: worker search costs, skill acquisition costs, and adaptation costs.

Worker search costs are any costs associated with finding a new job. They may include the value of time unemployed, if any; costs of interviewing; and the actual costs of addressing letters and typing résumés. **Skill acquisition costs** reflect the sacrifices made by those in the job market to develop new human capital; i.e. to retool in response to perceived market forces. **Adaptation costs** include any relocation costs and the value of any sacrificed employment benefits such as pensions.

The existence of search costs, skill acquisition costs and adaptation costs is the reason that w_{keep} will be less than w_{alt}. Since w_{keep} represents the lowest wage necessary to keep Noel in his current job it must be equal to:

$$w_{keep} = w_{alt} - \text{(search costs)} - \text{(skill acquisition costs)} - \text{(adaptation costs)}$$

Noel's current employer does not have to pay him the alternative wage that he could earn elsewhere because he cannot earn that wage elsewhere 'for free'. The quasi-rents earned by Noel are then equal to $(w-w_{keep})$. Worker search costs, skill acquisition costs and adaptation costs will vary greatly by individual; as such, we refrain from putting hypothetical values on them. It stands to reason, however, that within some occupations these costs could be substantial.

Different kinds of decisions can be analyzed with economic rents and quasi-rents. In most of this chapter we will be concerned with quasi-rents. The rationale is that quasi-rents are what is lost, in competitive markets, if an agent is forced to exit. Although rents can exist only temporarily in a competitive economy, quasi-rents are much more common. Quasi-rents are created whenever specialized non-salvageable investments are made; for example, when an individual works for an organization and is asked to carry out a task that cannot be transferred outside of the firm. Having made this investment, the individual will earn a higher wage than she can earn in the next-best alternative. If an individual has invested in an activity that cannot be recovered if she leaves, this person is now earning a quasi-rent. Quasi-rents therefore have the potential to be widely useful for providing incentives.

Distribution effects

Efficiency in exchange may also be affected by **distribution effects**, which refer to who has, or gets, what resources according to the terms of an exchange. Distributional issues manifest themselves in two ways. Some party to a transaction may not be able to 'afford' their part of an efficient allocation of resources. Also possible is a situation where the benefits (or costs) of production are shared in such a way as to lead to inefficient outcomes.

We can very easily contrive an example of how one party's ability to afford their part of an efficient transaction can have efficiency implications. Suppose that, as part of your job, you are required to use a laptop computer. Furthermore, both you and your employee are well aware that the performance, and perhaps the very survival, of your computer depends on how well it is cared for. The machine's performance may depend, for example, on how often the battery is permitted to run down completely, or on how many times it is used as an umbrella by a forgetful employee. These facts are recognized by both you and your employer; the only unresolved issue is who should own the laptop.

This situation is nothing more than the moral hazard problem encountered in Chapter 8. The efficient solution is probably for the employee to own the laptop, because only then can the proper incentives be created for the employee to be diligent in caring for the computer. Now, how can distributional issues affect this situation? Distributional issues become important if the employee lacks the financial resources to purchase the laptop. It is not enough for the firm to purchase the computer for the employee; if the machine breaks because of poor maintenance, the employee can rationally always ask for another one.

A second example of the importance of distributional effects and efficiency is provided by analyzing the wages paid to workers; or, in other words, how the benefits of production are shared between the factors of production.

Distribution is the mechanism by which the gross domestic product (GDP) is spread between individuals and groups in the economy. The functional allocation of income refers to the distribution of the GDP between the owners of land, labour, capital and entrepreneurial ability. One of the first attempts to explain the distribution of income according to 'natural law' was developed by the distinguished American economist John Bates Clark in 1893.

This type of analysis rests upon a supposition known as the marginal productivity theory of income distribution, a concept we will consider in greater detail in Chapter 12. This thinking suggests that an employer will not pay more for a unit of input – whether it be a person or an acre of land – than it is worth to the firm. Economic analysis based on this theory ignores several distributional issues.[3]

In many developing countries, the marginal revenue product of workers may be very low, implying meagre wages. In some cases the pay may not be enough to sustain a worker, much less his family and children. This was certainly the case in England during the Industrial Revolution, when children as young as age 6 would be found working in the mills because their fathers did not earn a wage high enough to feed all members of the family. Similarly, in many developing countries it is common to find children of a very young age working. If workers were paid a higher wage, their children could go to school, eat a more nutritious diet and ensure a more productive future.

Such practices certainly exist in today's world and are, in fact, perfectly consistent with the marginal productivity theory of income distribution. However, history has taught us that the long-run prospects of such economic and social structures are not good. Clearly, exploited workers in all nations are a sure sign that the interests of long-run efficiency dictate a higher wage paid to workers.

C. Economic rents going to a fixed factor

Payments to land

In economic analysis, it is useful to think in terms of rents as being captured by some entity. Both economic and quasi-rents are said to 'go' to some factor of production or, equivalently, to some party of the exchange. Economists began studying rents by examining the 'extra' benefits going to fixed factors of production. In later years, it became known that both economic and quasi-rents could be captured by non-fixed factors of production. In this section, our purpose is to explore rents going to a fixed factor. This will shed light on the non-fixed factor cases studied in the next section.

In a competitive economy there are no economic rents. The reason is clear. In a competitive setting, positive economic profits attract entrants who eliminate all rents in the long run. The obvious exception is, of course, if a factor of production is in inelastic (i.e. fixed) supply, in which case rents may exist in the long run.

As recently as a century ago virtually all economics texts devoted much space to land. This is easy to understand because most people worked the land for a living. David Ricardo, a leading English economist of the 19th century, argued that land is both original and indestructible. His arguments were based on three assumptions (Ricardo, 1817):

1 the amount of land available is fixed;
2 land used for growing corn (the generic term in England for all grains) has no alternative uses;
3 a landlord would prefer to receive any payment for the use of the land rather than to leave it idle and receive nothing.

The supply curve of land is then perfectly inelastic or vertical. Its price is determined by the height of the demand curve. Rather than leaving the land to grow grass, the landlord would willingly supply the same amount of land at a lower price. In fact, the landlord would accept any price determined by the demand curve.

The resulting payment is an economic rent, and will be determined by the productivity of land for farming. If demand rises, rents will rise; if demand declines, rents will decline. Notice that, if the land truly cannot be converted to another purpose, then the payments received by the farmer are also quasi-rents.

Monopoly power and barriers to entry

Rents can also go to fixed factors other than land. In most other cases, what is required to earn a rent is **monopoly power** in the provision of some good or service. Every instance of monopoly power, by definition, can be traced back to some operative **entry barrier**, or some device that keeps other firms out of the market.

Economies of scale, or continuous reduction in producer unit costs, represent a significant barrier to entry in many industries (see Box 1.4 in Chapter 1 entitled '(still) The importance of size'). Usually, economies of scale involve large fixed costs in production. The functioning of economies of scale as an entry barrier is fairly easy to see: the large fixed costs keep potential entrants away.

Suppose that one firm producing in an industry is able to exploit economies of scale in production, it can then produce a large number of units at very low per-unit costs. A second firm could hope, at best, to capture half of the industry demand if the second firm uses a similar production technology. Can the second firm expect to survive?

The first firm will fight (i.e. compete on price) so long as it is earning quasi-rents; i.e. charging a price greater than average variable costs of production (avc). The second firm is competing for economic rents, so its lowest price can be expected to be average total cost (atc). Given the large fixed costs usually involved in economies of scale, the difference between avc and atc is likely to be fairly large. In short, it will be very difficult for a second firm to enter the industry. Thus, economies of scale can represent a significant barrier to entry and earn the owners of the underlying capital significant economic rents and quasi-rents.

Economies of scope are said to exist when the total cost of producing two related outputs within the same firm is lower than when the outputs are produced separately. They represent an entry barrier in much the same way as do economies of scale.

Many other legal and structural barriers to entry exist as well. Franchises play a critical role in assigning market territories to individuals. Evidence of these rents is the recent selling of the Baltimore Orioles for $176 million and the Philadelphia Eagles for $156 million. Patents and copyrights play the same type of role. In the United States, the patent system gives the inventor of a new product or process exclusive right to sell the product for 17 years.

One commonly overlooked source of economic rents and quasi-rents concerns the old real estate adage 'location is everything'. The basic difference between two parcels of land is, of course, where they are located. Retail outlets prefer easily accessible sites; financial services firms prefer locations in central cities – to facilitate face to face contact with others in their own and the legal and banking communities.

Each of these instances involves rents going to a resource that is fixed, or even 'limited' supply, and relies on some associated monopoly power. Although instructive, these cases provide a limited basis for analysis owing to their fixed nature. More managerial insights are provided when our attention shifts to rents earned by the non-fixed factors of production.

D. Rents and non-specific investments

Worker shirking: An example

Mary Smith graduated from Cambridge University in 1985 with an undergraduate degree in economics, soon landing a job with a major City investment bank. She was delighted. During the summer of 1985 she moved down to London to a small but nice apartment in fashionable Chelsea.

Like most entry-level positions at financial institutions, Mary's job was demanding. She put in long hours learning a job, meeting deadlines and learning her way around the office. After a few years Mary was promoted and her career at the bank was looking bright. Then, in her late twenties, Mary met Tom (a successful stockbroker) on a weekend in Paris. Before long they were married and moved into a larger apartment.

As Mary turned 30 she and many of her friends from college started think-ing about having children and starting a family. Mary became pregnant and had a beautiful baby boy. She took only six weeks off from work. Then, Tom and Mary found a day care centre near home and Mary returned to work.

Things became difficult for Mary and her family very soon. With a new baby at home, Tom and Mary found that time was constrained. Much of their time was spent caring for the infant, working and keeping up their apartment. They had little time for each other, let alone for social and recreational inter-ests. Up to a point they managed. However, the demands on their time were tremendous. Tom and Mary soon began having difficult discussions about how they could improve their situation. One option was for one of them to quit their job; this raised serious questions about having an adequate family income and also about the large investments made in their human capital. They also considered other options.

One solution to Tom and Mary's problem would be for Mary to shirk at work, saving her energy for her family. In other words, Mary should put in less effort at the office so that she would have enough energy to take care of the baby, her husband and the apartment. The value of the extra energy and time devoted to her family would contribute to the economic and quasi-rents earned by Mary in her job.

This situation was faced by millions of employers as the female labour force participation rate of married women (many with small children) exploded dur-ing the 1980s. How did employers and employees react to this situation? How can employers prevent workers from shirking? In this case, part-time work or 'job-sharing' might seem to be an obvious solution. However, part-time work is unusual in highly paid, responsible positions such as Mary's.

As discussed in Chapter 8, one solution is to institute a pay-for-performance policy. We know the drawbacks of such a solution. First, all **monitoring** is very costly, especially at the individual worker level. It makes little economic sense to hire someone to monitor the efforts of a bus driver, a house cleaner or a clerk. Secondly, monitoring is also imperfect and subject to random influ-ences in a number of ways. These random influences may be so severe as to undermine the value of the agreement to both the worker and the firm.

One solution: Efficiency wages

How might firms deal with the principal–agent problem when direct supervi-sion is costly, difficult and open to possible error? One approach, the **effi-ciency wage model**, has been popularized by two economists, Carl Shapiro and Joseph Stiglitz (1984).[4] The logic of the efficiency wage model is straight-forward: pay workers an economic rent to reward good behaviour. In all fair-ness we must point out that the efficiency wage model is a working hypothesis in economics providing one explanation for the determination of wages. The efficiency wage model is very intuitive and allows us to illustrate how economic rents can be used by managers.

What the efficiency wage model does essentially is perform a benefit–cost comparison from the worker's perspective. More specifically, we isolate the decision of the worker: should he shirk or not? The efficiency wage model attempts to identify the costs and the benefits of shirking, and assumes that, if the costs of shirking exceed the benefits, then the worker will not shirk. In order to conduct our analysis we will have to introduce some notation.

Let w be the wage the employee is paid in his current employment. Let w_{alt} be the wage the employee could get if he looked for another job in the current employment market. In order to keep our analysis focused, assume that w_{alt}, the alternative wage, is already discounted to take into account worker search costs, adaptation costs and skill acquisition costs.

Let R be the amount that the employee could gain by shirking on the job. This gain might take the form of larger utility from increased leisure obtained by working shorter hours than agreed, or simply reduced pressures from responding less diligently to demands at work (this option was considered by Mary and Tom earlier). Let p be the probability that shirking is detected and the employee is fired for his actions. Let X be the number of time-periods over which the employment is expected to carry into the future. If the employee is hired for only one period, then X is 1. If there is to be continuing employment, then X can take any value greater than 1.

The basic outline of the efficiency wage model is quite straightforward. Monitoring is costly for the employer, so the firm knows that it cannot always observe the actions of the employee. Knowing this, the rational employee must decide whether to shirk or not. This decision is made by the employee in a rational way, where the costs of shirking are compared with the benefits of shirking. The problem facing the employer is then to recognize this and offer the worker a wage such that shirking is not a rational employee choice.

The gains from shirking are the easiest to identify. We assume that these gains are given by R. The costs of shirking are a little harder to identify because they are not experienced by the worker with certainty. Before accounting for the probabilistic qualities of the cost of shirking, let us examine what is lost if the worker's shirking is detected and he is fired.

Put simply, the worker stands to lose the quasi-rents associated with his employment. These quasi-rents are given by $(w-w_{alt})$.[5] If the employment situation is to carry over X periods, then the cost to the worker of shirking, if detected but ignoring the discounting of future wages, is

$$X\,(w-w_{alt})$$

We now turn our attention to the probabilistic aspect of getting caught shirking. Although the worker cannot be certain of getting caught and losing X $(w-w_{alt})$, the worker does know the expected value of being caught and fired. The expected costs of shirking are then:

$$pX\ (w{-}w_{\text{alt}})$$

In the worker's decision-making, he will shirk if shirking is in his interests. In other words, shirking will occur if the benefits of shirking, R, exceed the expected costs of shirking, $pX\ (w{-}w_{\text{alt}})$. Mathematically we would then say that shirking will occur if

$$R > pX\ (w{-}w_{\text{alt}})$$

The possibility of earning the quasi-rent $(w{-}w_{\text{alt}})$ makes the job valuable to the employee and also makes being fired an outcome to be avoided.

Even for most honest people, repeated and substantial temptations to cheat combined with ambiguity about what is right and wrong are likely to result in occasional cheating. What is an **efficient** response by an organization to this situation? There is one efficient approach suggested by the efficiency wage model.

Basically, the organization must consider what its options are. Only two variables in the above question are under the firm's control: p and w. Each of these affects the expected costs to the employee of shirking: increases in either will raise the expected costs to the employee of shirking. Let us consider the effects of each of these decision variables separately, holding one constant while we consider the other.

The wage chosen by the organization can cause workers to choose not to shirk. Consider the inequality above expressed as an equality:

$$R = pX\ (w{-}w_{\text{alt}})$$

If the wage set by the organization, w, is chosen so that the above equality holds, then workers will be indifferent between shirking and 'behaving'. If we solve this equality for w, then we have found the minimum wage necessary to encourage workers not to shirk. We call this wage the efficiency wage, w_e.

$$w_e = w_{\text{alt}} + R/(Xp)$$

Notice that the efficiency wage, w_e, exceeds the alternative or opportunity wage w_{alt} (recall that we have discounted w_{alt} to account for search and other 'new job' costs) by the amount $R/(Xp)$. Thus, the efficiency wage offers a quasi-rent. Efficiency wages include this quasi-rent to attract and hold workers in a particular employment, provided the higher pay is designed to induce higher productivity. By paying an efficiency wage when employer monitoring is costly, the firm establishes a financial reward for honest behaviour from its employees, and so discourages them from shirking (see Box 9.1).

The second option open to organizations to forestall cheating is to choose a different level for p, the probability of detecting and firing employees for exhibiting shirking behaviour. A larger value for p will raise the expected costs of shirking for employees and encourage their good behaviour.

Raising p, however, may be costly, perhaps exorbitantly so. Recall that, in the setting of the efficiency wage model, monitoring is costly; if it were not, a

Box 9.1 Efficiency wages at the Ford Motor Company

In 1914, Ford Motor Company made headlines by offering auto workers $5.00 per day, up from $2.50 a day. This was at a time when average wages in similar industries were between $2.00 and $3.00 a day.

Before 1913, automobile manufacturing required skilled workers. However, the assembly line changed all of that. Now work was repetitive and boring. As the automobile plants changed, turnover increased sharply and productivity fell.

In order to reduce the high level of turnover, the company offered an efficiency wage. The rationale was that the higher wage rate would increase efficiency. Only workers who had been at Ford for six months were eligible for the $5.00 a day wage. Within a few days 10,000 workers applied for work.

Although Henry Ford was attacked for it, the policy worked. According to historians, the $5.00 a day wage raised the value of the job to Ford workers. The labour turnover rate plummeted and in 1914 labour productivity at Ford was an estimated 50 per cent higher. So the increased productivity more than offset the increased wage. In sum, Ford's experience with the $5.00 an hour wage is consistent with efficiency wage theory. That is, in some cases efficiency wages may reduce principal–agent problems.

(See Raff and Summers, 1987)

performance incentive scheme could be used if it solved some of the measurement problems discussed in Chapter 8.

One clear-cut managerial interpretation from the efficiency wage model is that wages and monitoring may be substitutes. Recall the expression for the efficiency wage:

$$w_e = w_{alt} + R/(Xp)$$

First notice that w_e and p appear on opposite sides of the equation. The second thing to notice is that p appears in the denominator of a term added to the right-hand side. The organization's goal is to encourage workers not to shirk. One way to accomplish this, holding monitoring effort constant, is to raise the wages paid to workers. A second way to accomplish this is to increase p. Notice that if p is increased the expression $R/(Xp)$ gets smaller, implying a smaller efficiency wage. However, there is also a cost, say $C(p)$. It is in this sense that monitoring and wages are substitute tools in the manager's toolbox in encouraging proper behaviour by employees.

The fast food industry provides an interesting test of the efficiency wage model. The fast food business, as every college student knows, consists of a number of chains, such as McDonald's, Burger King, and others. Each of these chains has a large number of outlets, some of which are managed by the company, while others are owned and managed by independent business people operating under a franchise agreement.

To the consumer, the ownership form is unknown and of little importance. All stores within a chain appear to be similar. Each has the same architecture, the menu is identical and quality is consistent. In fact, a Big Mac looks and tastes the same in New York, Tokyo, London and Moscow. Who knows, Joe's Diner may serve better food, but you know exactly what you get at McDonald's. Moreover, the restaurants are similar in another aspect: they draw employment from the local labour market.

These restaurants differ, however, in one crucial aspect. The company-owned restaurants are managed by salaried employees, whereas the franchise units are managed by their owners. The owner has no control over the menu, interior decoration, suppliers of food stuffs or pricing policies, but he does choose the compensation packages and conditions of employment offered to employees. He is the one who decides to pay workers £4.75 an hour or £3.25 an hour. He also sets conditions for fringe benefits and hours of work, and makes the hiring and firing decisions. Most importantly, he is also the residual claimant for the income generated by the organization. In other words, he is the one who will reap the profits or suffer the losses.

An important aspect of management's job is to monitor and train the supervisory and non-managerial staff. Traditional economic theory would suggest that the franchisee who collects the residual income will monitor more intensely and train more effectively than will a salaried manager. As we saw above, efficiency wage theory would suggest an inverse relationship between monitoring intensity and the efficiency wage. Companies will pay higher wages in their outlets than franchisees in theirs. The higher wage makes the job more valuable and therefore the workers more productive.

Data from two fast food surveys suggest that in 1985 wages for a sample of supervisors were 8.9 per cent higher in company restaurants and 1.7 percent higher for full-time workers. A second survey found that company restaurants were less likely to hire workers at the minimum wage than were franchise restaurants. Company restaurants were also more willing to increase fringe benefits, for example free meals. Preventing workers from taking free meals is very difficult, especially at restaurants such as McDonald's where most marketing efforts are targeted towards the demographic group from which both employees and customers are drawn.

We can sum up our argument so far as follows. As an incentive not to shirk workers must be offered a higher wage than the competitive wage. If workers are fired for shirking they will face a decrease in wages. If the difference between wages is large enough, workers will be induced to be productive, and the firm will not have a problem with shirking. The wage at which no shirking occurs is called the efficiency wage.

E. The importance of reputation

Contractual honesty

For as long as traders can recall, successful commerce has demanded that people honour their contracts. As Adam Smith wrote more than 200 years ago: 'When a person makes perhaps 20 contracts a day, he cannot gain so much by endeavouring to impose on his neighbours, as the very appearance of a cheat would make him lose. When people seldom deal with one another, we find that they are somewhat disposed to cheat, because they can gain more by a smart trick than they can lose by the injury which it does to their character.' According to Adam Smith, the greater a merchant's volume of business, the greater the incentive to act honestly in order to protect his valuable business reputation.

In many business situations, conditions arise that we did not anticipate. Transactions can be classified according to how decisions are made in these circumstances. In the short run, there are no long, involved contracts. You buy fish in the spot market. When the fish 'stinks', the parties bargain among themselves. An alternative to the spot market is to establish a long-run relational contract, stipulating a governance structure (such as discussed in Chapter 7) where some designated party has the final word.

When you accept a job, you agree to follow whatever direction is given within some socially acceptable limits in exchange for some fixed hourly wage or salary. If you take a job at McDonald's you agree to cook hamburgers, make milk shakes or clean the toilet depending on what is needed. However, you should not have to clean the toilet every day, and be the only one to do it. The supervisor can exercise discretion in assigning tasks, and the employee must rely on the supervisor to do it fairly.

The disputes that arise in these situations are often connected with ambiguity about what kinds of discretionary behaviour are honest or appropriate. Let us assume that, although it is not possible to write complete contracts to cover all situations, it is possible for parties close to the transaction to determine whether the person with authority has done the right thing. This is a basic requirement of any system of reputation.

Although it may be impossible to specify in advance how the decision maker should behave in every possible situation, it may nevertheless be possible for those involved to decide afterward whether the parties had behaved honourably. In reality, however, perceptions of circumstances frequently conflict. Parties differ about what was the right thing to do. Even when people agree about the circumstances, they often disagree about each alternative. The problem is often compounded when a third party is involved because it is very difficult for outsiders to settle disputes. The cost and difficulty of making those judgements, and the need for them to be made repeatedly by a series of outsiders, undermine the effectiveness of a system of trust based on reputation alone.

Corporate Culture

Corporate culture is one way to enhance the efficiency of a system of reputation within an organization. **Corporate culture** is a set of routines for decision-making and shared expectations that employees are taught and the stories and related devices used to convey those expectations. The corporate culture provides a set of principles and procedures for judging right behaviour and resolving legitimate disputes. Because the principles to be communicated have to be simple and easily understood no one culture can work well for all organizations.

Sometimes these rules just evolve. Academia can offer some interesting instances of corporate culture. For example, some universities or departments have a strong research culture and put pressure on newcomers to conform, whereas others do not.

Retail businesses try to cultivate a corporate culture that says the customer is always right. In a small grocery store in Vermont there is a sign outside the store. The first line reads: 'The customer is always right.' The second line reads: 'If in doubt read the first line again.' Macy's, the US department store chain, is famous for accepting returned merchandise without asking questions. In New York City, it became common during the 1980s for people to buy a dress for a Saturday party and then return the dress on Monday.

Why is it important to offer trust in business? The answer is that offering trust maintains a person's or organization's reputation for honesty. In the world of business, a reputation for honesty can be a valuable asset because it can attract trading partners. It is expensive and time consuming to write detailed contracts. A good reputation can often allow a business deal to be closed with only a hand shake instead of incurring the expenses associated with crossing all the t's.

Reputation and market discipline

One interesting aspect of reputation is that, in markets where the competitive model introduced in Chapters 2 and 3 may not be applicable, reputation can serve as a disciplining mechanism working against unscrupulous, or unethical, producers. For example, in the absence of a trusted mechanic, people commonly ask their friends for the names of garages with which they have had some good experiences. Some corporations place great emphasis on their reputations and will go to great lengths to protect them. One advertising slogan used by the Sears department store in 1994 was 'Solid as Sears', an attempt to create an image of a trustworthy seller in the minds of consumers. In short, in markets where information is scarce, reputation is often relied upon as a substitute.

Along these same lines, reputation can be seen as a potential solution to the *ex ante* and *ex post* contracting problems outlined in Chapters 7 and 8. With respect to moral hazard, reputation may serve to make credible a claim by the agent that 'I will not shirk'. Likewise, regarding the hold-up problem under conditions of asset specificity, a reputation may amount to one party believing the others when they claim to be 'committed'.

Institutionalized reputation?

We also see instances where organizations attempt to 'institutionalize' reputation. In urban areas, for example, it is not uncommon for there to be an association of used car dealers. On a broader scale, some professional organizations have, as a part of their functioning, a practice of certifying members as being qualified or 'competent', perhaps even developing criteria to rate the efforts of their members. The British Medical Association is one such organization. In order to practise medicine in the United Kingdom it is necessary to be certified by the BMA. Similar institutions exist for accountants, lawyers, teachers and members of other professions in most countries.

These attempts at 'institutionalizing' reputation potentially suffer on one critical incentive dimension. The individuals who certify professional practices often stand to gain from the very reputation their organization is trying to create.

F. Rent-seeking behaviour

A dark side to rents

Up to this point we have examined how rents can have a positive influence on organizations. In other words, they can be used to increase efficiency. There is also a negative side to the existence of quasi-rents in organizations. The presence of rents in an organization can create incentives to attempt to reallocate these rents. Quite often these attempts at reallocating rents do not increase total value and may even decrease it. Economists consider such activities to be pure costs. Activities that serve no social function other than to transfer rents or quasi-rents have come to be called rent-seeking and directly unproductive activities.

A very simple example can illustrate **rent-seeking behaviour**. Suppose that the government gives out monopolies, and that it gives them away free. For example, a contract to build a new fighter aircraft, such as the Eurofighter being developed by Britain, Germany, Italy and Spain with a long history of cost overrun, can be very lucrative. The companies winning the contract will start to earn substantial economic rents due to their monopoly position. The lobbying activity for these contracts is extensive and such efforts typically involve huge expenditures trying to influence the decision makers.

Economists would call these costs **influence costs**, an attempt to alter the distribution of rents in an exchange situation. Such influence costs are **directly unproductive activities** because they fail to create value. Influence costs refer not only to the costs incurred by trying to alter the distribution of costs and compensation in an organization, but also to the costs associated with making inefficient choices when exposed to another party's influence.

Rent-seeking activities in private organizations have received much less attention than in government. In neoclassical theory there are no good jobs and bad jobs. The wages that workers can earn are the same in all jobs. If two jobs are the same, then they will pay the same. If one job is less pleasant than another, it will pay more. Thus, if it takes more education to be an engineer than a truck driver, the engineer will make more. If wages were really determined in this way, there would be no problem of organizational policies. People would not care about these decisions because all changes would be compensated for in their wages and salaries. However, the world of organizations is much more complicated, as we have already seen. There are quasi-rents within organizations and real resources are allocated as each group fights for a larger share of the organizational pie. Whenever individuals are asked to make specific investments in their jobs, quasi-rents are created. Firms will be led to offer higher pay whenever good performance is called for and monitoring is difficult. Especially talented workers may be given higher wages, and workers who go through a training programme will receive higher wages.

Influence activities

In order for influence activities to take place, two conditions have to be met. First, the affected parties must have open channels of communication to decision makers. Secondly, decisions have to be made that will affect the distribution of costs and compensation in the organization. Your university is a good example of an organization that meets the first condition. Universities are organizations that pride themselves on being open to all parties concerned and seek consensus governance.

Consider the case of General Motors and the influence activities and rent-seeking behaviour of its labour unions. In the early 1990s, the company had been plagued by expensive labour contracts, declining demand, sliding market share, negative press, big restructuring charges and the loss of $2 billion in 1993. The company desired to close four of its assembly plants, forcing workers into early retirement. The inducements offered by GM were enormous. Workers at the plants scheduled for closure would be able to retire as young as age 50 and receive vouchers of $10,000 toward the purchase of a new GM car plus more than $3,000 in cash to cover taxes, according to union officials. Unlike a normal retirement programme, these workers would be able to take another job without reducing their GM pensions.

However, the rank and file has resisted these efforts at every turn. Why? Because these severance benefits, seemingly generous, were substantially less than the economic and quasi-rents earned by continuing workers. The numerous labour laws that allow unionization and enforce collective bargaining create the first condition for influence activities: open channels of communication. The second condition, that decisions affecting the distribution of costs and compensation in the organization have been made, is met because of the recent financial problems faced by GM. In 1993, General Motors agreed to delay shutting down two factories and cancel the sale of a union-represented unit.

Influence activities are not limited to current employees. In 1993, IBM was in the midst of the worst business crisis in its history. Once the world's most profitable corporation, IBM had had to eliminate 180,000 of its 405,000 jobs. These moves were necessary because IBM had lost $8.37 billion that year. However, IBM still maintained an elaborate system of perks for its employees, despite the losses. In May of 1993 IBM staged its 'Golden Circle', a celebration for 330 of its best salespeople and their spouses. The money-losing computer giant rented a museum and treated everyone to veal and salmon, a five-act circus, casino games, and a live performance by Liza Minelli.

Should IBM employees receive such rents when thousands of people are being laid off, and shareholders are also asked to sacrifice through lower stock prices and dividends? IBM was long considered the safest of the blue chip stocks. Its steadily rising share price and generous dividend made it the mainstay of thousands of investors' portfolios. IBM's stock had lost nearly 75 per cent of its value in the six years prior to 1993. In 1993 IBM further hurt shareholders by chopping its annual dividend 79 per cent to $1 a share. Management's decision to continue to reward existing employees with rents lowers the return to existing stockholders. Employees who will be laid off from the company's mainframe computer spend time lobbying to have the rules changed that affect the distribution of rents within IBM.

There are two elements of influence costs that must be balanced to arrive at an optimal decision in any situation. First, opening the decision process to individuals whose own interests are at stake increases influence costs. This is true of either the professor who has to teach more, or the employees at IBM who will be laid off. Secondly, these influence costs must be balanced with the improved information that accompanies more participation. We will now examine the way in which influence costs can be reduced in organizations. One is to limit communication in an organization and the other is to limit the distributional implications of decisions.

Minimizing influence costs

It is important to design organizations that minimize influence costs. For example, if the Economics Department wants to hire more faculty because all of its professors are too busy doing research to teach, the dean can say no. However, this does not preclude the chairperson from making an appointment, with the dean and other university administrators to discuss the matter over and over thereby increasing influence costs. What is needed in organizations is a formal or informal method to curtail these types of discussions. 'Politicking' is an expensive process.

One effective way to control 'politicking' is to limit information. For example, most organizations keep salary information secret. Without salary information it is more difficult to build a case for yourself. However, this is difficult in a democratic society. For example, in most public institutions salaries are public information. Likewise, the earnings of top managers in large publicly traded firms are common knowledge. Controlling influence costs by limiting information is costly because useful information is often eliminated as well. In the former Soviet Union, copy machines were kept under lock and key. The reason was to keep information that could be used against the system private.

One way to limit the impact of adverse decisions is to limit the distribution of rents across potential competitors as much as possible. An excellent example is provided by the higher education system in Germany. There, most professors are civil servants and their salaries are determined by neither good teaching nor good research, but rather by years of service.

Such a pay system is frequently adopted in large corporations as well. Another approach is to offer employees group performance incentives; this approach can also foster cooperation and improve productivity.

A Japanese approach

Several detailed studies of Japanese firms support the notion that efficiency is enhanced by limiting influence activities. Some interesting characteristics have been institutionalized into Japanese organizations. These include long-term employment, flexible teamwork, narrow pay differentials across similar workers, and wages tied heavily to seniority. Plant-level union and cooperative non-adversarial bargaining allows flexible, informal agreements, and long-term employment in large firms encourages specific skill and career development for blue-collar team workers.

Internally, the Japanese firm and associated company unions maintain consensual, participatory labour and management relations, which substantially reduce the supervision and hierarchical control costs associated with traditional American firms. Less well known, perhaps, is the role of the implicit equity stake held by Japanese employees. High levels of firm-specific skill, together with much steeper age–earnings schedules than in the United States and a substantial lump-sum payment on retirement all combine to reduce mobility and impose considerable losses on core employees in the event of bankruptcy or dismissal for unsatisfactory performance.

Sometimes companies attempt to involve their workers more deeply in decision-making. One of the ways to lessen the differences in interests between workers and management is the **employee stock ownership plan** (ESOP). By making employees shareholders, firms with ESOPs hope to make the workers as a group more accepting of organizational changes, more willing to be flexible in accommodating labour-saving arrangements, and more forthcoming with suggestions about how to improve operations.

G. Chapter summary and key ideas

In classical economics, all works devoted much space to the issue of rent. Land is original and indestructible and the supply and location are clearly scarce. If demand rises, rents will rise, and if demand declines, rents will decline. Rent therefore is not a cost of production but a return in excess of total cost.

In neoclassical economics, rent is defined as a return in excess of what is needed to attract a resource into an activity. In a competitive economy there are no rents. In a perfectly competitive labour market all workers are paid the equilibrium wage. This wage is required to get the last worker to supply her labour. The other workers earn rents because their wage is greater than what would be needed to get them to work.

Employment is often a situation of a double moral hazard within the context of the principal–agent problem. Pay-for-performance plans are most capable of solving the principal–agent problem in those circumstances where individual output can be readily measured. But in many jobs measuring and assessing individual output are at best difficult and at worst impossible. The efficiency wage model suggests that firms pay an amount above the market clearing wage as a way to reduce employee shirking. The higher wage increases the relative value of the job as viewed by each worker. If workers are fired for shirking, they will face a decrease in wages. If the difference between wages is large enough, workers will be induced to be more productive, thus increasing efficiency, and the firm will not have a problem with shirking. The wage at which no shirking occurs is the efficiency wage.

The distinction between rents and quasi-rents is important. A rent is the portion of earnings in excess of the minimum amount needed to attract a worker to accept a particular job, or for a firm to enter an industry. A quasi-rent is the portion of earnings in excess of the minimum amount needed to prevent an agent from quitting her job. The crucial difference is that, whereas rents are defined in terms of decisions to enter an industry or job, quasi-rents are defined in terms of a decision to exit a job or industry. In most of this chapter we have been concerned with quasi-rents. It is quasi-rents that agents stand to lose if forced to exit an industry.

The existence of quasi-rents tempts people in organizations to compete for them. The attempt to reallocate economic rents between agents has no positive benefits. Activities that serve no social function other than to transfer rents are called rent-seeking activities. These activities have an economic cost. The costs are known as influence costs. Influence activities take place if two conditions are met. First, decisions have to be made that will affect the distribution of costs and wages in the organization. Secondly, the affected parties must have information and open channels of communication to decision makers.

There are at least two elements of influence costs that must be balanced. Opening the decision process to individuals whose interests are at stake increases influence costs. However, those influence costs must be balanced with the improved information that accompanies more participation. How to limit influence cost in organizations is an important aspect of organizational design.

One effective way to control politicking is to limit information. Controlling influence costs by limiting information is costly because useful information is often also eliminated. The other way to limit influence costs is to limit the impact of adverse decisions by limiting the distribution of rent across potential competitors. Participatory management is an attempt to do just that.

Japanese firms and their associated company unions practise participatory management. Key features include long-term employment, flexible teamwork, narrow pay differentials, limited outside opportunities, and job rotation. The workers also have an implicit equity stake in the company. High levels of firm-specific skill, together with much steeper age–earnings schedules than in the United States and a substantial lump-sum payment on retirement, all combine to reduce mobility and influence costs.

Appendix A: The difference between rents and quasi-rents

To understand the difference between rents and quasi-rents let us examine Figure 9.1. Under what conditions will a firm enter or exit an industry? This depends on the equilibrium condition. In long-run equilibrium under perfectly competitive conditions the firm will produce where marginal revenue, *MR*, equals marginal cost, *MC*. In long-run equilibrium, marginal revenue will equal marginal cost, average total cost, and price.

As long as price is equal to average total cost, there will be no incentive for other firms to enter the industry. In other words, economic rents will be zero. In Figure 9.1, the price that makes entry just profitable is p_{atc} where price is equal to average total cost. Any price above p_{atc} will make it profitable to enter. The price that makes exit uncomfortable is p_{avc}. P_{avc} is where price is just equal to average variable cost. At any price lower than p_{avc} the firm would not even cover all variable costs, and its losses would exceed its total fixed cost. For the firm not to exit the industry, p_{atc} must be greater than p_{avc}. These are quasi-rents. Thus, it is possible for a firm to be making an economic loss (price less

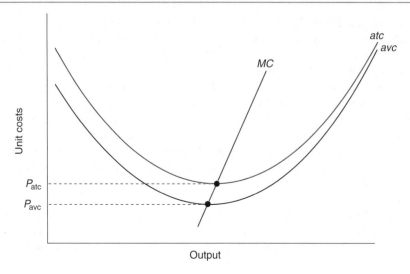

Figure 9.1 Competitive firms, entry decisions

than average total cost) and still be earning a quasi-rent. The difference between rents and quasi-rents arises from the presence of fixed costs that must be incurred to enter the market but that cannot be salvaged by an existing firm that chooses to exit. For this reason quasi-rents are always at least as great as rents.

Appendix B: Numerical example of efficiency wages

Assume that a worker is currently being paid 35,000 c.u. per year and that, if fired, his best wage is 30,000 c.u. This worker is earning a quasi-rent of 5,000 c.u.

Does it make sense for the worker to shirk? For simplicity assume that the employment situation is expected to last only one period, so that $X = 1$. Let us suppose that the worker could gain 500 c.u. by shirking and that the probability of getting caught and fired is equal to 0.05. In terms of our efficiency wage model, then:

$$w = 35,000 \text{ c.u.} \qquad w_{alt} = 30,000 \text{ c.u.}$$
$$p = 0.05 \qquad R = 500 \text{ c.u.}$$

The expected costs of shirking are 0.05(35,000–30,000), or 250 c.u. The expected costs of shirking are less than the gains from shirking; in fact the expected costs are one-half of the gains of 500 c.u.

What wage in this example will discourage shirking? We need to calculate the efficiency wage of w_e. This calculation is shown below:

$$w_e = 30,000 + 500/(0.05) = 40,000 \text{ c.u.}$$

Key words

adaptation costs	influence costs
corporate culture	marginal productivity theory
directly unproductive activities	monitoring
distribution effects	monopoly power
economic rents	opportunity costs
economies of scale	quasi-rents
economies of scope	rent-seeking behaviour
efficiency wage model	skill acquisition costs
efficient	sunk costs
employee stock ownership plan	worker search costs
entry barrier	

Questions and problems for review and discussion

1 Limits on a party's ability to pay cash damages are a common reason
for distribution and efficiency to be linked. Criminals are usually
punished for their crimes with prison terms, rather than through a
form of restriction. Some societies rely on whipping, ostracism and
even death. These forms of punishment result in a net reduction in
total welfare.
   (a) Evaluate the following claim: 'Social efficiency should require that
       victims receive some financial compensation from those who have
       harmed them.'
   (b) Can you provide any rationale for the lack of legal support for
       victim remuneration for certain crimes?
   (c) Can you provide any rationale for two systems of justice in the
       United Kingdom, one civil and the other criminal? Why are some
       offences classified as civil and result in remuneration via law suits?
2 Consider an industry in which an existing producer exploits significant
economies of scale. Usually, economies of scale are associated with
very large fixed costs of production.
   (a) Explain why these economies of scale represent a significant entry
       barrier.
   (b) Explain how these rents can be protected from being captured by
       entrants. In your explanation consider two firms, incumbent and
       entrant. Explain what the economic rents and quasi-rents are for
       each firm.
3 A common complaint of university students is that professors seem too

remote and uninterested in teaching them. How do university systems of compensation, promotion, tenure and pay rises contribute to the problem?

4 Firms that employ skilled workers are very conscious of the wages being paid by other employers and where they fit in the distribution of wages. In fact many surveys are done each year (and sold to business) of the compensation being paid in different geographical areas and industries to different types of employees.

   (a) Is this consistent with the standard labour market story of classical economics in which workers are paid a wage equal to the value of their marginal products?

   (b) How can this phenomenon be explained in the context of the efficiency wages model?

5 Under what types of conditions would you expect a firm to pay its workers an efficiency wage as opposed to an incentive-based wage?

6 In your opinion, can repeated dealings solve the problems of moral hazard in a contracting environment?

Notes

1 As of 1997 no professional football player had managed to earn more than $1 million per game; however, that boundary may have fallen by the time this book is printed.

2 The average total costs given by p_{atc} are those associated with the optimal level of production found by equating marginal revenue with the firm's marginal cost.

3 This point is made much more eloquently in the quotation at the beginning of this chapter.

4 An earlier version was proposed by Schlicht (1978).

5 Recall that we have discounted the alternative wage, w_{alt}, to take account of the costs associated with changing jobs. If we had not adjusted w_{alt} in this way, then our analysis would be based on economic rather than quasi-rents. We follow Milgrom and Roberts (1992) here.

References

Clark, J. B. (1893), *The Distribution of Wealth*, New York: Macmillan.

Milgrom, J. and P. Roberts (1992), *Economics, Organization and Management*, Englewood Cliffs, NJ: Prentice Hall.

Raff, D. M. G. and L. Summers (1987), 'Did Henry Ford pay efficiency wages?' *Journal of Labor Economics*, October, pp. 57–86.

Ricardo, D. (1817), *The Principles of Political Economy and Taxation*.

Schlicht, E. (1978), 'Labour turnover, wages structure, and natural unemployment', *Zeitschrift für die gesamte Staatswissenschaft*, 134, pp. 337–46.

Shapiro, C. and J. Stiglitz (1984), 'Equilibrium unemployment as a worker discipline device', *American Economic Review*, 74, pp. 433–44.

Smith, A. (1964), *Lectures on Justice, Revenue and Arms*, ed. Edwin Cannan, New York: Augustus M. Kelley, 1964.

Weber, M. (1925), *The Protestant Ethic and the Spirit of Capitalism*, New York: Scribner.

PART THREE
Organization, ownership and control

Theory of investment and financial markets

A. Chapter outline and student goals

All economies have markets for consumer goods, and we tend to focus on these. Equally or even more important are the financial markets where firms acquire capital. Indeed, financial markets are regarded as crucial components of a capitalist economy, closely related to the vital function of decentralized investment. The details of modern financial markets, enormous as they are in both scale and scope, are studied in specialized courses and texts on finance. In this brief chapter we can only outline some of the most basic and fundamental ideas, particularly as they relate to the problems of imperfect and asymmetric information that we emphasize throughout this text.

In recent years some of the most cherished economic principles of optimal investment and efficient financial markets have been challenged both by new theories and also by a steady stream of 'anomalies' or unexplained events in financial markets. The most spectacular of these anomalies was perhaps the stock market crash of October 1987, which did not appear to be accompanied by any bad news or change in **fundamentals**, that is, change in expected future cash flows or dividends. Most introductory texts avoid awkward empirical facts that disturb the established wisdom they are expounding, and controversial new theories are often ignored for similar reasons. However, the new developments in finance and investment are so important and far-reaching that a basic understanding of the issues is imperative for students and practitioners. Here we present elementary introductions to several of the most exciting new developments, alerting readers to the pitfalls involved in exclusive reliance on traditional approaches.

In the next section, we provide an elementary account of present values and the separation of consumption and investment decisions – the basic building blocks of the theory of finance and investment. The intuitive **Modigliani–Miller theorems** are discussed, showing that the value of a firm is determined by cash flow, irrespective of the 'bundling' or allocation of this flow to dividends and interest on debt. The major new development in this area comes from the insight that most **investment is irreversible** to some extent, and this combines with uncertainty over future returns to yield an option value for wait-

331

ing, or postponing investment until more information is available. With these realistic complications it is no longer true that all projects with positive present value should be undertaken, as we show with a simple numerical example.

Classical views of risk and return are then discussed, followed by the efficiency of financial markets in the next section. A major challenge to the traditional faith has come from growing evidence that financial markets fluctuate more than can be justified by changes in fundamentals alone. One reason put forward in the financial literature to explain **excess volatility** of asset prices is the notion that people 'overreact' to unexpected news events. The hypothesis that investors react to psychological factors goes back at least as far as Keynes' *General Theory* of 1936. Modern **behavioural finance** has began systematically to incorporate such factors. However it is recent *empirical* findings that have encouraged economists to study the influence of irrational or **noise traders**, responding to fads or fashions and generating excess volatility. Although a few individuals seem to be able to 'beat the market' over long periods, trading in existing securities is mainly a zero-sum game. Extensive resources are invested in rent-seeking, or the search for information that will affect market prices before others have access to – or the ability to act on – this information. There is little social benefit from this kind of competition, and most new investment is funded not by the stock market but rather through retained profits and credit. The main remaining function and justification of the stock market, to provide a market for corporate control, is discussed in Chapter 11 below.

The final section deals with the peculiarities of credit markets. Owing to informational asymmetry and moral hazard, equilibrium usually requires collateral and some kind of credit rationing to avoid adverse selection of high-risk borrowers. Interest rates are only one component of the 'price' of credit. As in other financial markets, there is evidence of **short termism**, or lack of long-term relationships between firms and suppliers of capital, particularly in the United Kingdom, which exacerbates informational asymmetry and also may have deleterious macroeconomic consequences.

After reading this chapter you should be able to:

- calculate the discounted net present value of an investment;
- understand why consumption and investment decisions can be separated if capital markets are perfect;
- describe the most important financial securities in use;
- explain why only cash flows, and not the debt–equity ratio, determine the value of a firm in perfect markets;
- evaluate the option benefit of postponing an irreversible investment in order to resolve some uncertainty;
- understand the reasons why diversification can reduce risk;
- form a judgement on claims that financial markets are efficient;

- describe some of the evidence for 'excess volatility' of the stock market;
- enumerate some of the social costs of the stock market;
- discuss 'short-termism' in financial markets;
- appreciate the necessity of collateral in credit markets.

B. Classical investment and modern developments

Present values

Investment means any current spending in order to obtain future returns. Fundamental to all analysis of investment is the evaluation of future cash flows in terms of current income. This is done by discounting, or present value calculation. In principle the idea of discounting future receipts is extremely simple and natural. To start with, however, the even simpler idea of future values is the most convenient concept to begin the analysis. Suppose you possess 100 units of some currency, say pounds or dollars, francs or ECUs, and invest today in a savings account at 10 per cent per year. One year hence, the bank would repay you the principal plus interest or $(1 + 0.1) \times 100 = 110$ units of the currency. The future value of 100 is 110 after one year when the rate of interest is 10 per cent, and after two years it is $(1.1)^2 \times 100 = 121$.

With these simple numbers we can immediately write down the present value of 110 due one year in the future, discounted at the rate of 10 per cent. The present value is just 100, the amount that would grow to the sum of money due in the future period. Similarly the present value of 121 two years hence is also 100. Quite generally, we can calculate the present value of Y received T years ahead, at the rate of discount or interest, r. The formula is:

$$PV(Y) = \frac{Y}{(1 + r)^T}$$

Why is this the present value of Y? Because if $PV(Y)$ was invested today at r per cent, then after T years we would have just $(1+r)^T \times PV(Y) = Y$, or the original sum of money again.

Now most real-world investment projects involve a sequence of outlays at various times, followed by returns at later dates. Directly comparing sums of money at different times is like comparing apples and pears – you can't just add them up to get a useful result. But by calculating present values according to the formula above we can express all future expenditure and income in terms of compatible units of our particular currency today. Only by comparing such present values to obtain the **net present value** (NPV) of the whole project can a financial or investment manager make sensible decisions on which projects to pursue.

Suppose then that our manager needs to invest X_1 after one year, X_2 after two years and X_3 after three years. The returns are estimated as Y_3 after three years, Y_4 after four years. Then the net present value of the project according to our formula is:

$$\text{NPV} = -\frac{X_1}{1+r} - \frac{X_2}{(1+r)^2} - \frac{X_3}{(1+r)^3} + \frac{Y_3}{(1+r)^3} + \frac{Y_4}{(1+r)^4}$$

If *NPV* is positive, the project yields a surplus or profit that raises the value of the firm. For example, if the expenditures X_i for $i = 1, 2, 3$ were borrowed from a bank, they could be paid back with part of the proceeds Y_3, leaving a positive net final value. To see this formally, multiply *NPV* by $(1+r)^4$, which is then also positive when *NPV* is > 0, giving

$$FV = NPV \times (1+r)^4 = -X_1 \times (1+r)^3 - X_2 \times (1+r)^2 - X_3 \times (1+r) + Y_3 \times (1+r) + Y$$

where the first three terms represent repayment of loans (principal plus interest). In practice of course, there is likely to be considerable uncertainty about the magnitude of the returns from any particular investment project. Expected values or 'certainty-equivalents' may still be used in the above formula to give a useful guide, but, if investments have elements of sunk cost or irreversibility, then present-value calculations may no longer give the correct signals to managers. We take up these problems at the end of this section.

The separation of consumption and investment

Consider next the case of a self-employed individual or entrepreneur who wishes to make various investments in her business. Does she have to cut back on her personal consumption every time she buys a new computer for the office? Personal experience and anecdotal evidence might suggest the answer is 'yes', but with perfect capital markets this is not so. With unrestricted borrowing and lending possibilities, the consumption and investment decisions depend only on interest rates and returns, and their timing is independent.

To see this, first assume that borrowing is impossible, so investments have to be made out of personal savings. To invest more, prior consumption has to be reduced. If the cash flow from the business is initially small, then investment is constrained by the necessity of maintaining some positive level of consumption. The entrepreneur or household is said to be 'liquidity constrained'. If there are good investment opportunities that the entrepreneur could pursue if funds were available, then such constraints are inefficient and wasteful. Investment projects that are not irreversible should be carried out whenever their net present value is positive, but this is possible only if the appropriate loans or other forms of funding are made available by a bank or some other institution or a wealthy individual. There is indeed considerable evidence that small businesses in particular would like to invest more than they actually do.

If the sequence of all investments in the business were known or estimated in advance, say as $X_1, X_2, \ldots, X_T$, and the returns were $Y_1, Y_2, \ldots, Y_T$, then the (net present) value of the business, V, could be defined simply as

$$V = \sum_{t=1}^{T} (Y_t - X_t) / (1+r)^t$$

Note that T is the planning horizon and that subscript or superscript 't' denotes one of the 1, 2, 3, $\ldots$, T periods. Ignoring the amount of her own working time spent on different projects, the owner should choose the sequence of investments that maximizes the value of her business, V.

This sounds obvious, particularly if the entrepreneur wishes to sell the whole or part of the business. But it is useful to see how she can also maximize her consumption possibilities in this case provided there are no liquidity constraints or restrictions on borrowing. Even without selling the firm, any stream of consumption expenditures, say $C_1, C_2, \ldots, C_T$ with present value at most V, can be funded out of firm profits. This is the only restriction; the timing of outlays C_t need not bear any relation to current profits $Y_t - X_t$.

The easiest way to understand the constraints on consumption is to assume that all outlays are funded by borrowing, leaving a total debt, D, as the final value of the consumption stream, say

$$D = C_1(1+r)^T + C_2(1+r)^{T-1} + \ldots + C_T$$

Then $D/(1+r)^T$ is just the present value of the (stream of) consumption choices. The final value of the firm is just $V(1+r)^T$, which would be the wealth accruing at T if all profits were invested at the interest rate, r. If D exceeded $V(1+r)^T$, then the entrepreneur would be left with unpaid debt or negative net worth, owing to excessive consumption. Any $D \leq V(1+r)^T$ is feasible without leaving any final debt unpaid. This is equivalent to the present value of consumption not exceeding the present value of the firm, or

$$\frac{D}{(1+r)^T} \leq V$$

as was claimed.

The fact that perfect capital markets allow individual consumption and investment timing decisions to be unconnected (except for the present or final value constraints) is called the Fisher separation theorem, after American economist Irving Fisher. It explains why the shareholders of a large corporation should want managers to maximize the current value of the shares, which is the value of the firm. Because shares entitle their holders to dividend payments rather than cash flows, the value of the corporation is just the present value of all expected future dividends. For the owner–entrepreneur of our example, the situation in practice is complicated by the time that she has to spend actually managing her own firm and making difficult decisions. Business growth and success may bring psychic as well as financial rewards, but too much time spent working – making decisions – leaves too little time for consumption activity. The owner–manager has to balance conflicting goals and demands on her time, perhaps maximizing a complex utility function of job satisfaction, leisure, consumption and other variables in addition to the present value of her firm, or even preferring maximum growth subject to some minimum level of profitability.

However, the overwhelming difficulty in most present value calculations is that future returns from investment are *not* known exactly and estimates may be wide of the mark. The longer the time horizon, the greater the uncertainty in general, so that managers are often tempted to demand quick returns and neglect projects that promise to pay off only in the distant future. The higher the interest rate, r, used to discount future receipts, the less important do these future receipts become in the present value formula. Thus high interest rates that raise the cost of borrowing may also encourage 'short-termism'.[1]

Financial securities

We have mentioned borrowing for investment or consumption purposes, and in fact debt, or obligations to pay fixed interest and the principal of the loan at given dates, is one of the most widely traded financial securities. Both corporate and government bonds are forms of debt, conveniently divided up into small units or denominations that offer highly liquid and relatively safe investments for even small individual savers. Bonds vary widely in their maturity or time to repayment of the principal and in the coupon or interest rate guaranteed.

Of course, corporations (and even governments) can fail to meet their obligations and default on their debt and interest payments. Bonds are ranked by major credit-rating agencies according to the reputation for credit-worthiness of the issuing company, starting with AAA for those with the best reputation. Downgrading a firm by a major credit-rating agency such as Moody's, say from AAA to ABB, means that the price of the bonds will fall. The investor who buys cheaper bonds receives a higher return from the fixed interest payments in compensation for the suspected greater risk.

There are even zero bonds, which provide no *regular* interest but simply promise to pay a fixed sum at some future date, say 100 ECU in the year 2000. The current price of such a bond, say P, will be less than the final value, so the implied rate of return, r, on an investment P can be calculated by

$$P(1+r)^T = 100$$

over a period of T years.

Some debt takes the form of bank loans such as mortgages and other forms of credit to generally small borrowers, which are not divided up and traded. Creditors demand security or collateral for personal and business loans, often in the form of a claim on the property or tangible assets of the business. When the borrower is unable to meet fixed interest payments, the bank may claim the assets that were named as collateral, evicting home owners for example, in order to sell the property quickly and secure as much as possible of the loan principal. In the recession of the early 1990s in the United Kingdom, banks frequently repossessed the homes of defaulting mortgage holders, so that the resulting sales and auctions put strong downward pressure on property prices, reducing individuals' wealth and exacerbating the recession.

The other main class of financial securities consists of equity shares of publicly traded companies. The shares entitle holders to dividends, which are set by top management; in bad times, dividends may not be paid, and creditors have prior claims on the firm's assets in case of default. Shareholders thus receive only the part of the residual income of the firm that management is willing to declare as a dividend. In return they usually have voting rights and the right to appoint the board of directors. Preferred shares without voting rights offer higher or guaranteed dividends, like bonds, even when no dividend is paid on ordinary shares, but creditors still have priority over preferred shareholders. Other classes of securities such as convertible preferred shares can be converted into ordinary shares in certain circumstances.

The Modigliani–Miller theorems

A classical proposition about the financial structure of the firm results if we abstract from the problems of bankruptcy and default. In place of our previous focus on the choice of real investment made by managers in the firm, we now consider the financing decision, or the choice of financial securities (essentially debt or equity) needed to fund a given total amount, or stream of investments over time. Existing owners of the firm's equity will want to minimize the cost of new investment in terms of interest and dividends that have to be paid to raise the required funds.

It used to be thought that too much debt relative to equity, manifested by an excessive debt–equity ratio, raised the cost of capital in two ways. The danger of default would rise, and also the increased variability of residual profits might reduce share prices and the total value of the firm, even in the absence of default.

In practice of course, one cannot separate the risk of default from the risk due to more volatile profits, but the achievement of the Modigliani–Miller theorems (Modigliani and Miller, 1958) was to demonstrate a logical flaw in the traditional view, a result that has become one of the most celebrated in the theory of finance.[2] The basic argument is surprisingly simple. An investor can always hold both debt and equity securities in the same proportions as they are issued by the firm, say a fixed fraction of the firm's total debt and equity. The investor thus always receives the same fraction of the firm's total profits, whatever the debt–equity ratio. The only effect of an increase in the debt–equity ratio is to raise the investor's interest receipts and reduce the dividend payments. Total profit, and hence any fixed share of total profit claimed by an investor, is unaffected. When investors hold differing mixtures of debt and equity, an individual can always offset a change in the firm's debt–equity ratio by a corresponding portfolio adjustment that maintains the same share of total profit.

A second Modigliani–Miller theorem extends the argument to the dividend policy of the firm. Assume the firm has a given sequence of investment over time, and that both firms and investors have the same access to credit markets. Then the firm's dividend policy can have no effect on its value.

To see this, recall that the value of the firm is the present value of all future profits. A higher dividend today means that borrowing must increase to finance investment, so future dividends fall when the extra debt is repaid. The present value of future profits is unchanged, and must remain equal to the present value of all future dividend payments. Neither is affected by the timing of dividends. Similarly, the investor's consumption is unaffected by dividend policy; the present value of consumption from ownership of the firm is always equal to the value of the firm.

These theoretical results actually serve to highlight the many practical reasons that financial structure and dividend policy *do* matter for firms and investors. The risk of costly bankruptcy does increase with debt, other things being equal. Incentives for managers may also change, however, as we discuss in the next chapter. Dividends and capital gains are taxed at different rates in many countries.

Financial economists have developed a variety of theories of investment decisions under risk. For example, a portfolio, which is a collection of securities or assets held by an investor, can be chosen to reduce risk if returns from individual securities held are negatively correlated. The theoretical models generally require knowledge of some parameters such as the mean and variance of the returns from securities. In practice, these parameters may only be estimated from historical values, which then give only imperfect guidance for future realizations.

Both common sense and theory suggest that a risky investment needs to offer a higher expected or mean return in order to compensate for the 'downside' risk of abnormally low returns. Equity holders receive an equity premium, or excess return, in the long run over the risk-free market rate for short-term government bonds. In the short run, of course, this does not help the equity holder faced with falling share prices, particularly if liquidity constraints or unexpected financial pressures enforce a premature sale of stock.

The detailed models of risky investment are covered in finance texts but, even after allowing for risk, the most important conclusions of classical investment theory remain. Provided expected future returns are discounted at an appropriately higher rate than the riskless market rate of interest, then the positivity of present value remains the correct criterion for (reversible) investment decisions. When there are no restrictions on borrowing and lending, the consumer is always better off as a stockholder when firm value is maximized. Since this is true whatever the desired timing of consumption outlays, there can be unanimity among diverse shareholders over the goals of the firms. This consensus, in turn, provides the economic foundation for the separation of ownership and management. Owners of a firm's equity need not be concerned with the details of investment projects, as long their present value is positive. All such projects will then maximize the owners' wealth, irrespective of the firm's borrowing and dividend decisions, according to Modigliani and Miller.

Irreversible investment: A problem for theory

Investment is one of the most volatile components of gross national product (GNP), with changes in investment playing a major role in triggering recession or initiating recovery. Predicting future investment behaviour is clearly of vital importance for government policy and for business forecasting and decision-making. Yet, as a leading expert, MIT economist Robert Pindyck, points out, 'the investment behaviour of firms, in industries and countries remains poorly understood'. Econometric models based on the classical theory outlined above 'have had limited success in explaining and predicting changes in investment spending, and we lack a clear explanation of why some countries or industries invest more than others' (Pindyck, 1991, p. 1110).

Pathbreaking recent developments in the theory of investment have remedied two serious problems in the standard theories, and are currently offering important new insights as well as the promise of major progress in future. The first problem is that most investment expenditures are largely irreversible, that is they represent **sunk costs** that cannot be recovered. The second problem not faced in the traditional view is that investment can usually be delayed, giving the investor an opportunity to collect improved information about prices, costs and market opportunities before committing specific resources.

The rapidly growing literature on new theories of investment shows that the ability to delay an irreversible investment project can have profound effects on the investment decision. In particular, the standard neoclassical model of investment is undermined, and the net present value rule to invest in a project when the present value of expected future net returns is positive is no longer valid. Since this rule is still almost universally taught in business texts and courses, it is important to spell out the conditions for its incorrectness.

The first question to clarify is when an investment expenditure is really a sunk cost, and thus irreversible. The usual reason is that the investment takes the form of firm-specific or industry-specific capital. Advertising, for example, is obviously firm specific and an irreversible, sunk cost. Tangible capital may be firm specific or industry specific. Even in the latter case, a decline in demand is likely to affect the whole industry and thus reduce the resale value of any capital equipment.

Even non-specific capital goods usually represent partly irreversible investments owing to the 'lemons' problem of moral hazard. New cars or office equipment in general use still lose a substantial portion of their initial value after only a few days, because buyers often cannot observe whether the equipment was badly treated or whether faults have appeared. There are also ubiquitous transaction costs of buying and selling, or hiring and firing, that generate positive adjustment costs or partial irreversibility of investment, for both firms and private individuals.

The option to delay an investment expenditure is almost always available; indeed, the optimal timing of investment is itself an important variable that is often considered in a strategic context. Delay usually involves obvious costs such as the risk of entry by competitors, or just the forgone cash flows or benefits, but these costs must be weighed against the advantages of waiting for new information.

An irreversible investment opportunity can be compared to a financial call option. This is a security that gives the right, over some period of time, to buy an asset at some predetermined price. Exercising the option is irreversible, because it is impossible to get back the exercise price, although the asset purchased can of course be resold. Similarly, a firm with an investment opportunity has the option to spend money (equivalent to the 'exercise price') at some point in time in order to acquire a capital asset. The asset can be resold, though perhaps at a loss, but the act of investment itself is irreversible. The initial option or opportunity to invest is valuable because of the expected future returns from the asset. The option also allows optimal timing of the investment to change as new information is obtained.

Investment opportunities are generated by knowledge in the first instance, a form of human capital that may be used to design new products or processes or implement strategies for market expansion through acquisition and merger. Realizing these opportunities then requires additional investment, such as exercising the call option. But any expenditure at a point in time 'kills' the option of delaying that particular outlay to take advantage of more favourable circumstances or better information, when some costs are sunk and so irretrievable.

To illustrate the importance of the opportunity cost of losing the option to postpone investment we consider a simple numerical example. An irreversible investment (say to build a new specialized factory) costs 88 c.u. and generates an uncertain return of 242 c.u. a year later, with probability $\frac{1}{2}$. The project may also fail and yield 0, with probability $\frac{1}{2}$. The expected net present value of investing now at a 10 per cent interest rate is given by:

$$NPV = -88 + \frac{1}{2}\left(\frac{242}{1.1}\right)$$
$$\cong -88 + 110$$
$$= 22$$

According to this standard criterion, the investment, which has positive *NPV*, should be made. However this calculation neglects the option value of waiting. Suppose the state of demand becomes known with certainty after a year, yielding a return of either 244 in the subsequent period in the good state, or 0 otherwise. By waiting for one year and then *only* investing in the good state, the expected *NPV* is now increased by the option value, so:

$$\text{NPV}_0 = \frac{1}{2} \left(\frac{88}{1.1} + \frac{242}{(1.1)^2} \right)$$

$$= \frac{1}{2} (-80 + 200)$$

$$= 60$$

Using the opportunity of waiting to resolve uncertainty nearly triples the expected present value of the investment, because the investment 'option' will be exercised only in the good state. This expected cost saving more than outweighs the delayed return.

Comparing the two values of $NPV = 22$, and $NVP_0 = 60$, the difference (given by $60 - 22 = 38$) can be regarded as the value of the option of postponing an irreversible investment. Clearly these simple examples could be extended in various ways to make them more realistic. A longer or even infinite stream of returns could be considered, new information might shift probabilities rather than yielding certainty, and so on. The calculations become much more complicated, as shown in advanced treatments, but the basic principle remains valid.

The irreversibility of investment explains why firms seem to require 'hurdle' rates of return on investment projects that are much higher than interest rates, without assuming an implausibly large risk premium. Instead, the rate of return has to be high enough to cover both the conventional cost of capital and also the option value of delaying an investment project.

Risk and return

Other things being equal, investors prefer safer assets. A risky investment will have to offer a higher return than a safe asset in order to compensate for undesirable risk, when these are the only choices available. In reality of course, there are a large number of different assets with widely varying degrees and types of risk. In particular, many risks are negatively correlated in some way. For example, if demand shifts from beer to wine, brewers suffer but vineyards prosper. Holding a portfolio of assets or shares whose risks are negatively related in this way represents a kind of home-made insurance policy, and reduces the overall risk faced by the rational investor.

This approach forms the basis for the modern theories of capital asset pricing developed in finance texts. The prices of assets or securities such as company shares depend on the returns required. If the returns from an asset are positively correlated with the optimal market portfolio, then this asset adds risk and requires a higher return than a safe investment such as a riskless government bond. However, if an asset's returns are negatively related to the whole portfolio, then purchasing this asset *reduces* overall risk, even though it may itself be quite risky. The holder of the **diversified portfolio** will thus be willing to accept a lower-than-riskless return from the negatively correlated security or asset because this asset is now providing some insurance or reduction of overall portfolio risk.

Accepting a lower return is equivalent to paying a higher price for the asset, and theories of this kind are widely used to evaluate security prices. However, there are fundamental problems involved with calculations based upon *expected* future returns, because expectations may be mistaken. Taste may shift from beer and wine to soft drinks or spirits, and reverse the negative correlation that was expected. Another problem is that the returns from many widely held assets such as consumer durables and property are difficult to observe or quantify, because they consist of intangible services. The risks associated with new products and ventures such as high-tech start-ups are particularly difficult to evaluate, because there is then no past record to provide even a guideline for expected future value and return. Not surprisingly, such investments are regarded as among the most risky, prudentially avoided by all but specialized professionals such as venture capitalists.

C.   Financial markets

Efficient markets

Until the 1980s, organized markets for financial securities and foreign exchange were regarded as efficient in the sense that prices were determined by 'fundamentals' and rational expectations, which quickly incorporated new information. The semi-strong form of the **efficient market hypothesis** (EMH) maintained that current stock prices reflected all publicly available information at any time. Future prices were therefore not predictable from past price movements or any other public information. According to this logic, it followed that chartists or technical analysts who claimed the ability to forecast price movements from patterns in previous prices were simply charlatans. More generally it was impossible to earn above-average returns without access to inside information. The strong form of the EMH argued that even inside information would 'quickly' be reflected in current prices, and this has received some support from 'event studies' in recent years. Unexpected changes in earnings of particular companies were often found to be preceded by corresponding stock price changes. More precisely, stock prices would, for example, begin to rise before public announcement of the new profit figures but after internal reports by company accountants had been completed. Similarly, the stock price of target companies in takeover bids tends to rise *before* public announcement of the bid. These observations suggest that either insider trading (which is illegal in the United States, where most studies were based) and/or leakage of inside information is widespread.

Large and rapid capital gains are thus attainable by those who respond most quickly to new information, including news of technological breakthroughs or decisive experiments of commercial relevance. The huge potential profit from being ahead in the race to act upon 'news' encourages a substantial amount of socially unproductive activity by highly talented individuals. It is important to realize that efforts to be 'first mover' affect only the *distribution* of rents or capital gains, and are quite distinct from productive activity devoted to *producing* information, such as R&D or the search for profitable acquisitions or new markets. Ironically, then, evidence for the strong EMH is also evidence for socially wasteful activity generated by such markets.

Excess volatility

The central tenet of market efficiency is that the value of securities is determined by fundamentals rather than by volatile market sentiments or fads. In the case of shares, fundamental value is determined by the NPV of future expected dividends. Although there are sometimes unexpected changes in dividends, on average or in the long run expectations based on enormous research efforts into company prospects should not be persistently and systematically off the mark.

This belief was demolished in a seminal paper by Robert Shiller in 1981 (see also Shiller, 1989), who showed that the real present value of future dividends had been following a fairly constant trend over long periods while stock prices fluctuated widely. Theoretically this could be explained by the alternating impact of good and bad 'news' which exaggerates or underestimates future prospects. However, subsequent research has failed to find evidence that news can account for much of observed volatility. The crash of October 1987, for example, seemed to occur in the absence of any adverse news. Shiller's work was one of the starting points of a research programme on behavioural finance, which seeks to enrich simple models of market behaviour with more realistic accounts of the ways in which real people actually behave. This research programme, combined with recent empirical evidence of predictable components in share price changes, has produced many insights as well as uncovering more puzzling 'anomalies' in financial markets that still defy convincing explanation.[3]

There is growing agreement that one of the keys to understanding financial markets is the influence of so-called 'noise traders'. These are individuals who do not follow fundamental analysis but rather buy or sell on the advice of friends and neighbours, market gurus, charlatans or astrologers. They are inclined to follow short-term trends or rumours of what the 'smart money' is doing, and thus can amplify overall movements into large fluctuations. Rational investors cannot ignore the effects of noise traders either. Noise traders are likely to be prone to shifting fads and sentiments, which create additional risk in the markets by causing temporary but possibly lengthy deviations from fundamental values. An alternative explanation for excess volatility is that expected returns seem to vary with the business cycle.

Among the anomalies or deviations from efficient markets that have emerged is the phenomenon of mean reversion. High-performance or low-performance stocks tend to revert to average returns over time, and markets appear to overreact to current events and news. Thus, in contrast to EMH, past price movements do have some power to predict future movements. However, the effects usually seem to be too small to provide profitable trading opportunities in the long run when all costs are considered.

In a remarkable new development of this line of research, University of Exeter economists George Bulkley and Richard Harris find that professional stock market analysts' forecasts of long-run company earnings growth in the United States are systematically biased. High projections are exaggerated, and low forecasts too pessimistic on average. Furthermore, these irrational forecasts do influence stock prices, in the sense that, after adjusting for risk, 'stock returns are positively correlated with analysts' forecast errors over the same period'. (Bulkley and Harris, 1997, pp. 359–71). This result in turn implies that the actual forecasts provided by analysts are negatively correlated with excess returns from stocks over the next five years. Bulkley and Harris also show that a 'contrarian' investment strategy on this basis, using only publicly available information, could have beaten the market and earned above-normal returns.

Another interesting development of recent years has been the discovery that expectations can be 'self-fulfilling', leading to systematic deviations from fundamental values, even when traders are fully rational. This can give rise to speculative but **rational bubbles**. As long as traders believe with some positive probability that prices may still rise, it can be optimal to hold an overvalued security until the bubble 'bursts'. The rise of the Tokyo stock market and urban property prices in Japan to dizzy heights little related to fundamentals in the late 1980s seems to fit this pattern. Together, the possibility of rational bubbles and the probability that many market participants are less than boundedly rational (or even downright irrational) seriously undermine the core belief of market efficiency.

Beating the market

The most robust prediction of the EMH seems to be the impossibility of obtaining above-average returns on the stock market using only publicly available information. Funds that pay high salaries to their managers for buying winners and selling losers tend to underperform the market on average. Thus over the five years to the end of 1995, the Financial Times All-Share Index of UK publicly traded shares returned 107 per cent, whereas the average UK growth trust (or fund) returned 82 per cent.

To reduce the costs of management and trading, a growing number of tracker funds simply buy and hold a wide portfolio of shares that represent the index they are 'tracking'. These funds provide maximum diversification at minimum administrative cost, unattainable for most private investors. It is perhaps no coincidence that these funds are gaining popularity after prolonged upward trends on many stock markets.

It must also be pointed out that some fund managers do outperform the market for extended periods, and not only in rising markets. Some individuals have also managed to beat the market systematically enough to become billionaires. Hungarian–American investor George Soros is one famous example; his speculation against the pound in effect forced the British currency out of the European Monetary System in 1992. The Quantum Fund, founded and managed by Soros, has produced an average annual return of 35 per cent over the 27 years since its inception in 1968. Though helped by the fund's off-shore, tax-haven status, this performance is all the more remarkable because it is not based on a few lucky hits. In contrast to some successful long-term investors, Soros and his managerial team trade with great frequency, completing thousands of transactions annually in search of even the smallest margins (*Investors Chronicle*, 26 January–1 February 1996). Anglo-French financier Sir James Goldsmith was another remarkably successful investor, who retired from business to become a Member of the European Parliament at Strasbourg, founder of Britain's Referendum Party, and a radical opponent of European monetary union and of free trade.[4] Just how a handful of individuals manage to achieve such improbably long runs of 'good luck', or indeed whether it is just luck or some rare ability, remain open questions.

The inefficiency of the stock market?

Substantial changes in stock prices seem to occur without 'news' or change in fundamentals. As in many other markets, fashions seem to shift unpredictably and sometimes dramatically. Considerable resources are spent on rent-seeking competition to obtain inside information, a form of competition that does not yield social benefits. Once regarded as the best-established empirical proposition in economics, the EMH is now under attack from all kinds of evidence from financial and currency markets, as well as new, more realistic psychologically based theories about how real people actually behave in markets.

To conclude this section, we now turn to the question of how the social benefits of the stock market relate to the costs, in order to consider whether or not the institution is socially efficient. A decade ago, this question would have sounded heretical in some countries, but not in others. The United Kingdom has about 2,000 publicly traded companies compared with fewer than 700 in France or Germany, and over 6,000 in the United States. The United Kingdom and the United States are often described as stock market dominated economies compared with continental Europe and Japan, where the role of the stock market is much less important.

In spite of these differences, there is one striking similarity in the function of stock markets across all countries, a similarity that has undermined the traditional claim for the stock market's role as a provider of industrial capital. In fact, the major proportion of business investment in all countries is *not* provided in the form of new equity by the stock market. Internal funds provide the largest share (80–90 per cent), followed by bank credit, and in the United States equity was a *negative* source of capital as many firms bought back outstanding shares to raise prices during the 1980s.

If the stock market is not a major provider of new investment capital, what functions remain? The stock market does provide a liquid market for owners of existing equity capital, who can always sell at short notice. However, the excess volatility of share prices increases the risk of holding shares and of short-term sales. Most economists believe the main function of the stock market should be to provide a market for corporate control, so that underperforming management can be removed, if necessary by a hostile takeover. The virtual absence of hostile takeovers in Japan, Germany and other successful economies raises problems for this view, which we shall discuss in the next chapter.

There is also evidence that the influence of the stock market in the Anglo-American economies encourages excessive attention by managers to short-term profit results, with a consequent neglect of long-term investment. This 'market myopia' was demonstrated most directly by Miles (1993), who showed that cash flows accruing five years in the future were discounted at much higher rates (up to twice as high) than more immediate returns. Although these results could theoretically be explained by varying risk premia, this alternative is not very plausible. There are, of course, also fluctuating fashions for high-technology stocks that do value, or even overvalue, long-term expectations, but there is also a wealth of ancedotal evidence for pervasive market pressures on most managers to maintain short-run earnings (see Miles, 1993, and Jacobs, 1991).

Joseph Stiglitz, a leading economist who was chairman of US President Clinton's Council of Economic Advisers, points out that

> Firms take actions that appear to increase after-tax earnings even when those actions at the same time increase the present discounted value of the tax liabilities. . . . Many firms did not use accelerated depreciation for the same reason. . . . But less reliance on stock markets might induce boards of directors to place more reliance on direct observation, on comparisons with other firms in the industry. (Stiglitz, 1994, pp. 95–6).

Stiglitz re-emphasizes the famous analogy between the stock market and a beauty contest that was originally put forward by J. M. Keynes. Here the problem is to guess not who is 'really' the most beautiful contestant, 'but who the other judges will judge to be the most beautiful. Thus resources are allocated to obtaining information not about the fundamentals but about perceptions.'

> More generally, much of the expenditure on information collected on the stock market has little, if any, social value. For stocks that are already traded, there is a zero-sum game. The gains of one party are at the expense of the other. The quest is to find information that will affect market price slightly before others do. (Stiglitz, 1994, p. 94)

'Going public' or offering shares for sale on the stock market can bring substantial capital gains to entrepreneurs or the founders of new firms. Realizing these gains by selling a sizeable block of shares can depress the price, however, if the market interprets the sale as a signal that the original owner(s) consider the shares to be overvalued. If they do not retain a majority holding, the firm may be vulnerable to takeover, perhaps by some larger competitor keen to obtain access to new technology. When corporate cultures do not mix, valuable human resources may be lost in this process of acquisition or merger. These questions are pursued further in the next chapter; where we consider whether the 'market for corporate control' can discipline the managers of large corporations with no dominating stockholders, and enforce efficient behaviour.

D. Credit markets

Collateral

For most people, obtaining a mortgage to buy a house is the largest financial transaction in which they will ever participate. This importance carries over to the economy as a whole, because mortgage interest rates and the state of the property market and construction industry are important cyclical indicators. The market for all kinds of credit – commercial and personal loans as well as mortgages – is one of the most important financial markets, and one that has a more direct impact on most people's economic welfare than other financial markets.

Yet credit 'markets' differ fundamentally from other markets. A given interest rate or 'price of credit' does not mean that a borrower can obtain any amount of credit at that rate. Instead, terms of the loan have to be negotiated individually, and these include the quantity of credit, mode of repayment and duration of the loan, and, most importantly, the security or 'collateral' offered to the lender. Credit transactions are thus much more complicated than simple commodity purchase.

The basic problem with a loan contract is that repayment, of principal and of interest, is deferred to future dates. Without some security that can be claimed by the lender, the borrower may default or break the contractual agreement and leave the creditor to bear the loss of a 'bad' or unpaid debt. In property mortgage transactions, the title deeds to the property are usually retained by the bank or creditor until repayment is complete. To provide complete security, the value of the property held as collateral should exceed the mortgage debt. The borrower thus needs some equity in the investment to make up the difference. Of course, if market prices fall rapidly during the lifetime of the loan, then the property owner can be left with negative equity, or debt obligations in excess of the property value. If adverse circumstances, such as job loss and unemployment, impair the mortgage holder's ability to repay her debt, then the creditor may repossess the property, evict the defaulting debtor and sell the property to recover as much as possible of the original loan principal.

During the recession of the early 1990s, repossession and distress sales of residential property became common in parts of the United Kingdom, particularly in the South East, where property prices had risen rapidly in the speculative boom of the late 1980s. The collapse of the boom and onset of recession left many home owners with negative equity and often without a job as well. Precipitate action by banks and loan companies, repossessing and selling by auction the homes of unlucky mortgage holders, was widely considered to have accelerated the collapse of house prices and prolonged the recession.

Rapid response by individual creditors may well have been the optimal reaction to the expectation of falling prices. Delay by any one lender could mean still lower proceeds from sale. However, if creditor response had been coordinated and defaulting householders given more time to find new jobs, then house price deflation might have been much less severe. The banks would then have ended up with smaller losses than they incurred through uncoordinated individual action, and the recession would also have been shortened.

Adverse selection and credit rationing

Markets where buyers are rationed or limited in the quantity obtainable at the prevailing price are usually associated with price controls. Thus it might be argued that deregulation and the freedom to adjust interest rates might be able to attain equilibrium in credit markets without rationing. In fact there is no evidence of this happening anywhere. And new theories of **adverse selection** with asymmetric information show that credit rationing is an essential part of credit market equilibrium rather than being due to any arbitrary imposed rigidity (see the discussion in Chapter 7). The boom-and-bust cycles of the 1980s in British and American credit and property markets followed precipitate and ill-prepared deregulation.

The problem is that higher interest rates are likely to deter investors with relatively safe projects that yield low rates of return. With riskier projects, the investor profits if he is lucky, and the creditor is likely to lose out if the project fails. The market value of collateral may drop unexpectedly, as in the case of the UK property market, imposing a loss on the creditor. It is not always possible to identify the risky loan applicants in advance, in spite of considerable efforts by lenders to screen their customers and eliminate the worst risks. In this situation, higher interest rates may just raise the proportion of undetectable (*ex ante*) high risks in the creditor's loan portfolio, and this effect can easily offset the greater return from borrowers who do not default.

For the economy as a whole, higher interest rates do tend to reduce the total demand for credit and thus help to restrain economic activity when inflation accelerates during a boom. On the other hand, lowering interest rates to stimulate recovery from recession may be less effective. If business prospects are poor and people are worried about the security of their jobs, simply lowering interest rates may not be sufficient to encourage much additional borrowing and investment.

There is evidence that small businesses and new start-ups are often unable to borrow as much as they would like to expand their business, even when prospects are good, basically because creditors regard them as too risky. Larger firms, unless they are already saddled with excessive debt, can usually offer sufficient security to obtain extra credit, probably on more favourable terms as well (see Fazzari *et al.*, 1988).

Most kinds of credit rationing and constraints are due to lenders' limited information. Banks specialize in providing relatively safe loans with low expenditure on obtaining information, usually restricted to fairly routine questionnaires. At the other extreme, venture capitalists become experts in particular market areas in order to judge the risks of providing equity capital with little in the way of security. Frequent small payoffs or losses have to be balanced by the occasional big winner, so this type of investor tries to identify long-term potential rather than seeking to avoid risk altogether, as in the credit market.

Short-termism again

Though exact quantification is difficult, it is generally accepted that there is considerably more short-term lending in the United Kingdom and the United States than in Germany and Japan. Short-term loans are less risky than long-term commitments in an otherwise similar context, for the obvious reason that uncertainty increases as the time horizon lengthens. However the risks of long-term credit can be mitigated by improving the information available to the creditor. One way of achieving this goal is to maintain long-term business relationships, so that information accumulates while personal contacts and trust are built up. This is precisely the way in which many firms in Germany and Japan have developed relationships with their 'main banks' and other institutional investors, reinforced by the presence of bank directors on company boards and equity holdings by the banks. Enhanced information about company prospects thus reduces the risk of long-term loan contracts, which in turn allows investors more scope for pursuing long-term projects.

In part, the problem lies in a different tradition of Anglo-American bank regulation, designed to protect depositors and separate investment from commercial banking. The unfortunate consequence is that managers may concentrate unduly on investments that promise a rapid payoff, while neglecting 'long-range' projects. Surveys show that British managers generally require much higher internal rates of return (or, equivalently, shorter payback periods) than continental European managers. Credit markets and managerial attitudes thus seem to exacerbate the tendency towards short-termism in the stock market dominated economies of the United Kingdom and the United States (Commission on Public Policy and British Business, 1997). In spite of all the evidence to the contrary, many financial economists still claim that stock markets are efficient and that short-termism is a myth.

E. Chapter summary and key ideas

This chapter has developed the key building blocks of classical and modern investment and finance theory at a very elementary, introductory level. The notion of present discounted values forms the foundation, leading naturally to classical separation (Fisher) and irrelevance (Modigliani and Miller) theorems, for which we provide simple, intuitive arguments. Acclaimed as the most important development in the theory of investment since Fisher's classic work, the role of irreversible investment with uncertainty and the option value of delaying investment to obtain more information are presented with the help of a simple numerical example.

Another far-reaching development of recent years has been the growing body of evidence, as well as new theories, challenging the classical hypothesis of efficient financial markets. Movements in stock prices such as the crash of 1987 are difficult to explain by changes in fundamentals. Fads and fashions seem to affect financial as well as other markets, though none of this offers easy ways to 'beat the market'. Disturbing from a policy perspective is the observation that markets seem to discount future cash flows at higher rates than more immediate flows, which could bias managers in the stock market dominated Anglo-American economies to neglect long-term investment.

Most worrying of all are the enormous resources invested in rent-seeking, information-gathering activity, in order to profit from price changes in financial markets. Most stock market and foreign exchange transactions are thus speculative, unrelated to new investment or international trade, and so essentially part of a zero-sum game. Although a few individuals can net profits running into billions, the social value of the efforts to emulate them by myriads of less successful traders is minimal. And credit markets are subject to their own problems of adverse selection and short-term lending by creditors, with adverse cyclical effects such as the collapse of the British property boom in 1989–90.

Key words

adverse selection	irreversible investment
behavioural finance	Modigliani–Miller theorems
debt	net present value
diversified portfolio	noise traders
efficient market hypothesis	rational bubble
excess volatility	short-termism
fundamentals	sunk costs

Questions and problems for review and discussion

1 Calculate the present value of 1 billion ECU after 100 years at discount rates of 1, 2, 5 and 10 per cent.
2 Explain why informational asymmetry and moral hazard lead to liquidity constraints or restrictions on borrowing by both consumers and businesses.
3 Construct your own numerical example of an irreversible investment with uncertain outcome, and calculate the option value of postponing the investment.
4 Explain the conditions under which a diversified portfolio reduces investment risk. What is the flow in the analogous argument that was used to justify conglomerate diversification?
5 How efficient do you think financial markets are? Justify your answer.
6 The price of shares in new high-tech companies is notoriously volatile, generating substantial risk for investors. What fundamental factors are likely to be involved? Do you think that 'fashions' in high-tech stocks are likely to be more or less influential in driving volatility than in the market for mature companies?
7 If the stock market is largely a zero-sum game, how would you attempt to estimate all the social costs of this institution?
8 Compare and describe the various ways in which financial markets in the United Kingdom and the United States are said to be 'short-termist'.
9 What are the costs and benefits of the use of collateral in credit markets?
10 Is credit rationing evidence that credit markets are not functioning efficiently? Explain your answer.

Notes

1 General problems of 'short-termism' are discussed later in this chapter. They seem often to be related to a fundamental psychological tendency to exaggerate the importance of current or recent events in decision-making, one of the reasons for 'quasi-rational' rather than perfectly rational behaviour in many economic situations, for which evidence is accumulating (Thaler, 1993).
2 The authors later both received Nobel prizes.
3 See the exciting collection of work by a pioneer of the field, Richard Thaler (1993).
4 See Goldsmith (1994). In this series of wide-ranging interviews Goldsmith emphasized the neglected social and environmental costs of trade, intensive agriculture, nuclear energy and policy centralization in the European Union.

References

Bulkley, G. and R. Harris (1997), 'Irrational analysts' expectations as a cause of excess volatility in stock prices', *Economic Journal*, 107, pp. 359–71.

Commission on Public Policy and British Business (1977), 'U.K. company myopia', in *Promoting Prosperity: A Business Agenda for Britain*, London: Vintage Books.

Fazzari, S. M., R. G. Hubbard and B. C. Peterson (1988), 'Financing constraints and corporate investment', *Brookings Papers*, pp. 141–95.

Goldsmith, J. (1994), *The Trap*, London: Macmillan.

Jacobs, M. T. (1991), *Short Term America*, Boston: Harvard Business School Press.

Miles, D. (1993), 'Testing for short termism in the UK stockmarket', *Economic Journal*, 103, pp. 1379–96.

Modigliani, F. and M. H. Miller (1958), 'The cost of capital, corporation finance, and the theory of investment', *American Economic Review*, 48, pp. 261–97.

Pindyck, R. S. (1991), 'Irreversiblilty, uncertainty and investment', *Journal of Economic Literature*, 29, pp. 1110–48.

Shiller, R. J. (1981), 'The excess volatility of stock prices', *American Economic Review*, 71, pp. 421–36.

Shiller, R. J. (1989), *Market Volatility*, Cambridge, Mass.: MIT Press.

Stiglitz, J. E. (1994), *Whither Socialism?*, Cambridge, Mass.: MIT Press.

Thaler, R. (1993), *Advances in Behavioral Finance*, New York: Russell Sage Foundation.

Ownership and control of the corporation

> Outside Shareholders are stupid and impertinent – stupid because they give
> their funds to somebody else without adequate control, and impertinent
> because they clamour for a dividend as a reward for their stupidity.
> (Statement attributed to German banker Carl Fürstenberg [1850–1933] by
> Martin Hellwig, 1995, p. 198)

A. Chapter outline and student goals

Ownership and control have obvious meanings in everyday life.[1] Owning a
house or a car implies the right to 'control' or determine the use (for what
and by whom) of these assets, subject of course to all the relevant legal restrictions that do often impose severe constraints. Indeed, ownership is essentially
defined as the right of use. This familiar terminology has been widely extended
to more complicated situations, and the shareholders of a large corporation
are also usually referred to as the 'owners'. However, if you are but one of
many shareholders in a large corporation, this does definitely not mean that
you can walk into the head office and start telling people what to do. In fact,
as a small shareholder there is very little that you can do, except sell your
shares if disgruntled, or otherwise hang on to them and collect your dividend
payments, if any, and hope for the best.

The common meaning of ownership has become dramatically diluted in the
case of multiple shareholdings. The consequences of this dilution for the control or governance of corporate enterprise have been the subject of intense
debate by economists and legal scholars, as well as policy makers, for more
than half a century. In this chapter we review the various strands of this debate,
and we shall see how corporate governance has evolved into very different
institutions in different countries. This diversity has not yet been reflected in
the dominating theoretical paradigm, which was mainly developed in the
United States with somewhat parochial disregard for experience elsewhere.

We start with the standard model of corporate governance, which abstracts
from the problems of diluted ownership by focusing on the shareholders as a
collective. The pioneering work by Berle and Means revealed the inadequacy

353

of this approach by showing just how widely dispersed the stock ownership of most large American corporations had become by the 1930s. Various models of the typical Anglo-American managerial firm were developed in the post-war decades, while little attention was paid to differing institutions of governance in continental Europe. A useful conceptual framework for analyzing the varieties of firm organization found in theory and practice is derived from the terms 'residual income' and 'residual control'. Intuitively these refer to the cash flow remaining after all contractual payments have been made, and to the discretionary power for decision-making after meeting all prior commitments and legal obligations, respectively. Much of our exposition, as well as previous debate, concerns the 'unbundling' of these residual rights in large organizations with multiple 'ownership', and consequent complications.

These problems do not, of course, arise in a firm with a single (residual) owner–manager, and so can be regarded as an inevitable consequence of the growth in scale of enterprise to the ubiquitous giant modern corporation. The professional top management or chief executive of a corporation with widely dispersed shareholders, and hence no dominant 'owner', appear to have residual control without necessarily any significant ownership stake at all. However the stock market does provide a market for corporate control that allows the takeover of poorly performing companies. The acquiring firm must generally obtain a majority of the shares of the target company, and can then replace unwanted or underperforming managers and directors.

Just how well this mechanism for enforcing efficient corporate governance has actually worked in the stock market or 'outsider' dominated economies of the United Kingdom and United States is a matter of considerable controversy. In the traditionally faster-growing economies of Japan, Germany and other European countries, large shareholdings by associated banks and other corporations are part of long-term, relationship investing that maintains insider control. Hostile takeovers are practically unknown in these countries, though friendly mergers have also been increasing.

Encouraged by the wave of management buyouts in the 1980s, Anglo-American financial economists have argued that concentrated ownership and insider control represent the best solution to the problems of corporate governance. However, they have ignored the essential role of employee stakeholders in continental European and Japanese firms. Workers with firm-specific skills are everywhere likely to share organizational rents or residual income, which they are liable to lose in case of job loss, bankruptcy or corporate takeover. Employees thus also share the residual risk of outside equity holders. As human capital becomes generally more important with technological progress, progressive employers everywhere are increasingly recognizing that 'our wealth is in our people'. Such firms become more like partnerships with employee involvement, shareholding or profit-sharing as human capital becomes the dominant factor of production. While such stakeholder firms are still exceptional in the Anglo-American economies, Japanese and continental systems of corporate governance have institutionalized the role of employee stakeholders in various ways that complement the higher general levels of skill and training in these countries. Although some aspects of Japanese productive organization such as lean production and teamwork have been widely adopted in today's integrated global economy, the recognition of human capital-owners as legitimate stakeholders in the goals of the firm, as well as shareholders, is still widely resisted.

After reading this chapter you should be able to:

- understand the many meanings of ownership and control;
- explain the separation of ownership and control in 'managerial' firms;
- judge the effects of takeovers and mergers on firm performance;
- compare the role of company directors in different countries;
- recognize the interests of employee stakeholders in the success of the firm;
- evaluate claims that the only legitimate goal of the corporation is to maximize shareholder value;
- compare Anglo-American with German–Japanese systems of corporate governance.

B. The separation of ownership and control

In the classical entrepreneurial firm, ownership and control were combined in the one person of entrepreneur–founder and current general manager who hired a few helpers. As these firms evolved and grew, outside shareholders might supply additional capital, and an employed manager might replace the founder or his heirs. In spite of warnings by the classical economists Adam Smith and J. S. Mill, the old concepts were still regarded as adequate for the new situation as firms grew larger in the first industrial revolution.

The basic model of corporate governance

Extending the multiplicity of ownership from the quite common cases of partnerships with several partners to the joint stock companies that emerged in the latter part of the nineteenth century seemed straightforward at first. The new 'owners' had limited liability, in contrast to partners, thus encouraging outside shareholders with no managerial role in the business. However they were still 'owners' who appropriated the residual income after all factors of production had been paid the going rate. Even if not active in management themselves, the new owners appointed the directors, who in turn hired and monitored the managers, and thus the owners apparently also retained ultimate or residual control as well.

Some capital is often supplied by creditors who receive a contractual rate of interest, but normally have no control rights. This situation changes abruptly if the firm is unlucky, or badly managed, and is thus unable to meet contractual interest and debt-repayment obligations. In such a case of default, there is no residual income left for shareholders and insufficient cash flow for debt service. The creditors are now residual claimants, who have the first claim on the firm's resources before any payment to shareholders can be made. It is thus appropriate for basic residual control to be transferred to creditors in case of default, in order to maximise their chances of repayment.

Because shareholders have limited liability, they will have no more interest in the business when the value of their shares or expected dividends has fallen to zero. Creditors then can have no more claims on shareholders and must themselves assume responsibility to rescue as much as possible of the company and their loans. Since these objectives may conflict, the usual practice is for an interim, outside manager such as an official receiver or administrator to be appointed with the explicit task of organizing a rescue package that maintains as much as possible of the original organization as a going concern. Liquidation of the company and piecemeal sale of all physical assets might satisfy creditors, but ensures that shareholders and employees lose out, and is thus only the last resort when all else has failed and no part of the business can be salvaged as a going concern.

In Anglo-American law and business practice, the power of banks and cartels has always been traditionally suspect, and even publicly quoted corporations were largely regarded as private contractual arrangements, much like any small limited liability company. Regulation concentrated on averting explicit fraud and overt misrepresentation, but left the details of governance mainly to the parties involved. British law did recognize the corporation as a legal individual with an identity distinct from its personal members and stakeholders, but this distinction was not developed as in continental law, where it formed the basis for much more detailed administrative regulation of the corporation and its responsibility to various stakeholders (and not just shareholders). Given this broader responsibility, major bank involvement and the anti-competitive nature of cooperative ventures and cartels were seen as far less threatening to the general welfare.

Berle and Means

It was not until the 1932 publication of a landmark study by the American lawyer Adolf Berle and the economist Gardiner Means that the efficiency of the basic, traditional model of the corporation was systematically challenged. Berle and Means showed that most large US corporations had such widely dispersed ownership that no individual shareholder was likely to have much influence, so that residual control was in effect in the hands of top management and directors, who were often nominated by management as well. Ownership rights had been unbundled and reduced to the claim on dividends, which were actually set at the discretion of top management.

If owners had little voice in the governance of their corporation, the exit option of selling shares also had limitations; the stock market crash of 1929 showed that share prices could fall too fast for many people to react promptly enough. Berle and Means sparked off a debate that has continued in the English-speaking economies until the present time. Indeed, the slower post-war growth of these countries compared with continental and Far Eastern rivals has intensified discussion of corporate governance and, more recently, interest in alternative models.

Many economists wedded to notions of competitive markets and their beneficial consequences were reluctant to accept Berle and Mean's thesis, and indeed ignored their findings. It was only in the 1960s that economic theorists rediscovered the problems identified by Berle and Means under the label of principal and agent theory, as part of the emerging economics of imperfect information.

The managerial firm

A generation after Berle and Means, economists thus began to take seriously the idea of firms that were run by managers, primarily in their own interest. Stockholders who received stable or steadily growing dividends were seen as closer to bond holders, while management tended to reinvest the residual income left after paying both contractual interest and expected dividends. As Japanese products began their rapid penetration of Western markets, the hypothesis of 'growth maximization' became an alternative to maximization of shareholder value in various models of the firm that were driven by managerial preferences and only loosely constrained by competitive forces and the need to pay 'adequate' and reliable dividends.

Economists such as William Baumol and Dennis Mueller found that the returns to investment of internal funds were often lower than the market rate of interest, particularly for older and less innovative firms in stagnating markets.[2] Such investment would actually reduce the value of shares, and owners would have been better served by higher dividend payouts. Internal cash flow that cannot be invested profitably inside the firm, to earn a return above opportunity cost, is often referred to as **free cash flow**. Instead of returning free cash flow to shareholders in the form of dividends, managers often pursued conglomerate mergers and acquisitions in apparently unrelated lines of business, claiming elusive synergy effects or benefits from diversification to reduce the risks of specialization. Since shareholders could themselves easily diversify their own portfolios, the latter argument was not obviously consistent with Anglo-American business leaders' repeatedly proclaimed dedication to shareholder value maximization.

In the turbulent post-Opec years, older conglomerates from earlier merger waves began to unravel. In the United Kingdom and the United States only a handful of conglomerates have survived and maintained market leadership with their internal capital markets. Companies such as General Electric, believed to owe much to an exceptional chief executive, remain rare exceptions. In contrast, most leading large Japanese corporations and many in continental Europe are conglomerates. And friendly mergers in the same industry, such as the recent (1996) combination of rival Swiss pharmaceutical giants Sandoz and Ciba, have been greeted enthusiastically by shareholders and commentators, who in this case can look forward to the cost savings from cutting 13,500 jobs or 10 per cent of the existing workforce. Novartis, as the new company is called, is predicted to be the first of several such major 'rationalizations' in the ever-more expensive business of developing and marketing specialized drugs (*Financial Times*, 8 March 1996).

The market for corporate control

Although managers obviously made the decisions on how to allocate residual income after all contractual commitments and payments had been made, economists argued that this residual control right was itself subject to market discipline. Even if existing stockholders were too widely dispersed to exert much control, bad management would lead to falling share prices that should encourage some corporate raider to obtain a controlling stake. After a change of management, assets could be put to better use and value maximized again.

According to Oliver Williamson (1975), one of the ways conglomerates or multidivisional corporations could improve the performance of their components was by use of the internal capital market. Williamson argues that, since informational asymmetries between outside investors and managers were likely to inhibit investment, the head office of a large diversified holding could direct internally generated funds to their most profitable use with the help of all the inside information available to managers.

Event studies of acquisitions generally showed a rise in the share price of the acquired firm, apparently suggesting gains in efficiency and a well-functioning market for corporate control, although owners of the acquiring firm did not appear to benefit. However, the theory predicted that acquired firms should be underperforming, and this was not supported by the empirical evidence. On average, acquired firms seemed to have been performing as well as non-acquired but otherwise similar companies (see Nickell, 1995). Another problem with the market for corporate control, at least until the 1980s, was that sheer size rather than performance was actually the best protection against takeover. Since larger firms usually acquired smaller firms, the best policy for managers seeking to preserve their independence might after all be the strategy of growth maximization rather than value maximization.

Box 11.1 The rise and fall of Hanson

Britain's fifteenth-largest company announced its break-up into four separate companies in January 1996, after over 30 years of ruthless acquisition and conglomerate growth. Shareholders achieved spectacular gains in the early years as drastic downsizing and divestment cut costs and boosted the return on capital. Lord Hanson was repeatedly voted Britain's most admired businessman, not least by (then) Prime Minister Margaret Thatcher, whose admiration was enthusiastically reciprocated.

In recent years the opportunities for rapid gains from undervalued targets dwindled, and Hanson's performance was disappointing. The company has substantially underperformed on the London stock market over the past 10 years. However, this has not deterred Lord Hanson and his senior colleagues from continuing to reward themselves with some of the biggest pay packets in Britain – no less than £1.37 million for the company founder in 1995.

Over the past decade Hanson has downsized its UK employment from 50,000 to 16,000 and remained a major corporate donor to the British Conservative Party. Hanson has been described as a 'role model to 1980s managers, someone whose ruthless dedication to short term earnings growth was widely admired and emulated. . . . But the admirers are dwindling. History will judge that the company's greatest – perhaps only – beneficiaries were Lord Hanson and his early shareholders, the City and the Conservative Party, in that order.'

(*The Independent on Sunday*, 4 February 1996).

Management buyouts

The decade of the 1980s began with a severe recession following the second major Opec oil-price hike. At the same time, global markets and competition were expanding, and technology was advancing rapidly, particularly in the fields of information and communications. The former high-flying conglomerates began to falter and fail in the new environment. The explosive growth of new technology and markets was forcing business to concentrate on core competencies and exposing fatal flaws in the corporate empire-building growth strategies of earlier decades. Very few of the diversified conglomerates retained market or product leadership. In the United States, General Electric, an example that was less diversified than most, seemed to owe much of its persistent success to its charismatic leader, Jack Welch, CEO since 1981. In Britain, the archetypal Hanson holding led by Lord Hanson finally split into four separate companies in 1996 as acquisitions faltered and the share price continued to lag behind the market index.

Major developments in financial technology were rapidly eroding the protection against takeover that size had long afforded. High-yielding, high-risk bonds known as **junk bonds** could be offered in exchange for part of the equity of the target firm by a raider with much smaller assets. The resulting organization had a higher debt–equity ratio, and could then often be broken up into constituents that were separately valued at more than the original, diversified conglomerate.

Transactions of this kind are called **leveraged buyouts** (LBOs) or **management buyouts** (MBOs), because they raise the share of debt (leverage, or gearing in British terms) to a high percentage of total assets. Remaining equity is usually held by a small group of venture capitalists, and management of the new organization typically holds a much higher proportion of total equity than is usual in widely owned public corporations. In MBOs, the takeover is initiated by a team of management insiders with backing from outside investors.

In direct contradiction to Williamson's theory of internal capital markets, many MBOs were led by the managers of some particularly successful corporate division that was receiving inadequate support from corporate headquarters. The new entities created were essentially highly indebted private partnerships that were supposed to solve the agency problems of ownership and control in a number of ways.

First, the legacy of unbridled growth and uncontrolled management, in the form of peripheral or unprofitable subsidiaries, was divested or 'spun off'. This allowed the new team to focus on the firm's core competencies – areas where managerial expertise and development potential were strongest. Secondly, top managers who held a high proportion of their personal wealth in the form of shares in their business were much more likely to act entrepreneurially like classical (small) owner–managers, working hard to maximize value rather than growth. Thirdly, this incentive was reinforced by the small number of outside shareholders with relatively large holdings. These owners would be represented on the board of directors and have a strong interest in monitoring managerial performance, as well as the power to replace the CEO quickly if necessary. Fourthly, an important new strategic role was ascribed to high levels of debt, contradicting the irrelevance propositions of Modigliani and Miller. If existing or projected cash flow was largely committed to debt service, then managerial discretion to engage in wasteful investment would be constrained. New investment would be subject to the scrutiny of the capital markets and the agency costs of free cash flow could be avoided. In addition, the threat of bankruptcy and job loss, traditionally seen as a disadvantage of high indebtedness, was now believed to provide an additional incentive for managerial effort.

Initially, the predictions of the theory seemed to be confirmed. MBOs in particular showed significant productivity gains following restructuring. Financial economists, as eager to follow fashion as the financial markets themselves, became euphoric, and one long-standing enthusiast for the benefits of merger and acquisitions activity even claimed that the public corporation had been superseded by the leveraged private company, and was due for extinction like the once-dominant dinosaurs (see Jensen, 1989).

More sober analysis by two eminent Harvard economists, Andrei Schleiffer and Laurence Summers (now under-secretary to the US Treasury), pointed out that short-term productivity gains could be obtained by enforced transfers from one set of stakeholders to another (see Schleiffer and Summers, 1988). For example, if implicit contracts with employees and suppliers who have made firm-specific investments are broken, costs can be cut when markets or technologies change, and measured productivity enhanced. The gains to shareholders are offset by losses to other parties that are more difficult to quantify, and have been generally ignored by financial economists.

These losses are by no means insignificant. Extensive downsizing and re-engineering or restructuring follows most buyouts and mergers. Apart from the 'sunset' or declining industries such as steel and ship building, where total employment has fallen dramatically, job losses have been concentrated among white-collar, primary workers who traditionally expected reasonably secure employment and career progression. What is widely perceived as 'breach of trust', the breaking of implicit agreements, is also believed to have had serious effects on employee loyalty and commitment by many observers. Workers who have kept their jobs have usually had to accept increased work loads and longer hours under the implicit threat to their security. Not surprisingly in such circumstances, for example the almost 50 per cent reduction in white-collar employment at British Telecom in the 10 years after privatization, measured productivity and profitability rise steeply.

To go beyond the narrow accounting and finance perspective, however, we need to consider not the only the disutility of increased stress, work loads and insecurity for remaining white-collar employees. Those who lose their jobs may be even worse off because their investments in firm-specific skills become obsolete. These losses have been recently estimated for a large sample of individuals in the United States, with average declines in total pay and benefits following job loss and re-employment of about 20 per cent (see Jacobson *et al.*, 1993).[3] The loss was greater for older workers as might be expected. Blair (1995) estimates that the returns to specific human capital in the United States are of similar magnitude to total pre-tax profits or owner's residual income. With such substantial loss of quasi-rents by displaced workers after downsizing, some portion of the measured productivity gain must be reinterpreted as a transfer from workers who have been terminated to shareholders. This transfer must be added to the shareholders' gains from an increased work load for remaining workers already mentioned. Whether net efficiency gains have been achieved in any particular case of corporate restructuring thus requires much more than the usual accounting or stock price data to decide.

With the onset of recession in the early 1990s, many heavily indebted companies were hit by the old-fashioned problems of default and bankruptcy that an earlier generation of financial analysts had emphasized. To reduce these risks, some highly leveraged partnerships began to go public again, reversing the previous trend. In the post-recession, mid-1990s, the argument for mergers and acquisitions changed yet again. As a leading British consultant and business economist, John Kay (1996), puts it: 'The emphasis is on partnerships and alliances, integration and related diversification, on industry restructuring. Strategic logic is the key buzzword.'

The effects of mergers

The market for corporate control differs from other markets in fundamental ways. While market shares of competing companies change gradually, control, Kay points out, 'is an all or nothing business'. Also the control market suffers from highly asymmetric information. You can take a used car for a trial run, but you cannot trial-run a target company, and many buyers end up getting taken for a ride! The 'winner's curse' that affects many bidding markets with asymmetric information is particularly prevalent in the market for control. Thus successful bidders may simply be those who were willing to pay too much – which is why they succeed. And good buys may remain unrecognized. Kay (1996) concludes that:

> The largely random incidence of the takeover process means that it is very far from being the source of corporate accountability and effective discipline on management behaviour that the text book model of the market for corporate control suggests.

In a similar vein, *Business Week* (30 October, 1995) and Mercer Management Consulting have conducted an 'exhaustive analysis' of mergers and acquisitions, and found that even the new strategic deals mostly fall below expectations and 'fail to deliver'. Kay notes that companies actually divest much of what they purchase, and that surveys asking firms whether acquisitions had been successful elicit only about 50 per cent positive responses.

C. Managerial constraints and incentives

There is no doubt that the top management of large corporations hold residual control for most of the time. However there may be dramatic change after a takeover or a financial crisis, and, when there is a dominating owner, managerial discretion may be much more tightly constrained. In any case it is useful now to consider the managerial function and reward system in more detail.

Managerial rewards and goals

The best-established empirical fact about top managers' pay is that total compensation is closely related to the size of the firm. This relationship, which holds in all countries, can be motivated in various ways. Larger organizations usually have more layers of management hierarchy, and to motivate effort at each level it may be necessary to offer significantly more pay at the next level, in the form of a 'prize' in the promotion 'tournament'. This structure would obviously lead to a correlation between size and chief executive compensation. It can also be argued that larger organizations are more difficult to manage, and hence require the most able managers, who have to be paid the market rate in order to retain their services. The observed correlation should thus be inherently stable.

However, a conflict of interest clearly arises. Small outside shareholders would like management to maximize the value of the firm. But, for example by making acquisitions that are unprofitable on average, top managers can increase both the size of the firm and their own compensation. Given the very unpredictable nature of merger outcomes, it is difficult for outsiders to be sure that managers are not simply looking for economies of scale or distribution or some other expected but elusive synergy.

Anglo-American companies now try to link compensation to share value with stock options or bonus payments that are profit related. However, these incentives do not completely remove the conflict. The managers of a larger firm can expect to receive more valuable options, a higher basic salary and other payments, so there is still a trade-off between value maximization and excessive growth.

The merger and aquisition game also offers unique thrills of the chase as non-pecuniary rewards for ambitious chief executives. As Kay (1996) puts it, 'Nothing else puts your picture and your pronouncements on the front page, nothing else offers so easy a way to expand your empire and emphasize your roles.' As well as prestige, sheer size also provides more of the untaxed benefits such as executive jets and lavish head offices that perhaps more profitable but smaller organizations could not afford.

In Britain and America, chief executive compensation rose much faster than average pay throughout the 1980s and 1990s, in the United Kingdom by about 20 per cent per year. At the same time, many companies were introducing performance-related pay, stock options and bonus schemes designed to align managerial incentives and shareholders' interests. However, detailed studies show the connection between top managerial pay and performance to be tenuous at best. And, after 1988, the link broke down in Britain altogether, when very large executive pay increases appeared to be unrelated to performance, which was frequently dismal during the subsequent recession (Gregg *et al.*, 1993).

The pay package used to reward chief executives and managing directors is often decided by a compensation committee that is either beholden to or appointed by the chief executive himself. Mounting public concern over the system and the size of chief executive pay rises has led to some stormy scenes at shareholders' annual general meetings but little evidence of any concrete action to alleviate the problems so far.

In continental Europe and Japan, managerial salaries do not seem to have grown faster than average pay, and indeed chief executives in these countries tend to earn far less than their US counterparts today. Stock options are little used and performance-related bonus plans are much less important, with no obviously detrimental effects on firm performance.

Concentrated ownership

A solution to these problems that is widely favoured by economists is concentrated share ownership. If a few individuals or firms hold a majority or substantial minorities of a company's outstanding shares, then they should have the incentive to monitor management performance closely. However, large shareholders may not necessarily prefer pure value-maximizing as the exclusive goal of the firm. Wealthy shareholders can afford to indulge their own personal preferences, which may include the prestige attached to acquisition and size, disseminating their political views or propagating their favourite product or hobby. The closer the involvement of outsiders with top management, the more likely these outsiders are to share in at least some of the perks of management and the non-pecuniary rewards of growth.

Large corporations are today so large that even very wealthy individuals can hold only a small proportion of the shares. Substantial owners are thus usually banks and other corporations, particularly in continental European countries and Japan. But these 'owners' are then themselves companies with managers who have their own goals. Many banks, for example, have widely dispersed shareholders. Again, then, there seems little reason for these large institutional shareholders to try to enforce a strictly value-maximizing policy.

In the United Kingdom and the United States, institutional shareholders often deliberately eschew any close relationship with companies whose shares form part of their portfolio. Instead, a policy of active market trading is followed in order to maximize financial returns, though, ironically, most portfolio and fund managers seem to underperform the stock market, as described in the previous chapter. In any case, this kind of arm's-length investment is not designed directly to influence company management. Rather, the market for corporate control is relied upon to discipline management, though, as we have seen, this market is subject to many imperfections.

The board of directors

The most direct link between shareholders and top management consists of the outside or non-executive directors. They form part of the single-tier, Anglo-American board, which also includes the chief executive or managing director. According to some reform proposals, outside directors should form the majority and should also be substantial stockholders. Their duty is then to monitor firms' performance, replace the chief executive if necessary and generally ensure the priority of shareholders' interests.

In practice, board members are often appointed by the CEO, and may themselves be executives from companies that are dependent on the CEO in some way through trading or financial links. The independence and impartiality of directors are thus often open to question. However, in response to mounting criticism in recent years over the failure of the internal control mechanism in large corporations, boards have sometimes taken decisive action to remove a troubled CEO. For example, the chief executives of IBM, General Motors, American Express, Westinghouse and, most recently, Apple have all been ousted by their boards. However, even such decisive action is often perceived to be too late to prevent substantial and avoidable damage.

Outside directors are dependent on the chief executive for their information, and even for the agenda of board meetings. Combining the role of chief executive with that of board chairman further enhances the CEO's power and impedes the monitoring function of outside directors. Some of these problems are avoided by the two-tier German board system, where an upper, **supervisory board** is explicitly charged with appointing the lower, management board and approving major strategic decisions. However the split into supervisory and managerial functions is only one aspect of German corporate governance, which we discuss in detail in the next section.

D. The stakeholder firm

The goals of the firm

Much economic theorizing and policy-making is still based upon the idea of a perfectly competitive economy, or at least some close approximation to the traditional model. A basic result is that, when all factors of production have been paid their marginal product, there is no profit or surplus left over in equilibrium, so total output is divided between the factor imputs, including labour and capital. Uncertainty in practice destroys this neat division of output, so that some capital is usually supplied by equity shareholders in exchange for a claim on the residual income left over after all wages, interest on debt and other contractual payments have been made. In this story, the equity holders appear to bear all the risk, because other payments are 'fixed' or 'contractual'. In this case, shareholders should have ultimate or residual control in order to maximize efficiency and the value of the firm. Other parties, such as management or workers, would otherwise be tempted to waste resources at the cost of equity holders.

This justification for the supremacy of shareholders' interests in large corporations, where ownership and management are separated, depends upon a number of implicit assumptions that are rarely made explicit in any detail. First and most obviously, creditors bear the risks of bankruptcy because shareholders have limited liability. It is true that, in the event of default, creditors do assume residual control, but clearly decisions taken prior to any actual default, such as risky but potentially highly profitable investment projects, can offer the chance of high returns to shareholders while shifting the cost of failure on the down side to debtholders. In principle, debt covenants can be written that restrict managerial discretion to shift the risk burden in this manner, but in practice the usual informational asymmetry limits the efficacy of such safeguards, and even the most tangible collateral can quickly lose value, as recent property price collapses have shown.

Perhaps the most serious implicit assumption of the competitive model is the notion that employees who lose their job when a firm runs into trouble can quickly find alternative employment at similar wages. As we have seen, displaced American workers suffer on average a loss of 20 per cent of their earnings, and European workers, who are generally believed to be less mobile than their US counterparts, are likely to suffer even greater losses. Employees thus quite clearly share the entrepreneurial risk of firm failure or declining demand.

In addition to the loss of future wages, many displaced workers suffer long spells of unemployment before finally finding a new job, while some, particularly older job losers, never succeed in obtaining permanent employment again. These facts have long been better known to employees than to academic economists in the neoclassical tradition of perfectly competitive markets. If labour markets were really competitive, expected risks of various kinds, such as job loss and accidents, should lead to higher pay in the form of compensating differentials. However, the widely observed segmentation of labour markets into primary and secondary sectors often leads to lower pay for the most risky and unsafe jobs that are common in secondary markets. In recent years, too, unexpected shocks have hit primary and white-collar jobs, as not only the workforce but also the future earnings prospects and wealth of specifically skilled workers have been sometimes drastically downsized.

In earlier stages of industrialization, prior to the post-war revolution in information technology, the pace of technological change was much slower than today. Standardized skills and training were more likely to be general than specific, in view of the much smaller range of products and technologies then existing. When most people still finished their schooling at the age of 14 or earlier, and unskilled manual labour was in much greater demand than it is today, human capital formed a relatively small proportion of national wealth. What is referred to by historians as the 'age of capital' up to, say, World War I, meant the age of *tangible* capital in the form of machines and buildings. The second half of the twentieth century has become the age of *human* capital, whereas many of the institutions and theories of corporate governance hail from the earlier age when tangible-capital owners were the predominant risk bearers. As Blair (1995, p. 238) puts it:

Investments in human capital are most likely to be important in technology-intensive or service-oriented enterprises, where most of the value added comes from innovation, product customization, or specialized services. These kinds of enterprises account for a growing share of economic activity . . . In such enterprises employees whose skills are specialized to the company will inevitably bear some of the risk associated with the enterprise, and this fact gives them a 'stake' in the company that is at risk in exactly the same way as the stake held by shareholders.

And two leading organizational economists come to similar conclusions in their pathbreaking text:

With high levels of firm-specific human capital, the decisions taken by the firm place risks on employees' human assets that are comparable to those borne by investors in physical capital. Protecting the value of this human capital then requires that employees' interests figure into the firm's decision making. (Milgrom and Roberts, 1992, p. 351)

In spite of such well-reasoned, authoritative conclusions and an enormous interest in Japanese management in the English-speaking economies over the past two decades, the narrow financial view that share value is the only legitimate goal of the firm still dominates academic discussion in the United Kingdom and the United States. One argument against incorporation of employee interests in the goals of the firm is that these interests are very difficult to quantify. Diluting the supremacy – and discipline – of shareholder value maximization with nebulous concerns about unmeasurable human capital would, it is claimed, essentially amount to a licence for top management to follow its *own* interests, to the cost of both shareholders and employees. This argument illustrates a familiar problem in the theory of agency and incentives. Objectives that are difficult to measure or monitor are indeed likely to be neglected. However, this result only *explains* – but in no way justifies – the neglect of what may be very important factors. As the importance of human capital in the advanced economies increases, so too does the *cost* of neglecting human capital in the objectives of the firm.

As was argued in the previous section, there is a wealth of evidence that the goals of the Anglo-American corporation are still primarily managerial goals, often biased towards excessive growth and (until recently) diversification. The market for corporate control is inherently imperfect, and acquired firms are not on average found to be underperforming their markets. The rhetoric of shareholder supremacy has been compared to the claims made for the now defunct socialism of Eastern Europe by Kay and Silberston (1995, pp. 87, 94).

Socialist bureaucrats purported to exercise power on behalf of the workers . . . The managers of many large British and American companies similarly defend their positions by claiming to act in the interest of the shareholders . . .

In the stultified authoritarian regimes of eastern Europe, the rhetoric of popular democracy was used to provide spurious legitimacy for self interested behaviour. The creation of supposedly independent remuneration committees by large companies in Britain and the United States has had precisely the same effect. The independence is generally a sham and the institution has proved to be a mechanism not for restraining excess but for justifying it.

The increasing emphasis on shareholder value in Anglo-American boardrooms has led to a proliferation of stock options and other profit-related bonus pay schemes for top management. The problem is that such reward systems encourage management to increase short-term profitability, which is most easily done at the expense of long-term international competitiveness and market share. As Peter Doyle of Warwick Business School puts it, 'achieving a temporary hike in profits can set up a chief executive for life' (*Financial Times*, 25 October 1996). Doyle notes how easy it is to boost temporary profits by raising prices and cutting investment, in addition to ubiquitous downsizing. But such strategies usually undermine the foundations for long-term, enduring market success – and even survival. As Doyle points out,

> The focus on cutting costs to boost return on capital employed led to the loss of 3m jobs in UK manufacturing industry between 1973 and 1996. UK profitability did jump but the cost was a sharp drop in its share of world markets. By contrast, manufacturing output rose in Japan, Italy, Germany, France and the US by an average of more than 40 per cent. Many of the UK businesses that boasted rapid profit recoveries in the 1970s and 1980s are now no longer around. They sacrificed long-run survival and international competitiveness for the applause of short-term profits.

Corporate governance and economic performance in Germany

The idea that concentrated stock ownership and long-term relationship investing as observed in Germany and Japan serve to align managerial behaviour and corporate goals more closely with shareholder interests is rejected by most experts with experience of those countries. As Kay and Silberston emphasize, public corporations in Germany are not regarded as exclusively private contractual arrangements as in Britain, requiring legal protection for shareholders only against outright fraud. Instead, the corporation is explicitly treated by the law in Germany as a social organization with obligations to employee and other stakeholders, and is subject to close regulation. Modern codetermination law is a natural expression of these concerns.

Concentrated share ownership of the largest German public corporations (*Aktiengesellschaften*) is usually held by banks and other companies. Their top managers, who sit on corporate boards, are not themselves large shareholders. Although profits are certainly regarded as important, not least because retained earnings are the main source of investment funds as in other countries, neither managers nor shareholders claim that firms should be run exclusively in the interests of shareholders.

There is a greater proportion of owner-managed small and medium-sized firms in Germany (***Mittelstand***) than in the United Kingdom, and owners often secure control by issuing non-voting preferred shares to outsiders. There is no evidence that wealth maximization is the exclusive goal of such owners either. Family and company traditions, status in the local community and personal reputation seem to play an important role. The virtual absence of the threat of hostile takeover for usually closely held (large and small) firms in Germany removes the main external pressure impinging on Anglo-American managers (in addition, of course, to competitive forces in the product market).

The most important departure from American and British corporate governance is undoubtedly the German system of **codetermination**. Essentially, this provides a formal legal framework that defines the role of employee stakeholders through two main bodies. The upper or supervisory board of directors (*Aufsichtsrat*) of large public companies (with over 2,000 employees) consists of equal numbers of employee and union representatives on one side, and shareholders' representatives on the other. The chairman of the board is nominated by the owners, and has an extra, casting vote in case of a tie. To the surprise of observers from more adversarial traditions, however, the casting vote is rarely used because most board decisions are agreed unanimously.

The supervisory board has to appoint members of the executive or top management board (*Vorstand*), and approve major strategic decisions. Agreement and consensus can usually be reached because the supervisory board's mandate is akin to trusteeship: to promote the interests of 'the enterprise' as a legal and social entity in its own right, rather than to constitute a bargaining forum between opposing parties.

The other arm of codetermination is the plant-level works council (*Betriebsrat*), which five or more employees are entitled to elect. The **works council** has far-reaching, legally defined rights of information, consultation and negotiation on most personnel-related management issues. Both works council and board members have traditionally been excluded from collective bargaining over wages and working time, and this division of labour is widely believed to have been chiefly responsible for the generally cooperative attitude of works councillors and labour representatives on the supervisory board.

The most divisive issues are naturally those that are concerned with the distribution of rents, such as basic wages and working time. These of course have always been the main concern of collective bargaining, and in Germany are negotiated at the regional level between employer and union representatives. Agreements are binding for all members of the employers' federation, though large corporations have often paid more than the industry standard (wage drift), and special local agreements at enterprise level have been proliferating since reunification.

Codetermination was originally imposed on the West German coal and steel industry after the war as an attempt to extend political democracy to these key heavy industries by the allied occupation authorities. Various extensions of codetermination laws were generally opposed by management, but are now widely accepted by all parties involved as promising superior employee 'voice' and labour–management communication channels than either exclusively union representation or the non-union model favoured by many Anglo-American managers.

Codetermination has attracted increasing attention from academics in the United States and elsewhere concerned with competitiveness in the global economy (see Kochan and Osterman, 1994; Turner, 1991). There is widespread agreement that the institutions of codetermination cannot be judged in isolation from other, complementary institutions of the German economy. Simply transplanting works councils or employee directors into lagging companies elsewhere without other fundamental changes is unlikely to be a panacea.

Most importantly, the extremely high standard and broad coverage of vocational training through apprenticeships and parallel state-supplied schooling have provided about two-thirds of the blue-collar workforce with high skills and qualifications, compared with only one-third in Britain. With this background, codetermination has undoubtedly helped to elevate human resource management (HRM) to a major component of top-level management in German companies, generally with much greater prestige and importance than in the United Kingdom or the United States. The result has been more rapid diffusion of new technology and flexible work systems, as well as a worldwide reputation for product quality that has maintained Germany's share of world exports at close to US levels until recently and well ahead of Japan. At the same time, Britain's share has declined to below 5 per cent, half of Germany's, in spite of a substantial decline in the value of the pound relative to the mark (DM) by late 1996. Subsequent weakening of the DM should help German exports, while the stronger pound in 1997 is worrying British exporters.

The German model of corporate governance has come under attack in the wake of mounting problems after reunification, including well-publicised events such as record losses at Daimler-Benz and the apparent failure of bank supervision before spectacular collapses of the Metalgesellschaft (a large conglomerate) and the Schneider property group. Daimler's problems began when the supervisory board, including, as main bank and dominant shareholder, Deutsche Bank, allowed the prestige car maker to go on an acquisition spree in the 1980s and transform itself into a diversified conglomerate. Like most earlier attempts of this kind, Daimler's dash for diversified growth plunged the company into the red, though the overvalued mark had undoubtedly exacerbated the problems of their aerospace subsidiaries. However, profits recovered to DM 2.4 billion in 1996, as restructuring reduced employment and share prices soared.

Not surprisingly after the unexpected losses at Daimler and persistently low profitability at Siemens, these and other German corporations have announced greater emphasis on shareholder value. Such announcements have been interpreted by some, particularly English-speaking, observers as a welcome and long overdue shift towards Anglo-American governance and goals. On the other hand, the problems faced by Daimler seem to be largely the *result* of pursuing a transatlantic acquisition strategy. In spite of employment protection, Daimler and most other large corporations in Germany (and other EU countries) have been reducing their payroll through natural attrition and outsourcing production to lower-wage countries. As profits recovered after the recession of the early 1990s, the German stock market boomed while unemployment approached 5 million by 1997.

Interestingly, criticism has focused on bank representatives and their role as supervisory board members, rather than on employee representation. Although suggestions for reform of the *Aufsichtsrat* abound, they do not usually include any rollback of codetermination or the basic two-tier system. Although German boards and managers are no more immune than any others to serious errors of judgement on occasion, there is no evidence that the system itself is failing under the growing strains on the Germany economy.

A major cause of these strains was the policy of West German unions in their push for rapid growth of East German wages towards parity with Western levels. Together with the collapse of market outlets in Eastern Europe, this policy devastated employment in eastern Germany, and much of the job loss was not included in official unemployment statistics, which topped the 4 million mark for the whole country by 1996 (FitzRoy and Funke, 1998). Massive subsidies for the East amounting to 6 per cent of German GNP have pushed up federal taxes and precipitated fiscal crisis.

Although employers are burdened with some of the highest real wages in the EU and substantial non-wage labour costs of taxation to support generous welfare programmes, productivity advances have also been remarkable as lean production and outsourcing to low-wage countries are extended. However, service sector and part-time employment, at 56 and 17 per cent respectively, lag behind other European countries, and unemployment is likely to grow even as some corporate profits rebound after recession and cumulative downsizing. Smaller firms have been particularly hard hit by uniformly high regional wage increases, though movement towards flexibility is beginning.

The success of many smaller German firms under these conditions has been remarkable. Specialized and well established in a narrow market segment, small firms often supply a dominant share of the world market for their particular product, such as Steiner Optik, with 80 per cent of the global market for military field glasses. Reputation for product quality and innovation rather than price competition is decisive in these cases. German consultant Hermann Simon reviews many fascinating examples in his 1996 book *Hidden Champions*, and argues that these companies have long practised the 'modern' lean manufacturing and participative management that Anglo-American companies have only recently begun to adopt from Japan. Worker loyalty and involvement are also maintained with a commitment to avoid downsizing, while closely held family ownership insulates these firms from takeover threats and short-term market pressures.

The German labour market is often viewed as rigid and over-regulated, hampered by a legacy of interventionist governments and all-powerful unions. Like many caricatures, this one does contain elements of truth, which, however, need careful clarification. For example, Klaus Zwickel, new head of the largest metal workers' union, IG Metall, has offered a wage freeze in exchange for job creation, and union opposition to more flexible working time has dwindled. In spite of employment protection laws and a required generous redundancy payment that has to be negotiated with the works council, German firms do eventually adjust employment to changing demand conditions as completely as US employers. However, work-sharing and short weeks are used to cushion the initial impact of negative shocks and allow long-term employment adjustment in response to permanent demand shifts rather than transitory fluctuations. Unnecessary job loss through temporary layoffs is thus avoided and employees on short weeks have time to search for alternative employment when the downturn is protracted (see Abrahan and Houseman, 1993; Simon, 1996).

Some of the costs of adjustment have been shifted to taxpayers through widespread use of early retirement, and Germany has not matched the success of Swedish labour market policy. Rather than drifting into long-term unemployment and welfare dependency, displaced workers in Sweden are required to undergo retraining and, if necessary, relocation to new employment. This policy helped to keep Swedish unemployment at very low levels of 3 per cent or less throughout the 1970s and 1980s, until the macro-crisis of the 1990s.

Over-regulation of the retail and service sectors and subsidization of innumerable special interest groups that are mostly neither poor nor deserving are serious problems in Germany, and radical reform is not facilitated by the decentralized, consensual democratic process that has worked so well in fostering social partnership. This is not evidence that the complementary institutions of corporate governance, codetermination and HRM have contributed to current problems; on the contrary, these institutions have undoubtedly played a major role in the country's remarkable economic success *in spite of* unnecessary political constraints and policy errors.

Comparing German and British track records

In the 1980s there was a significant acceleration of the growth of manufacturing productivity in the United Kingdom. This seems to have continued into the 1990s, albeit accompanied by a dramatic fall in manufacturing employment since

1979 and longer hours as well as greater effort for white-collar workers. However, some observers have compared the recent British and American productivity record with Germany and Japan's current economic problems, to conclude that Anglo-American corporate governance and deregulation represent a superior alternative to the 'corporatist' German or Japanese systems.

Restrictive union work rules and the oil-price shocks, combined with poor management, education and training, had left British manufacturing uncompetitive and overmanned by the end of the 1970s. The loss of about a third of manufacturing employment over the next 15 years, a decline unmatched in any other country or period, the influence of Japanese transplants, particularly in the automobile industry, and the associated spread of lean production techniques have all undoubtedly helped to boost productivity at a faster rate than previously. However, work loads and working time for many – particularly white-collar employees threatened by downsizing – also rose significantly, so real wage growth exaggerates the welfare gains.

International comparison of productivity levels achieved by the mid-1990s depends on the construction of purchasing power parity (PPP) indices. These allow real output to be compared, without relying on fluctuating official exchange rates. Such measures, which are published by Eurostat for the OECD, provide a concise indicator of a country's economic performance, and are one yardstick for comparing economic systems and the living standards they provide.

Although it is easy to count the kilos of biscuits or numbers of cars a country produces, such numbers are fairly meaningless without appropriate 'weighting' for quality. A satisfactory weighting must take into account the physical characteristics (and not just the relative prices) of the enormous variety of different goods produced in a modern economy. Pathbreaking recent work by Valerie Jarvis and Sig Prais (1995) at the National Institute of Economic and Social Research (NIESR) in London has shown that the standard PPP comparisons between British and Germany have seriously underestimated the quality differences between these countries. For representative producers, 'Top quality grades defined on the basis of physical characteristics (not prices) accounted for about a third of total German production of these products, but under a tenth of British production' (Jarvis and Prais, 1995, p. 26).

The NIESR team concludes that higher levels of skills and training in Germany have a dual influence on manufacturing quality. First, batch production of innovative and specialized high-quality products is facilitated by a more skilled and flexible workforce. British producers, by contrast, concentrate on longer runs of more standardized, simpler varieties, competing on price rather than quality.

Secondly, greater quality consciousness among German consumers is fostered by better practical education in general, and for retail assistants in particular. Higher real incomes and a more equitable income distribution than in the United Kingdom also encourage a broader-based demand for higher-quality goods.

Finally, the conclusion is that the quality-adjusted margin of German over British output per head should be *doubled* in comparison with most previous estimates, to about 50 per cent. With a smaller participation rate and shorter working time, this bonus is augmented in welfare terms by significantly greater leisure time in Germany. Furthermore, a much higher rate of public investment has left Germany (and also most other continental countries) with a far superior public infrastructure of transport facilities, schools, other public buildings and hospitals, which provide subsidized services accessible to most of the population.

Claims that Britain's stock market dominated, deregulated economy has almost caught up with Germany thus seem to be based on grossly inadequate statistics that do not account for the full extent of quality and public infrastructure differences. The paradox of Germany maintaining its high world market share of exports in spite of rising real wages and rapid currency appreciation – in other words, apparently declining competitiveness – would appear to be largely resolved. 'Is Germany sinking? Or would we be lucky to have the same problems?', asks *The Independent on Sunday* (21 January 1996, p. 17), and the affirmative answer to the second question is confirmed by casual observation of the two countries. Inept political response to the undoubtedly serious current problems may yet damage the foundations of the German model of corporate governance and HRM, but the fault will then be squarely in the political arena and not systemic, as superficial media reports and (previous) British government officials liked to claim.

Another striking indication of how far Britain has fallen behind its main competitors is provided in a report by Oxford Economic Forecasting and the Machine Tool Technologies Association ('The UK's Investment Performance', 1996). In 1992, British capital stock per worker was only about half of Japanese and German levels, and substantially less than stocks in France, Italy and the United States. This discrepancy, combined with lower skills, explains the United Kingdom's low wages.

The Japanese corporation

The Japanese corporation has long been perceived to be the archetypal stakeholder firm. Lifetime employment (albeit for only a third of the workforce), cooperative if not compliant enterprise unions, large profit-related bonus payments and the absence of strikes or hostile takeovers present a picture of oriental harmony unmatched by any European version of social democratic, corporatist industrial relations and codetermination. Even in the worst postwar recession, Japanese official unemployment remained at a third of European levels.

This situation is all the more remarkable when viewed against the background of often violent and bitter labour conflicts in pre-war and early post-war years, a historical record that is not obviously consistent with claims that Japanese economic organization is idiosyncratic and purely culturally based. The success of Japanese transplants, primarily in the very different cultural and economic climates of the deregulated United States and United Kingdom, seems to represent another counter-example. We return to the discussion of cultural factors in more detail below.

Surprising, too, is the lack of almost any formal legal framework for Japanese organization, say on the lines of codetermination. This has allowed the evolution of a dual economy, with a substantial secondary sector of small and usually family-run businesses paying low wages with few benefits and long hours. Although this sector bears the brunt of recession, extended family networks and firms do provide more protection for individuals than in the Anglo-American secondary sectors. Much underemployment is probably hidden through work sharing and labour hoarding.

Between the secondary sector and the giant corporations is a third sector of medium-sized companies forming clusters of subcontractors and suppliers to members of the major industrial groups (*keiretsu*). These firms gain stability and other benefits from close, long-term relationships with their main customers. Mutual shareholding and exchange of personnel as well as technical know-how are common. These factors encourage relationship-specific investment in skills and technology that is not subject to the risks of sudden obsolescence when, for example, a major contract is lost to a rival competitive bid. This happens frequently under the 'arm's length' market relationships that are usual in the United Kingdom and the United States, and reduces the incentive for productive specialization. Medium-sized firms subcontract and outsource to still smaller, secondary suppliers, increasingly in low-wage countries, and the pressure to cut costs is passed on down the tiers of suppliers.

At the centres of clusters of associated companies in the industrial groups are the best-known giant corporations such as Toyota or Hitachi, which are essentially final assemblers of components supplied by the network of subcontractors. Mutual shareholding is widespread among the larger associated companies, but total ownership of subsidiaries and vertical integration is rare. Main banks play an important role both as suppliers of credit and as equity holders. Mutual shareholdings cement trading relationships; both are for long-term benefits, and there is no reason for share value maximization to be a prime goal of large or small firms. Surveys of top managers of the largest Japanese corporations also suggest that shareholder interests rank relatively low on their list of priorities, which is dominated by the interests of employee and customer stakeholders.

The board of directors is usually dominated by insiders who have climbed the corporate hierarchy, while main banks and key corporate partners are also represented. Normally the chief executive chairs the board and appoints his own successor. In times of crisis, banks may intervene and replace top management as part of a rescue package. Banks are regarded as key outside monitors of corporate health, with not only their financial investment at stake but also their reputation, which is closely linked to the long-term success of their major trading partners and customers.

The job security expected by core male employees in large companies has no formal contractual or legal basis, but seems to have largely survived the severe recession of the early 1990s through extensive labour hoarding as well as reallocation of employees. These primary sector workers have attained Western wage levels, and enjoy extensive on-the-job training and promotion possibilities. Though women and employees of smaller firms are relatively underprivileged, with much lower pay, promotion prospects and effective job security, official unemployment remains far below Western levels. Although younger graduates may complain about the work ethic of lifetime commitment to a single company, Japan's main problems (like Germany's) are macroeconomic and political and not primarily related to the stakeholder objectives of Japanese firms.

The speculative 'overshooting' or appreciation of the yen to a clearly overvalued level with little relation to fundamentals is the primary culprit. The collapse of the property 'bubble boom' has also left many financial institutions with massive bad debts on their books, and the political system has been rocked by scandals and corruption that hamper decisive macro-policy measures to overcome recession. Nevertheless, by 1996, some relative decline in the value of the yen and growing consumer demand signalled that the worst was probably over.

Trust

Although aspects of lean production have been widely adopted by organizations in many countries, the Japanese and German systems of corporate governance and industrial organization remain quite distinctive despite all the pressures for convergence that are supposedly generated by the modern global economy. A powerful case for cultural determinants of economic organization and competitive advantage from trust has recently been made by Francis Fukuyama in a wide-ranging study of the 'social virtues' that neoclassical economics has neglected (Fukuyama, 1995). In subsequent work, a strong correlation between 'trust' expressed by survey respondents and economic performance has been found (Knack, 1996, p. 22).

As is well known, much economic activity in Japan takes place within the *keiretsu* networks of cooperating large corporations and successive tiers of smaller suppliers and subcontractors. Long-term relationships and highly specific assets are combined with the absence of any central authority to resolve disputes. Decisions must be based on consensus and trust, without the propensity to hold up and exploit bargaining weaknesses that Western economists might expect. Despite their adoption of Japanese internal organization, transplants in the West have not been able to replicate local (domestic) **supplier networks** with the same qualities, though some progress has been made with both transplant and domestic suppliers.

Fukuyama (1995, p. 205) argues: 'Networks based on reciprocal moral obligation have ramified throughout the Japanese economy because the degree of generalized trust possible among unrelated people is extraordinarily high.' This degree of trust is in turn traced back to the extent of 'spontaneous sociability' or informal cooperative organization common in pre-modern Japanese society. Fukuyama finds similar tendencies in Germany, where guild and craft traditions were adapted to modern industry with the help of codetermination, and sociability was fostered by a relatively decentralized pre-modern tradition of provincial rulers.

In low-trust societies such as France and Italy, by contrast, absolutist rulers suppressed spontaneous organization between non-kin groups. Trust was restricted to family members and cooperation in large firms or organizations usually required state intervention, leading to the prevalence of large state-owned corporations in these countries, as well as much more rigid hierarchies and more intense supervision in firm organization. Fukuyama even includes China among the 'familist' societies with dynamic small-firm and entrepreneurial sectors but few large private corporations; 'This suggests that the network structure of the Japanese economy will be only partially replicable, even in other high trust societies' (1995, p. 205).

Although trust can evolve through long association in some circumstances even in low-trust environments, there remain striking differences on average in corporate governance and organization across countries that are consistent with the cultural stories emphasized by Fukuyama and his forerunners. The small family firms, which can be innovative and dynamic when technology favours small scale in areas such as central Italy and southern China, usually run into problems of succession at some stage and are reluctant to employ professional top management. Large privately owned companies have rarely flourished in such familist environments. By contrast, the flourishing small business sectors in Germany or Japan were complemented at an early stage of development by large corporations linked by cooperative agreements into cartels, with the explicit support of government policy and large banks.

Inside the firm, the devolution of responsibility to highly skilled production workers on the shop floor, which has been part of the development of flexible and lean manufacturing, was a relatively natural consequence of high trust in Germany and Japan. Safeguarded by the institutions of codetermination or stakeholder commitments, these workers had not required the rigid job classifications and work rules spawned by low-trust, adversarial bargaining in other countries, such as France, Italy, Britain, or America. Trust thus economizes on opportunistic behaviour and reduces required supervisory and managerial tasks. A detailed comparison of French and German firms of similar size in the same sector revealed 42 white-collar workers for every 100 blue-collar workers in France, but only 36 in Germany. The ratio of average white- to blue-collar pay was 1.75 in France compared with 1.33 in Germany (Maurice *et al.*, 1986). Japanese pay structures are well known to be much more egalitarian than those in the United States or the United Kingdom.

It is important to realize that high trust within Japanese organizations and industrial groups does not imply the absence of competition *between* different groups. In fact, the most successful exporters have usually been firms that faced strong domestic competitors. Although national cultural habits such as trust and spontaneous sociability do seem to differ significantly it is also possible for international joint ventures involving very different cultures to succeed and to establish mutual trust and cooperation. Although the downside of high-trust societies such as Germany or Japan is lack of trust – and non-assimilation – of outsiders, joint ventures between them and the United States have been proliferating in high-technology areas in particular. Some of the most successful companies in the United States are noted for employee involvement, long-term employment, high trust and stakeholder goals.[4]

Cultural factors and social capital are not immutable or rigid barriers, though at the national level development may be a slow process over generations. However, as Fukuyama also emphasizes, erosion of painstakingly acquired social virtues can be alarmingly rapid. In the United States, the growth of family breakdown, crime, incarceration, inequality and litigation is an indicator of declining trust and community that could have serious economic consequences in the long run, going far beyond the immediate and direct costs of social pathology. In Europe, Britain has progressed farthest down the American route, combined with the traditional deep class divisions that also inhibit trust and cooperation between labour and management. British managers are thus, not surprisingly, the most outspoken opponents of any EU-wide extension of co-determination measures.

Rent-sharing and efficiency

The evidence for rent-sharing from the losses suffered by displaced workers who receive significantly lower pay in their new jobs has been summarized above. This evidence is complemented by the finding that wages are related to employer profits, even for non-unionized American workers. Rent-sharing is a natural result of collective bargaining but, in the absence of unions, efficiency wage theories suggest that pay above the opportunity cost of labour may well increase motivation and productivity.

Rent-sharing can thus actually reduce costs, a strategy that helps to maximize shareholder value. To illustrate the problems and conflicts that can arise, we present a simple numerical example, related to the discussion of these issues by Blair (1995, Chapter 7). Suppose an entrepreneur has invented a new machine that makes widgets more cheaply than before. The machine costs

95 c.u. to build. To learn how to operate the new technology, workers with appropriate initial qualifications require training and experience for one year. Their alternative wage or opportunity cost is $W_o = 1$ per year. In this novel situation, it may be necessary for the entrepreneur to pay for the specialized training. If she hires five workers, the total cost of training them, or the human capital investment, will be $H = 5$, so the entrepreneur's entire investment, representing all her savings plus loans from relatives, amounts to $I = 100$.

Suppose now the machine needs a team of five trained workers, who can produce 10 widgets per year. The market price of widgets is $P = 2$, giving a sales revenue of $S = 20$. Now, if their training was entirely specific, workers need in principle be paid only their opportunity wage, $W_o = 1$, but then they would have no reason to take care of the machinery or not to shirk whenever possible. We assume that doubling the wage to $W = 2$ maximizes the entrepreneur's utility, reducing time spent on monitoring the workers and maintenance outlays. This wage yields an optimal profit,[5] given by:

$$\pi = 20 - 2 \times 5$$
$$= 10$$

If the borrowing rate is 5 per cent per year, this annual return of 10 per cent on the initial investment, $I = 100$, gives a pure annual rent of 5 for the entrepreneur–owner, and an equal rent of 5 per annum for the workforce.

Next suppose that the widget market collapses for some reason, and the price falls to $P = 1$. Profit drops to $\pi = 10 - 10 = 0$. If the machine had a resale or surplus value of, say, 20, then clearly the entrepreneur would want to close down the business, terminating the five jobs and perhaps leaving the workers too old to obtain specialized training or other jobs. Now it would seem appropriate for the employees to renegotiate their rent-sharing wage contract, and to settle for a new wage, say $W = \frac{7}{5}$. The wage bill is now 7, leaving profit $\pi_1 = 10 - 7 = 3$. This represents a more attractive prospect than liquidating the business, since the resale proceeds of 20 would yield an annual income of only 1 at the going interest rate of 5 per cent. The entrepreneur would thus still get a positive quasi-rent of 2, while employee quasi-rents are now $7 - 5 = 2$, if the firm continues production.

In practice, of course, such significant wage reductions to save jobs are rarely observed. The threat of unemployment does put pressure on bargainers to moderate their wage demands, and recession does eventually slow down wage inflation, but this is a slow process, imposing severe costs in the form of lost jobs and output. Suppose, for example, that our entrepreneur could still produce six widgets with only two employees. If the wage was unchanged, profit would be

$$\pi_2 = 6 - 4 = 2$$

which is preferred to liquidation because a positive quasi-rent of $2 - 1 = 1$ remains.[6] The two remaining workers might well have to work harder for longer hours, so their utility, as distinct from their pecuniary rent, would decline after the sort of drastic downsizing, and perhaps re-engineering as well, that has become familiar.

Now observe that, as long as the marginal product of a worker exceeds the alternative wage of 1, downsizing is *not* socially efficient. If 4 workers could provide 8¾ widgets a year, the firm should maintain production of 10 with 5 employees after the price has fallen to 1, because the marginal product of the last worker is 1¼. The question remains why the efficient response of wage renegotiation is so difficult to attain.

The answer seems to lie at the borderline between the economics and the psychology of trust and bargaining. When there is low trust and asymmetric information between management and labour, 'concession bargaining' or re-negotiation could encourage management to make false or exaggerated claims about competitive pressures and the need for wage cuts, simply in order to increase profit. If adjustment is mainly through varying employment, it is more likely to be motivated by genuine changes in external factors. In a high-trust environment, on the other hand, Japanese managers and enterprise unions can share information. This policy has helped to avoid extensive job losses during Japan's worst recession in the 1990s, maintaining official unemployment at a third of the EU level. Germany's more centralized union bargaining mechanism has been much less successful in implementing wage flexibility, however. Just how Western firms could build up trust is our final topic.

A new view of governance

Respected business economists such as Margaret Blair and John Kay have begun to develop a new approach to the Anglo-American governance debate. Rather than seeking to enforce exclusive shareholder interests, they follow the high-trust tradition and example to argue for broader goals of the firm. Blair suggests total wealth maximization, including employee rents, as the appropriate goal. This would recognize the importance of specific human capital investment in the modern economy, which bears part of the residual risk and return. As Blair points out, defenders of shareholder value maximization fail to recognize the infeasibility of complete contracts that would remove labour's residual status. Kay follows a legal tradition that emphasizes corporate responsibility to various stakeholders and a trustee role for governance. As in many other occupations, top managers should be expected to balance the differing interest of shareholders, employees and customers and to be monitored by relatively independent outside directors.

However, even in a stakeholder firm, inflexible wages can create liquidity problems that prevent efficient maximization of total wealth. In Germany, in spite of relatively high trust, this problem of wage rigidity has helped to send unemployment on an upward spiral in the 1990s, so the specific question of creating institutions that combine trust with appropriate mechanisms for adjusting wages needs to be addressed.

Simply decentralizing bargaining in a low-trust environment, as in the United Kingdom in the 1980s, is unlikely to help. Unemployment peaked at the bottom of the recession in 1992 at much the same level as in previous recessions, and long-term British unemployment was about 10 times the rate in countries such as Austria and Sweden with coordinated, 'corporatist' bargaining institutions. This type of coordination may be more difficult in larger countries, but there is much that could be done at the enterprise level to foster flexibility in a stakeholder context.

Again, a number of different measures have been proposed that seem to be essentially complementary, rendering piecemeal reform rather ineffective. Profit-sharing in place of part of the fixed wage is one component, but does itself depend on high trust for acceptance, since otherwise accounting profits are too easily manipulated when employee representatives do not have access to the same information as management. In practice, profit-sharing bonuses are usually added on to normal wages, rather than replacing part of the wage.

A commitment to job security and work-sharing in the face of at least temporary declines will encourage all employees to accept more flexible pay, rather than playing off one group of privileged workers, who retain their jobs, against a minority who lose them. Employee involvement and participation in decision-making at various levels seem to be essential for building and maintaining trust. Only if informational asymmetries are minimized can a consensus on necessary measures in the face of adversity be reached. In Japan, for example, enterprise unions may be given access to company books when negotiating wages and bonus payments. Employee share ownership plans (ESOPs), which are widespread in Japan, should also help to reinforce stakeholder goals of total wealth maximization.

Western ESOPs often restrict employee voting rights, and were usually designed for tax reasons or to entrench management by blocking takeover bids. However, Blair suggests a more positive role for ESOPs. Instead of rent-sharing through higher fixed wage payments, workers could be paid their alternative wages, and receive rents in the forms of shares, perhaps held in a trust fund for some period or the duration of their employment. Shareholding of this kind would give employee shareholders votes comparable to the votes of outside shareholders. The efficient goal of total wealth maximization can then be implemented as total share value maximization, because only opportunity wages are counted as cost.

This scheme has considerable advantages over traditional forms of employee ownership. Workers do not require initial capital as in an employee buyout; specific training is paid for by the employer; and outside investors need not relinquish shares or voting rights. Where human capital is particularly important, as in high-technology industries, employee shareholders would hold a majority but could insure outside investors against some risks through preferential dividend payments. Default on debt obligations would be less likely owing to the lower fixed wage costs, so debt finance becomes less risky, in turn reducing outside equity requirements.

The role of the board of directors is crucial for appointing and monitoring top management, and without adequate representation of employee share-holders on the board (as under codetermination) total wealth maximization is likely to remain an illusive goal. In fact there are considerable obstacles to changes of governance systems. Existing management may fear more intense supervision from employee representatives, while outside shareholders are likely to worry about dilution of their equity and control rights, however inef-fective the latter may actually be in the present system.

Firms that maximize total wealth would not of course be immune to the pressures of structural and technological change, and fears are often voiced that **employee involvement** or codetermination rights hinder adjustment. The flexibility due to profit-related pay or share bonus schemes is likely to facili-tate adjustment, encouraging exit from declining industries or firms as total compensation falls. Involuntary redundancy may become necessary in some cases, and a combination of contractual redundancy payments with govern-ment-assisted retraining schemes to avoid long-term unemployment can min-imize the social losses of unavoidable separation.

None the less, Blair's rather pessimistic conclusions for the United States apply equally to the United Kingdom, and to some (varying) extent to most other countries as well:

> Such arrangements will not be adopted automatically (or) quickly, especially in times of rapid change when the development of governance structures that are responsive to the problems of today and tomorrow may be stymied by a ten-dency for all the parties involved to fight yesterday's war. In this regard, the great-est impediment to the development of new, more effective corporate governance arrangements may be the mindsets of many leaders among corporate manage-ment, labour, boards of directors, executives of financial institutions, and their lawyers. They, to a great degree, are stuck in an old model, in which sharehold-ers put up risk capital that is used to build the factory, workers are hired at their opportunity cost and paid fixed wages, and the job of management is to maxi-mize profits for shareholders. The typical business corporation of the 1990s does not look like this model, and the business corporation of the next century will be different yet again. All the different forms the corporation may take are not apparent yet, but it is a good bet that human capital will be at least as impor-tant to the wealth-creation process in the coming century as it is today, and prob-ably more so. The struggle is to design systems that simultaneously foster and protect such investments and attempt to maximize the returns to both human capital and physical capital. (Blair, 1995, p. 124)

E. Chapter summary and key ideas

This chapter has provided a brief summary of the main empirical findings and theoretical debates about ownership and control. Starting from Berle and Means' discovery in the 1930s of the separation of ownership and control in most large American corporations, the debate has progressed through a number of stages. Managerial corporations were found to be prone to wasteful growth and diversification, and most of the conglomerates built up by corporate raiders in the 1960s and 1970s later lost market leadership, declined or broke up.

The market for corporate control appeared to most Anglo-American economists to be the solution to what were now called agency problems of free cash flow. Leveraged and managerial buyouts in the 1980s improved productivity, with the help of high debt ratios that were supposed to discipline managers by enforcing the payout of surplus cash flow as interest to creditors.

However, recession in the early 1990s revealed the well-known dangers of excessive debt, and many highly leveraged constructions ran into trouble. The main beneficiaries of corporate takeovers seemed to be the top management of the acquiring firm and the shareholders of the acquired firm. The success of the German and Japanese economies, where hostile takeovers were essentially unknown, inspired interest in the virtues of concentrated ownership and long-term relationship investing by banks and trading partners as well as individuals. Substantial shareholders or their representatives on the board of directors should have a stronger incentive to monitor management and ensure that shareholders' interests were given priority, according to agency theory.

Although aspects of Japanese organization, particularly lean manufacturing, were widely implemented in the West following the successful example of the Japanese transplants, the concept of the stakeholder firm that underpinned cooperative labour relations in Germany and Japan was largely ignored, or explicitly rejected, for a long time elsewhere. Indeed, financial economists continue to claim that stockholders are the only residual income claimants and risk bearers in the firm, although displaced workers suffer substantial loss of their specific human capital and share of organizational rents.

As human capital becomes relatively more important in modern economies, so too does the residual risk-bearing role of employees with **specific skills**. Complete contracts and insurance are unfeasible, in contrast to the perfectly competitive factor markets with complete information on which the traditional theory is based. Shareholders receive only part of the residual, and efficiency requires maximization of total wealth including employee rent shares, rather than only shareholders' value.

The central role of human resource management in both German and Japanese corporations complements high-quality public education and apprenticeship systems. Cultural factors such as high levels of reciprocal trust and obligation help to maintain the networks of suppliers and subcontractors in the Japanese *keiretsu*, as well as cooperative labour relations inside the firm, without a formal, legal framework for corporate governance by stakeholder interests. In Germany, on the other hand, social partnership is codified in co-determination law and a highly regulated labour market. Regional wage-bargaining has proved to be less flexible than either enterprise unions in Japan or centralized bargaining in Scandinavia and other **corporatist economies**, generating serious problems that macro-policy mistakes, mismanaged reunification and currency appreciation have exacerbated.

In the United Kingdom and the United States, maximization of shareholder value is generally regarded as the only legitimate goal of the firm. As collective bargaining has declined in importance, wage and income inequality has increased rapidly, job security has dwindled and the proportion of temporary and part-time workers has also grown significantly. Two-thirds of the British manual workforce remains unskilled, and long-term unemployment is 10 times the level in Austria, Sweden or Japan. Richard Layard of the London School of Economics remarks that 'We have fallen into a different league from the main countries of Northern Europe as far as the attainments of our middle and less able young people are concerned' (1996, p. 5).

In the climate of low trust engendered by growing class divisions, inequality and insecurity, it becomes increasingly difficult for any one company to institute a culture of reciprocal trust and cooperation based on long-term employment, teamwork, involvement and HRM. Nevertheless, some of the most successful British and American firms have been able to develop high-trust, cooperative labour relations, with meaningful participation, ESOPs and stakeholder goals. The importance of teamwork and employee involvement in 'competing for the future' is being increasingly recognized, but effective implementation is difficult to achieve in a low-trust climate of frequent downsizing, when managerial or shareholder interests dominate human capital stakeholder claims. Just how these conflicts will be resolved in the low-trust economies remains unclear, as indeed does the future evolution of stakeholder economies under the mounting pressures from global competition.

Key words

codetermination	*Mittelstand*
corporatist economy	residual control
employee involvement	residual income
free cash flow	specific skills
junk bonds	supervisory board
keiretsu	works council
leveraged buyout	
management buyout	

Questions and problems for review and discussion

1 Describe the separation of ownership and control in large British and American corporations.
2 Evaluate the effects of mergers and acquisitions on various affected parties in the short and the long run.
3 How do management buyouts influence the incentives faced by managers?
4 Outline your own preferred scheme for determining top managerial pay in large companies, and compare your suggestion with current practice in the United Kingdom.
5 Do you think that concentrated ownership by institutions could solve the problem of separation of ownership and control? Supply some evidence.
6 Compare the goals of large firms in Germany, the United Kingdom and the United States.
7 Explain why employees often have an 'implicit' equity stake in the firm, in addition to the other stakeholders.
8 Discuss some of the most likely effects of explicit employee share ownership.
9 What lessons can you draw from Japanese corporate governance for Western firms?
10 Explain carefully the economic role of trust.
11 What is rent-sharing, and what are the main reasons that have been advanced for the adoption of rent-sharing?
12 Under what conditions does the maximization of shareholder value lead to socially efficient decisions by firms?

Notes

1 This chapter draws extensively on recent seminal works by Blair (1995) and by Kay and Silberston (1995). See also Kay (1996).
2 For a review of this and related work, see Mueller (1992).
3 Depending on the nature of the new job, some individuals may be able to accumulate new specific skills and recoup part of their loss. This clearly becomes more difficult with increasing age.
4 Interesting case studies are presented by Kochan and Osterman (1994) and Pfeffer (1994).
5 Note that this is not necessarily the maximum profit because the entrepreneur also gains utility from leisure.
6 Recall that the quasi-rent is the surplus over liquidation or exit from the market, which is the annual return of 1 from the scrap value of 20.

References

Abrahan, K. and S. Houseman (1993), *Job Security in America: Lessons from Germany*, Washington DC: Brookings Institution.

Berle, A. A. and G. C. Means (1932), *The Modern Corporation and Private Property*, New York: Macmillan.

Blair, M. (1995), *Ownership and Control*, Washington DC: Brookings Institution.

FitzRoy, F. and M. Funke (1998), 'Wages and employment in Eastern and Western Germany', *Regional Studies*.

Fukuyama, F. (1995), *Trust: The Social Virtues and the Foundations of Prosperity*, London: Hamish Hamilton.

Gregg, P., S. Machin and S. Szymanski (1993), 'The disappearing relationship between directors' pay and corporate performance', *British Journal of Industrial Relations*, 31, pp. 1–10.

Hellwig, M. (1995), 'Discussion', in H. Siebert, *Trends in Business Organization: Do Participation and Cooperation Increase Competitiveness?* Tübingen: Mohr, pp. 196–202.

Jacobson, L. S., R. J. La Londe and D. G. Sulliven (1993), 'Earnings losses of displaced workers', *American Economic Review*, 83, pp. 685–709.

Jarvis, V. and S. J. Prais (1995), 'The quality of manufactured goods in Britain and Germany', NIESR, Discussion Paper no. 88, December.

Jensen, M. (1989), 'The eclipse of the public corporation', *Harvard Business Review*, 67, pp. 61–74.

Kay, J. (1996), *The Business of Economics*, Oxford University Press.

Kay, J. (1996), 'Poor odds on the takeover lottery', *Financial Times*, 26 January.

Kay, J. and A. Silberston (1995), 'Corporate governance', *National Institute Economic Review*, August.

Knack, S. (1996), *Financial Times*, 26 June.

Kochan, T. and P. Osterman (1994), *The Mutual Gains Enterprise*, Boston:

Harvard Business School Press.

Layard, K. (1996), *Centre Piece*, February.

Maurice, M., F. Sellier and J.-J. Silvestre (1986), *The Social Foundations of Industrial Power: A Comparison of France and Germany*, Cambridge, Mass: MIT Press.

Milgrom, J. and P. Roberts (1992), *Economics, Organization and Management*, Englewood Cliffs, NJ: Prentice Hall.

Mueller, D. (1992), 'The corporation and the economist', *International Journal of Industrial Organization*.

Nickell, S. (1995), *The Performance of Companies*, Oxford: Blackwell.

Oxford Economic Forecasting and MTTA (1996), 'The UK's investment performance'.

Pfeffer, J. (1994), *Competitive Advantage Through People*, Boston: Harvard Business School Press.

Schleiffer, A. and L. H. Summers (1988), 'Breach of trust in hostile takeovers', in A. Auerbach (ed.), *Corporate Takeovers: Cause and Consequences*, Chicago: University of Chicago Press.

Simon, H. (1996), *Hidden Champions*, Boston: Harvard Business School Press.

Turner, L. (1991), *Democracy at Work: Changing World Markets and the Future of Labor Unions*, Ithaca, NY: Cornell University Press.

Williamson, O. (1975), *Markets and Hierarchies: Analysis and Anti-Trust Implications*, New York: Free Press.

PART FOUR

Managing human resources

CHAPTER

The employment relationship

A. Chapter outline and student goals

Employment is a major part of most people's lives in modern industrial economies, often taken for granted, yet never more important than when threatened – or replaced – by unemployment. Two-thirds of national incomes consist of wages and salaries for labour. Paradoxically, in market economies most people are rarely in the labour *market*, actually looking for a job; the overwhelming part of working time is spent inside some organization, interacting with other employees, or following instruction from some higher authority. Clearly the success of a business enterprise depends in large measure on the quality and quantity of work done by employees at all levels. For individuals, the quality of their whole lives depends not only on the pay packet taken home at the end of the week or month, but also on how good and how satisfying their job is in the time between pay-days, on the quality of working life.

For management, a crucial task is to hire the right people, pay them and motivate them appropriately, train them and develop necessary skills, in short to manage the **human resources** that increasingly form a company's prime asset. Workers may neglect their duties when nobody is watching them, so supervision is necessary (though costly) but can also alienate workers and even become counterproductive when supervisors are obtrusive and heavy-handed. Employees form social bonds with each other at the work place and can collude, either in opposition to management for the purpose of minimizing their work load, or alternatively in cooperation with managers and employers for mutual gain.

These complex ramifications of the employment relationship have long been familiar to effective managers, and have been much studied by academic and practical specialists in industrial relations. Karl Marx had already observed early in the nineteenth century that what employers purchased in any labour contract was only *potential* labour or 'labour power'. Actual, delivered performance on the job could hardly be precisely specified in advance, and so was generally a bone of contention between employer and employee. The modern economics of uncertainty and incomplete contracting has taken up many of these problems with the new methods and concepts introduced in previous chapters. The new approach is able to throw fresh light on existing, often puzzling practices, and also to offer guidance for better human resource management.

Before turning to the modern approaches, we summarize the traditional neoclassical view of the perfectly competitive market for homogeneous labour, a view that still has applications in macroeconomic analysis in spite of its obvious inadequacies. In the third section we consider the employment relationship in detail as an open-ended relationship that requires some form of authority to fill in the gaps and get the jobs done. The crucial role of human capital or resources in the relationship is also introduced to underline the position of the employee stakeholder.

Employment, instead of self-employment or entrepreneurship, provides at least partial insurance against some market risks – workers do not have to put up the capital to buy the machines they use, and hence bear the full risk of bankruptcy. The next section shows how employment relationships balance the goals of reducing risk while maintaining work incentives.

We then distinguish between primary and secondary, internal and external labour markets. The secondary sector consists of mainly unskilled workers, often in temporary or short-term employment, with high mobility, little chance of promotion and low wages and is closest to the neoclassical model. Highly skilled workers in the primary sector, by contrast, are usually offered promotion prospects through **internal job ladders** in their organization, a kind of internal labour 'market' that replaces the external market and takes over the task of allocating workers to appropriate jobs in the firm, as well as providing motivation and some security. Intangible factors such as fairness, reputation and trust are particularly important in the internal market as part of corporate culture. We also show how international differences in the institutions of the labour market help to explain persistent differences in rates of unemployment, and how the inexorable rise in unskilled unemployment everywhere is one of the most serious problems facing industrial countries.

In the last section we show how an increasingly uncertain economic environment is encouraging temporary and part-time employment, as well as eroding the relative security of qualified, primary sector employment relationships. As competitive pressures to cut costs in the short run intensify, long-term assets, such as worker loyalty and commitment, that were based on reciprocal obligations and security are being destroyed. This is particularly serious because competitive success in technological development and production of innovative new products depends to an ever greater degree upon human resources, cooperation and long-term investment.

After reading this chapter you should be able to:

- realize the limitations of aggregate labour market concepts such as the rate of unemployment;
- understand the importance of authority in the employment relationship, and sources of conflict in labour contracts;
- describe the insurance functions (and limits) of employment contracts and the role of human capital;
- distinguish between internal and external, primary and secondary labour markets, and provide examples of each category;
- explain how job ladders have supplemented the external labour market in large firms, and how they motivate employees at all levels of the organization;
- appreciate the role of reputation in facilitating the efficient matching of workers and complex tasks, or the assignment of human capital;
- show how mutual trust between labour and management can increase profits and foster technological progress.

B. The traditional neoclassical theory of labour market equilibrium

Labour markets used to be treated by economists much like any other competitive market for factors of production, such as those discussed in Chapter 3. Though it is now widely recognized that individual workers differ widely and need to be motivated in various ways, and that employers' knowledge of their workers' abilities and performance is usually imperfect, the classical concepts of labour demand and labour supply are still useful starting points, provided that they are used carefully. These concepts are certainly widely used, and so they form the topic of this section, illustrated with some simple examples.

The demand for labour

The classical firm faced a fixed price for each output and input at any point in time, determined by 'the market', or a demand curve for its product of finite elasticity (in the case of monopoly). Labour was usually taken to be a homogeneous commodity, say blue-collar workers all with the same training and skill levels, though various categories of worker could be incorporated. Implicitly it was also assumed, though seldom spelled out in detail, that these workers all performed the same tasks, at the same pace, for the same number of hours per week. Under these conditions the firm can calculate the extra revenue that would result from hiring one more worker (say for a week), when nothing else was changed. This is called the **marginal revenue product** per worker-week (and could also be obtained in a similar way for one extra hour of work or an extra year).

With the help of this concept, we can derive the firm's demand for labour schedule just like the demand for any other factor of production such as intermediate products, raw materials, energy or whatever, as described in Chapter 3. The profit-maximizing employer will hire additional labour until the marginal revenue product of the last worker is equal to his wage for the same time period, say a week. Thus, when the wage is constant, the marginal revenue product declines as more labour is hired in the usual way, because the amounts of other factors and capital equipment are held constant, and so less of them are available to be used by each worker. As the wage rises, any business establishment would hire fewer people, so we have obtained the familiar downward-sloping demand curve, just as for other inputs into production, or indeed for consumption. In principle we could now obtain the demand for each particular skill level or category of labour in the same way, and add up the demands by individual employers to obtain aggregate demand for each kind of labour at regional or national level.

The supply of labour

The standard theory of demand for labour as just another commodity clearly omits many aspects of the employment relationship that are of great importance to employers. In just what circumstances this theory provides a useful simplification and abstraction from real-world details remains controversial. Less controversial, however, is the neoclassical theory of labour supply. This theory is developed in texts on microeconomics and labour economics and will not be repeated here, but the basic idea is straightforward. Individuals and households, facing known wages and prices for consumer goods, simultaneously decide on the optimal combination of working hours and their purchases of goods and services for consumption. Some members of the household may of course choose not to take paid work at existing wages, but rather look after children or provide other family services at home. This is called the decision (not) to participate in the labour market, which is obviously prior to any decision about the quantity or hours of labour to supply.

At this point it should also be obvious that most employees who have decided to participate in the labour market do not themselves decide on their working time. Standard hours and even overtime decisions are made by employers, perhaps after collective bargaining with trade union representatives, and workers generally have to accept these decisions or quit the job. Because most employers offer very similar full-time, standard hours of work, choice is limited, and part-time jobs are usually restricted to relatively low-paying and low-skilled occupations.

Constraints of this kind do not invalidate the theory of labour supply, but they do complicate attempts by economists to look for empirical evidence for the theory. Since the basic theory of labour supply is generally accepted, this is not too serious.

Equilibrium and what it might mean

As with all other markets, the coordination of neoclassical supply and demand leads to labour market clearing or equilibrium, when supply equals demand at the equilibrium price or wage. It is the interpretation of this result in the face of persistent unemployment that has caused the greatest controversy over the relevance of the neoclassical theory of employment.

This is not just an academic argument, but a question that has profound and far-reaching consequences for economic policy and indeed for prosperity and welfare, as we now explain. The argument, in brief, is as follows. Critics point to slow adjustment of wages and persistent unemployment as evidence that labour markets are far from neoclassical equilibrium. The critics – often called New Keynesian economists – conclude that fairly generous unemployment benefits are required to avoid severe poverty among those unable to find work through no fault of their own. For moral hazard reasons that will be discussed later in this chapter, complete insurance against unemployment will not be viable, so the state must fund the transfer payments to those without work by taxation of employed people.

However, the neoclassical equilibrium view of labour markets can be defended by arguing that too generous unemployment benefits and excessive government regulation of the labour market provide the wrong incentives and encourage unemployment. Workers may prefer benefits to the alternative of accepting lower-paid or less desirable work, so the facts that appear to contradict equilibrium in the labour market may actually be caused by individuals responding to flawed government policy. This school of thought, which included the Thatcher government in the United Kingdom among its converts, favours lower welfare spending and taxation as the best recipe for higher employment and growth.

When confronted with historical evidence of even higher rates of unemployment in the Great Depression of the 1930s or during the many slumps of the nineteenth century, when benefits were minimal, defenders of the neoclassical theory have to admit that the labour market does differ in important respects from auction markets for commodities. Imperfect information about workers and employers leads to slow adjustment of wages and prolonged search activity between spells of employment. The resulting **frictional unemployment** is a necessary part of the process of matching workers with jobs in an uncertain, changing world. All economists would agree that governments can also make mistakes in macro-policy, setting interest rates too high or reducing expenditure too rapidly, and thus (at least temporarily) generate more unemployment than the minimum, unavoidable frictional level. The logical appeal of the neoclassical view is enhanced by psychological factors, such as the suspicion that arises naturally among those who are hard working (and well paid) that welfare recipients may be shirking or scrounging.

However, the debate is also complicated by recent labour market experience in Europe. Throughout the 1980s unemployment benefits became if anything *less* generous in most OECD countries, yet long-term joblessness in particular rose to unprecedented heights. In the United Kingdom the Thatcher government went furthest along the road of deregulation and benefit reduction. Although wage inequality rose sharply, so also did unemployment of unskilled workers, whose real incomes stagnated or declined. Similar tendencies are apparent in the unregulated US labour market.

At the end of this chapter we will understand where economists have reached a measure of consensus over recent labour market behaviour. Disagreement among academics and policy makers remains strongest about the *desirability* of different policies, about the merits of expected market and social outcomes of various policy measures. These judgements depend crucially on fine details of the employment relationship, details that are all too often glossed over in political or public and media debate. After covering some of this material in the rest of the chapter, we hope to be able to arrive at a better-informed basis for further evaluation of these important issues by the interested reader.

C. Dimensions of the employment relationship

The quantity of work and intensive margins

The number of workers to hire is the employment decision most emphasized in the neoclassical approach. However, there are other important dimensions of the employment relationship that have only recently been studied by economists. The most obvious **intensive margin** of employment is the number of hours per week that employees actually spend working. In the nineteenth-century heyday of classical economics, working hours, even for very young children, were often twice as long as current 35–40-hour weeks. Conditions for workers in early industrialization were graphically described in contemporary novels by Charles Dickens and in Emile Zola's later 'new realism', as well as in studies by Friedrich Engels, who was himself a successful entrepreneur in Victorian England, though he became better known as the long-time collaborator and financial backer of Marx.

Standard weekly working hours were usually similar or uniform over regions, and were left unchanged for long periods during which wages and employment might fluctuate considerably. Thus it was these latter, extensive margins that attracted most attention from economists and commentators at the time, and indeed ever since. Struggles by organized labour to obtain local or national reductions in standard hours were often even more protracted and more bitter than conflict over wages. To meet temporary increased demand, employers usually resorted to extra, overtime hours, paid at higher rates than standard hours, still a common practice today.

As real wages and incomes have risen rapidly in the post-war years in most European countries, workers have continued to press for shorter hours and also for longer vacations. In standard economic terminology, leisure is a normal good and wealthier workers with higher incomes demand more leisure, even though the opportunity cost of an extra hour of free time, which is just the real wage rate, has also increased. In economic jargon, the income effect dominates the substitution effect of rising cost. This is the typical response of full-time workers, but a contrasting situation can be observed in the US labour market, and also for many women.

In the United States, the real wages of unskilled male workers have declined dramatically, by 20–30 per cent, over the past 25 years, so that the poorest 10 per cent of American employees now earn only about half as much as their (West) German counterparts. In Europe, only the lowest-paid British workers have suffered a lack of growth in real income. Most women's pay and opportunities in the labour market have improved over time, tempting an increasing number of women into the labour market in all countries. The decision to participate in the labour force thus responds positively to wages and opportunity. However, to make ends meet, American male workers whose real wages have been falling cannot afford to work less, and their hours have not declined as in Europe, but have risen instead. Average vacations in the United States remain at less than half the typical 4–5 weeks enjoyed by Europeans of similar status (see Freeman, 1994a). Textbook treatments of the individual labour supply decision describe this behaviour by a so-called backward-bending labour supply curve, which contrasts with the 'upward-sloping' relationship between wages and labour supply found for women.

Finally, it is worth noting an interesting but usually neglected consequence of increased female participation in the labour market. As women spend less time doing non-market housework that is not explicitly paid for, they increasingly rely on market-provided services such as nursery or day-care for children and eating out. This tendency went furthest in Sweden, with one of the world's highest labour force participation rates for women. Many of these women are state employees, providing, for example, highly subsidized day-care for preschool children, whose mothers are also out at work! The system is expensive, though children, particularly from poorer families, gain long-term educational advantages from good pre-school care. However, the transfer of women from unpaid non-market work to the labour market simply inflates recorded national product (defined as aggregate pecuniary incomes), without increasing the quantity of services or working time supplied.

The quality of work: Incomplete and relational contracts

Another, but rather different and slightly less obviously missing, intensive margin in the neoclassical account of labour markets is the dimension or quality of individual effort or pace of work. Clearly this is a crucial determinant not only of productivity for the employer but also of worker fatigue and dissatisfaction. The simple neoclassical theory assumes, often implicitly, that both working time and effort are contractually predetermined, so that each worker's marginal revenue product per unit time is known. In fact, of course, the employment contract is the leading example of an incomplete and vague arrangement, for the reasons discussed in earlier chapters. Bounded rationality precludes the precise specification of more than a few possible contingencies in a formal, legally enforceable document, leaving the employee's duties ill defined in most cases.

As already noted long ago by Karl Marx but neglected by most economists until fairly recently, this inherent vagueness sets the stage for the endemic conflict between workers and employers that has affected industrial relations and societies so profoundly for two centuries. Many aspects of the employment relationship that we shall be studying can be understood as attempts to reduce the transaction costs arising from this conflict of interest in economic organization.

Under collective bargaining, unions and employers agree on a much more detailed contract than would be possible for individual workers. Although this may reduce the scope for conflict to some extent for the duration of the contract, the rigidities imposed by a detailed, formal agreement impose other costs, and union coverage has been declining in recent years, particularly in Britain and America.

The necessity of authority

Even in the most comprehensive contract, however, some decision-making mechanism has to be specified to limit the costs of recurrent bargaining in the face of possibly unforeseen contingencies. The obvious solution is to assign decision-making authority to the employer in case of doubt. This means that employees must agree to obey their boss's orders, unless these orders are illegal or explicitly contravene some explicit terms of the employment contract. If many workers object strongly to orders that they are given, then unions may organize a strike or some restrictive practice that limits effort and productivity (working to rule). Also, individuals can take legal action though the courts or invoke formal grievance procedures for settling a dispute, perhaps involving neutral outside arbitrators. Otherwise, a worker's ultimate defence is to quit, which is often possible without prior notice. On the other hand, the employer's ultimate threat or sanction is to sack the recalcitrant worker, though in European countries this may involve the costs of a legal battle and severance payment.

In the Marxian tradition, authority has usually been identified with superior power based on the employer's wealth and capital ownership. However, as we have seen, and as was first emphasized by Nobel Prize-winning political scientist, economist and wide-ranging scholar Herbert Simon (1951), *some* focus of authority in the employment relationship is an essential result of bounded rationality and uncertainty. In large organizations, **residual authority** over most employees is held by a boss or supervisor who is *not* the **residual income claimant** or owner of the enterprise, but who is also an employee, with a superior on the next hierarchical level. There are also efficiency arguments to explain this almost universal structure of organization, which we develop as follows.

First, it is usually appropriate for residual authority to be held by a single party, to avoid bargaining or conflict between bosses. Furthermore, this authority should always be held by the same party for all events unforeseen in the explicit contract, unless a change in the location of residual authority can be made conditional upon some verifiable event. This is what can actually happen in the case of default by a firm on debt obligations, when a court-appointed trustee (called the receiver in the United Kingdom) takes over ultimate authority in the firm from the owners. It is obvious that no single individual can *directly* assume ultimate decision-making authority for *all* the employees of a large organization. The role of a managerial hierarchy is thus clear. However, a more difficult question is who should appoint the boss at the top of the hierarchy? In the entrepreneurial firm this is easy: the founder who is still residual income claimant appoints the top manager, but is himself the ultimate residual decision-making authority. By contrast, in a large corporation with many widely dispersed outside stockholders, top management may own only a small proportion of outstanding shares. Managers are thus also formally salaried employees of the stockholders who receive the residual income. In practice, stockholders appoint a board of directors, who in turn hire the top manager and sometimes fire him, as they have done at IBM, General Motors and other major corporations in recent years.

We return to the problems of corporate governance in more detail in later chapters, but we can explain here why suppliers of capital are generally residual claimants and ultimate authority holders. Whereas the mobility of largely speculative financial capital flows in global markets has become notorious, fixed capital such as plant and equipment usually represents a more *specific asset*, specially designed and therefore immobilized for some particular purpose. In the event of bankruptcy and job loss, employees may find alternative employment, though usually at substantially lower wages, while the liquidation value of specific capital assets is likely to be very low indeed. It is the perceived greater risk of liquidation that motivates investors to demand the residual income, which offers a compensating upside potential for above-average profits when business booms.

Owners retain residual authority when contracts are incomplete, because any other party with residual authority, such as hired managers, would be tempted to use or abuse this authority for their own benefit, say by raising their salaries or perks, at the cost of residual income. However carefully contracts are written, there will always be some ways for holders of residual authority who are not (exclusive) residual income claimants to divert funds from the latter to themselves.

In certain kinds of organization such as professional partnerships, or universities, most of the capital consists of accumulated skills and experience in the form of employees' **human capital**. Any ability or knowledge that increases future productivity can usefully be regarded as some kind of human capital. Some skills are easily transferable from one work place to another, and thus are mobile or non-specific. However, a team of professionals, or individual skilled workers, may develop **specific human capital**, skills related to their business and each other, that are less than perfectly mobile. As developed in the previous chapter, any kind of capital asset, tangible or human, that is more productive in one particular use than in its next-best use earns a quasi-rent above its opportunity cost. Bankruptcy or liquidation of the team destroys these quasi-rents. Thus it makes sense for the team to claim residual income in the legal framework of a professional partnership and, by our logic above, also to share residual authority.

Of course, sharing decision-making authority could cause serious problems of conflicting interest unless the partnership was relatively homogeneous in terms of members' qualifications and goals. This tends to be true for teams of doctors, lawyers, accountants, architects or other professionals who frequently work in partnerships, so that residual income can be shared by simple rules, according to age and experience, while decision-making is relatively uncontroversial. Offices and computers or diagnostic equipment can be rented or leased, because these assets can easily be redeployed and are thus not at risk through bankruptcy.

Employee stakeholders and collective bargaining

The exclusive assignment of residual authority to the employer does not do justice to an important but neglected fact mentioned above. When workers at any level, blue collar or white collar, are *forced* to change jobs through downsizing or bankruptcy, they usually suffer a substantial wage reduction, as well as the costs of relocation and often a spell of unemployment. Brookings Institution economist Margaret Blair discusses this problem in her important study *Ownership and Control* (1995). She quotes Robert Topel's (1991) finding of an average 14 per cent wage reduction after job loss in the United States, with higher losses for older workers. The traditional view that shareholder–owners are the only risk bearers is therefore incorrect.

Employees are thus also stakeholders in their enterprise, who to some extent share the risks of failure by virtue of having acquired skills that were specifically valuable and specialized to their job or employer. As we shall see in the next section, the employment relationship does provide some partial insurance to employee stakeholders, but there remains a fundamental tension between the interests of specific human capital owners and the employer's residual authority in traditional capitalist firms. Historically two basically different responses to this tension have evolved.

The traditional response was the rise of organized labour in the form of trade unions, to represent and protect the interests of workers in bargaining with employers. After a history of often violent conflict, collective bargaining was generally recognized after World War II, though strikes caused frequent disruption, particularly in the adversarial Anglo-American tradition of industrial relations. Collective bargainers sought to protect vulnerable specific skills by restrictive work rules that tried to maintain elements of craft tradition against the progressively finer division of labour in Fordist mass production following the example of pioneer Henry Ford in the US automobile industry after World War I.

During the 1980s, collective bargaining came under attack in the United Kingdom and the United States, so that union coverage declined. Labour markets were deregulated in the belief that competitive forces would ensure efficiency according to neoclassical theory. One result of this process in the United States was a flood of employment-related litigation by employees who were now lacking any formal representation or 'voice' at work. The courts have become clogged with a backlog of cases, and employees without the resources required for legal action are severely disadvantaged.

A very different response has been developed in (West) Germany and other European countries, a response that does recognize the role of employee as stakeholder. In addition to collective bargaining between employers' and union representatives at industry and regional level over wages and working time, which applies to most employees independently of union membership, the German system of **codetermination** provides direct representation of labour interests at various levels of management. Elected employee representatives occupy half the seats on the top-level, supervisory board of directors of large public companies. Employees at all establishments with at least five workers are entitled to elect a **works council** that has far-reaching powers relating to personnel decisions. Although codetermination laws were initially opposed by business, there is now a consensus that the system has helped to maintain cooperative labour relations, partnership rather than confrontation in most areas of managerial decision-making. Working time and conditions are more regulated and adjustment of the workforce is relatively slow, but the proportion of skilled workers is much higher in Germany than in the United Kingdom or the United States. Although a systematic comparison of German institutions with those of other countries is reserved for Chapter 17, it may be

observed here that some of the most serious problems of the German economy, such as excessive non-wage labour costs due to a badly designed tax
system, and regulations that hamper entrepreneurial start-ups and self-
employment, are *not* related to the codetermination system.

In the United Kingdom, schemes of employee involvement and participation in job-related decision-making are positively correlated with productivity,
according to managers' subjective assessments in a large representative sample of companies (Fernie and Metcalf, 1995). Business, government and labour
are all generally agreed on the need for more employee involvement and commitment, though they differ on the appropriate means of achieving this goal.
Both business and government, however, strongly oppose any extension of
European legislation on work-place representation, such as works councils or
worker–directors.

The position of the employee as stakeholder is perhaps strongest in Japan,
though without codetermination laws and hence on a much more informal
basis than in Germany. Again deferring detailed discussion, we note that
Japanese transplants in the United Kingdom and elsewhere have transferred
many features of Japanese organization to their mainly local labour forces.
These workers have also been very rigorously selected (from numerous applicants, sometimes 100 or more for one vacancy) and trained, to achieve some
of the highest productivity levels in Europe, though without the benefit of collective bargaining or works councils! As usual in economics, it is difficult to
draw sharp or simple conclusions, because higher productivity could be due
to greater effort by more able and higher-paid workers.

Although the most common assignments of decision-making authority can
thus be explained in part at least on efficiency grounds, there is another possible explanation of some relevance, best discussed in connection with risk-
sharing in the next section.

D. The employment relationship as insurance and incentive

In the classical theory of employment, workers were always paid their marginal revenue product, which would vary with prices and demand shifts, so
that full employment should always hold. In practice, wages were much more
variable during early industrialization, but unemployment and layoffs were also
frequent, so the classical model did not fully explain employment behaviour
even in its heyday in the nineteenth century. These problems were recognized
by some pioneering economists long before the modern contractual approach
was developed.

Sticky wages and insurance

When wages gradually became less flexible or 'sticky' in the decades after World War I, a leading American economist of the time, Frank Knight (1985 [1921]), argued that entrepreneurs were less risk averse than workers and so bore the risk of fluctuating residual income while providing insurance by paying fixed wages. Massive unemployment during the Great Depression in the 1930s was unkind to that theory too, but the modern corporation certainly does allow shareholders to reduce the firm-specific risk by holding diversified portfolios of shares in many different firms. Since workers surely are risk averse, we may well ask why employment contracts do not resemble insurance contracts and maintain employees' income.

There are several different reasons, but most obviously an employer who guaranteed worker incomes would have no sanctions against lazy employees! If insurance was made conditional on workers obeying their boss's orders, it would be easy for the firm to cheat by claiming disobedience in some way that was hard for outsiders to verify. To break even, the employer would have to pay less than the worker's marginal revenue product in good times, to compensate for wages above productivity in bad times. But then it would be easy for workers to cheat by demanding higher wages or quitting when productivity was high and other jobs were more likely to be available.

There are also economy-wide risks, such as recession, that affect most employers simultaneously, so that complete insurance for workers is infeasible for all those reasons. However, various forms of partial insurance are regularly supplied by employers as part of the employment relationship, complemented by social security measures supplied by the state.

Today, wages of regular employers are rarely cut except in a crisis, and residual profits are indeed much more volatile than labour earnings. This can be interpreted as a form of partial insurance of the kind described by Knight, but the reasons go deeper. When employees earn more than the next-best opportunity for their firm-specific human capital, any formula for cutting wages in recession transfers these quasi-rents, which are difficult to measure precisely, from workers to employer. This redistribution raises the possibility of moral hazard, with costly bargaining or conflict when the employer, as residual decision maker, is tempted to renege on an implicit agreement. Simplified bargaining reduces transaction costs, and bargaining over a flexible wage, say one linked to productivity, is more complicated than the usual practice of bargaining over an hourly rate in fixed money terms. None the less, gain-sharing and profit-sharing agreements are quite common, and we will discuss them later.

Work-sharing and labour hoarding

Another fairly obvious form of partial insurance would seem to be work-sharing as an alternative to the temporary layoffs that are common in the United States. In fact, overtime hours are generally reduced before workers are laid off, and even a few exceptionally successful American companies such as Lincoln Electric offer an explicit contractual guarantee of permanent employment or 'no layoffs'. Other world-renowned US corporations such as Hewlett-Packard also institute shorter work-weeks for most employees in recession, rather than layoffs, though without a formal commitment. Instead, the practice of work-sharing is supported by an **implicit contract** or a firmly held expectation by all parties based on past practice.

Work-sharing in the form of shorter weekly working hours was quite common at the onset of the Great Depression in the early 1930s. However, as the downturn worsened, workers on short weeks and reduced incomes, even with unchanged hourly rates, began to feel the pinch and push for standard weeks again, or quit to obtain full-time work if their skills were mobile. In spite of minimal availability of unemployment benefits, work-sharing collapsed, swelling the dole queues and prolonging the depression as demand for consumer goods by the unemployed fell even further.

After World War II, American and British trade unions demanded protection for those who had been most vulnerable in the past. These were principally older workers with the most specific human capital or specialized skills accumulated after often many years with the same employer. 'Seniority protection' became the watchwords for collective bargains that stipulated layoffs by inverse seniority or tenure with the employer. The first workers to be laid off were the newest accessions to the firm according to the principle of LIFO (last in, first out), so that seniority afforded relative security.

In many continental European countries, partial employment insurance took a rather different form. Work-sharing became the main initial response to declining demand, and short-time (unemployment) benefits compensated for part of the reduction in weekly earnings. Little use is made of temporary layoffs, but only when the downturn in demand for products of a firm or industry is expected to be lasting is the workforce reduced. Substantial severance pay for workers who are dismissed is required by many collective bargains or by regulations at the national level in Germany, the Netherlands, Sweden and elsewhere. This form of partial insurance slows down the adjustment of the labour market to structural and cyclical change. Employers are also reluctant to hire new people on the upswing in view of possible future costs of severance pay, and may prefer to invest in labour-saving technology instead. Productivity in recession falls when workers who are not fully occupied remain on the payroll. Some degree of labour hoarding or underutilization of existing employees is universal simply because the transaction costs of instantaneous workforce adjustment would be too high. Clearly a greater amount of labour hoarding in countries such as Germany and Japan, where long-term employment is usual, does offer additional insurance to workers.

Although various rigidities and costs of adjustment of the labour force are believed by many economists to have contributed to persistently high levels of unemployment in Europe in the 1980s, the more stable employment offered by firms to their existing employees brings obvious benefits too. Less obviously, employers and employees are encouraged to make larger investments in specific human capital, because these investments become less risky when labour mobility is reduced. This effect is most pronounced in Japan, where large corporations offer implicit contracts for permanent employment to all full-time, male employees. Blue-collar workers are provided with unrivalled training and career-advancement opportunities. And they have every incentive for increasing productivity while knowing that their own jobs will not be threatened, and that they will share in the benefits through higher, seniority-related wages and promotion prospects. Japanese and German employment and industry will be treated in greater depth later. It does seem plausible that job security in these countries is related to provision of production-worker training and skill levels that are much higher on average than in the more mobile and less regulated labour markets of the United Kingdom and United States.

The age–wage profile

Older workers and those with longer tenure are generally paid more than younger workers, even when they are doing the same job, and this upward-sloping **age–wage profile** also represents a rather subtle form of insurance, as well as encouraging workers not to quit. When a new employee is first hired, the employer will be uncertain of her future productivity. If wage cuts are unacceptable for the moral hazard reasons mentioned above, initial wages will be set below the expected marginal productivity of all new hires. Wages can be raised according to performance as the employer learns about true productivity in the course of time, and even poor performers will have their wages raised enough to match their long-run productivity and total pay. The initial gap between wages and productivity 'insures' the worker against wage cuts in the future, and against the probable job loss that would result if wages were too high, while allowing the employer to avoid losses even on poor performers.

We expect the average age–wage profile to be steeper where the opportunities for training and skill development are greater. Thus it comes as no surprise that this relationship is steepest in Japan. If skills acquired are specific or difficult to transfer, postponement of higher wages in the form of quasi-rents on specific investment imposes risks on the employee. Job loss through dismissal or even bankruptcy of the employer causes greater loss of lifetime earnings in Japan than elsewhere. Precisely because of this threat, however, delayed quasi-rents provide an efficiency-wage type of incentive for workers to avoid dismissal, as discussed in the previous chapters, and to cooperate most effectively to avert bankruptcy, thus reducing the risk. However, at least an implicit assurance of work-sharing instead of layoffs will be required by employees who accept a very steep age–wage relationship.

Of course, a worker's productivity in a particular task or occupation will also change over time. As experience is gained, productivity usually rises for most occupations initially. However, maximum productivity is often attained at a fairly early age. Even when physical strength is not a requirement, opinion surveys of supervisors indicate that productivity in many occupations declines substantially as workers pass mid-career and grow older. Probably they also become less enthusiastic, losing hope of promotion when they remain stuck in the same job. None the less, pay continues to rise with age for the reasons given above. Clearly, older workers whose earnings have outstripped their productivity are particularly in need of the seniority protection discussed earlier. The findings also explain why such older workers have difficulty in obtaining new jobs if they become unemployed for some reason such as bankruptcy of the original employer. Owing to the problems with cutting wages discussed above, one can understand why most jobs are subject to compulsory retirement at age 65 or earlier, to avoid progressively less productive but relatively highly paid workers hanging on too long and retiring unpredictably.

Reputation as insurance

Another form of insurance for workers that is often emphasized is the **reputation** of the employer. Clearly employers, just like private individuals, can enhance the credibility of implicit contracts or informal promises by demonstrating a track record of compliance and good faith. Such a reputation reduces the need for legal or formal safeguards, and hence by reducing transaction costs represents a form of capital asset, often called 'good will'. In the labour market, a reputation as a good employer will attract the best job applicants, indeed usually more applicants than available openings. When this becomes well known, poor-quality applicants may not bother to apply, knowing their chances to be slim. In this way reputation provides a screening function, and encourages an efficient self-selection process that improves the average quality of the pool of applicants. This in turn lowers recruitment costs and increases the return on the employer's investments in human capital.

It would be a mistake, however, to deduce from this that competition will necessarily eliminate employers with bad reputations, as is sometimes claimed. Most people can point to an employer in their locality who is known to offer unpleasant working conditions, unsteady employment and low pay as well. Particularly in depressed areas or periods, those who lack qualifications or useful experience may have no choice but to accept badly paid, risky or unpleasant jobs. Their productivity may be low, but if wages are still lower the business

that employs them may survive and prosper in spite of a well-deserved reputation for harsh or unfair treatment, provided only that good jobs remain in
short supply. Just how such very different types of employer can coexist and
survive will be explored further in the next section.

E. Internal, primary and secondary markets

We have already mentioned the internal labour markets and job ladders within
organizations where most transfers from one task or occupation to another
take place. The neoclassical model of the external labour market was clearly
inadequate as a comprehensive description of labour allocation, but can be
further developed to complement internal markets in various ways. First, however it is useful to distinguish primary and secondary sectors (see Doeringer
and Piore, 1971, and also Solow, 1990). In the **primary labour market**, workers are skilled, enjoy promotion prospects or career advancement, and hold
relatively secure, well-paid and interesting jobs. Most primary workers are in
the internal labour markets of hierarchical organizations, but self-employed
professionals and craftspeople also belong to the primary sector.

Secondary labour markets, by contrast, are much closer to the classical
model. Here skills and job-security are minimal, wages are low and more variable, though not variable enough to eliminate unemployment, and work tends
to be monotonous or arduous. Examples are itinerant farm workers, casual
labour of all kinds, illegal immigrants and the lowest-paid blue- and white-collar employees who perform the unskilled work and menial tasks in most organizations, with little prospect of betterment or security. Some industries such
as textiles have a high proportion of secondary workers, and even Japanese
corporations employ some part-time and female labour on a secondary basis,
often as temporary help, without the commitment to long-term attachment or
career progression reserved for core employees.

Unions have helped to attain primary sector benefits of high pay and relative security even for unskilled assembly workers in some industries such as
automobiles. However, such highly paid but unskilled work in manufacturing
is being increasingly displaced throughout America and Europe by technical
progress, automation and cheaper imports from low-wage countries such as
Mexico and South-East Asia, using genuine secondary labour at a small fraction of the cost of Western wage rates. As *female*, often part-time employment
has grown dramatically in secondary service sectors in the English-speaking
world, unemployment has become a problem mainly for unskilled *male*
workers.

Traditionally, there has been more mobility between sectors in the New World
than in the Old. Young Americans often gained experience in a variety of secondary jobs before settling down to a primary career. Long-lasting jobs are common, particularly for older, male workers in *all* industrial countries. However,

loss of such a primary job when recession or bankruptcy overrides seniority protection can mean descent into the secondary sector and severe hardship. Unemployed primary workers usually search for another primary job before taking secondary employment or even abandoning the search for work. The loss of status and reputation in secondary jobs can worsen the chances for regaining primary employment, though long-term unemployment is equally damaging. The increasing importance of formal education and training qualifications has constricted the opportunities or ports of entry into many primary job ladders, excluding those individuals without the necessary formal training and credentials. However, expanding entrepreneurial and small-firm employment and self-employment have offered new opportunities in the primary sector as well as in secondary, temporary and part-time employment, particularly in the less regulated labour markets of the United Kingdom and the United States.

In contrast to the internal market, **external labour markets** receive most attention from economists and the media. Headline-grabbing changes in the number of people registered as unemployed prompt calls for policy action that governments ignore at their peril. Every year some people change their employer, often with a short interval of unemployment between jobs. School leavers and graduates enter the labour market for the first time, while the elderly and discouraged exit the labour market, sometimes returning to seek employment again later. Small changes in these substantial flows of individuals can generate large shifts in the stock of people out of work at any point in time. When aggregate demand weakens or productivity unexpectedly rises, it is the slow-down in hiring replacements for flows of quitters and retirees that first swells the ranks of the out-of-work.

The external labour market finally provides the environment in which internal labour markets have to operate. External pressures such as the threat of a longer spell of unemployment in recession, or the lengthier queue of job applicants, affect the morale and effort of existing employees. Rates of absenteeism and sickness may decline by half when jobs are most at risk in prolonged recession. However, in the day-to-day operations of most businesses and organizations it is in the internal labour market where most activity takes place and attention is focused.

Job assignment and the internal market

Long-term, enduring employment relationships in primary sector, **internal labour markets** imply restricted mobility across organizations. Since the appropriate assignment of workers to jobs is an important determinant of economic efficiency, growth and productivity, the internal market must offer major advantages to compensate for restricted mobility. Indeed, one of the fastest-growing and most successful economies, that of Japan, has come to rely most of all on the internal labour market.

There are three prominent benefits from long-term association with an organization and consequent reliance on internal mobility. First, there is greater scope for profitable investment in knowledge, skills and interpersonal relationships that are specific to the organization – firm-specific human capital. As well as raising productivity, such investment provides an incentive to remain with the same employer when the quasi-rents are shared, and this leads to other benefits.

The longer the expected duration of these rents, the greater the efficiency-wage incentive effect to avoid loss of the job and the quasi-rent. Supervision can thus be reduced, which in turn enhances workers' autonomy and job satisfaction. Longer time horizons also increase the importance of reputation, which helps to enforce implicit contracts and thus reduce the transaction costs of formal and explicit contracts.

Finally, longer tenure with an organization allows managers to accumulate more accurate information about their employees with experience, which in turn enables them to match jobs and workers more efficiently. Formal qualifications and references supplied by a job applicant from the external labour market provide some information for employers, but it is always incomplete. There is often no substitute for knowledge gained by supervisors and co-workers through close association over a period of perhaps many years.

Performance at simple, well-defined tasks is relatively easy to assess, so for this kind of work the gains from long-term association are minimized. Precisely these kinds of jobs characterize the secondary sector, which can thus function with high mobility and little specific human capital. The more complex and more specific the task, however, the greater is the cost of recruitment – locating and screening potential applicants – and of training on the job for new personnel. The benefits from long-term association in the internal labour market thus rise with the level and the specificity of the skills required.

Some highly skilled professionals such as traders in large financial markets for stocks, bonds or derivatives may conduct identical transactions for different employers, and thus are highly mobile. On the other hand, detailed knowledge of customer requirements represents a specialized asset that cannot be transferred to another employer unless, as sometimes happens, customers are wooed away and transferred as well. In this case the employee is functioning more like an entrepreneur or a subcontractor, whose assets consist of a loyal customer base. As a 'team', they are mobile and can seek the highest market return.

Promotion and job assignment

As knowledge of employee abilities is gained by managers in an internal labour market, and as employees accumulate organization-specific skills, the better performers can be assigned to more productive jobs. This assignment usually takes the form of promotion up an internal job ladder or hierarchy, rewarded at each stage or new rank by higher pay and prestige. To reduce bargaining, pay scales are usually related to job or positions, with well-defined criteria such as tenure or performance measures determining an individual's pay position on each scale. Entry is usually restricted to lower levels of the hierarchy, called **ports of entry**, partly because outsiders are unlikely to bring the requisite specific skills for higher-level positions, and also because allowing entry higher up in the hierarchy would impair the motivation and loyalty of existing employees in lower positions. Even when qualified outside candidates could be found, incentives for insiders are improved by excluding outsiders from competing.

Clearly, specific knowledge of an organization and appropriate abilities are nowhere more important than in the managerial hierarchy, particularly at high levels. Strategic decisions that set the future course of an organization are made by top management, so selection of the right people for these positions becomes crucial. Normally, performance at any one level plays a major role in deciding whom to promote to the next level of the hierarchy. It is usually easiest for supervisors to evaluate the performance of subordinates in the same hierarchy. These are also the candidates with the most specific knowledge of the functions that successful applicants will have to supervise in their new positions.

The possibility of promotion in an internal labour market is probably the most widely used incentive in modern economies where a majority of workers are in primary sector employment. However, promotion up an internal job ladder has one major drawback.

Hierarchical superiors and supervisors often seem to dislike the uncertainty and conflicts involved in performing subjective evaluations of their subordinates. Much effort has gone into developing formalized and 'objective' evaluation procedures as a basis for promotion and pay rises. Some subjective elements are often unavoidable, however, and this inevitably encourages internal politics or **influence activity**. Such activity is designed explicitly to gain the supervisor's favour, and indeed *may* coincide with organizational objectives. But perfect coincidence is generally unattainable. Making the boss's life easier rather than criticizing controversial decisions may generate a reputation for good interpersonal skills – a prerequisite for promotion and greater responsibility. On the other hand, a costly error in a superior's judgement may pass unchallenged by subordinates too eager to please. One way of limiting influence activity is to reduce superiors' discretion in promotion decisions by formal rules. The drawback again is that important information may be missed in unusual circumstances not foreseen by the rules.

Wages in internal labour markets

When mobility is reduced by specific skills, quasi-rents have to be shared between employee and employer, and there may not be a suitable market wage to serve as a benchmark. At the port of entry, people of similar qualification will expect similar lifetime rewards on average, but large differences among promotion and career patterns actually realized over time offer little guidance for setting pay in individual cases. Bargaining at each stage of the internal job ladder would expose immobilized employees to considerable risk from breach of any implicit agreement by unscrupulous employers. Indeed, with much uncertainty over true productivity and quasi-rents in large organizations, even honest attempts to reach a fair division can easily generate mutual mistrust and recrimination.

The rise of collective bargaining intensified the need to find objective criteria for wage-setting. Decisions had to be ultimately enforceable by arbitrators called in to settle disputes or by the courts. The solution that evolved in tandem with the development of modern industrial work organization early in the twentieth century was to set wages for well-defined standardized tasks or job classifications, as well as taking into account the age or seniority of workers.

The concern of management was to reduce costs by subdividing complex tasks into many precisely defined, routine operations. These could be performed by mainly unskilled or semi-skilled workers. Unions could bargain over wage scales for these standardized job classifications, which then protected workers from surreptitious pay cuts or increased work loads when the contract was in force. And wages for the same task could be more easily compared across organizations, further reducing the informational problems and costs of bargaining.

The lack of flexibility of this system began to cause serious problems when technological change accelerated in the 1970s. In Japan and Germany, wages were based on a combination of seniority and skills acquired, rather than on detailed job descriptions, providing an incentive for training and allowing more rapid redeployment of workers to satisfy shifts in demand and accommodate new technologies. However flexibility depends upon cooperation between labour and management, and the traditional adversarial bargaining and labour relations in the United States and United Kingdom began to have a negative effect on competitiveness in global markets.

In recent years, many Western employers have begun to reduce the number of job classifications, and to base wages upon skills and performance. Collective bargainers in the automobile industry and elsewhere have negotiated greater job security and severance pay in return for flexibility and productivity-related gains, rather than regular annual wage increases for all employers. At the same time, the steep decline of unionization and large-scale manufacturing in the United Kingdom and the United States in the 1980s reduced the scope of collective bargaining, and the dispersion of wages that were increasingly subject to individual negotiation rose.

Sometimes even specific skills can become valuable, for example to competitors or new entrants in an industry. These firms may seek to hire senior employees of incumbent rivals in order to imitate their technology or production methods. This raises difficult problems for wage policy in the internal labour market. If outside offers were always matched, this would create an incentive for employees deliberately to seek such offers as bargaining ploys, even when they have no intention of quitting. On the other hand, a policy of no response to outside offers may result in key personnel being sometimes lost. Promotion can be accelerated even with inflexible pay scales in order to retain valuable employees, and outside offers will be considered by most managers when making promotion decisions.

In spite of the importance of specific knowledge, chief executives of large organizations are sometimes replaced by outsiders in a crisis. As at IBM in 1993, the new CEO may even come from outside the industry, though this is unusual. When the crisis is deep rooted, it may be felt that insiders are unlikely to pursue the radical shake-up of the whole corporate culture that may be necessary. Without emotional bonds to co-workers, the newcomer may also be more ruthless in cutting staff and costs, though success is never certain when the crisis is deep enough.

In such a situation, when survival of the whole enterprise is at stake, substantial wage cuts may be negotiated between management and unions. At United Airlines in 1993, the agreement also included an employee stock ownership plan (ESOP), giving workers a share in future residual profits and decision-making authority. Such plans have become widespread in the United States and also in the United Kingdom, though often primarily for tax reasons or to prevent takeover.

We have seen why general, across-the-board wage cuts are unlikely unless a majority of employees are threatened with job loss. It might still be plausible to hire new workers at rates lower than those for existing employees when unemployment is high. Such 'two-tier' wage agreements have sometimes been tried during recession, but tend to generate problems between the **insiders**, or old employees, and new hires, or **outsiders**. In the course of time the outsiders become insiders who are expected to cooperate with the rest of the workforce, and pay differentials lead to resentment that can disrupt cooperation and teamwork.

Performance-related pay and profit-sharing

In many secondary jobs with little prospect of promotion, workers whose output is easy to measure have traditionally been paid according to what they produce, by a piece-rate instead of an hourly wage. Fruit pickers or salespeople who control the pace of their work can thus be given a flexible incentive to choose their optimal combination of effort and earnings. Where teamwork is important, group incentives depending on the output produced by the whole team have been introduced. And even white-collar employees are increasingly offered bonus payments and rewards related to some measure of their performance.

Particularly when technology or work tasks change, uncertainty arises over the appropriate piece-rate or bonus scheme. Information about the subjective cost of effort is asymmetric – only the worker has direct knowledge of this cost. When the job is idiosyncratic there may be no relevant market rate for comparison. Workers clearly have an incentive to exaggerate the effort required to produce a given output, and one way to do this is deliberately to slow down the pace of work. Weekly earnings for people in similar jobs are widely used as a benchmark so, by withholding effort, workers on piece-rates may succeed in obtaining higher rates of pay and hence 'normal' earnings with below-normal effort. With existing high piece-rates in this situation, greater effort and higher earnings might be preferred by workers. However, management might be expected to cut the piece-rate if earnings rose above standard levels, so workers are likely to cooperate and to try to prevent individuals from exceeding some informally established work norm. Social sanctions against 'rate-busters' by peer groups have frequently been observed in practice. Indeed, the whole process of designing and implementing performance-related pay schemes is plagued with uncertainty and conflict, which often outweigh the prospective benefits. Piece-rates are therefore usually only a small proportion of total pay, and their use has been declining for manual work.

In many white-collar and managerial jobs, 'output' may be hard to define and measure precisely. Some components, such as time spent in the office, are easy to measure, but other components such as the 'quality' of decisions or morale of subordinates are much harder to quantify and reward in the short run. Since performance-related pay necessarily rewards quantifiable performance, employees are tempted to neglect aspects of their tasks that are under-rewarded in their pay or bonus scheme. Long-term rewards through promotion to higher-paid or more prestigious positions, on the other hand, do allow superiors to accumulate a wide range of evidence on all aspects of performance before making these crucial decisions.

Rewarding performance by promotion differs from other rewards such as higher pay, because the number of higher-ranking positions is limited. For example, there is only one CEO in most companies, and many ambitious vice-presidents. Promotion is like a prize in a tournament, and close competitors who are unlucky may feel demoralized if they have worked extra hard in order to maximize their winning chances. Since the promotion tournament is repeated regularly, a loser in one round may nevertheless win in the next, however. Because performance does not have to be measured quantitatively as in a money–bonus formula, but only a rank ordering of candidates is required, the tournament system reduces some transaction costs and scope for errors.

On the other hand, there is a serious problem with competitive promotion whenever teamwork is important. One way of raising one's own relative standing may be to sabotage rivals' efforts in subtle ways, such as withholding important information. Competition can thus be divisive when there is interdependence of this kind. Particularly when the team is fairly small, a group bonus may be the most effective incentive in this case, so that peer group pressure is mobilized to discourage free-riding.

Some form of profit-sharing has long been used to motivate top management, but in recent years explicit profit-sharing, sometimes coupled with share ownership, has been offered to an increasing number of employees. In France, former President Charles de Gaulle viewed profit-sharing as a 'third way' of avoiding the endemic conflicts of capitalism and the centralized bureacracy of socialism, and encouraged the widespread establishment of such schemes. Tax incentives for profit-related pay were later introduced in the United Kingdom and the United States in the 1980s, in the belief that employee commitment to enterprise goals could thereby be strengthened. Sceptics noted that most employees in larger firms could hardly influence enterprise performance by their individual effort. Nevertheless, and perhaps somewhat surprisingly, many studies of profit-sharing firms in different countries show an increase in productivity after the introduction of profit-sharing, or evidence that profit-sharing causes the productivity gain. There is also evidence that schemes of this kind are most effective in conjunction with employee involvement or participation in work-place-related decision-making and a firm commitment to long-term employment or job-sharing (see Blinder, 1990, and Kruse, 1993).[1]

In the neoclassical model of competitive labour markets, wages should not be affected by firm profits. However, numerous recent studies show that individual wages and earnings are related to firm and industry profit levels even when personal and job characteristics are taken into account. Some kind of *implicit* profit- or rent-sharing thus seems to be widespread in industrial countries, in addition to the explicit schemes that governments have recently encouraged. As often in economics, these observations raise subtle issues of causality. Thus rent-sharing employers who pay higher wages will also attract 'better-quality' – perhaps 'better-looking' – job applicants. Many individual characteristics of this kind are not included in even the most comprehensive data sets. Thus it is always possible that at least some of the observed wage differential is a return or rent earned by, say, better-looking workers, or some other attribute that is unknown to the economist–observer but that is valued by managers or owners with market power. Of course, 'perfectly' competitive firms will have no surplus rents to share or to spend on better-looking workers. There is evidence that workers who move to a job in more profitable or more concentrated industries do gain higher wages, suggesting true rent-sharing, though again mobility may itself signal some other characteristic that employers value. And workers who lose their job in a high-wage industry suffer the largest wage cuts, which provides further support for rent-sharing.

Finally, it is important to realize that *extrinsic* motivation through pay or promotion can sometimes actually inhibit the *intrinsic* motivation provided by the challenge of doing an interesting job well. Bruno Frey summarizes evidence for this 'crowding out' effect, mainly from the psychological literature, in his book *Not for the Money Alone* (1997), which emphasizes subjective aspects of job satisfaction and cooperation that are often neglected by managers and economists.

Fairness and trust

Traditional economic theory assumed that individuals were selfish, so workers, for example, should care only about their own wages and work. However, a growing body of empirical evidence, including the prevalence of rent-sharing mentioned above, can be plausibly explained only if people are actually concerned about the *fairness* of economic outcomes, as well as their own narrowly defined rewards. According to the newer theories, workers are likely to feel that they have been treated unfairly if they do not receive a share in any above-normal profits. Workers who feel this way will be demotivated and tend to look for alternative employment in the long run. Thus they have less reason to acquire specific skills. Even a selfish employer may find that rent-sharing increases his own residual profit in the long run, while managers can personally benefit from an improved climate of industrial relations as well. Modern theories of fairness are thus intuitively quite compelling, and accord well with introspection and everyday observation, as well as offering the most plausible explanation for the results of sophisticated empirical and econometric investigations.

Recognition of a role for fairness does not of course exclude conflict. Workers may have a very different idea of what constitutes a fair distribution of rents from employers, and both sides can exploit uncertainty in bargaining. Just what is perceived to be a 'fair' distribution or solution to some conflict of interest seems to depend strongly on personal relationships between the parties, their reputations and the level of trust established.

Trust helps to increase flexibility and efficiency by allowing all parties to dispense with formal legally enforceable safeguards. As Nobel Prize-winning economist Kenneth Arrow wrote in his classic study *The Limits of Organization*: 'Trust is an important lubricant of a social system. It is extremely efficient; it saves a lot of trouble to have a fair degree of reliance on other people's word. Unfortunately this is not a commodity which can be bought very easily. If you have to buy it, you already have some doubts about what you've bought' (1974, p. 23; see also Gambetta, 1988). Political scientist Francis Fukuyama's major theory of trust as a foundation stone of social and economic efficiency was discussed in the previous chapter (Fukuyama, 1995).

The productive efficiency of internal labour markets is particularly dependent upon the intangible public good of trust. Only high trust allows rigid job classifications and pay scales as well as restrictive work rules to be dispensed with. Workers who believe they will be fairly treated and rewarded in the long run are less likely to shirk when their supervisor is not watching them, so monitoring may be less intensive. There is no incentive for workers to collude to restrain output when progressive pay and job security are ensured.

Without job security, some workers may lose their jobs when productivity rises. Then it may be rational for workers to collude and agree to reduce their efforts and productivity in subtle ways that go unnoticed by supervisors. In such a situation an individual worker could probably work harder to attract favourable attention and gain promotion. Such behaviour, however, might reveal the restraints practised by other workers and undermine their collusive strategy. Peer-group pressure, therefore, has often been used to maintain the norm of reduced work effort, just as in the case of conflict over piece-rates considered already.

In their concern to protect jobs that might be threatened by new technology or job design, union bargains have frequently formalized such restrictive practices or work rules, and thus reduced productivity. This problem has been avoided in Japan by providing an implicit contract for permanent employment in a high-trust environment. With career progression for blue-collar as well as white-collar workers, productivity gains benefit all employees. In this climate, work norms emphasize cooperation with management rather than opposition to bosses. Peer-group pressure can then limit shirking by individuals more effectively than can supervisors, who are not directly involved in the work process.

Efficiency of the internal labour market depends upon mobility within organizations. In Japan, workers learn to cooperate in teams and to master a wide range of tasks. If production in one plant is reduced, they also accept relocation to a different plant or occupation if necessary, unhindered by restrictive job classifications and working rules. This degree of internal mobility and flexibility is based upon trust that managers will not abuse their powers in the system, but continue to give all employees access to training and promotion possibilities.

Lack of trust, on the other hand, calls for limiting the discretion of workers, to minimize shirking and simplify supervision and to safeguard workers' pay and positions by restricting internal mobility and managerial discretion. Low trust means that conflicts are difficult to resolve internally, and that outsiders such as professional arbitrators or legal representatives appointed by the courts will be required. Outside parties have limited information for settling disputes, and need to rely on fairly precise and detailed descriptions of all workers' tasks. Such detailed descriptions in turn reduce the scope for discretion and autonomy at the work place, both for supervisors and for subordinates.

The intangible and elusive elements of reputation, the climates of trust and labour relations in an organization, are encapsuled in the notion of **corporate culture**. The very vagueness and open-ended nature of this concept has made it a favourite in the business press. Even economists, long dismissive of ideas that resisted quantification, have began to formalize beliefs and reputations with the tools of game theory and the mathematics of uncertainty. These models hardly begin to do justice to the pervasive scope and practical importance of 'climate' in an organization. Case-studies based on detailed descriptive accounts and survey results reveal remarkable differences in productivity between plants, even when capital equipment and labour skills are similar.

International comparisons are also striking in this regard, though of course national cultural differences interact with the corporate-culture factor and add further complications.

Top managerial pay

An increasingly contentious issue in recent years has been the total compensation of top managers and chief executives (CEOs) in large British and American companies. Salary and bonus payments including stock options of tens of millions of dollars for CEOs in many US corporations have caused resentment among shareholders and among employees who are often facing declining real wages and possible job loss through downsizing as well. During the 1980s the ratio of chief executive compensation to factory worker pay rose fivefold in the United Kingdom and the United States. Detailed studies have found only a very weak relationship between firm profitability and CEO compensation. Firm size has always been the main determinant of CEO rewards, while increasing international competition and scope of operations have been cited as reasons for the accelerating growth of CEO pay (see Crystal, 1992).

These developments have focused attention on the role of the board of directors, and reinforced suspicions that the board's control of CEOs often leaves something to be desired. The most notorious pay rises were received by the chief executives of privatized British utilities such as water, gas and electricity companies. These managers are hardly international high-flyers but usually simply long-standing former employees of old public utilities. They seem to have used their newly granted monopoly power in some cases to raise consumer charges, pay higher dividends to shareholders and salaries to themselves, as well as profit from increased share prices through generous option and bonus schemes. Investment has often been criticized as inadequate for future needs of the industries; and Conservative Prime Minister John Major was embarrassed by the public perception of large-scale rip-offs by corporate fat cats in the privatization programme that supporters claimed was a major success story of his administration's industrial policy. The privatized water utilities have generated most controversy. After record drought and heat during the summer of 1995, much of England suffered water rationing. Chief executives were paid annual salaries of £300,000 or more. In Belgium, which had an even hotter summer, there were no shortages, while top managers of the state-owned utilities earned only £55,000. Losses through leakage were much smaller than in England in a system that seems to put customers rather than shareholders first and offers better value at lower cost.

The credibility of international competition as a justification for CEO pay rises suffers from comparison with other European countries and Japan. Chief executive compensation in these countries has not generally grown faster than average wages, and is now only a small fraction, perhaps one-fifth, of the level in comparable US corporations. Little use is made of stock options and other bonus payments. Firm size is also the main determinant of top managerial pay, with profitability playing a minor role, which is less surprising given the employee stakeholder orientation of German and Japanese companies. Neither more rapid growth of managerial compensation nor explicit claims for stockholders' exclusive residual income status seem to have halted Britain's relative economic decline to one of Europe's 'low-wage' economies.

It could be argued that Japanese, German and other continental European managers are less mobile internationally (as well as nationally) than their Anglo-American counterparts, and hence less affected by US pay scales. The dramatic growth in pay scales, for whatever reasons, has coincided with drastic downsizing at major corporations, affecting many formerly secure white-collar and managerial employees. These and similar developments in the United Kingdom have not helped to remedy the lack of trust and the animosity that are so often the hallmark of Anglo-American labour relations, in contrast to the more cooperative labour–management relations that usually prevail in Germany and Japan.

Minimum wage legislation

Moving from the top to the bottom of the pay scale, we turn now to a policy issue that has generated renewed controversy lately. According to competitive neoclassical theory, minimum wage laws unambiguously reduced employment and were opposed by most economists. However, for an employer with power in, say, a local labour market, the situation can be different. With no minimum wage laws, the monopsonistic employer faces an increasing marginal cost for each additional employee that also implies a higher wage for all existing workers, when uniform wages are paid. An appropriate minimum wage means that employment can be expanded over some range without raising average wage costs. This can create an incentive to expand employment. Extensive recent research in the United States and the United Kingdom has shown generally negligible or even positive employment effects of small minimum-wage increases in a variety of markets and industries. As non-economists had long argued, the minimum wage seems to have mainly distributional effects, at least in the short run and within some limited range. Tracing long-term effects, which could be negative owing to exit from the industry by employers, is difficult in view of many other variables that change over time and influence the decision to enter or exit a particular market. Although there is no doubt that excessive wages do ultimately reduce employment, the recent research on the effects of changing minimum wages has cast considerable doubt on an almost universally held article of traditional economic faith (see Card and Krueger, 1995). In some situations the minimum wage may be obviously excessive. In France, with 25 per cent youth unemployment, an attempt to reduce the minimum wage by the Chirac government in 1995 was withdrawn after massive demonstrations by the insiders who had jobs and feared the redistributive effects of a cut.

F. The future of the employment relationship

Shifting risk and contingent labour

Established patterns of employment have come under increased pressure from conflicting forces in the turbulent 1990s. Most conspicuously, perhaps, the accelerating pace of technological change in many areas and the intensification of international competition have increased the uncertainty faced by business enterprise at all levels. To reduce the risks of long-term commitment in this environment, employers have been reducing their full time, core workforces and relying increasingly on contingent labour, that is on part-time, temporary and subcontracted workers. This reduces the cost of adjustment and raises the employer's flexibility in response to changing technology and demand; thus the tendency to use contingent workers can be observed in both private and public sectors in all Western economies. And even for those workers who are not explicitly part of the contingent labour force, the risk of job loss has grown dramatically, as employers find themselves unable to maintain long-term employment even for primary employees.

The other side of the coin is the effect of this shift on the workers themselves. Increased economy-wide risk is shifted from firms to individuals, in particular to new entrants to the labour force. Training and skills no longer guarantee the security of a primary sector career with a stable employer. Specific investments such as specialized skills or even home ownership become less attractive and individuals are likely to save more. Restrained household spending hampered recovery from recession in the early 1990s in the United Kingdom and other countries, though higher saving rates might have long-term benefits in the United States and United Kingdom, where savings and investment have been lower than in faster-growing economies.

The increasing demand for skill

Technology change is also putting opposing pressures on the labour market. Throughout the 1980s and 1990s, the demand for skilled labour increased in almost all branches of industry and trade, whereas the demand for unskilled work declined. The explosive expansion of information technology and automation have rendered many blue-collar jobs obsolete, including some skilled craft occupations. In 1970, half of OECD employment was white collar and half was blue collar. By 1990, there were twice as many white-collar as blue-collar employees. A few white-collar occupations need little qualification, but education and training requirements for most have risen substantially. The increased demand for skills is also reflected in rates of unemployment that decline everywhere for higher educational attainment. In the United States for example, with the most flexible wages, 12.6 per cent of those with less than a high school education were unemployed in 1993, compared with only 3.5 per cent of those with a batchelor degree. A blue-collar worker had roughly three times the probability of unemployment of a white-collar worker. Yet the real wages of American men with less than high school education declined by 23 per cent between 1972 and 1990 (see Freeman, 1995).

Declining real wages for most men, not only the low skilled, as well as a sharply widening degree of inequality, may have helped to keep US unemployment rates below European levels in the 1980s and 1990s. However, rising inequality and poverty have not had much of a beneficial effect on the UK labour market. By 1993, nearly one in four of working age men were *not* working, and the inactive who had left the labour force outnumbered the unemployed who were still seeking work. One-fifth of all working-age households had no wage-earner. Hidden unemployment or withdrawal from the labour market has increased rapidly in other countries too, so that official unemployment rates everywhere understate the problem. In the United Kingdom, part-time employment rose to 24 per cent by 1995, and in the Netherlands to 37.4 per cent, thus reducing official unemployment to only 6.4 per cent by 1997.

The experience of Germany suggests that education and training for lower-ability groups is an alternative to widening wage dispersion and inequality. German wage inequality has hardly increased, in striking contrast to the situation in the United Kingdom and the United States. Unemployment of those with low education has increased substantially in all countries, to similar levels in Germany and the United States and to much higher levels in the United Kingdom. In spite of their much higher wages, lower-skill groups in Germany have not suffered relatively more unemployment than the United States.

On the other hand, the distribution of educational attainment is much more compressed in Germany. The lowest-ability groups have significantly higher scores on comparable tests than in the United Kingdom and the United States. The proportion of the workforce with similar formal qualifications is twice as high in Germany as in the United Kingdom. It seems that better schooling for the less able, who are neglected in the Anglo-American system, has compensated for less (downward) wage flexibility and even kept the unskilled (as well as long-term) unemployment rates in Germany below British levels (Nickell, 1996).

Productivity and trade

Productivity of labour in manufacturing has tended to increase faster than demand for goods produced, so that employment in manufacturing has declined in most countries. Relatively unskilled jobs for men have been hardest hit in this sector. By contrast, the fastest employment growth has been in the personal and face-to-face services, which have taken up most of the rapid increase in female labour market activity.

Major international trade agreements such as GATT (General Agreement on Tariffs and Trade) and NAFTA (North American Free Trade Area) in 1995 have focused attention on another reason for the worsening job chances faced by men with low skills in the developed countries. University of Sussex economist Adrian Wood (1994) points out that exports of manufactured goods from developing countries in the Southern hemisphere and South-East Asia to the developed economies of Europe and North America have been growing very rapidly. These goods are made by workers whose wages are only a small percentage of wages in the European Union or United States. These workers are frequently employed by Western multinational corporations that have outsourced their domestic production to take advantage of these much lower wages but are often using modern technology. Well-publicised job losses in the high-wage countries caused by outsourcing or new production facilities in low-wage areas have generated popular opposition to expanding trade, particularly by union and labour representatives (see Wood, 1994, and Nickell, 1996).

Economists disagree about the precise extent to which import competition from low-wage countries has reduced the demand for low-skilled men, compared with the effects of new and changing technology. A dominating role for the latter is suggested by the fact that the shift towards skilled labour is equally marked in sectors producing non-traded goods and services. Nevertheless, import competition is likely to become increasingly important as trade liberalization in Eastern Europe progresses. These countries combine low wages with relatively high levels of education and training, so that even skilled workers in the West might be affected.

Flexibility

Most economists believe that the benefits from free trade in some sense outweigh the costs. Some would interpret this as meaning that the winners – including most consumers – could or should compensate the losers. However, the theory of **comparative advantage** (which goes back to classical economist David Ricardo) and its modern variants, which make the case for free trade, are silent on the distributional consequences. European policy makers, who view persistent high unemployment as one of their most serious problems, have found a new buzzword for the 1990s. More *flexible* employment practices and wages are widely believed to be necessary in order to compete effectively both with cheap imports and with the technological leadership of Japan and the United States.

Interestingly, the two leading economic powers offer very different examples of flexibility in practice. In Japan, one of the reasons for low unemployment has been flexible deployment of workers, particularly in large firms. High levels of training and widespread job rotation facilitate the movement of employees from one assignment or task to another, according to the requirements of rapidly changing product market demand and technology. As emphasized in comparative studies of industrial relations, such personnel flexibility depends upon a high degree of trust and cooperation between management and labour, so that workers can accept managerial discretion in job assignment without having to fear any subtle or long-term disadvantages such as loss of job security or of promotion opportunities.

By contrast, in the low-trust, adversarial labour relations typical of the United Kingdom or the United States, workers have traditionally been protected by detailed pay scales, work rules and job descriptions derived from collective bargaining. Although this rigid framework prevented employers from making use of changing market conditions as an excuse to move workers to lower-paid tasks, the alternative was often that specialized workers were laid off when demand for their particular, narrowly defined services declined.

Internal flexibility has been increasing as union coverage falls, but it is wage flexibility in the United States that has attracted most interest in Europe. While declining real wages for many workers have helped to keep total US unemployment at below-European levels, there is also concern over the social consequences and costs of widening wage dispersion, consequences that are also beginning to emerge in Britain, and which would be politically unacceptable in many other countries, particularly in north-western Europe. And declining or stagnant real wages for low-paid and unskilled American and British workers have *not* kept their unemployment rates below the rates for equivalent German workers, whose pay has kept up with skilled wages.

As Harvard economist Richard Freeman (1994b) points out, some 2 per cent of the total American male workforce was in prison in 1993, and another 5 per cent on probation. The prison population has grown by 8.5 per cent annually since 1980, and security guards represent the fastest-growing occupation. Many studies find inequality and low wages to be important factors in explaining high crime rates despite 'massive incarceration'.

These developments have put the employment relationship on the horns of a dilemma. Increasing market uncertainty and volatility put a premium on flexibility. However, internal flexibility as practised in Japan requires commitment and job security in a high-trust environment, attributes of the employment relationship that are directly and adversely affected by external market developments. As already pointed out, a popular response to this dilemma has been the growing use of contingent labour. This kind of employment offers flexibility and other cost savings, but inhibits the teamwork and specific human capital development together with employee involvement that the accelerating pace of change has made more important than ever before.

A new dualism?

Media reports about the 'demise of jobs' and the 'virtual corporation' are surely exaggerated. Self-employment has doubled in the United Kingdom since 1980, and large firms have been shrinking as peripheral activities are contracted out. The traditional secondary labour market has also been declining. Most importantly from our perspective, however, an increasing number of qualified, white-collar workers are subject to 'secondary-type' uncertainty and insecurity. This may be in the form of entrepreneurial uncertainty for the self-employed or the simple insecurity of the contingent worker.

These developments suggest that at least a partial solution to the employment dilemma described above may be emerging. A diminished number of highly skilled core employees will continue to enjoy relative job security, while involvement and teamwork together with profit-sharing and recognition as stakeholders extend among these core workers.

The enlarged secondary sector of contingent labour and many self-employed individuals includes an increasing number of qualified, white-collar and female workers. They share problems of employment insecurity and fluctuating earnings with the traditional secondary sector but, in contrast to the old classification, some of these new secondary workers should have career opportunities, albeit of a highly risky nature and depending upon their entrepreneurial energy and skills.

Finally and most worrying, the unskilled males and youth who would have found employment in the old secondary labour market, are already being relegated to the bottom of the social ladder and forming a new underclass, with little or no hope of finding legal employment. No less than 60 per cent of low-skilled youth were unemployed in Britain's most depressed regions in 1993.

There is widespread agreement on the need for more and better training and education, especially for the lower level of the ability distribution, which has traditionally been neglected, in the United Kingdom in particular. Reform of chaotic and uncoordinated welfare measures that have created perverse incentives to refuse low-paid work – the poverty trap – is another obvious priority for economists if not for politicians. In this connection, elements of Swedish-style 'workfare', instead of welfare without any obligations, look increasingly attractive.

In Sweden, the state has traditionally acted as employer of last resort for the low-skilled who have difficulty in finding market employment under the highly egalitarian Swedish wage system. Welfare payments are mainly dependent upon acceptance of a job offer after some interim period or on entry into a training programme. This system kept unemployment and poverty at very low levels, until recession and rising cyclical unemployment in the early 1990s put severe strain on an economy whose state sector and marginal tax burden were already the highest in Europe. However, according to most observers, there remains a political commitment to preserving the main achievements of the

Swedish welfare state, which include the virtual abolition of the poverty and homelessness that have grown so rapidly in the United Kingdom and the United States.

A contributing or complementary factor in the avoidance of unskilled unemployment in Sweden has probably been an egalitarian distribution of working time. Skilled workers in Sweden work much shorter hours than comparable employees in the United States and probably the United Kingdom and other countries too. This is partly due to high marginal tax rates, as well as generous sickness and parental leave, and is likely to have raised the demand for unskilled labour (see Björklund and Freeman, 1995).

This contrasts with a tendency for the working time of skilled white-collar and managerial workers to increase in the United Kingdom. As competition for the dwindling number of secure, core primary jobs intensifies, 'voluntary' longer hours become the most visible signal of the commitment and effort that many supervisors demand. As well as putting often severe strains on family and personal life, longer hours for skilled employees and self-employed individuals are likely to reduce aggregate labour market demand for the services of the low-skilled. Longer hours also reduce the hourly rate of pay for salaried, white-collar employees, who are often expected to work overtime without extra remuneration. On the other hand, some skilled blue-collar workers have traditionally been rewarded with higher rates of overtime pay as a flexible way of augmenting their weekly earnings. In this connection, a 1991 survey of UK employees revealed the remarkable fact that an average of about 7 weekly hours of overtime without pay were worked in that recession year, and about the same number of paid overtime hours. Although temporary overtime does serve as a 'buffer' to meet sudden extra demand, the very long average hours for many full-time workers probably contributed to high unemployment and job loss at the time.[2]

Casual observation might suggest that skilled and unskilled workers are poor substitutes or even complementary factors of production. In some cases, successful skilled entrepreneurs, for example, might create jobs for less skilled workers. However, most econometric studies show that capital and skilled labour are complements in production, and together substitute for unskilled labour in the medium to long run (see Hammermesh, 1993).

Relentless downward pressure on the employment prospects and wages of low-skill workers is set to continue or even intensify in the absence of a firm political commitment to support this group, as in Sweden. However, pressure on employers to cut costs by replacing older skilled and white-collar workers with younger, lower-paid substitutes is also eroding crucial aspects of the employment relationship. Long-term investment in specific skills and innovative new developments are likely to suffer when the employer cannot be trusted to reward loyalty and commitment with security. Short-term cost-cutting that violates implicit agreements or expectations and generates low trust can also destroy important long-term assets of employee motivation and involvement.

At the same time, increasing numbers of white-collar and managerial employees complain of rising work loads and longer hours, but feel compelled to acquiesce in a climate of pervasive insecurity.

The European consulting group International Survey Research has carried out regular surveys of employee satisfaction since 1990. Satisfaction increased from 1990 to 1997 in Switzerland, Spain and Italy, but Britain's flexible labour market saw the largest drop in satisfaction. The survey says:

> UK employees are markedly more critical of their company managements than they were, . . . and they are significantly more concerned both about the nature of their future with their companies, and indeed whether they have a future with them at all.

According to the *Financial Times*, this report should 'caution those who admire the flexible UK labour market model'. The report also concludes that perceptions of employment security are in 'free fall throughout Europe', with a 'profound effect' on attitudes towards employers and work (Taylor, 1997, p. 18).

G. Chapter summary and key ideas

In this chapter we have discussed the basic aspects of the employment contract, a relationship of dominating importance in working people's lives. The traditional or neoclassical view treated the demand and supply of labour as just another commodity, focusing on the number of workers in and out of work. These simple quantitative measures are still of some use as summary descriptions of the aggregate economy. The traditional approach, however, neglects qualitative aspects of work motivation and organization, as well as the intensive margins of working time and effort.

The modern view of the employment contract emphasizes the incompleteness of the relationship that results from bounded rationality and information costs. Incompleteness of the contract, in turn, requires the employer to hold residual authority for making decisions that are not explicitly covered by the contract. In some organizations, human capital in the form of employee skills is the most important kind of capital, so that employees themselves become holders of residual authority and income claims in the legal form of a partnership.

Workers cannot diversify their own human capital, and some aspects of employment contracts can be understood in terms of risk reduction or insurance for risk-averse employees. In particular, the residual authority usually held by the employer poses a perennial problem of moral hazard. Collective bargainers have sought to reduce this risk by detailed job descriptions that limit the scope of authority and by seniority protection for older, more vulnerable workers. Earnings are also related to seniority so that young workers are encouraged to work hard and avoid dismissal. Compulsory retirement becomes necessary, however, because the productivity of older workers usually declines, and wage cuts are problematic with asymmetric information and limited trust or moral hazard.

Even in modern economies there are some labour markets, called secondary labour markets, that resemble the classical model. Casual and other unskilled labour may be hired by the hour for simple tasks at wages that vary with supply and demand as in an auction or 'spot market'. The secondary market offers little in the way of promotion prospects or career advancement. Skilled and professional workers, by contrast, are in the primary labour market and generally face opportunities for promotion and career progression.

For primary employees, promotion possibilities are offered in the internal labour market or job ladders of all large, hierarchical organizations. Entry through the external labour market is often restricted to low-level positions, so that promotion to a better-paid, more responsible position is an important incentive reserved for insiders. Long-term association in the same internal labour market increases the reliability of information flows, enabling managers to assign workers to their most productive occupations. At the same time, employees can develop skills, including interpersonal relationships, that are specific to their organization. Such firm-specific human capital is less mobile in the external labour market, but can be rewarded and protected by the internal market.

The efficient functioning of the internal markets in which most (primary) workers spend much of their careers is greatly facilitated by intangible factors such as reputation and trust. Employees with specific human capital earn quasi-rents in excess of their opportunity cost, and these quasi-rents can be lost if an employer reneges on an implicit employment contract or invests unwisely. An employer's reputation can encourage employees to accept the risks of productive but specific investment in training and experience. Similarly a trusted worker requires less supervision, and in turn benefits from greater autonomy at work. Trust reduces the costs of monitoring and policing contracts of all kinds, but is most likely to develop through long-term association and shared goals or individual characteristics.

A number of interrelated developments of the 1980s and 1990s are now putting unprecedented strains on the institutions of the labour market. Technological change has shifted demand towards higher-skilled workers in most sectors. Growing imports of manufactured goods from low-wage countries have reinforced this tendency. Real wages and/or employment of the unskilled have fallen, unless policy has been specifically committed to providing support for this group, as most successfully in Sweden. Wage flexibility has been accompanied by growing poverty and crime in the United States and the United Kingdom.

Market volatility and uncertainty have also increased, as product life-cycles shrink and international competition intensifies. Faced with intense pressure to cut costs in the short run, firms have been downsizing and shedding even primary, white-collar employees, who had expected and enjoyed relative security in the past. Employee stakeholders who are forced to change jobs lose their job-specific investments and suffer substantial pay cuts on average. As reputations and trust are damaged, loyalty and cooperative relations suffer, and organizations can become *less* efficient in the long run.

Long-term, cooperative and high-trust employment relationships in the future are likely to be restricted to much smaller, core workforces, even in large, traditionally primary employers. Core workers may share firm rents and participate in decision-making, while enjoying much greater job security than a growing periphery of skilled but essentially contingent labour. Competition for a smaller number of secure, primary jobs is pushing up working time and pressure to perform for many white-collar employees, thus further depressing the demand for low-skill work. Service sectors are expanding their employment shares everywhere and offer some opportunities for relatively low-skill, and particularly female, workers.

Key words

age–wage profile	internal labour market
codetermination	insiders
comparative advantage	marginal revenue product
corporate culture	outsiders
external labour market	ports of entry
frictional unemployment	primary labour market
human capital	reputation
human resources	residual authority
implicit contract	residual income claimant
influence activity	secondary labour market
intensive margin	specific human capital
internal job ladder	works council

Questions and problems for review and discussion

1 Explain the necessity of authority in the employment relationship.
2 Why are the intensive margins of employment usually the most contentious?
3 Show that, even if employers were risk neutral, they would not supply complete insurance to risk-averse workers.
4 How would you explain that wages seldom fall in recession?
5 Distinguish carefully between primary and secondary labour markets.
6 What are the advantages of promotion over performance-related pay as an incentive?

7 Is it possible for profit-sharing to motivate the employees of a large firm? Supply reasons and evidence.

8 Is it rational for (a) employers and (b) employees to be concerned about fairness?

9 How do you explain the fact that top managers in Japan are paid much less than their US counterparts?

10 Discuss the advantages and disadvantages of 'lifetime' employment for core workers in large Japanese firms.

11 Summarize recent evidence on the effects of minimum wages.

12 Explain why job security has declined for many white-collar workers in recent years.

13 Would greater flexibility be able to solve the problems of unemployment for low-skilled workers in Europe?

14 Discuss the effects of international trade on European labour markets.

15 Should Britain adopt German-style codetermination?

Notes

1 Causality and selection issues are discussed by FitzRoy and Kraft (1995).

2 Two recent papers by David Marsden, of the Industrial Relations Department and Centre for Economic Performance of the London School of Economics, cover much of the material of this chapter. See Marsden (1995a, b).

References

Arrow, K. J. (1974), *The Limits of Organization*, New York: Norton.

Björklund, A. and R. B. Freeman (1995), 'Generating equality and eliminating poverty the Swedish way', Centre for Economic Performance, London School of Economics, D.P. No. 228, March.

Blair, M. (1995), *Ownership and Control*, Washington DC: Brookings Institute.

Blinder, Alan (ed.) (1990), *Paying for Productivity*, Washington DC: Brookings Institute.

Card, D. and A. Krueger (1995), *Myth and Measurement in the Labor Market*, Princeton, NJ: Princeton University Press.

Crystal, G. S. (1992), *In Search of Excess: The Overcompensation of American Executives*, New York: Norton.

Doeringer, P. and M. Piore (1971), *Internal Labor Markets and Manpower Analysis*, Lexington: D.C. Heath.

Fernie, S. and D. Metcalf (1995), 'Participation, contingent pay, representation and workplace performance: Evidence from Great Britain', Centre for Economic Performance, London School of Economics, D.P. No. 232, April.

FitzRoy, F. and K. Kraft (1995), 'On the choice of incentives in the firm', *Journal of Economic Behaviour and Organization*, 26, pp. 145–60.

Freeman, R. B. (1994a), *Working Under Different Rules*, New York: Russell Sage Foundation.

Freeman, R. B. (1994b), 'Crime and the labour market', Chapter 8 in J. Wilson and J. Petersilia (eds), *Crime*, San Francisco: ICS Press.

Freeman, R. B. (1995), 'Doing it right? The U.S. labour market response to the 1980s/1990s', Centre for Economic Performance, London School of Economics, D.P. No. 231, March.

Frey, B. (1997), *Not for the Money Alone*, London: Edward Elgar.

Fukuyama, F. (1995), *Trust: The Social Virtues and the Creation of Prosperity*, London: Hamish Hamilton.

Gambetta, D. (1988), *Trust: Making and Breaking Cooperative Relations*, Oxford: Blackwell.

Hammermesh, D. (1993), *Labor Demand*, Princeton, NJ: Princeton University Press.

Knight, F. H. (1985 [1921]), *Risk, Uncertainty and Profit*, Chicago: University of Chicago Press.

Kruse, D. (1993), *Profit-Sharing: Does It Make a Difference?* Michigan: Upjohn Institute.

Marsden, D. (1995a), 'The impact of industrial relations practices on employment and unemployment', Centre for Economic Performance, London School of Economics, D.P. No. 240.

Marsden, D. (1995b), 'Management practices and unemployment', Centre for Economic Performance, London School of Economics, D.P. No. 241.

Nickell, S. (1996), 'Sectoral structural change and the state of the labour market in Great Britain', Oxford University and CEP Discussion Paper No. 2, May.

Simon, H. (1951), 'A formal theory of the employment relationship', *Econometrica*, 19, pp. 293–305.

Solow, R. (1990), *The Labour Market as a Social Institution*, Oxford: Basil Blackwell.

Taylor, R. (1997), 'Europe's unhappy world of work', *Financial Times*, 14 May.

Topel, R. (1991), 'Specific capital, mobility and wages: Wages rise with job-security', *Journal of Political Economy*, 99, pp. 145–76.

Wood, A. (1994), *North–South Trade, Employment and Inequality: Changing Fortunes in a Skill Driven World*, Oxford: Clarendon Press.

The organization of work

We will win and you will lose. You cannot do anything about it because your failure is an internal disease. Your companies are based on Taylor's principles. Worse, your heads are taylorized too. You firmly believe that sound management means executives on the one side and workers on the other, on the one side men who think and on the other side men who can only work. For you, management is the art of smoothly transferring the executives' idea to the workers' hands.

   We have passed the Taylor stage. We are aware that business has become terribly complex. Survival is very uncertain in an environment filled with risk, the unexpected, and competition . . . We know that the intelligence of a few technocrats – even very bright ones – has become totally inadequate to face these challenges. Only the intellects of all employees can permit a company to live with the ups and downs and the requirements of the new environment. Yes, we will win and you will lose. For you are not able to rid your minds of the obsolete Taylorisms that we never had. (Konosuke Matsushita, 1988; quoted by Best, 1990)

A. Chapter outline and student goals

As we saw in the previous chapter, the neoclassical account of employment ignored the content of work as well as problems of motivation. Yet the founding father of modern economics, Adam Smith, first discussed the **division of labour** as the guiding principle for work organization in his *Wealth of Nations* in 1776. As the industrial revolution progressed over the next century, traditional craft-based manufacturing methods were gradually superseded. In the early years of the twentieth century, continuous-flow manufacturing, **Taylorism** and scientific management developed and led later to modern mass-production methods, with their extreme division of labour.

   For a long time, technological progress seemed to have only a rather limited impact on the organization of production work – technology was in the domain of engineers and managers, not blue-collar workers. In recent decades this has been changing. A large majority of the workforce now processes information or serves customers in the service sector, and a new revolution in the

431

organization of production work is under way. Demand for standardized, mass-produced articles has become an ever-smaller part of total demand. Product life-cycles and development time have shortened, and small batch production or customized products take an increasing share of global markets.

Technology has rendered some skills obsolete, such as those of the type-setter in the printing industry. But the flow of new products and processes depends on new, flexible skills and teamwork rather than rigid specialization and repetitive tasks. As trade barriers have fallen, traditional, unskilled assembly work has moved away from domestic producers to low-wage, emerging economies, principally in the Far East.

As former American Labour Secretary Robert Reich emphasized in his influential 1991 book, *The Work of Nations*, highly paid workers and managers in the United States and Europe can compete successfully only if they develop the skills and cooperative work organization needed for high value-added production. This also means abandoning many of the precepts developed by Frederick Taylor, the founder of scientific management, precepts that have become deeply entrenched in managerial practice and thought. The principles of Taylorism form the topic of the next section, where we see that Taylor's engineering approach to the design of individual work tasks had only limited success, though 'Taylorism' itself became almost synonymous with mass-production techniques.

In the third section we review the recent shift towards teamwork in work organization, often called 'post-Fordist' to underline the demise of the traditional assembly-line organization that Henry Ford had pioneered at the start of World War I. Although some of the rapid change in work organization that has been observed in the past decade or two has been primarily demand driven, technological change has also had a major impact. This is the subject of the fourth section, which concludes the main part of the chapter.

After reading this chapter, you should be able to:

- understand what Frederick Taylor wanted to do, and why it did not work out quite as he imagined;
- explain the effects of division of labour on assembly-line productivity and job satisfaction;
- list reasons for changes in the skill composition of the labour force and corresponding changes in work organization;
- appreciate the growing importance of teamwork and cooperative labour–management relations in modern production;
- describe the impact of modern information technology on job design;
- predict which sectors and occupations will probably continue to decline in coming years.

B. Taylorism and scientific management

Division of labour in the first industrial revolution

The foundation stone of **scientific management** was laid by Adam Smith at the beginning of the industrial revolution in England, more than two centuries ago. Smith illustrated his discussion of division of labour with the well-known example of pin-making. A craftsman could make whole pins by cutting and straightening the wire, pointing one end and putting a head on the other end. In large-scale production, however, the whole task could be divided up so that one workman spent all his time cutting wire, another specialized in putting heads on the pins, and so on. Altogether, as many as 18 workers, each engaged in one of the separate operations, could be combined if the demand for pins produced was large enough. This had several advantages. Each worker became more dextrous at his particular speciality, and spent less 'down time' between productive activities. Also, lower skill requirements for the individual tasks meant that each worker was paid a lower wage than the craftsman who could make a complete product. Smith also mentioned the major disadvantage of this division of labour. Workers who spent all their working lives performing simple repetitive tasks lost not only the craftman's pride in his work but eventually even their basic human sensibilities. 'The man whose whole life is spent in performing a few simple operations . . . generally becomes as stupid and ignorant as it is possible for a human creature to become' (Smith, 1976, p. 734).

The introduction of inventions such as the spinning jenny and the mechanical loom, which were combined with steam power in the textile factories of the nineteenth century, raised productivity dramatically. Women and children could tend the machinery, with little or no training, for long hours at subsistence wages. The enormous increases in productivity due to mechanization, technological progress and the division of labour did reduce prices and increase real wages in the long run. In engineering and heavy industry, craft traditions lasted longer, but were also crumbling in those traditionally male preserves at the beginning of the twentieth century when two major developments accelerated the process.

The beginning of Taylorism

Frederick Taylor was an engineer who not only believed that complex manual tasks could everywhere be subdivided into simple, routine operations. He also imagined that this process could be pursued *scientifically*, by precise measurement of every movement involved and elimination of all inessential components of the task. Taylor's programme originated in the problems with setting piece-rates. Since effort or subjective exertion could not be directly observed by overseers, workers could deliberately slow down the pace of work and restrain output in order to maintain favourable piece-rates and leisure-on-the-job. There was little incentive to boost productivity when higher output was 'rewarded' with rate cuts to keep earnings down to customary levels. Taylor believed that rates could be set 'objectively' on the basis of precisely measured tasks, thereby eliminating shirking by workers as well as conflict over rate-setting.

As might be expected, Taylor's rather utopian programme did not work according to plan, and his methods failed to eliminate conflict and shirking. On the contrary, workers fiercely resisted the introduction of scientific management through both union and informal organization. Truly objective measurement of tasks was in any case illusory when workers could dissemble and mislead the engineers. Although time-and-motion studies in various forms gradually diffused, and elements of Taylorism became commonplace in industry, the complete programme of scientific management was too extreme, and indeed was explicitly rejected by many companies.

Continuous-flow production and assembly

In fact, other developments that culminated in the years just before World War I turned out to be of greater practical relevance, in the form of continuous-flow production and machine-paced work. In the earlier mechanized textile mills, tasks were already largely dictated by the requirements of the power looms or spindles, but there was some flexibility – workers moved around and interacted with each other, and were also subject to the direct discipline of often autocratic or tyrannical foremen, who had the power to hire and fire. It was the early meat-packing industry in Chicago that pioneered continuous flow (in this case dissembly), with carcasses hanging from overhead conveyors, which were followed by the workmen who had to keep pace with the conveyor.

However, the most important innovation in work organization was the first modern assembly line, at Ford's Highland Park plant in 1914. For the first time, work in the form of a sub-assembly was brought to the worker at a fixed work station by a conveyor, while components for assembly were stockpiled at the station. Unproductive movement around the production area was eliminated, the speed of assembly was determined by the mechanical conveyor rather than an obtrusive foreman, and the number of supervisors required could be reduced far below customary levels.

At the same time, most craft skills and lengthy training requirements became superfluous for the simple assembly tasks performed by each operative. The famous $5-a-day efficiency wage, also introduced by Ford in 1914, drastically reduced employee turnover and ensured the compliance and docility of the workforce. This in turn made it possible to curtail the foreman's powers of arbitrary dismissal. It was the assembly line that thus set the pattern for work organiza-

tion for the next 50 years, run by a system of management that became 'bureaucratic' rather than 'scientific'. In retrospect, '**Fordism**' turned out to be a more
appropriate label for modern mass-production methods than 'Taylorism'.

Fordism and prosperity

As technology progressed, the division of labour on the assembly line was
refined, and workers were assisted – or in some cases replaced – by ever more
sophisticated tools and machinery. This increase in the capital equipment available per worker, as well as growing plant size, steadily increased the complexity
of managerial functions. Particularly after World War II the proportion of supervisors and other white-collar employees increased rapidly. On the other hand,
their fast-growing productivity meant that a declining proportion of production workers could meet society's needs for mass-produced and increasingly
standardized goods.

In the post-war decades of prosperity that lasted until the Opec oil-price shocks
of 1973–4, opposition to the Taylorist separation of planning and doing, at least
by organized labour, seemed finally to evaporate. The apparent triumph of
bureaucratic management and mass production was not due only to steadily rising real incomes for most workers. Precisely defined job classifications and pay
scales, with internal job ladders and promotion possibilities, provided career progression and long-term incentives for primary sector workers. Formalized grievance procedures offered protection against arbitrary decisions by superiors.
Seniority provided a degree of security and protection from layoffs for older
workers with the most firm-specific human capital. Although pioneered by collective bargainers in unionized firms, these benefits became widespread throughout the primary sector. Indeed, large-scale production with a relatively stable
workforce came to depend on the efficiency-enhancing properties of implicit
employment contracts of this kind, as we developed in the previous chapter.

In industries such as automobiles and steel, economies of scale led to domination by a few very large corporations in most industrial countries. With
much less foreign competition or fear of new entrants than in today's global
economy, price competition was largely avoided, to maintain oligopolistic rents
above the normal rate of return on capital. These rents were shared with well-
organized labour unions in these and other concentrated industries, giving the
most privileged blue-collar workers wages well above the national average for
unskilled or semi-skilled work.

Work and its discontents

Although high and growing levels of pay attracted job applicants and recon-
ciled employees to monotonous and repetitive tasks, there was also evidence

of increasing dissatisfaction with Fordist work organization, particularly in the most advanced and wealthiest US economy. A 1973 report to the US Secretary of Health, Education, and Welfare identified the problem as follows:

> Dull, repetitive, seemingly meaningless tasks, offering little challenge or auton-omy, are causing discontent among workers at all occupational levels. This is not so much because work itself has greatly changed; indeed, one of the main prob-lems is that work has not changed fast enough to keep up with the rapid and widescale changes in worker attributes, aspirations and values. A general increase in their educational and economic status has placed many American workers in a position where having an interesting job is now as important as having a job that pays well. (HEW, 1973, pp. xv–xvi)[1]

In Europe at this time the situation was rather different. Whereas industrial sociologists in France and Germany were concerned with work organization,[2] the unions' objective was to maintain the rapid growth of real wages, which had started from extremely low levels following war-time destruction of the industrial base. In Germany, union organization and the codetermination sys-tem were dominated by the relatively privileged and highly qualified skilled workers (*Facharbeiter*). Foreign 'guest workers', and women, were over-represented in semi-skilled assembly work, and had less influence on union policy. Cooperation with management to raise productivity and wages with-out losing jobs was of overriding importance to union leadership and its main constituency.

In Britain, France and Italy, traditional redistributive conflict and low-trust, adversarial relations predominated. Restrictive work rules maintained elements of craft production in the United Kingdom, and also held down productivity growth to much lower rates than were achieved by rival exporters. At this junc-ture, however, a number of other developments were beginning to threaten even the most visible elements of prosperity, such as pay and job security, in all industrial economies. The oil-price hike by newly formed Opec members in the year that the HEW report appeared turned public attention towards urgent macroeconomic issues. More fundamental problems, which have long since overtaken Opec to become central concerns of policy, were obscured and ignored by most observers. It is to these problems that we now turn.

C. Post-Fordism and lean production

The demise of Fordism

The productivity of the American system of mass production had become a model for the rest of the world and saturated domestic markets for consumer durables in the post-war era. By 1970, most US households had at least one car, and almost all possessed a TV set, washing machine, hi-fi and many other items that are still rare luxuries in much of the world. Low unit cost was achieved by spreading the substantial overheads or fixed costs of the corporate administrative and planning hierarchy over a lengthy production run. Introducing a new model typically involved years of design and planning followed by expensive retooling of the production facilities. Minor annual change or 'facelifting' was the preferred option.

When oil prices were doubled by Opec in 1973–4 and again in 1979, severe recession followed in all industrial countries as consumers postponed the replacement of their durable goods, sales plummeted and investment was delayed. When the US economy recovered, smaller, fuel-efficient automobiles from Japan and Europe became much more attractive and import shares grew rapidly. The long lead-time for producing new models began to handicap US producers, and their compact cars, when they finally appeared on the market, were generally a poor match for imported competitors. After two decades of massive investment, often unprecedented losses and increasing import penetration, there were finally signs of fundamental change in US manufacturing in the early 1990s, helped by an overvalued yen and at the cost of a steady decline in real wages for many American workers.

Toyota and the development of lean production

In the decade of the 1970s, imported Japanese cars increased their market share in the United States from 4.2 to 22.8 per cent. Even by 1980 though, Japanese auto workers were earning only half as much as their US equivalents, and this wage differential was widely seen as the root cause of Japanese success. But detailed studies showed that Japanese manufacturers were actually more efficient in terms of the labour-time needed to assemble a vehicle or other product. To understand how this advantage was achieved, we must go back to consider the development of post-war Japanese manufacturing and work organization, and contrast this development with the American system of mass production already described.

It was Toyota that had pioneered several of the key elements that made up the Japanese alternative to Taylorist–Fordist mass production. These included machines that stopped automatically in the event of malfunction or product defects. This allowed one worker to oversee several different machines, which in turn required a range of skills rather than the emphasis on specialization and repetition found in the Taylorist regime. Regular job rotation and cooperation in a working team with extended responsibilities for a particular area of production complemented technological developments.

Teamwork evolved out of an early post-war period of intense labour–management conflict, and was coupled with job security for core (male) employees of large companies. It was this organizational innovation that again allowed Toyota to press forward with **just-in-time** (JIT) or **'lean production'**, which minimized inventory costs and down-time and the underutilization of workers and machines. In this system there were no '**buffer stocks**' or inventories of components waiting at each assembly station. Instead, parts were ordered only when they were needed from other units or subcontractors, and prompt delivery was then essential. JIT manufacturing was clearly also very vulnerable to disruption by any group of workers in the chain of production, who could essentially bring the whole process to a halt. Cooperative rather than adversarial labour relations were thus a vital precondition for 'lean production'. The transformation of post-war conflict into consensual industrial relations, based upon enterprise unions, would hardly have been possible without the implicit contract offering the security of permanent employment.

Two experts on Japanese manufacturing methods, Martin Kenney and Richard Florida (1993), have emphasized the most fundamental distinction between Fordism and the modern, post-Fordist, Japanese system of production. Starting from very low levels of output in post-war reconstruction, Toyota and other companies could not hope to spread their overheads over long production runs as did their American competitors. Instead, the strategy adopted was one of continuous improvement (*kaizen*), or what Kenney and Florida call innovation-mediated production. Rather than designing and planning a new model independently of the production process, Toyota and others were able to integrate production workers into a system of continuously improving both the product and the manufacturing process.

Once again we can see the independence of the various elements of the post-Fordist Japanese organization of work. Continuous improvement would have been infeasible with workers who had mastered only simple, routinized operations. To harness the full potential of all production workers, scope for training and teamwork was necessary. Only with an extended knowledge of product and process could workers contribute to innovation themselves and to rapid implementation of design changes coming from associated engineers.

Furthermore, only job security could remove the threat of job loss from increased productivity, a threat that has traditionally inhibited blue-collar cooperation, and indeed often inspired resistance to change. In this context, teamwork becomes important to facilitate exchange of knowledge and continuous improvement. No less valuable, the team reduces supervision requirements. When workers face long-term career and promotion prospects related to the performance of their group and the whole enterprise, peer-group pressure becomes a powerful motivation to increase productivity, instead of helping to restrict output when rate reductions or job loss threaten individuals.

As Kenney and Florida (1993, p. 39) have summarized:

> Perhaps the key element of the Japanese industrial system is its ability to harness workers' knowledge as a source of value directly at the point of production . . . The team is a simultaneous source of motivation discipline and social control for team members, driving them to work harder and more collectively. In this way, workers are encouraged, stimulated and provided incentives to offer up their ideas and continuously improve the production process.

It is an irony of history that an important role in developing the *kaizen* system in Japan was played by an American statistician, W. E. Deming. Instead of Taylorist emphasis on cost reduction, often at the expense of quality, Deming introduced **statistical quality control** (SQC) to post-war Japanese industry as a tool for continuous upgrading of product quality. SQC had been propagated in America during the war, but was abandoned afterwards by the 'top-down rule-bound corporate bureaucracies', which preferred to intensify Taylorist management (Best, 1990, p. 159). Deming became a national hero in Japan after his methods were universally adopted. He criticized the dominance of accountants and accounting methods in American industry, which failed to capture the hidden costs of poor quality, such as erosion of customer loyalty. By contrast, 'statistical symbols and methods became in Japan a second language for everybody, *including hourly workers*' (cited by Best, 1990, p. 159; emphasis added).

Flexible manufacturing systems

The culmination of all these developments was the **flexible manufacturing system** (FMS), which linked computer-controlled work stations with automated material transport systems. Teams of skilled workers could produce small batches of customized or specialized items with minimal down-time between operations. Continuous improvement could be applied to a whole range of products, and lengthy production runs were no longer necessary to reap economies of scale. The JIT inventory system was particularly valuable in flexible mass production with frequently changing product specification, to avoid stockpiling many different kinds of components. Commitment and cooperation of the workforce, based on job security, were essential components of FMS.

Transplants

Following the dramatic growth of Japanese import penetration in the 1970s, the next decade saw an equally striking expansion of Japanese manufacturing **transplants** in the United States. The number of transplants increased five-fold, from 240 in 1980 to 1,275 in 1989. Many Western commentators had long insisted that Japanese manufacturing methods were 'culture bound', and hence not transferable to other countries. Certainly the early transplants in the United States and the United Kingdom seemed to provide support for this pessimistic view. However, later developments have shown that Japanese organization of work and production can be successful in other countries.

A striking early example was New United Motor Manufacturing, Inc. (NUMMI). In 1983, Toyota and General Motors (GM) announced this joint venture to build small cars in a disused GM assembly plant in Fremont, California. GM had abandoned operations here partly because of extremely high absenteeism (over 20 per cent) and appalling labour relations in general. Under Toyota management, most of the workers hired were former GM employees who had been laid off when the plant was closed two years previously. The agreement between NUMMI and the United Auto Workers stipulated teamwork with job rotation and participation in quality circle and *kaizen* programmes. A specific commitment to job security and no recourse to lay-offs (unless the future of the company was at stake) was included. This policy has been maintained through production downturns of up to 30 per cent.

Many transplants have chosen greenfield sites and recruited local labour that was not accustomed to Taylorist work organization. Even in such non-union settings, however, at least informal commitments to job security are usually made. All transplants have dramatically reduced the numerous, rigid job classifications that are customary in Fordist production. Since each team is responsible for a given segment of production and there is no slack labour, missing workers' tasks have to be filled in by other team members. Strong social pressures against absenteeism and tardiness that result are reinforced by strict rules on attendance. Without extra employees on the payroll merely to replace unscheduled absence from work, labour productivity benefits, and is not far from the level at parent plants in Japan.

In Europe, the best-known transplants are the Nissan, Honda and Toyota factories in the United Kingdom. These units have set new productivity standards for the European automotive industry, and Nissan (UK) has become Britain's biggest exporter. Honda's long-standing alliance with Rover helped that company to become the best-performing domestic car manufacturer, and Rover was taken over by the German prestige car maker BMW in 1995, with a very lean work organization and a greatly improved reputation for quality and reliability. As already described in Chapter 1, the transplants' considerable achievements have been made in spite of substantial problems with non-transplant suppliers.

Europe has seen no expansion of Japanese involvement in heavy industry comparable to the takeover of much of the US steel and tyre industries by Japanese firms, leading to a revitalization of parts of the former US '**Rust Belt**'. These industries were notorious for restrictive work practices in older unionized plants and histories of serious labour conflict. Striking improvements in various measures of performance have been recorded. The basic ideas of lean production and related movements such as total quality management, which apply to services as well as manufacturing, have gained wide acceptance beyond the automobile industry. The wheel has turned full circle since Japanese management and organization were dismissed, not so long ago, as 'culture bound' by Western observers. Instead, now in the 1990s, critical comments are rarely heard as competitive pressures from lower-wage producers intensify and many features of lean production are increasingly taken for granted.

The down side of lean production

Managers, economists and accountants pay most attention to easily measurable, money costs of production that directly affect the famous 'bottom line' accounting measures of annual or quarterly profits. However, there are also human costs of production that are more difficult to quantify and therefore attract less attention. Lean production and JIT delivery of components have removed inventory 'buffers' of materials and simultaneously cut down on human buffers, or labour that is not continuously utilized at 'maximum' capacity. In an interlinked, sequential production system the output flow depends on the weakest link, even if the number of individuals involved is large.

In the usual case of teamwork involving simultaneous or parallel contributions from a number of individuals, any slackening of effort by one person will have a negligible effect on total output when the size of the team is large. This gives rise to the free-rider problem, often used as an argument against group incentives such as profit-sharing. Lean production provides a drastic solution to this incentive problem by essentially placing responsibility for total output on each and every member of the team as one link in the chain of production. If one member of a team with no spare capacity is absent, there are two alternatives: either production is held up or neighbouring workers have to carry out the absent member's tasks in addition to their own. Absence or slacking by any individual thus have immediately felt consequences for co-workers. Loss of output can reduce any kind of bonus or incentive payment, and an additional work load causes serious problems for already stressed workers.

The specific organization of lean production thus mobilizes peer-group pressure to maintain effort and minimize shirking, which is precisely the opposite reaction to that obtained with piece-rates under low trust described in the previous section. The fragility or vulnerability of lean production to disruption clearly also requires cooperation and high trust between labour and management, the cornerstones of which have been job security for core, male employees and above-average wages incorporating a share of enterprise rents.

To earn these privileges, employees have to submit to an extremely fast pace of work, without respite from slack or 'imbalance' in other parts of the assembly process. Individual tasks are simple, repetitive and monotonous, as in Fordist production. Workers are required to perform a number of different tasks and contribute to continuous improvement, but skill requirements for individual tasks in automobile assembly remain low. There is no discretion for workers to vary the short, machine-paced work-cycle time, and, although all employees are empowered to stop the assembly line as a last resort, there is intense pressure from supervisors and co-workers alike to avoid delays and stoppage of any kind.

In an exhaustive comparison of Japanese and Swedish automobile manufacture, industrial sociologist and engineer Christian Berggren (1993) reports widespread discontent among Japanese carworkers in the early 1990s. Surveys

by the JAW (the national federation of unions in the Japanese automobile industry) revealed that 67 per cent were not satisfied with their working environments, 62 per cent thought the work was too routine, and only 4 per cent
would recommend their children get jobs in the automobile industry.

Long working hours are another bone of contention both in Japan and in
the transplants. As Berggren (1993, p. 52) put it, 'strictly speaking, lean production is not buffer-free. The long and flexible work times comprise the hidden reserve that is squeezed out in the production process.' Employees are
expected to work extended overtime at short notice, to avoid extra staffing or
delayed delivery.

For these reasons, the Japanese auto industry began to experience recruit-
ing problems before the major recession of the 1990s, problems that were
avoided by the transplants for various reasons. In the United Kingdom, greenfield sites were chosen for most transplants in areas with very high local unemployment. Exceptionally motivated staff were selected from 100 or more
applicants per job, and paid wages that were higher than usual in the region.
The wage premium enjoyed by most transplant employees and the lack of
comparable employment opportunities represent an obvious rent or 'efficiency
wage' of the kind discussed in Chapter 12. Less obviously, however, the intense
pressure by co-workers as well as supervisors to maintain the pace of production allows for no slack or respite from continuous effort. Much of the
-visible rent thus appears on closer scrutiny to represent a compensating payment for faster work, more effort and higher stress levels. Rotation among
repetitive tasks does not provide autonomy or intrinsically satisfying, skilled
work. Although Western enthusiasts for the productivity benefits of lean production have heralded a fundamental departure from Fordist mass production, critics have emphasized 'multi-tasking' rather than multi-skilling, and
'management by stress' instead of discretionary control over intrinsically
satisfying work.

D. Alternatives to lean production[3]

Volvo's Swedish trajectory

The only systematic attempts to develop an alternative to lean production, at
least in the traditional mass-production context of automobile assembly, were
pioneered by Volvo in Sweden in the 1970s and 1980s. The emergence of these
developments depended crucially on a number of unique features of the
Swedish economic system in general, and of the Volvo company in particular.

Throughout the post-war period until the crisis of the 1990s, Sweden
enjoyed essentially full employment, with the state functioning as an employer
of last resort, providing jobs for a growing number of women entering the
labour force and for others who failed to find employment in the private sector.

The powerful trade unions maintained an egalitarian, 'solidaristic' wage structure, with much smaller differentials for the automobile industry than were
customary in other countries. Discontent with monotonous, repetitive work
grew with post-war prosperity, as elsewhere, but Swedish employers could not
offer premium wages to compensate for the monotony of the assembly line,
nor was the threat of job loss any great incentive in an environment where
alternatives could quickly be found.

Faced with the disruptive effects of 100 per cent or more annual employee
turnover, the management of Sweden's largest automotive company decided
on a radical break with traditional mass-production methods. This decision
was facilitated by the fact that Volvo was a managerial firm in the classical
sense. There was no dominating ownership interest, but rather a large number of dispersed shareholders who allowed management considerable autonomy to pursue unorthodox ventures. Furthermore, the chief executive, Pehr
Gyllenhammar, was a strong personality with an unusual commitment to give
employees 'meaning and satisfaction' as well as variety without losing efficiency
in their work.

Teamwork at Kalmar

The result was a brand-new assembly plant at Kalmar, which opened in 1974
and attracted widespread interest. The plant was designed to provide a light
and airy environment where work was organized in teams responsible for
assembly tasks on intermittently moving carriers. This allowed extensive job
rotation, though individual tasks remained simple. After teething troubles and
modifications, the plant provided Volvo's best productivity performance
through the 1980s, but it remained small, with an annual output of 30,000
cars. Flexibility in responding to model and demand change, as well as car
quality, was also superior to results at Volvo's larger, conventional facility at
Torslanda near Gothenburg, which produced five times Kalmar's output.

However problems remained in the low-unemployment climate that kept
turnover uncomfortably high. Teams were not given autonomous control of
their carriers, which were controlled instead by centralized computers to maintain coordination, and the pace of work was intense. It was argued that the
Kalmar design had not been radical enough to fulfil the objectives of meaningful work and autonomy. Kalmar had been an exclusively management initiative designed without direct input or cooperation from the unions, but now
a new attempt got under way, this time in close cooperation with union representatives, to develop a fundamentally different production concept.

Integrated production at Uddevalla

For the first time, Volvo's new factory in the former shipbuilding town of Uddevalla abandoned the idea of a mechanically paced assembly line. Instead, some 40 parallel teams each assembled largely complete vehicles at fixed locations. This placed heavy demands on the mechanized materials delivery process, but held a number of major benefits for the working teams. First, production was holistic rather than fragmented; each worker was involved in assembling a complete final product, performing and rotating among a wide variety of tasks in the team over an extended cycle time of an hour or more.

Secondly, teams were given the power to control their own work pace, rather than having to keep up with the flow of a mechanically controlled line or carrier. This reduced stress and monotony, and further efforts were made to design tools, individual tasks and working positions ergonomically to minimize strains from repetitive or awkward motion. These innovations allowed the employment of women as blue-collar workers in auto assembly, hitherto a largely male preserve on account of the physical strains involved.

After starting production in 1987, productivity at Uddevalla gradually improved and turnover fell to an unprecedented low of 4 per cent by 1991. Though work had been specifically designed to provide 'meaning and satisfaction', productivity matched Volvo's traditional assembly at Gothenburg but remained far below Japanese transplant standards. Since Kalmar had required 10 years to realize its full potential, considerable further improvement could have been expected from the more innovative new design of Uddevalla beyond 1991, after only two complete years of operation. Nevertheless, both product quality and flexibility in model change were superior to other Volvo plants.

However, in 1991–2 Sweden was hit by the worst post-war recession and auto demand collapsed. As a result of the crisis, an alliance with Renault was planned, though later abandoned, and CEO Gyllenhammar stepped down. Volvo was left with massive overcapacity, so a divided management decided to centralize manufacturing operations with other functions in the largest facilities at Gothenburg, and Uddevalla was closed down in 1993.

Berggren (1993) has argued persuasively that this unfavourable constellation of external circumstances was to blame for the closure, rather than any inherent defects of the integrated production concept at Uddevalla. Other serious problems were the poor quality of components supplied by Gothenburg, and lack of coordination between design and production for the purpose of simplifying manufacture, as practised in Japan. Further evidence for the viability of integrated parallel assembly comes from the success of the bus and heavy-duty truck divisions of Volvo and its main competitor, Saab-Scania. Although on a much smaller scale than automobile production, the systematic use of integrated assembly has allowed the Swedish truck industry to remain at the top of the world productivity league, whereas all other sectors have declined relative to international leaders. A study by the McKinsey Global

Institute ascribes the problems in the rest of the Swedish economy primarily to lack of competition in the domestic market, in addition to serious errors in macroeconomic policy. Much less weight is given to the usually emphasized factors of high taxation and over-regulated labour markets (*Financial Times*, 8 September 1995, p. 2).

One overriding lesson has emerged from the various experiments with integrated production in Sweden. Although Henry Ford's 1924 claim that 'the average worker wants a job . . . in which he does not have to think' has often been reiterated by management spokespeople, careful surveys of the workers' own opinions reveal very different attitudes. '*In all factories and age groups, and at all educational levels, workers with monotonous jobs expressed a strong desire for more variety and better prospects for development*' (Berggren, 1993, pp. 203–4; emphasis in original). Furthermore, repetitive work has pronounced negative effects on long-term physical and mental health. In part, the costs of treating the delayed consequences of traditional assembly work are borne by society, in the form of an increased burden on the health care system and more early retirement and invalidity.

Berggren (1993, p. 10) has also marshalled evidence from his comparative studies of Swedish plants to show that 'the overwhelming feelings of boredom and tediousness on the line were not ameliorated by job rotation'. At one Volvo plant, '90 percent of the workers participated in extensive job rotation, yet 80 percent considered the work so monotonous as to be degrading'. In view of evidence of increasing discontent among Japanese workers, particularly in the automobile industry, it is surprising that standard accounts of lean production tend to ignore these problems. Researchers such as Womack, Jones and Roos have even denied, without any supporting evidence, that integrated production as at Uddevalla could provide greater job satisfaction than rotation among repetitive, short-cycle jobs in lean production. They described Uddevalla as 'a return full circle to Henry Ford's assembly hall of 1903' without ever having visited the plant, and also denied that such integrated production could ever match the productivity of conventional mass production. In fact, Uddevalla reached the productivity of Volvo's conventional assembly by 1991 (see Womack *et al.*, 1990, p. 101; cited by Berggren, 1993, p. 13).

As Berggren (1993, p. 251) has summarized, parts of the lean production 'package' represent 'irrefutable contributions' to efficiency. 'But other parts of the package . . . are closely linked to the regressive working conditions in the Japanese system, including the widespread fragmentation and intense machine pacing of human tasks; the rigid demands to fulfil production quotas . . .; then close surveillance of the individual and excessive regimentation of the work place, and the failure to adapt the working environment, ergonomic conditions, and work pace to long-term human requirements.'

Demands by Japanese unions for improvement in working conditions along the lines of the Swedish experiments have also been overtaken by the worst post-war recession. The overvalued yen until 1997 accelerated the trend to relocate manufacturing to low-wage countries. When unemployment and over-capacity threaten, competitiveness and saving jobs take precedence over the longer-term consideration of more meaningful work. As technological change continues to weaken the position of low-skill workers, work organization might be expected to evolve further along the lean production path, with little attention to 'human requirements'. Some aspects of modern technology suggest a more optimistic assessment, however, as we consider in the next section.

E. Technological change and the future of work

Computing and information technology

Spectacular progress in all areas of computing and communications has been having profound effects on conditions of work. However, perhaps surprisingly, there is considerable controversy about the overall direction and nature of these effects. On the one hand, there are widespread fears that 'automation' in office and clerical work as well as manufacturing is destroying jobs even faster than earlier eras of mechanization. And many existing jobs, it is claimed, are being deskilled as smart machines displace manual dexterity. These fears are supported by well-publicized examples of skilled crafts such as type-setting becoming obsolete and of redundancies in office or factory due to the vastly increased productivity of new technology.

On the other hand, there is no doubt about the shift in demand towards more qualified workers in all broad areas, which was discussed in the previous chapter. So how are today's students and workers to make sense of these apparently conflicting tendencies? As is so often the case, reality is more complex than most media reports allow. All the commentators are right in part. Skills and jobs are disappearing, but new skills and new jobs are required to operate and manufacture the new technology.

Skill and advanced technology

In a survey of British workers, qualifications and training requirements were uniformly higher for those using advanced technology than for those not using advanced technology across a wide range of occupations. More of those working with advanced technology felt that their skill requirements had increased over time, compared with those without (McLoughlin and Clark, 1994). Other dimensions of working with new technologies are more difficult to measure. Higher skill levels do not automatically imply greater job satisfaction. McLoughlin and Clark (1994, p. 150) conclude that computing and information technologies do 'eliminate or reduce the number of complex tasks requiring manual skills and abilities; second, they generate new complex tasks which require mental problem solving abilities and an understanding of system interdependencies'.

There has been much debate over the precise extent to which new technologies determine job content, and over the role and scope of management and organization in adapting technology to human needs. A long line of utopian novelists has seen automation of routine tasks with the help of benevolent robots as heralding the end of human drudgery. Even in Japan, however, the leading producer and user of robots for manufacturing, their use in routine assembly tasks has made only slow progress. Sceptics such as George Orwell, in his totalitarian vision *1984*, feared that information technology could be (mis)used to intensify surveillance and control.

Ironically, too, some of the highest technology is based on the most Taylorist organization of secondary labour. Silicon valley in California is a classical example of a dual labour market, with a highly paid primary sector of scientists and engineers that stands in marked contrast to production work such as chip manufacture. This work is repetitive, stressful and hazardous owing to widespread use of toxic materials. Pay for the frequently female and immigrant production workers is low, prospects for promotion are minimal, and turnover is high. Manufacture of high-technology components is increasingly moving to low-wage countries, and blue-collar employment in the OECD countries continues to decline, putting further pressure on the wages and working conditions of those who remain.

To automate or informate?

The scope for managerial discretion in the use of modern technologies has been highlighted by Shoshana Zuboff of the Harvard Business School. Zuboff (1988) argues that the *distribution* of information is crucial. In the traditional, Fordist organization, information was concentrated or monopolized by managers in the upper levels of hierarchical organizations to complement the rigid division of labour between decision-making and planning at the top and execution of tasks at the bottom. Automation in this context simply replaced some manual labour, whereas information technology would be a tool for management.

However, one of the main characteristics of computing and information technology is the dramatic decline in the costs of information processing and transmission. This cost decline favours decentralization rather than centralization. According to Zuboff, it is now feasible to **informate** an organization by providing workers at all levels with access to almost limitless information about the production process and any other aspect of the organization. Only the informated organization can harness the potential of *all* employees for problem-solving and flexible response to ever more complex product and process technologies.

Employee involvement (EI), empowerment and teamwork or the *kaizen* process of continuous improvement all depend upon the information available to workers throughout the organization. Greater efficiency is likely to require a breakdown of the information and control monopoly held by management in Fordist organization. But workers will also need more education and training to develop the 'mental problem-solving abilities' that are needed to realize the potential for involvement that cheap information offers.

In existing, 'top–down' organizations the fundamental decision for management is whether to 'automate or informate'. Different decisions are possible within the same set of technological constraints or parameters. Freeman (1995, p. 356) notes that 'UK employers have not developed EI programmes to the extent of American employers'. According to the UK Workplace Industrial Relations Survey, there was relatively little provision of information by management to employees. Freeman remarks that 'perhaps EI is better suited for the more educated American workforce. Perhaps British management recognises that works councils will come to the U.K. as part of the Social Chapter and will be the future mode of employee participation/representation' (1995, p. 356).

Freeman argues that, in the long run, successful EI will require some form of formal employee representation such as unions or works councils. The much greater strength of such institutions in continental Europe suggests that companies there are more likely to 'informate', whereas their British competitors just try to automate. It should be added that unions in the United Kingdom have often opposed new technology and changing work practices by trying to maintain obsolete, craft-based work rules that protected a privileged minority of skilled manual workers. Such attitudes have undoubtedly hastened the decline of Anglo-American confrontational union organization and bargaining.

Change in the Rust Belt

Even work in the most traditional heavy industries such as steelmaking, remote from the glamour of high tech, has been revolutionized by dramatic developments in process innovation. Pioneered by Japanese steel companies and implemented in their many transplants in the United States, these developments have transformed the old US Rust Belt. They have also set standards for steel producers everywhere, and rendered older facilities in Europe and elsewhere obsolete, leading to overcapacity in several countries.

In place of traditional batch production with separate casting, rolling, coating and other steps, cold-rolled steel can now be produced in an hour instead of days by salaried workers and engineers who never actually handle the steel. Instead, they monitor and control the automated transfer of steel through successive stages to final production of the finished rolls. The spotlessly clean environment of a modern steelworks is more like an oil refinery or a paper-mill, and seems to be a different world from the grime, noise, sweat and pollution of the old-fashioned 'dark satanic mills'. Communication and infor-mation technology has been used in this industry to 'informate' the few multi-skilled workers who are still needed, but the very efficiency and productivity of the new technology are also the down side – so few of these workers are needed, compared with the old labour intensive technology.

The service economy

Although automation has not reduced labour requirements so drastically in the production of more complex, finished products such as automobiles or computers, it is a commonplace that the share of employment in manufac-turing has been declining everywhere. But the dominance of the service sec-tors that has emerged in recent decades at the same time as the revolution in computing and information technology has also called into question the tra-ditional classifications into 'services' and 'manufacturing'.

Former US Labour Secretary Robert Reich (previously at Harvard's Kennedy School) has described the currently used classifications as 'archaic' in his best-selling book *The Work of Nations* (1991) and proposed an insight-ful new way of classifying what people actually do according to the skills required, the competition they face and other properties of the work. Reich starts by defining three broad categories of work that correspond to different competitive positions and calls them routine production services, in-person services, and symbolic-analytic services.

The first category of **routine production services** in Reich's wider sense includes the low-skill, repetitive manufacturing tasks typically performed by blue-collar workers, usually in secondary labour markets. But Reich includes routine, low-level supervisory and control functions performed by low-level managers and foremen, which involve routine checks of subordinates and enforcement of standard operating procedures. Furthermore, routine production services are not confined to the older or declining manufacturing industries. In spite of the hype and optimism surrounding computing and information technology, these industries require many routine workers who process raw data 'in much the same monotonous way that assembly line workers . . . processed piles of other raw materials' (Reich, 1991, p. 175).

Routine producers in high-tech industries are guided by standard proce-dures and rules that usually leave them with little discretion or autonomy. They are closely monitored, often with the aid of computers. Although basic liter-acy and some computational ability are usually required, reliability and will-ingness to take orders are the main qualifications. A high proportion of these workers are female, absenteeism and repetitive strain injuries are common and pay, often according to output, is low.

These routine production workers, whether male or female, in high-tech or Rust Belt, are the most endangered by competition from low-wage countries. Comprising perhaps a quarter of the workforce of advanced economies, they are the most easy to replace by workers in developing countries earning only a small percentage of wages in Europe or the United States.

In-person services, Reich's second category, 'also entail simple and repetitive tasks' and have fairly modest skill requirements. 'The big difference between in-person servers and routine producers is that these services must be provided person to person and thus are not sold world-wide.' The category includes retail sales, gastronomy, healthcare, and secretarial and all the myriad other services that have been growing disproportionately. 'A pleasant demeanour' is usually required for traditionally female, in-person servers (Reich, 1991, p. 176).

Finally, the **symbolic-analytic services** are activities requiring high levels of skill and education that involve abstraction, symbolic manipulation, problem-solving and the exercise of authority. Higher managerial and professional work usually belongs to this category. Pay depends primarily on the quality rather than the quantity or hours of work performed. These workers are in competition with similarly qualified people the world over, and although their earnings relative to other groups have been rising, particularly in the United Kingdom and the United States, their job security has declined in many cases.

Reich acknowledges that some traditional job categories such as secretarial and managerial overlap with more than one of his functional categories. However, the traditional designations date from times when these occupations were much more standardized, and often reveal little about the tasks being performed today. Reich excludes public sector employees such teachers and civil servants from his classification, noting that they are not directly subject to international competition. Another omitted category consists of the small but important group of skilled workers who require extensive training to work with their hands and tools rather than symbols and machines. They include craftspeople, technicians and maintenance engineers. This group provides a vital in-person service to anyone who uses complex technologies that are liable to malfunction, in home, factory or office. The extensive training required differentiates the skilled craftsperson from the majority of in-person servers, and includes problem-solving ability of the kind needed by symbolic analysts.

Significantly, the combination of theoretical and practical training for blue-collar workers that is supplied by the German apprenticeship system is underdeveloped in the United Kingdom and the United States. A fundamentally Taylorist ideology has hindered state support for a theoretical component of schooling in symbolic and problem-solving skills for blue-collar workers, who have not been through the higher levels of the full-time education system. Lack of such skills in Britain, where only one-third of the workforce have vocational or higher educational qualifications (compared with three-quarters in Germany), is widely viewed as a serious problem for the United Kingdom's declining manufacturing sector in particular.

While the majority of low-skilled in-person servers are not *directly* threatened by competition from low-wage countries, they are *indirectly* in competition with these areas. For routine production workers whose jobs have been outsourced to Mexico, Thailand or Poland are also potential suppliers of in-person services that require only low skills, particularly if they are female. The entry of these displaced workers into the service sector can only help to maintain downward pressure on wages there as well.

The apparent insulation from the effects of international competition afforded by the very nature of in-person services thus turns out to be more apparent than real. Of course, the middle-aged steelworker displaced by automation may find few takers for his brawn and muscle. But redundant young female routine production workers can easily transfer to retail sales or catering. Even high-level in-person providers of managerial and professional services are by no means immune. As Reich (1991, p. 184) concludes, 'in the emerging global economy, even the most impressive position in the most prestigious of organizations is vulnerable to worldwide competition if it entails easily replicated routines. The only true competitive advantage lies in skill in solving, identifying and brokering new problems.'

Whatever the precise classifications adopted, the dominating role of services in the modern economy should be clear. So too should the importance of international competition and modern technologies based on computing and information processing in shaping the contents of the jobs people do and the wages they earn. One of Adam Smith's many fruitful ideas was that people who perform less pleasant or more dangerous work should receive a **compensating differential** in the form of extra pay to compensate for less intrinsic job satisfaction. This idea receives some support among samples of people with similar qualifications in competitive markets. However, in comparing people with different skill levels, modern market forces are accentuating almost the opposite effect. As rewards and opportunities for those who perform repetitive and monotonous tasks are squeezed, the relative pay of the 'problem-solvers' with the most interesting and challenging jobs is rising. But these (growing) pay differentials understate the welfare effects of new technology in the global economy. Including job satisfaction or just some crude proxy for this difficult-to-measure attribute, we observe not compensation but enlargement of obvious differences. The widening welfare gap represents a future of 'lousy jobs' or no jobs at all for a growing underclass at the bottom of industrial society, and poses a growing threat to the social fabric. Although most evident, for different reasons, in the United States and Eastern Europe, these problems are now emerging in Western Europe as well, particularly in Britain.

F. Chapter summary and key ideas

Ever-increasing division of labour and specialization have accompanied and complemented technological progress, to generate the steady growth in productivity that industrial economies have enjoyed over most of their history. Throughout this development, old skills and occupations have become obsolete and new requirements have evolved. For half a century, the technical triumph of Fordist continuous-flow production condemned most blue-collar or manual production workers to monotonous and meaningless repetitive work tasks.

The remarkable Swedish experiments that sought to combine modern technology with integrated assembly by semi-autonomous teams of workers foundered in Sweden's most severe post-war recession in the early 1990s. However, by that time two or three other major developments were fundamentally changing the world of work and the organization of production.

First, perhaps, was the evolution of lean production, pioneered by Toyota in Japan. The elimination of slack and buffers in mass production, and the integration of all workers in teams under unrelenting pressure for continuous improvement in performance, generated phenomenal productivity gains. Competitive pressures and the example of Japanese transplants helped to spread the gospel of lean production and related ideas such as total quality management, **flexible manufacturing systems** and **employee involvement**.

These developments were also encouraged by the extraordinary advance of computing and information technologies in the two decades following Opec's first oil-price shock. The new technologies facilitated decentralization and flexibility by radically cutting the costs of information transmission and processing. Skill requirements to use these opportunities have been rising on average. However, monotonous and repetitive work, what Robert Reich calls routine production services, has not been eliminated by technological change. The products and the materials have changed since the heyday of Fordist production, but human dexterity, coupled with minimal literacy and computational skills, is still cheaper than advanced robotics and complete automation for many tasks.

This brings us to the final components of the forces that are revolutionizing the world of work as a new millennium approaches. Unlike the first two components, which originated in the advanced countries, the final new development came from the newly industrializing countries (NICs) of the Southern hemisphere, or the traditional 'third world'. As Northern capital and know-how have become more mobile, they have been combined with cheap labour in countries from Latin America to South Asia, and most recently in Eastern Europe as well, to produce cheap components and manufactured goods for export to the high-wage countries of the Northern hemisphere. The rapid growth of these exports and the outsourcing of production to the low-wage NICs is likely to continue unabated. Low-skill workers or 'routine producers' in the North will be unable to compete indefinitely with workers whose wages are only a fraction of their own.

In the long run, some convergence of wages in the NICs to the higher levels of advanced countries may be expected. However, this process may take a long time – too long for a generation or two of routine producers unable to find jobs that keep them out of poverty. The importance of education and training is clearly paramount. In-person services may absorb some of the displaced routine producers, though market forces alone are likely to push these services sector wages far below current European standards. Clearly the world of work faces unprecedented turmoil and problems in the foreseeable future, problems that will tax policy makers and managers to the limits of their ingenuity.

Key words

buffer stocks	*kaizen* (continuous improvement)
compensating differential	lean production
division of labour	outsourcing
employee involvement	routine production serves
flexible manufacturing system	Rust Belt
Fordism	scientific management
informate	statistical quality control
in-person services	symbolic-analytic services
integrated production	Taylorism
just-in-time manufacturing	transplants

Questions and problems for review and discussion

1 Explain the problems that arose in the practical application of Frederick Taylor's programme of scientific management.
2 Discuss the effects of division of labour on job satisfaction.
3 Characterize the system of manufacturing pioneered by Toyota, and contrast this system with traditional Fordism.
4 Why have Japanese transplants been so successful in the very different UK and US environments?
5 What were the main features of the Swedish integrated-production alternative to lean manufacturing?
6 How has the advance of computing and information technology affected the demand for skills?
7 Explain why teamwork and employee involvement have been growing in importance in recent years.
8 Discuss the differing impact of outsourcing and foreign competition on various kinds of services.

Notes

1 See also the perceptive early account by Bell (1970 [1956]).
2 For an influential example, see Kern and Schumann (1977).
3 This section is based on Berggren's (1993) path-breaking study.

References

Bell, D. (1970 [1926]),*Work and Its Discontents*, New York: League for Industrial Democracy.

Berggren, C. (1993), *The Volvo Experience*, London: Macmillan.

Best, M. (1990), *The New Competition*, Cambridge: Polity Press.

Deming, W. E. (1982), *Quality, Productivity and Competitive Position*, MIT Center for Advanced Engineering Study, Cambridge, Mass: MIT Press.

Freeman, R. B. (1995), 'Will the union phoenix rise again – in the U.K. or the U.S.?' *Scottish Journal of Political Economy*, 42, August.

HEW (1973), *Work in America*, Cambridge, Mass.: MIT Press.

Kenney, M. and R. Florida (1993), *Beyond Mass Production*, Oxford: Oxford University Press.

Kern, H. and M. Schumann (1977), *Industriearbeit und Arbeiterbewusstsein*, Frankfurt: Suhrkamp Verlag.

McLoughlin, I. and J. Clark (1994), *Technological Change at Work*, London: Open University Press.

Reich, R. (1991), *The Work of Nations*, New York: Simon & Schuster.

Smith, A. (1976 [1776]), *An Inquiry into the Nature and Causes of the Wealth of Nations*, Chicago: University of Chicago Press.

Womack, J. P., D. T. Jones and D. Roos (1990), *The Machine That Changed the World*, New York: Rawson.

Zuboff, S. (1988), *In the Age of the Smart Machine*, New York: Heinemann.

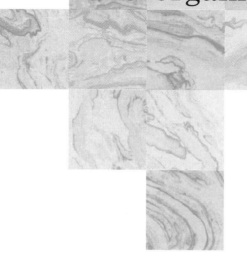

PART FIVE

Innovation, technology and organization

CHAPTER 14

Innovation and Technological Change

A. Chapter outline and student goals

The effects of technological change are pervasive in almost every sphere of modern life. As consumers we use an array of products and services, most of which were undreamed of a few decades ago. Producers in almost every industry face a stream of competing innovations that must be matched or improved upon to ensure survival. Most of the technologies that we use at work and leisure are far beyond the detailed comprehension of non-specialists, so we become even more dependent upon the services of expert advisers and technicians.

Economists have long pondered the causes and effects of technological change. For a long time the prevailing view stemmed from the famous Austrian– American economist Joseph Schumpeter. He argued that only large monopolistic firms, which possessed the market power to set prices above marginal cost, had the resources required for the systematic development of innovative new products. Schumpeter summarized the experience of the first half of the twentieth century, when most industrial research and development (R&D) was indeed carried out in specialized laboratories and centres operated by the largest firms. Pioneers included I. G. Farben and Siemens, leaders of the German chemical and electrical industries, followed by their competitors in the United States and other countries.

Many key inventions have of course been made by dedicated individuals, frequently eccentric 'loners' who would not fit into the organized labs of 'big science'. In recent decades there has been something of a resurgence of innovative activity by individuals and small firms, particularly in the United States, which retains scientific and technology leadership in many areas. Scientists and engineers frustrated with slow-moving corporate bureaucracy frequently leave their jobs to found new **entrepreneurial** firms that can develop and market their ideas more rapidly.

This process of new firm formation, particularly in high-technology areas, depends on the **venture capital** market provided by investors who are willing to back promising but unproven ideas for a share of the future profits. The risks of failure are high. Most new ideas or inventions never turn

457

into marketable products. The willingness to bear this kind of entrepreneurial risk is what seems to distinguish American investors, scientists and managers, who support the highest rate of new start-ups. Major US university research centres have also helped to stimulate entrepreneurial innovation with a supply of expertise and personnel. For example, faculty scientists and well-trained graduates from Stanford and Berkeley contribute to the prominence of Silicon Valley in California in high-technology entrepreneurship and innovation.

In Europe, the lack of such university research centres and above all the almost non-existent venture capital markets and much greater risk aversion by all parties leave little scope for entrepreneurial innovation. In Germany, corporate R&D has maintained high quality and export shares in traditional engineering and chemical products, but the newer information and biotechnologies have been neglected. Venture capital is scarce and new start-ups are rare.

Similar conditions prevail in Japan, with most R&D conducted by large corporations; yet, in contrast to Europe, Japan has succeeded in rivalling or even overtaking the United States in many high-tech areas. One of the reasons for this success appears to be the close relationship between R&D and production, which has helped Japanese firms convert innovations into best-selling new products on a remarkable scale. US venture capital markets offer enormous capital gains to entrepreneurs who pioneer a technological 'breakthrough' and then sell their stakes before putting the innovation into production. The process of developing a working product for large-scale manufacture may then be neglected. Britain, with an emerging venture capital market, has produced some high-tech entrepreneurs and Europe's largest biotechnology sector. However, some of these companies, whose shares have risen to spectacular heights on the stock market, are still years away from marketing their innovations in the form of a tested drug.

Government policy on science technology and the role of 'pure' or basic scientific research are often misunderstood but crucial components of the whole innovative process. Pure science today, by definition designed to advance fundamental knowledge with no economic payoff in the foreground, is the foundation of tomorrow's applied science and technological progress. The knowledge gained from basic research is a public good, with commercial benefits too uncertain and remote to be captured by private investors. There is thus a temptation for scientifically illiterate and short-termist politicians to cut back on the support of basic research that is performed mainly in universities. The United Kingdom has performed particularly badly in this respect, being the only OECD country to have suffered a real decline in government funding of civil R&D since 1981, a decline that has hit basic research particularly hard. With even government funding bodies demanding evidence of commercial benefits from research projects, there are worries that the pure science foundations of future progress – current university research and teaching – are being eroded. Nobel awards to UK scientists have dwindled sharply since the mid-1980s, while the flow of emigrants to better-funded centres in the United States has increased.

Government funding of applied science and technology is often criticized for picking losers rather than winners. A major portion of British, French and American government expenditure on R&D goes to military and nuclear energy projects. Large corporations and established research areas or centres typically grab the lion's share of public funding through their well-developed networks and lobbying activities. Nuclear power generation, faced with astronomical long-term costs of reactor decomissioning and waste disposal as well as widespread public opposition since Chernobyl, would be quite uncompetitive without enormous government outlays of taxpayers' money.

Although American research and scientific dominance remain unchallenged in many areas, the glamour and importance of high tech entrepreneurship in the United States have tended to obscure some of the social costs imposed by highly mobile scientific personnel and the competitive pursuit of scientific 'breakthroughs', which can generate huge capital gains for pioneers and venture capitalists but are still far removed from the production process.

In Japan, on the other hand, Schumpeter seems confirmed. Large corporations there do most of the R&D and innovation in relatively unbureaucratic, flexible organizations that maintain close contact with production. The Taylorist division of labour, which strictly separates scientific and research personnel from production workers in most Western firms, has been avoided in Japan. Production experience on the shop floor that is required of graduate engineers who later move to R&D helps to strengthen the *kaizen* process of continuous improvement and maintain a balance between product and process innovation. Surprisingly too, the lack of a strong academic tradition of basic research has not stopped the dramatic advance of Japanese high-tech manufacturing in many fields.

Europe, despite its political problems and lagging performance in the newer information and biotechnology industries, still has a major resource base in the form of highly skilled labour and varied research establishments. Combining and developing these assets to their most productive use have often been hindered rather than helped by government policies and priorities, but still offer growth potential for the future.

After reading this chapter you should be able to:

- understand more about the role of pure science in the development of technology;
- recognize the importance of R&D in generating productivity growth;
- follow the European debate about high tech deficits and policy;
- evaluate the costs and benefits of high tech entrepreneurship in the United States;
- compare Japanese, European and US prowess in technology and innovation.

B. Science and technology

The development of science

In spite of the dominating role of technology in our daily lives, many people do not appreciate the extent to which most practical innovations are based on advances in pure science. The advances are usually motivated by curiosity and the desire to understand fundamental laws of nature, sometimes with no inkling of practical applications that may take decades to realize.

Thus the Scottish physicist James Clark Maxwell developed the mathematical theory of electromagnetism nearly half a century before Marconi demonstrated the first radio transmission in 1896. Maxwell's equations are still the foundation of the vast and rapidly growing telecommunications industry, a development that Maxwell could never have imagined.

Even more momentous consequences for human affairs can follow from pure scientific endeavour. At the beginning of the twentieth century, the synthesis of ammonia from nitrogen and hydrogen was an outstanding unsolved problem that had defeated generations of chemists. A leading young German chemist, Fritz Haber, determined to tackle this problem with initially no thought of applications. For his success in 1909 Haber later received a Nobel prize, and the synthesis of ammonia provided the foundations for the chemical fertilizer industry.

Haber's breakthrough also provided the ammonia used to produce high explosives without imported raw materials. As another Nobel Prize winning chemist has written of Haber:

> By a terrible irony of fate, it is his apparently most beneficent invention, the synthesis of ammonia, which has also harmed the world unmeasurably. Without it, Germany would have run out of explosives once its long-planned blitz krieg against France failed. The war would have come to an early end and millions of young men would not have been slaughtered. In these circumstances Lenin might never have got to Russia, Hitler might not have come to power. (Perutz, 1996, p. 36)

Most scientific discoveries do not of course have such far-reaching consequences as the work of Maxwell or of Haber. Nevertheless, even basic researchers are increasingly aware of the rewards for successful applications, and few can afford to pursue knowledge with no consideration of its potential usefulness. The sheer scope and scale of technology and applied science today mean that promising results from fundamental research are more quickly developed to commercial fruition than previously.

The optimal balance between pure and applied science and the policy to achieve such an optimum are not easy to discern. Before the decline in government funding for non-military R&D under the Thatcher government of the

1980s, Britain had an excellent record in basic scientific research but a very poor history of commercial development. Conservative management, adversarial labour relations and a relatively unskilled workforce did not encourage the production of innovative and high-quality new products. In Japan, by contrast, there was no tradition of fundamental research. However, high levels of education, training and long-term, mainly industry-funded, R&D combined to generate a phenomenally successful stream of new products and processes. In the United States, 'spillovers' from leading university research centres seem to have played an important role in stimulating local concentrations of high-technology entrepreneurship such as Silicon Valley and many other less well-known clusters of innovative activity.[1]

The modern technology of global communication allows researchers to disseminate their latest results far more speedily and efficiently than before. However, the sheer quantity of available information, which has been growing exponentially and perhaps doubling every decade, tends to overload the bounded capacity of researchers to process this information. Face-to-face communication, including casual and informal interaction between people working on related problems, remains of great importance to most scientists, and helps to explain the geographical clustering of high-tech industries, which is most prominent in America though less important in much smaller European countries.

The production of innovation

Given the importance of innovation in modern economies, economists have devoted much effort to studying just how – and where – important innovations are actually produced, and precisely what they contribute in economic terms. Innovations can be classified as **product** or **process innovations**, the latter referring to innovations in the technology of production. An early measure of innovative activity was the number of **patents** issued annually in a particular industry or country. Patents provide incentives in the form of exclusive rights to exploit an innovation for a specified period of time. The problem with this measure is that many important innovations are not patented in order to avoid the required disclosure of details, which might enable a competitor to 'invent around' the original patent. Alternatively, to prevent such imitation, numerous closely related patents may be used to 'fence in' an innovation, so the number of patents is again poorly related to the number of innovations.

As R&D labs have proliferated and firms publish their expenditure on this primary input activity in the production of innovation, economists have also studied R&D as a type of investment that increases the future sales and productivity of firms and industries. Neither patent protection nor secrecy enables an inventor to capture all the returns from her innovation. Knowledge disseminates through many different channels, and sooner or later successful innovations will undermine the initial monopoly or exclusive supply position held by the producer of a new product. Owing to these spillovers, the **social returns** to R&D spending are likely to be greater than the **private returns** to the firm or individual innovator. Quantitative studies have confirmed this, and even found direct evidence of spillovers from R&D between countries, in addition to the effects of trade, that raise productivity.

Published R&D outlays are not a perfect indicator of inputs into the innovation process however. Small firms, in particular, perform much innovative activity in conjunction with production, and with no formal R&D budget or special facilities. The R&D statistics thus underestimate the total activity devoted to generating innovation. If Schumpeter was right and most technological progress is produced by the larger firms, which usually have explicit R&D budgets, this discrepancy would not matter much. However, recent research that directly measures innovative output has cast doubt on Schumpeter's hypothesis for some countries.

The number of innovations recorded in trade journals for a particular industry and time period provides a direct measure that overcomes many of the problems associated with proxies for innovation such as patents or R&D. The innovation count does not distinguish between major innovations and less important ones, but it seems to be the best measure currently available. It turns out that, in many American and British industries, small firms produce more innovations per employee than do large firms (see Acs and Audretsch, 1990). In high-tech industries, the number of innovations also increases less than proportionately with firm sales.

These results provide an interesting contrast with the conventional wisdom that R&D outputs increase more than proportionately with firm size. Thus large American firms seem to be less efficient in generating innovations from their R&D expenditure. However, small firms are also less likely to attempt the kind of innovations that require major investments, and in old 'low-tech' industries, where progress is simply more difficult to achieve, innovations do increase more than proportionately with sales.

In many modern high-tech areas, innovations can be made with relatively small facilities and outlays. Creative scientists and engineers with freedom to develop their ideas are the crucial input. In large organizations, creative individuals are often frustrated by bureaucratic controls and delays. The most successful innovators are usually promoted to administrative positions, and the profits from innovation accrue mainly to outside shareholders.

In contrast, the key scientists in small entrepreneurial start-ups are often major equity holders who participate directly in the commercial success of their ideas. With fewer hierarchical layers between researchers and top management, implementation of new initiatives tends to be speedier and less complicated. The down side, of course, is the risk of failure of even the most promising theoretical ideas and the lack of relative job security that is generally provided by larger firms.

Technology standards

Technological advances typically present a number of options to the market place where the benefits and costs of each form of the new technology must be carefully weighed. The winner in the market place is said to set the standard for that particular type of technology. The importance of winning this competition cannot be understated. In the early 1980s Bill Gates left IBM to found a new software company, Microsoft. How did Microsoft become the industry leader in PC application software? Bill Gates successfully became the one to set the standard for the exploding computer industry.

Economists have only recently become interested in the process of setting standards and we hope to provide some insights into this process. This question is neither new nor trivial to organizational economists. In the nineteenth century, the development of large-scale manufacturing was made possible by the adoption of technological standards for interchangeable parts.

Generally, a new technology becomes available in a number of formats. Consider the video games you may have in your home, and what factors come into play as the market decides between 16-bit and 32-bit formats. As the new computer technologies emerge in the business world, individuals are presented with options. Macintosh operating systems (platforms) feature user-friendly graphics and a 'click and point' menu-driven system of commands. The Macintosh platforms compete with Windows, MS-DOS and Unix-based operating systems. In such situations, a single producer usually 'wins' the competition in the long run and becomes the standard.

On closer inspection it becomes clear that the competition is not between individual products, but rather between **network systems** – referring to collections of two or more components together with an interface that allows the components to work together.[2] Some examples of systems are: staplers and staples, which together bind your homework together; petrol or diesel and cars, which yield transportation services; and your computer hardware and word-processing package, which together provide the service of transferring your writing into a more presentable form. The key features of competition between network systems are strong **consumption complementarities** between the components and the ability (or inability) to link together the components of different suppliers.

The market competition between network systems, as opposed to more limited competition between individual products, features three important issues: expectations, coordination and compatibility. Although it is not our purpose to explore this interesting area too deeply, a brief exposition of the central ideas should help us in understanding some of the issues important in shaping the technological environment in which firms operate.

Consumer expectations concerning the success of any network system are perhaps the most important force in the market. If a given network system, such as Windows software and its many applications programs, is thought to become popular then it is more likely to be adopted. Purchasers will be able to communicate with others purchasing that software, and are virtually guaranteed a 'wide' market in the future with relatively inexpensive upgrades and enhancements. Another example of network system competition involves credit cards: the usefulness of a card depends on how widely accepted it is.

Consumer expectations also cause network systems to generate **consumption externalities** of the type described in Chapter 5. Clearly my decision to adopt a particular network system enhances its value to others who already have adopted (or yet may adopt) that network system.

Network systems also pose coordination problems for relationships between firms, for the firms themselves, and for the relationship between a firm and its customers. A firm contemplating whether to develop a new computer architecture is forced to speculate about whether or not software will be provided to work on it. Perhaps the most well-known example of recognition of the coordination problem facing firms is IBM's strategy of allowing other software developers to write software applications that are compatible with its personal computers.

The compatibility problems facing providers of network systems are also important, causing decisions to be made concerning the future course of events in any market. Compatibility asks the question, 'Can a component designed to work in one system also function in another system?' Classic examples of incompatibility include: railroad cars that do not match the tracks, MS-DOS and Unix, and people speaking in different languages.

A wide variety of solutions exists to the consumer expectation, coordination and compatibility problems posed by network systems. If competing network systems are in existence, or even planned to exist, one obvious solution is cooperation. Throughout the 1980s and 1990s two nations led the world in the development of high-density television (HDTV): the United States and Japan. The Japanese committed early to an analog-based system.

In the United States, the Federal Communications Commission organized a competition between different firms vying to set the standards for the distribution of a digital-based HDTV signal. The result of this competition was the emergency of a 'Grand Alliance' of firms agreeing to share their technologies and split the licensing fees (see Box 1.3 in Chapter 1: 'High-Density Television: The Grand Alliance').

If cooperation is impossible to achieve then network systems will be largely incompatible. Some possible strategies have been observed by economists in such situations.

1 Firms may strive to build an 'early' lead (or at least the perception of one) in the competition with other network system suppliers. This may involve heavy use of 'penetration pricing', introductory classes and seminars, and consumer give-aways. Firms also often release very inflated sales figures showing an artificially high adoption rate.

2 Firms may attempt to obtain close and exclusive relationships with suppliers. In network system competition, a firm always wants complements for its product to be generously supplied, and complements for its rivals' products to be scarce. This suggests that firms may be more apt to integrate suppliers vertically in order to speed the adoption of product innovations while precluding others from enjoying them.
3 Firms may use elaborate product pre-announcements. The effect of these highly publicized announcements is to make existing competitors' products less desirable.

In short, the adoption of 'industry standards' for many of the technical advancements during the 1970–90 period was usually not a straightforward process. Many of the difficulties arose because of the network system characteristic of these goods and services.

European problems

High-tech entrepreneurial firms and new start-ups are much less common in continental Europe, though interestingly, small and medium-sized firms hold *larger* shares of output and employment than in the United Kingdom and the United States. The relationship between firm-size and innovation is less well researched on the continent however.

Europe is home to some leading large companies with strong innovation performance in areas such as pharmaceuticals (Switzerland, the United Kingdom), chemicals and electrical equipment (Germany, the Netherlands, Sweden). However, Table 14.1 shows the scale of Japanese and American

Table 14.1 Investing in the future

	Number of companies in the top 300 for R&D	Percentage of sales spent on R&D
Sweden	8	13.0
Switzerland	12	6.3
Netherlands	5	5.3
Japan	76	4.9
Germany	23	4.3
United States	123	4.2
France	20	4.0
United Kingdom	18	2.5
Average of top 300 companies		4.4

Source *New Scientist*, 6 July 1996, p. 10, from *The 1996 UK R&D Scoreboard*, Department of Trade and Industry.

dominance according to one measure. Among the 300 companies worldwide with the largest R&D budgets, two-thirds were US and Japanese based. Furthermore, the table shows that the 76 top Japanese companies spent 4.9 per cent of sales on R&D, compared with only 2.5 per cent for the 18 British firms in the top 300, and 4.3 per cent for the 23 German companies represented. The UK firms are dominated by pharmaceuticals, which perform about one-third of British industrial R&D, in particular the leaders Glaxo-Wellcome and SmithKline Beecham.

Comparisons of this kind understate the problems, however, because most European R&D and innovation is concentrated in the more traditional industries mentioned above. In the newer technologies such communications and information technology, biotechnology and even consumer electronics, Europe is seriously under-represented, and the leading American and Japanese competitors are dominant. Since these are the fastest-growing technology sectors, Europe's poor current showing bodes ill for the future unless major efforts are made to catch up.

In today's global economy, corporate and even national boundaries are becoming increasingly blurred. Keen to access Europe's enormous internal market and skilled labour resources, American and Japanese companies are forming joint ventures and strategic alliances with European corporations, thus helping to diffuse the most modern technological advances. In the meantime, markets for the 'older' engineering and chemical products are not disappearing, even if they do become relatively less important. International specialization is the traditional cornerstone of comparative advantage and trade. There is no reason for every high-tech sector to be equally represented in each region or national jurisdiction. Some of the political concerns still regularly heard are reminiscent of pre-war or cold war strategic autonomy arguments that motivated enormously wasteful subsidies to commercially non-viable sectors. Thus the wartime interruption of imports led successive post-war British governments to a drive for agricultural self-sufficiency, subsidizing intensive food production or 'factory farming' with little regard for the health of animals or consumers. This enormously expensive and destructive policy, which long predated the ill-reputed Common Agricultural Policy has culminated in the epidemic of 'mad cow disease' (BSE) and the emergence of human infection with a related version of Creuzfeld-Jakob Disease (CJD) after a long history of official disinformation, inadequate controls and denial of danger to consumers that has strained relations with continental partners.

Another genuine problem in Europe has been the lack of **venture capital** markets and entrepreneurial start-ups, in both high tech industries and other areas such as services. Scientists and engineers in established positions seem to be more risk averse than their America counterparts, and also face much greater problems trying to obtain credit or venture capital for a new enterprise. Unemployment in the European Union (EU) averages 11 per cent, twice the US level, and the process of downsizing large companies and outsourcing production to low-wage countries has only just begun in most EU countries.

While the share of self-employment doubled in Britain in the 1980s as manufacturing employment declined by a third, the job-creating impact of new high-tech enterprise, which was more common in the United Kingdom than elsewhere in Europe, has been minimal. Long-term unemployment is concentrated among unskilled men, who are the least likely to be employed in high-tech industries, so the undoubted – and considerable – benefits of an improved venture capital market will not include much of a contribution to Europe's most serious problem.

Government policy

Government policy towards science and technology has traditionally been torn between three conflicting goals. In one corner, and usually dominating, are the powerful lobbies for prestigious or well-established interest groups such as nuclear energy or military projects such as the American 'Star Wars', which obtain huge subsidies for commercially non-viable or scientifically infeasible programmes. Vague but emotionally compelling arguments about national interests and security have helped to channel a major portion of government R&D funds into non-productive but rent-preserving activities of this kind. Indeed, the long-run costs of nuclear waste disposal and reactor decommissioning, for example, have been swept under the carpet of official neglect and secrecy for future generations to pick up.

Becoming increasingly powerful are the red pencils wielded by finance ministers trying desperately to cut deficits and meet the **Maastricht Treaty** conditions for a European monetary union timetable of controversial utility and doubtful practicality. This process has gone furthest in eurosceptical Britain, raising serious concerns in the scientific community about the future of scientific education, not to mention the fate of a proud but crumbling tradition of excellence in basic research. However, the relatively short time horizon in political decision-making has put funding for basic science under pressure in other countries as well, albeit starting from more generous levels in many cases.

By far the weakest pole in the triad of influence facing government policy is a somewhat grudging recognition that basic or 'pure' science by definition has no certain or near-term payoff. Becoming ever more fragile is the official acceptance of a fundamental lesson from the history of scientific and technological progress, which is that the most abstract or apparently irrelevant advances may ultimately yield major practical payoffs (see Box 14.1). As competition for funding becomes more severe, low-risk projects with payoffs in the near future look most attractive to risk-averse bureaucrats and grant-givers, while the 'long shots' that offer larger but more distant rewards lose out.

This form of short-terminism could have serious consequences for competitiveness in the long run. Many studies have shown that the social returns to

Box 14.1 The eye of the lobster

Twenty years ago, Mike Land at Sussex University in England and Klaus Vogt, now at Freiburg University in Germany, independently discovered how the lobster's eye works. A bundle of numerous tiny facets reflect light off their walls and guide it to the retina at the back of the eye without needing a lens. This principle has been used to develop an X-ray telescope with a lens made up of millions of tiny lead glass tubes that focus the X-rays. Astronomers at the University of Leicester who pioneered this technique also hope to use the new lens to create a parallel or 'collimated' beam of X-rays for the fabrication of transistors and chips hundreds of times smaller than current microelectronic components. The new X-ray lithography could thus replace existing photolithography, which is limited by the much longer wavelength of visible light compared with X-rays.

The technology promises to revolutionize computing power and spawn a multi-billion dollar industry. And all because two biologists were intrigued by the curious optics of the lobster's eye and a bunch of astronomers adopted the idea for astronomy . . .

The politicians might remember how unpredictable is the path from basic research to billion-dollar industry. And we hope they will not choke on their lobster when they hear that no British company felt able to take up the Leicester group's new technology. It is to be developed in Massachusetts.

(*New Scientist*, 6 July 1996, p. 3)

R&D far exceed the private returns, as knowledge-spillovers and learning diffuse all the benefits of new discoveries and innovation. Because firms and inventors thus do not appropriate all the rewards from their (private) investment, the level of R&D will be below the socially optimal level without government support. This is just an example of overproduction of a partially public good – scientific knowledge – so that government subsidy is necessary for the efficient, socially optimal production of knowledge. There is also evidence of international spillovers, so that R&D in one country, say the United States, ultimately boosts productivity in trading partners through joint ventures and the exchange of goods and services that incorporate new knowledge and innovation.

Government policy toward science and technology varies considerably from country to country, and interacts with other national institutions and traditions, so that it is difficult to draw simple or clear-cut conclusions. Germany pioneered large-scale state involvement with a network of (basic) research centres, now called Max Planck Institutes after the founder of the quantum theory. The German technical universities, also founded in the nineteenth century, have always worked closely with industry but concentrated on applied research. These institutions combined with very high standards of education and training, particularly vocational training for the non-academic sector, to produce the superior quality of manufactured goods that has maintained Germany's export success despite some of the world's highest wages and non-wage labour costs.

In contrast to Germany and Japan, much of government R&D in Britain and France has been in support of a lingering global military posture and major arms export business, much of it to developing countries, and with relatively minor commercial spin-offs. Basic R&D in most other areas has been neglected, particularly in France but increasingly so in the United Kingdom, and scientific education and training have also lagged, as the brightest students turn to more lucrative business careers.

C. The breakthrough illusion[3] and the rise of Japan

Numerous industrial R&D laboratories were established in the United States in the early decades of the twentieth century.[4] Their close links with manufacturing, often located on factory sites, were essential for their role in developing advanced products such as the automatic transmission and colour TV for mass production after World War II, and for American technological leadership in the 1950s and 1960s. However, the very success of the US system of Fordist mass production in these post-war decades contributed ultimately to the demise of what two prominent experts on business organization, Richard Florida and Martin Kenney, have called the 'follow-through economy'.

The follow-through economy

The **follow-through economy** refers to the ability to follow important new scientific or technological discoveries (breakthroughs) with development of new products for mass production at competitive prices. The breakdown of the follow-through economy in the United States began in the 1960s and 1970s, with increasing specialization and hierarchical division of labour in the R&D lab.

There were two dimensions of this apparently natural extension of Taylorist management principles from the assembly line to the production of innovation. By functional specialization, corporations sought to make R&D as standardized and predictable as possible. Professional, 'scientific' management increasingly took control of research projects, and forced scientists and engineers to communicate through formal, bureaucratic channels. Projects were moved from one specialist division to the next, on assembly-line principles, so the creative freedom of each successive group was contained by prior decisions.

The other dimension of specialization was the physical relocation of R&D labs away from older production sites and their surrounding environmental degradation, to green suburban campuses. Production was also gradually moved, first to the Sunbelt and then to low-wage, third world countries. This relocation was supposed to provide R&D scientists with a more favourable environment, far from the factory floor and more conducive to innovation. Lack of contact between white-collar R&D workers producing innovations and blue-collar workers making the firm's products was entirely in accord with Taylorist principles of specialized division of labour.

In retrospect, the disconnection of R&D from downstream activities turned out to be disastrous. Corporations responded to various emerging problems by adding new layers of management to the bureaucracies that were already stifling the creativity of fragmented, over-specialized R&D units. The application of standard financial accounting criteria, which accompanied the bureaucracy, imposed a short-term orientation on the fundamentally long-term nature of most R&D. Job-hopping and high turnover among managers and even scientists further handicapped long-term R&D projects that incurred costs currently but were expected to yield returns only after the responsible manager or researcher had moved on.

Because manufacturing divisions of US corporations were also monitored and evaluated by the same short-term financial accounting criteria, they frequently lost interest in long-term developments. Distant R&D labs often no longer even attempted to deliver much-needed incremental product or process improvements. Instead of being used in domestic manufacturing, important innovations were sometimes simply sold off to competitors such as the Japanese! As Florida and Kenney have summarised: 'The path from R&D to manufacturing became a bureaucratic nightmare of "it's not my job", "that isn't my department", and "we can't do that". It became harder to get R&D projects going, more troublesome to complete them once they were started, and exceedingly difficult to transform innovations into products' (1991, p. 26).

The breakthrough economy

The new breakthrough economy emerged from this situation to exploit profitable new technological opportunities and growth areas that bureaucratic Fordist organizations were unable to take advantage of. The increasing frustration of R&D scientists and managers encouraged small groups with promising ideas to leave large firms such as IBM and form entrepreneurial start-ups. A vital role was played by the emerging new venture capital industry, which arose precisely to fill the funding gap between conception and realization of new market products and technologies.

The venture capitalist, often a wealthy individual or a small partnership, would supply a majority of equity or risk capital for the new start-up. Based on close personal knowledge of the individuals involved, financial and managerial advice was provided by venture capitalists with seats on the board and a close, hands-on relationship to the start-up. The entrepreneurial team themselves then supplied the rest of the equity capital from personal savings or loans from family or friends.

Free from the labyrinthine bureaucracy of large corporate R&D, scientists and engineers developed interactive teamwork with intensive, informal communication at all levels in the new start-ups. Motivated by their ownership stake, peer-group pressure from team members was sufficient to elicit high levels of efforts, with little formal or hierarchical monitoring. Innovation naturally blossomed in this 'hot-house' atmosphere of the new high-technology start-ups. Most of the major breakthroughs in computer technology, semiconductors and the emerging field of biotechnology came from entrepreneurial ventures of this kind.

The most important breakthroughs have generated enormous and well-publicized capital gains for founding entrepreneurs and venture capitalists. Such 'big hits' compensate the venture capitalists for the high incidence of start-ups that never take off or fail in their first few years. When start-ups are successful and go public, shares have soared on the stock exchange, sometimes years before marketing a new product based on the original innovation, and there is then a big temptation for the founders to sell out, or move on or retire. Process innovation and production of new products generally offer much less spectacular and less rapid rewards than the breakthrough discovery itself.

In fact, for a number of reasons, the breakthrough economy, although stimulating innovation, has not halted the relative decline of US high-technology manufacturing. One problem is that the separation of R&D and production has remained or even increased, as more and more production moves to low-wage countries in Asia or Latin America. The essential interaction between R&D and the productive process that is required for continuous improvement as practised by Japanese manufacturers is thus difficult to implement.

The breakthrough economy was made possible by the high mobility of American employees, but this very mobility also imposes severe costs on the system. Departure of one or two key team members can seriously disrupt a project, or even destroy the value of past investment in R&D. With annual employee turnover rates of 30–50 per cent common in Silicon Valley, long-term development projects are jeopardized, and even the survival of small firms is at risk when their most important human capital cannot be retained.

It was cooperative teamwork that gave new start-ups such a significant innovative lead over the old corporate R&D bureaucracies. Without continuity, teamwork loses much of its efficiency. Specialization and fragmentation may return to limit the damage from defection of workers who are knowledgeable about all aspects of a project. It is thus difficult to realize the full potential of teamwork in a highly mobile society.

In addition to teamwork in the firm, the other cornerstone of Japanese organization is the production network of core company and subcontractors, both involving long-term relationships and high trust. By contrast, the extreme mobility of high-technology workers at all levels mirrors the cut-throat competition and lack of cooperation between firms in the high-technology clusters of Silicon Valley, Boston's Route 128 and elsewhere. With no continuity even among key personnel, it becomes difficult for firms to establish enduring joint ventures or subcontracting agreements that are based on high-trust, personal relationships.

Much competition in high technology consists of 'patent races' and other contests to establish priority legal rights over breakthrough discoveries. In this climate, arm's-length market exchange and formal contracts are hedged with legal safeguards to protect firm-specific information from leaking to competitors. The extensive exchange of technical know-how, customary in Japanese networks, is thus blocked.

It is true that Silicon Valley and other clusters benefit from an infrastructure of legal, financial and other services geared to the requirements of high-technology enterprise. New start-ups are thus encouraged to locate in these areas, and also benefit from the proximity of major research universities such as Stanford, which in turn supply major scientific talent and consulting services. The most successful firms in Silicon Valley do enter into strategic alliances and form joint ventures, often with Japanese companies, and have succeeded in following breakthrough with competitive production – all this in spite of hypermobility and low trust. But litigation, particularly against small and new companies for alleged theft of intellectual property, has also increased explosively. As a prominent business economist, Bennett Harrison (1994) has noted, Silicon Valley has many different faces. In spite of all the problems that affect American industrial organization, Silicon Valley has survived recession and international competition in much better shape than its former rival district, Boston's Route 128.

However, the concentration on breakthrough R&D has also encouraged a new breed of **vulture capitalists**. These entrepreneurs specialize in personnel raids, hiring key individuals away from competitors in order to get ahead in the race for some promising new breakthrough. Start-ups may be launched largely on the basis of raids of this kind, which essentially transfer people and know-how from one enterprise to another, destroying nearly as much value as they create in the process.

It is often difficult for small firms, in particular, to match a raider's offer of increased compensation to a member of a cooperative team. Other team members will demand similar rewards, or cooperation is likely to suffer, and a uniform pay rise may be unaffordable. No less damaging than raids by outside, vulture capitalists is the flood of defections of employees from established high-technology companies. Too many 'copycat' start-ups in a fashionable field may swamp the market and destroy most of the newcomers' or existing firms' viability.

Raids, defections and start-ups are all ultimately driven by the lure of rapid gains in value or high returns on capital. Human capital is of primary importance in high technology, so investment in employee training and human capital is critical when technical progress implies rapid obsolescence of existing knowledge. However, the high turnover rates and risks of defection reduce the return on investment in human capital by employers, and thus discourage the kind of continuous training programmes common in Japanese industry.

The main social costs of hypermobility in US high technology can thus be summarized as underinvestment in human resources and disruption of ongoing R&D teamwork. Extreme mobility also fosters arm's-length relations among suppliers, breach of implicit contracts whenever opportune, low trust and little informal cooperation. The proliferation of small new start-ups pursuing every imaginable technological 'holy grail' generates a few big winners and a multitude of losers, another example of the 'winner-take-all' society that is widening inequality and eroding trust in the United States and the United Kingdom (see Frank and Cook, 1996).

Even the winners generally remain remote from production, uninterested in incremental product or process in improvement. The breakthrough model of innovation has had little impact on consumer products and traditional manufacturing. The consumer electronics industry has been overwhelmed by Japanese imports, and technological leadership in basic manufacturing such as steel and automobiles has been taken over by Japanese transplants in the United States.

Neglect of manufacturing by the breakthrough economy raises even more serious problems for the near future. Contracting out production to third world countries lowers cost in the short run, but actually transfers valuable know-how in the long run. Already by 1988, South Korea had overtaken West Germany to become the third-largest producer of semiconductors, after Japan and the United States. Based in part on learning from subcontracting, South Korea is developing a major high-technology sector. Conglomerates Samsung and LG have launched large new high-tech production facilities in the United Kingdom to gain a foothold in the European Union.

As the pace of technological progress and product cycles accelerates, continuous improvement of both product and production process became critical for competitive success. An increasingly global separation of production from innovation precludes the interaction between the two that has put high technology and other Japanese manufacturing so far ahead. Interaction and communication require a skilled and empowered workforce that can contribute its own detailed knowledge of the production process to continuous innovation. Third world and even domestic high technology manufacturing has replicated the Taylorist division of labour between semi-skilled, routinized production work, and professional teamwork to produce breakthrough innovation. Until this division is overcome, and the functions of manufacturing and R&D are integrated, it seems unlikely that the problems of the breakthrough economy can be overcome.

The Japanese capture of high technology

Japan's rise to pre-eminence in many branches of advanced manufacturing has been spectacular by any standards. Commercial R&D spending and employment grew by about 15 per cent a year until the recession of the 1990s, two-thirds funded by industry, to give the highest non-military and industry-financed R&D effort of any country. One example of the results of this policy is that Japan overtook the United States in production of data-processing equipment, after starting from a world market share of less than 10 per cent as recently as 1980. Similar developments could be charted for many other high-technology products, some of which were actually pioneered and developed in the United States. Table 14.2 documents Japan's overall success in high-tech exports, compared with declining shares for the United States and European countries.

The loss of follow-through capacity in US manufacturing has been described in the previous section. The key to Japanese success has been the integration of R&D with production, in large organizations, linked into stable networks that provide economies of scale and scope and synergy without bureaucracy. The role of government has been limited but, as already indicated at various points, the Japanese system of economic organization is far removed from the free market or *laissez-faire* ideology that become increasingly popular in the United States and United Kingdom during the 1980s. Instead of universal arm's-length competition between all firms, commitment and cooperation in workteams and supplier networks are the hallmark of Japanese economic organization. Table 14.3 shows Japan's increasing domination of even European patenting, and the United Kingdom's rapid decline.

A surprising difference between the patterns of innovation in Japan and the United States is the dominance of large firms in Japan. In spite of a much larger share of production by small firms in Japan, most innovation there is produced by giant corporations. By 1988, the three companies receiving the largest number of US patents were Hitachi, Toshiba and Canon, all ahead of American leaders GE and IBM, or Siemens in Germany. These and other top Japanese innovators have maintained a wide range of consumer and commercial product lines, which are closely related to take maximum advantage of

Table 14.2 Shares of world high-technology exports (%)

Country	1970–3	1988–9
United States	29.5	20.6
Japan	7.1	16.0
Germany	16.6	12.5
United Kingdom	10.1	7.6

Source *Science and Technology Indicators*, 1966.

Table 14.3 Share of patents granted by the European Patent Office

Country	1982	1985	1988	1991
United States	27.0	27.4	26.2	25.0
Germany	23.1	21.9	21.4	20.0
Japan	12.9	15.3	18.0	22.3
France	9.6	8.6	8.5	8.6
United Kingdom	8.5	7.7	7.2	5.2
Newly industrialized economies	0.1	0.1	0.2	0.4

Source Organization for Economic Co-operation and Development, *Using Patent Data as Science and Technology Indicators, Patent Manual 1994*, Paris, 1994, Table 6.

synergy in the application of their integrated R&D efforts. Japan now seems to have added a major breakthrough capacity to a successful follow-through capability.

High-technology start-ups in the United States have been successful in specialized development projects, but are often too small and narrowly focused to take advantage of the range of ideas and discoveries that can emerge as joint products from even a very specialized and targeted R&D effort. Large Japanese corporations can utilize the full spectrum of R&D output in their diversified production. This includes achieving synergistic benefits from a single innovation in a range of products, such as video displays in Watchman TVs and laptop computers.

Economies of scale also provide advantages in systems technologies. 'Mechatronics' is a new synthesis that combines mechanical and electronic systems in FMS, industrial robots and semiconductor fabrication, and cannot be developed by specialized companies lacking any one of the component skills. As well as cross-fertilization and communication between differing but related R&D projects, cross-subsidization helps to contain set-up costs and new product lines.

At this point, the crucial question arises: how have the Japanese avoided the stranglehold of bureaucratic, Taylorist management, which destroyed the follow-through capability of so many large US and other corporations? As so often in Japan, the answer lies both in the internal organization of firms and also in the relations between the firms of a productive network.

Inside firms, decentralized management and teamwork apply to R&D as well as to production. Most importantly, the two have remained integrated in various ways. R&D facilities are usually located close to assembly plants, and R&D projects are systematically pursued in cooperation with production personnel. R&D scientists and engineers usually transfer to production after 10 or 15 years, where they help to maintain close links between the two activities. The barriers erected between innovation and production by Fordist management in the United States are excluded by the most basic principles of productive organization in Japan.

The other part of the answer to our question follows essentially from the long-term nature of links between parent and supplier companies in Japanese production networks. Parent firms concentrate on core activities, without fear of hold-up by suppliers and without the necessity of totally owning or integrating with subsidiaries. As new projects or products evolve beyond the core activities that offer most synergy in the single, parent organization, they can be spun off to form associated but independent companies. Or new spin-offs can be created with personnel exchange and financial support from the parent until independence is attained in a permanent relationship, perhaps with part ownership.

This process is driven by consensus management in the parent company. It thus represents the polar opposite to the creation of new start-ups by frustrated R&D scientists from US corporations, who can disrupt ongoing projects by quitting suddenly, with possibly irreplaceable human capital and know-how. Instead of cooperating with their parent in the United States, the new start-ups usually try to transfer customers and business away from their old employer, and in turn can expect no assistance and perhaps costly litigation or other hostile manoeuvres as they renege on implicit contracts.

By concentrating on related activities that promise synergy at some stage, Japanese corporations can dispense with the layers of bureaucracy and high manager–worker ratios that stifle large US organizations. The latter can reduce costs in the short-run by simply downsizing, but they cannot reproduce consensus management and a commitment by all employees to continuous improvement without far-reaching changes. Indeed, as discussed in Chapter 1, downsizing has eroded worker loyalty and commitment, and is being criticized by former proponents such as Stephen Roach of Morgan Stanley Bank.

Japanese R&D teams are encouraged to use company resources to develop their own ideas. If these are promising they can enlarge their budgets and staff and create an internal 'start-up', without the costs of quitting the organization. Some of the most innovative US corporations, such as Hewlett-Packard and 3M, have also encouraged internal, **intrapreneurship** of this kind with some success. Suppliers and subsidiaries in Japan have their own R&D programmes, which also concentrate on product development. About 90 per cent of total R&D resources in Japan are devoted to product development. Close personnel and organizational links with production divisions throughout the development process allow products to be designed for easy manufacture. Production delays are thus minimized, so new or improved products can be marketed more rapidly than elsewhere.

The importance of 'first-mover' advantages in marketing high-technology products puts tremendous pressures on R&D teams in Japan, as in American start-ups. **Karoshi,** or death by overwork, has become a much discussed problem in Japan, matching the burn-out of hyper-mobile R&D workers sometimes observed in the United States.

Large US companies have attempted to emulate positive features of Japanese organization by forming strategic alliances with high-technology start-ups as a way of buying into new technologies without the uncertainties of the R&D process. With no expectation of long-term cooperation in most cases, these alliances often collapse in mutual recrimination or law suits, when the larger partner has in effect appropriated the start-up's technology. Direct acquisitions of start-ups also run into all the problems of overcentralized organization already discussed, and frequently stifle creativity or lead to loss of key researchers as corporate cultures clash. The competitive strength of Japanese networks depends on several complementary factors: decentralized internal organization, permanent employment and links between suppliers that allow optimal exchange of information and personnel without risks of hold-up or expropriation.

Given these comparative national advantages and failings, it is perhaps not surprising that large, bureaucratic European and US companies seeking synergistic rather than opportunistic alliances are turning to Japanese corporations. Japanese investment in joint ventures and high-technology start-ups in the United States has been growing, partly because US breakthrough technology can often be manufactured most effectively with Japanese production expertise. Japanese high-technology manufacturing, in turn, benefits from access to important discoveries that may generate improvements and new products, or to restricted EU markets. This trend continues the Japanese tradition of learning from foreign technology and building footholds in its main markets, but now on the basis of a formidable domestic R&D capacity that did not exist in early post-war years of pure imitation.

EU and US companies have also begun to imitate important aspects of Japanese organization, and the most successful have integrated some of the key complementarities such as decentralization and long-term employment, in spite of contrary pressures in the stock market dominated UK and US environments. This process has been accelerated by the rapid development of Japanese transplants. High-technology, automated steelworks have revolutionized this traditional, US Rust-Belt industry. Japanese automobile-assembly transplants have generated hundreds of transplant and (more recently) American and British suppliers using Japanese production and JIT delivery methods. Long-term relations, teamwork, joint problem-solving and other features of Japanese production networks have been replicated in the United States and the United Kingdom, demonstrating that these modes of organization are not culturally determined, as some observers have claimed.

As transplants have grown in numbers and importance, R&D functions have followed to maintain the close links between production and innovation that are so important throughout Japanese manufacturing. US steelmaking as well as rubber and tyres have also been fundamentally restructured and transformed by the technology transplants. Early consumer electronics assembly has been followed by high-technology electronics, and basic research labs have been set up in various innovation centres to attract high-quality US researchers.

Hope for Europe?

Recognition of the problems discussed here, at least, has now swept through the European Union. With a 'domestic' market larger than the North American and a highly trained labour force, the EU is likely to reap tremendous gains from a unifying market. Strategic alliances and joint ventures are proliferating, not only across internal national boundaries but particularly with Japanese and US leaders in the high-technology sectors that have been neglected in Europe.

The rapid development of Eastern Europe, with its low-wage, highly skilled labour, offers much scope for outsourcing and applying competitive pressure on Western Europe's highly paid workers. These pressures and deep recession in the early 1990s have kept wage increases below productivity gains in Germany and other major European countries. Downsizing and outsourcing are contributing to levels of unemployment in the EU that are on average 10–12 per cent, more than twice as high as in the United States. This persistent unemployment in turn puts a break on the rises in wages and non-wage costs that have reduced the competitiveness of German industry in particular.

A particular hurdle for high-technology industry in the EU is the relative lack of cooperation between research universities and the business sector. The famous high-technology clusters centred around major universities such as Stanford or MIT in the United States have hardly appeared, except for some smaller developments such as the Cambridge Science Park in England (see Box 14.2). In this as elsewhere, there are signs of change, however, as universities begin to overcome their traditional ivory-tower isolation under pressure from selectively targeted research funding.

There have been examples of successful industry–government cooperation, as with the European Airbus, which is now closing the gap with world aerospace leader Boeing, and has pioneered innovations such as the wide-body, twin jet engine design and the two-man, all-electronic cockpit.

Perhaps the most fundamental factor predicting European companies' ability to catch up in high technology has been revealed in a major research project by the private Council on Competitiveness and the Harvard Business School. As Bennett Harrison (1994, p. 184) reports, two leading American economists, Lawrence Summers (now Under-Secretary at the Treasury) and James Poterba (of MIT), interviewed CEOs of the largest firms in the United States, Japan, Germany and Britain. These researchers found varied and striking evidence of the short-term orientation of US management, and the much longer time horizon relevant for Japanese and German companies. In the United States, much higher rates of return on investment capital are required, 12 per cent in recent years, rates that far exceed the cost of capital. Potentially valuable investment projects, particularly long-term ones, are thus regularly ejected by these high 'hurdle rates'. The lower hurdles in Germany and Japan are matched by much higher proportions of GNP going into aggregate investment in these countries.

Box 14.2 Sophia Antipolis

Science parks are rare in Europe. Cambridge University has spawned a cluster of high-tech start-ups, but the prime example is near Nice in Southern France. Here a cluster of about 1000 firms employ some 16000 people around an extension of Nice University. Since its foundation in the late 1960s, the science park called Sophia Antipolis has grown rapidly, housing researchers for most high-tech areas attempting with varying success to bridge the gap between laboratory and market place. Major companies such as Thomson, Digital or Glaxo-Wellcome are represented alongside a host of small businesses. Reflecting both the problems and hopes of European high-tech industries, the impact of the cluster has been limited so far.

(Source *Financial Times*, 2 March 1994)

Most disturbing, even the nature of R&D projects reflects the short-termism of many US companies. Only 20 per cent of R&D projects were classified as long term by the American CEOs on average, whereas over 60 per cent or twice as many were described as explicitly long term by German top managers. This proportion exceeded even the Japanese share of 47 per cent long-term R&D projects, and points to relatively increasing technical sophistication of German products in the future.

University and other basic research is still strong in Germany and other EU countries, though funding problems are severe as governments try to meet the

Table 14.4 The growth in Europe's biotechnology industry, 1995–1996

	1995		1996		Percentage change	
	Europe	USA	Europe	USA	Europe	USA
Public companies						
Revenues (ECU m.)	297	6,960	433	9,040	46	30
R&D expenses (ECU m.)	158	3,440	243	3,760	54	9
Net loss (ECU m.)	73	1,840	54	1,760	−26	−4
No. of companies	28	260	49	294	75	13
No. of employees	2,958	60,000	5,315	73,000	80	22
Industry total						
Revenues (ECU m.)	1,471	10,160	1,721	11,680	17	15
R&D expenses (ECU m.)	1,252	6,160	1,508	6,320	20	3
Net loss (ECU m.)	1,206	3,680	1,113	3,750	−8	2
No. of companies	584	1,308	716	1,287	23	−2
No. of employees	17,200	108,000	27,500	118,000	60	9

Source 'The cloning of US success', *Financial Times*, 15 May 1997, p. 21.

stringent fiscal conditions of the Maastricht Treaty. However, European basic research is second only to American, and far ahead of Japanese efforts to promote fundamental scientific knowledge. EU firms can draw on this reservoir of knowledge for commercial application, particularly if they move further towards Japanese organizational flexibility and cooperation in production, and resist pressures for short-term shareholder value maximization.

A promising example is the European biotechnology industry, which is finally beginning to grow faster than its much larger American counterpart (see Table 14.4). Whereas US biotechnology employment grew by 9 per cent between 1995 and 1996 (reaching almost 120,000), European biotechnology grew an amazing 60 per cent (to approach 30,000). Sales and R&D outlays are now also growing faster in Europe, though again from much smaller bases. Britain has as many biotechnology companies as France and Germany combined, and Europe now has 700 companies in this sector, against 1,300 in the United States (of which 294 are quoted and often much larger than their European counterparts). However, venture capital involvement, joint ventures and government support are all increasing in European countries.

D. Chapter summary and key ideas

The production of innovation has evolved into surprisingly different patterns of organization in different countries. In post-war America, once-dominant large corporations such as IBM have come under growing competitive pressure from two different directions. At home, the unrivalled university-based research centres have combined with venture capitalists and frustrated corporate scientists to stimulate a stream of dynamic new enterprises, a few of which have grown spectacularly into the Apples and Microsofts of global fame.

From abroad, Japanese technologically based exports and transplants have conquered consumer electronics and increased market shares in many other sectors. This success is all the more surprising because Japan lacks the fundamental science base that complements industrial R&D in Europe as well as the United States. Furthermore, large Japanese corporations have maintained the close links between production and R&D that were lost in the United States as Taylorist organization encompassed white-collar workers as well as the shop floor. Bureaucratic ossification and frustration seem to have been avoided, leaving neither scope nor need for entrepreneurial start-ups and venture capitalists.

Europe's fledgling high-tech industries have stagnated between these two polar extremes for organizing innovation. Germany has maintained large export shares with high-quality but relatively 'low-tech' products in traditional sectors, whose continuing success, coupled with strong risk aversion among policy makers, managers, investors and researchers, seems to have kept the newer technologies on the back burner. Britain is a major competitor in global pharmaceuticals but little else; however, low wages, an unregulated labour market and the English language have generated Europe's largest flow of inward investment including South Korean and even German high-tech manufacturing, with a Siemens chip-making facility on Tyneside.

There is no reason for European institutions and industries to attempt to duplicate either Japanese or American patterns of innovation. As usual, developing core competencies is probably the best way forward, and this route can include learning from leading competitors but retaining national specialization and organizational diversity.

Key words

break through illusion	network system
consumption complementarities	patents
consumption externalities	private returns to R&D
entrepreneurship	process innovation
follow-through economy	product innovation
intrapreneurship	social returns to R&D
karoshi	venture capitalist
Maastricht Treaty	vulture capitalist

Questions and problems for review and discussion

1 What principles should guide government policy towards fundamental scientific research?
2 Discuss the role of technological progress in explaining economic growth.
3 Why does Europe lag behind Japan and the United States in high-tech innovation and manufacture?
4 Has government policy contributed to the high tech deficit of question 3?
5 Analyze the costs and benefits of the 'breakthrough economy'.
6 Compare the production of innovation in Japan and the United States.
7 Should European countries attempt to follow or emulate the United States or Japanese organization of high tech industries?
8 Write a case-study of a European innovation that has been successfully produced and marketed.

Notes

1 See Acs *et al.* (1996) for a review of recent work on spillovers from university-based R&D.
2 Two interesting articles serve as the basis for this discussion (Beson and Farrel, 1994; Katz and Shapiro, 1994). The articles are not overly technical and are written at a level that most undergraduates should understand.
3 See Florida and Kenney (1991).
4 This followed the pioneering development of R&D labs in Germany in the 1880s and 1890s, which were complemented by state-funded basic science research institutes and close links between industry and the new technical universities.

References

Acs, Z. and D. Audretsch (1990), *Innovation and Firm Size*, Cambridge, Mass: MIT Press.

Acs, Z., F. FitzRoy and I. Smith (1996), 'High technology employment: Wages and achieving R&D spillovers', Chapter 7 in Alice Belcher *et al.* (eds), *R&D Decisions*, London: Routledge.

Beson, S. M. and J. Farrel (1994), 'Choosing how to compete: strategies and tactics in standardization', *Journal of Economic Perspectives*, 8, pp. 117–32.

Florida, R. and M. Kenney (1991), *The Breakthrough Illusion*, New York: Basic Books.

Frank, R. and P. Cook (1996), *The Winner-Take-All Society*, New York: Free Press.

Harrison, B. (1994), *Lean and Mean*, New York: Basic Books.

Katz, M. L. and C. Shapiro (1994), 'Systems competition and network effects', *Journal of Economic Perspectives*, 8, pp. 93–116.

Perutz, M. F. (1996), 'The cabinet of Dr. Haber', *New York Review of Books*, 43, 20 June, pp. 31–6.

CHAPTER **15**

Flexible production technology and organization

> Manufacturing is undergoing a revolution. The mass production model is being replaced by a version of a flexible multiproduct firm that emphasizes quality and speedy response to market conditions while utilizing technologically advanced equipment and new forms of organization. (Milgrom and Roberts, 1990, p. 511)

A. Chapter outline and student goals

In this chapter we move our analysis into the organizations of today and analyze the actions, alternatives and strategies of the successful firms that either evolved under or were born into the new business environment. We by no means want to imply that the metamorphosis of business is complete. Product and process innovations will likely continue, bringing even further changes in organizational structures. Advances on the information technology front alone will probably eclipse today's machines.

In order to survive and prosper in the new economy of the **Information Age**, firms have had to completely rethink the strategies that worked in the past. The first aspect of this strategy is to position your firm in the global market place. This complex process involves discovering not only what your organization is good at, but what it is best at. Back in the 1770s, Adam Smith, the father of modern economics, lectured on the importance of the gains from specialization.

The 'back to basics' movement asks the question, 'What are your core competencies?' A **core competency** is an area of business in which an organization has not only a competitive advantage in producing a good or service, but also a similar advantage in developing new and related products. It refers to the strength of the firm, either technological or organizational, that allows it to do one thing cheaper, better and faster than any other firm in the world, and to build that one thing into a succession of high-quality, tailored products or services. In a dynamic environment, a firm's capacity to innovate, to introduce new products quickly and to manufacture them efficiently can be even more important than economies of scale.

483

The second aspect of the strategy prevailing in today's organizations is rebuilding the factory from scratch: introducing flexible manufacturing systems, robots, computer-controlled machine tools, quality control equipment, and much more. It also involves an upgrading of the labour force from semi-skilled workers to a much more broadly educated workforce. The strength of the labour force in the Information Age lies in their firm-specific human capital being complementary to the physical capital used by their firms.

The third aspect of this strategy is restructuring the organization itself. Much modern manufacturing technology cannot be fully exploited in yesterday's hierarchical organizations. Piecemeal changes are not enough; a complete overhaul of organizations is called for. Many firms began this process (either wittingly or not) in the early 1990s. This process usually unfortunately involved a downsizing as well.

Successful organizational evolution into today's competitive environment recognizes complementarities. Two activities in an organization are said to be complementary if one activity experiences feedbacks from changes in the other activity. Marketing and manufacturing are an example of this type of relationship. A marketing strategy based on a certain degree of customization, speed of order processing and after-sales follow-up may not be supported within the organization by a manufacturing capability that allows only large batches, has substantial costs in changing for variations in product and has a high defect rate. In practice, complementarities usually extend over several activities. A collection of activities is mutually complementary if doing more of any one activity increases (or at least does not decrease) the marginal profitability of each other activity in the group.

In this chapter we present a simplified version of a theoretical model developed by two economists from Stanford University, Paul Milgrom and John Roberts, which helps answer the question: 'How should the modern manufacturing firm be organized?' Theory suggests that: (1) an organization should not, over an extended period of time, have substantial volumes of both highly flexible and highly specialized equipment being used side by side; (2) because of complementarities it is relatively unprofitable to adopt only one part of a modern manufacturing strategy when the other components have barely begun to be put into place; and (3) a flatter organization is better suited to modern manufacturing technology than a vertically integrated one.

The job of management in organizations is to ensure coordination. The survival and success of organizations is crucially dependent on achieving effective coordination of the actions of the many individuals and subgroups in the organization. Management must make sure that they are all focusing their efforts on carrying out a feasible plan of action that will promote the organization's goals, and on ensuring that the plans are adjusted appropriately to remain feasible and appropriate as circumstances change. This chapter complements our discussion of work organization in Chapter 13.

After reading this chapter, you should be able to:

- explain why organization is important;
- explain what organizational economists mean when they use the term 'corporate strategy';
- provide a brief intuitive explanation of what is meant by manufacturing strategy;
- explain what core competencies are;
- explain why complementarities in production are important, regarding their impact on various activities conducted by modern organizations.

B. The development of production technology

Advances in computer technology have not only affected the ways in which we transfer and analyze information; they have also made possible an entirely new approach to how goods are actually made. The success of this new approach is leading to changes in firms and industries as we move from mass production technologies to flexible production technologies.[1] The impact on organizations has been enormous and we devote the whole of section D to a more thorough understanding of this impact. For now, we introduce the basic terminology and concepts in a historical context.

Transfer machines

One of the major technological advances in manufacturing during the 1930s resulted in the introduction of transfer machines. **Transfer machines** consist of a number of machines or work stations, each for a separate operation such as drilling or milling, organized to work together in such a fashion that a work piece is automatically put in place at one work station, operated on there, and then transferred to the next work station, and so on. Work is performed simultaneously at all work stations, and several operations may be performed simultaneously at each work station.

After World War II there was an increased use of mechanization in mass production. The first large-scale application of automation was at the Ford engine plant in Brook Park, Ohio. Ford tied together several large stationary transfer machines into a continuous system. The system inspired a succession of improved engine plants in the United States and became known as **Detroit automation** or 'Fordism'. While the development of automation continued into the early 1970s, the most important technological progress in the past 30 years appeared in an entirely different direction – the development of numerical controls.

Numerical controls

With the advent of numerical controls in the late 1940s, the potential emerged for reversing the 150-year technological trend in machine tools favouring large-scale production. The original development in numerical controls started around 1949, when the US Air Force began to use machine tools in the aircraft industry that could produce highly complex parts that were not only more accurate than those produced by conventional methods, but also less expensive. With financial support from the government, John Parsons and the Servomechanisms Laboratory at MIT developed prototypes by 1951. The first commercial **numerically controlled** (NC) **machines** were displayed in 1955 by the national Machine Tool Builders Association.

Although the major technological inventions for NC machines occurred at the end of the 1950s, they were not commercially applied until the late 1960s. The extensive diffusion of NC machines tools did not really begin until 1975, when the Japanese introduced the microcomputer-based numerical control unit, thus enabling **computer numerical control** (CNC) to be used. At this point two developments occurred that would forever change the organization of firms. First, the programmability and therefore flexibility of CNCs increased dramatically owing to the development of more powerful computers. Secondly, cheaper and more flexible numerical controllers in combination with other changes led to mass production of CNCs, resulting in drastically reduced prices. Taken together, these two developments meant that better, more powerful CNC manufacturing systems were more readily available.

The continued evolution of new flexible technologies has brought a host of various other flexible production techniques. It should be emphasized that reference to 'flexible technology' may include any of the various forms of flexible production, whereas any specific type, such as a stand-alone NC machine tool, is clearly distinct from, say, a flexible manufacturing system (FMS).

NC machines occupy an intermediate position between transfer machines and conventional hand-operated machines. Since the 1970s, there has been an increased emphasis on manufacturing larger and faster NC machines, thereby enhancing their competitiveness vis-à-vis transfer machines.

Flexible manufacturing systems

A **flexible manufacturing system** (FMS) consists of a programmable robotics material-handling system, a tool-changing system, and a central control system. An FMS serves the same purpose as a conventional automated production system. It can be more easily reprogrammed and made compatible with computer-aided design (CAD) and computer-aided manufacturing (CAM) technologies, rendering the overall system of production substantially more flexible than transfer machines. Subsequently the cost of small-volume production of complex parts has been reduced much more than that of large-volume production of standardized products. Such systems represent an enormous advantage for **small-batch production**.

An **industrial robot** is typically composed of three components. The first is a mechanical system of grippers or some other special-purpose device, such as a welding or painting mechanism. The second element is a 'Servo-System', which precisely controls the movement and positioning of the 'arms' of the robot. Finally, a computer control system is required to coordinate and direct the robot. Industrial robots are primarily used for material handling and machine loading, as well as for specific process functions such as spot and arc welding, spraying, finishing and assembly.

Computer-aided design (CAD) technologies involve an interactive computer terminal that designs product models as well as performs modifications and tests. In particular, CAD is used in computer graphics and simulation models. Computer-aided manufacturing systems typically involve applying CAD to control and actually perform manufacturing processes. **Computer-aided manufacture** (CAM) enables the integration of systems comprised of machine tools robots and other process machinery used in manufacturing. The mean cost of a CAD/CAM system fell from $400,000 in 1980 to $250,000 in 1985. However, using a microcomputer, smaller stand-alone CAD/CAM work stations cost as little as $10,000 in 1982.

C. Modern manufacturing strategy

What is modern manufacturing strategy? This question is best addressed by putting it in the context of what it evolved from, mass production. Under mass production, the strategy was simply to get bigger, achieving economies of scale

Old economy	New economy
Sprawling plant	Small factories
Verticle integration	Subcontracting
Economies of scale	Flexibility
Hierarchical organization	Flat organization
Organization men	Entrepreneurs
Grabbing market share	Creating new markets
Mass marketing	Niche marketing
Quality	Total quality management

Figure 15.1 Comparison of organizational aspects of the old and new economies.

so as to produce a standardized product of average quality at the lowest possible price.

However the problem is not whether companies should be bigger or smaller, but how they should be organized and managed. Figure 15.1 highlights the key differences between the so-called 'old economy' and the economy that now prevails in the Information Age. In 1989, *Business Week* asked, 'Is your company too big?' Years ago when foreign businessmen visited the United States they gravitated to Detroit and Pittsburgh. Today they trek to 'Silicon Valley' and 'Route 128 Boston'. The fact is that large American companies, in contrast to their Japanese competitiors, have usually failed to maintain their international leadership. The biggest companies are often neither the most innovative or the most profitable. In most industries the largest corporations fail even to attain the average rate of return in their industry. In order to survive in the new economy, firms have to rethink their existing strategy.

The first aspect of this strategy is to position yourself in the global market place. This involves discovering not only what you are good at, but what you are the best at. The 'back to basics' movement asks the question, 'What are your core competencies?' Core competency refers to the strength of the organization, either technological or organizational, that allows it to do something cheaper, better and faster than any other firm in the world.

In order to become more competitive today, many firms are becoming more flexible. They are broadening product lines and there is a widespread increased emphasis on quality, both through frequent product improvement and new product introductions, and through reduction in defects in manufacturing.[2]

The second aspect of this strategy is rebuilding the factory from scratch. An important aspect of this strategy has been the adoption of flexible manufacturing technologies. Flexible production technology allows a firm to design products more quickly, have shorter production runs and reduce inventories. It involves the introduction of modern manufacturing equipment, robots, computer-controlled machine tools, quality control equipment, and much more. It also involves an upgrading of the labour force from semi-skilled workers to a much more broadly educated workforce. These technologies, when used together, allow the organization to run faster and leaner, thereby competing more effectively.

An important feature of the discussions in the business press about flexible manufacturing is the frequent assertion that success requires starting from scratch. In order to move towards the factory of the future it is not enough to make small adjustments at the margin. In discussing the adoption of 'computer-integrated manufacturing' (CIM), the total overhaul of the organization's strategy is needed. In other words, you have to redesign the way in which you do business.

The third aspect of modern manufacturing strategy is restructuring the organization. Much modern manufacturing technology cannot be fully exploited in yesterday's organizations. Therefore, you must not only change the production technology, but overhaul the whole organization. However, the re-engineering of organizations involves important complementarities both within manufacturing and between functions, such as marketing and engineering.

From an organizational perspective, there are four key organizational characteristics behind the modern manufacturing strategy: more product differentiation, more subcontracting, team production and skilled labour.

The emergence of more flexible technology has enabled firms to accommodate the increased demand for more differentiated products. By increasing the use of modules, and making each module available with a variety of features, firms have been able to achieve an almost infinite variety of characteristics of the final product. The key here is flexible automation: it makes it possible to serve a variety of customer needs while spreading the design costs over larger output.

Flexible production technology gives the firm the option of producing in-house or subcontracting all or some of the components. The tendency in recent years seems to have been for the original manufacturer to focus on certain key components while subcontracting others. For example, in the case of Caterpillar, there are many common components in wheel loaders, wheel tractors and compactors. With careful design, these components can be made interchangeable from a manufacturing point of view, while at the same time offering the customer a choice of options. The subcontractor may very well have on-line electronic exchange of information with the contractor, making use of the investment in design already made by the original contractor and making it possible to make design changes quickly and cheaply, and to coordinate production via just-in-time delivery systems. In effect, flexible production reduces transaction costs with subcontractors.

As discussed in previous chapters, and in contrast to Fordist mass production, the complex equipment used in flexible production requires fewer workers; however, it also requires workers with higher levels of skill. Teamwork and quality control mean that workers take control of aspects of production and make decisions. Demand for skilled workers is increasing everywhere, and the untrained have a hard time finding any kind of work.

D. The economics of flexible manufacturing

Nearly every student in every business school has been exposed to the idea of the flexible manufacturing strategy. However, this exposure has been largely informal, based on examples and gained in the absence of any rigorously derived theoretical background. By no means do we wish to downplay the importance of informal learning involving numerous examples; rather, we hope to describe a powerful theoretical framework enabling the student to sort out the important issues and how these issues interact within the realm of modern manufacturing strategy. We do point out, however, that academic learning starts in the application of known theories and considers examples as empirical evidence in support of those theories.

In this section we hope to help to correct this shortcoming in the business literature by presenting a simplified version of a complete formal model specified by Paul Milgrom and John Roberts (1990). One thing this model makes abundantly clear is that business strategies in the modern manufacturing environment address both design and innovative attributes. Their approach is a price-theoretic supply-side one involving three major elements: exogenous (outside the firm) price changes, complementarities among the production capabilities of the firm, and non-convexities in these relationships between productive capabilities.

Technological progress

We can think of technological progress as lowering the price of certain inputs for a firm. Economists have long been concerned with the effect of input price changes on the mix of inputs chosen by a firm. In Chapter 4, we presented the traditional approach to this problem. Recall the single-firm condition of productive efficiency, which said that the ratio of input marginal products to input prices must be the same for all inputs used by the firm. Consider the case of two inputs K and L, and their prices, r and w respectively. The condition is then:

$$MP_{\mathrm{K}}\,/r = MP_{\mathrm{L}}\,/\,w$$

If the price of capital were to fall, the above equality would be violated and the left-hand side would become larger than the right. Efficient firm behaviour would require the firm to use relatively more capital and less labour in order to move the single-firm condition of productive efficiency back to an equality.

For firms adopting the modern flexible manufacturing systems, the problem was much more difficult than the change of a single input price. Given the advances in technology, when several inputs had to be changed the single condition of productive efficiency could no longer be counted on to provide clear guidance. Even more importantly, technological linkages were forged between different divisions of a modern manufacturing organization. Marketing and sales are, for example, more closely tied to happenings on the shop floor to help coordinate the ordering of complex tailored products with the firm's ability to produce them.

Put another way, in the new organizational structure many effects of changing input prices caused by technological advances arise because of **complementarities**. What are complementarities? Complementarities are said to exist between groups of activities in an organization if increases in the level of one activity cause an increase in the marginal returns to the other activities.

As an example, consider a firm with separate sales, design and manufacturing divisions. Computer-aided design (CAD) equipment lowers the cost of the 'design' input to the firm. Its impact need not stop there however. Some CAD systems prepare actual computer-coded instructions that can be read by programmable flexible manufacturing systems (FMS). The CAD system and the programmable FMS are then complementary to the firm and the adoption of the CAD system lowers the cost to the firm of installing and operating a programmable FMS. The impacts need not stop there because activities in the sales divison may also be affected. Sales departments can also use the CAD packages to create drawings and provide detailed technical information to customers.

It is one thing to understand that complementary relations exist between the divisions of a firm; it is quite another to gain an understanding of what form the complementarity relations actually take. One of the major contributions of the Milgrom and Roberts model of flexible manufacturing is that these relationships are not necessarily smooth and continuous. Instead they may be characterized as exhibiting 'jumps' because of non-convexities. A **non-convexity** implies that small changes in one organizational unit can have large impacts on other divisions in the organization. These impacts may be so large as to be overwhelming.

Suppose, for example, that a firm invests in a customer ordering system using the latest information technology. It allows orders to be placed quickly and accurately, providing detailed information on just how the customer would like the company's product tailored to its needs. If the firm lacks sufficient manufacturing flexibility, the adoption of quicker customer ordering capability may not be profitable for the firm if, for example, set-up costs resulting from modifications of the base product are high in the manufacturing process. However, it may be profitable for the firm also to invest in more manufacturing flexibility. If we think of complementarities as linkages between the organizational units of the firm, then non-convexities imply that these linkages can be extremely sensitive. A small change in one unit may require major investment or reorganization elsewhere.

Towards a formal model

We begin presenting the Milgrom and Roberts model by considering a firm producing and selling a product at a single point in time. We will then move the firm through a number of time periods over which the firm receives orders for differentiated products and manufactures them. In this way we will be able to build the model of the modern manufacturing firm, starting with a simple framework with which you are probably familiar.[3] In our presentation of the model there are two kinds of variables. Decision variables are the variables that the firm chooses after weighing the appropriate design and innovative attributes effects on corporate structure. In our notation, decision variables are represented as lower-case letters. Upper-case bold-faced letters will represent functional relationships and parameters in the model. The firm's demand function is denoted $\mathbf{D}$ for example and $\mathbf{T}$ represents time. The firm cannot influence either the functional relationships or the parameters in the model.

Following along our stepwise plan to explore the Milgrom and Roberts model, we examine the firm producing at an instant in time. The firm sells the output at a price of p, and incurs a direct marginal cost of production of c. The net revenue per unit is then $(p-c)$. The number of units demanded depends on the base demand for the product, $\mathbf{D}(p,\mathbf{T})$, and a demand shrinkage factor, $\mathbf{S}(a,\mathbf{W},b)$. Base demand, $\mathbf{D}(p,\mathbf{T})$, is defined as a function of unit price and calendar time. Demand shrinkage, $\mathbf{S}(a,\mathbf{W},b)$ is a function of a, representing order receipt and processing time, $\mathbf{W}$, representing expected wait for an order to be filled, and b, delivery time.

Base demand is assumed to be decreasing in unit price and increasing in calendar time, i.e. base demand grows over time. The demand shrinkage is included to capture the importance of quickly filling customers' needs and it is assumed that demand shrinks as a result of slower ordering, longer waits for production and drawn-out delivery times. The shrinkage factor $\mathbf{S}(a,\mathbf{W},b)$ can be thought of as a fraction between 0 and 1, speedier processing of orders, production and delivery times push $\mathbf{S}(a,\mathbf{W},b)$ towards 1.

For now, we can continue to ignore fixed costs of production and write out the firm's net incremental profits as equation (15.1):

$$(p - c)\ \mathbf{D}(p,\mathbf{T})\ \mathbf{S}(a,\mathbf{W},b) \tag{15.1}$$

The importance of speed is clear from the elements of equation (15.1). A firm having faster customer ordering, processing and delivery time will have larger revenues from any variant of the product sold. These 'speed' variables, along with the direct marginal costs of production, are, in effect, chosen by the firm when the firm adopts a manufacturing system with certain capabilities. Shortly, we will consider the cost elements of the model that reflect the fact that these choices are not made for free by the organization. Before we do, however, we need to add some measures of flexibility to the model, which we do by jumping to the next period.

Equation 15.1 represents an approximation of net incremental revenues for the firm at one point in time as it produces one variant of its base product. Let us now suppose that the firm receives an order for a second variation of its base product. We will consider explicitly the costs to the firm of changing production set-up to produce the variant called for in the new order.

Producing a changed product causes the firm to incur costs related to setting up the machinery and costs related to the design of the product variant. We define d as representing the design costs asssociated with producing a new product variant and s as the costs associated with changing the manufacturing machinery to produce the product variant. In our sequential development of the model of flexible manufacturing we will consider how the expression in equation (15.1) changes when a new order is received and processed. Including these costs in our model changes the net incremental profit to:

$$(p - c) \; \mathbf{D}(p,\mathbf{T}) \; \mathbf{S}(a,\mathbf{W},b) - (d + s) \qquad (15.2)$$

Essentially what we have done is take the earlier measure of net incremental profit and subtract away additional design and manufacturing costs, which appear as additional variable costs (i.e. they change as output changes).

At this point in developing our model of flexible manufacturing we need to consider the planning horizon of the firm. We will assume that the firm's planning horizon is sufficiently long so that many variations on the basic product are ordered and produced.[4] The number of product variations in the firm's planning horizon is denoted by n, which affects the structure of our model in several ways.

First, n should be included in our base demand function $\mathbf{D}$, which would become $\mathbf{D}(p,\mathbf{T},n)$. Base product demand is increasing in n, implying that customers are attracted, and demand increased, if a firm is known to be more flexible. Secondly, because our firm plans over several product variants and the expression in equation (15.2) deals with one product variation, we need to multiply this expression for a single product variant by the number of product variants over the firm's planning horizon. Thirdly, n will affect the expected wait for an order to be processed; basically, other things being equal, the larger n (the more product variants) the greater the wait for an order to be processed. Then the function $\mathbf{W}$ is rewritten as $\mathbf{W}(n)$. The effects of n on the firm's revenues over its planning horizon are somewhat offsetting. Revenues increase in n because of increased base demand and more production runs. Revenues decrease in n because the more set-ups the firm expects the longer the expected wait for an order to be processed.

The number of product variations also affects the variable cost structure of the firm because designing and manufacturing each product variant involves extra costs. According to our notation, each product variant costs d to design and s to actually produce, so n product variants will cost the firm $n \, (d + s)$.

The net incremental profit over the firm's planning horizon is then given by:

$$[(p - c) \; n] \; \mathbf{D}(p,\mathbf{T},n) \; \mathbf{S}[a,\mathbf{W}(n),b] - [n \, (d + s)] \qquad (15.3)$$

Considering the progression from equation (15.2) to equation (15.3), we can see the effects on net incremental profit of n as offsetting. As explained earlier, n can either increase or decrease firm revenues; additionally, n adds costs. The ultimate effect of the number of product variants on net incremental profit depends on the relative sizes of the effects of n on $\mathbf{D}$, $\mathbf{W}$ and the sizes of d and s.

One important aspect of the net incremental profit expression of equation (15.3) is the presence of complementarities. A clear connection exists between the marketing functions of the firm, the manufacturing functions of the firm and the design functions of the firm. Ordering and delivery speed directly affect revenues and are connected to both design activities (which cost d) and manufacturing activities.

The full effects of the integration of the different activities of the firm are illustrated when we add capital, or fixed, costs to the model. The fixed costs arise as the firm chooses from available technologies to be used in each division in pursuing its productive activities. It is within the fixed costs where the lower prices of the technological inputs implicitly appear. We consider the fixed costs to be determined by the firm's choice of its decision variables and time (T) rather than explicitly including the 'amount' of the inputs times their prices.

Our expression for capital costs is $K(c,a,b,s,d,n,T)$. Lower values for c, a, b, s and d raise capital costs. Thus the desirable traits of lower direct marginal costs of production – speedier ordering and delivery, smaller manufacturing set-up and design set-up costs – impose increased capital costs on the firm. Because capital costs increase in the number of product variants that the firm plans on producing, flexibility may be expensive. Finally, as time passes, technological advances will tend to decrease capital costs as new innovations are available for use as inputs by the firm.[5]

As an example of the relationship between capital costs and decision variables consider the following. A firm installs a computerized system allowing customers to place orders directly with little assistance from sales or marketing personnel; this system could transmit information directly to the factory or shop floor. The costs of installing such a system are capital costs. In our model it would allow the firm to enjoy lower values for a and s while increasing capital costs. CAD-CAM technologies have a similiar effect since they develop and exploit complementarities between design and manufacturing. Their adoption would raise capital costs, K, and lower s, c and d.

The total profit expression for the modern manufacturing firm is then seen to be:

$$[(p - c)\ n]\ \mathbf{D}(p,\mathbf{T},n)\ \mathbf{S}[a,\mathbf{W}(n),b] - [n\ (d + s)] - \mathbf{K}(c,a,b,s,d,n,\mathbf{T})\ (15.4)$$

There are two striking differences between this type of model and the one traditionally considered in economics. First, complementarities are explicitly included, affecting revenues, variable costs and fixed costs. In traditional economic analysis, fixed costs are created by resources devoted to organization, advertising, marketing and product design. This is not the case here. Secondly, fixed costs are jointly determined along with a firm's output decision. In the traditional model, fixed costs are largely ignored: for the perfectly competitive firm considered in Chapter 3, fixed costs play no role in determining the level of firm output.

Strategy is directly built into the model. We can use this model to identify and analyze many aspects of the trade-offs involved in the organization's choice of manufacturing strategy. The flexibility of design technology is modelled by

Box 15.1 Dictionary of model terms

Decision or choice variables:
- p unit price
- c direct marginal costs of production
- a order receipt and processing time
- b delivery time
- s set-up costs for manufacturing
- e design costs of set-ups
- n number of product variations

Parameters and functional forms:
- **D**   base demand for product a function of unit price and time
- **T**   a measure of calendar time
- **S**   demand shrinkage factor, based on time for order recipt, processing and delivery
- **W**   expected wait for a processed order to be filled

the variable d. The introduction of CAD technology in the design function of the firm lowers d, but may also put pressures on other aspects of the firm's operations such as sales and delivery, modelled by the variables a and b.

The flexibility of manufacturing equipment impacts the formation of a business strategy, some aspects of which are represented in the model. First, flexibility is often associated with low costs of routinely changing over from producing one good to another. Here, this effect is represented through lower values for the variable s. However, adopting such flexibility might involve costs of changing machinery over to produce new or redesigned products, thereby lowering the value of d.

The reader has probably already noticed that we say nothing about the effect of labour relations in this model. We point out, however, that an element of flexibility in modern manufacturing is associated with broadly trained workers and work rules that facilitate frequent changes in activities. In this context we may interpret investments in flexibility in terms of worker education and in industrial relations efforts, as well as in purchases of physical capital. In this environment, flexibility in employees is complementary with flexibility in capital equipment. This discussion is in fact complemented by Chapter 13, which focuses on the human resources aspects of work organization.

Obtaining a solution for this model is quite difficult, involving quite advanced mathematical techniques. Calculus-based constrained optimization techniques cannot be applied because of the non-convexities in the complementary relationships between the activities of the various functional areas, or divisions, of the organization. However, important insights that are in accordance with recent behaviour by a variety of business organizations are contained in the solution. Thus, we can draw useful conclusions from the specified solution of the model of flexible manufacturing.

The model predicts that technological advances over time will cause a number of changes in organizations as they adopt numerous process innovations embodying advances in information technology. Because of the complementarities present in production, we would expect to see organizational changes reflect linkages between various areas of function within firms. In particular, the formal solution obtained by Milgrom and Roberts is consistent with:

- lower prices of output and marginal costs of production,
- more frequent product redesigns and improvements,
- higher quality in production and fewer defects in final products,
- widespread use of information technology, enabling customers to place detailed orders,
- smaller production batch sizes, caused by more frequent set-ups in manufacturing and lower inventory levels,
- smaller costs associated with product redesigns.

Although these characteristics of the solution to the model are interesting and useful in understanding organizational behaviour, the model is even more useful for what it implies about organizational evolution. Specifically, it suggests that, even if environmental changes occur gradually, the adoption of new technologies will be more erratic for two reasons.

First, the operating divisions are affected by complementarities. The theory suggests that we should not see an extended period of time during which one component of the firm's strategy is in place and the other components have barely begun to be put into place.

Secondly, the complementarities discussed above are quite possibly governed by non-convexities. Facing the problem of obtaining the optimal organizational structure, managers realize that the optimal solution may be discontinuous. This result means that it is unprofitable to be stuck with a mixture of highly dedicated and highly flexible production equipment. Explicitly, Milgrom and Roberts' theoretical model suggests that it will be unprofitable to operate with substantial volumes of both highly flexible and highly specialized equipment side by side.

 ## E. Vertical governance structures

The role of transaction costs

Many economists have studied the role of transaction cost considerations in forming agreements between economic agents. The initial groundwork was laid by the Nobel Prize-winning economist Ronald Coase in his 1937 paper. Coase introduced the idea of **transaction costs** and argued that efficiency would dictate that contractual arrangements would be crafted in ways to minimize them. According to the Coasian logic, individuals and organizations would choose a contractual format, termed a 'governance structure', from a wide variety of possibilities.

At one extreme, transactions could take place within a 'market'. This extreme is the realm of most traditional theoretical economic analysis and was summarized in Chapters 2, 3 and 4 of this book. In this ultra-competitive world there is perfect information, lots of competition and little, if any, room for opportunism. At the other extreme is the possibility that transactions could occur entirely within an organization. If the transaction costs were too high in terms of informational asymmetries, selection problems or asset specificity, then, in some dimensions, organizations could be self-sufficient.

One of the major topics considered in Chapter 6 of this book was the role of transaction costs in the 'make-or-buy' decision of firms. The back to basics approach being taken by many businesses today usually involves the innovative and design attributes in the make-or-buy decision. As an organization focuses its efforts more and more on what it perceives to be its core competencies, it must craft agreements for other organizations to conduct necessary, but ancillary, functions.

The large, mass-producing firms that dominated manufacturing earlier in the twentieth century had a highly vertically integrated structure out of necessity. Mass producers had to exploit economies of scale extensively because of the massive fixed investments required. This made stability in input and output markets a primary concern to the mass producer. The presence of transaction costs in many of the exchanges required to run the machinery of mass production directly threatened this stability. The easiest, and most efficient, solution was ownership and a corporate governance structure emerged that featured a high degree of vertical integration.

Markets and hierarchies

In the 1970s, some economists began to conclude that the mass production system in place in the United States was soon to be tested by more efficient organizational patterns being observed in other countries. This led to the exploration of alternative theories of the firm. One of these perspectives of firm behaviour was based on transaction cost analysis. This train of thought was picked up by Oliver Williamson in his 1975 work, *Markets and Hierarchies*. Williamson follows a 'comparative institutional' perspective in which there is a wide range of institutional arrangements that can be used to govern transactions between economic agents. Governance structures emerge in response to various transactional considerations.

According to Williamson's view, the boundary between a firm and a market provides a very rough distinction between the two primary institutional arrangements used by economic agents seeking to promote efficiency in defining the relationships between them. One type is the spot market transaction, where buyer and seller come together at one point in time and exchange. A second alternative is for buyer and seller to craft their relationship with a complex long-term contract. For any given transaction, the chosen governance structure could be either of these two extremes, or lie somewhere in the middle.

Of all the different sources of transaction costs, asset specificity has the clearest implications for the form of governance structure chosen by firms. When specialized assets are required, spot market transactions can be ruled out. The reasoning relies on expectations of opportunistic behaviour and on investments in bargaining position that are inefficient. Investment by firms is seen as creating, at most, a stream of economic rents, and, at least, a stream of quasi-rents. The threat that these rents and quasi-rents may be appropriated by other parties will lead to investment at less than the efficient level (the level that would occur in the absence of any transaction costs). Making a relationship-specific investment transfers an *ex ante* situation that may be competitive into an *ex post* bargaining situation that is not competitive and is, in fact a bilateral monopoly.

This leaves two forms of governance structure to consider: ownership and long-term relational contracting, as described in Chapter 7. In an environment where technologies are rapidly changing, resulting in lower capital (fixed) costs of firms, demand for customized products is growing and competition in quality is forcing firms to focus on their core competencies, ownership will not provide what is necessary for organizations to organize economic activity efficiently. By its very nature, investment in new technology is a risky proposition for firms.

Uncertainties exist as to the applicability of the equipment; further, firms have reason to fear an even better application of technology being introduced that will make their recent investment unable to compete in terms of quality and cost. In this the Information Age, capital costs are far less of a barrier to entry than they were in the past. In fact, several studies have found that capital costs are less of a barrier to entry than advertising (Acs and Audretsch, 1990, Chapter 5). Thus, not only is it possible that an innovation will take place that eliminates your cost advantage; a competitor will likely be able to afford the innovation. In a sense, the same factors that raise the costs of ownership encourage the use of long-term relational contracts.

Any long-term relational contract must accomplish two things. First, it must maintain a degree of trust in the contractual relationship. Second, it must preserve individual and joint incentives. This is possible given the nature of flexible manufacturing technology, which, by its nature, represents a far less specific, or specialized, investment and also a smaller capital outlay. In terms of the contracting theory presented in Chapter 7, there is less fear that the stream of economic and quasi-rents generated by the act of investing will be appropriated via some form of *ex post* contractual opportunism.

The make-or-buy decision

These forces will affect both the firm hiring an outside supplier to produce a component and the outside supplier itself. The changing technologies and resultant emergence of the flexible manufacturing strategy then work to eliminate at least some, if not most, of the transaction costs associated with investing in specific assets. Given that markets are demanding high-quality, specialized goods, firms are able to concentrate on their own area of expertise in production, farming out the production of components to subcontractors or outside suppliers. The mechanics behind the make-or-buy decision have changed, and efficiency dictates that more firms pursue the buy option.

Box 15.2 Make or buy

The next manufacturing revolution is under way, and companies are bringing airplanes, cars, even kitchen stoves to market faster and cheaper by leaning on their suppliers to help engineer and bankroll new products.

This revolution goes far beyond the changes of the 1980s, when manufacturers attacked their high labour costs by shifting production to suppliers with lower labour costs. New manufacturers are slashing product-development expenses by farming out the tasks to suppliers – in essence, evolving from manufacturers to orchestrators that harmonize their suppliers' work.

Meanwhile, the suppliers, which once did little more than bang out parts as cheaply as possible, are hiring hundreds of engineers to staff new research and development departments.

Using the new approach, Whirlpool Corp. is cooking up its first gas range without hiring engineers to create the gas burner system; instead, the design work is being done by Eaton Corporation, a supplier that already makes gas valves and regulators for other appliance manufacturers. Whirlpool expects to get its new range to market several months sooner this way.

At Chrysler Corp., skilful use of parts suppliers to design everything from car seats to drive shafts has enabled it to spend consistently less money than its competitors do to develop new vehicles. It is a key factor behind the auto makers's strong comeback in the past three years.

(Source 'Manufacturers use suppliers to help them develop new products', *Wall Street Journal,* 19 December 1994, p. 1.)

The implications for organization structure are fairly clear and general at this point in our discussion and consistent with what is observed in successful, flexible firms today. Firms will concentrate on their core competencies. Where cost or quality disadvantages exist, outside suppliers will be asked to provide inputs or components. In such an organization there must necessarily be a centralized managerial effort whose primary task is (after identification of core competencies) to coordinate the activities of the firm with the activities, expertise and abilities of its outside suppliers.

In mass production industries, while they were vertically integrated, the decision of centralized versus decentralized decision-making was a decision variable. Some firms were more centralized than others. With flexible manufacturing technologies, however, the modern firm must be controlled from the centre, in order to coordinate its internal and external activities.

In Chapter 16 we take this line of reasoning to the next logical level, focusing on the formation of strategic alliances. As organizations in the advanced industrial economies moved from primarily mass production to the flexible manufacturing strategy with less vertical governance, the boundaries between firms became increasingly blurred. As we consider a number of relational contracts between firms in the next chapter, the boundaries between firms will become increasingly blurred once again.

F. Chapter summary and key ideas

This chapter has analyzed the strategies that modern manufacturing firms pursue to compete effectively in a global market place. Strategic planning by organizations is a complex process asking a simple question: 'How should resources be allocated and organized within a firm?' Organizational strategy is a blueprint for accomplishing an efficient allocation of corporate resources.

There are certain elements of coherence or fit evident in a good strategy. One common element is sharing information. Only when information is spread across the organization and all parties share a common view of the organization's goals can successful strategic planning be conducted. These elements make it important to coordinate the actions of various parts of the organization closely through some centralized structure. The three inputs into organizational design are: economies of scale, economies of scope and core competencies.

Modern manufacturing strategy involves the firm rethinking its existing strategy in order to survive in the new economy. The first aspect of this strategy is to position yourself in the global market place. The second aspect of this strategy is rebuilding the factory from scratch. The third aspect of modern manufacturing strategy is restructuring the organization. Much modern manufacturing technology cannot be fully exploited in yesterday's organizations. From an organizational perspective there are four key organizational characteristics behind the modern manufacturing strategy: product differentiation, subcontracting, team production and skilled labour.

This strategy is necessary because technological progress lowers input prices to the firm. However, the lowering of several prices across different divisions of the firm no longer gives clear indications of what strategies to pursue. In the new organizational structure, there are many effects of changing input prices because of complementarities. These complementarities exist between groups of activities if increases in the level of one activity cause an increase in the marginal returns to other activities.

It is one thing to understand that complementarities exist; it is another to gain an understanding of what form they will actually take. These relationships are not necessarily smooth and continuous. Non-convexities imply discontinuities, so that even small changes in one organizational unit can have large impacts on other activities or divisions in the organization. Modern manufacturing strategy implies that we should not see extended periods of time when one component of the firm's strategy is in place and the other components have barely begun to be put in place. One implication is that it is unprofitable to be stuck with a mixture of dedicated and non-dedicated equipment. Another implication of the model is that firms will rely less on vertical relationships than in the past.

Key words

complementarities	Information Age
computer-aided design	innovation
computer-aided manufacture	internal coordination
computer numerical control	manufacturing strategy
core competency	non-convexity
design decisions	numerically controlled
Detroit automation	machine
economies of scale	organizational strategy
economies of scope	restructuring
flexible manufacturing	small-batch production
system	transaction costs
imperfect information	transfer machines
industrial robot	

Questions and problems for review and discussion

1 (a) In your own words, describe what economists mean by the term complementarities as applied to production. Give an example in line with your description.

   (b) In your own words, describe what economists mean by the term core competency. Give an example in line with your description.

2 Consider equation 15.1. Describe each of the following pieces of the equation appearing below as fully as you can.

   (a) $(p{-}c)$

   (b) $D(p, T)$

   (c) $S(a, W, b)$

   Questions 3 and 4 refer to equation 15.3 which shows the flexible manufacturing firm's net incremental profit function over the planning horizon as:

$$[(p{-}c)n] \; D(p,T,n) \; S[a,W(n),b] - [n(d{+}s)]$$

3 One of the most important features of the flexible   manufacturing systems is that the process by which firms organize economic activity is characterized by non-convexities.

   (a) In your own words, define the term non-convexities as used in this context.

   (b) Explain the relationship between the two concepts of non-convexities and complementarities. In your explanation adopt the framework that the former describes the latter.

   (c) Explain, using the two terms above, why it is maintained by organizational economists that in order to operationalize the flexible manfacturing system, the entire organization must be re-created.

4 (a) Explain what the expected customer wait function, W, is and its relationship to n.

   (b) The first additive term in the firm's net incremental profit function (everything except $n \times (d{+}e)$) is an expression for net revenue. Explain what happens in terms of direct changes to this net revenue expression if the following occur:

      i.   an increase in p.

      ii. an increase in n.

      iii. a decrease in a.

5 Considering the entire expression for net incremental profits, what will happen if n is increased? In your explanation identify each separate effect on the equation and all its components of an increase in n.

6 One of the findings of the flexible manufacturing model presented in

Chapter 15 is its prediction that firms adopting flexible technologies will have less formal vertical governance.

(a) What is vertical governance?

(b) Why is it a prediction of the material in Chapter 15 that firms will have less formal vertical governance?

7 There are two firms making similar products and competing in some output market. The first employs a flexible manufacturing strategy while the second relies on a more traditional production technology. In which firm would we expect to see a more centralized management structure? Explain why.

Notes

1 This section is adapted from Acs and Audretsch (1990).

2 Total quality management, which many people associate with Japan, was invented in Bell Labs in the 1920s and became central to American war production. (The occupying Americans taught it to the Japanese in the 1940s, who then retaught it to their teachers in the 1970s.)

3 It is only fair to point out that the presentation here is much simpler than that advanced by Milgrom and Roberts (1990). However, we maintain the essential components. The actual Milgrom and Roberts model is quite abstract and involves mathematical techniques beyond the calculus-based techniques usually used in economic analysis.

4 We make two major simplifications of the Milgrom and Roberts model in this step. First we assume that the number of different product variants produced equals the number of set-ups done by the firm. Additionally we simplify by assuming that the number of set-ups equals the expected number of improvements per product. This simplification is consistent with our second assumption, which is that the firm does not hold inventory, selling all that is produced.

5 A number of extensions to this basic model suggest themselves. Milgrom and Roberts include a variable depicting wastage costs per set-up, and allow for inventory accumulation. Also interesting would be the representation of a firm's ability to raise capital to buy the newer technologies. Empirical results in this area are mixed. A truly complete model would explicitly consider the labour dimension in flexible manufacturing. This would prove tremendously difficult as it would involve a statement of the relationship between labour input, new technologies, and output.

References

Acs, Z. J., and D. B. Audretsch (1990), *Innovation and Firm Size*, Cambridge, Mass.: The MIT Press.

Business Week (1989), 'Is your company too big?' 27 March, pp. 46–53.

Coase, R. (1937), 'The nature of the firm', *Economica*, 4, pp. 386–405.

Milgrom, J. and P. Roberts (1990), 'The economics of modern manufacturing: Technology, strategy, and organization', *American Economic Review*, 80, pp. 511–28.

Williamson, O. (1975), *Markets and Hierarchies: Analysis and Antitrust Implications*, New York: Free Press.

CHAPTER

The economics of strategy

[T]he core corporation is no longer a 'big' business, but neither is it merely a collection of smaller ones. Rather, it is an enterprise web. Its center provides strategic insight and binds the threads together. Yet points on the web often have sufficient autonomy to create profitable connections to other webs. There is no 'inside' or 'outside' the corporation, but only different distances from its strategic center. (Reich, 1992, pp. 95–6)

In the short run, a company's competitiveness derives from the price performance attributes of current products. But the survivors of the first wave of global competition, Western and Japanese alike, are all converging on similar and formidable standards for product cost and quality – minimum hurdles for continued competition, but less and less important as sources of differential advantage. In the long run, competitiveness derives from an ability to build, at lower cost and more speedily than competitors, the core competencies that spawn unanticipated products. The real sources of advantage are to be found in management's ability to consolidate corporatewide technologies and production skills into competencies that empower individual businesses to adapt quickly to changing opportunities. (Prahalad and Hamel, 1990, p. 81)

A. Chapter outline and student goals

If we put the study of corporate organization into a historical perspective we have to conclude that change is the only constant: organizations change when their environments and the technologies they use change. Furthermore, as firms accumulate information and experience about what kinds of organizations work best for particular tasks, the speed of change quickens. During the nineteenth century, the key environmental changes were the development of unified national markets linked by rail transport and the concurrent development of technologies necessary to engage in large-scale production. The much-heralded mass production system was developed first and furthest in the United States, and thrived on the inherent stability provided in the period after World War II in the input and output markets. Highly vertically integrated

505

firms came to dominate the world economy, owing much of their competitive advantage to economies of scale and scope.

The situation remained well in hand until the mid-1970s when the need for most organizations to change became apparent. The formation of the Organization of Petroleum Exporting Countries (Opec) raised crude oil prices by about 400 per cent. On the output side, many Western mass producers found great difficulty competing with emerging Japanese competitors who benefited from technological advances. Not only were the new technologies cheaper, resulting in a smaller minimum efficient scale of operations; the new technologies were also more flexible in tailoring products more closely towards individual customer needs.

The most successful corporations that are evolving today are usually quite different from those that preceded them 25 or 30 years ago. Whereas the older firms focussed on a strategy that exploited economies of scale and scope, the newer firms emphasize cost advantages from using flexible production technologies. The high degree of **vertical integration** has also, by and large, lost importance as the premier way to organize economic activity. The winners in today's economy are quite often flatter and more reliant on outsiders.

All of this is to say that corporate strategies are undergoing a tremendous metamorphosis. A successful **corporate strategy** will address four key overlapping and complementary areas: the boundaries of the firm, the competiveness of the market, a determination of the firm's competitive advantage, and the way in which the firm chooses to organize its productive resources. None of these areas can be considered in isolation from the others; or, put another way, a successful firm will have found the 'right' answer to questions in each of these four areas. We can, however, focus most of our attention in this chapter on the last of these four areas, dealing with the others in turn.

Perhaps the most important change in the business environment today concerns the rise of an alternative governance (or organizational) structure: the strategic alliance. Strategic alliances include equity purchases, licensing and marketing agreements, research contracts, and joint ventures. Quite often a corporation is involved in a series of these strategic alliances. Famous examples of strategic alliances and production networks are the supplier relations of the Japanese automobile firms and other manufacturers.

Strategic alliances allow participants to enjoy the benefits of both vertical integration and market transactions. This type of governance structure may also encourage economic efficiency because it allows participants to specialize in the area(s) in which their competitive advantage lies.

After reading this chapter you should be able to:

- list the four areas that a corporate strategy must address and understand the complementary relationship between each of the areas;
- understand that setting corporate strategy requires consideration of problems involving design and innovative attributes;
- explain what economies of scale and scope are and their importance as strategic tools;
- understand the importance of determining an organization's core competency;
- appreciate that corporate strategy involves choosing the appropriate governance structure to organize economic activity;
- explain what a strategic alliance is, understanding it as a hybrid between market exchange and integrated hierarchies;
- explain how, in many industries, economic activity represents a web linking customers, suppliers and competitors.

B. Internationalization, organization and competitiveness

Change in Eastern Europe, 1995

On 9 November 1989, the Berlin Wall collapsed and, for the first time in nearly a half a century, Eastern Europe would feel the winds of economic competition.[1] Not only would these formerly communist nations be competing with what used to be West Germany, they would be forced to go head to head with the United States, Japan, the four tigers of Asia, and the whole developing world. Almost overnight they had to contend with a system of world prices for almost every known commodity from oil to bananas; prices that were largely absent in their former economic systems.

Under communist rule, the strategies of these nationalized companies were somewhat similar to the strategies adopted earlier by the large mass-producing firms in Western Europe, the United States and the United Kingdom. Their purpose was simple: take advantage of economies of scale. A deep underlying adherence to the principle that there are significant economies to be reaped from large-scale production was embedded in the socialist world. Large units of production were viewed as the most efficient means for transforming inputs into outputs, and any deviation from mass production was viewed socially and politically as a wasteful use of resources. However, drastic environmental changes occurred. These changes are best highlighted by Johnson, Kotchen and Loveman (1995): p.53

Imagine a large, vertically integrated company with no marketing or sales department and no distribution channels. Suppose that for decades this company was
so insulated from competition that it was able to survive with products of poor
quality and outdated, inefficient production systems. Imagine that it grew bloated
with excess employees and was heavily weighted down with debt. Such a company, confronting competition from around the globe, is a company with tremendous challenges. Add to its list of infirmities limited access to new capital,
ambiguous enterprise governance, and an unfamiliarity with competitive markets, and you have summed up the circumstances facing most large state enterprises in postcommunist countries. Although large Western companies have faced
difficult conditions when deregulation or new competition has forced dramatic
change, many have had the protection of considerable market power and few
have been afflicted with such a daunting list of serious problems.

The economies of Eastern Europe face great problems in moving to a more
market-oriented system. They need to redraft laws to allow for new forms of
economic organization. They must determine property rights and decide who
will be allowed to own the currently state-owned enterprises. They have to find
managers to run their enterprises. They must decide on competition and regulation policies.

A tale of two shipyards

During Poland's communist era, the national shipbuilding industry was dominated by six shipyards.[2] The market served by the Polish shipyards was not
completely determined by competitive forces, but rather by political ones. The
Polish shipyards' major customers were Eastern bloc countries, particularly the
former Soviet Union. The government's influence in shipbuilding operations
was pervasive. The incentives faced by the communist managers at the Polish
shipyards led them to be far more concerned with size and versatility than
with product focus or cost control. By producing a variety of ships, they were
unable to develop world-class expertise or world-class manufacturing efficiency
in any one particular model.

As a result of the collapse of the Soviet Union, government funding was withdrawn from state-owned enterprises throughout the region, and East European
shipping companies could no longer afford to buy ships produced in the Polish
yards. By 1990, the shipyards' primary client, the Soviet Union, was in a state
of economic disarray. The central government was bankrupt and the country
had been transformed into a conglomeration of republics. The disappearance
of the Soviet market resulted in the demise of Comecon, perhaps the largest
of Poland's six shipyards, and wrenching output declines and staggering financial setbacks at Gdansk and Szchecin, two of Poland larger shipyards.

The responses to this changing environment by the managers of the Gdansk
and Szchecin shipyards were quite different. We briefly consider each below,
because important lessons on managing economic organizations in the mod-

ern world economy can be gained by considering their responses to a changing environment.

The Gdansk shipyard

Supported by government subsidies and Soviet clients, the 146 acre Lenin shipyard was a self-contained industrial city in the 1970s. With a workforce of 17,000, the yard produced over 30 ships a year. Its product portfolio was extraordinarily diverse. Not only did the yard assemble ships, it manufactured almost all internal components and even served as a supplier of diesel engines and boilers to other Polish shipyards. In other words, there was very little business available in terms of outside suppliers; the highly vertically integrated structure encouraged by government pretty much precluded their existence.

In 1990, the Polish government and the Ministry of Industry recommended the privatization of the shipyard. The management continued to pursue a high-wage, high-employment managerial policy very similar to that used in the 1970s. The new management was reluctant to make rapid reductions in the size of the shipbuilding operation. Moreover the management focused on a strategy of increasing revenues instead of profits. This was because of the size of the facility. Fixed costs played a more important role than variable costs. So by simply producing more ships – that is, by increasing revenues – management would be able to spread the fixed cost over a larger production base, which would naturally increase the profitability of each project.

Since the plant was operating at less than full capacity, the goal was to build more ships. This idea was in line with management's reluctance to release labour. The high wages paid to workers were justified on the grounds that the work was demanding. The shipyard continued to operate a vast infrastructure of workers' amenities including hotels, health spas, day care services and a sports club.

The Gdansk management team argued that ship building belonged within the realm of government rather than in the uncompromising world of a free market, calling for a continuance of the government financial support it received during the communist era. The shipyard had contracts for ships ordered by the former Soviet Union; the ships were built but never delivered because of the collapse of the Soviet economy. Gdansk management argued that the government should provide unlimited loans to cover the expenses incurred in building the ships, even without a buyer. Moreover, they could not understand why the shipyard's main government contact had become the Ministry of Privatization and not the Ministry of Industry.

The Gdansk management team believed that their shipyard would be unable to find investors. In sum, the new strategy for profitability was a complete product line, a focus on economies of scale and government support. The only problem with this strategy was that, though it had worked before, it was not consistent with the new environment facing the shipyard.

The Szchecin shipyard

Events at the Szchecin shipyard closely mirrored those at the Gdansk ship-yard prior to the introduction of economic reforms in Poland. However, the restructuring strategy pursued by management resulted in fundamental dif-ferences in operations and performance. Management pursued a strategy of reducing the company's massive debt and streamlining the yard's wasteful pro-duction operation by allowing the yard to pursue its core competency in con-tainer ships.

While trying to reduce debt, the company started to implement a sweeping change in production operations. The shipyard would try to become interna-tionally competitive by de-emphasizing its portfolio of products, minimizing production cycle time, restructuring wages, and shifting markets from the East to the West. Management felt that it was important to develop a product niche and focused all production capacity on container ships.

This proved to be a wise choice. By 1993 almost all of the orders coming in to Szchecin shipyard were for container ships. Once the product focus was set, management turned its attention to reducing the time required to build a single vessel. This strategy served two purposes. First, by reducing cycle time, the firm would have to borrow less money for shorter periods. Secondly, shorter production cycles would attract customers who needed ships to be delivered quickly, a growing population in the competitive market place. By restructur-ing the labour force they were able to cut production time to less than a year.

A key component of management's strategy to reduce cycle time was the overhaul of the shipyard's compensation system. A form of internal labour market and teamwork was set up. Management assigned each shipyard worker to a professional qualification category that reflected occupational training and total years of work experience. An hourly wage was then assigned to employ-ees in each qualification category, with higher wages being allocated to more highly qualified workers. Employees could advance to higher qualification classes by passing a series of occupational exams. All workers were required to work 8 hours per day, and no overtime was permitted.

The shipyard's production workers were divided into workers' brigades, each of which was directed by a foreman and assigned specific tasks by shipyard management. Each job was carefully analyzed and a fixed number of hours were assigned. Workers' brigades were expected to complete their assignments within the time-frame established by the engineering department. Tasks not finished in this specified time-frame were completed in the worker's own time.

Besides restructuring its labour force, the Szchecin shipyard directed its mar-keting efforts westward, where there was a larger demand for container ships. By focusing on a single type of ship rather than on several types, the firm reaped gains from specialization and became even more efficient because of its larger experience base. In effect, the Szchecin shipyard management chose to concentrate on building on what it identified as its core competency, con-tainer ships. Additionally, the shipyard cut non-production costs.

Gdansk and Szchecin embarked on the difficult path of restructuring with very different management strategies. The degree to which a restructured state-owned company can compete effectively in fiercely competitive international markets is perhaps the most important indicator of the success of its restructuring programme. By 1993 Szchecin shipyard had emerged as Poland's most successful shipbuilder. The success can be attributed to the firm's competitive advantage: container ship expertise, an extraordinarily rapid production cycle, and the relatively low cost of Polish labour.

C. The role of management in coordinating strategy

Four complementary areas

The study of organization is not about how boxes are arranged on a tree of authority, but about how people and other resources are coordinated and motivated to get things done. The course of events at the two Polish shipyards considered in the previous section makes this point quite clearly.

A successful corporate strategy will address four key overlapping and complementary areas: the boundaries of the firm, the competiveness of the market, a determination of its competitive advantage, and the way in which the firm chooses to organize its productive resources. None of these areas can be considered in isolation from the others; or, put another way, a successful firm will have found the 'right' answer to questions in each of these four areas.

Strategic planning by organizations is a complex process addressing a simple question: 'How should the resources available to the firm be allocated to best conduct the economic activity that the firm organizes?' Strategic management then represents a drive for efficiency in organizations. The role of management in encouraging efficiency is first to arrange the resources of the corporation in the best possible way. Following that, the task of management is to coordinate and motivate the pieces of the organization so that, as a whole, efficiency is maintained. Organizational strategy then is a blueprint for accomplishing an efficient allocation of corporate resources.

Design and innovative decisions

We can characterize some of the problems faced in strategic decision-making by the availability of information to the organization. Some aspects of the organizational puzzle have what organizational theorists call **design attributes**. Organizational problems have design attributes if two conditions hold. First, there is a great deal of information available within the organization concerning the nature of the best organizational structure or optimal solution for the firm. Secondly, a small mistake made in spelling out the solution can prove very costly because the effects of that mistake spread through the various activities of the firm. Other aspects of the organizational puzzle have what organizational theorists call **innovative attributes,** when information concerning the best organizational structure is not available within the organization.

Certain elements of fit evidenced in a good strategy recognize both design and innovative decision attributes. The one common element in the solution to each of these types of problem involves sharing information throughout the organization. The design attributes involve spreading existing information. The innovative attributes involve one party in the organization acquiring the information from outside and distributing it within the organization. Only when the information is spread across the organization and all parties share a common view of the organization's goals can successful strategic planning be conducted.

These elements make it important to coordinate the actions of various parts of the organization closely through some centralized structure. All of these factors work against using prices (such as transfer prices) or other very decentralized means of coordination. The design and innovative decision attributes instead favour direct communication, top–down command and other more systematic, centralized control systems.

D. Strategic managerial tools and concepts

Achieving strategic goals

Addressing the four areas necessary for a successful corporate strategy is not an easy task. The world is full of companies that had, at one time, great visions of their future success. In this section we explore some important concepts useful to managers in addressing the question of strategy. Some of these concepts involve strictly design issues facing corporations, some involve strictly innovative issues; others involve both design and innovative attributes. We must stress that none of these strategic management devices should be considered in isolation; rather each must be viewed as complementary to the others.

Economies of scale

Economies of scale arise in the production of a good or service in which average unit costs decline as output expands. Remember that returns to scale have to do with the slope of the long-run average total costs curve. If long-run unit costs fall as output expands, we say that there are increasing returns to scale, or, more simply, economies of scale. Dis-economies of scale are said to exist if long-run average costs increase as output expands.

Within any given firm, two factors contribute to the presence of economies of scale. Some of the variable factors of production may be experiencing diminishing marginal productivity. As additional units of variable inputs are added to the production process, costs (the numerator of average costs) increase at a constant rate, and output (the denominator of average costs) increases at a decreasing rate. The ratio of costs to output then decreases. Economies of scale may also be present if fixed costs are large relative to market demand and unit variable costs. In this case, average costs will diminish as output expands and the fixed costs of production are spread over more and more units.

If there are dis-economies of scale then any given increase in output can be obtained only by a proportionately larger increase in input usage. When production is characterized in this way, if demand is large it will generally be optimal to divide production among a number of smaller units in order to keep total costs relatively low.

Operational scale is a design variable because it meets two conditions. First, it has predictable implications for the various parts of the organization, and, secondly, the cost of mistakes associated with incorrect perceptions of scale by other parts of the organization can be very high. By making sure that its managers share common expectations about what it is trying to do, the firm takes an important step towards coordinating their plans and behaviour. The operational scale chosen by the organization clearly affects each of the four strategic areas; this choice will also affect decisions made in a number of other areas such as sales force size, order-processing technology and administrative support offices.

Economies of scope

Most firms produce more than one good, instead choosing to produce a set of goods related in terms of their physical design or even sharing a common key component. **Economies of scope** exist in production if it is less expensive to produce a set of goods together than separately. The concept of economies of scope helps us understand why different activities are often undertaken by the same firms.

In the airline industry, most domestic carriers everywhere recognize that economies of scope exist in providing airline services. If scheduled flights converge on one city in a particular region in a hub and spoke pattern, there are certain economies of scope in serving other, smaller cities in that region. The economies of scope may arise in terms of reservations, scheduling, baggage handling, aircraft maintenance, advertising and plane scheduling. Economies of scope are also apparent in industries more geared to hard goods production. Mercedes Benz and its divisions produce cars; they also produce trucks. The production of both cars and trucks relies on much the same technical expertise, shared components and marketing know-how. Arguing against the break-up of the American telephone monopoly AT&T in the early 1980s, many economists warned that important economies of scope existed between local and long-distance telephone services and research in telecommunications.

From the managerial perspective, economies of scope offer both a blessing and a curse. On the up side, even when a firm operates at too small an output to enjoy significant economies of scale for a single output, it may benefit from producing certain key components used in each of several products. On the down side, economies of scope involve greater coordination within the multi-product firm across its various product lines.

Core competency

One of the basic building blocks in understanding international trade is the principle of comparative advantage, a concept that has much in common with the idea of core competencies applied to firms. Country A will export good X to country B, which will, in turn, export good Y to country A. The United States exports heavy construction machinery and computer systems programming services because it can produce these more cheaply in terms of goods not produced than can other countries. Brazil and Columbia export coffee and cocaine because they are better at producing those things than, say, the United States or European Union countries. As heavy construction machinery becomes more advanced and powerful, and as new blends of coffee are created, it is likely that the United States and Brazil, respectively, will continue to export these goods.

A similar concept exists for economic organizations. **Core competencies** are said to exist when an organization not only has an advantage in producing a good or service; but also has an advantage in producing new, related products. That is, one kind of scale economy that a firm may enjoy occurs at the level of product development: acquiring generalized technical, marketing or other expertise in the necessary skills required to design and market new products in a set of related markets.

Core competencies affect corporate strategy as a problem that has both design and innovative attributes. In a dynamic environment, a firm's capacity to introduce new products and to manufacture them efficiently can be even more important than the economies of scale and scope it achieves in making its existing product line. In that setting, a strategy of developing scale and scope economies translates into one of building the core competencies of a firm. We saw the importance of this in the example concerning the Szchecin shipyards in Poland.

In their classic article relating core competencies to organizational strategies, Prahalad and Hamel (1990) provide three criteria that can be applied to identify core competencies in a company. First, in order for a skill or ability in an area to be a core competency, it must provide potential access to a wide variety of markets. Competency in electronic displays, for example, would lead to market possibilities in desktop and laptop computers, calculators, video cameras and automobile dashboards. Secondly, a core competency in an area must add significant value to the product for the consumer. Thirdly, it must be difficult for existing and potential competitors to duplicate the core competency. In this sense, a core competency is a 'natural' ability. One of the major points that Prahalad and Hamel make is that establishing and maintaining a core competency is a long-term effort by an organization; at times this may be at odds with short-term goals and objectives.

Recall that in Chapter 7 we introduced the concepts of *ex ante*, meaning before the fact, and *ex post*, meaning after the fact. The managerial challenges of core competencies are best illustrated by noting that core competency is an *ex ante* concept. When a firm is building core competencies to manufacture a set of products, it is doing so for a series of products that do not yet exist. In other words, a firm is investing in key technologies, key people and key machinery, on the gamble that it can consistently develop a successful new product line.

Governance structure

The setting of a corporate strategy involves the pursuit of how best to organize economic activity. At the heart of this effort is the attempt by the firm to determine its optimal governance structure, principally its degree of vertical integration. At first glance, this issue seems to be synonymous with determining what business a firm should be in. On further examination, it becomes clear that the determination of the best governance structure refers to the following two questions: 'Of all the resources necessary to organize a particular economic activity, which should we own?' and 'How should the activities of our resources and people be coordinated and motivated?' Of course, these are somewhat different from the corporate governance questions relating to ownership and control of the whole corporation that were emphasized in Chapter 11.

Whether or not to outsource is a strategy question with both design and innovative attributes. Attention must be paid to the ability of one, or another, firm to achieve economies of scale and scope. The firm may be better off permitting others to achieve some of the benefits of size if the others are willing to share in those gains. Firms must also be concerned with the possibility of high transaction costs in using outside suppliers if the exchanges are to be made in less than competitive markets. If specific commitments are required by either your firm or the supplier, opportunistic behaviour may result. It is also possible that significant agency problems could arise when activities are outsourced. On the other hand, the decision to outsource may in fact be motivated by a desire to shed divisions in which agency problems currently dominate. Recall that one of the biggest issues in the negotiations in the autumn of 1996 between the United Auto Workers, an American labour union, and the Big Three US car companies involved this very issue.

Formation of strategic alliances

One of the most important tools available on which to base a corporate strategy is the use of strategic alliances. A **strategic alliance** occurs when one party cooperates with another in order to organize economic activity. Two of the most often cited benefits of pursuing a strategic alliance are the lower risks involved in financing a new venture and the lessening of the necessary capital for any single participant. Strategic alliances may take many forms, including equity purchases, licensing and marketing agreements, research contracts, on-line information exchanges and joint ventures. Quite often a corporation is involved in a series of these strategic alliances, the terms 'production network' and 'alliance group' describing a related grouping of strategic alliances. Some famous examples of strategic alliances and production networks are the supplier networks of the Japanese automobile firms and other manufacturers, or the Emilia-Romagna region of Italy, and 'Silicon Valley'.

In the best possible light, strategic alliances allow participants to enjoy the benefits of both vertical integration and market transactions while avoiding some of the difficulties of each. In a capitalistic market economy, as pointed out by Adam Smith over 200 years ago, there are tremendous benefits to specialization in production. On the organizational level, we may view activities in which firms specialize as being their core competencies. In this light, then, a successful strategic alliance will blend the component core competencies of two or more firms in such a way that the value created by this aggregation will exceed the sum of its parts. At times, large vertically integrated firms have had trouble coordinating their component activities, let alone becoming world class in any of them.

Since partners in a strategic alliance interact without the benefit of common ownership, this union is not, by design, permanent. The strategic alliance partners must respect competitive forces. If Motorola and Fujitsu form a strategic alliance with Sun MicroSystems, with Motorola supplying electronic components and Fujitsu providing a visual display, both Motorola and Fujitsu must be wary of the cost and quality of the goods offered in the market place by Kubota and Sony if they expect to remain in good standing with Sun MicroSystems.

A very recent 'snapshot' of strategic alliance activity provided by Graham Vickery (1996) stresses that these collaborative arrangements between firms are somewhat clustered when we consider the source country of the collaborating firms, the industries the involved firms are in, the local geographical concentration of the newly created entities, and the motives for creating the arrangement. Within certain high-technology industries there is a long, well-documented pattern of the clustering of new activities. Some of the better-known examples include biotechnology in San Francisco, scientific instruments in Cambridge, UK, and musical instruments in Hamamatsu, Japan. In other, more traditional industries, certainly those that are more labour intensive and competitive, the proximity of many similar types of firms appears to provide each of them with a certain synergy; examples include textile production in particular areas of Italy and furniture production in North Carolina, USA. Service industries also exhibit similar benefits of geographical aggregation or agglomeration. Some particular examples that are fairly well known include financial services in New York and London, and motion picture creation in cities such as Los Angeles. Geographical concentration occurs particularly because of localization economies, where the external advantages of being in the same area may arise for many reasons. In a cluster of similar firms there may be specialized suppliers and contractors, customers, a good technological infrastructure and training resources, a suitable and competent labour force, and an extensive network of outsourcers (vertical disintegration). For many of these reasons, geographical clustering may have certain efficiency-enhancing properties.

In terms of a contribution to a synthesized organizational strategy, there are many benefits to the involved firms of participating in a strategic alliance. These collaborative agreements can, to a certain extent, mitigate a lack of capital, make technology available and allow greater access to capital markets. Some empirical evidence is presented in Table 16.1, which shows the motivations, by industry, for the formation of strategic alliances between 1980 and 1989.[3]

Table 16.1 Motivation for high-tech strategic alliances, 1980–9

Industry	Number of alliances	Cost of venture and risks (%)	Access to capital (%)	Technology complemen-tarity (%)	Increase speed of innovation (%)	Access to basic R&D(%)	Market concerns (%)
				Motivation			
Biotechnology	847	1	13	35	31	10	28
New materials technology	430	1	3	38	32	11	47
Information technology	1,660	4	2	33	31	3	49
Computers	198	1	2	28	22	2	61
Industrial automation	278	0	3	41	32	4	38
Microelectronics	383	3	3	33	33	5	58
Software	344	1	4	38	36	2	35
Telecommunications	366	11	2	28	28	1	51
Other	91	1	0	29	28	2	59

Alliance capitalism

The spread of alliances in the West and the concurrent move towards vertical disintegration follow patterns established earlier in Japan. Networks or tiers of subcontractors and the degree of high-trust, long-term cooperation with the large corporations such as Toyota that mainly perform final assembly are seen as key components of Japanese economic success. Indeed, *Alliance Capitalism* was the title chosen by Gerlach for his important 1992 book about Japanese industrial organization, and Western competitiors have been steadily following suit. As usual, the United States has been the Western pioneer of new strategic concepts such as alliance capitalism, disintegrating, outsourcing and downsizing more rapidly and extensively than European rivals, so again most of Europe seems to occupy an intermediate organizational position between the two leading industrial economies.

E. The theoretical underpinnings of strategic alliances

Throughout this entire textbook we have stressed that firms exist as a collection of contracts whose purpose is to organize economic activity. Accordingly, the fundamental building block of firms is contracts. Difficulties experienced in crafting these contracts – transaction costs – prove interesting to us not in and of themselves but because of the way in which they influence the format of the contracts crafted by firms to organize themselves.

Alternative governance structures

We term the organizational form chosen by a firm its governance structure, at the heart of which lies the make-or-buy decision facing the firm. One of the basic arguments in a transaction cost approach to organizational economics is that spot market transactions, as a form of governance structure, fall victim to contracting problems. A comparison of organizational styles through recent history reveals that successful corporations in the new economy heeded Adam Smith's advice and specialized in production according to their perceived core competencies. Somewhere along the way to today's successful organizational forms, ownership became a far less attractive option as a governance structure. We note that one compelling reason that ownership was also made less attractive is that the new flexible manufacturing technologies not only are less specific; they were less expensive. This lower cost enables other organizations to emerge that can specialize in their own areas of core competency.

According to these reasons, efficiency leads to an arrangement of firms similar to a network where producers band together with suppliers through strategic alliances. This development is in accordance with established economic theories: the Coase theorem of Chapter 5 and the constrained efficiency postulate from Chapter 6. One loose paraphrasing of the **Coase theorem** is that, if transaction costs are zero, then individuals will be led to act efficiently. The **constrained efficiency postulate** is somewhat weaker, arguing that individuals will act so as to *tend* to efficiency, given their limited information, resources and bounded rationality.

Strategic alliances and transaction costs

Strategic alliances do not eliminate transaction costs; instead, they represent a form of organizing economic activity that tends towards efficiency. Strategic alliances are chosen today as the most efficient way to organize economic activity because of fundamental changes in the business environment: the widespread adoption of flexible manufacturing technology, the back to basics movement in firms towards their core competencies, and the emergence of a more market-oriented philosophy guiding firms.

As firms specialize in production they become more innovative and more cost efficient and produce higher-quality goods. When Adam Smith spoke of the gains from specialization in the 1770s, his comments referred to activities within a single firm. Strategic alliances are the governance structure that permits this specialization to happen across firms.

Strategic alliances represent incomplete, relational contracts as described in Chapter 7. Trust is an essential building block in these relationships; a reputation for fairness and honesty is crucial. However, additional stability is provided by the environment in which these relationships are developed. The incentives in the environment of the new economy work together with trust to initiate many of the transaction costs that typically give rise to contracting problems. We next consider some of the main types of contracting problems and the way in which strategic alliances minimize their impact in the new economy to allow the benefits of specialization to occur.

For the large mass-producing firms, stability of inputs and a reliable output market were primary concerns; thus the optimal governance structure featured ownership and a large degree of vertical integration. Outside suppliers were leery of making highly specialized investments for fear of being held up or made victim of other post-contractual opportunism by the contracting firm. Ironically, the contracting firms held the same fears about their outside suppliers. In modern manufacturing, the threat of being held up is much smaller because the underlying investments capitalizing new, technologically aided and flexible production techniques are far less specific.

In general, in a production network composed of numerous strategic alliances, any form of reneging is not likely to occur because of the importance of reputation. In the network, firms become specialized, so that their long-term survival requires a steady stream of contracting partners. Once a reputation for being 'dishonest' or 'unfair' is established, that future stream of contracting partners is no longer guaranteed. In the examples to come, describing organizations in Silicon Valley and Japan, we see evidence that institutional devices exist to develop and spread reputations.

Hold-ups and moral hazard

The two major forms of post-contractual opportunism were outlined in Chapters 7 and 8: the hold-up and moral hazard. One solution to these sources of transaction costs is, in general, some market-disciplining device. With strategic alliances, reputation serves as one form of market-disciplining device. A second is offered by the typical widespread availability of information within productive networks and the fact that strategic alliances are by no means exclusive. By this we mean that a company A may have a strategic alliance with firm X where firm X produces a key component of firm A's output. Very likely, firm X will have a similar relationship with other firms B, . . ., producing similar components. Furthermore, both A and B will know about firm X's relationships and may discuss firm X's performance. Any feeling that firm X is shirking in its duties or exploiting some specificity will be quickly spread between and by the two contracting firms.

Another aspect of strategic alliances that may help diminish transaction costs arising is the agency nature of these relationships, in that bounded rationality may be less of a problem than in simple arm's-length contracting. Both the contracting firm and the subcontractor have knowledge of both firms' manufacturing processes and of the technological questions that arise in fulfilling the contractor's request. It is unlikely then that the subcontractor will be able to 'stonewall' or mislead the contractor by claiming problems with some terribly advanced technological issue.

The use of strategic alliances has two clear implications for the management charged with formulating the corporation's strategy. First, the intrafirm coordination costs will decrease. The firm is not required to purchase as many assets or to hire the workers to operate and manage them if organizations outside the firm play a larger role in designing, producing and shipping output. What this implies is that interfirm coordination becomes more important, which leads to the second implication for organizational management.

As explained in Chapter 15, there is an increased need in organizations adopting modern, flexible techniques for more centralized management. Only a centralized management scheme can consistently gather and process the information required to develop a strategy that advances the organization's interests. The issues facing management are large and broad: What are our core competencies? What should we produce? Who should we seek out as partners? On what terms? The answer to any one of these questions clearly depends on the answers to all the others. Thus, an efficient, coherent reply can come only from a centralized management scheme.

F. The alliance revolution

A business ecosystem

Businesses unite now in vastly different ways today than they did in the past. Joint ventures were originally oriented towards a collaborative effort between two companies; today alliances generally have numerous participants. Part of the reason for this is that companies have come to realize that competing in a global market place requires specialization or the pursuit of a core competence. Another compelling factor encouraging the formation of strategic alliances is the growing complexity of products and services. The vast majority of products contain separable components that individually incorporate wholly distinct and specialized technologies. In such an environment, vertical integration may be neither possible or desirable. Specialization and economies of scale are very convincing factors.

In the 1990s, business strategists have embraced this new, emerging environment, likening it to an ecosystem, a concept borrowed from the biological sciences. Some of the concepts currently used shed valuable insights on the choice of strategy in a world where strategic alliances proliferate.[4]

Firms openly speak of the concept of **co-evolution** under which a company can create new businesses, markets and industries by working with direct competitors, customers and suppliers. Co-evolution could only survive in industries where there is room for other than dominant players, in which technology is quickly changing, and where a suitable degree of trust exists among related firms. Opportunities for profitable partnering are termed 'white-space opportunities', which are described as new areas of niched market opportunities that do not naturally match the skills, abilities and competencies of existing companies. In industries where most activity is the result of a mix of collaborative efforts, the term 'business ecosystem' is used to describe a system in which companies work cooperatively and competitively to support new products, satisfy customers and create the next round of innovation in market segments. Because they mark evolving trends in business strategy, these concepts are extremely important to organizational economists. We now turn our attention to two interesting issues surrounding the firms and alliances that make up business ecosystems: what is known about their characteristics, and the special role they play in encouraging innovation.

Factors in alliance formation

Benjamin Gomes-Casseres (1994) has provided the seminal work on the characteristics of alliance groups.[5] These characteristics are consistent with the motives determined for strategic alliances in Table 16.1. This listing is by no means complete, nor are all characteristics equally important in different industries.

- **Collaboration may substitute for firm size.** Alliance networks often arise to allow participants to enjoy some of the benefits of 'bigness' – two examples of which are economies of scale or market concentration.
- **Alliances are pieced together.** Strategic alliances do not instantly arise; rather, they are pieced together as the initial partners come to understand their needs and competencies better.
- **A complete composition.** Successful strategic alliances have memberships that ensure coverage of all technologies and markets necessary to produce the product. This characteristic is especially important in high-technology markets where the competition between different products will result in the setting of the industry standard.
- **Internal competition.** Firms within alliances may very well be in competition with each other. An alliance that, for example, produces entire, functioning computer systems may have more than two chip foundries. They will not, however, contain 200 chip foundries. The idea is that competition should be healthy within the alliance. Equally important is the competition between members outside the alliance, which should not be of the intense, direct variety. A healthy competitive atmosphere within the alliance will allow greater group flexibility and increased innovation and secure a stable supply.

Good for innovation?

The bulk of the world's strategic alliances are found in the high-tech industries, those that rely heavily on seemingly continuous innovation. This has led researchers to address the possibility that there is some factor unique to strategic alliances that tends to encourage innovation. Two US economists, Henry W. Chesbrough and David J. Teece (1996), have recently developed an answer to this question that relies on the role of incentives. Within a highly virtual framework, such as within an alliance, most activity is coordinated through the market place, where incentives are simply more powerful than within a more vertically integrated company. William Joy, a vice-president of R&D at Sun MicroSystems, explains it this way: 'Not all the smart people [in the workstation industry] work for Sun.' A developer of workstation software who is outside of Sun could ultimately obtain greater rewards by selling software to Sun customers directly than by working as a software developer within Sun. That independent software developer would then be expected to work harder and faster and to take more risks than a software developer working within Sun MicroSystems.

Chesbrough and Teece are quick to point out the obvious drawback to participating in a more virtual system. The same incentives that make market exchange so powerful also leave it vulnerable because the higher rewards and risk taking make coordination among parties through the market place more difficult. In such an environment, characterized also by opportunism, bounded rationality and the unpredictability of technical advances, disputes between once friendly partners may arise, stifling attempts to coordinate development activity. By way of contrast, more vertically integrated organization schemes under centralized management are better at settling conflicts and coordinating the activities necessary for innovation. The drawback, of course, to a more vertically integrated structure is that it offers far weaker incentives to take risks. The job of management then is to find its organization's best position in the trade-off between a lowering of incentives to take risks and a heightened ability to settle conflicts and coordinate activities as the degree of vertical integration increases.

G. Strategic alliances in biotechnology

You can't make mother's milk from scratch

Marteck Biosciences is a biotechnology company headquartered in Columbia, Maryland. Originally spun off from Martin Marietta, Marteck went public in 1993, and is traded on the NASDAQ index. The company has 70 full-time employees and is working in several product areas. Marteck's mission is to be the leading biotechnology company in the world, on the basis of its core competency: growing algae, commonly referred to as seaweed. Its corporate strategy is to exploit its core competencies in developing algae-based products and to form alliances with other companies to complement its own strengths.

Breastfeeding is good for babies. There are certain amino acids (the building blocks of protein) in mother's milk that are not available in infant formula. Studies of childhood development have shown that these particular acids are directly linked to intelligence in children. The market problem is that not all mothers are able, owing to physical or time challenges, to breastfeed their children and must rely on infant formula. Adding the amino acids found in mother's milk to infant formula could be a multi-million dollar market. Marteck has developed an algae-based derivative that replicates the amino acids in mother's milk.

Like most biotechnology companies, Marteck was not able to exploit its core competencies alone. The company did not have the financial, regulatory or marketing skills needed to capitalize on its ability and grow. Therefore, like many young biotechnology companies, Marteck's corporate strategy was to rely on strategic alliances to achieve its goals.

A major hurdle in the production of the infant formula additive is that it has to be manufactured in large enough quantities to satisfy global market demand. Marteck did not have the facilities to manufacture the product. Therefore it entered into a strategic alliance with a large fermentation company in the Midwest to manufacture the product in large quantities. It formed a second strategic alliance with several large producers of baby formula to market the product. The product will be directly added to infant formula and Marteck will receive a royalty from each bottle and can of infant formula sold.

Marteck did not make one of the major mistakes of many biotechnology companies. It never licensed, or let others use, its proprietary technology. The company maintained proprietary control of its core competency, and cooperated with other organizations that complemented its unique strengths.

Marteck will continue to develop its core competencies in algae and to develop new products that will find a place in the global market. In each case it will seek out partners with core competencies that complement its own.

In the biotechnology industry, strategic alliance is the name of the game. Many biotech companies in the United States, Japan, the United Kingdom and elsewhere form strategic alliances with both domestic and foreign companies. As of 1989, 46 publicly traded American biotechnology firms had an average of six corporate partners each. The search for suitable partners that truly allow biotech companies to integrate core competencies is not confined to the United States. The average number of foreign alliances for each US biotechnology company in 1989 was 3.5, which includes an average of 2.1 alliances with European firms and 1.4 deals with companies based in Asia, usually with the Japanese.

Biotech: Allying with whom

Half a dozen US biotechnology companies have forged an extraordinary number of foreign ties: Chiron, Biogen and Genentech lead the way, as seen in Tables 16.2 and 16.3. The data reveal several different strategies for foreign strategic alliances: some US firms have emphasized European accords, while others have stressed Asian over European alliances.

Three common types of strategic alliance are equity arrangements, joint ventures and marketing deals. Because of the risky nature of their specialized businesses and their small size, biotechnology companies are always looking for capital. Selling equity to major US and foreign corporations has always been an important part of this fund-raising, often accompanying strategic marketing or distribution deals. Equity investment gives a corporation much-needed

Table 16.2 Breakdown of alliances made by US biotech firms with foreign partners

Total number of alliances	With European partners	With Asian partners
1	28	18
2	9	11
3	4	2
4	0	3
5	0	0
6	0	1
7	3	0
8 +	1	0

Source US Office of Technology Assessment (1992), Table 4.7.

Table 16.3 Listing of strategic alliances of some US biotech companies, 1989

US company	European deals	Asian deals	Foreign deals
Amgen	1	4	5
Biogen	8	7	15
Bio-Response	0	0	0
Bio-Technology General	0	4	4
California Biotechnology	3	2	5
Centocor	4	4	8
Chiron	12	4	16
Cytogen	1	0	1
Damon Biotech	1	0	1
Ecogen	0	0	0
Genentech	7	6	13
Genetics Institute	6	3	9
Genex	3	1	4
Immunex	5	0	5
Plant Genetics	1	3	4
Repligen	4	1	5
Synergen	1	0	1
Vestar	3	0	3
Xoma	3	0	3

Source US Office of Technology Assessment (1992), Table 4.8.

cash in exchange for part ownership. For example, Nova Pharmaceutical Corporation, headquartered in Baltimore, Maryland, sold $10 million worth of Nova shares in 1987 to Celanese for partial ownership.

With the exception of complete acquisition, the most intimate relationship two companies can have is a joint venture. In most cases, these arrangements consist of both parties contributing a core competency. In biotechnology, the genetic engineering company invariably contributes the necessary technology, while the partner contributes financing and marketing skills. For most biotechnology companies, joint ventures are almost always preferred over licensing arrangements because they give the start-up firm the opportunity to finance internal infrastructure and a share of profits rather than receiving only a small royalty on eventual sales.

Licensing agreements are also very popular in biotechnology companies. Despite their popularity, they do not receive rave reviews from biotechnology executives. These arrangements, if made exclusively to raise cash before the product is ready, put the company at a negotiating disadvantage from the beginning. However, if a firm has already created a product that has potential, like Marteck in the above example, then licensing can be of great benefit to the firm because it is guaranteed a stream of income in the future and does not have to give up either technology or equity.

H. Production networks in computers

A silicon-based ecosystem

For years the large computer manufacturers in the United States such as IBM had structures featuring a high degree of vertical integration.[6] This method of production, which survived well into the 1980s, was characterized by slow-moving technology and stable product lines. The firm designed and produced not only the final product but also all of the technologically sophisticated components and sub-systems in-house. Subcontractors were used only to meet surges in boom times and were relegated to standard inputs.

Competitive conditions in the computer industry have changed drastically since the 1970s. The cost of bringing new products to market has increased while the pace of new product introduction and technological change has accelerated. In this newer, more competitive market, products have to be brought to market in a matter of months instead of years. This change in the business environment forced IBM to rely on outside suppliers to an unprecedented extent in the early 1980s in order to bring a personal computer to the market rapidly.

Growing technological complexity has raised the cost of developing new products. Computer systems today include central processing units, operating systems, power supplies, storage systems, and much more. Customers seek increased performance in all aspects of the product, making it virtually impossible for one firm to stay at the forefront of all these technologies.

Firms, out of necessity, must therefore focus on what they do best, their core competencies, and acquire the rest. This represents a fundamental shift away from vertical integration. When Sun Microsystems was established in 1982 it decided to focus on designing hardware and software work stations, and to limit manufacturing to prototypes, final assembly and testing. All components for the work stations were purchased. The management of Sun Microsystems understood the issues quite clearly. A vertically integrated structure was possible, but Sun would face great difficulties remaining competitive in a number of separate areas. Sun Microsystems recognized that there were hundreds of specialty shops in Silicon Valley investing heavily in staying at the leading edge in the design and manufacturing of microprocessors, disk drives, printed circuit boards and other pieces of computer hardware. Relying on outside suppliers reduces Sun's overheads and ensures that the firm's work stations use state-of-the art technology.

The guiding principle of Sun, like that of most new Silicon Valley systems firms, is to concentrate its expertise and resources on coordinating the design and assembly of a final system. This is the core competency of many of these firms, and Sun Microsystems was able to advance only those technologies critical to the firm's main line of business. This is not to say that the principle of bounded rationality did not apply to Sun; rather, the limits of Sun's bounded rationality were reduced owing to changes in the underlying technologies and industry structure.

In fact, some firms explicitly recognize their reliance on suppliers and foster their development. Apple Computers' venture capital arm makes minority investments in promising firms that offer complementary technologies.

This trend towards more of a reliance on decentralizing activities in the firm and on productive networks is not limited to small or new firms seeking to avoid fixed investments. Even Hewlett-Packard, which designs and manufactures chips, printed circuit boards, disk drives and many other peripherals, has restructured to gain flexibility.

The network of integrated computer producers extends beyond the system firms and their immediate suppliers. Silicon Valley's suppliers of electronic components and sub-systems are themselves vertically desegregated to spread the risks of chip-making. The cost and risks of developing new computer systems are spread across networks of autonomous but interdependent firms in Silicon Valley. In an environment that demands rapid new product introduction and continual technological change, no one firm has the core competency to design and manufacture the computer on its own.

The more specialized these computers and their components become, the more organizations are drawn into partnerships with their suppliers. And as they are increasingly treated as equals in a joint process of designing, developing and manufacturing innovative systems, the suppliers themselves become innovative and capital-intensive producers of differentiated products hiring their own outside suppliers. In other words, another layer is added to the productive web of firms.

Silicon Valley system firms now view their relationships with suppliers more as long-term investments rather than as short-term procurement relationships. They recognize collaboration with suppliers as a way to speed the pace of new product introductions and improve product quality and performance. In order to keep the interfirm coordination and management costs small, most organizations build relationships with a few suppliers to supply most of their components.

These relationships are based on shared recognition of the need to ensure the success of a final product. Epitomizing the trust between partners, long-term business plans are commonly shared, as are confidential sales forecasts and cost information. The sharing of sales forecasts allows suppliers to plan investment levels. Spreading the knowledge concerning cost structures encourages a fair negotiation of prices high enough to yield suppliers a fair return on their investments and low enough to keep the systems firm competitive.

These relationships obviously transcend simply handling an order placed by a customer. In the early stages of product development, engineers from the systems firms and parts suppliers explore issues of technical feasibility and share product visions. Throughout the whole process, communication is vital as the boundaries between firms become increasingly blurred. Interestingly enough, in these strategic alliances, the way that firms interact with each other is not much different from the way departments in a vertically integrated firm interact. The key difference is that, in a strategic alliance, the systems firm and the suppliers treat each other as customers and not as corporate overhead.

Although in many of these alliances non-disclosure agreements and contracts are normally signed, few believe that they really matter. What does seem present is a mutually shared concern for the long-term health of the other firms. According to Apple Computers' manager of purchasing:

> We have found you don't always need a formal contract . . . If you develop trust with your suppliers, you don't need armies of attorneys . . . In order for us to be successful in the future, we have to develop better working relationships, better trusting relationships, than just hounding vendors for price decreases on an annual basis. (Cohodas, 1986).

Although these relationships are often remarkably close, both parties are careful to preserve their own autonomy. Most Silicon Valley firms will not allow their business to account for more than 20 per cent of a supplier's product and prefer that no customer occupy such a position. Suppliers are thus forced to find outside customers, which ensures that the loss of a single account will not put them out of business.

Intensifying competition and the high mobility of scientists and engineers strain alliances and other forms of cooperation, because key employees can carry crucial know-how with them when changing jobs. One result has been a growing flood of litigation to protect proprietory technology and other commercially valuable knowledge. These factors, and the concomitant erosion of trust in American society, have raised the costs of cooperation in Silicon Valley and other centres of US high technology.

I. Chapter summary and key ideas

The importance of strategy to organizations is well documented by the recent course of events in corporate America and Britain. By the early 1980s, as once-leading US companies found themselves battered by global competitors and more nimble entrepreneurs, the cerebral strategizing of the past seemed a luxurious relic from a more prosperous bygone era. Instead of weaving elegant stratagems, companies were scrambling to improve quality, to restructure, to downsize and to re-engineer. Cutting costs, streamlining and right-sizing were taken for granted. Now, in the United States as elsewhere, the pure efficiency approach, once vehemently embraced, is being abandoned. Why? There are many reasons; the one that is most relevant to us is that the pure efficiency approach failed to generate distinct competitive advantages in the companies that followed this path.

In many of today's most competitive global industries, firm strategies are being developed that encourage specialization as the route to high-quality, low-cost provision of goods and services. These strategies determine the boundaries of the firm, the competiveness of the market in which they operate, the core competency of the firm and the way in which the firm chooses to organize its productive resources.

Every organization must decide where to place itself in the make-or-buy decision. This will decide to what extent the firm will be vertically integrated. Between the two extremes of vertical integration and markets lies strategic alliances. Today's business strategists recognize the importance of collaborative efforts and individual firm specializations, speaking of co-evolution, white-space opportunities and a business ecosystem within a particular industry.

Key words

business ecosystem	economies of scale
co-evolution	economies of scope
Coase theorem	innovative attributes
constrained efficiency	joint venture
postulate	production network
core competency	strategic alliance
corporate strategy	trust
design attributes	vertical integration

Questions and problems for review and discussion

1 In the second section of Chapter 16 concerning competitiveness a
  brief narrative is given about the course of events at two Polish
  shipyards in the early 1990s.
  (a) Give a brief description of the broad environment facing the
      Polish shipbuilding industry at the time.
  (b) How is the response by the Szchecin yard different from the
      response at the Gdansk yard?
2 (a) Name the four areas addressed by a successful corporate strategy.
  (b) Using an example of a firm that you view as a success do the
      following:
      i. Explain why you feel that this firm is a success.
      ii. Explain the relationships among the four areas of a successful
          corporate strategy.
3 Explain the differences between organizational problems with design
  attributes and those with innovative attributes. Provide an example of
  each.
4 (a) Provide a layman's definition of the term *core competency*.
  (b) Draw a parallel between the concept of a firm's core competency
      and a country's trading advantage along the lines of comparative
      advantage.
5 True, false, or uncertain: When economic activity is organized within a
  strategic alliance rather than within a firm there are more market
  incentives to encourage innovation?
6 Discuss the ways in which strategic alliances serve as a substitute for
  vertical integration as described in this chapter.

Notes

1 This section is adapted from Johnson and Loveman (1994, ch. 1) and Johnson *et
  al.* (1995).
2 This section is adapted from Johnson and Loveman (1994, ch. 1).
3 These data are from Hagedoorn and Schakenraad (1991), cited in Vickery (1996,
  p. 114).
4 There are many places where the interested reader can go to explore this important
  topic. Perhaps the best accessible is Byrne (1996).
5 A related case authored by Benjamin Gomes-Casseres and Krista McQuade illustrates many of the issues associated with strategic alliances: Mips Computer Systems
  (A), Harvard Business School # 9-792-055.
6 This section is adapted from Saxenian (1991).

References

Byrne, J. (1996), 'Strategic planning', *Business Week*, 26 August, pp. 46–52.

Chesbrough, H. W. and D. J. Teece (1996), 'When is virtual virtuous?', *Harvard Business Review*, January–February, pp. 65–73.

Cohodas, M. (1986), 'How Apple buys electronics', *Electronics Purchasing*, November.

Gerlach, M. (1992), *Alliance Capitalism*, Los Angeles: University of California Press.

Gomes-Casseres, B. (1994), 'Group versus group: How alliance networks compete', *Harvard Business Review*, July–August, pp. 4–11.

Gomes-Casseres, B. and K. McQuade (1996), Mips Computer Systems (A), Harvard Business School, No. 9-792-055.

Hagedoorn, J. and J. Schakenraad (1991), *The Role of Inter-firm Cooperation Agreements in the Globalization of the Economy and Technology*, Brussels: FAST.

Johnson, S. and G. Loveman (1994), *Starting Over*, Cambridge, Mass.: Harvard University Press.

Johnson, S. D., T. Kotchen and G. Loveman (1995), 'How one Polish shipyard became a market competitor', *Harvard Business Review*, November–December, pp. 53–74.

Pralahad, C. K. and G. Hamel (1990), 'The core competence of the corporation', *Harvard Business Review*, May–June, pp. 79–91.

Reich, R. B. (1992), *The Work of Nations*, New York: Knopf.

Saxenian, A. (1991), 'The origin and dynamics of production networks in Silicon Valley', *Research Policy*, 20, pp. 423–37.

US Office of Technology Assessment (1992), *Biotechnology in a Global Economy*, Washington DC: OTA.

Vickery, G., with C. Casadio (1996), 'The globalization of investment and trade', in J. de la Mothe and G. Paquet (eds), *Evolutionary Economics and the New International Political Economy*, London: Cassel.

CHAPTER

International comparison of economic organization

A. Chapter outline and student goals

Throughout this text we have emphasized international comparison of differing economic institutions. A key issue is the comparative performance of the relatively deregulated and 'flexible' stock market dominated Anglo-American economies and the contrasting continental European systems. A third focus is the Japanese economy, in many ways closer to the European model, but of course also distinctive.

Modern managers in today's global economy need to understand the fundamental differences between economic systems. In spite of multinational corporations, the proliferation of joint ventures and strategic alliances and much discussion of 'convergence', national institutional cultures and identities remain distinctive and important. Without attempting to do justice to the diversity of European institutions, we continue to focus in this summary review on the Germany economy as the best-known European contrast to Anglo-American institutions.

In this chapter we shall thus highlight the key country-specific aspects of interest – that is, the many similarities and differences between the Anglo-American, German and Japanese economies. Starting with manufacturing, the US tradition of mass production, Taylorism and emphasis on exploiting economies of scale is already familiar from our accounts in Chapters 13 and 14. The organization of production in German firms has evolved in a somewhat different way. The strong craft tradition in that country and the powerful labour union organizations, backed by extensive legislation and generally favourable government and public attitudes, remain major environmental influences to the present day. Small and medium-sized owner-managed entrepreneurial firms have a much larger share of total manufacturing in Germany than in the United States or the United Kingdom. A comprehensive state-supported system of vocational education and training has provided Germany with the most highly skilled blue-collar labour force in Europe . This combination gave Germany a head start in the development of flexible manufacturing in Europe. For many years, Germany not Japan was the largest exporter of manufactured goods. Strategic alliances and long-term relationships with

533

subcontractors are common-place in Germany, among both large corporations and smaller companies.

The most striking differences between the three systems being considered here are apparent in the area of labour relations. The Anglo-American tradition of adversarial, conflict-ridden labour–management relations becomes increasingly dysfunctional as companies strive to implement flexible manufacturing systems. By contrast, Germany has a long tradition of institutionalized cooperation between labour and management. For traditional British or American managers, having to consult a powerful works councils at plant level or answer to worker representatives on the board of directors represents a topsy-turvy world. However, we shall see that these institutions of codetermination have had major benefits (though also some costs) in the German model of productive organization.

In another contrast to extensive German laws on codetermination and labour relations, the Japanese system of lifetime employment for core employees in large corporations is a purely informal arrangement, without explicit contractual basis or legal enforcement. Combined with relatively weak outside stockholder control of large Japanese companies, security of job tenure makes employees more like residual income claimants than workers in an American firm. Japanese firms do not seem to want to maximize stockholder value, as Western theories say they should. Instead they seem to be operated in the interests of all their stakeholders, primarily employees and customers. This has far-reaching consequences that we discuss in more detail below, but it is one lesson from Japan that managers and owners in most other countries are not enthusiastic about. Perhaps, however, it is a lesson that does have some relevance for the newly emerging market economies in Eastern Europe.

Consistent with the importance of employee stakeholders in Japan and Germany, corporate control or 'governance' in these countries is organized on quite different lines from the United States and the United Kingdom. Hostile takeovers, for example, are almost unknown and the stock market plays only a relatively minor role. Banks are legally permitted to be major stockholders of German and Japanese corporations, and bank directors play an important role on many corporate boards. Mutual shareholdings by members of strategic alliances are commonly used to cement their common interest rather than for purely financial reasons. Anglo-American economists extol the salutary disciplinary effect on corporate managers that should be exerted by the threat of hostile takeover. However, German and Japanese managers have been remarkably successful without this threat. Furthermore, incentives such as stock options, which are considered essential to motivate American managers, are conspicuously absent in the German and Japanese reward structure. And the salaries received by top Japanese and German managers are only a small fraction of equivalent American salaries.

International differences in scientific and technological progress, particularly in the fields of high technology, have captured popular imagination and attracted much attention from policy makers in government and industry. The US economic system offers enormous rewards for scientific and, especially, technological breakthrough. Much talent is thus drawn into pioneering innovative entrepreneurial activity. However, in recent years the United States has lagged increasingly far behind Japan in its ability to translate these breakthroughs into marketable and competitive products. The Japanese emphasis on teamwork rather than individual breakthroughs has put production and process innovation at centre stage. Starting with consumer electronics and photo optics, Japanese development of follow-through innovation and perfection of the production process has allowed Japan to take over leadership from the United States in one high-tech industry after another. In most cases the fundamental ideas have come from the United States or elsewhere. Throughout this period, basic research in Japanese universities and industry has been relatively undistinguished.

German experience with high technology and innovation forms a contrasting and instructive example. In spite of substantial educational and organizational advantages, German manufacturing has been falling behind in most high-technology areas. Part of the reason can be found in traditional German pre-eminence in the fields of engineering and chemicals, which led to neglect of the newer high-technology industries. The 1980s were a decade of export successes, which led to complacency among managers and unions, and rising costs, which were exacerbated by the burdens of reunification. In the final part of the chapter, we explore the future prospects for innovation among the major players in the new global economy.

B. International patterns of production

Whereas technology knows no frontiers, and advanced products are made by all the developed economies, the organization of production varies to a surprising degree across countries. We have already described the evolution of Taylorism and Fordist mass production in the United States as the dominant industrial paradigm up to the 1960s. By this time, however, Toyota and other Japanese manufacturers had begun to develop flexible manufacturing systems and teamwork, which were to replace the American model as the dominant system of manufacturing . Between these polar cases, different traditions and environments in Europe produced different patterns of production. In Germany in particular, a strong craft tradition and a large sector of small and medium-sized firms, the *Mittelstand,* helped to propel that country from the ruins of war to the continent's leading economic power. In this section we compare some of the salient features of manufacturing and the organization of production in these three countries.

US firms

Henry Ford's introduction of the assembly line in 1914 must rank as one of the great industrial innovations of the twentieth century. Unnecessary human movement and skills were minimized by mechanically transporting partially assembled units from one fixed work station to the next. In America's huge domestic market, linked by a superb transportation infrastructure, economies of scale could be realized to the full. By the 1960s, advanced durable goods were being mass produced at unprecedentedly low prices, albeit at the cost of repetitive and mind-numbing work tasks for employees on the line. However, scale economies allowed workers to be held at these jobs by the highest industrial wages in the world, which included an element of rent-sharing by oligopolistic producers in markets that were not yet penetrated by foreign competitors.

The stable macroeconomic environment necessary for the smooth functioning of this system was disturbed by a number of shocks in the 1970s. Oil-price hikes initiated by the Opec oil-producing countries pushed the industrial economies into recession and inflation. Gas-guzzling US automobiles suddenly became vulnerable to cheaper and more economical imports. Less spectacularly but more generally, both shifting patterns of demand for manufactured goods and the patterns of technological change began to favour smaller and more flexible production units. As Japanese and other imports conquered one US market after another, standards in production technology came to be set by Japanese-owned and Japanese-managed subsidiaries or **transplants** in the United States. These transplants showed that Japanese productive organization was not culture bound, but could be eminently competitive while employing American workers, even in the old industrial heartland, or Rust Belt, of the Midwest.

To compete both domestically and internationally, American firms have begun to adopt principles of flexible manufacturing and the new Japanese-style work practices. Just how far this process has gone is shown by a 1992 survey on the use of flexible work organization (Osterman, 1994). Some 35 per cent of establishments with more than 50 employees made substantial use of teamwork, job rotation and total quality management. Significantly, these practices were particularly common in internationally competitive sectors and among manufacturers that emphasized product variety and quality rather than simply competition on the basis of low costs. Remaining low-wage, routinized assembly work will continue to be shifted to the lower-wage countries of Latin America and East Asia. Although the transformation of American manufacturing to flexible production still has some way to go, export shares and productivity have surged ahead in the 1990s, boosted by the overvalued yen and declining or stagnating real wages for most workers.

Much of the productivity growth in the United States (and the United Kingdom) comes from massive investment in information technology machines that replace back-office or routine workers in the growing service sector. As downsizing reduces payroll costs and boosts measured profits and productivity, remaining knowledge workers face ever higher workloads with a technology that allows them to remain 'on-line' virtually 24 hours a day. Stephen Roach of Morgan Stanley bank, formerly a leading proponent of downsizing, now complains of 'increasingly hollow companies' that may lose out in the long run to less short-termist competitors (Roach, 1996).

The German firm

The success of major German corporations such as Mercedes, BMW and Siemens in international markets has made them well known the world over as brand names synonymous with German quality and workmanship. Much less well known is Germany's relatively large and stable sector of small and medium-sized firms, the *Mittelstand*. These firms are usually privately or family owned, and have frequently established world leadership in niche markets, particularly in the fields of engineering and metalworking. The concentration of these small and medium-sized firms is particularly strong in south-western Germany, where they have flourished with the support of a carefully targeted industrial policy by local government. This policy includes an excellent system of technical and vocational education and training, government-supported research institutions and selective grants for promising research and development projects. Entrepreneurial families cooperate with each other and with labour unions, or as subcontractors for large companies, on the basis of high trust and personal reputation.

Germany's relatively large sector of small and medium-sized firms is more stable than the corresponding sectors in the United States and the United Kingdom. This is only partly due to macroeconomic stability up to 1990. In addition, for a variety of reasons, there is both less entry into – and less exit from – the small and medium-sized firm sector. New start-ups are relatively rare in Germany, owing partly to a more regulated labour market and also to the relatively undeveloped venture capital market. Managers in large corporations have had rather secure jobs in a fairly low-risk environment and have been reluctant to leave this environment for the risks of new ventures. The flow of managerial and scientific talent that has fuelled the formation and growth of small entrepreneurial start-ups in the United States is thus largely absent in Germany.

On the other hand, there has also been less rapid exit from the small-firm sector in Germany because of the lack of empire-building corporate raiders and predators. It is also the case that total manufacturing employment in Germany has declined more slowly than that in all the other main economies except Japan. It should be noted at this point that the service sector has also grown relatively slowly in Germany, in part because of uniformly high wages, in strongly unionized and regulated labour markets, which have impeded the rapid growth of low-wage service jobs as in the United States.

The craft tradition has remained remarkably strong in industrialized Germany, and has retained a pervasive influence on manufacturing in that country. Reasons may be found in Germany's late start with industrialization, the important role of scientific education and training throughout the process of industrialization, as well as centralized corporatist bargaining with strong labour unions. At the political level, extensive regulation and legislation have encouraged the craft tradition and maintained a dominating role for government in education and training at all levels. This tradition-bound system has been criticized for being bureaucratic and inflexible. Craft-based qualifications and regulation of entry have often failed to keep up with technical progress, particularly in services. New start-ups, self-employment and other entrepreneurial entry, as well as part-time employment have thus been hindered and participation in the labour force kept below the levels found in the United States, the United Kingdom and Scandinavia.

On the positive side, there is little doubt that the combination of the craft tradition with heavy government involvement in the training system has produced what is probably the most highly skilled blue-collar labour force in Europe. Some two-thirds of the German workforce possess vocational qualifications, compared with one-third or less in the United Kingdom and the United States. Most teenagers (90 per cent) either are in full-time schooling, leading on to higher education, or combine apprentice training in industry with part-time schooling. Skilled workers who obtain certification as master craftsmen frequently move on to take responsible positions in lower-level management, positions that would be reserved for graduates with higher education in the Anglo-American system. In Britain, vocational training for those who do not enter higher education has been seriously neglected, leaving a growing, almost unemployable 'underclass', and a still-widening skill gap in comparison with Germany and, indeed, most other European countries.

If what is sometimes called 'lower education' in Germany clearly leads most other countries, it must also be emphasized that *higher* education in Germany suffers from serious problems. The once-dominant state university system is now overcrowded, bureaucratic and inefficient. Students often take six years or more to obtain their first degree. Only a handful of small and undistinguished private universities compete with the state-run institutions of higher education in Germany. Attempts to reform the latter have so far made as little headway as the rather haphazard efforts to reform 'lower' education and training in the United States and the United Kingdom.

The Japanese firm

The origins of what has become known as the characteristically Japanese organization of production can be found in two independent developments of the early post-war years. First was the use of machines that stopped automatically in the event of faults or defects and that were arranged in configurations that enabled one operator, with the appropriate multiple skills, to tend more than one machine. Related to this was the *kanban* or order-card system for coordinating production by direct communication between related units, by which components were ordered directly as and when needed. This system had considerable advantages over the top–down, command system of centralized production and component scheduling in US, Fordist mass production. These developments were pioneered by Taichi Ohno at Toyota Motors, but rapidly spread to other companies.

The other foundation of modern Japanese manufacturing grew, paradoxically, out of intense labour–management conflict. This led to the establishment of less radical enterprise unions and an implicit agreement to respect managerial rights to direct the enterprise. In return, blue-collar workers gained job security – the expectation of permanent employment. This **implicit contract** with labour soon turned out to possess important complementarities with the multi-skilling requirements of the technological organization.

Employers quickly realized that they could invest in training without fear of losing their investment when workers quit to join competing companies. The build-up of multiple skills in turn encouraged decentralization under the *kanban* system. Workers were increasingly able to perform maintenance and quality-control operations, which were separated from production work under the traditional Taylorist division of labour in Fordist manufacturing.

The stage was now set for the evolution of what is often described as the most important feature of Japanese-type production. With job security, workers had no incentive to resist reorganization for increased productivity, because they had no need to fear job loss. Skill-sharing, cooperation and job rotation defined the teamwork that naturally complemented the decentralized, flexible technology pioneered by Toyota. The just-in-time (JIT) practice of ordering component parts exactly when required, rather than building up inventories, helped to reduce costs. Most importantly, the integrated work teams of multi-skilled, highly motivated individual employees embodied the dedication and flexibility that were the essential foundation for the development of flexible manufacturing systems (FMS).

Transfer of workers or job rotation, both within teams and within the whole plant, equipped workers with the range of knowledge required for two functions that were unheard of in Fordist production. Rapid response in coping with new products as well as developments in the production process becomes increasingly valuable as the pace of technical change quickens and product life-cycles shorten. Workers also become empowered to contribute their production-related skills to a process of continuous improvement or *kaizen*. This strategy, based on an organization of flexible work teams, stands in radical contrast to the Taylorist separation of planning and doing on which American mass production was based.

Because many managerial tasks were devolved to the shop floor, blue-collar workers could rise to lower-level managerial positions. The integration of production and management was thus fostered by personnel movement, rather than rigid specialization. Suggestions for improvement were encouraged from all employees as part of the *kaizen* process. All affected parties participate in discussion of specific decisions to reach a consensus, resulting in more rapid implementation by informed and committed participants.

Japanese productive organization thus seems to have evolved from a confluence of historical accidents, rather than as a result of specifically Japanese cultural factors. The export of Japanese organization principles in the form of numerous successful transplants in several countries is further evidence of their general viability.

Another important structural element of the Japanese system is the highly developed network of end-users and suppliers, which actually blurs the boundaries of the individual firm. This is the famous subcontracting system, practised not only in the automobile industry as described in Chapter 14 but throughout Japanese manufacturing. As an alternative to both arm's-length market contracting and vertical integration hierarchy, the parent or core company acts as a final assembler. A high proportion of components are delivered by closely located and often partially owned first-tier suppliers. These, in turn, depend upon second-tier suppliers for their components, which are served by numerous tertiary subcontractors.

Relations within the production network in many ways are the mirror image of teamwork inside the firm. The just-in-time (JIT) delivery system puts a premium on reliability, which is maintained by long-term relationships, personnel sharing, partial ownership or shareholding, joint product development and intensive communication and knowledge-sharing. The long-term nature of cooperation reduces the risks attendant upon exchange of scientific and technological information. Relation-specific investment is fostered, and the hold-up problem is attenuated by maintaining dual or multiple suppliers in many cases, as well as by the importance of reputations that would be lost in case of opportunism.

On the other hand, the maintained separate identity of firms in the network reduces the problems of bureaucracy and influence activity (or rent-seeking) that plague large vertically integrated organizations. JIT delivery does render the system vulnerable to strikes or other labour conflicts, so the system is hardly compatible with adversarial labour relations. With cooperative relations based on permanent employment for core workers, both work teams and supplier networks have powerful incentive effects. Team members' peer-group pressure maintains a high work pace and long hours, while core companies impose exacting standards on suppliers, reinforced by some competition between multiple sources.

Small firms with fewer than 100 employees account for about one-third of total Japanese employment but pay only just over half the average wage of large firms. However, small Japanese firms have the largest share of manufacturing employment among all advanced economies, and are spared the risks of arm's-length market contracting and cut-throat competition, which produce much higher bankruptcy and exit rates in the more turbulent US environment. Small subsidiaries can specialize with core-company support, and without the risk of hold-up and hostile takeover that accompanies highly specialized assets in a short-term market context. On the other hand, key employees are unlikely to defect from Japanese companies that strongly discourage job-hopping and impose sanctions on opportunistic knowledge-hoarding. It is therefore less risky for Japanese employers to encourage knowledge-sharing and to build up aggregate human capital, which in turn accelerates the *kaizen* process.

Not only are there fewer exits from the small-firm sector in Japan, but there are also few new start-ups by disgruntled managers and engineers from large corporations, of the kind that have become common in the United States. We argue below that even in the fields of high technology this has not proved to be a handicap for Japan. Rather to the contrary, large firms there have concentrated on synergy-producing activities. When employment is permanent, long-term development can be pursued without the risk of losing key team-players to competitors, moves that can destroy the potential of many years of investment. Decentralized management in large companies has combined with a network of specialized but independent suppliers to reduce problems of bureaucratic hierarchy and keep large organizations efficient, in a way that runs counter to much recent experience in the United States.

However, the resurgence of US high-tech and manufacturing exports in the 1990s, while Japan was mired in its worst post-war recession, has led to growing criticism of the 'Japanese model'. Inefficient retail and agricultural sectors clearly need reform, and a growing number of American-trained managers favour US-style flexibility and mobility. Although the yen had declined from its peak by 1997, pressure from low-cost rivals such as China and Korea is growing, and it remains to be seen how Japanese corporations and other institutions will react and evolve.

C. International patterns of human resource management

International differences between even developed economies are nowhere more striking than in the areas of human resource management and the operation of labour markets. Hiring a new worker, firing an existing worker or simply reallocating an employee from one position to another are simple managerial tasks that are subject to quite different constraints, conventions and rules in different countries. Understanding these differences can help managers to avoid major pitfalls in international business. In labour relations, as in other aspects of economic organization, important lessons can be learnt from long experience under different rules in other countries.

Adversarial labour relations

Relations between management and labour are traditionally described as 'adversarial' in the United Kingdom and the United States. This does not just mean that more days are lost through strikes than in Germany or Japan. Adversarial labour relations have many more subtle and perhaps even more important manifestations that are less obviously visible. A pervasive 'them-and-us' attitude in the workforce is inimical to productive cooperation and team-work, the essential components of modern flexible manufacturing. Mutual suspicion and lack of trust encourage closer supervision and more intensive monitoring. Workers who feel they are not trusted are in turn encouraged to act accordingly, for example by colluding to outwit supervisors and managers. An example that has often been observed in the history of industrial relations is the following. Workers on piece-rates or some form of merit pay, particularly with a new product or process, may believe that rates will be lowered if their productivity and hence their earnings become too high. In this situation, it thus behoves workers deliberately to *restrict* output and earnings, rather than choosing their optimal pace of work at the current rate of pay. An individual who broke ranks and worked harder than the rest (at his individually optimal pace) might signal to management that output was being deliberately restrained. To avoid revealing this collusive strategy, social sanctions against 'rate-busters', as such individuals are called, have been frequently observed with performance-related pay of any kind. Even payment of a group bonus will not necessarily solve the problem, when management cannot be trusted to allow workers to retain the fruits of their own efforts.

It is interesting to trace the evolution of current adversarial labour management relations to the development of labour markets and institutions in the United States. Early industrialization of the United States was greatly facilitated by a flow of immigrants from the Old World, willing and eager to work hard for low wages wherever jobs beckoned. Markets were competitive and labour was mobile. Workers who quit or who were fired could easily be replaced. In this climate, there was little reason for commitment by either employer or employee. Firms' specific investments in training and human capital were relatively risky in this highly mobile labour market. Instead, ambitious workers looked for professional qualifications, which would be recognized by employers right across the country. Employers for their part were encouraged by scientific management to standardize tasks at all levels and to hire workers with appropriate and recognized qualifications as and when they were needed.

Ironically, many of these tendencies were actually reinforced by the growing power of unions in the decades of prosperity following tighter labour markets in World War II and the Korean War. The giant, capital-intensive corporations of the US industrial heartland (which later became the Rust Belt) faced stable and growing markets for steel, automobiles and other products. There were few competitors, and fewer imports, so that profits were consistently high. The sheer scale of their operation encouraged union organization, and high oligopolistic profits allowed the payment of premium wages. The unions also gained a measure of job security for their most senior members, with the help of agreements that stipulated layoffs according to inverse seniority. In time of recession, the youngest and most junior workers were the first to be laid off, so that if recessions were not too deep the majority of more senior workers could look forward to relative job security. At the same time, basically adversarial attitudes required collective bargaining agreements that could be monitored by union representatives and if necessary taken to outside arbitrators and the courts of law for enforcement. Pay rates were negotiated for numerous standardized tasks and job classifications. Promotion through internal job ladders to higher-paid classifications offered incentives to workers that were less susceptible to opportunistic manipulation or strategic collusion by employers or employees.

As the implicit price for these gains, unions conceded to management absolute rights of decision-making in the often disputed areas of employment, work organization and technology. Although formalized grievance procedures were established to deal with overt abuses of managerial authority, there was no attempt by even the most powerful unions to challenge this authority with any kind of employee empowerment or participation in managerial decision-making. The fundamental Taylorist division of labour between the planning and the doing of tasks was thus cemented in a highly bureaucratic and inflexible organization of labour in the giant manufacturing corporations. This lack of flexibility was no great handicap in the heyday of mass production, but even then bureaucratic organization and adversarial management–labour relations took their toll in the form of unnecessarily high costs, which accelerated import penetration and the decline of traditional American mass production manufacturing.

To supervise workers with little loyalty or commitment to their organization, American industry needed a higher ratio of managerial employees to production workers than its new rivals in Japan and Germany. As levels of education and aspiration rose during the prosperous 1960s, so too did rates of absenteeism and general disaffection with routinized, repetitive work. Product and process innovation were hampered by restrictive working rules and job classifications, which were originally designed to protect the craft-based jobs of the most senior union members.

Most seriously and fundamentally perhaps, collective bargaining and labour–management relations were regarded as primarily part of a distributional conflict, concerned with sharing a pie rather than increasing the size of the pie available for sharing. Few economists doubted that the legitimate goal of the firm was to maximize shareholder value, which implied minimizing costs, including labour costs, for a giving output. Some managers might sacrifice shareholder value for the sake of corporate empire-building and bloated compensation for themselves, but even they paid lip-service to the supremacy of stockholder interests. Employees were generally treated like any other factor of production – expendable, mobile and with no legitimate stake in the goals of the organization. There was little acknowledgement of the role of stakeholders such as customers and employees, whose interests dominate among the goals of the Japanese corporation. It is ironic to contrast this traditional view with two studies of the most successful US companies today.[1] These are companies that emphasize the interests of all their stakeholders, employees, customers and owners, and thereby do more for shareholder value than those firms that concentrate exclusively on the traditional goals of maximizing profits and stockholder value. A notable example is Hewlett-Packard, which by any standards is one of the most innovative companies in the United States or indeed in the world, and which has had a long tradition of Japanese-style permanent employment, with cooperative rather than adversarial labour relations. Many other examples show that adversarial labour relations and distributional conflict can block or delay the transition to flexible manufacturing. Although there are also such examples in Britain, UK policy in recent years has attempted to follow the American model and has resisted continental influence.

Codetermination in Germany

Codetermination is perhaps the best known and distinctive feature of German industrial relations. Codetermination was introduced by the allied occupational authorities after World War II, in a deliberate attempt to impose democratic control on the traditional core heavy industries of steelmaking and coalmining. Codetermination has two quite distinct components. The original and best-known institutional arm of codetermination was to give labour representatives seats on the board of directors of large corporations. In German law, the board of directors of a public company is quite distinct from top management. The board of directors or **supervisory board**, as it is called, consists only of outside directors, whose main task is to appoint the top management board, which is responsible for the day-to-day running of the company. The supervisory board must also be consulted on major strategic decisions, such as new acquisitions or plant closure. We describe the system of labour representation on supervisory boards, and its effect on the performance of German corporations, in more detail below.

The second institutional arm of codetermination is the **works council** at plant level. The employees of any plant or business employing more than five people are entitled to elect a works council or committee, which has far-reaching and carefully defined legal powers. This institution has no parallel under Anglo-

American company law, but varieties of works councils can be found in most continental European countries. The works council is formally and legally quite separate from union organization, and is explicitly prohibited from participating in any way in wage-bargaining. The powers of the works council are mainly restricted to personnel and job-related areas of decision-making.

A broadest requirement is for advance information on all personnel-related matters, including layoffs, short-time working, overtime working and any changes in technology and work organization. In addition to these information requirements, the works council has to be consulted on any substantive changes in working practice and on any changes at all in employment. In the case of layoffs, management must negotiate an agreement with the works council on the individual workers affected and agree on severance payment for them, called a **social plan**.

Though these powers may make the works council sound like an American or British manager's nightmare, this is not the way the institution has worked in practice. In addition to their formidable rights under German law, works councils also have carefully defined legal responsibilities. Councils actually have the right to veto managerial decisions on personnel matters, but they are also expressly prohibited from using their veto rights in any way that would endanger the prosperity or survival of their organization. Works councils were not designed as institutions to give workers extra leverage in distributional conflict with managers and owners. Rather, councils are required to *cooperate* with managers towards the overall success of their companies. Works councils, and codetermination in general, are thus part of a philosophy of company law and business organization that differs significantly from the adversarial Anglo-American tradition. The philosophy of cooperation among the major stakeholders in a productive organization under codetermination is so different from the Anglo-American tradition that it is frequently misunderstood by academic economists, business leaders and politicians.

As an example of this attitude, Britain has rejected out of hand any extension of continental works councils throughout the European Union to include British business. At the same time, hostility towards codetermination is accompanied by lack of any detailed knowledge of how the system has actually worked in Germany and other continental countries. Although German managers sometimes complain of the constraints imposed on them by codetermination laws, innumerable studies have shown that their cooperation with works councils has been productive and beneficial in a number of ways. One explicit indicator has been the very low incidence of overt conflict, such as strikes and lockouts, in German industry. Perhaps even more important, codetermination is generally considered to have facilitated rapid technological change and productivity growth. Works councils that are trusted by the labour force have gained cooperation in implementing changes, which might otherwise be blocked or delayed by adversarial attitudes. Although charismatic entrepreneurs or managers may do as well or better without the constraints of works

councils and codetermination, such individuals are exceptional, and most organizations do seem to benefit from the legal framework of codetermination and
in particular the works councils.

It is important to emphasize that codetermination law has complemented
existing German company law in a fairly natural manner. German top managers are legally required to consider the interests of all their major stakeholders and not just the interests of owners. Though managers routinely
opposed the introduction and various extensions of codetermination, they now
(with a few exceptions) generally defend the principles of cooperative
labour–management relations. On the other hand, simply transferring legal
codetermination rights into owner- or manager-oriented American or British
organizations might initially exacerbate adversarial relations and conflicts.
Perhaps we have here another example of the organizational complementarities discussed in previous chapters. To attain benefits from continental-style
codetermination may well require more fundamental reorientation of the one-
dimensional goals of the traditional Anglo-American firm.

In spite of the formal independence of codetermination and union organization, there is also a strong complementarity between the two institutions in
Germany. In large companies at least, works councils are dominated by union
members. Unions are also concerned with employment stability, working time
and working conditions, as well as with wages. Collective bargaining at regional
and industry levels is between union and employer representatives. Agreed
wage scales are for skill groups rather than detailed job classifications and are
applicable for all employers who belong to the employers' federation. The most
bitter conflicts have undoubtedly been with unions over wages and working
time, rather than within the institutions of codetermination. In spite of rhetoric
by union officials about class struggle and redistribution, most settlements in
the history of the post-war German economy have been regarded as moderate and non-inflationary, at least in retrospect. Only after reunification in 1990
was moderation abandoned at least in the East, and West German unions
helped to push the wages of East German workers up to levels far exceeding
their productivity of one-half to one-third of Western levels. The collapse of
Eastern markets in the former Soviet Union and elsewhere then dealt the final
blow to the economy of former East Germany, and deprived most industrial
workers of their jobs there. German and other corporatist continental unions
have traditionally opposed concessionary bargains for ailing firms or even
regions, but local workforces are increasingly negotiating more flexible deals.
There has been much less growth of wage inequality than in the less corporatist, or more decentralized, bargaining systems of America and Britain, but
lavish welfare support is coming under increased pressure in Germany, France,
Sweden and elsewhere.

This policy has had both costs and benefits for the whole German economy. The expansion of relatively low-paid and part-time service sector jobs,
particularly for women, has been much slower than in the United States.

Participation in the labour force, especially by women, is much lower than in Scandinavia or in the United States. But many of the problems of over-regulation and high cost in German labour markets are due to government legislation rather than to union bargaining. Taxes on labour to pay for social security (known as non-wage labour costs) form a higher proportion of total labour costs than in many other countries. For example, legislation rooted in craft traditions has impeded entry by new start-ups and self-employment in the service sector. Legislation has also failed to keep up with new technology, which often renders traditional skills and qualifications superfluous. None the less, the German system of vocational training, run with the backing of unions and employers, remains the envy of other European countries and provides one of the world's most skilled labour forces. And it is skilled blue-collar work-ers who typically represent labour in the organs of codetermination.

Labour representation on the supervisory boards of large corporations forms perhaps the most visible and most contentious part of the codetermination system. Initial legislation after the war required half the seats on the boards of steel and coal companies to be occupied by labour representatives. The chair of the board, representing owners, was given a second or casting vote to break the deadlock in the event of an equally split vote. This system of **almost parity** was extended to all public companies with more than 2,000 employees in 1976, extending labour's representation from their previous one-third of the board. These changes, and indeed codetermination in general, may have generated some costs by delaying the adjustment of the labour force in the face of shift-ing or declining demand. As in Japan, German firms tend to react with shorter working weeks to sudden downturns, and temporary layoffs are rare. Greater job security does, however, encourage more investment in firm-specific skills and training, although in the long run German employment adjusts to demand in much the same way as in the United States. The cooperation between labour representatives and other managers on corporate boards is generally described as productive and harmonious. Confrontations are extremely rare and most decisions are actually reached unanimously, even if they are sometimes pre-ceded by heated discussion. Although it is extremely difficult to quantify the effects of board representation by labour, most observers agree that codeter-mination has contributed to cooperative labour relations and rapidly growing productivity. There is no hard evidence that employee protection or codeter-mination have increased unemployment, in contrast to claims by politicians and the media.

Comparative studies of plants making the same product with similar capi-tal equipment have shown labour productivity and real wages in the German plants to be much greater than in the British plants (Prais, 1990).[2] The higher proportion of highly skilled blue-collar workers in the German plants seems to be partly responsible for the difference. However, it is also important that the most-skilled German blue-collar workers, or master craftsmen, are empow-ered to take decisions and perform crucial maintenance tasks that would be the prerogative of specialized engineers or members of management in Britain or the United States.

The former skilled workers who sit on Germany's corporate boards and cooperate with senior bankers and other outside directors represent the most visible pinnacle of the German system of industrial relations. However, they form only one of a number of complementary institutional components, and works councils may be even more important in day-to-day practice. Where labour mobility is often limited by strong local traditions and attachments, and where most blue-collar workers are well trained and skilled, it seems natural to include representation of all employee stakeholders in the management and decision-making process of the firm. The 1980s decade of growing prosperity, followed by the shock and the policy errors after unification, as well as a distorted, overgrown structure of government subsidy and regulation, have all left a legacy of serious problems. Provided a degree of social consensus can be maintained under current strains, cooperative, non-adversarial labour relations in the framework of codetermination offer more hope than any other system for overcoming current difficulties.

Lifetime employment in Japan

In the West perhaps the best-known distinguishing feature of the Japanese economy is the system of lifetime or permanent employment. The limitations of the system are less well known, but it is true that male employees, particularly of large corporations, start work after leaving high school or university and expect to remain with the same employer for the rest of their career, until early retirement at around the age of 55. After retirement, many continue to work for associated companies or subcontractors at lower rates of pay until 65 or older. There are no formal contracts for lifetime employment in Japan. Instead there is an *implicit* agreement or mutually held expectation that jobs are secure. For most women and for part-time and casual workers, there is no expectation of job security. These groups form the secondary labour market in Japan, with variable employment, low wages and usually manual work with few prospects of career advancement. Core primary workers in the large corporations represent only about one-third of the Japanese labour force. The rest work in small and medium-sized companies and family firms and in self-employment, particularly in retailing and agriculture. Wages are substantially lower and much more variable in these intermediate sectors, but there is still a commitment to long-term employment and there is less mobility than in US labour markets.

The severe recession of the early 1990s put the system of lifetime employment under considerable strain. Recruitment of fresh graduates to the major employers has dwindled to a small fraction of the normal intake. However, there have been no large-scale redundancies or layoffs of the kind that have become commonplace in the United States. Instead, critics argue that there is substantial employment of individuals, with many white-collar workers having become functionally superfluous and being retained simply to honour implicit agreements. Overall, the rates of registered unemployment have remained extremely low by international standards in Japan.

Lifetime employment in the primary sector of large corporations clearly encourages investment in firm-specific skills and training. With less risk of job loss, Japanese employees can accept a steeper age–earnings profile than occurs in the United States. Young employees receive low rates of pay, but even blue-collar workers are offered extensive training and career development opportunities. Pay rises rapidly with seniority, while qualification, promotion and outstanding performance bring additional rewards.

Growth of the Japanese firm translates into career advancement for most employees. On the other hand, bankruptcy or job loss would deprive workers of the high earnings they expect towards the end of their career as well as of the substantial lump sum, amounting to two or three years' final salary, that is usually paid out on retirement. Another unique feature of Japanese employment, is the twice-annual bonus payment, averaging about 25 per cent of annual earnings, which is often more closely related to current profitability than to regular wages or salary.

Wages themselves are determined by annual bargaining with enterprise unions. Wage bargains have been generally responsive to economic conditions and the prosperity of the employer. Wages are particularly flexible in the small and family firms, which in any case are closer to partnerships than to conventional employers, and this has helped to maintain low levels of unemployment in the economy as a whole. In large firms, extensive overtime working at premium rates of pay is the first to be reduced when demand declines. This then has the effect of reducing *average* wage levels substantially. For all these reasons, employees in large Japanese firms are also closer to being residual income claimants, or partners, than is conventional labour as a factor of production in a typical British or American company. Wage and bonus flexibility implies that all workers share firm-specific rents with the stockholders who are the formal residual claimants. Employee share ownership plans (ESOPs) are also widespread in Japan but, even without them, employees are more like part-owners, with consequent commitment and loyalty towards their employer, attitudes that are conspicuous by their absence under the adversarial labour–management relationships so common in the United States and Britain.

The employment relationship in Japan is thus characterized by high levels of trust and cooperation, such as are normally found only in successful partnerships in Western economies. There is no need for the hundreds of detailed job classifications used in American collective bargaining agreements to protect workers from surreptitious down-grading and pay cuts by opportunistic managers. Pay related to qualification and skills did in fact greatly facilitate the pioneering development of flexible manufacturing systems in Japan, which has already been described.

High trust and worker commitment are fostered through long-term association of work teams and co-workers under lifetime employment. As would be expected in a partnership, decision-making in the firm is consensual and decentralized, rather than authoritarian and centralized. All workers are expected to contribute to team success and the process of continuous improvement. Top managers circulate draft plans for major decisions through the hierarchy for comment and stamp of approval. Achieving agreement on an important issue in a Japanese organization can thus be a fairly lengthy process. By contrast, a central planner, or the chief executive who has ultimate authority in a Western corporation, can issue commands and directives that may go unchallenged by subordinates and should theoretically be implemented without delay. In practice however, implementation, particularly of important decisions, may proceed more rapidly and smoothly in Japanese organizations precisely because of prior consensus on the measures involved. In more authoritarian, centralized organizations, the devil that lurks in every detail, coupled with opposition by subordinates, may combine to delay or sabotage the implementation of even the best-laid and best-intentioned plans.

Can Japanese organization work in Eastern Europe?

The emerging market economies of Eastern Europe, having dismantled central planning, are now faced with the task of building new forms of economic organization more or less from scratch. The first generation of Eastern reformers, as well as their Western advisers, favoured so-called 'shock therapy'. This implied the quickest possible transition to a largely unregulated market economy, where labour could be hired and fired at will, without any of the legal rights or long-term implicit agreements that shape labour relations in Europe and Japan. This approach has run into severe political opposition, particularly in Russia. Large-scale close-down of too many former state-owned enterprises could, it is feared, generate mass unemployment and political anarchy.

Privatization in Russia has proceeded by giving employees of former state-owned enterprises vouchers for preferential purchase of new enterprise shares. Widespread employee ownership has thus established a legal basis for at least one aspect of Japanese organization, namely residual claimant status for Russian employees. Clearly, employees' rights will have to accommodate incentives for outside investors to provide the new capital that is necessary for the survival of these enterprises. Widespread reallocation of labour from the former military and heavy industrial sectors will be necessary before long-term employment relations become possible. Remaining employees in former state-owned enterprises will have to make major and prolonged sacrifices before viable new production for a market economy is developed. It is perhaps not implausible that the long-term rewards offered by ownership status will do more to encourage wage restraint and enterprise survival than the conventional process of collective bargaining. The experience with the wage explosion in former East Germany, following reunification in 1990 and leading to the demise of much of East German industry, does lend support to this interpretation.

American-style adversarial labour relations in Eastern Europe are likely to fuel political instability and extremism. However, the informal consensus and high trust that characterize Japanese labour relations can hardly be created overnight in a fragile and very different environment. Elements of the German codetermination system described above, which provide a more formal framework for cooperation between labour representatives and management or capital owners, might help to ease the pain of transition in Eastern Europe. Even cautious Eastern reformers will have to continue to walk a political tightrope, so it is to be hoped that they and their Western advises will not ignore the lessons from the development of labour relations in the post-war German and Japanese economies (see Acs and FitzRoy, 1994).[3]

D. International patterns of corporate control

As business becomes global, national boundaries in many ways become less important, but major differences remain between countries in the laws and institutions that govern the way business can operate. It thus becomes more important than ever for international managers and entrepreneurs to understand these differences, which reflect all aspects of economic organization. Government regulation of business everywhere receives much media attention, and experience with differing laws and institutions in other countries can provide valuable guidance and lessons for domestic policy. National, cultural traditions shape the institutions of economic life, and simply transplanting one particular institution into a very different setting, which lacks perhaps a host of complementary factors, may have unexpected and undesirable consequences. Thus it is important for both managers and policy makers to be aware of the main patterns of international economic organization.

Just as labour markets are more regulated or constrained by custom in German and Japan, so too are capital markets and the market for corporate control. The stock market is much less important in these and other continental European countries, and the banks have maintained a considerably more important role than in the United Kingdom or the United States. The tradition of reliance on free markets in the recent Anglo-American tradition has left the hostile takeover as the ultimate control on managerial behaviour. By contrast, hostile takeovers are essentially unknown in Germany and Japan, and top managers in these countries earn but a small fraction of the total compensation paid to American managers. Top managers are not obviously less efficient in Germany and Japan, so this comparison adds fuel to the debate over the role and effectiveness of the takeover mechanism in the United States and in the similar environment of the United Kingdom.

The role of the banks in Japan and Germany

Systems of corporate control and finance in Japan and Germany are usually described as bank based, in contrast to market-based systems in the United States and also the United Kingdom. However, recent research suggests that banks are less important in Germany than previously believed. According to this work, the most significant difference between market-based US and other systems lies in the differing patterns of ownership between countries. Banks play the most important role in Japan, and are influential, though not as dominant as often claimed, in Germany.

In Japan, the key position of main banks for individual companies or corporate networks (**keiretsu**) has been well documented. Main banks maintain long-term relationships and supply a higher proportion of debt capital than in other countries. Banks also hold equity shares of their main customers. Most importantly, main banks are likely to take an active part in restructuring or rescue of ailing firms at a time of financial crises. Long-term association and regular personnel interchange, including directors, give the main bank an informational advantage over other outsiders. Combined debt and equity holding removes any incentive to favour one party at the expense of the other, say by initiating bankruptcy proceedings that might satisfy senior, secured creditors while expropriating junior debt and equity holders. There is empirical evidence that firms with a main bank connection are more likely to survive financial crises in some, perhaps restructured, form or other.

Until the major recession of the early 1990s, growing prosperity had steadily reduced the dependence of Japanese firms on bank finance, enabling them to fund an increasing proportion of investment with retained earnings. However, bank relationships have bounced back to assume considerable importance for the growing tide of insolvencies and necessary restructuring during the severest post-war recession.

In addition to banks, most large stockholders of Japanese firms are other companies, but in particular they are usually companies with close trading relations. Their equity holdings are infrequently adjusted and are not held for short-term financial returns. Instead, they serve to align the objectives of trading partners and hence reduce incentives for opportunistic breach of trust or implicit contract. With a majority of their equity closely held in this way, Japanese firms are not threatened by hostile takeovers or corporate raiders. Long-term investment strategies can thus be followed with less risk of disruption.

Although there is some exchange of personnel, including directors, between banks and major stockholders of companies, most directors are insiders, drawn from the company's own top management. Thus there is little *formal* outside control of chief executives of large Japanese corporations. However, the corporate culture of decision-making by consensus does impose informal constraints on top management. Employee stakeholders have no explicit representation on the board of directors, but surveys suggest that their interests are usually put before those of outside stockholders by top managers in Japan.

Smaller firms and subcontractors in production networks are often partially owned by the parent or core corporation. Again, such ownership complements the primary trading relationship without the costs of bureaucracy and hierarchy involved in a vertically integrated or completely owned subsidiary.

In some ways, the structure of German banking relationships is quite similar to the Japanese. Most companies maintain long-term connections with a particular bank, called a **Hausbank**. Bank directors sit on the supervisory boards of large corporations, and banks hold substantial equity stakes in many companies. In the aggregate, however, debt finance has been almost as unimportant in Germany as in the United States, with most investment being internally financed. Furthermore, banks play only a minor role in restructuring companies in financial distress in Germany, and have no involvement in day-to-day management. Bank representatives are often influential in choosing the chief executive or chair, as well as other members of the management board, which is the essential function of the supervisory board of outside directors.

Although the board members have access to internal company data, they meet infrequently (once or twice a year) and are largely dependent on information provided by top management. In several well-publicized cases, a steady deterioration in corporate performance went unnoticed and unchecked for several years, leading to the takeover of ailing electrical giant AEG by Daimler Benz, or to the restructuring of insolvent metals conglomerate Metallgesellschaft. Top managers of the Big Three universal banks – Deutsche, Dresdner and Commerz – sit on well over 100 corporate supervisory boards and thus wield considerable economic power. The widely dispersed shareholdings of the major banks mean that there is little overt control by outsiders.

Banks do control more of the votes at shareholders' meetings than is implied by their own stockholdings. The reason for this is the proxy votes given to the bank by private stockholders, whose shares are held on deposit by the banks as part of their stockbroking function. However, German law gives considerable power to minority holdings of 25 per cent, which allows them to block or veto majority stockholders' decisions. Bank (or other) majority holdings are thus less decisive than under US law.

This brings us to what recent writers have found to be the most important difference between Anglo-American and German–Japanese systems of corporate governance (Edwards and Fischer, 1994). In Germany, only a relatively small proportion of companies are publicly quoted. The smaller UK economy has about five times as many listed corporations as Germany. Most German companies are privately held or family owned. However, most large listed corporations *except* the banks have concentrated institutional ownership. That is, at least one (usually institutional) stockholder has at least 25 per cent of the shares. In contrast, most publicly quoted companies in the United States have widely dispersed, mainly individual ownership.

The classical problem of separation of ownership as residual income claim and effective or residual control thus does not seem to arise to any great extent for non-financial institutions in Germany or in Japan. It should be emphasized, though, that most corporate ownership in these countries is by other corporations. The managers of these companies may have quite different goals from individuals who hold equity stakes for purely financial gains. German and Japanese top managerial salaries are closely related to firm size and only very weakly responsive to profitability measures. Top managers are also paid a small fraction, perhaps one-fifth, of comparable US compensation. Bonuses related to performance are relatively unimportant, and stock options or large holdings by top managers are almost unknown. Finally, the threat of hostile takeover is practically non-existent. Concentrated institutional equity holding in both Germany and Japan represents long-term relationships. However, German holdings are not as closely related to trading relationships as in Japanese industrial groups. As noted above, the large banks are the major exception to the rule of concentrated ownership, and all have, in fact, widely dispersed ownership.

The large banks in Germany are thus quintessential managerial corporations. Top managers of other big firms sit on their boards to form a system of interlocking directorships. Non-bank management is ultimately controlled by the managers of banks and of other, non-financial corporations with large equity stakes. This system does not suffer from the pervasive 'short-termism' of the stock market based system of corporate governance in the United States. Stable equity holdings and interlocking directorships favour long-term investment as in Japan. Parity labour representation on supervisory boards under German codetermination ensures that employee-stakeholder interests are respected. The German system of corporate governance does seem to avoid the major weaknesses of the stock market based US and UK systems, though it does not always function effectively and has come under growing criticism in recent years.

Do takeovers enforce efficiency?

By most measures the Japanese and German economies have outpaced the UK economy. The interesting question remains, however, how well does the hostile takeover mechanism work to enforce efficiency? This question has been the subject of much research and controversy. General agreement on a number of stylized facts has emerged. First, the shareholders of *acquired* firms generally benefit from substantial increases in their share prices. On the other hand, the stockholders of *acquiring* firms benefit little, because their share prices show little or no appreciation after a successful takeover bid. Given the very close correlation between firm size and top managerial compensation, the chief executives of acquiring firms almost certainly make substantial gains. Furthermore, the stock prices of acquired firms tend to show abnormal gains *before* takeover bids are announced, which suggests the practice of (illegal) insider trading. There is little evidence of improved performance by acquired companies on average, while aggressive acquirers spend less on R&D and innovate less than firms that are less active in the takeover market.[4]

Among the most successful takeovers have been those of related or complementary businesses, which aid the development of core competency. Management buyouts and corporate restructuring that involves the divestiture of peripheral lines of business also seem to improve corporate performance, at least in the medium term. However, most of this kind of activity has been too recent to provide long-term observations of its effects. The mere threat of takeover has often been cited as a major incentive for managerial performance. However, the threat of hostile takeover has also prompted considerable efforts at managerial entrenchment. Numerous legal defences have been put in place by wary managers in recent years, designed to thwart potential takeover bids, and incurring considerable cost.

Even if the stockholders of acquired and acquiring companies benefit in the aggregate, there is no guarantee that these gains do not come at the cost of other stakeholders such as employees and customers. Since these stakeholders often depend on implicit contracts rather than formal and legally enforceable agreements, there is a danger that acquiring firms may renege on these implicit contracts and inflict costs that are difficult to observe and cannot be recouped. Prior to the spread of managerial entrenchment, the unrestricted takeover mechanism undoubtedly provided incentives for ambitious managers to pursue empire-building and wasteful diversification. Incompetent management teams could also be replaced, and synergistic mergers and acquisitions have undoubtedly taken place. The difficulty of observing many of the possible costs and benefits makes it hard to arrive at an overall conclusion on the effectivity of the threat of takeover in promoting efficiency in the United States or the United Kingdom, but considerable doubt remains in view of pressure for short-term stock market performance.

As an alternative to takeovers, outside directors on the boards of the largest US corporations have taken an increasingly activist stance in recent years. The chief executives of troubled giants such as General Motors or IBM have been replaced without the necessity of takeover bids or restructuring. Whether these board-led changes of top management will prove adequate in the long run remains to be seen. A more active role for boards of directors in response to widespread stockholder dissatisfaction with the performance of many US and

UK corporations means that less reliance need be placed on the takeover mechanism. At the same time, cooperative joint ventures between different companies offer an increasingly attractive alternative to outright acquisition in many cases.

E. International patterns of innovation

Technological progress and innovation are important determinants of international competitiveness, productivity growth and living standards. The rapid expansion of high-technology sectors and the pervasive impact of their products have focused intense academic, policy and popular interest on the process of innovation. The race for scientific and technical breakthroughs now attracts media attention of the kind that used to be reserved for sporting contests.

A long history of successful, pioneering discoveries or breakthroughs in many fields of modern technology in the United States, contrasts with rapidly growing market shares for more and more high-technology products attained by Japanese companies. US industrial supremacy was once based on pioneering innovation. This ability to translate breakthroughs into marketable products has been increasingly captured by Japanese manufacturers. The resurgence of US manufacturing and high technology in some areas in the 1990s, while the Japanese economy suffered serious recession, has led some observers to conclude that the Japanese economy has run out of steam, but this seems premature.

The breakthrough illusion

Whereas large industrial R&D labs were pioneered in Germany and the United States, the dominance of the giant corporations in America in the 1960s and 1970s led to an increasingly bureaucratic organization of R&D that became ever more remote from the production process. The integration of production and innovation in the Japanese *kaizen* process of continuous improvement turned out to be more than a match for the sluggish response of hitherto sheltered US producers in many sectors of industry.

As large companies lost market shares in America, frustrated scientists and managers were leaving (still) market leaders such as IBM in droves, to set up their own new entrepreneurial ventures. Although many failed to develop or market their ideas, a successful breakthrough could generate vast fortunes for the founding entrepreneurs. While Silicon Valley, and other centres, prospered on this 'breakthrough' principle, the routine manufacture and refinement of products based on the innovative breakthrough were usually less rewarding and consequently often neglected (see Florida and Kenney, 1991).

The ruthless pursuit of technological breakthrough and instant capital gains led to hypermobility among top scientists and engineers, often disrupting the painstaking teamwork and synergy that took years to build up and unleashing a flood of litigation to reclaim damages and protect proprietary knowledge. However, small new entrepreneurial firms were often much more flexible than larger competitors, and could motivate employees with potentially valuable ownership stakes. Particularly in newer areas such as biotechnology, innovative leadership in the United States was taken over by the entrepreneurial start-ups.

Japanese and European innovation

This situation stands in marked contrast to the organization of innovation in Japan. Most R&D there is conducted by large firms, which have avoided many of the problems besetting corporate R&D in other countries. The close personnel and organizational links between production and R&D have been a major source of competitive advantage, complemented by long-term employment relationships that maintain continuity and avoid the costs of hypermobility.

In Germany, long-term employment is also common, and industrial R&D is backed by state-funded research centres and a strong tradition of university-based fundamental scientific research as in the United States, but lacking in Japan. Although Germany's traditional leadership in engineering and chemicals has been maintained, the new high-tech industries such as biotechnology and much of electronics have lagged far behind the United States and Japan. This is symptomatic of other, less scientifically and technically advanced European countries, but is being addressed by proliferating joint ventures and alliances with Japanese and US companies eager to gain a foothold in the world's largest unified market.

A lack of venture capital and entrepreneurial risk taking does not seem to have handicapped Japanese technological advance, but is often criticized in Germany and other European countries, where corporate bureacracy may be less conducive to creative innovation than it is in Japan. Britain has the most developed venture capital market in Europe and more entrepreneurial activity, partly fuelled by downsizing of large corporations and the drastic decline of manufacturing employment. However, foreign inward investment in high-tech and other manufacturing has had a much larger impact, and even Siemens is building its latest chip-making facility on Tyneside, attracted by the high flexibility and low cost of labour in Britain.

Innovation and R&D have been organized on very different lines in the countries with active programmes. Whereas international cooperation flourishes, there is little sign of convergence in the organization of R&D. Both Japan and Europe remain as far as ever from the entrepreneurial high-tech culture of the United States, but with very varying degrees of success. Japan employs twice as many scientists and engineers in R&D per head of population as the United Kingdom, more even than the United States, the second-most intensive employer of scientists and engineers. There is a widening gap between Britain's stagnant R&D employment and the increasing intensity of scientists and engineers in Germany, Japan and the United States.

F. Chapter summary and key ideas

This chapter has summarized the key international comparisons that were emphasized throughout our previous discussions of manufacturing, human resources, financial markets and corporate governance. As usual, the natural focus on contrasting Anglo-American, German and Japanese economic systems has been retained. This focus hardly does justice to European diversity, and indeed Germany, with the best-developed systems of worker participation and training in Europe, is by no means typical in all respects. However, our choice of examples does serve to highlight the most salient differences between more and less regulated market approaches.

Any discussion of international organizational patterns culminates naturally with the question of convergence. Will the erosion of national economic boundaries and the forces of global markets impose uniform rules on economic actors? Popular as this idea has become, national institutions and customs still seem to attract much popular support. While lavish welfare expenditure in Germany, Sweden, France and other countries comes under heavy attack in the run-up to European monetary union, there is little criticism in Germany of the unique institutions of codetermination. For all the European rhetoric about labour market flexibility, there is strong opposition to importing Anglo-American inequality and the attendant social costs of a large and deprived underclass.

As another example of apparent barriers to convergence, German vocational training has been widely extolled but little imitated. Employee involvement (and share ownership) have made only slow progress internationally, despite their complementary role in lean manufacturing. More generally, inefficient practices seem to survive global market pressures for surprisingly long periods. Put differently, the costs of adjustment or barriers to change in established customs are high. In the long run, of course, small evolutionary steps accumulate to generate major structural change, of a kind that is often hard to predict from current trends.

Key words

adversarial labour relations	*kanban*
almost parity	*keiretsu*
breakthrough illusion	*Mittelstand*
codetermination	social plan
Hausbank	supervisory board
implicit contract	transplants
kaizen	works council

Notes

1 See books by best-selling management author Robert Waterman (1994) and by Stanford Business School's Jeffrey Pfeffer (1994).
2 Aggregate comparisons of British and German output and wages have underestimated the higher average quality of German products, and hence the real productivity differential. When correctly measured, real German wages seem to be about 50 per cent higher than corresponding British wages, owing partly to the higher average quality of consumption goods in Germany. See Jarvis and Prais (1995).
3 Uvalic and Vaughan Whitehead (1997) provide a detailed account of employee ownership in transition. Much supporting evidence for employee ownership in transition economics is given by ILO (1997).
4 This has been established in a large-scale study by Hitt (1996).

References

Acs, Z. and F. R. FitzRoy (1994), 'A constitution for privatizing large eastern enterprise', *The Economics of Transition*, 2, pp. 83–94.

Edwards, J. and K. Fischer (1994), *Banks, Finance and Investment in Germany*, Cambridge: Cambridge University Press.

Florida, R. and M. Kenney (1991), *The Breakthrough Illusion*, New York: Basic Books.

Hitt, M. (1996), 'The market for corporate control and firm innovation', *Academy of Management Journal*, 39(6).

ILO (International Labour Office, Central and East European Team, Budapest) (1997), *Experts' Policy Report: Employee Ownership in Privatization*.

Jarvis, V. and S. J. Prais (1995), 'The Quality of Manufactured Goods in Britain and Germany', NIESR Discussion Paper no. 88, December 1995.

Osterman, P. (1994), 'How common is work place tranformation and who adopts it?' *Industrial and Labour Relations Review*, 47, pp. 173–88.

Pfeffer, J. (1994), *Competitive Advantage Through People*, Boston: Harvard Business School Press.

Prais, S. J. (ed.) (1990), *Productivity, Education and Training*, London: NIESR.

Roach, S. (1996), 'The hollowing of smokestack America', *Harvard Business Review*, November–December.

Uvalic, M. and D. Vaughan Whitehead (ed) (1997), *Privatization Surprises in Transition Economics*, Edward Elgar.

Waterman, R. (1994), *What America Does Right*, New York: Norton.

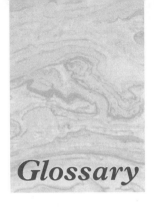

Glossary

acquisition An arrangement in which the assets and liabilities of the seller are absorbed into those of the buyer.

adaptation costs Part of the implicit or explicit costs to workers to find a new job if it is necessary to relocate or to give up any employment benefits such as pensions.

adjustable rate mortgage A type of secured debt on private homes that allows the interest rate on the unpaid balance to vary through time according to some specified index or other criteria.

adverse selection A form of pre-contractual, or *ex ante*, opportunism in which one party has private information at the time of negotiation that potentially reduces the value of the contract to the other party.

age–wage profile The relationship between the wage earned by an employee at a given firm and various points in time (perhaps corresponding to that employee's age), typically assuming that higher wages are earned at higher ages.

agency costs A general name given to the costs involved in monitoring the behaviour of some party acting on your behalf.

allocative efficiency Refers to the economy's ability to produce the quantities of the good and services that consumers desire to buy.

almost parity An institutional component of the codetermination system in Germany in which workers are granted by law one-half of the seats on corporate supervisory boards, 'almost' because the chair of the board, representing ownership interests, is given two votes to break a deadlock.

arc elasticity A measure of the resilience to price changes measured over a range on a given demand curve.

asset specificity One dimension of transaction costs; refers to the degree to which a resource is committed to a specific task and thus cannot be redeployed to alternative uses without a substantial reduction in its value.

asymmetric information The relative holdings of data by individuals, when at least one party to an agreement has superior knowledge of some dimension of the agreement.

at-will employment Employment situations in free economies; workers are

561

employed (or sacked) at the will of the employer and employees voluntarily work.

authority relationship An arrangement in which one party has the right, within reasonable bounds, to direct the behaviour of, punish and reward other parties.

average fixed cost Fixed costs of production divided by the number of units produced.

average product The total product, or output, divided by the number of units of a given input employed.

average total cost The total cost of production including explicit and implicit components at any level of output divided by the number of units produced; equals average variable plus average fixed cost.

average variable cost Total variable cost divided by the number of units produced.

bankruptcy A situation in which a firm is unable to pay its bills and must go out of business, shareholders lose their investments, creditors have a long fight to recover debt, and managers may lose credibility.

barriers to entry Anything, either physical, institutional, or the result of some decision process that makes it prohibitive for new firms to enter a market; it is necessary if incumbent firms are to maintain monopoly power.

behavioural finance Modern approach to financial markets that goes beyond simple economic rationality to include psychological subtleties.

Bertrand competition When the competition between two or more firms is characterized by each firm assuming that the price(s) of its rival(s) are fixed; a very severe form of competition characterized by price wars.

block booking A pricing strategy in which sellers with some market power group similar goods together and offer them as a package to less informed buyers.

blocked pricing A pricing practice that is a case of second degree price discrimination, when a firm with market power charges higher prices for the first units of a good bought and lower prices for later units.

board of directors Shareholder-elected officials who act in the interest of the owners in a corporation's internal control mechanism.

book value One way to place a value on a firm; the historical accounting valuation of the firm's assets including accumulated depreciation charges and owners' equity.

bounded rationality A property common to parties involved in economic exchange which implies that economic agents act with less than perfect information; arises because information is costly to acquire and process; that is, transaction costs will prevent parties from becoming fully informed.

brand name capital specificity A form of asset specificity that refers to becoming affiliated with a well-known brand name and thus less free to pursue other opportunities.

breakthrough illusion The notion that scientific or technological advances (breakthrough) are sufficient to gain competitive advantage, even when developed and production are neglected.

buffer stocks Stocks held to cushion fluctuations in supply or demand.

business ecosystems Interrelationships between a business, its suppliers, trading partners and customers.

business re-engineering A form of business reorganization often embracing techniques such as teamwork, employee training in multiple skills and worker empowerment.

business unit strategy The way the firm competes in a given line of business.

capital structure The mix of debt and equity financing chosen by a firm; the higher the ratio of debt to equity, the more leveraged the firm.

capped option A form of corporate executive compensation involving a standard option with a certain strike price and a limit on the share price the executive can cash in on.

carrot method A way to deal with the incentive problem facing managers by attempting to encourage individual responsibility by linking employee pay to performance.

cartel Group of firms in the same industry that cooperate in order to maintain (high) prices or market shares.

change in demand A shift from one demand curve to another reflecting a change in one of the non-price determinants of demand.

change in quantity demanded The movement along a given demand curve in response to a change in the good's price.

change in quantity supplied The movement along a given supply curve in response to a change in the good's price.

change in supply A shift from one supply curve to another reflecting a change in one of the non-price determinants of supply.

Coase theorem A proposition that, if legal, strategic or informational barriers to bargaining are absent and if property rights are clearly defined, people can always negotiate an efficient outcome.

codetermination The process permeating every aspect of labour–management relations in Germany; the assigning of workers to seats on corporate boards and establishment of works councils at individual plants.

co-evolution A process through which social learning on the part of organizations interacts with changes in the environment, in unforseeable ways.

collateral Tangible assets pledged by a borrower as security in case of default or inability to repay loan.

collusion Agreement or cooperation amongst individuals or firms to further their own goals at the cost of others.

commercial mortgage A common form of debt secured by fixed property.

commitment Determination or promise to follow a particular course of action.

comparative advantage A theory used to explain international trading patterns; countries choose what to produce by determining those goods in whose production they have an advantage (in terms of the opportunity cost of other, lost outputs) over other countries.

comparative statics The comparison of two different equilibrium points.

compensating differential Pay the difference required to compensate for unpleasant or dangerous work.

complementarities The relationships between groups of activities in an organization in that one activity experiences feedbacks from changes in the other activity.

computer-aided design (CAD) The use of computers to speed up design, involving an interactive computer terminal and product models and the ability to perform modification and tests.

computer-aided manufacture (CAM) The use of computers to speed up the manufacturing process by connecting computers to machine tools, enabling the integration of systems of numerically controlled machine tools, robots and other process machinery used in manufacturing.

computer numerical control (CNC) A machine that has as its basis a minicomputer and occupies an intermediate position between transfer machines and conventional hand-operated machine tools.

concentration Economic term referring to the importance of large products in a market; said to increase when fewer, larger producers dominate a market.

constant returns to scale A situation in production where increasing inputs by x per cent will result in increasing output by x per cent. If inputs are doubled, for example, output will double.

constrained efficiency postulate A hypothesis that states that, if individuals are able voluntarily to bargain to an enforceable allocation, then the result will tend to be efficient, subject to their generally limited information and resources and bounded rationality.

consumer surplus The difference between what final users are willing to pay for a good and what they actually pay.

consumption complementarities The process in which two related products or goods are used together; use of one complements the use of the other.

consumption externalities Created when the use of a good by one party affects the use of that good by another party. *See* externalities.

contestability An economic concept stating that economic rents can be earned only if others are precluded from securing them by some process such as market bidding or industry entry.

contract An interlocking set of mutual promises enforceable and acknowl-edged by some disinterested third party; generally specifies actions that each party will take; may assign decision-making powers.

contract curve The locus of points in a production Edgeworth box which represent tangencies of each firm's isoquants at the prevailing input price ratio.

convertible preferred shares (stock) Preferred shares with a right to conversion to ordinary shares at a later date.

cooperation In business terminology, partnerships with businesses in similar industries.

coordination costs A broad category of transaction costs entailing the determination of prices, the costs of acquiring information concerning the location, quality, reputation and availability of different parties, and other costs associated with allocating workers to specific tasks and with bringing transaction participants together.

core competency An area of business in which an organization has a competitive advantage not only in producing a good or service but also in developing new and related products.

corporate control The process by which society, through markets or regulatory means, exerts some authority on a business entity.

corporate culture A set of routines for decision-making and shared expectations that employees are taught as well as the stories and related devices used to convey those expectations; provides a set of principles and procedures for judging behaviour and resolving legitimate disputes.

corporate governance The way in which the contracts are arranged that tie the individual units in an organization together; degree of vertical integration.

corporate strategy The determination of which business activities the firm will undertake.

corporation A legal entity recognized by and subject to the various laws in the state in which it is created; a dominant form of organizing economic activity because of the limited liability of its owners.

corporatist economy Arrangement whereby representatives of organized labour, business and government agree informally or formally on eco-nomic policy.

co-specialized assets Two resources that are most productive when used together and lose much of their value in the absence of the other.

credibility Plausibility of claims or promises.

cross-price elasticity of demand The percentage change in the quantity demanded of a good that results from a 1 per cent change in the price of another good, all other things being equal.

cross subsidization Using profits from one line of business to cover losses in another.

deadweight loss The area of consumer and producer surplus lost due to the presence of a monopoly seller in a market.

debt A form of financing a firm; represents an agreement requiring regular payments; provides no element of corporate control to the providers of the loan.

decentralization A process taking place in corporations in which the functions of command and control are redistributed and more independent business units emerge.

deconglomeration The act of returning a form to its original competencies; the breaking up of firms into many lines of business.

decreasing returns to scale When an X per cent increase (decrease) in all inputs causes output to increase (decrease) by only Y per cent where X is greater than Y.

dedicated asset specificity form of asset specificity involving investment in general-purpose assets made at the behest of a particular transaction partner.

demand The quantity of a good or service that consumers are willing and able to purchase.

demand curve The graphical depiction of the relationship between quantity demanded and price, holding all other factors affecting consumer behaviour constant.

demand function An explicit mathematical or graphical relationship between the price of a good and the quantity demanded.

derived demand Requirement of a good or service not for itself but for what it can produce.

design attributes Some characteristics of a problem in formulating corporate strategy involving information that is generally available in the firm; an inefficient choice will have wide ramifications throughout the organization.

design decisions Choices made by organizations involving the way in which economic activity will be arranged when a small mistake will have large implications in future periods.

Detroit automation A method of factory mechanization pioneered by Ford Motor Co. at its engine plant in Brook Park, Ohio; linking several large transfer machines in a continuous system; also referred to as Fordism.

differentiated products In a market where the wares of one seller are different, but not substantially so, from the wares of (an)other seller(s); the wares fulfil the same basic function but vary in at least one dimension.

dimensions of transaction costs A breakdown of transaction costs into five types: asset specificity; assessment of the benefits of the transaction; complexity and uncertainty; familiarity with the transaction; and relationship to other transactions.

diminishing marginal productivity A generally accepted theory in economics stating that the marginal product of an input to the production process eventually declines as more units of that input are added to the production process.

direct demand Requirement of a good or service for the utility, or satisfaction, that good itself directly provides.

directly unproductive activities Actions that individuals take to change the allocation of rents within an organization; do not necessarily create value for the organization.

disequilibrium A situation in which quantity demanded and quantity supplied differ, unleashing forces to bring them into equilibrium.

distribution effects A force affecting efficient exchange pertaining to who has, or gets, what resources; can refer to a party's ability either to 'afford' its portion of an efficient allocation or to share the value created within firms.

diversified portfolio Collection of assets with differing or uncorrelated risks.

division of labour Separation of tasks into a large number of different component activities.

dominant strategy One course of action which always yields the decision maker a greater payoff than all other courses of action, whatever other parties do.

downsizing A process by which a corporation reduces the number of its employees, leaves a line of business, sells off assets, or any combination of the three.

economic rents A term used by economists to describe 'extra' payments going to a resource; more specifically the benefits from an activity going to a resource in excess of what is needed to attract that resource to that activity; in a sense representing 'something for nothing'.

economies of scale The result of physically combining inputs to form outputs that continually reduce producer unit costs over the relevant range of demand.

economies of scope The results of physically combining inputs to form outputs that produce two or more related outputs within the same firm; implies lower unit costs for each output than if produced separately.

Edgeworth box A graphical depiction of the total amount of two factors of production going to the production of two outputs.

efficiency A term describing the potential outcome of some exchange-based activity from which any change increasing one party's well-being necessarily causes a reduction in the well-being of one other party.

efficiency principle The proposition that people can bargain effectively to implement and enforce their decisions, resulting in outcomes that are efficient.

efficiency wage model A working hypothesis attempting to explain compensation patterns in labour markets; especially useful because it addresses measurement costs and predicts that managers will reward good behaviour by workers with economic rents.

efficient An economic arrangement is said to be efficient if it is impossible, given available resources, to implement an alternative arrangement under which all parties involved are at least as well off.

efficient market hypothesis The proposition that prices in security markets fully and accurately reflect all information relevant to forecasting future returns.

elastic demand The percentage change in quantity demanded of a good in response to a 1 per cent change in price that is higher than one in magnitude.

employee involvement Inclusion of production or other non-managerial employees in some area of managerial decision making.

employee stock ownership plan (ESOP) When the employees of a firm obtain equities in their organization and actively participate in management.

employment relationship A long-term relational contract existing between a firm and its employees featuring gradually rising wages; intended to create incentives for workers to accumulate firm-specific human capital and develop loyalty.

endogenous barriers Obstacles to entry into an industry which are deliberately created by incumbents, such as brand loyalty or excess capacity.

entrepreneurial regime Describes the availability of information necessary for innovation; is said to exist if the information available to potential innovators exists outside of existing firms.

entrepreneurship Private initiative to start a business venture.

entry barrier Some device keeping other sellers from freely entering a market, including economies of scale and scope, control of a key resource or location, or a patent or copyright.

equilibrium A state in an economic or physical system within which there are no forces affecting change; the price and quantity that such demand equals supply.

equilibrium price The single price at which the quantity demanded and the quantity supplied of a good or service balance.

equity A form of financing a firm; represents a stake in a corporation made by an investor who obtains some rights to dictate the policies and operation of that firm.

evolutionary economic A theory of economic organization and industrial structure that focuses on change; the primary assumptions are (1) firms satisfy rather than maximize, relying on routines and decision rules in doing so, (2) the competitive environment rewards success, and (3) any industry is not likely to be in equilibrium at any point in time.

ex ante A Latin phrase that translates roughly as 'before the fact'.

excess volatility Fluctuations in share prices that exceed the range plausibility justifiable by future dividend payments.

exchange efficiency When the allocation of goods and services in the economy is such that, for all consumers, no one consumer can be made better off without making someone else worse off.

exclusive dealing A contracting device that restricts one party's ability to freely contract with other than stipulated parties.

exclusive territories In which a single distributor is the only one allowed to sell a particular product.

exit One choice that share owners have if they are unhappy with the performance of the company in which they have shares. To exist, they simply sell their shares.

exogenous barriers The need for a resource or access to a resource that is necessary to enter a market because of the physical nature of the production, distribution, or sale of a good.

explicit collusion A formal agreement in written or verbal form among a group of rivals that restricts the individual decision making of any single agent.

explicit contract Dealings occur under a specified, existing contract.

ex post A Latin phrase that translates roughly as 'after the fact'; used in describing contracting situations after the agreement has been reached.

external contract An agreement between the firm and parties lacking an ownership or employment interest.

external labour market Labour market outside of a particular firm or organization.

externalities Costs (negative) or benefits (positive) imposed involuntarily on another party not regulated by any system of prices.

final goods Outputs produced in an economic system sold directly to consumers without further processing.

financial restructuring The alteration of a firm's debt–equity ratio without changing its assets.

firm Cooperative interaction and agreement among any number of people, in order to produce some marketable output, define a firm.

firm-specific human capital A term describing employee-acquired skills and knowledge that have greater value in their current employing organization.

first-degree price discrimination When each consumer is charged a price exactly equal to the value of the product for the consumer (no surplus).

fixed cost A cost incurred by the firm that does not vary with output.

fixed input An input that does not vary with output, such as land area of a factory site.

fixed proportion production A technology that does not allow substitution or varying input ratios.

flexible manufacturing system (FMS) A process typically consisting of multiple work stations, an automated material-handling system and a supervision system through computer controls; often relies on computer-aided manufacturing technology.

follow-through economy The institutions that turn basic technological breakthroughs into marketable products.

Fordism Mass production with moving assembly line as pioneered by Henry Ford.

free cash flow Funds existing in an organization that do not have to be paid out to workers, for materials, to suppliers or to service debt.

free-rider problem The difficulty in eliciting true willingness to pay for a public good whose enjoyment by non-payers cannot readily be prevented.

frictional unemployment Unemployment of those moving between jobs or searching for new jobs.

fundamentals Real factors such as future profits that should ultimately determine stock prices.

fungible An economic description of something with a very general purpose that can be crafted to meet very unique individual needs and circumstances.

game Any exchange environment or otherwise competitive environment in which participants must choose a course of action when there is a large degree of uncertainty regarding what choices other participants might make.

game theory The formal modeling of a game highlighting the interaction resulting from choices made by all the players.

general equilibrium analysis A method of enquiry that simultaneously determines the prices and quantities in all markets.

general-purpose human capital The stock of skills and abilities possessed by a worker that are usable in a number of applications.

globalization The process by which investment and technology occur on an international scale; is directly tied to foreign investment; most of the world's trade occurs within multinational corporations.

golden parachutes Contracts that promise large severance payments to employees who lose or leave their job shortly after and because of a change in corporate control.

governance structure The contractual format chosen to manage a transaction, ranging from a simple spot market transaction to complex, long-term relational contracts to ownership.

greenmail Payment by a corporation to a potential corporate raider to induce her to give up the attempted takeover.

gross domestic product (GDP) The total money value of the goods and services produced by the residents of a country in a given time period;

frequently used by economists to measure output in a national economy because it accounts for the 'openness' of economic activity.

gross national product (GNP) A measure of the incomes of the residents of a country including incomes earned abroad but excluding payments made to those abroad.

hard science A natural science such as physics, biology or chemistry.

Hausbank The name given to the primary bank of a German corporation.

Herfindahl index Sum of the squared market shares of firms in an industry.

hold-up A form of *ex post* opportunism arising because of asset specificity that involves exploiting in the inflexibility of one party to a transaction.

horizon problem A potential mismatch between the planning horizon of the decision maker and those affected by her decision.

horizontal differentiation When producers make a product that is at least slightly different from that made by competing producers but roughly the same quality.

horizontal equity The concept in an organization that wages be similar across workers.

horizontal integration One dimension of firm strategy that determines the firm's horizontal boundaries, which basically determine the business in which the firm should be engaged.

horizontal restrictions A type of endogenous entry barrier said to occur when different firms selling competing products act to reduce current and future competition in the marketplace.

hostile takeover One firm taken over by a second without the cooperation of the management of the first firm.

human asset specificity When individuals develop skills with narrow applications.

human capital The amount of knowledge, skills, education, training and experience held by an individual enabling that person to become more productive, earn higher future incomes, lead a more meaningful life, and have improved decision-making ability.

human resource management A field specializing in developing policies to administer the relationship between firms and workers.

idiosyncratic exchange A particular type of relational interchange between contracting partners (usually long term) in which, once the general nature of the relationship is established, neither party has an incentive to engage in opportunistic behaviour; said to be self-enforcing.

imperfect commitment A situation resulting in transaction costs; occurs when the parties come to an agreement that one or both would later like to abandon.

imperfect information Less than complete or accurate data held by at least some buyer or seller.

implicit contract A type of agreement with no formal statement of the terms and conditions agreed to by the parties.

inalienability problem A difficulty occurring in organizations where the net benefits from a business relationship cannot be sold by those currently holding the rights to those benefits.

incentive problem A difficulty in an environment facing the manager of a firm who must motivate and coordinate employees, possibly in a team production context.

income elasticity of demand The percentage change in the quantity demanded of some good resulting from a 1 per cent increase in income.

incomplete contracts Agreements that fail fully to specify actions under every conceivable course of events.

incomplete information A situation where economic agents have data that are not accurate or complete.

increasing returns A relationship between costs and input usage by the firm in which additional units of input yield successively more to output, resulting in declining average costs over a wide range of output.

increasing returns to scale A situation in production where increasing inputs by x per cent will result in increasing output by more than x per cent. If inputs are doubled, for example, output will more than double. Increasing returns to scale will put pressure on unit costs to decline as output expands.

indifference curve A depiction of all combinations of two goods or services that yield the same satisfaction to the household.

industrial divide The moment in history when the path of technological development itself is at issue; a 'pointer' that demarcates a period before and after a significant change in the way firms organize economic activity.

industrial robot A machine typically composed of components: a mechanical special-purpose device, a 'servo-system' that controls movement of the device, and a computer control system that coordinates the machine within its industrial environment.

industrial system The relationship between firms' internal organization and their connection to one another and to the social structures and institutions in their particular localities.

inelastic demand When the percentage change in the quantity demanded of a good divided by the percentage change in price is less than one in magnitude.

influence costs Costs associated with rent-seeking behaviour; occur when one party attempts to alter the distribution of costs and compensation in a contractual setting; or when decision makers make inefficient decisions because of their exposure to rent-seeking behaviour.

informate To supply with abundant information.

Information Age A time period described by the replacement of traditional raw materials in the manufacturing process with knowledge.

informational asymmetries When the amount and/or quality of data held by parties to an exchange differs, or is believed to differ.

innovation A process that begins with an invention, proceeds with its development, and results in the introduction of a new product, process or service.

innovative attributes Some characteristics of a problem in formulating corporate strategy involving information that is not available within the organization.

in-person services Tasks which require face-to-face interaction with customers.

inputs Any resource used in the production of an economic good or service.

insiders Current employees of firms or organizations.

integrated production Includes manufacture rather than purchase of components used.

intensive margins Utilization of production factors, such as hours of work per day.

intermediate good Output subject to later processing before ultimately being sold to consumers.

internal contract An agreement limited to parties within a firm; typically vague with some amount of latitude given to each of the involved parties.

internal control One of the ways in which firms in a capitalistic economy face demands for efficient behaviour; refers to the authority and conduct of that authority by boards of directors acting in the interests of stock-holders.

internal coordination Coordination in an organization or group without external intervention.

internal job ladder Sequence of career positions or moves in an organization hierarchy or structure.

internal labour markets Career paths and so-called job ladders within organizations where wages are tied to jobs and employees are rewarded by moving up to higher-paying slots.

international joint venture An undertaking in which one party is head-quartered in a different country.

internationalization A situation in which the demand for an output is international as opposed to national or just regional.

intrapreneurship Entrepreneurial activity within organizations.

investment The current expenditure of resources that produces a stream of benefits over a future period creating an asset.

irreversible investment Investment with no alternative use or resale value.

isocost line The combinations of two inputs that cost the same amount.

isoquant The combinations of two inputs that yield the same output.

joint ventures Two or more legally distinct organizations, each of which actively participates beyond an investment role, such as in the decision-making activities of the mutually owned entity.

junk bonds Interest-bearing securities issued by corporations to finance their activities, usually involving a merger or acquisition, which have a very high risk of default.

just-in-time manufacturing system A production system in which outside suppliers work closely with large firms to provide parts on a rigid schedule eliminating the need for all firms to carry large inventories.

kaizen A strategy widely adopted in Japanese firms empowering workers to contribute their skills in an atmosphere of continuous process improvement; can include: teamwork, quality circles, job rotation and flexible work teams.

kanban A characteristic of Japanese production that implies a high degree of coordination and communication between related units; emulated in the United States.

karoshi A Japanese word meaning roughly 'death by overwork'; a particular problem in high-tech industries owing to the importance of speed.

keiretsu The name given to a group of related firms in Japan that dominate the Japanese economy; usually consists of independent firms with close financial and technological links, possibly a shared name.

law of diminishing marginal productivity As the use of an input to the production process increases (while other inputs remain constant), the additional output produced will eventually decrease.

law of diminishing marginal returns A general principle in economics which says that for any activity as additional units of that activity are conducted, the return on those additional units of activity will decline.

law of diminishing returns A premise that increasing amounts of a variable factor applied to a given amount of a fixed factor will add increasingly less to output.

lean production Minimizes down time, inventories, waste, etc.

learning curve Path of declining unit cost for new products as a manufacturer learns to overcome initial problems.

lease When a resource is put in the control of a party without an ownership interest.

leveraged buyout Acquisition of a firm through heavy use of debt.

logical positivism A method of enquiry adhered to by most economists.

long run A term used to describe the time frame over which all inputs to the production process are not in fixed supply to the firm.

long-run equilibrium A situation in which the firm earns zero profits in competitive markets because the correct number of firms are active, each producing at minimum average total cost such that industry supply and demand are balanced.

Maastricht Treaty Foundation agreement for European Monetary Union (EMU).

make-or-buy decision The choice a firm must make about whether it should make an intermediate good in-house or secure it in some market.

management buyout The purchase of a firm by its managers; often leveraged because it is accomplished with heavy debt.

managerial misbehaviour The imperfect monitoring and conflicting incentives of the owners of a firm and its managers characterized by unjustifiably high salaries and maximizing something other than shareholder wealth.

manufacturing strategy A plan to position a firm in the global market place.

marginal cost The increase in the total costs of production resulting from raising output by one unit.

marginal product The change in total product, or output, resulting from the use of one more unit of a variable factor, other things being equal.

marginal productivity theory A premise in economics stipulating that all factors of production be paid the value of their marginal contribution to output.

marginal rate of substitution The rate at which consumers are willing to substitute units of one good for another, holding utility levels constant.

marginal rate of technical substitution (MRTS) Provides a measure of the amount of capital that must be added when one less unit of labour is used to keep output constant.

marginal revenue The change in total revenue resulting from the sale of one more unit of output; equal to price for perfectly competitive firms.

marginal revenue product The market value of the output produced when the firm uses one more unit of a variable input in the production process, holding all else constant.

market The interaction of one or more buyers with one or more sellers.

market discipline A functioning, competitive market prevailing if enough buyers (sellers) learn of a particular seller's (buyer's) poor behaviour so as to curtail that seller's activities; punishment for 'bad' behaviour.

market failure A malfunction in a market mechanism that results in an allocation of resources that is not efficient.

market for corporate control When investors try to become aware of and purchase corporations that are undervalued due to poor management or use of assets; theoretically promotes efficient behaviour by the managers of a firm.

market power When a buyer or a seller can influence the market price by their actions.

market structure Size distribution and modes of competition between firms in an industry.

market value The total worth of all of the firm's outstanding shares minus the amount of debt.

mean reversion Tendency of stock prices to fluctuate around some long run trend or mean.

measurement costs In economic terms, expenses incurred by contracting parties attempting to become fully informed; a sub-class of the broader concept of transaction costs.

merger An arrangement in which the assets and liabilities of the seller are absorbed into those of the buyer.

minimum efficient scale As output expands for the firm, that level of output at which the average total costs of production are minimized.

minimum supply price The smallest amount that a seller will accept in exchange for the good or service that she sells.

Mittelstand German industrial organization featuring a large sector of small and medium-sized firms.

Modigliani–Miller theorems An approach to classical finance consisting of two theorems: the first states that a firm's market value is independent of its capital structure; the second states that the total market value of the firm is independent of the way it finances its dividends.

monitoring The act of observing the actions and behaviour of contracting partners.

monopolistic competition Competition between producers of non-identical or differentiated goods.

monopoly A type of market structure in which there is a single seller facing the market demand function; potentially the most profitable of all market structures.

monopoly power Control held by a seller in economic exchange; if the seller can, to any degree, ignore the prices of other sellers in the market; the demand curve has a negative slope to it.

moral hazard An *ex post* contracting situation and source of transaction costs that occurs when one party's actions are imperfectly observable and when the incentives of the parties may be less than perfectly aligned.

mortgage bond A type of debt for firms secured by fixed assets.

motivation costs A broad category of transaction costs that have a basis in incomplete information; most important areas are imperfect monitoring of behaviour and ensuring that others remain committed.

multidivisional firm A type of organization producing more than one output for market.

N-firm concentration ratio A numerical measure of market concentration by sellers, equals the sum of the largest N firms' market shares.

Nash Equilibrium Any set of actions or strategies for the players in a game in which each player is doing the best it can, given the actions of its opponent.

natural monopoly A monopoly that is created when there are large fixed costs in production; serves as a basis for one of the principal reasons for the regulation of public utility companies.

net present value An amount of money to be received in the future and considered equal to its value today.

network externality A term equivalent to consumption externality; refers to the value to one party of other parties' choice of a particular good or service.

network system In economic terms refers to two or more components of a system that are complementary, or work together.

noise traders Participants in organized markets such as stock markets who are ill informed or irrational and thus create disturbances (noise) such as excess volatility.

non-convexities A characteristic of the relationship between inputs or activities within an organization implying that small changes in one activity will cause increasingly larger changes in other, related activities.

non-cooperative games Situations where participants pursue independent strategies, without explicit coordination or cooperation.

non-excludability The concept that, once a good is produced, it is impossible to prohibit others from consuming it.

non-rivalrous consumption The process by which one party's usage of a good or resource does not detract from its full enjoyment by other parties.

normative economics Questions with some moral or ethical basis.

numerically controlled machine A mechanical tool that can be controlled by a computer.

oligopoly Markets with a few (large) competitors who take each others' reactions into account.

operating curves Plot the relationship between long run costs and level of output.

opportunism The policy of taking advantage of an informational asymmetry in the pursuit of self-interest; it is a central assumption of transaction cost economics.

opportunistic behaviour Action taken when one party to an agreement acts in her own selfish interests, even at the expense of other parties involved in the agreement.

opportunity cost The value of the next-best alternative to an action.

opportunity cost of capital The rate of return measuring the next-best return available for the funds a firm has for investment.

option swaps A form of compensating CEOs in the form of stock in the corporation; occurring when a company issues a stock option in exchange for a previously issued stock option.

organizational strategy A blueprint for accomplishing an efficient allocation of corporate resources.

outputs The result of some effort to organize production.

outsiders Individuals *not* employed in a particular organization or group.

outsourcing Purchase of inputs from outside suppliers rather than production of them.

ownership The right to decide by whom, how, when, for how long and under what conditions an asset will be used.

partial equilibrium analysis Economic analysis that examines events in one market in isolation from all other markets.

partnership A type of firm in the economic system that consists of two or more persons associating to conduct non-corporate business.

patent Right to profit from an invention without imitation for a given period of time.

pay compression The concept that the wages in an organization are similar across all workers.

payoff matrix Array of rewards received by 'players' or participants in some interactive situation, according to actions taken.

perfect competition An arrangement of buyers and sellers in which there is perfect information, a homogeneous product, similar firms and free entry and exit.

perfect information When every participant (and potential participant) in a market becomes aware of every price, product specification and buyer and seller location at no cost.

physical asset specificity A particular investment in machinery or equipment that has one narrowly defined purpose.

planning curves Plot the relationship between long-run costs and level of output.

players Those economic agents engaged in competition of some sort where there is uncertainty regarding the courses of action taken by others.

point elasticity The percentage change in quantity demanded divided by the percentage change in price defined at a single point on a given demand function.

poison pill A defence against corporate takeover that can take many forms, each of which increases the cost to the acquirer and decreases the value of the firm taken over.

port of entry Position in organizational hierarchy where newly hired employees start to work.

positive economics The science of explaining what is and predicting what is to be.

precommitment contracts The practice by incumbent firms in an industry of precluding potential entrants assets or the rights to assets necessary to the production of a good.

preferred shares (stock) Shares with priority dividend claims but no voting rights.

price discrimination Charging different prices to different goods for highly similar goods; when the goods differ the prices do too by more than any cost difference in providing the good.

primary labour market Sectors of skilled jobs offering career progression and, traditionally, more security than unskilled, casual work.

principal–agent problem The recognition of the consequences of separating ownership and control in various transactions; the principal is the controlling authority, the agent is paid to act for the principal.

principle of risk-sharing The concept behind every insurance policy and financial diversification strategy that the sharing of independent risks of a single party reduces the total cost of bearing those risks.

prisoners' dilemma game Classic example of a situation where individual (selfish) rationality leads to a worse outcome for all than altruistic behaviour.

private costs Costs borne by the initiator of some activity.

private placement A way for a firm to raise funds by issuing debt to an identified investor; this type of debt is not made available to the general public.

private returns to R&D Rewards reaped by the investor in R&D.

process innovation A change in the way a product is made, or a service is provided, that improves quality and/or lowers cost.

producer surplus The area above the supply curve and below the market price; represents the difference between the minimum amount the seller will accept for any given unit sold and its actual price.

product innovation A concept closely affiliated with basic new knowledge and products.

product life-cycle The series of stages experienced by an output: introduction, growth, maturity and decline.

product mix efficiency A condition for overall efficiency and maximization of social well-being in an economic system; requires that all products produced are sold, or, in other words, that all markets clear.

product tie-in Creating a link between the sale of one good or service and the sale of (an)other good(s).

production The process of turning inputs into outputs featuring numerous fixed and numerous variable inputs.

production efficiency Attainment of maximum output from given inputs (no waste).

production function The characteristic behaviour between the inputs of the production process and the resulting output; indicates the firm's maximum attainable output for every specified combination of inputs.

production network A form of production that exists between markets and hierarchies.

production possibilities frontier The combination of two goods that an economy can produce by fully utilizing all of its resources including technology.

productive efficiency A condition of production by firms that is reached when the production of one output cannot be increased without a corresponding reduction in the production of another good.

productivity A measure of output, or other result, per unit of effort expended in obtaining it.

profit maximization The process of achieving the largest profits possible; requires that the marginal revenue of the firm equal the marginal cost at a point where marginal costs are increasing; the goal of the firm in neoclassical economics.

property rights Ownership.

proxy When one's actions are taken for, or substitute for, another's; when stockholders grant others their voting rights for a limited time dealing with a specified issue.

public good An economic good for which markets fail; defined by two properties: non-rivalrous consumption and non-excludability.

public issue When a firm raises funds through the creation of new shares of stock and makes these issues available to the general public.

quasi-rents The benefits from an activity going to a resource in excess of the minimum required to keep a resource in the current situation; in organizations, relevant for analyzing the exit decision of a resource.

rational bubble Speculative boom driven by self-fulfilling expectations.

rationality The principle that individuals and firms act in a consistent manner.

reaction function Choice of output or other variable by a firm in response to the choices made by competitors.

real An economic measure expressed in currency units defined in some base period; adjusted for inflation.

regulatory forbearance A policy of the US federal government during the early 1980s that permitted economically insolvent deposit-taking institutions to continue to operate.

relational contracting Agreement, incomplete in nature, for failing to specify actions fully in every possible set of circumstances; typically includes an agreement on broad goals and objectives and mechanisms for dispute resolution.

reload option A form of executive compensation in a corporation allowing the CEO and other executives to collect the profits that they would have received had they exercised their option on the day during the option period that would have earned them the highest profits.

reneging A form of *ex post* opportunism said by economists to occur when one or more parties to an agreement simply refuse to honour it.

rent Return from an activity above the minimum required to attract resources to that activity.

rent-seeking behaviour An attempt by some interested party to alter the allocation of rents in a contractual agreement; in general, does not create value within the organization.

reputation Recognition viewed by economists as part of an organization's or individual's capital stock; based on past behaviour and, more importantly, on others' perception of that behaviour.

resale price maintenance The setting of retail prices by manufacturers.

reservation price The maximum amount a buyer would be willing to pay for an item, given preferences, incomes and the prices of other goods.

reservation reward The minimum amount for which an individual will voluntarily work; observed to vary by an individual's age and qualifications.

reservation reward profile The relationship between an individual's reservation reward and various points in time (perhaps corresponding to age); typically assumed to be higher at more advanced ages.

residual authority See residual right of control.

residual income claimant A person or organization that controls an asset and has the opportunity to employ the asset how it wishes; may be entitled to the economic rents or profits generated by that asset.

residual return Mandated by state and federal laws, the payments to individuals who own stock in a corporation.

residual right of control A benefit given to stock owners by a corporation giving them some influence on the activities of the corporation through the election of a board of directors.

resource allocation The distribution of limited resources efficiently or in a way that maximizes some fixed objective.

restrictive practice A set of actions taken by sellers in the market place to restrict competition.

restructuring The act of changing the resources available to a firm and/or altering the lines of business a firm is in; changing the way a firm chooses to organize economic activity, or those activities themselves.

returns to scale Refers to the relationship between uniform percentage increases in the inputs available to a firm and the percentage change in output.

risk averse A person who wishes not to face risks and is willing to pay some explicit or implicit amount to have the risk removed; a person who prefers a certain deal over an uncertain deal with equal expected value.

routine production services Routine and unskilled blue- or white-collar jobs.

routinized regime Describes the availability of information necessary for innovation, if the information necessary for innovation exists only in established, existing firms.

Rust Belt Region of traditional heavy industry in the middle west of the USA.

scale economies The property of some production processes when average unit costs decline as the number of units produced increases.

scientific management A management's style for supervising workers featuring extensive task specialization, a detailed set of rules and frequent evaluation of individual performance.

scientific method A way of thinking about problems and formulating a solution.

scope economies The results of physically combining inputs to form outputs that produce two or more related outputs within the same firm; implies lower unit costs for each good than if each was produced separately.

screening A potential solution to adverse selection that occurs when the uninformed parties to a contract undertake activities to cause the informed parties to distinguish between themselves in regard to some unobservable characteristics.

secondary market An institution allowing for the debt and equities of firms to be bought and sold.

second-degree price discrimination Dependence on unit price on the number of units purchased.

secondary labour market Market for unskilled and often short-term labour with little job security or career prospects.

secured debt Form of financing backed by an existing asset that acts as collateral.

self-selection A type of behaviour usually in response to some screening activity that causes some percentage of a larger group of potential trading partners to identify themselves as desirable candidates for exchange.

separation of ownership and control A property of publicly held corporations; one group of shareholders owns the firm and a second group of managers runs the firm.

shareholder activism Vigorous action taken when shareholders become so dissatisfied with the actions of the corporation's management that they actively attempt to influence, or even eliminate, management; occurs because of the separation of ownership and control.

shirking A form of *ex post* opportunistic behaviour arising because of imperfect monitoring; one party puts in less effort than it otherwise might if its actions were perfectly observable.

shortage A situation in which the quantity demanded of a good or service is greater than the quantity supplied.

short run A term to describe the period of time in which the firm is not free to vary all its factors of production.

short-run equilibrium A situation in which the firm has no incentive to change its level, or mix, of outputs and the number of firms in the markets is fixed.

short-termism Focus on short-term profits at the cost of long-term investment.

shut-down point The minimum price that a firm will produce output for in the short run, equal to average variable cost at the chosen level of output; further decreases in price cause losses larger than fixed costs.

signalling A way to reduce inefficiencies caused by adverse selection; the better-informed party may give indications of unobservable, but desirable, characteristics.

single firm conditions of productive efficiency When a firm produces efficiently the ratio of marginal products to input prices for all inputs must be equal.

site specificity A form of asset specificity; the condition of being limited to a particular location.

skill acquisition costs The cost borne by workers as they gain new knowledge and skills to change jobs; that is, the costs of building new human capital.

small-batch production One property of flexible manufacturing when a very small number of units can be produced at a very low cost per unit.

social costs The total costs borne by all members of society, including those not directly participating in that activity.

social indifference curve Shows all combinations of goods and services produced in the economy that yield society the same level of well-being.

social plan One element of codetermination in Germany requiring that the works council agrees on severance pay for redundant workers.

social returns to R&D Total benefit to society from R&D; may exceed private returns when there are external effects.

soft science The study of the interactions resulting from human behaviour.

sole proprietorship A type of firm in the economic system owned by a single individual.

specialization The division of tasks on the basis of comparative advantage.

specific skills Skills only relevant in some particular job or organization.

specific human capital see specific skills.

standard option CEO compensation that gives the holder the right to purchase a specific number of shares of the company's stock at a specified target price.

statistical quality control Sampling output to estimate average quality.

stick method A way for managers to solve the incentive problem in a team production context by forcing the employee to act by making threats in a specified way.

strategic In an exchange, or otherwise competitive environment, one party's choices not only affects other parties, the choices also affect the choices made by the other parties.

strategic alliance An association to exploit the unique strength of two or more companies whose core competencies are complementary when neither partner has the ability, or the desire, to acquire the other party's unique strength.

strategic misrepresentation A situation in which one party may try to benefit by being less than truthful about their assessment of an exchange situation; employed to increase bargaining power.

strategy Choice of action under all possible circumstances.

sunk costs Costs that can never be recouped once they are paid; irrelevant for decision makers.

supervisory board The German corporate construct that best corresponds to a board of directors in a US firm; comprised only of outsiders; hires top management.

supply The quantity of a good or service that producers are willing to produce.

supply curve The graphical depiction of the relationship between quantity supplied and price, holding all other factors affecting producer behaviour constant.

supply function An explicit mathematical or graphical relationship between the price of a good and the quantity supplied.

surplus An amount that remains when the quantity demanded of a good or service is less than the quantity supplied.

symbolic analytic services Work which requires a high level of skill and analytical ability.

synergies When the combined effect of two activities is greater than their sum taken separately; agglomerations.

tacit collusion Collusion without explicit communication or agreement.

takeover market commercial activity by a number of investors seeking a corporation undervalued because of poor management to buy, replace management, and raise its value.

Taylorism A management style for supervising production commonly used in mass-producing firms: (1) specialize each job through the simplification of individual tasks, (2) devise predetermined rules coordinating the separate tasks, and (3) evaluate the individual performance through a detailed monitoring system.

team production A form of making output that requires the simultaneous efforts of more than one individual.

technological efficiency This is attained when it is impossible to increase (physical) output without more inputs, so 'no waste' is implied but no relative cost considerations are involved.

theory An unproven explanation of observation.

third-degree price discrimination Separating customers into two or more subgroups based on differences in their elasticities of demand, and charging a higher price to the group whose demand is less elastic.

total cost Inclusive expenses (both implicit and explicit) of producing any given level of output; includes opportunity cost.

total factor productivity Output produced per unit of input employed when total input is an index of three individual inputs: labour, capital and materials.

total market value The amount of cash needed to purchase a firm free and clear; an amount equal to the market value of the firm's equities plus all debt.

total product A relationship between output and variations in one input.

total quality management (TQM) A philosophy practised by an entire organization working together with an interdepartmental collective responsibility for the quality of products and services.

total revenue Price times quantity.

total value The economic concept of a transaction as the total benefit of the exchange; may include regularly defined profits of firms and consumer surplus, elements of risk minimization, strategic gains, and non-market benefits.

total value maximization A goal of economic behaviour to increase to a maximum the total value surrounding a transaction.

tracker fund A fund that mimics some index of stock market performance such as the Dow Jones or FTSE 100 by holding the market portfolio.

transaction costs Costs incurred in exchange, either explicit or implicit, above and beyond contracted prices, including the acquisition of costly information, monitoring performance and committing specific assets.

transfer machines A number of smaller machines or work stations committed to a specific task and organized so that a piece of work is immediately transferred to the next work station.

transplants Japanese-owned and/or managed subsidiaries operating in the United States.

trust Belief in partner's honesty or goodwill.

two-part tariff A form of pricing, considered discriminatory, under which buyers are charged both an entry fee and a usage fee.

underwriter An entity who sells bonds in a public offering; often helps in many areas of issuing bonds.

unitary elasticity of demand When the percentage change in the quantity demanded of a good divided by the percentage change in the price of the good are equal and their ratio equals 1 in magnitude.

unsecured debt Liability supported only by the borrower's credit worthiness.

value maximization When the management of a corporation acts to maximize the market value of outstanding shares (equities) so as to transfer the maximum value to the owners of those shares.

variable cost All costs incurred in production by firms that vary directly with output.

variable input Input that varies with quantity of output, such as production labour.

venture capital High risk equity stake in new enterprise.

vertical differentiation When producers of differentiated products allow their products to differ along quality, or perceived quality lines.

vertical integration The process in which either one of the input sources or one of the output buyers of the firm is moved inside the firm.

vertical restrictions When one firm buys another's goods or services and this relationship is exploited by either the buyer or seller to preclude further entry into the market.

virtual corporation A temporary network of companies that come together quickly to exploit changing market conditions under which companies can share costs, skills and access to global markets, with each partner contributing what it does best.

'voice' One choice that share owners have if they are unhappy with the performance of the company in which they have shares. They exercise voice if they express their dissatisfaction, attempting to alter management style.

vulture capitalists Some entrepreneurs who specialize in raiding high-tech firms, hiring away their best talents as a basis for starting a new firm.

wealth maximization When the management of a corporation acts to increase the assets under corporate ownership; maximizes the book value of the firm.

welfare triangle A graphical device in a supply and demand context showing the gains from trade as the sum of consumer and producer surplus.

worker search costs Expenses that employees incur when looking for a new job; including the value of time unemployed, interviewing, and efforts in contacting potential employers.

works council A group within the firm under codetermination in Germany that has certain decision-making powers in management issues related to personal decisions.

x-inefficiency The operation of a firm less efficiently than could occur given technical constraints.

Index